Seventeenth-Century English Prose

The Borzoi Anthology
of 17th-Century English Literature

GENERAL EDITOR

Joseph A. Mazzeo
Columbia University

Seventeenth-Century English Poetry (Vols. I & II)

EDITED BY *MIRIAM K. STARKMAN*
Queens College of The City University of New York

Seventeenth-Century English Prose (Vol. III)

EDITED BY *DAVID NOVARR, Cornell University*

Literary Criticism of Seventeenth-Century England (Vol. IV)

EDITED BY *EDWARD W. TAYLER, Columbia University*

Religious Prose of Seventeenth-Century England (Vol. V)

EDITED BY *ANNE DAVIDSON FERRY, Harvard University*

Seventeenth-Century

English Prose

E D I T E D   B Y

David Novarr
CORNELL UNIVERSITY

ALFRED · A · KNOPF
NEW YORK
1967

Preface

The purpose of this volume is to set forth sizable selections of literary prose by Bacon, Burton, Walton, Browne, Bunyan, and Pepys, and to represent the major prose genres of the century—essay, character, short life, and epistle. Each selection is presented in an authoritative text. Original spelling has been followed, but *i, j, u, v, vv,* and long *s* have been made to conform to modern usage, abbreviations have usually been expanded, and obvious errors in printing have been silently corrected. Original punctuation has been retained except in a few places where it confuses or misleads. The text used for each selection has been specified, often in considerable detail, in the second paragraph of the Biographical and Bibliographical Notes at the end of the book. The first paragraph of these Notes chronicles very briefly the main details of an author's career; the last paragraph is a short and selective index to the most useful editions and biographical and critical studies.

In accordance with the method used in the series of which this book is a part, annotation has, on the whole, been rigidly confined to the translation of all foreign words, phrases, and passages, and to glossing all words which may be troublesome to a modern reader. The symbol * before a footnote indicates that a marginal note or a footnote in the original text is reproduced. Where the superscript symbol § appears next to a word, the word appears in the Glossary at the back of the book. A statement about glossing procedure precedes the Glossary.

The Introduction tries to open up the special nature of seventeenth-century literary prose by considering the prose styles of the century, by defining the domain of literary prose in the century, and by describing its most popular literary genres.

I wish particularly to acknowledge the kindnesses of my friends at the Cornell University Library, who not only provided me with a useful apartment in their own large house, but were also daily cherishers of my studies. For a multiplicity of favors, I am indebted to the Avery Architectural Library at Columbia, the Beinecke Rare Book and Manuscript Library at Yale, the Bodleian Library, the Folger Shakespeare Library, the Henry E. Huntington Library, and the Public Record Office. The American Philosophical Association, the Clarendon Press, and G. Bell & Sons have kindly permitted me to use material under copyright. My work has been facilitated by a grant from the funds generously made available to the Department of English at Cornell by an anonymous donor. To my wife, who is now rather less certain that good deeds bring their own reward, I owe thanks and much more.

Contents

III Izaak Walton

IV Sir Thomas Browne

V John Bunyan

VI Samuel Pepys

VII Essays

VIII Characters

Dorothy Osborne, Letters to William Temple

John Aubrey

Sir George Etherege

Seventeenth-Century
English Prose

§

*This gloss mark § indicates a word to be found
in the Glossary at the end of the book.*

Introduction

I

Tis an admirable thing to see how some People will labour to finde out term's that may Obscure a plaine sence, like a gentleman I knew, whoe would never say the weather grew cold, but that Winter began to salute us. I have noe patience for such Coxcomb's and cannot blame an old Uncle of mine that threw the Standish at his mans head because he writt a letter for him where instead of sayeing (as his Master bid him) that hee would have writ himself but that hee had the Goute in his hand; hee sayed that the Goute in his hand would not permitt him to put pen to paper; the ffellow thought hee had mended it Mightily and that putting pen to paper was much better then plaine writeing.

Dorothy Osborne's commendation of plain writing, in a letter dated 1653, falls easily on our ears; we approve her sentiments and find agreeable her own plain, direct, clear expression. Her statement and her way of stating it conform to modern criteria for good expository prose. Some thirty years before Miss Osborne wrote, Robert Burton had announced his reliance on plain style: since he had neither time to revise his book nor money for secretarial help, he "was therefore enforced, as a Bear doth her whelps, to bring forth this confused lump":

> I had not time to lick it into form, as she doth her yong ones, but even so to publish it, as it was first written, *quicquid in buccam*

venit, in an extemporean stile, as I do commonly all other exercises, *effudi quicquid dictavit genius meus,* out of a confused company of notes, and writ with as small deliberation as I do ordinarily speak, without all affectation of big words, fustian phrases, jingling terms, tropes, strong lines, that like *Acestes* arrows caught fire as they flew, strains of wit, brave heats, elogies, hyperbolical exornations, elegancies, &c. which many so much affect. I am *aquæ potor,* drink no wine at all, which so much improves our modern wits, a loose, plain, rude writer, *ficum voco ficum, & ligonem ligonem,* and as free, as loose, *idem calamo quod in mente,* I call a spade a spade, *animis hæc scribo, non auribus,* I respect matter, not words; remembring that of *Cardan, verba propter res, non res propter verba:* and seeking with *Seneca, quid scribam, non quemadmodum,* rather what, then how to write. For as *Philo* thinks, *He that is conversant about matter, neglects words, and those that excell in this art of speaking, have no profound learning,*

> *Verba nitent phaleris, at nullas verba medullas*
> *Intus habent—*

Besides, it was the observation of that wise *Seneca, when you see a fellow carefull about his words, and neat in his speech, know this for a certaintie, that mans mind is busied about toyes, there's no soliditie in him. Non est ornamentum virile concinnitas:* as he said of a nightingale,

> *—vox es, præterea nihil, &c.*

I am therefore in this point a professed disciple of *Apollonius,* a scholar of *Socrates,* I neglect phrases, and labor wholly to inform my readers understanding, not to please his ear; 'tis not my study or intent to compose neatly, which an Orator requires, but to express my self readily & plainly as it happens.

For all his emphasis on plainness, on matter rather than words, Burton's sentences are, in their short units, catalogues, Latin tags, and staccato rhythms, jarringly affected for a modern reader. His style seems obtrusive; it calls attention to itself in a way that Miss Osborne's does not; the extemporary speaking voice is here, but it overwhelms the ideas it expresses. For us Burton has a strange way of calling a spade a spade; we are conscious of a style at work. The style is not totally unfamiliar: it has something of what has been called "the nervous transcriptive spontaneous faculty" of avant-garde prose, but that prose does not yet fall naturally on our ears. Miss Osborne's prose, except for a few old-fashioned words, presents its subject matter like plate glass in a shop window; we are unaware of its rhetorical structure. It seems totally unmannered. Precision of meaning is never subordinated to effect; in fact, we are not conscious of effect at all.

We take for granted such prose as Dorothy Osborne's; we barely recognize it as a style. It is immediately intelligible, unpretentious and low-pitched, practical and unpedantic, more colloquial than formal, dependent on speech rhythms, not poetic prosody; it is simple rather than ornate, lively and temperate, easy, rapid, direct, intellectually serene. It has been the workaday prose of English letters for three hundred years, the prose of Hobbes and Bishop Sprat, of Goldsmith and Boswell, of Wordsworth and Arnold, of Shaw and Chesterton, of T. S. Eliot and Bertrand Russell, of Marquand and *The New Yorker,* of Jacques Barzun and Gilbert Highet and James Reston and Dwight MacDonald. It is, of course, the prose which derives from Dryden. When Dr. Johnson said that Dryden's style could not easily be imitated, either seriously or ludicrously, he focused mainly on its resistance to parody: "for being always equable and always varied, it has no prominent or discriminative characters. The beauty who is totally free from disproportion of parts and features cannot be ridiculed by an overcharged resemblance." He had already complimented the consummate craftsmanship necessary to the fashioning of such a style when he had written of Dryden's critical prefaces:

> They have not the formality of a settled style, in which the first half of the sentence betrays the other. The clauses are never balanced, nor the periods modelled; every word seems to drop by chance, though it falls into its proper place. Nothing is cold or languid; the whole is airy, animated, and vigorous; what is little is gay; what is great, is splendid. He may be thought to mention himself too freely; but while he forces himself upon our esteem, we cannot refuse him to stand high in his own. Every thing is excused by the play of images and the spriteliness of expression. Though all is easy, nothing is feeble; though all seems careless, there is

nothing harsh; and though, since his earlier works, more than a century has passed, they have nothing yet uncouth or obsolete.

He who writes much, will not easily escape a manner, such a recurrence of particular modes as may be easily noted. Dryden is always *another and the same,* he does not exhibit a second time the same elegancies in the same form, nor appears to have any art other than that of expressing with clearness what he thinks with vigour.

Dr. Johnson's own prose does not, of course, reproduce the qualities he so admired in Dryden's. We are aware, even in two short paragraphs, of the firmness and formality and polish of his manner. The balanced phrases, the parallel structures, both produce and reinforce an attitude which is considered, magisterial, dogmatic. Johnson hearkens back to a style even older than Burton's, the Ciceronian style which characterized fine Elizabethan prose rather the Senecan mode that dominated most of the seventeenth century before the Restoration. Burton describes the Ciceronian style in describing how his own differs from it. It is *composed neatly,* according to oratorical requirements; its cadences are harmonious and sonorous, its structure and its ideas are planned, shaped, polished. It is written with great deliberation; it has been licked into form. According to Burton, it is more concerned with words than with matter; his own outpouring of such words as *fustian, tropes, strong, strains, brave, hyperbolical, elegancies* shows his antagonism to a style which is heightened, eloquent, overconsciously rhetorical.

Burton's dissatisfaction, like that of some of the generation of writers before him, stemmed from a feeling that Ciceronianism encouraged verbal felicity at the expense of refined analysis of a subject and deep penetration into it. Like Bacon, he probably felt that the polish and rotundity of the style were often only a slick veneer. Bacon had thought that the Ciceronian mode of delivering knowledge was "Magistrall and peremptorie; and not ingenuous and faithfull; in a sort, as may be soonest beleeved; and not easiliest examined" and he had announced that knowledge ought to be "delivered and intimated, if it were possible, *In the same Methode wherein it was invented.*" Some such feeling provided ammunition for the deliberate exploding

of the Ciceronian periodic sentence, for the displacement of
balance and symmetry by disproportion and asymmetry. Two
forms of the Senecan "amble" replaced the dignified, even,
pompous, Ciceronian gait. Formalistically, the "curt" style attained a hovering, imaginative order rather than a conclusive
and logical one by the brevity of its parts, by the asymmetry
of members of a rhetorical period in length or grammatical form
or degree of literalness, by the omission of ordinary syntactic
ligatures; the "loose" style reached the same end by its heavy
use of coordinating conjunctions, absolute participial construc-
tions, and parentheses. One was pithy, terse, abrupt, succinct;
the other was associational and digressive. In both, emphasis
was on expressiveness, not expression, or, at least, on the expression of expressiveness. Both reflected, or gave the impression
of reflecting, not a mind at rest, secure that it had communicated its conviction, but a mind in motion, in the process of
thinking something through; not a mind that moved in complete equipoise toward a logical conclusion, but one that moved
laboriously and energetically toward an imaginative realization
or resolution. The Senecan style is emergent, exploratory, experimental. It reflects a mind which stops, broods, turns on
itself, sees one facet of an idea and then another, responds
now with wit and now with emotion, here with reason and there
with passion. The result is writing which is intimate, personal,
introspective, which reveals individuality and personality because it puts a premium on private searching rather than on
public expression—or *seems* to. After it had become fashionable, Bacon himself complained that it might be abused, constructed by artifice, so that "every passage seemes more witty
and waighty than indeed it is." Though Bacon and the Senecans
had insisted that the Ciceronians were more inclined to "copie,
than weight," toward words and expression rather than matter,
the Senecan style indulged in fullness of rhetorical expression
even as the earlier style had; it merely exploited other rhetorical
techniques. (Nor, of course, did Bacon and the Senecans cut
themselves off from the persuasiveness and authority of the
Ciceronian period; the Senecan style is rarely unadulterated.)
It substituted a rhetorical copiousness of its own for the *copia*

of Ciceronianism. And, like the Ciceronians, the Senecans, too, sought in their own way for statement that was full, exhaustive, authoritative.

The above remarks will serve to remind us that prose style is something more than the sum of its formalist elements, that it is somehow linked to a writer's outlook, his view of his own role, his values and assumptions. Professor Morris Croll, upon whose work all discussion of seventeenth-century prose style depends, himself sees style as representative of habit of mind. The curt style bears the marks of sententiousness, penetrating wit, Stoic intensity; the loose style reveals an author's dislike of formalism, his roving and self-exploratory curiosity, his skeptical tendency. Since the two styles are not always easily distinguishable, since they are frequently found side by side in the same work, they together reflect, for Croll, the dominant attitudes of the century. Croll sees the Senecan style as the tool forged "to conduct an experimental investigation of the moral realities" of the time.

To call a spade a spade is not, then, merely a matter of precision of diction. A spade is, after all, what a man makes of it. A spade is a spade and no other thing only as the result of a narrowing of focus, a simplification. The efficient, clear, serene style of Dryden, the style which has subsequently dominated English letters, is a magnificent achievement, but, we may suggest, it reflects an outlook more limited, less complex, than that of the style it supplanted.

When the century opened, the proper study of mankind was thought to be man, but it was hardly considered presumptuous to scan God. Since the dignity of man stemmed from the spark of divinity in him, since his very rationality linked him with God in a congruent and harmonious universe, all study of man was inevitably related to study of God in all His manifestations. The starry heavens above were not the exclusive domain of the astronomers but part of the natural province of every man. The human situation and human conduct were inevitably connected to the Divine, and all study of the human condition took place within the framework of the Divine. A little learning was not only a dangerous thing but a disastrous one. To drink deeply

of the Pierian spring was not enough without immersion in the
waters of Jordan. Behind the Alps on Alps loomed the Delectable
Mountains, and tomes of casuistry had not yet been relegated
to the moon. The century's ideal of *copia* was more than fullness
of expression and accumulation of authorities; it was a large
scale religious and philosophical view, a view which narrowed
as the century wore on.

Bacon had thought that his new program would redound to
the greater glory of God and man; it drifted instead toward empirical naturalism. Early in the century, even *scientia* (knowledge of the world) was thought limited; it must be bolstered by
sapientia (knowledge of this world and the next; wisdom).
Later, *scientia* diminished into science. Natural philosophy had
once been the handmaid of moral philosophy; increasingly, it
served only itself. Sir Thomas Browne conceived of his profession as the study of "life and death"; for him the function of the
physician was not only to preserve the living and keep men out
of urns; it was, equally, to make the dead live and to discourse of
human fragments—he did not merely practice medicine. Early
in the century, all roads pointed to or from heaven, and all of
them were paved with hard questions; later, men were more concerned with things than with heaven, and Dryden could say that
"the things we must believe, are few, and plain." Search for the
truth was replaced by reliance on common sense. Wit had once
been the edge of the mind which pried into hidden places; it became the pointed expression of commonplaces. Manly pursuit of
the good gave way to the gentlemanly pursuit of good taste; development of self was followed by refinement of manners. We are
marvelously amused by the grace of Millamant when she says
that she "may by degrees dwindle into a wife"; in Congreve's
world, she is the absolute mistress of manners and nearest of
kin to virtue. It is not so amusing to witness the fall from grace,
as Spenser's concept of magnificence and Milton's man of complete and generous education dwindle into Congreve's Mirabell.

We are likely to underestimate the nature of the compliment
Dryden paid Sir John Suckling when he praised him for expressing "so much the Conversation of a Gentleman." Although
Dryden admitted that Shakespeare had "an universal mind,
which comprehended all characters and passions," he thought

nonetheless that Beaumont and Fletcher "understood and imitated the Conversation of Gentlemen much better" than Shakespeare, and he believed that the English language had arrived
at its highest perfection in them. He ascribed the advantage
which poets and playwrights of his age had over Jacobean writers to the "gallantry and civility" of his age and to the fact that
writers were now "conversant in courts." Professor James Sutherland has recently said that Dryden's own prose is in the main
"a slightly formalized variation of the conversation of gentlemen," and he has provided us with a "character" of the Restoration gentleman:

> The gentleman converses with ease, and with an absence of em-
> phasis that may at times become a conscious and studied under-
> emphasis, but is more often the natural expression of his poise and
> detachment. He is imperturbable, nothing puts him out or leads
> him to quicken his pace; indeed, a certain nonchalance and a cas-
> ual way of making the most devastating remarks are characteristic
> of him, for if he is always polite he is never mealy-mouthed, and
> has no middle-class inhibitions. He will never betray too great
> eagerness or ride his ideas too hard or insist too absolutely, for that
> is to be a bore; he will not consciously exploit his own personality
> or indulge in eccentricity or whimsies, for that is to be selfish, to
> think too much about himself. On all occasions, like a good host,
> he will consult the convenience and pleasure of those he is enter-
> taining; and he will therefore try to express himself clearly and
> politely and unpedantically. If he can manage it (and if he can't
> he won't try) he will make his points with a witty turn of thought
> and phrase. He will not dogmatize, or proselytize, or appeal en-
> tirely to the emotions; for to do so is the mark of the ignorant zealot
> and the godly fanatic, of whom no Restoration gentleman wished
> to be reminded.[1]

The gentleman is easy to live with, nor ought we denigrate the
skill and discipline by which he has attained his ease. But commitment is as much a virtue as detachment is; in some circumstances nonchalance may not only be indecorous, but sinful.
Mere casualness and politeness can be more boring than eagerness and insistence; real intellectual passion rarely bores. There
is need in the world for clarity; unfortunately, all things worth

[1] *On English Prose* (1957), pp. 67–68; reprinted by permission of the University of Toronto Press.

discussing are not always clear. We may admire verve, confidence, urbanity, but not if they utterly exclude self-searching and humility. What we call natural or plain prose is convenient and pleasant; we would not willingly do without it. It does entail, however, a loss as well as a gain. It leaves something out, and we would not be without the prose of Dr. Johnson, Carlyle, Henry James, Faulkner, or the prose which is the product of the best seventeenth-century minds.

II

In quite the same way as the dominance of Dryden's prose style represents a narrowing of outlook, so the growth and importance of the novel as a literary genre have narrowed our view of what literature is. We have the novel in mind when we separate prose into fiction and non-fiction. We split prose into that which is "creative" and that which is "expository." We try to determine whether the intent of a work is primarily aesthetic or primarily didactic, whether it means to call attention to how it has rendered its "content" or whether it seeks a transparent medium. We would categorize one work as primarily expressive, connotative, imaginative, and another as primarily referential, denotative, informational. We equate fiction with invention, falseness, unreality, and non-fiction with facts, truth, reality. We say that biography is a craft, not an art. We understand that a historian must be selective in the facts he uses, but we say at the same time that to suggest he has manipulated facts to produce symmetry of structure would be grounds for libel.

In this context, the prose masterpieces of the seventeenth century, those works tested by "length of duration and continuance of esteem" are, on the whole, non-fiction. Richard Hooker wrote *Of the Laws of Ecclesiasticall Polity* before the turn of the century, and its perfected parts were published in 1593 and 1597, but since Books VI and VIII were first published in 1648 and Book VII in 1662, since prior to the Restoration it was considered, in Fuller's words, "an *Old-Almanack* grown out of date," we may start our list of masterpieces with it. It was one of many defenses of the Anglican Church, written at a time when there was no market for books about church discipline, especially for those presenting the views of the Established Church, but, though its printing was privately subsidized, it towered over run-of-the-mill treatises. Hooker grounded his discussion of church government, liturgy and ceremonies, church lands, and kingship on a consideration of the nature of law and the nature of man. His general approbation of episcopacy, church prerogatives, and limited constitutional monarchy may not be plain and clear, but it stems from the application of profound historical awareness, a grasp of the classical and Christian traditions, and skill in political philosophy. In like fashion, the King James Version of the Bible was but one of a long line of translations of the Scriptures into English and into other vernaculars, but it is the only one to have held the hearts and minds of men for centuries (though it was never specifically authorized by official pronouncement and though in America it had to overcome devotion to the Geneva version). The circumstances of the translation would seem to have insured disaster: some fifty scholars had their hands in it; they seem to have worked consciously for an old-fashioned flavor in their reliance on the words and rhythms of Tyndale and Coverdale; they had among them only one man who has any kind of literary reputation, Lancelot Andrewes. One critic has indeed suggested that "the Bible is the grand proof in English that in the greatest writing literary beauty is not a main object but a by-product." Of one thing we may be sure: several years of intense and dedicated labor went into the translation. The translators wholly believed that they were opening up the word of God about the way of life and of salvation, and they worked at a time when the good life and life eternal were immediate and pressing realities, not merely one part of the Sunday-school curriculum, and when the Bible was The Book, not merely a single archetypal structure or one of several definitive myths.

Other prose masterpieces of the century have subjects which seem equally unpromising for "literary" works. Burton's *Anatomy of Melancholy* is a compendium of the causes of melancholy, its manifestations and kinds, and its cures; its title page states that these subjects are "*Philosophically, Medicinally, Historically, Opened and Cut Up.*" In *Religio Medici*, Thomas Browne, a young provincial doctor, examines the nature of his religious beliefs. *Areopagitica* is an unlicensed pamphlet in which Milton objects to the Parliament's enforcement of an ordinance which forced pamphlets and books to be licensed before they were printed. Hobbes's *Leviathan, or the Matter, Forme and Power of a Commonwealth Ecclesiasticall and Civil,* is a logically deduced volume of political theory which frightened and provoked even those who agreed with its doctrine of the absolute authority of the state because of its naturalistic view of man and its depression of the place of the Church. Walton tells the reader of *The Compleat Angler* that the more useful part of his book is on "the nature and breeding, seasons and catching of fish." In his *True Historical Narrative of the Rebellion and Civil Wars,* first published in 1702–04, Sir Edward Hyde combined an account of events and of the men who shaped them, written during the 1640's when he was Charles I's Chancellor of the Exchequer, with an autobiography written in the late 1660's when he was the Earl of Clarendon, Charles II's banished Lord Chancellor. If he avoided abstract issues, he avoided, too, the perils of immediacy and self-justification to produce a wise and moving work. *The Pilgrim's Progress,* the most nearly novelistic book on our list, first appeared in 1678, written, strangely enough, by a man who considered himself the chief of sinners, a man whose first book was called *Some Gospel Truths Opened* and who also wrote in 1678 a volume called *Come and Welcome to Jesus Christ.* John Bunyan tells us that he first loved the historical parts of the Bible; even in *Grace Abounding,* where he would be *"plain and simple, and lay down the thing as it was,"* he had turned the straight and narrow way into a gap in a wall on a mountain; in *The Pilgrim's Progress,* he tells the story of Christian on the high road to Heaven in a continuous allegory which objectifies and concretizes his own spiritual journey. John Locke also saw himself as "clearing the ground a little," but he thought it necessary "to examine our own abilities, and see what *objects* our understandings were, or were not, fitted to deal with." *An Essay Concerning Human Understanding* is a coolly argued epistemological treatise.

Are all these works literary masterpieces because they were written "about something" with "style"? Shall we put them into the category of descriptive writings which have survived by virtue of their interesting verbal patterns after their value as a representation of facts has faded? Is it true that the religion of one age is the literary entertainment of the next? It seems fair to assume that a literary element was not imposed on these works by time alone. If they are literature today, they were literature yesterday, and they were literature then because their authors did not think that there was an irrevocable divorce between religion and literature or between a literary work and one that was about something.

Professor Northrop Frye has recently helped us understand what we always felt—that many seventeenth-century works are intrinsically in the literary domain—by treating the novel as one form of fiction and by reminding us that the word "fiction" means etymologically something made for its own sake. His classification of fiction into novel, romance, confession, and anatomy, and his demonstration of the mixing of these forms, makes room in the house of literature for many occupants, and if he excludes biography and history, he does not put up a "No Vacancy" sign. "All structures in words," he says, "are partly rhetorical, and hence literary," and he says, further, "Whether a thing is a work of art or not is determined by convention, social acceptance, and the work of criticism in the broadest sense."

Professor Frye finds, for example, the literary ancestry of Burton in Rabelais and Erasmus and, ultimately, in Lucian. He sees Burton as working in the specific medium of the Menippean satire, as presenting a vision of the world in terms of a single intellectual pattern as he is now satirical, now fanciful, now moral. He shows that Burton, like other Menippean satirists, relies heavily on digression and on dialogue (though the symposium in the *Anatomy of Melancholy* is one constructed out of books). Burton's all-embracing conception of melancholy allows him, Frye explains, to study human society by concentrating not on people but on mental attitudes, ideas, theories; and his "creative treatment of exhaustive erudition" allows him to overwhelm the philosophical pedantry which preferred theory to practice and imposed oversimplified ideals on experience. The result is "the most comprehensive survey of human life in one book that English literature had seen since Chaucer." In like fashion, Frye says, Walton's *The Compleat Angler* organizes the world through a dialogue on "the doctrine and discipline of angling"; it is an anatomy "because of its mixture of prose and verse, its rural *cena* setting, its dialogue form, its deipnosophistical interest in food, and its gentle Menippean raillery of a society which considers everything more important than fishing and yet has discovered very few better things to do."

Professor Frye's critical frame, his placing of these works within a generic structure, illuminates Burton's work and Walton's for us as readers by setting them in a literary context. The seventeenth century was, of course, very much conscious of genre theory, especially in poetry, and during the century this consciousness grew and developed to receive its theoretical culmination when Dryden, "the father of English criticism," addressed himself to such forms as dramatic poesy, the historical poem, the verse epistle, epic, and satire. Even in prose, the sermon and the devotion demanded attention to rules, and the century developed its own forms, as we shall see, in the essay and the character. But not all prose writers, then as now, started writing with a well-defined genre in mind. Many men, particularly those who did not make a career of writing, even those amateurs who were self-conscious about their role as writer, did not sit down to write in a firmly fixed form but were at most vaguely aware of a vague tradition. It is useful for us to view *Hydriotaphia* as a combination of anatomy and essay, but Sir Thomas Browne probably had neither form in mind. He seems, rather, to have started writing an archeological report about fifty-four urns recently unearthed in Walsingham; his subject expanded as he sought to provide a historical context, and, finally, as the urns worked to shape the imagination of the potter, he moved into the rarer altitude of meditation. In *Grace Abounding*, Bunyan, imprisoned, wished nevertheless to fulfill his duty to his congregation; he wrote his autobiography so that, as he says, "*if God will, others may be put in remembrance of what he hath done for their Souls, by reading his work upon me.*" He may indeed have written a self-justificatory intellectualized confession, one that in its gross pattern even resembles other confessional Puritan documents, but it is not likely that he conceived of his task in just those terms.

So, Burton did not identify himself with Erasmus or with Lucian, but with Democritus: he would find out the seat of melancholy, "whence it proceeds, and how it was engendred in mens bodies, to the intent he might better cure it in himself, by his writings and observations teach others how to prevent and avoid it." Although Sir William Osler called the *Anatomy* the greatest medical treatise ever written by a layman, Professor Lawrence Babb has shown that less than a quarter of the book is strictly devoted to medicine, physiology, psychology, and psychiatry. Between the first and sixth editions, Burton never rearranged his technical material and never added substantially to it, though he increased the book by about sixty per cent. His additions show that his interest was primarily in amplifying his own commentary, in introducing new illustrations and quotations in the nontechnical passages. His nearest sources and analogues are treatises on the passions, the moral psychologies of the time, whose purpose was not to impart knowledge but to increase that self-knowledge which is necessary to self-control and to virtuous conduct. Burton started out to write a psychological treatise, Professor Babb suggests, but his consideration of the comprehensive nature of the causes of melancholy caused him to move beyond physiology and formal psychology, and the primary theme of his book became the examination of the conditions of human life. He saw, too, that medical therapy dealt inadequately with the basic psychological and social causes of universal melancholy, and he therefore tried to set forth rational principles for the conduct of life and the reordering of society. Burton knew from experience that one did not arrive directly at peace of mind by positive thinking, and he avoided the snares which appeal to modern divines who would be physicians. His method was indirect, digressive, agglomerative, and his accumulating stories and quotations magnified follies into absurdity. Above all else, Burton knew that distressing thoughts must not be combatted but diverted. His own book, full of "dextrous interlarding" (the term is Anthony à Wood's), provided therapeutic diversion for himself and for his readers.

So, too, it is doubtful that Walton set out to produce a formal anatomy, that his love for good recipes and good talk has any direct relation to *The Deipnosophists* of Athenaeus. A recent study by John R. Cooper shows that the *Compleat Angler* can be read with profit in the context of the georgic, the pastoral, or the philosophical dialogue, but though all these exerted some pull on Walton, they were not uppermost in his mind. Walton says that he did not undertake to write the *Angler* to please himself; he was probably asked to write the book by his friend and publisher Richard Marriot, who so admired Thomas Barker's *The Art of Angling* that he bought the rights to it and published an edition even after he had published the *Angler*. It is likely that Marriot did not get quite what he wanted from Walton until the second edition of the *Angler*, when the text was increased by fifty per cent, most of it practical fishing instruction probably given to Walton by well-intentioned anglers. Walton himself modestly says in his prefatory address to the reader that he hopes to provide profit or pleasure, that he has made "a recreation, of a recreation," and that he has "in severall places mixt some innocent Mirth." The address is followed by a notice in which Walton says that he has "not observed a method" in his discourse, and for "easier finding out some particular things which are spoken of" he provides a table of contents by chapter to show what fish he has discussed. Since Walton says parenthetically in his address that "no man is born an *Artist* nor an *Angler*," his statement that he did not observe a method means only that he did not follow the logical method of practical instruction. For Walton, fishing was—his subtitle tells us—the contemplative man's recreation, and his interest in angling was as much philosophical as it was piscatorial. His purpose was didactic, but he was more interested in moral instruction than in fish: he was fishing for men's hearts and minds. Walton's "method" was to create an ideal world in which milkmaids sang like nightingales and in which fishermen had the fresh holiness of primitive Christians. To counteract the discord of the Puritan world he lived in, he presented Piscator's world of peace, patience, and calm content, where the catechism was plain and unperplexed, where the old Service Book was in use, where Kit Marlowe and Sir Walter Raleigh were writing "old fashioned

Poetry, but choicely good, . . . much better then that now in
fashion in this Critical age," where men cast off their business
and studied to be quiet.

The Anatomy of Melancholy is more than a treatise on melancholy written with style and the *Compleat Angler* is more than
an outmoded fishing manual written with verbal felicity. To
say this is not, of course, to deny that Burton and Walton were
interested in ideas and equally interested in rendering ideas
effectively. Both their books may be generally characterized as
Menippean satires or anatomies, but their genre is more accidental than purposeful. Each is a fictive work, a work made for
its own sake in the image of its maker. Burton might have said
with Walton that "the whole discourse is a kind of picture of
my owne disposition." Each book reflects its author, not the
divine who would be a physician, not the angler, but the whole
man; the subjects are not merely melancholy and angling but
these in the totality of the human condition. Each writer conceived a work not limited by its specialized subject, but, given
the nature of his outlook, extended the frame of the subject so
that it was more than professionally significant, of value to all
men. Each brought all his resources to bear on his book, not just
his reason and intelligence, but his imagination. And when
Walton qualified his statement that his book reflected his disposition by saying that the reflection held at least for "such
daies and times as I allow my self, when honest *Nat.* and R. R.
and I go a fishing together," he indicated that intelligence and
imagination were consciously tempered by artistic discipline and
control.

Like *The Anatomy of Melancholy* and *The Compleat Angler,*
Areopagitica, it is possible to say, was not designed with a
primarily literary intention, but Milton, like any cultivated
seventeenth-century author, would not have categorized his work
as "literary" and "non-literary." Milton was supremely aware of
the theory of genres; he differentiated the production of his
right hand from that of his left hand, but, after all, both derived from the same mind. His purpose in *Areopagitica* was
immediate and practical, but his mind conceived of his job in
terms of its universal relevance. He wrote a propagandistic
pamphlet, but his model was the classical oration. His outlook,

his frame of reference, made it improbable that he would write in a non-literary manner even about such subjects as licensing and divorce and education.

The prose masterpieces of the seventeenth century are, then, fictive works. To use Helen Gardner's criteria, they appeal to our intellects, to our sense of order and harmony, to our experience as human beings. Their appeal is rational, aesthetic, moral. Specialized though some of their subjects may be, they move beyond the logic and elegance which characterize the best writing "on" a subject; they have moral significance. In terms which the century took over from Augustine, they are books which make their appeal to man's rational soul: they jog the memory, increase the understanding, and influence the will. By so doing, they are directives toward that wisdom in man which is the image of the increate wisdom of God.

III

Some of the pedestrian writers of prose narratives in the seventeenth century may have thought that they too were writing such directives, but their feeble attempts were mundanely conceived; others were interested neither in this world nor in the next but in a titillating, exotic never-never land. As a genre, the prose narrative stagnated in the century. It is fair to say that it was not considered seriously as a literary form by serious men of letters. Milton would no more have thought of writing a novel than Chaucer of writing a play. The level of reality, the depth of characterization, the technical virtuosity in Aphra Behn's *The Wandring Beauty* of 1698 differ very little from those in Nicholas Breton's *Wit's Trenchmour*, written a century earlier, and, as a matter of fact, most of the novelistic works popular in the seventeenth century were written in the sixteenth; *Reynard the Fox*, which had ten issues or editions in the seventeenth century, was first printed by Caxton in 1481. It was not until the eighteenth century, when learning became increasingly specialized and professionalized and when it was no longer considered so intrinsically related to conduct, that the novel became a subtle exploratory instrument of moral philosophy. Still, to say that the seventeenth-century novel was not in-

terested in morality would be to mislead completely; it was interested in very little else. The trouble was that it sought to be
popularly moral, and, of course, it was moralistic.

The novel was not, however, the primary dispenser of popular
morality. It has been estimated that forty per cent of the books
printed in England between 1480 and 1640 were religious and
that the percentage was higher still between 1600 and 1640.
Increasingly, as it became necessary to gain popular support in
the controversies between Catholicism and Protestantism and
between Anglicanism and Nonconformity, theological disputations intended by learned commentators for others like themselves gave way to popular exposition, and doctrinal admonitions
and animadversions to moral guides. Arthur Dent's *Plain Man's
Pathway to Heaven* (1601) was reprinted thirty times in the
century; Bishop Lewis Bayly's *Practice of Piety*, published about
a decade later, seems to have gone through some seventy impressions and editions; Michael Sparke offered readers *Crumbs
of Comfort* about 1623 and the same crumbs were cast on the
waters forty-one times more in the next thirty-three years;
Richard Allestree's *The Whole Duty of Man* (1658) had at least
twenty-four impressions and editions before 1700. Plain and
familiar accounts of contemplations upon the principal passages
of Holy Story were turned into short rules for the good life.
The pensive man was told what to practice and he had a "practicall" catechism made for him. He could choose among innumerable devotions, meditations, cases of conscience, and manuals of
conduct, and he could not have digested or swallowed or even
tasted a small portion of the sermons which were printed. So
many books of divinity there were, Burton says, "so many commentators, treatises, pamphlets, expositions, sermons, that whole
teemes of oxen cannot draw them; and had I been as forward
and ambitious as some others, I might have haply printed a
sermon at *Pauls-Cross*, a sermon in St. *Maries Oxon*, a sermon
in *Christ-Church*, or a sermon before the right honorable, right
reverend, a sermon before the right worshipful, a sermon in
latine, in english, a sermon with a name, a sermon without,
a sermon, a sermon, &c. But I have been ever as desirous to suppresse my labours in this kinde, as others have been to presse
and publish theirs."

Even in 1590 Spenser had complained, in writing to Sir Walter
Raleigh about the *Faerie Queene*, that some readers "had rather
have good discipline delivered plainly in way of precepts, or
sermoned at large, as they use, then thus clowdily enwrapped
in Allegoricall devises." His allegorical romance was too sophisticated and too subtle for the growing middle class public. Although it had taken thirteen editions (and a sequel) of *Euphues,*
Lyly's weakly narrative discussion of morals and manners, to
satisfy gentlemanly and gentlewomanly readers between 1578
and the end of the century, ten editions took care of seventeenth-
century readers, and the last of these appeared in 1636. Sidney's
Arcadia was one of the most popular novelistic works of the
seventeenth century, but it was not reprinted in the last quarter
of the century. Its popularity points up the great demand for
romance (even fashionable readers were entranced by the
French heroic romances "whose heroes neither eat, nor drink,
nor sleep, for love," and "too much love can never be a fault");
it was not, however, strange and lurid enough, not exciting and
exotic enough for the middle class audience that clamored for
the chivalry of *Valentine and Orson,* Greene's *Pandosto,* Emanuel Forde's *Parismus* and *The Famous History of Montelyon,
Knight of the Oracle*, Richard Johnson's *Seven Champions of
Christendom*, and the exploits of Friar Bacon, Dr. Faustus, and
Jack of Newbury.

If the *Faerie Queene* was too cloudily enwrapped in allegorical devices for the taste of seventeenth-century readers, the
fables of Aesop were not. Some fifty English and Latin versions
and editions, the bulk of them printed after 1650, testify to the
popularity of the story with a moral. The old *Gesta Romanorum,*
a collection of pseudo-historical and pseudo-devotional tales,
remained in favor in Richard Robinson's sixteenth-century version. A little religious allegory, Richard Bernard's *Isle of Man*
(1626), with an exorbitant number of moral abstractions for
characters, had more editions in the century than any novelistic
work except *The Pilgrim's Progress*, in which, too, a transpar-
ently abstract conception utterly controls character. The very
title of John Reynolds' *The Triumphs of Gods Revenege Against
the Crying and Execrable Sinne of Murther* (1621) shows the
exploitation of narrative for moral purpose, and its five original

tales were added to, reprinted, imitated, pirated, and abridged.

So firmly rooted in the fabulous and the exemplary was the novelistic writing of the century that one would never guess from its novels that the century had any real interest in personality, in personal relationships, in character as it manifested itself in society. The tales and mere fables give no indication of the scope and depth of the achievement of Elizabethan and Jacobean poetry and drama as they probed the tics and tropisms of the individual man, as they examined the relations between one man and others, as they investigated the effect of a man on circumstances or of circumstances on a man. In *An Anatomie of the World*, Donne gave voice to the prevailing outlook that "every man alone thinkes he hath got / To be a Phoenix, and that there can bee / None of that kind, of which he is, but hee," and he did so in a poem so frequently interpreted as a personal tribute to Elizabeth Drury that he had to insist that he had "the Idea of a Woman" in mind. The dramatists explored the universal in the human predicament by insightful representation of the concrete and particular; they tested and qualified and illuminated the abstractions of morality by focusing not on "man," but on Lear or Volpone or Bosola or Penthea. The behavior of man was studied not alone on the road from Eden or on the pathway to heaven but in Mr. Frankford's home and at Bartholomew Fair. Conduct was not measured directly by moral categories but was examined in terms of manners, and sometimes conduct was measured by manners alone. Although the novelistic writing of the century produced only the crudest of narratives and the barest semblance of people (some of it the raw material of the drama), other prose genres, especially the essay, the character, and the biography, not only reflected contemporary interest in character and personality but provided means and methods for the exploration of man as a moral and social being.

If the intellectual efforts of the century seem to have been directed at remedying the deficiencies of knowledge which Bacon set forth in *The Advancement of Learning* (1605), so too the cultivation of particular prose genres may seem almost to have stemmed from Bacon's opinions and proposals. Bacon had said, "a substantiall and severe Collection of the *Heteroclites,* or *Irregulars* of *Nature,* well examined & described I find not: specially not with due rejection of fables, and popular Errors," and Sir Thomas Browne set out in *Pseudodoxia Epidemica* (1646) to fill that gap. In his *Holy and Profane State,* Fuller's concern for the principles of conduct, for practical divinity and even more practical secular behavior, seems to have stemmed from Bacon, but his aim was more didactic and ethical than analytic. Even Burton's *Anatomy of Melancholy* seems based in part on Bacon's statement that medicine considers the *"causes of Diseases, with the occasions or impulsions: The Diseases themselves,* with the *Accidents:* and the *Cures,* with the *Preservations"* and on his proposal that men examine *"how, and how farre the humours and affects of the bodie, doe alter or worke upon the mind;* or againe, *how and how farre the passions, or apprehensions of the minde, doe alter or worke upon the bodie";* but Burton had no real familiarity with Bacon's directions for learning nor was his approach the experimental one which Bacon advocated. Bacon's program for knowledge was seminal for some works, directive and suggestive for others. His relation to the development of the chief prose genres of the century was also of both kinds.

The end and term of natural philosophy, Bacon says, is the knowledge of ourselves, and in moral philosophy, as elsewhere, he advocates particularity and practicality, common sense and experience. Since he thinks that in studying moral philosophy, as in all things which are practical, "we ought to cast up our account, what is in our power, and what not," the first article of this knowledge is "to set downe Sound and true distributions and descriptions of the several characters & tempers of mens Natures and dispositions," and to Bacon this means an objective examination which includes knowing exactly "all the conditions of the *Serpent:* his basenesse and going upon his bellye, his volubility and lubricity, his envy and stinge, and the rest; that is all fourmes and Natures of evill." Bacon seems almost to be propounding a program for the character writers of the century, but he reveals an intent more precise and serious than theirs when he praises the poets and the writers of histories as the best doctors of the knowledge of the affections or passions: "where we may finde painted fourth with greate life, How affections are kindled and incyted: and how pacified and refrained: and how againe Conteyned from Act, & furder degree: how they disclose themselves, how they work, how they varye, how they gather and fortifie, how they are inwrapped one within another, and howe they doe fighte and encounter one with another." Again, the history of lives, Bacon says, excels the history of a time (a chronicle) in its profit and use, and well-written lives, "propounding to themselves a person to represent, in whom actions both greater and smaller, publique & private, have a commixture, must of necessitie containe a more true, native, and lively representation" than chronicles. Bacon would not limit the writing of lives to accounts of sovereign princes or absolute commanders; there are "many worthy personages, that deserve better then dispersed report, or barren *Elogies*." When he said, "I doe finde strange that these times have so little esteemed the vertues of the times, as that the Writings of lives should be no more frequent," he encouraged the examination of the lives of worthy men and gave justification for and impetus to the writing of biography.

For Bacon, moreover, Human Philosophy or Humanity has two parts: "The one considereth Man *segregate, or distributively:* The other *congregate* or *in societie,*" and he saw deficiencies particularly in one branch of what he called man's "conjugate" or "Civile" knowledge. "Conversation," or the wisdom of discreet social behavior, Bacon thought, had been sufficiently and elegantly handled, and "Government," or the wisdom of statecraft, had been in part examined, but "Negotiation," or the wisdom of business, had been neglected. Bacon focused, then, both in *The Advancement of Learning* and in his essays on providing insight into the affairs of the world, into all the occasions "incident to mans life." He even describes in *The Advancement* the method of his essays, though their method is *not* the one he praises most highly for an examination of ordinary human nature as it works in active daily life. The *fittest* form of writing about negotiation is, he says, "*discourse upon Histories or Examples,*" not parables, aphorisms, or fables. He prefers induction from particulars where "the discourse attendeth upon the Example," and since the written lives of men are particularly conversant in private actions, they are useful material for the discourse of business. Even more useful are wise and weighty letters, which afford more direct and particular representation of business than do lives. ("Letters of Affaires from such as Manage them, or are privie to them, are of all others the best instructions for History, and to a diligent reader, the best Histories in themselves," Bacon said, and he thought that the letters of wise men, whether they be "Advertisments, Advises, Directions, Propositions, Peticions, Commendatorie, Expostulatorie, Satisfactorie, of Complement, of Pleasure, of Discourse, and all other passages of Action," were the best of all the words of men.) In *The Advancement of Learning*, however, Bacon had illustrated the sort of knowledge he advocated about the affairs of men by quoting a number of the "sentences pollitique" of Solomon and by adding to them his own brief observations, though he thought that "it hath beene too much taken into Custome, out of a fewe *Axiomes* or Observations, uppon any Subjecte, to make a solemne, and formall Art; filling it with some Discourses, and illustratinge it with Examples; and digesting it into a sensible *Methode*." This description is not far removed from Bacon's approach to the essay in 1625, when he added to the title of his original *Essaies* the words *or Counsels, Civill and Morall;* some of his original anti-Ciceronian bias against method disappeared in his desire to persuade.

The first ten *Essaies* of 1597 were more aphoristic, as though Bacon had put together with a minimum of comment groups of related apophthegms taken from a commonplace book. The virtues of writing in aphorisms Bacon explained in *The Advancement:* they cannot be made "but of the pyth and heart of Sciences: for discourse of illustration is cut off, Recitalles of Examples are cut off: Discourse of Connexion and order is cut off; Descriptions of Practize are cutte off; So there remayneth nothinge to fill the *Aphorismes,* but some good quantitie of Observation: And therefore no man can suffice, nor in reason will attempt to write *Aphorismes,* but hee that is sound and grounded." Two further advantages of aphoristic writing are consonant with Bacon's preference for the Senecan mode: "*Methodes* are more fit to winne Consent or beleefe, but lesse fit to point to Action; for they carrie a kinde of Demonstration in

Orbe or Circle, one part illuminating another; and therefore
satisfie. But particulars beeing dispersed, doe best agree with
dispersed directions. And lastlye, *Aphorismes*, representing a
knowledge broken, doe invite men to enquire further; whereas
Methodes carrying the shewe of a Totall, doe secure men, as if
they were at furthest." Bacon originally intended his essays as
invitations to further inquiry and as pointers to action. For him
the essay was an analytic tool which probed by virtue of its con-
centrated insight, original or derived. His essays are, therefore,
objective and detached (in outlook as well as in style), and their
pragmatism and expediency are rooted in what he considered
to be the wisdom of the ancients and in his own cool observation of men as he saw them in the world of affairs. When Bacon
thought to dedicate the *Essaies* of 1612 to Prince Henry, he said
of the term "essay," "The word is late, but the thing is auncient.
For *Senacaes* Epistles to *Lucilius*, yf one marke them well, are
but *Essaies*,—That is dispersed Meditacons, thoughe conveyed
in the forme of Epistles." The phrase "dispersed Meditacons,"
echoing as it does the "particulars beeing dispersed" Bacon had
used to describe aphorisms in *The Advancement,* is an indication that he conceived of the essay as encapsulated wisdom,
that he meant something different from Dr. Johnson when
Johnson defined the essay as "a loose sally of the mind; an
irregular indigested piece; not a regular and orderly composition."

Johnson had in mind the numerous tentative speculations
about this or that which flourished late in the seventeenth century (and perhaps also the essays of Addison, Steele, and Pope),
the forbears of our modern As-I-Like-It pieces of literary criticism, newspaper editorials, syndicated columns, and magazine
articles, which stemmed more or less from *Les Essaies* of Montaigne. Bacon had merely used Montaigne's term; it is likely that
he would have wanted experimental evidence for Montaigne's
statement that "chaque homme porte la forme entiere de l'hu-
maine condition" [2] and his aim was far from Montaigne's "je
me suis presenté moy-mesmes à moy, pour argument et pour
subject." [3] Late in 1600, however, Sir William Cornwallis wrote

---

[2] Each man has in himself the entire configuration of the human condition.
[3] I presented myself to myself as argument and as subject.

in the first of his *Essayes,* "Truly, I neede no other example
then myne owne life," and, despite his debts to Seneca and
Plato, the familiar, personal, confessional essay was born in
England. "I holde," Cornwallis wrote in "Of Essaies and Bookes"
(1601), "neither *Plutarche's* nor none of those auncient short
manner of writings nor *Montaigne's* nor such of this latter time
to bee rightly tearmed Essayes; for though they be short, yet
they are strong and able to endure the sharpest tryall. But mine
are Essayes, who am but newly bound Prentise to the inquisition
of knowledge and use these papers as a Painter's boy a board,
that is trying to bring his hand and his fancie acquainted. It is
a maner of writing wel befitting undigested motions, or a head
not knowing his strength." The discursive self-revelatory essay
is, however, far less frequent in the century than the short
piece of personal opinion made as strong as possible to endure
sharp trial, the small discourse which persuades to piety, or the
short argument which demonstrates the wit of the writer. Meditations and contemplations, reflections and resolves, paradoxes
and problems are all related to the essayistic tendency of the
century.

Much of the epistolary writing of the century is also related
to the essay, for many of its letters are hardly so familiar as
their headings and closes would seem to indicate. Joseph Hall
wrote in 1607 when he dedicated his *Epistles* to Prince Henry,
"Your Grace shal herein perceive a new fashion of discourse,
by Epistles; new to our language, usual to others: and (as
Noveltie is never without some plea of use) more free, more
familiar. Thus, we do but talke with our friends by our pen,
and expresse our selves no whit lesse easily; some-what more
digestedly." Two-thirds of Hall's letters deal with religious questions and he is far more interested in getting published his
opinions on various matters than he is in the person to whom
he addresses a letter. Donne differentiated the familiar letter
from homilies and meditations, "apparitions, and ghosts" of
letters, and the publication in 1651 of his *Letters to Severall
Persons of Honour* (and in 1659 of Suckling's identically entitled volume) reflects contemporary interest in the familiar
letter, but many of Donne's letters are beautifully contrived
essays, and a handful of them was first published with his

Poems (1633) as examples of epistolary elegance, almost as a manual of cultivated courtly letter writing. Formularies which treated letter writing as a legitimate branch of the study of rhetoric were, of course, popular in the Renaissance (they were used in seventeenth-century schools), and the first manual of letter writing in England, William Fulwood's *The Enimie of Idleness* (1586), thoroughly derivative though it was, had gone through nine editions by 1621. Original "presidentiall" letters, which provided precedents for imitation, were introduced into the manual by Angel Day in his *The English Secretorie* (1586); it is a short step to Nicholas Breton's *A Poste with a Packet of Madde Letters* (1602) where the intent is more to amuse than to instruct. Breton's rather puerile and unwitty volume was reprinted throughout the century, but with the publication in 1640 of John Massinger's *The Secretary in Fashion* (a translation of Jean Puget de la Serre's *Le Secretaire à la Mode*), the fashionable letter book emphasized the rules of civility and the art of gentlemanly elegance. The continued popularity of the manuals in the century (and by its end there were even texts for business letters) shows the receptiveness of the century to the epistolary form, and the success which Howell's *Familiar Letters* achieved might have been predicted from the vogue earlier in the century for transcribing and collecting familiar letters by eminent hands along with copies of poems. Like Joseph Hall, Howell was not so much interested in writing epistles as he was in making use of the epistolary form. He exploited his readers' desire for an awareness of the person behind the words, for the presentation of information and instruction in a form that seemed natural and immediate. It is no wonder, then, that before the end of the century, even tracts and arguments were being cast into epistolary form. In 1662, the Bishop of Winchester vindicated himself from the calumny of Richard Baxter in a "Letter to a Friend," and the distempers of the present time were discussed in modest and peaceable letters from a quiet and conformable citizen of London to two busy and factious shopkeepers in Coventry. Milton on education, Sanderson on the case of the liturgy, Locke on toleration, Dryden on all the literary concerns in his dedications and prefaces—all used the epistolary form, and John Evelyn was either applying a very limited view or an impossibly high standard when he wrote about 1690 (in a letter) that there were "few tolerable letters of our own country."

The character was the most idiosyncratic and most popular minor prose genre of the century, but it has affinities to the essay at one extreme and to biography at the other. In what may have been the first English book of characters published, *Characters of Vertues and Vices* (1608), Joseph Hall, who was as adept at spotting a new trend for sophisticated readers as Breton was for a more general public, reveals that he sometimes regarded his characters of virtues as abstractions, as definitions of virtues rather than as portraits of kinds of virtuous men. In his table of contents, some of his titles resemble Bacon's: *"Of True-Friendship," "Of Faith," "Character of Wisdome"*; in his text he used more personal forms: *"The True Friend,"* "The Characterism of the *Faithfull man,"* "Character of the Wise Man." Donne's "Essay of Valour" was printed with the Overburian characters (see p. 517), and John Earle's collection of characters, *Micro-cosmographie,* was subtitled *a Peece of the World Discovered in Essayes and Characters.* The genre of the character had been well established by Theophrastus when he wrote his thirty sketches of moral qualities embodied in representative Athenian figures early in the third century B.C.: he briefly defined the dominant quality of the character and related objectively, through significant detail, what he did, what he said, what he looked like. The Overburian description of "What a Character Is" (1616) already mentioned squaring out a character "by our English levell," and a "pure" character is a rarity; the character was alternately realistic or romantic, witty or didactic or both. The character by our English level moved from that of Theophrastus in two main ways. First, Hall's "The Good Magistrate" broadened the range of the character by dealing with a "virtue" and with a type in a particular position in society rather than one dominated by a particular quality (all the surviving sketches of Theophrastus characterize "vices" and only one deals with social place), and increasingly the English character examined social and professional types and civil business in their relation to morality. Second, either because the English character writers recognized what they shared with Jonson in his ex-

posure of humours and affectations or because their standard
of good was not Theophrastus' temperate man of the golden
mean but the idealized man of Christian ethics, they exploited
satire and wit, and they did so with such generosity that they
called attention to what they were doing. Within two years of
its appearance, Hall's book was translated into French, the first
English book of literary interest to be accorded such recognition.
Earle's original collection of fifty-four (in 1628) had grown to
seventy-eight by 1633 and was printed a dozen times in the
century. The twenty-one characters in the Overburian collection
of 1614 grew to eighty-two in the eleventh impression (1622)
and had gone through seventeen impressions by 1664; in the
following year, a book by Ralph Johnson gave rules to school-
boys interested in making characters. It is impossible to estimate
the number produced in the century, but they appear wherever
one looks—in prose and in verse: Cleveland on a London diurnal, Marvell on Holland, Evelyn on England, Glanvill on a
coffee-house, Halifax on a trimmer, Sir Kenelm Digby on his
wife, Traherne on the "less Principal Vertues," "Hudibras"
Butler on two hundred subjects, even Milton in "L'Allegro" and
"Il Penseroso," and Dryden on Zimri and company.

In its diagnosis and analysis of traits, the character was
primarily an instrument of moral philosophy or of social criticism, but it got at morals through manners and it relied on
portraiture. Its details of action and speech were generally ordered to illustrate an ideal of goodness or badness, but they
managed also to vivify a type. Its purpose was most often judgment of a type, but its particularity fostered recognition of an
individual. In its increasing concern with follies rather than
vices, in its increasing emphasis on lapses from rational standards of civilized behavior, it provoked interest in ephemeral sub-
types of men. So it would seem to be close to biography. Still, its
primary focus was on static types, not on individual temperament; it encouraged too neat an explanation of character as well
as the blurring of individuality when it heightened various colors
"by one shadowing"; and it led some writers to believe that a
biography could be easily constructed by merely tacking a character to a chronicle.

It is difficult to evaluate the interplay between the character and biography because the character, though it started as a relatively fixed genre, was not only fiercely exploited but also became a habitual mode of thought. On the other hand, the many varieties of biography were expressive of a movement toward a genre. Only when a form or concept attains some measure of individuality and independence does it demand a new description, and the word "biography" did not enter the language until 1661. When Bishop Gauden first used the term "biographers" in 1662, he placed parentheses about it and defined it as writers of lives, and still the word was so strange to the printer that he spelled it "Biogrrphers." The medieval view of life-writing made it an ancillary of religion and of history, and the hagiographic impulse to use lives as examples of holy living and holy dying continued into the seventeenth century; so, too, historiographers tended to equate the story of a king with the history of his reign and to moralize on the fall of illustrious men. Occasionally, writers represented the details of individual temperament so vividly or delineated character through events so successfully that they broke through the conventional frames, as in the sixteenth century George Cavendish had in his *Life of Cardinal Wolsey* and William Roper in his *Life of Sir Thomas More*. It was not mere accident, however, that these lives were not printed until the seventeenth century. Fuller was responsive to his time when he wrote *The History of the Worthies of England* (published 1662) and also when he announced that he did so not only to gain some glory to God, to memorialize the dead and provide examples for the living, but also to entertain his reader with delight and—he was not ashamed to profess publicly—to procure some honest profit for himself.

The increasing esteem which the century had for biography is evident in the story of the publication of Walton's lives. He wrote his *Life of Donne* because he thought that Donne's sermons ought not be published without the customary life, and his seventeen folio pages are a preface to the 826 pages of *LXXX Sermons* (1640). His *Life of Sir Henry Wotton* was also a prefatory life, overshadowed by the bulk of Wotton's literary remains in *Reliquiae Wottonianae* (1651; other editions in 1654, 1672, 1685). In 1658, Walton's publisher prevailed upon him to allow the publication of the *Life of Donne* without the support of Donne's sermons, and this expanded and revised life was the first of Walton's lives put forth independently. Walton's life of Hooker was commissioned by Archbishop Sheldon, and it is clearly the main item in the volume called *The Life of Mr. Rich. Hooker* (1665), though there is some supplementary material not by Walton. His life of Hooker was so much esteemed as a fitting representation of the man (and as a proper assessment of the authenticity of various books of the *Ecclesiasticall Polity*) that it replaced Bishop Gauden's life as a preface to Hooker's *Works* (1666; reprinted 1676 and 1682). The *Life of Herbert* Walton had written to be included in a projected collection of his *Lives* (1670), but the publisher first issued it independently, probably without Walton's knowledge, and it was used, too, this time with Walton's permission, as an introduction to Herbert's *The Temple* (10th ed., 1674; 11th eds., 1678 [1679] and 1695). The collection of four lives was successful enough to warrant another edition in 1675. Walton's last life, the *Life of Dr. Sanderson, Late Bishop of Lincoln,* was independently published in 1678 (and here some of Sanderson's tracts provide supplementary evidence for points raised by the *Life*), and it prefaced editions of Sanderson's *Sermons* in 1681 and 1686 (re-issued 1689). The progression from mere adjunct to an intrinsically valuable property, from preface to the dignity of a collection, reflects, to be sure, the growth of Walton's own reputation as a writer, but it reflects, too, the change in the status of biography in the century.

Anthony à Wood tells us that John Hales, "the best critic of the last age," affirmed that "he had not seen a life written with more advantage to the subject, or more reputation to the writer" than Walton's *Life of Donne*. That life is, by the time Walton had revised it three times, his closest approach to hagiography; his purpose in biography was always didactic, but his aim was generally more polemical than ethical and each life after the *Donne* had a thesis. In the *Wotton,* Walton sought to present in the 1650's a lesson about the evils of religious wrangling; in the *Hooker,* he wrote a corrective of Gauden's portrait, claimed Hooker as a champion of the High Church, and pulled Hooker's doctrines into harmony with those of the Restoration Church; Herbert is the prototype of the good parson, and Walton wrote a guide to the practices and obligations of a minister and an argument proving that the Church was a worthy profession for men of the highest station, education, and abilities; the *Sanderson* demonstrates the past and present dangers of Nonconformity. Walton's theses, however, do not generally usurp the position of importance in the *Lives*, nor do they invalidate his portraiture. The polemical cast of the *Lives* drove him more than an ethical purpose would have toward respect for significant narrative and accurate detail. If his detail is sometimes not so arresting as Aubrey's (and no one's is), it is yet concrete and illuminating, and his awareness of the need for chronological development and his insight into fact made it possible for him to write lives rather than sketches and mere remarks. Walton's probings into temperament were limited both by his own emotional and intellectual capacities and by the age's relatively uncomplex formal psychology, but we recognize his subjects as persons. That, for him, affection was pre-requisite to biography, that his point of view seems to us idealized so that the lives are panegyrical, are not such deficiencies as we may suppose, for his view of man was still characteristic in his time, though that view was changing. The century never arrived at the point of believing that men were not merely human, but all too human; it never produced the Stracheyan biography of belittlement, but it took a step in that direction. Dryden, indeed, was merely making a distinction between history and biography when he said in 1683 (in his *Life of Plutarch*) that in history "you are conducted only into the rooms of state" and that in biography "you are led into the private Lodgings of the Heroe: You see him in his undress, and are made familiar with his most private actions and conversations. . . . The Pageantry of Life is taken away; you see the poor reasonable Animal, as naked as ever nature made him; are made acquainted with his Passions and his Follies, and find the *Demy-God* a *Man*." Dryden's view of men gives us back our own picture, but it goes some way toward explaining why he felt that Nature had to be exalted, consciously "wrought up to a higher pitch" in a serious drama. And it starts to explain, too, why the result of such an attitude and such a procedure could produce in Almanzor only a papier-mâché Achilles.

IV

When Bacon applied the wisdom of Solomon to civil business, he made quite clear his awareness that the same wisdom might be applied "to a more divine use." He saw, too, that "morrall Philosophye propoundeth to it selfe the framing of Internall goodnesse: But civile knowledge requireth onelye an Externall goodnesse." And he said that "such as are accomplished in that honor of urbanity, please themselves in name, and seldome aspire to higher vertue"; focus on discretion of behavior was, for him, "a great Theefe of Meditation." When he made his analysis of the "small Globe of the Intellectuall world," he did not consider it complete until he surveyed the realm of divinity, "the Sabaoth and port of all mens labours and peregrinations." Bacon's own work exemplifies the premium which the earlier part of the century placed on both "compleat-ness" and "anatomy." Even in religion, however, the catholicism and comprehensiveness that Donne sought in satire and in sonnet had devolved to Catholicism and to Comprehension, and even Comprehension was limited to the embracing of particular sects on uncompromising terms. When Donne wrote his *Anatomie of the World,* he had one eye on the progress of the soul. In character, in essay, in biography, the focus narrowed to an anatomy of man, often without the breadth of the examinations by Earle and Bacon. The concerns of Mr. Pepys in his diary, his marvelous zest for the things of this world (despite an occasional "God forgive me"), and his magnificently reportorial outlook (which glosses over the deficiency of his imagination) are far more typical of the times than the concerns and outlook of *Grace Abounding* and far more representative of the marginalia of literature in which the century is so rich.

Of these, we may say gratefully what Browne said of his urns: "Time which antiquates Antiquities, and hath an art to make dust of all things, hath yet spared these *minor* Monuments." The prose literature of the century is not, however, to be measured by the remnants of history, the private records and evidences which have casually escaped the shipwreck of time, charming though these may be. Nor is it to be measured solely by its popular prose genres, for these might persuade us that writers agreed with Samuel Daniel when he said, "I had rather be Maister of a small peece handsomely contrived, than of vaste roomes ill proportioned and unfurnished." Daniel's alternatives express his own trouble with large structures; they are not the only possible ones. The century's respect for vast rooms is evident even in a selective list of the men whose works were wholly or in part made into English: Homer and Virgil; Plato and Aeschylus; Augustine and Boethius; Boccaccio, Machiavelli, and Tasso; Rabelais and Montaigne; Cervantes; Corneille, Racine, Molière. In poetry and in drama, in *Paradise Lost* and in *Lear* and in *Volpone*, its own vastest rooms were proportioned and furnished beyond compare. Its primary genius is here, but it has its share, too, of major prose monuments produced by men who refused to diminish their dimension.[4]

4 I am particularly indebted in the Introduction to the following works: Douglas Bush, *English Literature in the Earlier Seventeenth Century*, 2nd ed. (Oxford, 1962); Morris W. Croll, "The Baroque Style in Prose," in *Studies in English Philology: A Miscellany in Honor of Frederick Klaeber*, ed. Kemp Malone and Martin B. Rudd (Minneapolis, 1929); Northrop Frye, *Anatomy of Criticism* (Princeton, 1957); Charles C. Mish, "Best Sellers in Seventeenth-Century Fiction," *Papers of the Bibliographical Society of America*, XLVII (1953), 356–373; Jean Robertson, *The Art of Letter Writing* (London, 1942); James Sutherland, *On English Prose* (Toronto, 1957).

I

Francis Bacon

FROM

The Essayes or Counsels,
Civill and Morall

OF TRUTH

I

What *is Truth;* said jesting *Pilate;* And would not stay for an Answer. Certainly there be, that delight in Giddinesse; And count it a Bondage, to fix a Beleefe; Affecting§ Free-will in Thinking, as well as in Acting. And though the Sects of Philosophers of that Kinde[1] be gone, yet there remaine certaine discoursing§ Wits, which are of the same veines, though there be not so much Bloud in them, as was in those of the Ancients. But it is not onely the Difficultie, and Labour, which Men take in finding out of *Truth;* Nor againe, that when it is found, it imposeth§ upon mens Thoughts; that doth bring *Lies* in favour: But a naturall,

[1] The Greek Skeptics.

though corrupt Love, of the *Lie* it selfe. One of the later Schoole
of the Grecians, examineth the matter, and is at a stand,[§] to
thinke what should be in it, that men should love *Lies;* Where
neither they make for Pleasure, as with Poets; Nor for Advantage, as with the Merchant; but for the *Lies* sake. But I cannot
tell: This same *Truth*, is a Naked, and Open day light, that doth
not shew, the Masques, and Mummeries, and Triumphs[§] of the
world, halfe so Stately, and daintily, as Candle-lights. *Truth* may
perhaps come to the price of a Pearle, that sheweth best by day:
But it will not rise, to the price of a Diamond, or Carbuncle, that
sheweth best in varied lights. A mixture of a *Lie* doth ever adde
Pleasure. Doth any man doubt, that if there were taken out of
Mens Mindes, Vaine Opinions, Flattering Hopes, False valua-
tions, Imaginations as[§] one would, and the like; but it would
leave the Mindes, of a Number of Men, poore shrunken Things;
full of Melancholy, and Indisposition, and unpleasing to themselves? One of the Fathers, in great Severity, called Poesie,
Vinum Dæmonum;[2] because it filleth the Imagination, and yet
it is, but with the shadow of a *Lie*. But it is not the *Lie*, that
passeth through the Minde, but the *Lie* that sinketh in, and
setleth in it, that doth the hurt, such as we spake of before. But
howsoever these things are thus, in mens depraved Judgements,
and Affections,[§] yet *Truth*, which onely doth judge it selfe,
teacheth, that the Inquirie of *Truth*, which is the Love-making,
or Wooing of it; The knowledge of *Truth*, which is the Presence
of it; and the Beleefe of *Truth*, which is the Enjoying of it; is
the Soveraigne Good of humane Nature. The first Creature of
God, in the workes of the Dayes, was the Light of the Sense; The
last, was the Light of Reason; And his Sabbath Worke, ever since,
is the Illumination of his Spirit. First he breathed Light, upon
the Face, of the Matter or Chaos; Then he breathed Light, into
the Face of Man; and still[§] he breatheth and inspireth Light,
into the Face of his Chosen. The Poet, that beautified the Sect,[3]
that was otherwise inferiour to the rest, saith yet excellently
well: *It is a pleasure to stand upon the shore, and to see ships
tost upon the Sea: A pleasure to stand in the window of a Castle,
and to see a Battaile, and the Adventures thereof, below: But*

---

2 The wine of devils.
3 The Epicurean poet, Lucretius.

no pleasure is comparable, to the standing, upon the vantage ground of Truth: (A hill not to be commanded,§ and where the Ayre is alwaies cleare and serene;) *And to see the Errours, and Wandrings, and Mists, and Tempests, in the vale below:* So alwaies, that this prospect, be with Pitty, and not with Swelling, or Pride. Certainly, it is Heaven upon Earth, to have a Mans Minde Move in Charitie, Rest in Providence, and Turne upon the Poles of *Truth.*

To passe from Theologicall, and Philosophicall *Truth,* to the *Truth* of civill Businesse; It will be acknowledged, even by those, that practize it not, that cleare and Round§ dealing, is the Honour of Mans Nature; And that Mixture of Falshood, is like Allay in Coyne of Gold and Silver; which may make the Metall worke the better, but it embaseth it. For these winding, and crooked courses, are the Goings of the Serpent; which goeth basely upon the belly, and not upon the Feet. There is no Vice, that doth so cover a Man with Shame, as to be found false, and perfidious. And therefore *Mountaigny* saith prettily, when he enquired the reason, why the word of the *Lie,* should be such a Disgrace, and such an Odious Charge? Saith he, *If it be well weighed, To say that a man lieth, is as much to say, as that he is brave towards God, and a Coward towards men.* For a *Lie* faces God, and shrinkes from Man. Surely the Wickednesse of Falshood, and Breach of Faith, cannot possibly be so highly expressed, as in that it shall be the last Peale, to call the Judgements of God, upon the Generations of Men, It being foretold, that when Christ commeth, *He shall not find Faith upon the Earth.*

OF DEATH

II

Men feare *Death,* as Children feare to goe in the darke: And as that Natural Feare in Children, is increased with Tales, so is the other. Certainly, the Contemplation of *Death,* as the *wages of sinne,* and Passage to another world, is Holy, and Religious; But the Feare of it, as a Tribute due unto Nature, is weake. Yet in Religious Meditations, there is sometimes, Mixture of Vanitie, and of Superstition. You shal reade, in some of the Friars Books

of *Mortification,* that a man should thinke with himselfe, what
the Paine is, if he have but his Fingers end Pressed, or Tortured;
And thereby imagine, what the Paines of *Death* are, when the
whole Body, is corrupted and dissolved; when many times, *Death*
passeth with lesse paine, then the Torture of a Limme: For the
most vitall parts, are not the quickest of Sense.§ And by him,
that spake onely as a Philosopher, and Naturall Man, it was well
said; *Pompa Mortis magis terret, quàm Mors ipsa.*[4] Groanes and
Convulsions, and a discoloured Face, and Friends weeping, and
Blackes, and Obsequies, and the like, shew *Death* Terrible. It is
worthy the observing, that there is no passion in the minde of
man, so weake, but it Mates,§ and Masters, the Feare of *Death:*
And therefore Death, is no such terrible Enemie, when a man
hath so many Attendants, about him, that can winne the combat of him. *Revenge* triumphs over *Death; Love* slights it; *Honour* aspireth to it; *Griefe* flieth to it; *Feare* pre-occupateth§ it;
Nay we reade, after *Otho* the Emperour had slaine himselfe,
Pitty (which is the tenderest of Affections) provoked many to
die, out of meere compassion to their Soveraigne, and as the
truest sort of Followers. Nay *Seneca* addes *Nicenesse*§ and *Saciety;*§ *Cogita quam diù eadem feceris; Mori velle, non tantùm
Fortis, aut Miser, sed etiàm Fastidiosus potest.*[5] A man would die,
though he were neither valiant, nor miserable, onely upon a
wearinesse to doe the same thing, so oft over and over. It is no
lesse worthy to observe, how little Alteration, in good Spirits,
the Approaches of *Death* make; for they appeare, to be the
same Men, till the last Instant. *Augustus Cæsar* died in a Complement; *Livia, Conjugii nostri memor, vive & vale.*[6] *Tiberius* in
dissimulation; As *Tacitus* saith of him; *Jam Tiberium Vires,
& Corpus, non Dissimulatio, deserebant.*[7] *Vespasian* in a Jest;
Sitting upon the Stoole,§ *Ut puto Deus fio.*[8] *Galba* with a Sentence;§ *Feri, si ex re sit populi Romani;*[9] Holding forth his
Necke. *Septimius Severus* in dispatch; *Adeste, si quid mihi restat*

---

[4] The accompaniments of death are more frightful than death itself. (Bacon is
probably thinking of Seneca.)
[5] Consider how long you have done the same thing; a man may wish to die not
only because he is brave, or wretched, but also because he is disdainful of life.
[6] Livia, mindful of our married life, live on, and fare thee well.
[7] His physical powers were leaving Tiberius, but not his power of dissimulation.
[8] As I think (*or* cleanse myself), I am becoming a god.
[9] Strike, if it is for the good of the Roman people.

agendum.[1] And the like. Certainly, the *Stoikes* bestowed too much cost§ upon *Death*, and by their great preparations, made it appeare more fearefull. Better saith he, *Qui Finem Vitæ extremum inter Munera ponat Naturæ.*[2] It is as Naturall to die, as to be borne; And to a little Infant, perhaps, the one, is as painfull, as the other. He that dies in an earnest Pursuit, is like one that is wounded in hot Bloud; who, for the time, scarce feeles the Hurt; And therefore, a Minde fixt, and bent upon somewhat, that is good, doth avert the Dolors of *Death:* But above all, beleeve it, the sweetest Canticle is, *Nunc dimittis;*[3] when a Man hath obtained worthy Ends, and Expectations. *Death* hath this also; That it openeth the Gate, to good Fame, and extinguisheth Envie.

—*Extinctus amabitur idem.*[4]

OF ADVERSITIE

V

It was an high speech of *Seneca*, (after the manner of the Stoickes) *That the good things, which belong to Prosperity, are to be wished; but the good things, that belong to Adversity, are to be admired. Bona Rerum Secundarum, Optabilia; Adversarum, Mirabilia.* Certainly if Miracles, be the Command over Nature, they appeare most in Adversity. It is yet a higher speech of his, then the other, (much too high for a Heathen) *It is true greatnesse, to have in one, the Frailty of a Man, & the Security of a God. Verè magnum, habere Fragilitatem Hominis, Securitatem Dei.* This would have done better in Poesy; where Transcendences are more allowed. And the Poets indeed, have beene busy with it; For it is, in effect, the thing, which is figured§ in that Strange Fiction, of the Ancient Poets, which seemeth not to be without mystery; Nay, and to have some approach, to the State of a Christian: That *Hercules, when hee went to unbinde Prometheus,* (by whom Human Nature is represented) *sailed the length of the great Ocean, in an Earthen Pot, or Pitcher:*

1 Come quickly if there is more for me to do.
2 Who considers the end of life as one of nature's gifts.
3 Now lettest thou thy servant depart in peace.
4 The same man will be loved when he's dead.

Lively§ describing Christian Resolution; that faileth, in the fraile
Barke of the Flesh, thorow the Waves of the World. But to
speake in§ a Meane. The Vertue of *Prosperitie*, is Temperance;
The Vertue of *Adversity*, is Fortitude: which in Morals is the
more Heroicall Vertue. *Prosperity* is the Blessing of the Old
Testament; *Adversity* is the Blessing of the New; which carrieth
the greater Benediction, and the Clearer Revelation of Gods
Favour. Yet, even in the old Testament, if you Listen to *Davids*
Harpe, you shall heare as many Herselike Ayres, as Carols: And
the Pencill of the holy Ghost, hath laboured more, in describing,
the Afflictions of *Job*, than the Felicities of *Salomon*. *Prosperity*
is not without many Feares and Distastes;§ And *Adversity* is not
without Comforts and Hopes. Wee see in Needle-workes, and
Imbroideries, It is more pleasing, to have a Lively Worke, upon
a Sad and Solemne Grounde; then to have a Darke and Melancholy Worke, upon a Lightsome Ground: Judge therfore, of
the Pleasure of the Heart, by the Pleasure of the Eye. Certainly,
Vertue is like pretious Odours, most fragrant, when they are
incensed,§ or crushed: For *Prosperity* doth best discover Vice;
But *Adversity* doth best discover Vertue.

OF PARENTS AND CHILDREN

VII

The Joyes of *Parents* are Secret; And so are their Griefes, and
Feares: They cannot utter the one; Nor they will not utter the
other. *Children* sweeten Labours; But they make Misfortunes
more bitter: They increase the Cares of Life; but they mitigate
the Remembrance of Death. The Perpetuity by Generation is
common to Beasts; But Memory, Merit, and Noble workes, are
proper to Men: And surely a Man shall see, the Noblest workes,
and Foundations, have proceeded from *Childlesse Men*; which
have sought to expresse the Images of their Minds; where those
of their Bodies have failed: So the care of Posterity, is most in
them, that have no Posterity. They that are the first Raisers of
their Houses, are most Indulgent towards their *Children*; Beholding them, as the Continuance, not only of their kinde, but
of their Worke; And so both *Children*, and *Creatures*.

The difference in Affection, of *Parents*, towards their severall *Children*, is many times unequall; And sometimes unworthy; Especially in the *mother;* As Salomon saith; *A wise sonne re-joyceth the Father; but an ungracious sonne shames the Mother.* A Man shall see, where there is a House full of *Children*, one or two, of the Eldest, respected, and the Youngest made wantons; But in the middest, some that are, as it were forgotten, who, many times, neverthelesse, prove the best. The Illiberalitie[§] of *Parents*, in allowance towards their *Children*, is an harmefull Errour; Makes them base; Acquaints them with Shifts;[§] Makes them sort[§] with meane Company; And makes them surfet more, when they come to Plenty: And therefore, the Proofe is best, when Men keepe their Authority towards their *Children*, but not their Purse. Men have a foolish manner (both *Parents*, and Schoole-masters, and Servants) in creating and breeding an Emulation between Brothers, during *Childhood*, which many times sorteth to Discord, when they are Men; And disturbeth Families. The *Italians* make little difference betweene *Children*, and Nephewes, or neere Kinsfolkes; But so they be of the Lumpe, they care not, though they passe not through their owne Body. And, to say Truth, in Nature, it is much a like matter; In so much, that we see a Nephew, sometimes, resembleth an Uncle, or a Kinsman, more then his owne *Parent;* As the Bloud happens. Let *Parents* choose betimes, the Vocations, and Courses, they meane their Children should take; For then they are most flexible; And let them not too much apply themselves, to the Disposition of their *Children*, as thinking they will take best to that, which they have most Minde to. It is true, that if the Affection or Aptnesse of the *Children*, be Extraordinary, then it is good, not to crosse it; But generally, the Precept is good; *Optimum elige, suave & facile illud faciet Consuetudo.*[5] *Younger Brothers* are commonly Fortunate, but seldome or never, where the *Elder* are disinherited.

[5] Choose the best; habit will make it pleasant and easy.

OF MARRIAGE AND SINGLE LIFE
VIII

He that hath *Wife* and *Children,* hath given Hostages to Fortune; For they are Impediments, to great Enterprises, either of Vertue, or Mischiefe. Certainly, the best workes, and of greatest Merit for the Publike, have proceeded from the *unmarried,* or *Childlesse Men;* which, both in Affection, and Meanes, have married and endowed the Publike. Yet it were great Reason, that those that have *Children,* should have greatest care of future times; unto which, they know, they must transmit, their dearest pledges.

Some there are, who though they lead a *Single Life,* yet their Thoughts doe end with themselves, and account future Times, Impertinences.[§] Nay, there are some other, that account *Wife* and *Children,* but as Bills of charges. Nay more, there are some foolish rich covetous Men, that take a pride in having no *Children,* because they may be thought, so much the richer. For perhaps, they have heard some talke; *Such an one is a great rich Man;* And another except to it; *Yea, but he hath a great charge of Children:* As if it were an Abatement to his Riches. But the most ordinary cause of a *Single Life,* is Liberty; especially, in certaine Selfe-pleasing, and humorous[§] Mindes, which are so sensible of every restraint, as they will goe neare, to thinke their Girdles, and Garters, to be Bonds and Shackles. *Unmarried Men* are best Friends; best Masters; best Servants; but not alwayes best Subjects; For they are light to runne away; And almost all Fugitives are of that Condition. A *Single Life* doth well with Church men: For Charity will hardly water the Ground, where it must first fill a Poole. It is indifferent for Judges and Magistrates: For if they be facile,[§] and corrupt, you shall have a Servant, five times worse than a *Wife.* For Souldiers, I finde the Generalls commonly in their Hortatives, put Men in minde of their *Wives and Children.* And I thinke the Despising of *Marriage,* amongst the Turkes, maketh the vulgar souldier more base. Certainly, *Wife* and *Children,* are a kinde of Discipline of Humanity: And *single Men,* though they be many times more Charitable, because their Meanes are lesse exhaust;

yet, on the other side, they are more cruell, and hard hearted, (good to make severe Inquisitors) because their Tendernesse, is not so oft called upon. Grave Natures, led by Custome, and therfore constant, are commonly loving *Husbands;* As was said of *Ulysses; Vetulam suam prætulit Immortalitati.*[6] Chast Women are often Proud, and froward,§ as Presuming upon the merit of their Chastity. It is one of the best Bonds, both of Chastity and Obedience, in the *Wife,* if She thinke her *Husband* Wise; which She will never doe, if She finde him *Jealous. Wives* are young Mens Mistresses; Companions for middle Age; and old Mens Nurses. So as a Man may have a Quarrell§ to marry, when he will. But yet, he was reputed one of the wise Men, that made Answer to the Question; When a Man should marry? *A young Man not yet, an Elder Man not at all.* It is often seene, that bad *Husbands,* have very good *Wives;* whether it be, that it rayseth the Price of their *Husbands* Kindnesse, when it comes; Or that the *Wives* take a Pride, in their Patience. But this never failes, if the bad *Husbands* were of their owne choosing, against their Friends consent; For then, they will be sure, to make good their owne Folly.

OF LOVE

X

The Stage is more beholding§ to *Love,* then the Life of Man. For as to the Stage, *Love* is ever matter of Comedies, and now and then of Tragedies: But in Life, it doth much mischiefe: Sometimes like a *Syren;* Sometimes like a *Fury.* You may observe, that amongst all the great and worthy Persons, (whereof the memory remaineth, either Ancient or Recent) there is not One, that hath beene transported, to the mad degree of *Love:* which shewes, that great Spirits, and great Businesse, doe keepe out this weake Passion. You must except, neverthelesse, *Marcus Antonius* the halfe Partner of the Empire of Rome; and *Appius Claudius* the *Decemvir,* and Law-giver; Whereof the former, was indeed a Voluptuous Man, and Inordinate; but the latter, was an Austere, and wise man: And therefore it seemes (though

6 He preferred his old wife to immortality.

rarely) that Love can finde entrance, not only into an open Heart; but also into a Heart well fortified; if watch be not well kept. It is a poore Saying of *Epicurus; Satis magnum Alter Alteri Theatrum sumus:*[7] As if Man, made for the contemplation of Heaven, and all Noble Objects, should doe nothing, but kneele before a little Idoll, and make himselfe subject, though not of the Mouth (as Beasts are) yet of the Eye; which was given him for higher Purposes. It is a strange Thing, to note the Excesse of this Passion; And how it braves,[§] the Nature, and value of things; by this, that the Speaking in a Perpetuall *Hyperbole,* is comely in nothing, but in *Love.* Neither is it meerely in the Phrase; For whereas it hath beene well said, that the Arch-flatterer, with whom all the petty Flatterers have Intelligence, is a Mans Selfe; Certainly, the *Lover* is more. For there was never Proud Man, thought so absurdly well of himselfe, as the *Lover* doth of the Person *loved:* And therefore, it was well said; *That it is impossible to love, and to be wise.* Neither doth this weaknesse appeare to others onely, and not to the Party *Loved;* But to the *Loved,* most of all: except the *Love* be reciproque. For, it is a true Rule, that *Love* is ever rewarded, either with the Reciproque, or with an inward, and secret Contempt. By how much the more, Men ought to beware of this Passion, which loseth not only other things, but it selfe. As for the other losses, the Poets Relation, doth well figure them; That he that preferred *Helena,* quitted the Gifts of *Juno,* and *Pallas.* For whosoever esteemeth too much of Amorous Affection, quitteth both Riches, and Wisedome. This Passion, hath his Flouds, in the very times of Weaknesse; which are, great *Prosperitie;* and great *Adversitie;* though this latter hath beene lesse observed. Both which times kindle *Love,* and make it more fervent, and therefore shew it to be the Childe of Folly. They doe best, who, if they cannot but admit *Love,* yet make it keepe Quarter:[§] And sever it wholly, from their serious Affaires, and Actions of life: For if it checke[§] once with Businesse, it troubleth Mens Fortunes, and maketh Men, that they can, no wayes be true, to their owne Ends. I know not how, but Martiall Men, are given to *Love:* I thinke it is, but as they are given to *Wine;* For *Perils,* commonly aske, to be paid in *Pleas-*

[7] Each of us is to the other a large enough theater.

ures. There is in Mans Nature, a secret Inclination, and Motion, towards *love* of others; which, if it be not spent, upon some one, or a few, doth naturally spread it selfe, towards many; and maketh men become Humane, and Charitable; As it is seene sometime in Friars. Nuptiall *love* maketh Mankinde; Friendly *love* perfecteth it; but Wanton *love* Corrupteth, and Imbaseth it.

OF GREAT PLACE

XI

Men in *Great Place,* are thrice *Servants:* Servants of the Soveraigne or State; Servants of Fame; and Servants of Businesse. So as they have no Freedome; neither in their Persons; nor in their Actions; nor in their Times. It is a strange desire, to seeke Power, and to lose Libertie; Or to seeke Power over others, and to loose Power over a Mans Selfe. The Rising unto *Place* is Laborious; And by Paines Men come to greater Paines; And it is sometimes base; And by Indignities,§ Men come to Dignities. The standing is slippery, and the Regresse, is either a downefall, or at least an Eclipse, which is a Melancholy Thing. *Cùm non sis, qui fueris, non esse, cur velis vivere.*[8] Nay, retire Men cannot, when they would; neither will they, when it were Reason: But are impatient of privatenesse,§ even in Age, and Sicknesse, which require the Shadow: Like old Townesmen, that will be still sitting at their Street doore; though thereby they offer Age to Scorne. Certainly Great Persons, had need to borrow other Mens Opinions; to thinke themselves happy; For if they judge by their owne Feeling; they cannot finde it: But if they thinke with themselves, what other men thinke of them, and that other men would faine be as they are, then they are happy, as it were by report; When perhaps they finde the Contrary within. For they are the first, that finde their owne Griefs; though they be the last, that finde their owne Faults. Certainly, Men in Great Fortunes, are strangers to themselves, and while they are in the pusle§ of businesse, they have no time to tend their Health, either of Body, or Minde. *Illi Mors gravis incubat, qui notus*

---

8 When you are no longer what you were, you no longer wish to live.

nimis omnibus, ignotus moritur sibi.[9] In *Place,* There is License
to doe Good, and Evill; wherof the latter is a Curse; For in Evill,
the best condition is, not to will; The Second, not to Can.[§] But
Power to doe good, is the true and lawfull End of Aspiring. For
good Thoughts (though God accept them,) yet towards men,
are little better than good Dreames; Except they put in Act;
And that cannot be without Power, and Place; As the Vantage,
and Commanding Ground. Merit, and good Works, is the End
of Mans Motion; And Conscience[§] of the same, is the Accomplishment of Mans Rest. For if a Man, can be Partaker of
Gods Theater,[§] he shall likewise be Partaker of Gods Rest. *Et
conversus Deus, ut aspiceret Opera, quæ fecerunt manus suæ,
vidit quod omnia essent bona nimis;*[1] And then the Sabbath. In
the Discharge of thy *Place,* set before thee the best Examples;
For Imitation, is a Globe[§] of Precepts. And after a time, set before thee, thine owne Example; And examine thy selfe strictly,
whether thou didst not best at first. Neglect not also the Examples of those, that have carried themselves ill, in the same *Place:*
Not to set off thy selfe, by taxing[§] their Memory; but to direct
thy selfe, what to avoid. Reforme therfore, without Braverie,[§]
or Scandall,[§] of former Times, and Persons; but yet set it downe
to thy selfe, as well to create good Presidents,[§] as to follow them.
Reduce things, to the first Institution,[§] and observe, wherin, and
how, they have degenerate; but yet aske Counsell of both Times;
Of the Ancient Time, what is best; and of the Latter Time, what
is fittest. Seeke to make thy Course Regular; that Men may know
before hand, what they may expect: But be not too positive, and
peremptorie; And expresse thy selfe well, when thou disgressest
from thy Rule. Preserve the Right of thy *Place;* but stirre not
questions of Jurisdiction: And rather assume thy Right, in Silence, and *de facto,*[2] then voice it, with Claimes, and Challenges.
Preserve likewise, the Rights of Inferiour *Places;* And thinke it
more Honour to direct in chiefe, then to be busie in all. Embrace,
and invite Helps, and Advices, touching the Execution of thy
Place; And doe not drive away such, as bring thee Information,
as Medlers; but accept of them in good part. The vices of *Au-*

[9] Death seems hard to him who dies too well known to all men but unknown to
himself.
[1] And God saw every thing that he had made, and, behold, it was very good.
[2] As a matter of course.

thoritie are chiefly foure: *Delaies; Corruption; Roughnesse;*§ and
Facilitie.§ For *Delaies;* Give easie Accesse; Keepe times appointed; Goe through with that which is in hand; And interlace§
not businesse, but of necessitie. For *Corruption;* Doe not onely
binde thine owne Hands, or thy Servants hands, from taking;
but binde the hands of Sutours also from offring. For Integritie
used doth the one; but Integritie professed, and with a manifest
detestation of Bribery, doth the other. And avoid not onely the
Fault, but the Suspicion. Whosoever is found variable, and
changeth manifestly, without manifest Cause, giveth Suspicion
of *Corruption.* Therefore, alwayes, when thou changest thine
Opinion, or Course, professe it plainly, and declare it, together
with the Reasons, that move thee to change; And doe not thinke
to steale§ it. A Servant, or a Favorite, if hee be inward,§ and no
other apparant Cause of Esteeme, is commonly thought but a
By-way, to close§ *Corruption.* For *Roughnesse;* It is a needlesse
cause of *Discontent: Severitie* breedeth Feare, but *Roughnesse*
breedeth Hate. Even Reproofes from Authoritie, ought to be
Grave, and not Taunting. As for *Facilitie;* It is worse then
Bribery. For *Bribes* come but now and then; But if Importunitie,
or Idle Respects§ lead a Man, he shall never be without. As
Salomon saith; *To respect Persons, is not good; For such a man
will transgresse for a peece of Bread.* It is most true, that was
anciently spoken; *A place sheweth the Man:* And it sheweth
some to the better, and some to the worse: *Omnium consensu,
capax Imperii, nisi imperasset;*[3] saith *Tacitus* of *Galba:* but of
Vespasian he saith; *Solus Imperantium Vespasianus mutatus in
melius.*[4] Though the one was meant of Sufficiencie,§ the other
of Manners, and Affection.§ It is an assured Signe, of a worthy
and generous Spirit, whom *Honour* amends. For *Honour* is, or
should be, the Place of Vertue: And as in Nature, Things move
violently to their Place, and calmely in their Place: So Vertue
in Ambition is violent, in Authority setled and calme. All Rising
to *Great Place,* is by a winding Staire: And if there be Factions,
it is good, to side§ a Mans selfe, whilest hee is in the Rising; and
to ballance Himselfe, when hee is placed. Use the Memory of

---

[3] In everyone's opinion, a man fit for empire if he had not been emperor.
[4] Of all the emperors, only Vespasian changed for the better (after he came to power).

thy Predecessour fairely, and tenderly; For if thou dost not, it is a Debt, will sure be paid, when thou art gone. If thou have Colleagues, respect them, and rather call them, when they looke not for it, then exclude them, when they have reason to looke to be called. Be not too sensible,§ or too remembring, of thy Place, in Conversation, and private Answers to Suitors; But let it rather be said; *When he sits in Place, he is another Man.*

OF ATHEISME
XVI

I had rather beleeve all the Fables in the *Legend,*[5] and the *Talmud,* and the *Alcoran,* then that this universall Frame, is without a Minde. And therefore, God never wrought Miracle, to convince§ *Atheisme,* because his Ordinary Works convince it. It is true, that a little Philosophy inclineth Mans Minde to *Atheisme;* But depth in Philosophy, bringeth Mens Mindes about to *Religion:* For while the Minde of Man, looketh upon Second Causes Scattered, it may sometimes rest in them, and goe no further: But when it beholdeth, the Chaine of them, Confederate and Linked together, it must needs flie to *Providence,* and *Deitie.* Nay even that *Schoole,* which is most accused of *Atheisme,* doth most demonstrate *Religion;* That is, the *Schoole* of *Leucippus,* and *Democritus,* and *Epicurus.* For it is a thousand times more Credible, that foure Mutable Elements, and one Immutable Fift Essence, duly and Eternally placed, need no God; then that an Army, of Infinite small Portions, or Seedes unplaced, should have produced this Order, and Beauty, without a Divine Marshall. The Scripture saith; *The Foole hath said in his Heart, there is no God:* It is not said; *The Foole hath thought in his Heart:* So as, he rather saith it by rote to himselfe, as that he would have, then that he can throughly beleeve it, or be perswaded of it. For none deny there is a *God,* but those, for whom it maketh§ that there were no *God.* It appeareth in nothing more, that *Atheisme* is rather in the *Lip,* then in the *Heart* of Man, then by this; That *Atheists* will ever be talking of that their Opinion, as if they fainted in it, within themselves, and would

5 *The Golden Legend,* a popular collection of saints' lives and miracles.

be glad to be strengthned, by the Consent of others: Nay more,
you shall have *Atheists* strive to get *Disciples*, as it fareth with
other *Sects*: And, which is most of all, you shall have of them,
that will suffer for *Atheisme*, and not recant; Wheras, if they
did truly thinke, that there were no such Thing as *God*, why
should they trouble themselves? *Epicurus* is charged, that he
did but dissemble, for his credits sake, when he affirmed; There
were *Blessed Natures*, but such as enjoyed themselves, without
having respect to the Government of the World. Wherein, they
say, he did temporize; though in secret, he thought, there was
no *God*. But certainly, he is traduced; For his Words are Noble
and Divine: *Non Deos vulgi negare profanum; sed vulgi Opin-*
iones Diis applicare profanum.[6] *Plato* could have said no more.
And although, he had the Confidence, to deny the *Administra-*
tion, he had not the Power to deny the *Nature*. The *Indians* of
the *West*, have Names for their particular *Gods*, though they
have no name for *God*: As if the *Heathens*, should have had the
Names *Jupiter, Apollo, Mars*, &c. But not the Word *Deus*:
which shewes, that even those Barbarous People, have the Notion, though they have not the Latitude, and Extent of it. So
that against *Atheists*, the very Savages take part, with the very
subtillest Philosophers. The Contemplative *Atheist* is rare; A
Diagoras, a *Bion*, a *Lucian* perhaps, and some others; And yet
they seeme to be more then they are; For that, all that Impugne
a received *Religion*, or *Superstition*, are by the adverse Part,
branded with the Name of *Atheists*. But the great *Atheists*, indeed, are *Hypocrites;* which are ever Handling Holy Things,
but without Feeling. So as they must needs be cauterized in the
End. The *Causes* of *Atheisme* are; *Divisions* in *Religion*, if they
be many; For any one maine Division, addeth Zeale to both
Sides; But many Divisions introduce *Atheisme*. Another is,
Scandall of *Priests;* When it is come to that, which S. *Bernard*
saith; *Non est jam dicere, ut Populus, sic Sacerdos: quia nec*
sic Populus, ut Sacerdos.[7] A third is, Custome of *Profane Scoff-*
ing in *Holy Matters;* which doth, by little and little, deface the
Reverence of Religion. And lastly, *Learned Times*, specially

6 It is not profane to refuse to believe in the people's gods, but it is profane to
believe of the gods what the people believe of them.
7 Now it cannot be said, the priest is as the people; for the people are not so bad
as the priest.

with Peace, and Prosperity: For Troubles and Adversities doe more bow Mens Mindes to *Religion*. They that deny a *God*, destroy Mans Nobility: For certainly, Man is of Kinne to the Beasts, by his Body; And if, he be not of Kinne to *God*, by his Spirit, he is a Base and Ignoble Creature. It destroies likewise Magnanimity, and the Raising of Humane Nature: For take an Example of a Dog; And mark what a Generosity, and Courage he will put on, when he findes himselfe maintained,[§] by a Man; who to him is in Stead of a *God*, or *Melior Natura*:[8] which courage is manifestly such, as that Creature, without that Confidence, of a better Nature, than his owne, could never attaine. So Man, when he resteth and assureth himselfe, upon divine Protection, and Favour, gathereth a Force and Faith; which Humane Nature, in it selfe, could not obtaine. Therefore, as *Atheisme* is in all respects hatefull, so in this, that it depriveth humane Nature, of the Meanes, to exalt it selfe, above Humane Frailty. As it is in particular Persons, so it is in Nations: Never was there such a *State*, for Magnanimity, as *Rome*: Of this State heare what *Cicero* saith; *Quam volumus, licet, patres conscripti, nos amemus, tamen nec numero Hispanos, nec robore Gallos, nec calliditate Pœnos, nec artibus Græcos, nec denique hoc ipso huius Gentis & Terræ domestico nativoque sensu Italos ipsos & Latinos; sed Pietate, ac Religione, atque hâc unâ Sapientiâ, quod Deorum Immortalium Numine, omnia regi, gubernarique perspeximus, omnes Gentes Nationesque superavimus.*[9]

OF TRAVAILE

XVIII

Travile in the younger Sort, is a Part of Education; In the Elder, a Part of Experience. He that *travaileth* into a Country, before he hath some Entrance into the Language, goeth to *Schoole*,

---

8 A better nature.

9 However good an opinion we have of ourselves, O senators, we have not surpassed the Spaniards in population, the Gauls in strength, the Carthaginians in cunning, the Greeks in arts, or, finally, the Italians and Latins themselves in the homely and native sense which belongs to this race and land; but in piety, in religion, and in the special wisdom of perceiving that all things are ruled and governed by the will of the Immortal Gods, we have surpassed all races and nations.

and not to *Travaile*. That Young Men travaile under some Tutor, or grave Servant, I allow[s] well; So that he be such a one, that hath the Language, and hath been in the Country before; whereby he may be able to tell them, what Things are worthy to be seene in the Country where they goe; what Acquaintances they are to seeke; What Exercises or discipline[s] the Place yeeldeth. For else young Men shall goe hooded, and looke abroad little. It is a strange Thing, that in Sea voyages, where there is nothing to be seene, but Sky and Sea, Men should make Diaries; but in *Land-Travile*, wherein so much is to be observed, for the most part, they omit it; As if Chance, were fitter to be registred, then Observation. Let Diaries, therefore, be brought in use. The Things to be seene and observed are: The Courts of Princes, specially when they give Audience to Ambassadours: The Courts of Justice, while they sit and heare Causes: And so of Consistories Ecclesiasticke: The Churches, and Monasteries, with the Monuments which are therein extant: The Wals and Fortifications of Cities and Townes; And so the Havens & Harbours: Antiquities, and Ruines: Libraries; Colledges, Disputations,[s] and Lectures, where any are: Shipping and Navies: Houses, and Gardens of State, and Pleasure, neare great Cities: Armories: Arsenals: Magazens:[s] Exchanges: Burses;[s] Ware-houses: Exercises of Horsemanship; Fencing; Trayning of Souldiers; and the like: Comedies; Such wherunto the better Sort of persons doe resort; Treasuries of Jewels, and Robes; Cabinets, and Rarities: And to conclude, whatsoever is memorable in the Places; where they goe. After all which, the Tutors or Servants, ought to make diligent Enquirie. As for Triumphs; Masques; Feasts; Weddings; Funeralls; Capitall Executions; and such Shewes; Men need not to be put in minde of them; Yet are they not to be neglected. If you will have a Young Man, to put his *Travaile*, into a little Roome, and in short time, to gather much, this you must doe. First, as was said, he must have some Entrance into the Language, before he goeth. Then he must have such a Servant, or Tutor, as knoweth the Country, as was likewise said. Let him carry with him also some Card[s] or Booke describing the Country, where he travelleth; which will be a good Key to his Enquiry. Let him keepe also a Diary. Let him not stay long in one Citty, or Towne; More or lesse as the place deserveth, but not long:

Nay, when he stayeth in one City or Towne, let him change his
Lodging, from one End and Part of the Towne, to another;
which is a great Adamant[§] of Acquaintance. Let him sequester
himselfe from the Company of his Country men, and diet in
such Places, where there is good Company of the Nation, where
he travaileth. Let him upon his Removes, from one place to another, procure Recommendation, to some person of Quality,
residing in the Place, whither he removeth; that he may use his
Favour, in those things, he desireth to see or know. Thus he
may abridge his *Travaile*, with much profit. As for the acquaintance, which is to be sought in *Travaile;* That which is
most of all profitable, is Acquaintance with the Secretaries, and
Employd Men of Ambassadours; For so in *Travailing* in one
Country he shall sucke the Experience of many. Let him also
see and visit, Eminent Persons, in all Kindes, which are of great
Name abroad; That he may be able to tell, how the Life agreeth
with the Fame. For Quarels, they are with Care and Discretion
to be avoided: They are, commonly, for Mistresses; Health;[§]
Place, and Words. And let a Man beware, how he keepeth Company, with Cholerick and Quarelsome Persons; for they will en-
gage him into their owne Quarels. When a *Travailer* returneth
home, let him not leave the Countries, where he hath *Traviled*,
altogether behinde him; But maintaine a Correspondence, by
letters, with those of his Acquaintance, which are of most Worth.
And let his *Travaile* appeare rather in his Discourse, then in his
Apparrell, or Gesture: And in his Discourse, let him be rather
advised in his Answers, then forwards[§] to tell Stories: And let
it appeare, that he doth not change his Country[§] Manners, for
those of Foraigne Parts; But onely, prick[§] in some Flowers, of
that he hath Learned abroad, into the Customes of his owne
Country.

OF CUNNING

XXII

We take *Cunning* for a Sinister or Crooked Wisedome. And certainly, there is great difference, between a *Cunning* Man, and
a *Wise* Man; Not onely in Point of Honesty, but in point of

Ability. There be that can packe the Cards, and yet cannot play well; So there are some, that are good in Canvasses,§ and Factions, that are otherwise Weake Men. Againe, it is one thing to understand Persons, and another thing to understand Matters; For many are perfect in Mens Humours, that are not greatly Capable of the Reall Part of Businesse; Which is the Constitution of one, that hath studied Men, more then Bookes. Such Men are fitter for Practise, then for Counsell; And they are good but in their own Alley: Turne them to New Men, and they have lost their Ayme; So as the old Rule, to know a Foole from a Wise Man; *Mitte ambos nudos ad ignotos, & videbis;*[1] doth scarce hold for them. And because these *Cunning Men,* are like Haberdashers of Small Wares, it is not amisse to set forth their Shop.

It is a point of *Cunning;* to wait upon him, with whom you speake, with your eye; As the Jesuites give it in precept: For there be many Wise Men, that have Secret Hearts, and Transparant Countenances. Yet this would§ be done, with a demure Abasing of your Eye sometimes, as the Jesuites also doe use.

Another is, that when you have any thing to obtaine of present dispatch, you entertaine, and amuse the party, with whom you deale, with some other Discourse; That he be not too much awake, to make Objections. I knew a *Counsellor* and *Secretary,* that never came to *Queene Elizabeth* of *England,* with Bills to signe, but he would alwaies first put her into some discourse of Estate, that she mought§ the lesse minde the Bills.

The like Surprize, may be made, by Moving things, when the Party is in haste, and cannot stay, to consider advisedly, of that is moved.

If a man would crosse a Businesse, that he doubts some other would handsomely and effectually move, let him pretend to wish it well, and move it himselfe, in such sort, as may foile it.

The breaking off, in the midst of that, one was about to say, as if he tooke himselfe up, breeds a greater Appetite in him, with whom you conferre, to know more.

And because it workes better, when any thing seemeth to be gotten from you by Question, then if you offer it of your selfe, you may lay a Bait for a Question, by shewing another Visage and Countenance, then you are wont; To the end, to give Oc-

1 Send them both naked to strangers, and you shall see.

casion, for the party to aske, what the Matter is of the Change? As *Nehemias* did; *And I had not before that time been sad before the King.*

In Things, that are tender and unpleasing, it is good to breake the Ice, by some whose Words are of lesse weight, and to reserve the more weighty Voice, to come in, as by chance, so that he may be asked the Question upon the others Speech. As *Narcissus* did, in relating to *Claudius,* the Marriage of *Messalina* and *Silius.*

In things, that a Man would not be seen in, himselfe; It is a Point of *Cunning,* to borrow the Name of the World; As to say; *The World sayes,* Or, *There is a speech abroad.*

I knew one, that when he wrote a Letter, he would put that which was most Materiall, in the *Post-script,* as if it had been a By-matter.

I knew another, that when he came to have Speech, he would passe over that, that he intended most, and goe forth, and come backe againe, and speake of it, as of a Thing, that he had almost forgot.

Some procure themselves, to be surprized, at such times, as it is like, the party that they work upon, will suddenly come upon them: And to be found with a Letter in their hand, or doing somewhat which they are not accustomed; To the end, they may be apposed§ of those things, which of themselves they are desirous to utter.

It is a Point of *Cunning,* to let fall those Words, in a Mans owne Name, which he would have another Man learne, and use, and thereupon take Advantage. I knew two, that were Competitors, for the Secretaries Place, in *Queene Elizabeths* time, and yet kept good Quarter betweene themselves; And would conferre, one with another, upon the Businesse; And the one of them said, That to be a Secretary, in the *Declination of a Monarchy,* was a Ticklish Thing, and that he did not affect it. The other, straight caught up those Words, and discoursed with divers of his Friends, that he had no reason to desire to be Secretary, in the *Declination of a Monarchy.* The first Man tooke hold of it, and found Meanes, it was told the *Queene;* Who hearing of a *Declination of a Monarchy,* tooke it so ill, as she would never after heare of the others Suit.

There is a *Cunning*, which we in *England* call, *The Turning of the Cat in the Pan;* which is, when that which a Man sayes to another, he laies it, as if Another had said it to him. And to say Truth, it is not easie, when such a Matter passed between two, to make it appeare, from which of them, it first moved and began.

It is a way, that some men have, to glaunce and dart at Others, by Justifying themselves, by Negatives; As to say, *This I doe not:* As *Tigillinus* did towards *Burrhus; Se non diversas spes, sed Incolumitatem Imperatoris simplicitèr spectare.*[2]

Some have in readinesse, so many Tales and Stories, as there is Nothing, they would insinuate, but they can wrap it into a Tale; which serveth both to keepe themselves more in Guard, and to make others carry it, with more Pleasure.

It is a good Point of *Cunning*, for a Man, to shape the Answer he would have, in his owne Words, and Propositions; For it makes the other Party sticke[§] the lesse.

It is strange, how long some Men will lie in wait, to speake somewhat, they desire to say; And how farre about they will fetch; And how many other Matters they will beat over, to come neare it. It is a Thing of great Patience, but yet of much Use.

A sudden, bold, and unexpected Question, doth many times surprise a Man, and lay him open. Like to him, that having changed his Name, and walking in *Pauls*,[§] Another suddenly came behind him, and called him by his true Name, whereat straightwaies he looked backe.

But these Small Wares, and Petty Points of *Cunning*, are infinite: And it were a good deed, to make a List of them: For that nothing doth more hurt in a State, then that *Cunning Men* passe for *Wise*.

But certainly, some there are, that know the Resorts[§] and Falls[§] of Businesse, that cannot sinke into the Maine of it: Like a House, that hath convenient Staires, and Entries, but never a faire Roome. Therfore, you shall see them finde out pretty Looses[§] in the Conclusion, but are no waies able to Examine, or debate Matters. And yet commonly they take advantage of their Inability, and would be thought Wits of direction. Some build

2 That he had not several hopes to rest on, but looked simply to the safety of the Emperor.

rather upon the Abusing of others, and (as we now say;) *Putting Tricks upon them;* Then upon Soundnesse of their own proceedings. But *Salomon* saith; *Prudens advertit ad Gressus suos: Stultus divertit ad Dolos.*[3]

OF INNOVATIONS

XXIV

As the Births of Living Creatures, at first, are ill shapen: So are all *Innovations,* which are the Births of Time. Yet notwithstanding, as Those that first bring Honour into their Family, are commonly more worthy, then most that succeed: So the first President[§] (if it be good) is seldome attained by Imitation. For Ill, to Mans Nature, as it stands perverted, hath a Naturall Motion, strongest in Continuance: But Good, as a Forced Motion, strongest at first. Surely every *Medicine* is an *Innovation;* And he that will not apply New Remedies, must expect New Evils: For Time is the greatest *Innovatour:* And if Time, of[§] course, alter Things to the worse, and Wisedome, and Counsell shall not alter them to the better, what shall be the End? It is true, that what is setled by Custome, though it be not good, yet at least it is fit. And those Things, which have long gone together, are as it were confederate within themselves: Whereas New Things peece[§] not so well; But though they helpe by their utility, yet they trouble, by their Inconformity. Besides, they are like *Strangers;* more Admired, and lesse Favoured. All this is true, if Time stood still; which contrariwise moveth so round, that a Froward Retention of Custome, is as turbulent a Thing, as an *Innovation:* And they that Reverence too much Old Times, are but a Scorne to the New. It were good therefore, that Men in their *Innovations,* would follow the Example of Time it selfe; which indeed *Innovateth* greatly, but quietly, and by degrees, scarce to be perceived: For otherwise, whatsoever is New, is unlooked for; And ever it mends Some, and paires[§] Other: And he that is holpen, takes it for a Fortune, and thanks the Time; And he that is hurt, for a wrong, and imputeth it to the Author. It is good also, not to try Experiments in States;

[3] The simple believeth every word: but the prudent man looketh well to his going.

Except the Necessity be Urgent, or the utility Evident: And well
to beware, that it be the Reformation, that draweth on the
Change; And not the desire of Change, that pretendeth[§] the Reformation. And lastly, that the *Novelty*, though it be not rejected,
yet be held for a Suspect: And, as the Scripture saith; *That we
make a stand upon the Ancient Way, and then looke about us,
and discover, what is the straight, and right way, and so to walke
in it.*

OF FRENDSHIP

XXVII

It had beene hard for him[4] that spake it, to have put more Truth
and untruth together, in few Words, then in that Speech; *Whosoever is delighted in solitude, is either a wilde Beast, or a God.* For
it is most true, that a Naturall and Secret Hatred, and Aversation[§] towards *Society*, in any Man, hath somewhat of the Savage
Beast; But it is most Untrue, that it should have any Character,
at all, of the Divine Nature; Except it proceed, not out of a Pleasure in *Solitude*, but out of a Love and desire, to sequester a
Mans Selfe, for a Higher Conversation[§]: Such as is found, to
have been falsely and fainedly, in some of the Heathen; as *Epi-
menides* the Candian, *Numa* the Roman, *Empedocles* the Sicilian, and *Apollonius* of Tyana; And truly and really, in divers of
the Ancient Hermits, and Holy Fathers of the Church. But little
doe Men perceive, what *Solitude* is, and how farre it extendeth.
For a Crowd is not Company; And Faces are but a Gallery of
Pictures; And Talke but a *Tinckling Cymball*, where there is no
Love. The Latine Adage meeteth[§] with it a little; *Magna Civitas,
Magna solitudo;*[5] Because in a great Towne, *Friends* are scattered; So that there is not that Fellowship, for the most Part,
which is in lesse *Neighbourhoods*. But we may goe further, and
affirme most truly; That it is a meere, and miserable *Solitude*, to
want true *Friends*; without which the World is but a Wilder-
nesse: And even in this sense also of *Solitude*, whosoever in the

4 Aristotle, *Politics.*
5 A great city, a great solitude.

Frame of his Nature and Affections, is unfit for *Friendship,* he taketh it of the Beast, and not from Humanity.

A principall *Fruit* of *Friendship,* is the Ease and Discharge of the Fulnesse and Swellings of the Heart, which Passions of all kinds doe cause and induce. We know Diseases of Stoppings, and Suffocations, are the most dangerous in the body; And it is not much otherwise in the Minde: You may take *Sarza*[§] to open the Liver; *Steele*[§] to open the Spleene; *Flowers*[§] of *Sulphur* for the Lungs; *Castoreum* for the Braine; But no Receipt[§] openeth the Heart, but a true *Frend,* to whom you may impart, Griefes, Joyes, Feares, Hopes, Suspicions, Counsels, and whatsoever lieth upon the Heart, to oppresse it, in a kind of Civill Shrift or Confession.

It is a Strange Thing to observe, how high a Rate, Great Kings and Monarchs, do set upon this *Fruit* of *Friendship,* wherof we speake: So great, as they purchase it, many times, at the hazard of their owne Safety, and Greatnesse. For Princes, in regard of the distance of their Fortune, from that of their Subjects & Servants, cannot gather this *Fruit;* Except (to make Themselves capable thereof) they raise some Persons, to be as it were Companions, and almost Equals to themselves, which many times sorteth to Inconvenience. The Moderne Languages give unto such Persons, the Name of *Favorites,* or *Privadoes;* As if it were Matter of Grace, or Conversation. But the Roman Name attaineth the true use, and Cause thereof; Naming them *Participes Curarum;*[6] For it is that, which tieth the knot. And we see plainly, that this hath been done, not by Weake and Passionate *Princes* onely, but by the Wisest, and most Politique that ever reigned; Who have oftentimes joyned to themselves, some of their Servants; Whom both Themselves have called *Frends;* And allowed Others likewise to call them in the same manner; Using the Word which is received between Private Men.

L. Sylla, when he commanded *Rome,* raised *Pompey* (after surnamed the *Great*) to that Heigth, that *Pompey* vaunted Himselfe for *Sylla's* Overmatch. For when he had carried the *Consulship* for a Frend of his, against the pursuit of *Sylla,* and that *Sylla* did a little resent[§] thereat, and began to speake great, *Pompey* turned upon him againe, and in effect bad him be quiet; *For that more Men adored the Sunne Rising, then the Sunne setting.*

6 Partners in cares.

With *Julius Cæsar, Decimus Brutus* had obtained that Interest, as he set him downe, in his Testament, for Heire in Remainder, after his *Nephew*. And this was the Man, that had power with him, to draw him forth to his death. For when *Cæsar* would have discharged the Senate, in regard of some ill Presages, and specially a Dreame of *Calpurnia;* This Man lifted him gently by the Arme, out of his Chaire, telling him, he hoped he would not dismisse the Senate, till his wife had dreamt a better Dreame. And it seemeth, his favour was so great, as *Antonius* in a Letter, which is recited§ *Verbatìm*, in one of *Cicero's Philippiques*, calleth him *Venefica, Witch;* As if he had enchanted *Cæsar*. *Augustus* raised *Agrippa* (though of meane Birth) to that Heighth, as when he consulted with *Mæcenas*, about the Marriage of his Daughter *Julia, Mæcenas* tooke the Liberty to tell him; *That he must either marry his Daughter to Agrippa, or take away his life, there was no third way, he had made him so great*. With *Tiberius Cæsar, Sejanus* had ascended to that Height, as they Two were tearmed and reckoned, as a Paire of Frends. *Tiberius* in a Letter to him saith; *Hæc pro Amiticiâ nostrâ non occultavi:*[7] And the whole Senate, dedicated an Altar to *Frendship*, as to a *Goddesse*, in respect of the great Dearenesse of *Frendship*, between them Two. The like or more was between *Septimius Severus*, and *Plautianus*. For he forced his Eldest Sonne to marry the Daughter of *Plautianus;* And would often maintaine *Plautianus*, in doing Affronts to his Son: And did write also in a Letter to the Senate, by these Words; *I love the Man so well, as I wish he may over-live§ me*. Now if these Princes, had beene as a *Trajan*, or a *Marcus Aurelius*, A Man might have thought, that this had proceeded of an abundant Goodnesse of Nature; But being Men so Wise, of such Strength and Severitie of minde, and so Extreme Lovers of Themselves, as all these were; It proveth most plainly, that they found their owne Felicitie (though as great as ever happened to Mortall Men) but as an Halfe Peece, except they mought have a *Frend* to make it Entire: And yet, which is more, they were *Princes*, that had Wives, Sonnes, Nephews; And yet all these could not supply the Comfort of *Frendship*.

It is not to be forgotten, what *Commineus* observeth, of his first Master *Duke Charles* the *Hardy;* Namely, that hee would

7 Because of our friendship, I have not concealed these things from you.

communicate his Secrets with none; And least of all, those Secrets, which troubled him most. Whereupon he goeth on, and
saith, That towards his Latter time; *That closenesse did impaire,
and a little perish his understanding.* Surely *Commineus* mought
have made the same Judgement also, if it had pleased him, of his
Second Master *Lewis* the Eleventh, whose closenesse was indeed
his Tormentour. The Parable of *Pythagoras* is darke, but true;
Cor ne edito; Eat not the Heart. Certainly, if a Man would give
it a hard Phrase, Those that want *Frends* to open themselves
unto, are Canniballs of their owne *Hearts.* But one Thing is most
Admirable, (wherewith I will conclude this first *Fruit* of *frendship*) which is, that this Communicating of a Mans Selfe to his
Frend, works two contrarie Effects; For it redoubleth *Joyes,* and
cutteth *Griefes* in Halfes. For there is no Man, that imparteth his
Joyes to his *Frend,* but he *joyeth* the more; And no Man, that
imparteth his *Griefes* to his *Frend,* but hee *grieveth* the lesse. So
that it is, in Truth of Operation upon a Mans Minde, of like
vertue, as the *Alchymists* use to attribute to their Stone, for Mans
Bodie; That it worketh all Contrary Effects, but still to the Good,
and Benefit of Nature. But yet, without praying[§] in Aid of *Alchymists,* there is a manifest Image of this, in the ordinarie course of
Nature. For in Bodies, *Union* strengthneth and cherisheth any
Naturall Action; And, on the other side, weakneth and dulleth
any violent Impression: And even so is it of Minds.

The second *Fruit of Frendship,* is Healthfull and Soveraigne
for the *Understanding,* as the first is for the *Affections.* For
Frendship maketh indeed a *faire Day* in the *Affections,* from
Storme and Tempests: But it maketh *Day-light* in the *Understanding,* out of Darknesse & Confusion of Thoughts. Neither is
this to be understood, onely of Faithfull Counsell, which a Man
receiveth from his *Frend;* But before you come to that, certaine
it is, that whosoever hath his Minde fraught, with many Thoughts,
his Wits and Understanding doe clarifie and breake[§] up, in the
Communicating and discoursing with Another: He tosseth his
Thoughts, more easily; He marshalleth them more orderly; He
seeth how they looke when they are turned into Words; Finally,
He waxeth wiser then Himselfe; And that more by an Houres discourse, then by a Dayes Meditation. It was well said by *Themistocles* to the King of *Persia; That speech was like Cloth of Arras,*

opened, and put abroad; Whereby the Imagery doth appeare in Figure; whereas in Thoughts, they lie but as in Packs.[§] Neither is this Second *Fruit* of *Frendship,* in opening the *Understanding,* restrained onely to such *Frends,* as are able to give a Man Counsell: (They indeed are best) But even, without that, a Man learneth of Himselfe, and bringeth his owne Thoughts to Light, and whetteth his Wits as against a Stone, which it selfe cuts not. In a word, a Man were better relate[§] himselfe, to a Statua, or Picture, then to suffer his Thoughts to passe in smother.

Adde now, to make this Second *Fruit* of *Frendship* compleat, that other Point, which lieth more open, and falleth within Vulgar Observation; which is *Faithfull Counsell* from a *Frend.* Heraclitus saith well, in one of his Ænigmaes; *Dry*[§] *Light is ever the best.* And certaine it is, that the Light, that a man receiveth, by Counsell from Another, is Drier, and purer, then that which commeth from his owne Understanding, and Judgement; which is ever infused and drenched in his Affections and Customes. So as, there is as much difference, betweene the *Counsell,* that a *Frend* giveth, and that a Man giveth himselfe, as there is between the *Counsell* of a *Frend,* and of a *Flatterer.* For there is no such *Flatterer,* as is a Mans Selfe; And there is no such Remedy, against *Flattery* of a Mans Selfe, as the Liberty of a *Frend. Counsell* is of two Sorts; The one concerning *Manners,* the other concerning *Businesse.* For the First; The best Preservative to keep the Minde in Health, is the faithfull *Admonition* of a *Frend.* The Calling of a Mans Selfe, to a Strict Account, is a Medicine, sometime, too Piercing and Corrosive. Reading good Bookes of *Morality,* is a little Flat, and Dead. Observing our Faults in Others, is sometimes unproper for our Case. But the best Receipt (best (I say) to worke, and best to take) is the Admonition of a *Frend.* It is a strange thing to behold, what grosse Errours, and extreme Absurdities, Many (especially of the greater Sort) doe commit, for want of a *Frend,* to tell them of them; To the great dammage, both of their Fame, & Fortune. For, as S. *James* saith, they are as Men, *that looke sometimes into a Glasse, and presently forget their own Shape, & Favour.*[§] As for *Businesse,* a Man may think, if he will, that two Eyes see no more then one; Or that a Gamester[§] seeth alwaies more then a Looker on; Or that a Man in Anger, is as Wise as he, that hath said over the foure and twenty

Letters;[8] Or that Musket may be shot off, aswell upon the Arme, as upon a Rest; And such other fond[§] and high Imaginations, to thinke Himselfe All in All. But when all is done, the Helpe of good *Counsell*, is that, which setteth *Businesse* straight. And if any Man thinke, that he will take *Counsell*, but it shall be by Peeces; Asking *Counsell* in one Businesse of one Man, and in another Businesse of another Man; It is well, (that is to say, better perhaps then if he asked none at all;) but he runneth two dangers: One, that he shall not be faithfully counselled; For it is a rare Thing, except it be from a perfect and entire *Frend*, to have Counsell given, but such as shalbe bowed and crooked to some ends, which he hath that giveth it. The other, that he shall have Counsell given, hurtfull, and unsafe, (though with good Meaning) and mixt, partly of Mischiefe, and partly of Remedy: Even as if you would call a Physician, that is thought good, for the Cure of the Disease, you complaine of, but is unacquainted with your body; And therefore, may put you in way for a present Cure, but overthroweth your Health in some other kinde; And so cure the Disease, and kill the Patient. But a *Frend*, that is wholly acquainted with a Mans Estate, will beware by furthering any present *Businesse*, how he dasheth upon other Inconvenience. And therefore, rest not upon *Scattered Counsels;* They will rather distract, and Misleade, then Settle, and Direct.

And these two Noble *Fruits of Frendship;* (*Peace in the Affections*, and *Support of the Judgement*,) followeth the last *Fruit;* which is like the *Pomgranat,* full of many kernels; I meane *Aid,* and *Bearing a Part,* in all *Actions,* and *Occasions.* Here, the best Way, to represent to life the manifold use of *Frendship,* is to cast and see, how many Things there are, which a Man cannot doe Himselfe; And then it will appeare, that it was a Sparing Speech of the Ancients, to say, *That a Frend is another Himselfe:* For that a *Frend* is farre more then *Himselfe.* Men have their Time, and die many times in desire of some Things, which they principally take to Heart; The Bestowing[§] of a Child, The Finishing of a Worke, Or the like. If a Man have a true *Frend,* he may rest almost secure, that the Care of those Things, will continue after Him. So that a Man hath as it were two Lives in his desires.

---

[8] The alphabet; *i* and *j* were regarded as one letter, as were *u* and *v*. (We would say "count to ten.")

A Man hath a Body, and that Body is confined to a Place; But where *Frendship* is, all Offices of Life, are as it were granted to Him, and his Deputy. For he may exercise them by his *Frend*. How many Things are there, which a Man cannot, with any Face or Comelines, say or doe Himselfe? A Man can scare alledge his owne Merits with modesty, much lesse extoll them: A man cannot sometimes brooke to Supplicate or Beg: And a number of the like. But all these Things, are Gracefull in a *Frends* Mouth, which are Blushing in a Mans Owne. So againe, a Mans Person hath many proper Relations, which he cannot put off. A Man cannot speake to his Sonne, but as a Father; To his Wife, but as a Husband; To his Enemy, but upon Termes: whereas a *Frend* may speak, as the Case requires, and not as it sorteth with the Person. But to enumerate these Things were endlesse: I have given the Rule, where a Man cannot fitly play his owne Part: If he have not a *Frend*, he may quit the Stage.

OF DISCOURSE

XXXII

Some in their *Discourse*, desire rather Commendation of Wit, in being able to hold all Arguments, then of Judgment, in discerning what is True: As if it were a Praise, to know what might be Said, and not what should be Thought. Some have certaine Common Places, and Theames, wherein they are good, and want Variety: Which kinde of Poverty is for the most part Tedious, and when it is once perceived Ridiculous. The Honourablest Part of Talke, is to give§ the Occasion; And againe to Moderate§ and passe to somewhat else; For then a Man leads the Daunce. It is good, in *Discourse*, and Speech of Conversation, to vary, and entermingle Speech, of the present Occasion with Arguments; Tales with Reasons; Asking of Questions, with telling of Opinions; and Jest with Earnest: For it is a dull Thing to Tire, and, as we say now, to Jade, any Thing too farre. As for Jest, there be certaine Things, which ought to be priviledged from it; Namely Religion, Matters of State, Great Persons, Any Mans present Businesse of Importance, And any Case that deserveth Pitty. Yet there be some, that thinke their Wits have been asleepe; Except they dart out some-

what, that is Piquant, and to the Quicke: That is a Vaine,§ which
would be brideled; *Parce Puer stimulis, & fortiùs utere Loris.*[9]
And generally, Men ought to finde the difference, between Salt-
nesse and Bitternesse. Certainly, he that hath a Satyricall vaine,
as he maketh others afraid of his Wit, so he had need be afraid
of others Memory. He that questioneth much, shall learne much,
and content much; But especially, if he apply his Questions, to
the Skill of the Persons, whom he asketh: For he shall give them
occasion, to please themselves in Speaking, and himselfe shall
continually gather Knowledge. But let his Questions, not be
troublesome; For that is fit for a Poser.§ And let him be sure, to
leave other Men their Turnes to speak. Nay, if there be any, that
would raigne, and take up all the time, let him finde meanes to
take them off, and to bring Others on; As Musicians use to doe,
with those, that dance too long Galliards. If you dissemble sometimes your knowledge, of that you are thought to know; you shall
be thought another time, to know that, you know not. Speach of a
Mans Selfe ought to be seldome, and well chosen. I knew One,
was wont to say, in Scorne; *He must needs be a Wise Man, he
speakes so much of Himselfe:* And there is but one Case, wherein
a Man may Commend Himselfe, with good Grace; And that is in
commending Vertue in Another; Especially, if it be such a Vertue, whereunto Himselfe pretendeth. Speech of§ Touch towards
Others, should be sparingly used: For *Discourse* ought to be as a
Field, without comming home to any Man. I knew two *Noblemen,* of the West Part of *England;* Whereof the one was given to
Scoffe, but kept ever Royal Cheere in his House: The other,
would aske of those, that had beene at the Others Table; *Tell
truely, was there never a Flout or drie§ Blow given;* To which the
Guest would answer; *Such and such a Thing passed:* The Lord
would say; *I thought he would marre a good Dinner. Discretion
of Speech,* is more then *Eloquence;* And to speak agreeably§ to
him, with whom we deale, is more then to speake in good Words,
or in good Order. A good continued Speech, without a good
Speech of Interlocution,§ shews Slownesse: And a Good Reply, or
Second Speech, without a good Setled Speech, sheweth Shallow-
nesse and Weaknesse. As we see in Beasts, that those that are
Weakest in the Course, are yet Nimblest in the Turne: As it is

[9] Spare the whip, boy, and use the reins more firmly.

betwixt the Grey-hound, & the Hare. To use too many Circumstances,§ ere one come to the Matter, is Wearisome; To use none
at all, is Blunt.

OF MASQUES AND TRIUMPHS
XXXVII

These Things are but Toyes, to come amongst such Serious Observations. But yet, since Princes will have such Things, it is better, they should be Graced with Elegancy, then Daubed with Cost.
Dancing to Song, is a Thing of great State, and Pleasure. I understand it, that the Song be in Quire,§ placed aloft, and accompanied with some broken§ Musicke: And the Ditty fitted to the
Device.§ *Acting in Song,* especially in *Dialogues,* hath an extreme
Good Grace: I say *Acting,* not *Dancing,* (For that is a Meane and
Vulgar Thing;) And the *Voices* of the *Dialogue,* would be Strong
and Manly, (A Base, and a Tenour; No Treble;) and the *Ditty*
High and Tragicall; Not nice§ or Dainty. *Severall Quires,* placed
one over against another, and taking the Voice by Catches,§ *An-
theme* wise, give great Pleasure. *Turning Dances* into *Figure,§*
is a childish Curiosity. And generally, let it be noted, that those
Things, which I here set downe, are such, as doe naturally take
the Sense, and not respect Petty Wonderments. It is true, the
Alterations of Scenes, so it be quietly, and without Noise, are
Things of great Beauty, and Pleasure: For they feed and relieve
the Eye, before it be full of the same Object. Let the *Scenes*
abound with *Light,* specially *Coloured* and *Varied:* And let the
Masquers, or any other, that are to come down from the *Scene,*
have some Motions, upon the *Scene* it selfe, before their Comming down: For it drawes the Eye strangely, & makes it with great
pleasure, to desire to see that, it cannot perfectly discerne. Let
the *Songs* be *Loud,* and *Cheerefull,* and not *Chirpings,* or *Pulings.*
Let the *Musicke* likewise, be *Sharpe,* and *Loud,* and *Well Placed.*
The *Colours,* that shew best by Candlelight, are; White, Carna-
tion, and a Kinde of Sea-Water-Greene; And *Oes,§* or *Spangs,§* as
they are of no great Cost, so they are of most Glory. As for *Rich
Embroidery,* it is lost, and not Discerned. Let the *Sutes* of the
Masquers, be Gracefull, and such as become the Person, when

the Vizars[§] are off: Not after Examples of Knowne Attires; Turks,
Soldiers, Mariners, and the like. Let *Antimasques* not be long;
They have been commonly of Fooles, Satyres, Baboones, Wilde-
Men, Antiques, Beasts, Sprites, Witches, Ethiopes, Pigmies, Tur-
quets,[§] Nimphs, Rusticks, Cupids, Statua's Moving, and the like.
As for *Angels,* it is not Comicall enough, to put them in *Anti-
Masques;* And any Thing that is hideous, as Devils, Giants, is on
the other side as unfit. But chiefly, let the *Musicke* of them, be
Recreative,[§] and with some strange Changes. Some *Sweet Odours,*
suddenly comming forth, without any drops falling, are, in such
a Company, as there is Steame and Heate, Things of great Pleasure; & Refreshment. *Double Masques,* one of Men, another of
Ladies, addeth State, and Variety. But All is Nothing, except the
Roome be kept Cleare, and Neat.

For *Justs,*[§] and *Tourneys,*[§] and *Barriers;*[§] The Glories of them,
are chiefly in the Chariots, wherein the Challengers make their
Entry; Especially if they be drawne with Strange Beasts; As
Lions, Beares, Cammels, and the like: Or in the Devices of their
Entrance; Or in the Bravery[§] of their Liveries; Or in the Goodly
Furniture[§] of their Horses, and Armour. But enough of these
Toyes.

OF NATURE IN MEN

XXXVIII

Nature is Often Hidden; Sometimes Overcome; Seldome Extin-
guished. Force maketh *Nature* more violent in the Returne:
Doctrine and Discourse maketh *Nature* less Importune:[§] But
Custome onely doth alter and subdue *Nature*. Hee that seeketh
Victory over his *Nature,* let him not set Himselfe too great, nor
too small Tasks: For the first, will make him dejected by often
Faylings; And the Second will make him a small Proceeder,
though by often Prevailings. And at the first, let him practise
with Helps, as Swimmers doe with Bladders, or Rushes: But after
a Time, let him practise with disadvantages, as Dancers doe
with thick Shooes. For it breeds great Perfection, if the Practise
be harder then the use. Where *Nature* is Mighty, and therefore

the Victory hard, the Degrees had need be; First to Stay and Arrest *Nature* in Time; Like to Him, that would say over the Foure and Twenty Letters, when he was Angry: Then to Goe lesse in Quantity; As if one should, in forbearing Wine, come from Drinking Healths, to a Draught at a Meale: And lastly, to Discontinue altogether. But if a Man have the Fortitude, and Resolution, to enfranchise Himselfe at once, that is the best;

> *Optimus ille Animi Vindex, lædentia pectus*
> *Vincula qui rupit, dedoluitque semel.*[1]

Neither is the Ancient Rule amisse, to bend *Nature* as a Wand, to a Contrary Extreme, whereby to set it right: Understanding it, where the Contrary Extreme is no Vice. Let not a man force a Habit upon himselfe, with a Perpetuall Continuance, but with some Intermission. For both the Pause, reinforceth the new Onset; And if a Man, that is not perfect, be ever in Practise, he shall as well practise his Errours, as his Abilities; And induce one Habite of both: And there is no Meanes to helpe this, but by Seasonable Intermissions. But let not a Man trust his Victorie over his *Nature* too farre; For *Nature* will lay buried a great Time, and yet revive, upon the Occasion or Temptation. Like as it was with *Æsopes Damosell*, turned from a Catt to a Woman; who sate very demurely, at the Boards End, till a Mouse ranne before her. Therefore let a Man, either avoid the Occasion altogether; Or put Himselfe often to it, that hee may be little moved with it. A Mans *Nature* is best perceived in Privatenesse, for there is no Affectation; In Passion, for that putteth a Man out of his Precepts; And in a new Case or Experiment, for there Custome leaveth him. They are happie Men, whose *Natures* sort§ with their Vocations; Otherwise they may say, *Multùm Incola fuit Anima mea:*[2] when they converse§ in those Things, they doe not Affect.§ In Studies, whatsoever a Man commandeth upon himselfe, let him set Houres for it: But whatsoever is agreeable to his *Nature*, let him take no Care, for any set Times: For his Thoughts, will flie to it of Themselves; So as the Spaces of§ other

---

1 He is the best liberator of his spirit who breaks the chains that gall his breast and gets rid of his grief once and for all.
2 My soul hath long dwelt with him that hateth peace.

Businesse, or Studies, will suffice. A Mans *Nature* runnes either
to Herbes, or Weeds; Therefore let him seasonably Water the
One, and Destroy the Other.

OF YOUTH AND AGE

XLII

A Man that is *Young in yeares,* may be Old in Houres, if he have
lost no Time. But that happeneth rarely. Generally, *youth* is like
the first Cogitations, not so Wise as the Second. For there is a
youth in thoughts as well as in Ages. And yet the Invention of
Young Men, is more lively, then that of Old: And Imaginations
streame into their Mindes better, and, as it were, more Divinely.
Natures that have much Heat, and great and violent desires and
Perturbations, are not ripe for Action, till they have passed the
Meridian of their yeares: As it was with *Julius Cæsar, & Septimius
Severus.* Of the latter of whom, it is said; *Juventutem egit, Errori-
bus, imò Furoribus, plenam.*[3] And yet he was the Ablest Emper-
our, almost, of all the List. But Reposed Natures may doe well in
Youth. As it is seene, in *Augustus Cæsar, Cosmus* Duke of *Flor-
ence, Gaston de Fois,* and others. On the other side, Heate and
Vivacity in *Age,* is an Excellent Composition§ for Businesse.
Young Men, are Fitter to Invent, then to Judge; Fitter for Execution, then for Counsell; And Fitter for New Projects, then for
Setled Businesse. For the Experience of *Age,* in Things that fall
within the compasse of it, directeth them; But in New Things,
abuseth§ them. The Errours of *Young Men* are the Ruine of Businesse; But the Errours of *Aged Men* amount but to this; That
more might have beene done, or sooner. *Young Men,* in the Conduct, and Mannage of Actions, Embrace more then they can
Hold, Stirre more then they can Quiet; Fly to the End, without
Consideration of the Meanes, and Degrees; Pursue some few
Principles, which they have chanced upon absurdly;§ Care§ not
to Innovate, which draws unknowne Inconveniences; Use Extreme Remedies at first; And, that which doubleth all Errours,
will not acknowledge or retract them; Like an unready§ Horse,
that will neither Stop, nor Turne. *Men* of *Age,* Object too much,

[3] His youth was full of errors, even of madnesses.

Consult too long, Adventure too little, Repent too soone, and seldome drive Businesse home to the full Period;§ But content themselves with a Mediocrity of Successe. Certainly, it is good to compound Employments of both; For that will be Good for the *Present*, because the Vertues of either *Age*, may correct the defects of both: And good for Succession, that *Young Men* may be Learners, while *Men* in *Age* are Actours: And lastly, Good for *Externe Accidents*, because Authority followeth *Old Men*, And Favour and Popularity *Youth*. But for the Morall Part, perhaps *Youth* will have the preheminence, as *Age* hath for the Politique. A certaine *Rabbine*,§ upon the Text; *Your Young Men shall see visions, and your Old Men shall dreame dreames;* Inferreth, that *Young Men* are admitted nearer to God then *Old;* Because *Vision* is a clearer Revelation, then a *Dreame*. And certainly, the more a Man drinketh of the World, the more it intoxicateth; And *Age* doth profit rather in the Powers of Understanding, then in the Vertues of the Will and Affections. There be some have an Over-early Ripenesse in their yeares, which fadeth betimes: These are first, Such as have Brittle Wits, the Edge whereof is soone turned; Such as was *Hermogenes* the *Rhetorician*, whose Books are exceeding Subtill; Who afterwards waxed Stupid. A Second Sort is of those, that have some naturall Dispositions, which have better Grace in *Youth*, then in *Age:* Such as is a fluent and Luxuriant Speech; which becomes *Youth* well, but not *Age:* So *Tully*§ saith of *Hortensius; Idem manebat, neque idem decebat.*[4] The third is of such, as take too high a Straine at the First; And are Magnanimous, more then Tract§ of yeares can uphold. As was *Scipio Affricanus*, of whom *Livy* saith in effect; *Ultima primis cedebant.*[5]

OF GARDENS

XLVI

God *Almightie* first Planted a *Garden*. And indeed, it is the Purest of Humane pleasures. It is the Greatest Refreshment to the Spirits of Man; Without which, *Buildings* and *Pallaces* are but Grosse Handy-works: And a Man shall ever see, that when Ages

---

[4] He remained the same, when the same was not becoming.
[5] His last actions were not equal to his first.

grow to Civility and Elegancie, Men come to *Build Stately,* sooner
then to *Garden Finely:* As if *Gardening* were the Greater Perfection. I doe hold it, in the Royall Ordering of *Gardens,* there ought
to be *Gardens,* for all the *Moneths* in the Yeare: In which, severally, Things of Beautie, may be then in Season. For *December,*
and *January,* and the Latter Part of *November,* you must take
such Things, as are Greene all Winter; Holly; Ivy; Bayes; Juniper; Cipresse Trees; Eugh; Pine-Apple-Trees;§ Firre-Trees; Rose-
Mary; Lavander; Periwinckle, the White, the Purple, and the
Blewe; Germander; Flagges;§ Orenge-Trees; Limon-Trees; And
Mirtles, if they be stooved;§ & Sweet Marjoram warme§ set. There
followeth, for the latter Part of *January,* and *February,* the Me-
zerion§ Tree, which then blossomes; Crocus Vernus, both the Yel-
low, and the Gray; Prime-Roses; Anemones; The Early Tulippa;
Hiacynthus Orientalis; Chamaïris;§ Frettellaria.§ For *March,*
There come Violets, specially the Single Blew, which are the
Earliest; The Yellow Daffadill; The Dazie; The Almond-Tree in
Blossome; The Peach-Tree in Blossome; The Cornelian-Tree in
Blossome; Sweet-Briar. In *Aprill* follow, The Double white Violet;
The Wall-flower; The Stock-Gilly-Flower; The Couslip; Flower-
De-lices,§ and Lillies of all Natures; Rose-mary Flowers; The
Tulippa; The Double Piony; The Pale Daffadill; The French
Honny-Suckle; The Cherry-Tree in Blossome; The Dammasin,§
and Plum-Trees in Blossome; The White-Thorne§ in Leafe; The
Lelacke Tree. In *May,* and *June,* come Pincks of all sorts, Spe-
cially the Blush Pincke; Roses of all kinds, except the Muske,
which comes later; Hony-Suckles; Strawberries; Buglosse; Col-
umbine; The French Mary-gold; Flos§ Africanus; Cherry-Tree in
Fruit; Ribes;§ Figges in Fruit; Raspes;§ Vine Flowers; Lavender
in Flowers; The Sweet Satyrian,§ with the White Flower; Herba§
Muscaria; Lilium§ Convallium; The Apple-tree in Blossome. In
July, come Gilly-Flowers of all Varieties; Muske Roses; The Lime-
Tree in blossome; Early Peares, and Plummes in Fruit; Ginnit-
ings;§ Quadlins.§ In *August,* come Plummes of all sorts in Fruit;
Peares; Apricockes; Berberies; Filberds; Muske-Melons; Monks
Hoods, of all colours. In *September,* come Grapes; Apples; Pop-
pies of all colours; Peaches; Melo-Cotones;§ Nectarines; Cornel-
ians; Wardens;§ Quinces. In *October,* and the beginning of
November, come Sarvices;§ Medlars; Bullises;§ Roses Cut or Re-

moved to come late; Hollyokes;§ and such like. These Particulars
are for the *Climate* of *London;* But my meaning is Perceived, that
you may have *Ver Perpetuum,*[6] as the Place affords.

And because, the *Breath* of Flowers, is farre Sweeter in the
Aire, (where it comes and Goes, like the Warbling of Musick)
then in the hand, therfore nothing is more fit for that delight,
then to know, what be the *Flowers,* and *Plants,* that doe best
perfume the Aire. Roses Damask & Red, are fast§ Flowers of
their Smels; So that; you may walke by a whole Row of them,
and finde Nothing of their Sweetnesse; Yea though it be, in a
Mornings Dew. Bayes likewise yeeld no Smell, as they grow. Rose-
mary little; Nor Sweet-Marjoram. That, which above all Others,
yeelds the *Sweetest Smell* in the *Aire,* is the Violet; Specially the
White-double-Violet, which comes twice a Yeare; About the middle of *Aprill,* and about *Bartholomew-tide.* Next to that is, the
Muske-Rose. Then the Strawberry Leaves dying, which [yield] a
most Excellent Cordiall§ Smell. Then the Flower of the Vines;
It is a little dust, like the dust of a Bent,§ which growes upon the
Cluster, in the First comming forth. Then Sweet Briar. Then
Wall-Flowers, which are very Delightfull, to be set under a Par-
ler, or Lower Chamber Window. Then Pincks, and Gilly-Flowers,
specially the Matted Pinck, & Clove Gilly-flower. Then the
Flowers of the Lime tree. Then the Hony-Suckles, so they be
somewhat a farre off. Of Beane Flowers I speake not, because
they are Field Flowers. But those which *Perfume* the Aire most
delightfully, not *passed by* as the rest, but being *Troden upon*
and *Crushed,* are Three: That is Burnet, Wilde-Time, and Wa-
ter-Mints. Therefore, you are to set whole Allies of them, to have
the Pleasure, when you walke or tread.

For *Gardens,* (Speaking of those, which are indeed *Prince-like,*
as we have done of *Buildings*[7]) the Contents, ought not well to
be, under *Thirty Acres of Ground;* And to be divided into three
Parts: A *Greene* in the Entrance; A *Heath* or *Desart* in the Going
forth; And the *Maine Garden* in the midst; Besides *Alleys,* on
both Sides. And I like well, that Foure Acres of Ground, be assigned to the *Greene;* Six to the *Heath;* Foure and Foure to either
Side; And Twelve to the *Maine Garden.* The Greene hath two

6 Perpetual spring.
7 The subject of Essay XLV.

pleasures; The one, because nothing is more Pleasant to the Eye, then Greene Grasse kept finely shorne; The other, because it will give you a faire Alley in the midst, by which you may go in front upon a *Stately Hedge*, which is to inclose the *Garden*. But, because the Alley will be long, and in great Heat of the Yeare, or Day, you ought not to buy the shade in the *Garden*, by Going in the Sunne thorow the *Greene*, therefore you are, of either *Side* the *Greene*, to Plant a *Covert Alley*, upon Carpenters Worke, about Twelve Foot in Height, by which you may goe in Shade, into the *Garden*. As for the Making of *Knots*, or *Figures*, with *Divers Coloured Earths*, that they may lie under the Windowes of the House, on that Side, which the *Garden* stands, they be but Toyes: You may see as good Sights, many times, in Tarts. The *Garden* is best to be Square; Incompassed, on all the Foure Sides, with a *Stately Arched Hedge*. The *Arches* to be upon *Pillars*, of Carpenters Worke, of some Ten Foot high, and Six Foot broad: And the *Spaces* between, of the same Dimension, with the *Breadth* of the *Arch*. Over the *Arches*, let there bee an *Entire Hedge*, of some Foure Foot High, framed also upon Carpenters Worke: And upon the *Upper Hedge*, over every *Arch*, a little *Turret*, with a *Belly*, enough to receive a *Cage* of *Birds*: And over every *Space*, betweene the *Arches*, some other little *Figure*, with Broad Plates of *Round Coloured Glasse*, gilt, for the *Sunne*, to Play upon. But this *Hedge* I entend to be, raised upon a *Bancke*, not Steepe, but gently Slope, of some Six Foot, set all with *Flowers*. Also I understand, that this *Square* of the *Garden*, should not be the whole Breadth of the Ground, but to leave, on either Side, Ground enough, for diversity of *Side Alleys*: Unto which, the Two *Covert Alleys* of the *Greene*, may deliver you. But there must be, no *Alleys* with *Hedges*, at either *End*, of this great *Inclosure*: Not at the *Hither End*, for letting⁵ your Prospect upon this Faire Hedge from the *Greene*; Nor at the *Further End*, for letting your Prospect from the Hedge, through the Arches, upon the *Heath*.

For the Ordering of the Ground, within the *Great Hedge*, I leave it to Variety of Device; Advising neverthelesse, that whatsoever forme you cast it into, first it be not too Busie, or full of Worke. Wherein I, for my part, doe not like *Images Cut out* in *Juniper*, or other *Garden stuffe*: They be for Children. *Little low*

Hedges, Round, like Welts,§ with some Pretty *Pyramides,* I like well: And in some Places, *Faire Columnes* upon Frames of Carpenters Worke. I would also, have the *Alleys,* Spacious and Faire. You may have *Closer Alleys* upon the *Side Grounds,* but none in the *Maine Garden.* I wish also, in the very Middle, a *Faire Mount,* with three Ascents, and Alleys, enough for foure to walke a breast; Which I would have to be Perfect Circles, without any Bulwarkes, or Imbosments; And the *Whole Mount,* to be Thirty Foot high; And some fine *Banquetting House,* with some *Chimneys* neatly cast, and without too much *Glasse.*

For *Fountaines,* they are a great Beauty, and Refreshment; But *Pooles* marre all, and make the *Garden* unwholsome, and full of Flies, and Frogs. *Fountaines* I intend to be of two Natures: The One, that *Sprinckleth* or *Spouteth Water;* The Other a *Faire Receipt§* of *Water,* of some Thirty or Forty Foot Square, but without Fish, or Slime, or Mud. For the first, the *Ornaments* of *Images Gilt,* or of *Marble,* which are in use, doe well: But the maine Matter is, so to Convey the Water, as it never Stay, either in the Bowles, or in the Cesterne; That the Water be never by Rest *Discoloured, Greene,* or *Red,* or the like; Or gather any *Mossinesse* or *Putrefaction.* Besides that, it is to be cleansed every day by the Hand. Also some *Steps* up to it, and some *Fine Pavement* about it, doth well. As for the other Kinde of *Fountaine,* which we may call a *Bathing Poole,* it may admit much Curiosity, and Beauty; wherewith we will not trouble our selves: As, that the Bottome be finely Paved, And with Images: The sides likewise; And withall Embellished with Coloured Glasse, and such Things of Lustre; Encompassed also, with fine Railes of Low Statua's. But the Maine Point is the same, which we mentioned, in the former Kinde of *Fountaine;* which is, that the *Water* be in *Perpetuall Motion,* Fed by a Water higher then the *Poole,* and Delivered into it by faire Spouts, and then discharged away under Ground, by some Equalitie of Bores, that it stay little. And for fine Devices, of Arching Water without Spilling, and Making it rise in severall Formes, (of Feathers, Drinking Glasses, Canopies, and the like,) they be pretty things to looke on, but Nothing to Health and Sweetnesse.

For the *Heath,* which was the Third Part of our Plot, I wish it to be framed, as much as may be, to a *Naturall wildnesse. Trees*

I would have none in it; But some *Thickets*, made onely of *Sweet-Briar*, and *Honny-suckle*, and some *Wilde Vine* amongst; And the Ground set with *Violets, Strawberries*, and *Prime-Roses*. For these are Sweet, and prosper in the Shade. And these to be in the *Heath*, here and there, not in any Order. I like also little *Heaps*, in the Nature of *Mole-hils*, (such as are in *Wilde Heaths*) to be set, some with Wilde Thyme; Some with Pincks; Some with Germander, that gives a good Flower to the Eye; Some with Periwinckle; Some with Violets; Some with Strawberries; Some with Couslips; Some with Daisies; Some with Red-Roses; Some with Lilium Convallium; Some with Sweet-Williams Red; Some with Beares-Foot;§ And the like Low Flowers, being withal Sweet, and Sightly. Part of which *Heapes*, to be with *Standards*,§ of little *Bushes*, prickt§ upon their Top, and Part without. The *Standards* to be Roses; Juniper; Holly; Beare-berries (but here and there, because of the Smell of their Blossome;) Red Currans; Goose-berries; Rose-Mary; Bayes; Sweet-Briar; and such like. But these *Standards*, to be kept with Cutting, that they grow not out of Course.

For the *Side Grounds*, you are to fill them with *Varietie* of *Alleys*, Private, to give a full Shade; Some of them, wheresoever the Sun be. You are to frame some of them likewise for Shelter, that when the Wind blows Sharpe, you may walke, as in a Gallery. And those Alleys must be likewise hedged, at both Ends, to keepe out the Wind; And these *Closer Alleys*, must bee ever finely Gravelled, and no Grasse, because of Going wet. In many of these *Alleys* likewise, you are to set *Fruit-Trees* of all Sorts; As well upon the Walles, as in Ranges.§ And this would be generally observed, that the *Borders*, wherin you plant your *Fruit-Trees*, be Faire and Large, and Low, and not Steepe; And Set with *Fine Flowers*, but thin and sparingly, lest they Deceive§ the *Trees*. At the End of both the *Side Grounds*, I would have a *Mount* of some Pretty Height, leaving the Wall of the Enclosure Brest high, to looke abroad into the Fields.

For the *Maine Garden*, I doe not Deny, but there should be some Faire *Alleys*, ranged on both Sides, with *Fruit Trees;* And some Pretty *Tufts* of *Fruit Trees*, And *Arbours* with *Seats,* set in some Decent Order; But these to be, by no Meanes, set too thicke; But to leave the *Maine Garden,* so as it be not close, but the Aire Open and Free. For as for *Shade,* I would have you rest, upon the *Alleys* of the *Side Grounds,* there to walke, if you be Disposed, in the Heat of the Yeare, or day; But to make Account, that the *Maine Garden,* is for the more Temperate Parts of the yeare; And in the Heat of Summer, for the Morning, and the Evening, or Over-cast Dayes.

For *Aviaries,* I like them not, except they be of that Largenesse, as they may be *Turffed,* and have *Living Plants,* and *Bushes,* set in them; That the *Birds* may have more Scope, and Naturall Neastling, and that no *Foulenesse* appeare, in the *Floare* of the *Aviary.* So I have made a Platforme[§] of a *Princely Garden,* Partly by Precept, Partly by Drawing, not a Modell, but some generall Lines of it; And in this I have spared for no Cost. But it is Nothing, for *Great Princes,* that for the most Part, taking Advice with Workmen, with no Lesse Cost, set their Things together; And sometimes adde *Statua's,* and such Things, for State, and Magnificence, but nothing to the true Pleasure of a *Garden.*

OF NEGOCIATING

XLVII

It is generally better to *deale* by Speech, then by Letter; And by the Mediation of a Third, then by a Mans Selfe. Letters are good, when a Man would draw an Answer by Letter backe againe; Or when it may serve, for a Mans Justification, afterwards to produce his owne Letter; Or where it may be Danger to be interrupted, or heard by Peeces. To *deale in Person* is good, when a Mans Face breedeth Regard, as Commonly with Inferiours; Or in Tender[§] Cases, where a Mans Eye, upon the Countenance of him with whom he speaketh, may give him a Direction, how farre to goe: And generally, where a Man will reserve to himselfe Libertie, either to Disavow, or to Expound. In Choice of *Instruments,* it is better, to choose Men of a Plainer Sort, that are like to doe that, that is committed to them, and to report back again faithfully the Successe; Then those, that are Cunning to Contrive out of other Mens Businesse, somewhat to grace themselves; And will helpe[§] the Matter, in Report, for

Satisfaction sake. Use also, such Persons, as affect the Businesse,
wherin they are Employed; For that quickneth[§] much; And such,
as are Fit for the Matter; As Bold Men for Expostulation, Faire
spoken Men for Perswasion, Craftie Men for Enquiry and Observation, Froward and Absurd Men for Businesse that doth not
well beare[§] out it Selfe. Use also such, as have beene Luckie,
and Prevailed before in Things wherein you have Emploied
them; For that breeds Confidence, and they will strive to maintaine their Prescription.[§] It is better, to sound a Person, with
whom one *Deales*, a farre off, then to fall upon the Point at
first; Except you meane to surprize him by some Short Question.
It is better *Dealing* with Men in Appetite, then with those that
are where they would be. If a Man *Deale* with another upon
Conditions, the Start or First Performance is all; Which a Man
cannot reasonably Demaund, except either the Nature of the
Thing be such, which must goe before; Or Else a Man can
perswade the other Partie, that hee shall still need him, in some
other Thing; Or else that he be counted the Honester Man. All
Practise,[§] is to *Discover*,[§] or to *Worke*.[§] Men *Discover* themselves,
in Trust; In Passion; At unawares; And of Necessitie, when
they would have somewhat done, and cannot finde an apt Pretext. If you would *Worke* any Man, you must either know his
Nature, and Fashions, and so Lead him; Or his Ends, and so
Perswade him; Or his Weaknesse, and Disadvantages, and so
Awe him; or those that have Interest in him, and so Governe
him. In *Dealing* with Cunning Persons, we must ever Consider
their Ends, to interpret their Speeches; And it is good, to say
little to them, and that which they least looke for. In all *Nego-
ciations* of Difficultie, a Man may not looke, to Sowe and Reape
at once; But must Prepare Businesse, and so Ripen it by Degrees.

OF STUDIES

L

Studies serve for Delight, for Ornament, and for Ability. Their
Chiefe Use for Delight, is in Privatenesse and Retiring; For
Ornament, is in Discourse; And for Ability, is in the Judgement
and Disposition of Businesse. For Expert[§] Men can Execute,

and perhaps Judge of particulars, one by one; But the generall Counsels, and the Plots, and Marshalling of Affaires, come best from those that are *Learned*. To spend too much Time in *Studies*, is Sloth; To use them too much for Ornament, is Affectation; To make Judgement wholly by their Rules is the Humour of a Scholler. They perfect[§] Nature, and are perfected by Experience: For Naturall Abilities, are like Naturall Plants, that need Proyning[§] by *Study*: And *Studies* themselves, doe give forth Directions too much at Large, except they be bounded in by experience. Crafty Men Contemne *Studies;* Simple Men Admire[§] them; and Wise Men Use them: For they teach not their owne Use; But that is a Wisdome without them, and above them, won by Observation. Reade not to Contradict, and Confute; Nor to Beleeve and Take for granted; Nor to Finde Talke and Discourse; But to weigh and Consider. Some *Bookes* are to be Tasted, Others to be Swallowed, and Some Few to be Chewed and Digested: That is, some *Bookes* are to be read onely in Parts; Others to be read but not Curiously;[§] And some Few to be read wholly, and with Diligence and Attention. Some *Bookes* also may be read by Deputy, and Extracts made of them by Others: But that would[§] be, onely in the lesse important Arguments, and the Meaner Sort of *Bookes:* else distilled *Bookes,* are like Common distilled Waters, Flashy[§] things. Reading maketh a Full man; Conference a Ready Man; And Writing an Exact Man. And therefore, If a Man Write little, he had need have a Great memory; If he Conferre little, he had need have a Present Wit; And if he Reade litle, he had need have much Cunning, to seeme to know that, he doth not. *Histories* make men Wise; *Poets* Witty; The *Mathematicks* Subtill; *Naturall Philosophy* deepe; *Morall* Grave; *Logick* and *Rhetorick* Able to Contend. *Abeunt studia in Mores.*[8] Nay there is no Stond[§] or Impediment in the Wit, but may be wrought out by Fit *Studies:* Like as Diseases of the Body, may have Appropriate Exercises. Bowling is good for the Stone and Reines;[§] Shooting for the Lungs and Breast; Gentle Walking for the Stomacke; Riding for the Head; And the like. So if a Mans Wit be Wandring, let him *Study* the *Mathematicks;* For in Demonstrations, if his Wit be called away never so little, he must begin again: If his Wit be not Apt to distin-

8 Studies change into character.

guish or find differences, let him *Study* the *Schoole-men;* For they are *Cymini sectores.*[9] If he be not Apt to beat[s] over Matters, and to call up one Thing, to Prove and Illustrate another, let him *Study* the *Lawyers Cases:* So every Defect of the Minde, may have a Speciall Receit.

OF JUDICATURE

LVI

Judges ought to remember, that their Office is *Jus dicere,* and not *Jus dare; To Interpret Law,* and not to *Make Law,* or *Give Law.* Else will it be like the Authority, claimed by the *Church* of *Rome;* which under pretext of Exposition of Scripture, doth not sticke[s] to Adde and Alter; And to Pronounce that, which they doe not Finde; And by *Shew* of *Antiquitie,* to introduce *Noveltie. Judges* ought to be more Learned, then Wittie; More Reverend, then Plausible;[s] And more Advised, then Confident. Above all Things, Integritie is their Portion, and Proper Vertue. *Cursed* (saith the Law) *is hee that removeth the Land-marke.* The Mislaier of a *Meere Stone* is to blame. But it is the Unjust *Judge,* that is the Capitall Remover of Land-markes, when he Defineth amisse of Lands and Propertie. One Foule Sentence, doth more Hurt, then many Foule Examples. For these doe but Corrupt the Streame; The other Corrupteth the Fountaine. So saith *Salomon; Fons turbatus, & Vena corrupta, est Justus cadens in causâ suâ coram Adversario.*[1] The Office of *Judges,* may have Reference, Unto the *Parties that sue;* Unto the *Advocates that Plead;* Unto the *Clerkes* and *Ministers of Justice* underneath them; And to the *Soveraigne* or *State* above them.

First, for the *Causes* or *Parties that Sue. There be* (saith the Scripture) *that turne Judgement into Worme-wood;* And surely, there be also, that turne it into *Vinegar;* For Injustice maketh it Bitter, and Delaies make it Soure. The Principall Dutie of a *Judge,* is to suppresse Force and Fraud; whereof Force is the more Pernicious, when it is Open; And Fraud, when it is Close

---

9 Carvers of cumin seed (hair splitters).
1 A righteous man falling down before the wicked is as a troubled fountain, and a corrupt spring.

and Disguised. Adde thereto Contentious Suits, which ought to
be spewed out, as the Surfet of Courts. A *Judge* ought to prepare his Way to a Just Sentence, as *God* useth to prepare his
Way, by *Raising Valleys,* and *Taking downe Hills:* So when there
appeareth on either side, an High Hand; Violent Prosecution,
Cunning Advantages taken, Combination,§ Power, Great Counsell, then is the Vertue of a *Judge* seene, to make Inequalitie
Equall; That he may plant his *Judgement,* as upon an Even
Ground. *Qui fortitèr emungit, elicit sanguinem;*[2] And where
the Wine-Presse is hard wrought, it yeelds a harsh Wine, that
tastes of the Grape-stone. *Judges* must beware of Hard Con-
structions,§ and Strained Inferences; For there is no Worse Torture, then the Torture of Lawes. Specially in case of Lawes
Penall, they ought to have Care, that that which was meant
for Terrour, be not turned into Rigour; And that they bring not
upon the People, that Shower, whereof the Scripture speaketh:
Pluet super eos Laqueos:[3] For Penall Lawes Pressed, are a
Shower of Snares upon the People. Therefore, let *Penall Lawes,*
if they have beene Sleepers of long, or if they be growne unfit
for the present Time, be by Wise *Judges* confined in the Execution; *Judicis Officium est, ut Res, ita Tempora Rerum,* &c.[4] In
Causes of *Life* and *Death; Judges* ought (as farre as the Law
permitteth) in Justice to remember Mercy; And to Cast a Severe
Eye upon the Example, but a Mercifull Eye upon the Person.

Secondly, for the *Advocates* and *Counsell that Plead:* Patience
and Gravitie of Hearing, is an Essentiall Part of Justice; And
an Over-speaking *Judge* is no *well tuned Cymball.* It is no Grace
to a *Judge,* first to finde that, which hee might have heard, in
due time, from the Barre; or to shew Quicknesse of Conceit§ in
Cutting off Evidence or Counsell too short; Or to prevent§ Information, by Questions though Pertinent. The Parts of a *Judge*
in Hearing are Foure: To direct the Evidence; To Moderate
Length, Repetition, or Impertinency of Speech; To Recapitulate,
Select, and Collate, the Materiall Points of that, which hath
beene said; And to Give the Rule or Sentence. Whatsoever is
above these, is too much; And proceedeth, Either of Glory and

2 The wringing of the nose bringeth forth blood.
3 Upon the wicked he shall rain snares, fire and brimstone, and an horrible
tempest.
4 Just as a judge must consider the matter, so he must consider the times.

willingnesse to Speake; Or of Impatience to Heare; Or of Short-
nesse of Memorie; Or of Want of a Staid and Equall[§] Attention.
It is a Strange Thing to see, that the Boldnesse of *Advocates,*
should prevaile with *Judges;* Whereas they should imitate *God,*
in whose Seat they sit; who *represseth the Presumptuous,* and
giveth Grace to the Modest. But it is more Strange, that *Judges*
should have Noted Favourites; Which cannot but Cause Multi-
plication of Fees, and Suspicion of By-waies. There is due from
the *Judge,* to the *Advocate,* some Commendation and Gracing,[§]
where *Causes* are well Handled, and faire Pleaded; Especially
towards the Side which obtaineth not; For that upholds, in the
Client, the Reputation of his *Counsell,* and beats[§] downe, in him,
the Conceit[§] of his *Cause.* There is likewise due to the *Publique,*
a Civill Reprehension of *Advocates,* where there appeareth Cunning Counsel, Grosse Neglect, Slight Information, Indiscreet
Pressing, or an Over-bold Defence. And let not the *Counsell* at
the Barre, chop[§] with the *Judge,* nor winde himselfe into the
handling of the *Cause* anew, after the *Judge* hath Declared his
Sentence: But on the other side, Let not the *Judge* meet the
Cause halfe Way; Nor give Occasion to the Partie to say; *His
Counsell or Proofes were not heard.*

Thirdly, for that that concernes *Clerks,* and *Ministers.* The
Place of *Justice,* is an Hallowed Place; And therefore, not only
the Bench, but the Foot-pace,[§] and Precincts, and Purprise[§]
thereof, ought to be preserved without Scandall and Corruption.
For certainly, *Grapes,* (as the *Scripture* saith) *will not be gathered of Thornes or Thistles:* Neither can *Justice* yeeld her Fruit
with Sweetnesse, amongst the Briars and Brambles, of Catching[§]
and Poling[§] *Clerkes* and *Ministers.* The Attendance of Courts is
subject to Foure bad Instruments. First, Certaine Persons, that
are Sowers of Suits; which make the Court swell, and the Country pine. The Second Sort is of those, that ingage Courts, in
Quarells of Jurisdiction, and are not truly *Amici Curiæ,*[5] but
Parasiti Curiæ;[6] in puffing a Court up beyond her Bounds, for
their owne Scraps, and Advantage. The Third Sort is of those,
that may be accounted, the Left Hands of Courts; Persons that
are full of Nimble and Sinister Trickes and Shifts, whereby they

5 Friends of the court.
6 Parasites of the court.

pervert the Plaine and Direct Courses of *Courts*, and bring *Justice* into Oblique Lines and Labyrinths. And the Fourth is, the Poler and Exacter of Fees; which justifies the Common Resemblance of the *Courts* of *Justice*, to the *Bush*, whereunto while the Sheepe flies for defence in Wether, hee is sure to loose Part of his Fleece. On the other side, an *Ancient Clerke*, skilfull in Presidents, Wary in Proceeding, and Understanding in the *Businesse* of the *Court*, is an excellent Finger of a *Court*; And doth many times point the way to the *Judge* himselfe.

Fourthly, for that which may concerne the *Soveraigne* and *Estate*. *Judges* ought above all to remember the Conclusion of the *Roman Twelve Tables; Salus Populi Suprema Lex;*[7] And to know, that Lawes, except they bee in Order to that End, are but Things Captious, and Oracles not well Inspired. Therefore it is an Happie Thing in a *State*, when *Kings* and *States* doe often Consult with *Judges*; And againe, when *Judges* doe often Consult with the *King* and *State*: The one, when there is Matter of Law, intervenient in Businesse of State; The other, when there is some Consideration of State, intervenient in Matter of Law. For many times, the Things Deduced to *Judgement*, may bee *Meum* and *Tuum*,[8] when the Reason and Consequence thereof, may Trench to Point of Estate: I call Matter of Estate, not onely the parts of *Soveraigntie*, but whatsoever introduceth any Great Alteration, or Dangerous president; Or Concerneth manifestly any great Portion of People. And let no Man weakly conceive, that Just Laws, and True Policie, have any *Antipathie*: For they are like the Spirits, and Sinewes, that One moves with the Other. Let *Judges* also remember, that *Salomons Throne*, was supported by Lions, on both Sides; Let them be Lions, but yet Lions under the Throne; Being circumspect, that they doe not checke, or oppose any Points of *Soveraigntie*. Let not *Judges* also, be so Ignorant of their owne Right, as to thinke, there is not left to them, as a Principall Part of their Office, a Wise Use, and application of Lawes. For they may remember, what the *Apostle* saith, of a Greater *Law*, then theirs; *Nos scimus quia Lex bona est, modò quis eâ utatur Legitimè.*[9]

---

7 The welfare of the people is the supreme law.
8 Mine and thine.
9 But we know that the law is good, if a man use it lawfully.

OF VICISSITUDE OF THINGS

LVIII

Salomon saith; *There is no New Thing upon the Earth.* So that as *Plato* had an Imagination; *That all Knowledge was but Remembrance:* So *Salomon* giveth his Sentence; *That all Noveltie is but Oblivion.* Whereby you may see, that the River of *Lethe*, runneth as well above Ground, as below. There is an abstruse Astrologer that saith; *If it were not, for two things, that are Constant; (The one is, that the Fixed Starres ever stand at like distance, one from another, and never come nearer together, nor goe further asunder; The other, that the Diurnall Motion perpetually keepeth Time:) No Individuall would last one Moment.* Certain it is, that the *Matter*, is in a Perpetuall Flux, and never at a Stay. The great Winding-sheets, that burie all Things in Oblivion, are two; *Deluges*, and *Earth-quakes*. As for *Conflagrations*, and great *Droughts*, they doe not meerely dispeople, and destroy. *Phaetons* Carre went but a day. And the *Three yeares Drought*, in the time of *Elias*,§ was but Particular, and left People Alive. As for the great *Burnings by Lightnings*, which are often in the *West Indies*, they are but narrow. But in the other two Destructions, by *Deluge*, and *Earth-quake*, it is further to be noted, that the Remnant of People, which hap to be reserved,§ are commonly Ignorant and Mountanous People, that can give no Account, of the Time past: So that the Oblivion is all one, as if none had beene left. If you consider well, of the People of the *West Indies*, it is very probable, that they are a Newer, or a Younger People, then the People of the Old World. And it is much more likely, that the Destruction, that hath heretofore been there, was not by *Earth-quakes*, (As the *Ægyptian* Priest told *Solon*, concerning the Island of *Atlantis; That it was swallowed by an Earth-quake;*) But rather, that it was desolated, by a Particular *Deluge*. For *Earth-quakes* are seldome in those Parts. But on the other side, they have such *Powring Rivers*, as the *Rivers* of *Asia*, and *Affrick*, and *Europe*, are but Brookes to them. Their *Andes* likewise, or Mountaines, are farre higher, then those with us; Whereby it seemes, that the Remnants of Generation of Men, were, in such a Particular *Deluge*, saved.

As for the Observation, that *Macciavel* hath, that the *Jealousie* of *Sects*, doth much extinguish the Memory of Things; Traducing *Gregory* the *Great*, that he did, what in him lay, to extinguish all Heathen Antiquities; I doe not finde, that those Zeales, doe any great Effects, nor last long: As it appeared in the Succession of *Sabinian*, who did revive the former Antiquities.

The *Vicissitude* or *Mutations*, in the *Superiour Globe*, are no fit Matter, for this present Argument. It may be, *Plato's great*[s] *Yeare*, if the World should last so long, would have some Effect; Not in renewing the State of like Individuals (for that is the Fume[s] of those, that conceive the Celestiall Bodies, have more accurate Influences, upon these Things below, then indeed they have) but in grosse. *Comets*, out[s] of question, have likewise Power and Effect, over the Grosse and Masse of Things: But they are rather gazed upon, and waited[s] upon in their Journey, then wisely observed in their Effects; Specially in their Respective Effects; That is, what Kinde of *Comet*, for Magnitude, Colour, Version[s] of the Beames, Placing in the Region of Heaven, or Lasting, produceth what Kinde of Effects.

There is a Toy, which I have heard, and I would not have it given[s] over, but waited upon a little. They say, it is observed, in the *Low Countries* (I know not in what Part) that Every Five and Thirtie yeeres, The same Kinde and Sute[s] of Yeers and Weathers, comes about againe: As Great Frosts, Great Wet, Great Droughts, Warme Winters, Summers with little Heat, and the like: And they call it the *Prime*. It is a Thing, I doe the rather mention, because computing backwards, I have found some Concurrence.

But to leave these Points of *Nature*, and to come to *Men*. The greatest *Vicissitude* of Things amongst *Men*, is the *Vicissitude* of *Sects*, and *Religions*. For those Orbs rule in Mens Minds most. The True *Religion* is *built upon the Rocke*; The Rest are tost upon the Waves of Time. To speake therefore, of the *Causes* of New *Sects*; And to give some *Counsell* concerning them; As farre, as the Weaknesse of Humane Judgement, can give stay to so great Revolutions.

When the *Religion* formerly received, is rent by Discords; And when the Holinesse of the Professours[s] of *Religion* is decayed, and full of Scandall; And withall the Times be Stupid, Ignorant, and Barbarous; you may doubt[§] the Springing up of a *New Sect;* If then also there should arise, any Extravagant and Strange Spirit, to make himselfe Authour thereof. All which Points held, when *Mahomet* published his *Law.* If a *New Sect* have not two Properties, feare it not: For it will not spread. The one is, the Supplanting, or the opposing, of Authority established: For Nothing is more Popular then that. The other is, the Giving Licence to Pleasures, and a Voluptuous Life. For as for *Speculative Heresies* (such as were in Ancient Times the *Arrians,* and now the *Arminians*) though they worke mightily upon Mens Wits, yet they doe not produce any great Alterations in States; except it be by the Helpe of Civill Occasions. There be three Manner of Plantations of *New Sects.* By the Power of *Signes* and *Miracles:* By the *Eloquence and Wisedome* of *Speech* and *Perswasion:* And by the *Sword.* For *Martyrdomes,* I reckon them amongst *Miracles;* Because they seeme to exceed, the Strength of Human Nature: And I may doe the like of *Superlative* and *Admirable Holinesse* of *Life.* Surely, there is no better Way, to stop the Rising of *New Sects,* and *Schismes;* then To reforme Abuses; To compound[§] the smaller Differences; To proceed mildly, and not with Sanguinary Persecutions; And rather to take off the principall Authours, by Winning and Advancing them, then to enrage them by Violence and Bitternesse.

The *Changes* and *Vicissitude* in *Warres* are many; But chiefly in three Things; In the *Seats* or *Stages* of the *Warre;* In the *Weapons;* And in the *Manner* of the *Conduct. Warres* in ancient Time, seemed more to move from *East* to *West:* For the *Persians, Assyrians, Arabians, Tartars,* (which were the Invaders) were all Easterne People. It is true, the *Gaules* were Westerne; But we reade but of two Incursions of theirs; The one to *Gallo-Grecia,* the other to *Rome.* But *East* and *West* have no certaine Points of Heaven: And no more have the *Warres,* either from the *East,* or *West,* any Certainty of Observation. But *North* and *South* are fixed: And it hath seldome or never been seene, that the farre Southern People have invaded the Northern, but contrariwise. Whereby it is manifest, that the *Northern Tract* of the World, is in Nature the more Martiall Region: Be it, in respect of the Stars of that Hemisphere; Or of the great Continents that are upon the *North,* whereas the *South Part,* for ought that is knowne, is almost all Sea; Or (which is most apparent) of the Cold of the *Northern* Parts, which is that, which without Aid of Discipline, doth make the Bodies hardest, and the Courages warmest.

Upon the *Breaking* and *Shivering* of a great *State* and *Empire*, you may be sure to have *Warres*. For great Empires, while they stand, doe enervate and destroy the Forces of the Natives, which they have subdued, resting upon their owne Protecting Forces: And then when they faile also, all goes to ruine, and they become a Prey. So was it, in the Decay of the *Roman Empire;* And likewise, in the *Empire* of *Almaigne,* after *Charles* the Great, every Bird taking a Fether; And were not unlike to befall to *Spaine,* if it should break. The great *Accessions* and *Unions* of *Kingdomes,* doe likewise stirre up *Warres*. For when a State growes to an Over-power, it is like a great Floud, that will be sure to overflow. As it hath been seene, in the States of *Rome, Turky, Spaine,* and others. Looke when the World hath fewest *Barbarous Peoples,* but such as commonly will not marry or generate, except they know meanes to live; (As it is almost every where at this day, except *Tartary*) there is no Danger of Inundations of People: But when there be *great Shoales* of *People,* which goe on to populate, without foreseeing Meanes of Life and Sustentation, it is of Necessity, that once in an Age or two, they discharge a Portion of their People upon other Nations: Which the ancient *Northern People,* were wont to doe by Lot: Casting Lots, what Part should stay at home, and what should seeke their Fortunes. When a *Warre-like State* growes *Soft* and *Effeminate,* they may be sure of a *Warre*. For commonly such States are growne rich, in the time of their Degenerating; And so the Prey inviteth, and their Decay in Valour encourageth a Warre.

As for the *Weapons,* it hardly falleth under Rule and Observation: yet we see, even they have *Returnes* and *Vicissitudes*. For certain it is, that *Ordnance* was known in the Citty of the *Oxidrakes* in *India;* And was that, which the *Macedonians* called Thunder and Lightning, and Magicke. And it is well knowne, that the use of *Ordnance* hath been in *China,* above 2000 yeares. The Conditions of *Weapons,* & their Improvement are; First, The Fetching a farre off: For that outruns the Danger:

As it is seene in *Ordnance* and *Muskets*. Secondly, the Strength of the Percussion; wherin likewise *Ordnance* doe exceed all Arietations,[§] and ancient Inventions. The third is, the commodious use of them: As that they may serve in all Wethers; That the Carriage may be Light and Manageable; and the like.

For the *Conduct* of the *Warre:* At the first, Men rested extremely upon *Number:* They did put the Warres likewise upon *Maine Force,* and *Valour;* Pointing Dayes for Pitched Fields, and so trying it out, upon an even Match: And they were more ignorant in *Ranging*[§] and *Arraying*[§] their *Battailes.* After they grew to rest upon *Number,* rather Competent, then Vast: They grew to *Advantages,* of *Place, Cunning Diversions,* and the like: And they grew more skilful in the *Ordering* of their *Battailes.*

In the *Youth* of a *State, Armes* doe flourish; In the *Middle Age* of a *State, Learning;* And then both of them together for a time: In the *Declining Age* of a *State, Mechanicall Arts* and *Merchandize. Learning* hath his Infancy, when it is but beginning, and almost Childish: Then his Youth, when it is Luxuriant and Juvenile: Then his Strength of yeares, when it is Solide and Reduced:[§] And lastly, his old Age, when it waxeth Dry and Exhaust. But it is not good, to looke too long, upon these turning Wheeles of *Vicissitude,* lest we become Giddy. As for the *Philology* of them, that is but a Circle of Tales, and therefore not fit for this Writing.

II

Robert Burton

FROM

The Anatomy of Melancholy

DEMOCRITUS JUNIOR TO THE READER.

Gentle Reader, I presume thou wilt be very inquisitive to know what antick§ or personate§ actor this is, that so insolently intrudes upon this common theatre, to the worlds view, arrogating another mans name, whence he is, why he doth it, and what he hath to say; Although, as he[1] said, *Primum si noluero, non respondebo, quis coacturus est?*[2] I am a free man born, and may chuse whether I will tell, who can compel me? If I be

---

1 *Seneca in ludo in mortem Claudii Cæsaris.* [Seneca, in his satire on the death of Claudius Caesar.] (All the marginal notes on Burton's first two pages are reproduced as footnotes; thereafter they are omitted.)
2 In the first place, if I don't want to answer, I won't; who will make me? (Here, as elsewhere, Burton provides his own translation or paraphrase in the words which follow. To illustrate his customary practice, I have translated all the Latin on his first two pages of text. Thereafter, whenever the Latin is not translated in a footnote, it may be assumed that Burton gives an English version.)

urged, I will as readily reply as that *Egyptian* in *Plutarch*,[3] when a curious fellow would needs know what he had in his basket, *Quum vides velatam, quid inquiris in rem absconditam?*[4] It was therefore covered, because he should not know what was in it. Seek not after that which is hid, if the contents please thee, *and be for thy use, suppose* the Man in the Moon, *or whom thou wilt to be the Author;*[5] I would not willingly be known. Yet in some sort to give thee satisfaction, which is more then I need, I will shew a reason, both of this usurped name, title, and subject. And first of the name of *Democritus;* lest any man by reason of it, should be deceived, expecting a pasquil, a satyre, some ridiculous treatise (as I my self should have done) some prodigious tenent,[§] or paradox of the earths motion, of infinite Worlds, *in infinito vacuo, ex fortuit â atomorum collisione,* in an infinite waste, so caused by an accidental collision of Motes in the Sun, all which *Democritus* held, *Epicurus* and their Master *Lucippus* of old maintained, and are lately revived by *Copernicus, Brunus,* and some others. Besides it hath been always an ordinary custom, as *Gellius* observes,[6] *for later Writers and impostors, to broach many absurd and insolent fictions, under the name of so noble a philosopher as* Democritus, *to get themselves credit, and by that means the more to be respected,* as artificers usually do, *Novo qui marmori ascribunt Praxitelem suo.*[7] Tis not so with me.

> *Non hic Centauros, non Gorgonas, Harpyasque*
> *Invenies, hominem pagina nostra sapit.*[8]
> No *Centaures* here, or *Gorgons* look to finde,
> My subject is of man, and humane kinde.

Thou thy self art the subject of my discourse.

> *Quicquid agunt homines, votum, timor, ira, voluptas,*
> *Gaudia, discursus, nostri farrago libelli.*[9]

3 *Lib. de curiositate.* ["On Curiosity," *Moralia.*]
4 When you see the cover, why ask about what's hidden?
5 *Modò hæc tibi usui sint, quemvis auctorem fingito. Wecker.* [If these things are useful to you, suppose whomever you please to be the author.]
6 *Lib.* 10 c. 12. *Multa à malè feriatis in Democriti nomine commenta data, nobilitatis authoritatisque eius perfugio utentibus.* [Book 10, chap. 12. Many fictions are produced under the name of Democritus by malicious idlers who use the protection of his nobility and authority.]
7 Who sign Praxiteles' name on a new marble statue of their own.
8 *Martialis lib.* 10. *epigr.* 14. [Martial, *Epigrams*, X. 14 (properly 4).]
9 *Juv. Sat.* 1. [Juvenal, Satire 1.]

What ere men do, vows, fears, in ire, in sport,
Joys, wandrings, are the sum of my report.

My intent is no otherwise to use his name, then *Mercurius
Gallobelgicus, Mercurius Britannicus,* use the name of *Mercurie,
Democritus Christianus,*[1] &c. Although there be some other circumstances, for which I have masked my self under this visard,
and some peculiar respects, which I cannot so well expresse,
untill I have set down a brief character of this our *Democritus,*
what he was, with an Epitome of his life.

Democritus, as he is described by *Hippocrates*[2] and *Laertius,*[3]
was a little wearish⁵ old man, very melancholy by nature, averse
from company in his latter daies, and much given to solitarinesse,[4] a famous Philosopher in his age,[5] *cœvus*[6] with *Socrates,*
wholly addicted to his studies at the last, and to a private life,
writ many excellent works, a great Divine, according to the
divinity of those times, an expert Physitian, a Politician, an
excellent Mathematician, as *Diacosmus*[7] and the rest of his
works do witnesse. He was much delighted with the studies of
Husbandry, saith *Columella,*[8] and often I finde him cited by
Constantinus[9] and others treating of that subject. He knew the
natures, differences of all beasts, plants, fishes, birds; and, as
some say, could understand the tunes and voyces of them.[1] In
a word, he was *omnifariàm doctus,*[2] a generall scholar, a great
student; and to the intent he might better contemplate, I find

---

1 *Auth. Pet. Besseo edit. Coloniæ* 1616. [Written by Pierre de Besse, published
at Cologne, 1616.]
2 *Hip. Epist. Damaget.* [Hippocrates, *Epistles* (to Damagetus).]
3 *Laert. lib.* 9. [Diogenes Laertius, *Lives of the Philosophers,* Book 9.]
4 *Hortulo sibi cellulam seligens, ibique seipsum includens, vixit solitarius.*
[Choosing for himself a little concealed place in a little garden and confining
himself there, he lived alone.]
5 *Floruit Olympiade* 80, 700. *annis post Troiam.* [He flourished at the time of
the eightieth Olympiad, seven hundred years after the Trojan War.]
6 Contemporary.
7 *Diacos. quod cunctis operibus facilè excellit. Laert.* [*Diacosmos,* which easily
excels all other works. Diogenes Laertius.]
8 *Col. lib.* 1 c. 1. [Lucius Junius Moderatus Columella, Book 1, chap. 1.]
9 *Const. lib. de agric. passim.* [Constantine VII (Porphyrogenitus), *Husbandry.*]
1 *Volucrum voces & linguas intelligere se dicit Abderitanus. Ep. Hip.* [The
Abderite says that he understands the voices and languages of flying creatures.
Hippocrates, *Epistles.*]
2 Learned in everything.

it related by some,[3] that he put out his eys, and was in his old age voluntarily blinde, yet saw more then all Greece besides, and writ of every subject,[4] *Nihil in toto opificio naturæ, de quo non scripsit.*[5] A man of an excellent wit, profound conceit; and to attain knowledg the better in his yonger years, he travelled to *Egypt* and *Athens*,[6] to confer with learned men, *admired of some, despised of others.*[7] After a wandering life, he setled at *Abdera,* a town in *Thrace,* and was sent for thither to be their Law-maker, Recorder or town-clerk as some will; or as others, he was there bred and born. Howsoever it was, there he lived at last in a garden in the suburbs, wholy betaking himself to his studies, and a private life, *saving that sometimes he would walk down to the haven,*[8] *and laugh heartily at such variety of ridiculous objects, which there he saw.*[9] Such a one was *Democritus.*

But in the mean time, how doth this concern me, or upon what reference do I usurp his habit? I confesse indeed that to compare my self unto him for ought I have yet said, were both impudency and arrogancie. I do not presume to make any parallel, *Antistat mihi millibus trecentis,*[1] *parvus sum, nullus sum, altum nec spiro, nec spero.*[2] Yet thus much I wil say of my self, and that I hope without all suspition of pride, or self-conceit, I have lived a silent, sedentary, solitary, private life, *mihi & musis,*[3] in the University as long almost as *Xenocrates*

3 *Sabellicus exempl. lib.* 10. *oculis se privavit, ut melius contemplationi operam daret, sublimi vir ingenio, profundæ cogitationis, &c.* [Marcus Antonius Coccius Sabellicus, *Examples, in Ten Books.* He put out his eyes so that he could better devote his effort to contemplation; a man of sublime genius, of profound intellectual force.]
4 *Naturalia, Moralia, Mathematica, liberales disciplinas, artiumque omnium peritiam callebat.* [He was skilled in natural history, ethics, mathematics, liberal studies and the knowledge of all arts.]
5 There is nothing in all of nature's working of which he has not written.
6 *Veni Athenas, et nemo me novit.* [I came to Athens, and no one knew me.]
7 *Idem contemptui & admirationi habitus.* [Held at the same time in contempt and admiration.]
8 *Solebat ad portam ambulare, et inde, &c. Hip. Ep. Dameg.* [He was accustomed to walk to the city gates, and from there. . . . Hippocrates, *Epistles* (to Damagetus).]
9 *Perpetuo risu pulmonem agitare solebat Democritus.* Juv. Sat. 7. [Democritus always shook with laughter. Juvenal, Satire 7 (properly 10).]
1 *Non sum dignus præstare matellam. Mart.* [I am not fit to hand him a chamber-pot. Martial.]
2 He excels me in 300,000 ways; I am insignificant; I am nothing; I neither aspire to greatness nor hope for it.
3 For myself and my studies.

in *Athens, ad senectam ferè*,[4] to learn wisdom as he did, penned up most part in my study. For I have been brought up a student in the most florishing Colledge of *Europe, Augustissimo collegio*,[5] and can brag with *Jovius*, almost, *in eâ luce domicilii Vaticani, totius orbis celeberrimi, per 37. annos multa opportunaque didici*;[6] for 30 years I have continued (having the use of as good Libraries as ever he had) a scholar, and would be therefore loth, either by living as a drone, to be an unprofitable or unworthy a Member of so learned and noble a societie, or to write that which should be any way dishonourable to such a royal and ample foundation. Something I have done, though by my profession a Divine, yet *turbine raptus ingenii*, as he [Scaliger] said, out of a running wit, an unconstant, unsetled mind, I had a great desire, (not able to attain to a superficial skil in any) to have some smattering in all, to be *aliquis in omnibus, nullus in singulis*,[7] which *Plato* commends, out of him *Lipsius* approves and furthers, *as fit to be imprinted in all curious wits, not be a slave of one science, or dwell altogether in one subject, as most do, but to rove abroad*, centum puer artium,[8] *to have an oar in every mans boat, to taste of every dish, and sip of every cup*, which saith *Montaigne*, was well performed by *Aristotle* and his learned countrey-man *Adrian Turnebus*. This roving humor (though not with like successe) I have ever had, & like a ranging spaniel, that barks at every bird he sees, leaving his game, I have followed all, saving that which I should, & may justly complain, and truly, *qui ubique est, nusquam est*,[9] which *Gesner did in modesty*, that I have read many books, but to little purpose, for want of good method, I have confusedly tumbled over divers authors in our Libraries, with small profit for want of art, order, memory, judgment. I never travelled but in Map or Card,[8] in which my unconfined thoughts have freely expatiated, as having ever been especialy delighted with the study of *Cosmography. Saturn* was Lord of my geniture, culminating, &c. and *Mars* principal *significator* of manners, in partile conjunction with

4 Nearly to old age.
5 *Christ-church in Oxford.
6 In that splendor of a Vatican habitation, the most distinguished in the world, I have spent thirty-seven full and advantageous years.
7 Somebody in everything, nobody in anything.
8 A servant of a hundred arts.
9 He who is everywhere is nowhere.

mine *Ascendent;* both fortunate in their houses, &c. I am not poor,
I am not rich; *nihil est, nihil deest,* I have little, I want nothing:
all my treasure is in *Minerva's* tower. Greater preferment as I
could never get, so am I not in debt for it, I have a competency
(*Laus Deo*)[1] from my noble and munificent Patrons, though I
live still a Collegiat student, as *Democritus* in his garden, and
lead a monastique life, *ipse mihi theatrum,*[2] sequestred from
those tumults and troubles of the world, *Et tanquam in specula
positus,* (as he [Heinsius] said) in some high place above you
all, like *Stoicus Sapiens, omnia sæcula, præterita presentiaque
videns, uno velut intuitu,*[3] I hear and see what is done abroad,
how others run, ride, turmoil, and macerate themselves in court
and countrey, far from those wrangling Law suits, *aulæ vani-
tatem, fori ambitionem,*[4] *ridere mecum soleo:* I laugh at all, *only
secure, lest my suit go amiss, my ships perish,* corn and cattle
miscarry, trade decay, *I have no wife nor children good or bad
to provide for.* A meer spectator of other mens fortunes and
adventures, and how they act their parts, which me thinks are
diversely presented unto me, as from a common theatre or scene.
I hear new news every day, and those ordinary rumors of war,
plagues, fires, inundations, thefts, murders, massacres, meteors,
comets, spectrums,§ prodigies, apparitions, of towns taken, cities
besieged in *France, Germany, Turky, Persia, Poland, &c.* daily
musters and preparations, and such like, which these tempestu-
ous times afford, battles fought, so many men slain, monomachies,§ shipwracks, piracies, and sea-fights, peace, leagues,
stratagems, and fresh alarums. A vast confusion of vows, wishes,
actions, edicts, petitions, lawsuits, pleas, laws, proclamations,
complaints, grievances are daily brought to our ears. New books
every day, pamphlets, currantoes,§ stories, whole catalogues of
volumes of all sorts, new paradoxes, opinions, schisms, heresies,
controversies in philosophie, religion, &c. Now come tidings of
weddings, maskings, mummeries, entertainments, jubilies, em-
bassies, tilts and tournaments, trophies, triumphs, revels, sports,
playes: Then again, as in a new shifted scene, treason, cheating tricks, robberies, enormous vilanies in all kindes, funerals,

1 Praise God.
2 Sufficient entertainment to myself.
3 Like the wise Stoic, seeing all ages, past and present, as at one glance.
4 The vanity of a court, the ambition of public life.

burials, death of Princes, new discoveries, expeditions; now comical, then tragical matters. To day we heare of new Lords and officers created, to morrow of some great men deposed, and then again of fresh honors conferred; one is let loose, another imprisoned; one purchaseth, another breaketh: he thrives, his neighbor turns bankrupt; now plenty, then again dearth and famine; one runs, another rides, wrangles, laughs, weeps, &c. Thus I daily hear, and such like, both private and publick news, amidst the gallantry and misery of the world; jollitie, pride, perplexities and cares, simplicity and vilany; subtletie, knavery, candor and integrity, mutually mixt and offering themselves, I rub on *privus privatus*,[5] as I have still lived, so I now continue, *statu quo prius,* left to a solitary life, and mine own domestick discontents: saving that sometimes, *ne quid mentiar,*[6] as *Diogenes* went into the city, and *Democritus* to the haven to see fashions, I did for my recreation now and then walk abroad, look into the world, and could not choose but make some little observation, *non tam sagax observator, ac simplex recitator,*[7] not as they did to scoffe or laugh at all, but with a mixt passion.

Bilem sæpè, jocum vestri movêre tumultus.[8]

I did sometime laugh and scoff with *Lucian,* and satyrically tax[s] with *Menippus,* lament with *Heraclitus,* sometimes again I was *petulanti splene chachinno,*[9] and then again, *urere bilis jecur,*[1] I was much moved to see that abuse which I could not amend. In which passion howsoever I may sympathize with him or them, tis for no such respect I shroud my self under his name, but either in an unknown habit, to assume a little more liberty and freedom of speech, or if you will needs know, for that reason and only respect, which *Hippocrates relates* at large in his Epistle to *Damegetus,* wherein he doth expresse, how coming to visit him one day, he found *Democritus* in his garden at *Abdera,* in the suburbs, under a shady bower, with a book on his knees, busie at his study, sometimes writing, somtime walk-

5 In strict privacy.
6 Not to tell a lie.
7 Not so wise an observer as a simple narrator.
8 Oft have your passions roused my rage or mirth.
9 Jeering with petulant spleen.
1 Burning with wrath.

ing. The subject of his book was melancholy and madness, about him lay the carcasses of many several beasts, newly by him cut up and anatomized, not that he did contemn Gods creatures, as he told *Hippocrates,* but to finde out the seat of this *atra bilis,* or melancholy, whence it proceeds, and how it was engendred in mens bodies, to the intent he might better cure it in himself, by his writings and observations teach others how to prevent and avoid it. Which good intent of his, *Hippocrates* highly commended: *Democritus Junior* is therfore bold to imitate, & because he left it unperfect, & it is now lost, *quasi succenturiator Democriti,*[2] to revive again, prosecute[§] and finish in this treatise.

You have had a reason of the name; If the title and inscription offend your gravity, were it a sufficient justification to accuse others, I could produce many sober treatises, even sermons themselves, which in their fronts carry more phantastical names. Howsoever it is a kinde of policie in these daies, to prefix a phantastical title to a book which is to be sold: For as Larks come down to a day-net,[§] many vain readers will tarry and stand gazing like silly passengers,[§] at an antick picture in a painters shop, that will not look at a judicious peece. And indeed as *Scaliger* observes, *nothing more invites a reader then an argument unlooked for, unthought of, and sels better than a scurrile pamphlet,* tum maxime cum novitas excitat palatum.[3] Many men, saith *Gellius, are very conceited in their inscriptions,* and able (as *Plinie* quotes out of *Seneca*) to make him loyter by the way, *that went in hast to fetch a mid-wife for his daughter, now ready to lie down.* For my part I have honourable presidents[§] for this which I have done: I will cite one for all, *Anthonie Zara Pap. Episc.*[4] his Anatomie of wit, in four sections, members, subsections, &c. to be read in our Libraries.

If any man except against the matter or manner of treating of this my subject, and will demand a reason of it, I can alleage more then one, I write of melancholy, by being busie to avoid melancholy. There is no greater cause of melancholy then idlenesse, *no better cure then businesse,* as *Rhasis* holds: and howbeit, *stultus labor est ineptiarum,* to be busied in toyes is to

---

2 As a substitute for Democritus.
3 Especially when its novelty sharpens the appetite.
4 Bishop of Pavia. (In fact, Zara was Bishop of Pedena.)

small purpose, yet hear that divine *Seneca,* better *aliud agere quam nihil,* better do to no end than nothing. I writ therefore, and busied my self in this playing labour, *otiosaque diligentiâ ut vitarem torporem feriandi*[5] with *Vectius* in *Macrobius,* atque otium in utile verterem negotium.[6]

————*Simul & jucunda & idonea dicere vitæ,*
Lectorem delectando simul atque monendo.[7]

To this end I write, like them, saith *Lucian,* that *recite to trees, and declaim to pillars for want of auditors:* as *Paulus Ægineta* ingeniously confesseth, *not that any thing was unknown or omitted, but to exercise my self,* which course if some took, I think it would be good for their bodies, and much better for their souls; or peradventure as others do, for fame, to shew my self (*Scire tuum nihil est, nisi te scire hoc sciat alter.*)[8] I might be of *Thucydidis* opinion, *to know a thing and not to expresse it, is all one as if he knew it not.* When I first took this task in hand, & *quod ait ille, impellente genio negotium suscepi,*[9] this I aimed at; *vel ut lenirem animum scribendo,* to ease my minde by writing, for I had *gravidum cor, fœtum caput,*[1] a kind of impostume[§] in my head, which I was very desirous to be unladen of, and could imagin no fitter evacuation then this. Besides I might not well refrain, for *ubi dolor, ibi digitus,*[2] one must needs scratch where it itches. I was not a little offended with this maladie, shall I say my Mistris *melancholy,* my *Ægeria,* or my *malus genius,*[3] & for that cause as he that is stung with a scorpion, I would expel *clavum clavo,*[4] comfort one sorrow with another, idlenes with idlenes, *ut ex viperâ Theriacum,* make an Antidote out of that which was the prime cause of my disease. Or as he did, of whom *Felix Plater* speaks, that thought he had some of *Aristophanes* frogs in his belly, still crying *Brecececex, coax, coax, oop, oop,* and for that cause studied

---

[5] In order to avoid the sluggishness of inactivity.
[6] And to turn my leisure to useful business.
[7] At once to profit and to please / And teach the reader at his ease.
[8] Your knowledge is nothing unless someone knows that you know it.
[9] And, as he [Jovius] says, undertook the work at the urging of my talent.
[1] A heavy heart, a teeming head.
[2] Where there is pain, there is a finger.
[3] Evil Genius.
[4] One nail with another.

physick seven years, and travelled over most part of *Europe* to ease himself: To do my self good I turned over such physicians as our libraries would afford, or my private friends impart, and have taken this pains. And why not? *Cardan* professeth he writ his book *De consolatione* after his sons death, to comfort himself; so did *Tully*§ write of the same subject with like intent after his daughters departure, if it be his at least, or some impostors put out in his name, which *Lipsius* probably suspects. Concerning my self, I can peradventure affirm with *Marius* in *Salust, that which others hear or reade of, I felt, and practised my self, they get their knowledge by books, I mine by melancholizing, Experto crede* Roberto.[5] Something I can speak out of experience, *ærumnabilis experientia me docuit*,[6] and with her [Dido] in the Poet, *Haud ignara mali miseris succurrere disco*.[7] I would help others out of a fellow-feeling, and as that vertuous Lady did of old, *being a leper her self, bestow all her portion to build an Hospital for Lepers*, I will spend my time and knowledge, which are my greatest fortunes, for the common good of all.

Yea but you will infer that this is *actum agere,* an unnecessary work, *cramben bis coctam apponere*,[8] the same again and again in other words. To what purpose? *Nothing is omitted that may well be said,* so thought *Lucian* in the like theam. How many excellent Physitians have written just Volumes and elaborate tracts of this subject? no news here, that which I have is stoln from others, *Dicitque mihi mea pagina fur es*.[9] If that severe doom§ of *Synesius* be true, *It is a greater offence to steal dead mens labours, than their clothes,* what shall become of most Writers? I hold up my hand at the bar amongst others, and am guilty of felonie in this kinde, *habes confitentem reum*,[1] I am content to be pressed§ with the rest. Tis most true, *tenet insanabile multos scribendi cacoethes*,[2] and *there is no end of writing of books,* as the Wise-man found of old, in this scribling age, especially wherein *the number of books is without number,*

---

5 Trust the experienced Robert.
6 Painful experience has taught me.
7 Not unschooled in woe, I have learned to succor the woeful.
8 To serve a reheated dish.
9 And my page says to me, "You are a thief."
1 You have the confession of the defendant.
2 Many are possessed by an incurable passion for writing.

(as a worthy man saith) *presses be oppressed,* and out of an itching humor, that every man hath to shew himself, desirous of fame and honor (*scribimus indocti doctique* ———)[3] he will write no matter what, and scrape together it boots not whence. *Bewitched with this desire of fame, etiam mediis in morbis,*[4] to the disparagement of their health, and scarce able to hold a pen, they must say something, *and get themselves a name,* saith *Scaliger, though it be to the down-fall and ruine of many others.* To be counted writers, *scriptores ut salutentur,* to be thought and held *Polymathes* and *Polyhistors, apud imperitum vulgus ob ventosæ nomen artis,*[5] to get a paper-kingdom: *nulla spe quæstus sed amplâ famæ,*[6] in this precipitate,[8] ambitious age, *nunc ut est sæculum, inter immaturam eruditionem, ambitiosum & præceps* (tis *Scaligers* censure) and they that are scarce auditors, *vix auditores,* must be masters and teachers, before they be capable and fit hearers. They will rush into all learning, *togatam, armatam,*[7] divine, humane authors, rake over all *Indexes* & Pamphlets for notes, as our merchants do strange havens for traffick, write great Tomes, *Cum non sint re vera doctiores, sed loquaciores,* when as they are not therby better scholars, but greater praters. They commonly pretend publike good, but as *Gesner* observes, tis pride and vanity that eggs them on, no news or ought worthy of note, but the same in other terms. *Ne feriarentur fortasse typographi, vel ideo scribendum est aliquid ut se vixisse testentur.*[8] As Apothecaries we make new mixtures every day, pour out of one vessel into another; and as those old *Romans* rob'd all the cities of the world, to set out their bad sited *Rome,* we skim off the cream of other mens wits, pick the choice flowers of their till'd gardens to set out our own sterill plots. *Castrant alios ut libros suos per se graciles alieno adipe suffarcinant* (so *Jovius* inveighs) They lard their lean books with the fat of others works. *Ineruditi fures,*[9] &c. A fault that every Writer findes, as I do now, and yet faulty them-

---

3 We all write, learned and unlearned.
4 Even in the midst of illness.
5 To get a name for worthless talent among the ignorant masses.
6 With no hope of gain but great hope of fame.
7 Civil, military.
8 They must write something so that the printers may perhaps not take a holiday or so that they may prove they have been alive.
9 Illiterate thieves.

selves, *Trium literarum homines*,[1] all theeves; they pilfer out
of old Writers to stuffe up their new Comments, scrape *Ennius*
dung-hils, and out of *Democritus* pit, as I have done. By which
means it comes to passe, *that not only libraries and shops are
full of our putid*[§] *papers, but every close-stool and jakes, Scribunt
carmina quæ legunt cacantes;*[2] they serve to put under pies, to
lap[§] spice in, and keep rost-meat from burning. With us in
France, saith *Scaliger, every man hath liberty to write, but few
ability. Heretofore learning was graced by judicious scholars,
but now noble sciences are vilified by base and illiterate scriblers*,
that either write for vain-glory, need, to get money, or as Parasites to flatter and collogue with some great men, they put out
burras, quisquiliásque ineptiasque.[3] *Amongst so many thousand
Authors you shall scarse finde one, by reading of whom you
shall be any whit better, but rather much worse, quibus inficitur
potiùs, quàm perficitur*, by which he is rather infected than any
way perfected.

> ———*Qui talia legit,*
> *Quid didicit tandem, quid scit nisi somnia, nugas?*[4]

So that oftentimes it fals out (which *Challimachus* taxed of
old) a great Book is a great mischief. *Cardan* findes fault with
French men and Germans, for their scribling in no purpose,
non inquit ab edendo deterreo, modo novum aliquid inveniant,
he doth not bar them to write, so that it be some new invention
of their own; but we weave the same web still, twist the same
rope again and again, or if it be a new invention, tis but some
bauble or toy which idle fellows write, for as idle fellows to
read, and who so cannot invent? *He must have a barren wit,
that in this scribling age can forge nothing. Princes shew their
armies, rich men vaunt their buildings, souldiers their manhood, and scholars vent their toyes*, they must read, they must
hear whether they will or no.

> *Et quodcunque semel chartis illeverit, omnes*
> *Gestiet à furno redeuntes scire lacuque,*

1 Men of three letters, i.e., thieves.
2 They write songs which are read on the toilet.
3 Nonsense, rubbish, and trifles.
4 What has he learned who scans such themes? / What does he know but
trifling dreams?

Et pueros & anus——
What once is said and writ, all men must know,
Old wives and children as they come and go.

What a company of Poets hath this year brought out, as *Pliny*
complains to *Sossius Sinesius; This April every day some or
other have recited.* What a catalogue of new books all this year,
all this age (I say) have our *Frank-furt* Marts, our domestick
Marts brought out? Twice a year, *Proferunt se nova ingenia &
ostentant,* we stretch our wits out, and set them to sale, *magno
conatu nihil agimus.*⁵ So that which *Gesner* much desires, if a
speedy reformation be not had, by some Princes Edicts and
grave Supervisors, to restrain this liberty, it will run on *in infinitum. Quis tam avidus librorum helluo,*⁶ Who can read them?
As already, we shall have a vast *Chaos* and confusion of Books,
we are oppressed with them, our eyes ake with reading, our
fingers with turning. For my part I am one of the number, *nos
numerus sumus,* I do not deny it, I have only this of *Macrobius*
to say for my self, *Omne meum, nihil meum,* tis all mine, and
none mine. As a good house-wife out of divers fleeces weaves
one peece of cloth, a Bee gathers wax and honey out of many
flowers, and makes a new bundel of all,

*Floriferis ut apes in saltibus omnia libant,*⁷

I have laboriously collected this *Cento* out of divers Writers, and
that *sine injuriâ,* I have wronged no authors, but given every
man his own; which *Hierom* so much commends in *Nepotian,*
he stole not whole verses, pages, tracts, as some do now a daies,
concealing their Authors names, but still said this was *Cyprians,*
that *Lactantius,* that *Hillarius,* so said *Minucius Felix,* so *Victorinus,* thus far *Arnobius:* I cite and quote mine Authors (which
howsoever some illiterate scriblers account pedantical, as a cloke
of ignorance, and opposite to their affected fine stile, I must and
will use) *sumpsi, non surripui;*⁸ and what *Varro Lib. 6. de re
rust.*⁹ speaks of Bees, *minimè maleficæ, nullius opus vellicantes*

---

5 With great effort we attain nothing.
6 Who is so greedy a glutton for books?
7 As bees in flowery glades sip every plant.
8 I have borrowed, not stolen.
9 In Book 6 of *On Rustic Matters.*

faciunt deterius,[1] I can say of my self, whom have I injured?
The matter is theirs most part, and yet mine, *apparet unde
sumptum sit* (which *Seneca* approves) *aliud tamen quàm unde
sumptum sit apparet,*[2] which nature doth with the aliment of
our bodies incorporate, digest, assimulate, I do *conquoquere
quod hausi,* dispose of what I take. I make them pay tribute, to
set out this my *Macaronicon,*[§] the method only is mine own, I
must usurp that of *Wecker è Ter.*[3] *nihil dictum quod non dictum
priùs, methodus sola artificem ostendit,* we can say nothing but
what hath been said, the composition and method is ours only,
& shews a Scholar. *Oribasius, Ætius, Avicenna,* have all out of
Galen, but to their own method, *diverso stilo, non diversâ fide,*[4]
our Poets steal from *Homer,* he spews, saith *Ælian,* they lick it
up. Divines use *Austins* words *verbatim* still, and our Story-
dressers do as much, he that comes last is commonly best,

> ———*donec quid grandius ætas*
> *Postera sorsque ferat melior.*———[5]

Though there were many Giants of old in Physick and Philosophy, yet I say with *Didacus Stella, A dwarf standing on the
shoulders of a Giant may see farther then a Giant himself;* I
may likely add, alter, and see farther then my predecessors;
And it is no greater prejudice for me to endite[§] after others,
then for *Ælianus Montaltus* that famous Physitian, to write
de morbis capitis[6] after *Jason Pratensis, Heurnius, Hildesheim,
&c.* Many horses to run in a race, one Logician, one Rhetorician,
after another. Oppose then what thou wilt,

> *Allatres licet usque nos & usque,*
> *Et gannitibus improbis lacessas.*[7]

I solve it thus. And for those other faults of barbarism,[§] *Dorick*
dialect, extemporanean stile, tautologies, apish imitation, a rap-
sodie of rags gathered together from several dung-hils, excre-

---

[1] They are not at all malicious; they injure nothing they take honey from.
[2] It's clear what it is taken from, yet it appears as something other than that it
is taken from.
[3] From Tertullian.
[4] In a different style, but not with a different instrument.
[5] Until a later age and better luck produce something grander.
[6] About diseases of the head.
[7] You may bark at me incessantly / And snarl at me violently.

ments of authors, toyes and fopperies confusedly tumbled out,
without art, invention, judgement, wit, learning, harsh, raw,
rude, phantastical, absurd, insolent, indiscreet, ill-composed, indigested, vain, scurrile, idle, dull and dry; I confesse all (tis
partly affected) thou canst not think worse of me then I do
of my self. 'Tis not worth the reading, I yield it, I desire thee
not to lose time in perusing so vain a subject, I should be peradventure loth my self to reade him or thee so writing, tis not
operæ pretium.[8] All I say, is this, that I have presidents for it,
which *Isocrates* cals *perfugium iis qui peccant,*[9] others as absurd, vain, idle, illiterate, &c. *Nonnulli alii idem fecerunt,*
others have done as much, it may be more, and perhaps thou
thy self, *Novimus & qui te, &c.*[1] we have all our faults; *scimus,
& hanc veniam, &c.*[2] thou censurest me, so have I done others,
and may do thee, *Cædimus inque vicem, &c.*[3] tis *lex talionis,
quid pro quo.*[4] Go now censure, criticize, scoffe and rail.

> *Nasutus sis usque licet, sis denique nasus:*
> *Non potes in nugas dicere plura meas,*
> *Ipse ego quàm dixi, &c.*
> Wer'st thou all scoffs and flouts, a very *Momus.*
> Then we our selves, thou canst not say worse of us.

Thus, as when women scold, have I cried whore first, and in
some mens censures, I am afraid I have overshot my self, *Laudare se vani, vituperare stulti,*[5] as I do not arrogate, I will not
derogate. *Primus vestrûm non sum, nec imus,* I am none of the
best, I am none of the meanest of you. As I am an inch, or so
many feet, so many parasanges, after him or him, I may be peradventure an ace[8] before thee. Be it therefore as it is, wel or ill, I
have assayed, put my self upon the stage, I must abide the censure, I may not escape it. It is most true, *stylus virum arguit,* our
stile bewrayes us, & as hunters find their game by the trace, so is
a mans *genius* descried by his works, *Multò meliùs ex sermone*

---

8 Worth while.
9 A refuge for sinners.
1 We know someone who has seen you.
2 We know, and beg pardon.
3 We cut to pieces, and in turn, etc.
4 The law of retaliation, tit for tat.
5 The vain praise themselves; the foolish censure themselves.

quàm lineamentis, de moribus hominum judicamus;[6] 'twas old *Cato's* rule. I have laid my self open (I know it) in this treatise, turned mine inside outward, I shall be censured, I doubt not, for to say truth with *Erasmus, nihil morosius hominum judiciis,* there's naught so peevish as mens judgments, yet this is some comfort, *ut palata, sic judicia,* our censures are as various as our palats.

> *Tres mihi convive prope dissentire videntur*
> *Poscentes vario multum diversa palato, &c.*[7]

Our writings are as so many dishes, our readers guests, our books like beauty, that which one admires, another rejects; so are we approved as men fancies are inclined.

> *Pro captu lectoris habent sua fata libelli.*[8]

That which is most pleasing to one is *amaracum sui,*[9] most harsh to another. *Quot homines, tot sententiæ,* so many men, so many mindes: that which thou condemnest he commends.

> *Quod petis, id sane est invisum acidumque duobus.*[1]

He respects matter, thou art wholly for words, he loves a loose and free stile, thou art all for neat composition, strong lines, hyperboles, allogories; he desires a fine frontispiece, entising pictures, such as *Hieron. Natali* the Jesuit hath cut[§] to the Dominicals,[§] to draw on the Readers attention, which thou rejectest; that which one admires, another explodes[§] as most absurd and ridiculous. If it be not point blank to his humor, his method, his conceit, *Si quid forsan omissum, quod is animo conceperit, si qua dictio, &c.* If ought be omitted, or added, which he likes, or dislikes, thou art *mancipium paucæ lectionis,*[2] an idiot, an asse, *nullus es,* or *plagiarius,*[3] a trifler, a trivant,[§] thou art an idle fellow; or else tis a thing of meer industry, a collection without wit or invention, a very toy. *Facilia sic putant omnes quæ jam facta,*

---

6 We judge much better about a man's character by his conversation than by his appearance.
7 They seem to me to differ like three guests / Whose different palates require different food.
8 The fate of books depends on the fancy of the reader.
9 Like marjoram to a sow.
1 What you like is sour and repulsive to two others.
2 An ill-read slave.
3 You're a nobody or a plagiary.

nec de salebris cogitant, ubi via strata,[4] so men are valued, their labours vilified by fellows of no worth themselves; as things of nought, who could not have done as much? *unusquisque abundat sensu suo,* every man abounds in his own sense; and whilest each particular party is so affected, how should one please all?

> *Quid dem, quid non dem? Renuis tu quod jubet ille.*[5]

How shall I hope to expresse my self to each mans humor and conceit, or to give satisfaction to all? Some understand too little, some too much, *Qui similiter in legendos libros, atque in salutandos homines irruunt, non cogitantes quales, sed quibus vestibus induti sint,*[6] as *Austin* observes, not regarding what, but who write, *orexin habet authoris celebritas,*[7] not valuing the mettle, but stamp that is upon it, *Cantharum aspiciunt, non quid in eo.*[8] If he be not rich, in great place, polite and brave, a great doctor,[§] or full fraught with grand titles, though never so well qualified, he is a dunce, but as *Baronius* hath it of Cardinal *Caraffa's* works, he is a meer hog that rejects any man for his poverty. Some are too partial, as friends to overween,[§] others come with a prejudice to carp, vilifie, detract, and scoffe; (*qui de me forsan, quicquid est, omni contemptu contemptius judicant*[9]) some as bees for honey, some as spiders to gather poyson. What shall I do in this case? As a dutch[§] host, if you come to an Inn in *Germany,* and dislike your fare, diet, lodging, &c. replies in a surly tone, *aliud tibi quæras diversorium,* if you like not this, get you to another Inn: I resolve, if you like not my writing, go reade something else. I do not much esteem thy censure, take thy course, tis not as thou wilt, nor as I wil, but when we have both done, that of *Plinius Secundus* to *Trajan* will prove true, *Every mans witty labour takes not, except the matter, subject, occasion, and some commending favorite happen to it.* If I be taxed, exploded by thee and some such, I shall haply be approved and commended

---

4 When a thing has been done, people think it easy; when the road is smooth, they don't think about the rough spots.
5 What shall I serve, and what not? You refuse what he orders.
6 They rush into the reading of books in the same way that they decide whom to say hello to, not knowing the thing itself but the cover.
7 The fame of the author creates the demand.
8 They look at the tankard, not what's in it.
9 Who judge whatever I've done as completely beneath contempt.

by others, & so have been (*Expertus loquor*[1]) and may truly say
with *Jovius* in like case (*absit verbo jactantia*) *heroum quorun-
dam, pontificum, & virorum nobilium familiaritatem & amici-
tiam, gratasque gratias, & multorum bene laudatorum laudes
sum inde promeritus*,[2] as I have been honoured by some worthy
men, so have I been vilified by others, and shall be. At the first
publishing of this book; (which *Probus* of *Persius'* satyrs) *editum
librum continuò mirari homines, atque avidè deripere cœperunt*,[3]
I may in some sort apply to this my work, The first, second, and
third edition were suddenly gone, eagerly read, & as I have said,
not so much approved by some, as scornfully rejected by others.
But it was *Democritus* his fortune, *Idem admirationi & irrisioni
habitus*.[4] Twas *Seneca's* fate, that superintendent[§] of wit, learning, judgement, *ad stuporem doctus*,[5] the best of *Greek* and
Latine writers, in *Plutarch's* opinion; That *renowned corrector of
vice*, as *Fabius* terms him, *and painful[§] omniscious[§] philosopher,
that writ so excellently and admirably well*, could not please all
parties, or escape censure: How is he vilified by *Caligula, A. Gellius, Fabius*, and *Lipsius* himself, his chief propugner[§]? *In eo
pleraque pernitiosa*,[6] saith the same *Fabius*, many childish tracts
and sentences he hath, *sermo illaboratus*, too negligent often,
and remisse, as *A. Gellius* observes, *oratio vulgaris & protrita,
dicaces & ineptæ sententiæ, eruditio plebeia*,[7] an homely shallow
writer as he is. *In partibus spinas & fastidia habet*,[8] saith *Lipsius*,
and as in all his other works, so especially in his epistles, *aliæ in
argutiis & ineptiis occupantur, intricatus alicubi, & parum com-
positus, sine copiâ rerum hoc fecit*,[9] he jumbles up many things
together immethodically, after the Stoicks fashion, *parum or-
dinavit, multa accumulavit, &c.*[1] If *Seneca* be thus lashed, and

---

[1] I speak from experience.
[2] Without boasting, I have earned the intimacy and friendship of some eminent
military men, clergymen, and noblemen, and have had pleasant favors from
them, and the praises of many men who were highly praised themselves.
[3] When the book first appeared, people began both to admire it and to pick
holes in it eagerly.
[4] He was the object both of admiration and of scorn.
[5] Unbelievably learned.
[6] Corrupting, for the most part.
[7] A homely and trite style, far-fetched and foolish ideas, common learning.
[8] In some places, he perplexes and disgusts.
[9] Some are full of puzzles and trifles; in some he is involved and disorganized;
and he does this without wealth of content.
[1] He did little organizing; he accumulated much.

many famous men that I could name, what shall I expect? How
shall I that am *vix umbra tanti philosophi,*[2] hope to please? *No
man so absolute, Erasmus holds, to satisfie all, except antiquity,
prescription, &c. set*[§] *a bar.* But as I have proved in *Seneca,* this
will not alwayes take place, how shall I evade? Tis the common
doom of all writers, I must (I say) abide it, I seek not applause;
Non ego ventosæ venor suffragia plebis;[3] again, *non sum adeo
informis,*[4] I would not be vilified.

> ——*laudatus abunde,*
> *Non fastiditus si tibi lector ero.*[5]

I fear good mens censures, and to their favorable acceptance I
submit my labors,

> ——*& linguas Mancipiorum*
> *Contemno,* ——[6]

As the barking of a dog, I securely contemn those malicious and
scurrile obloquies, flouts, calumnies of railers and detractors, I
scorn the rest. What therefore I have said, *pro tenuitate meâ*[7] I
have said.

One or two things yet I was desirous to have amended if I
could, concerning the manner of handling this my subject, for
which I must apologize, *deprecari,* and upon better advice give
the friendly reader notice: It was not mine intent to prostitute
my muse in *English,* or to divulge *secreta Minerva,*[8] but to have
exposed this more contract[§] in *Latine,* if I could have got it
printed. Any scurrile pamphlet is welcome to our mercenarie
Stationers in *English,* they print all,

> ——*cuduntque libellos*
> *In quorum foliis vix simia nuda cacaret;*[9]

But in *Latine* they will not deal; which is one of the reasons
Nicholas Car in his oration of the paucity of *English* writers,

2 Hardly the shadow of so great a philosopher.
3 I don't seek out the support of the fickle crowd.
4 I am not so ugly.
5 I shall have praise enough if you don't despise me, worthy reader.
6 I despise the talk of slaves.
7 To the best of my poor ability.
8 The secrets of Minerva.
9 They grind out pamphlets with the leaves of which even a destitute monkey
wouldn't wipe himself.

gives, that so many flourishing wits are smothered in oblivion, ly dead and buried in this our nation. Another main fault is, that I have not revised the copy, and amended the stile, which now flows remisly, as it was first conceived, but my leasure would not permit, *Feci nec quod potui, nec quod volui,* I confesse it is neither as I would, or as it should be.

> *Cùm relego scripsisse pudet, quia plurima cerno*
> *Me quoque quæ fuerant judice digna lini.*
> When I peruse this tract which I have writ,
> I am abash'd, and much I hold unfit.

Et quod gravissimum,[1] in the matter it self, many things I disallow at this present, which when I writ, *Non eadem est ætas, non mens;*[2] I would willingly retract much, &c. but tis too late, I can only crave pardon now for what is amisse.

I might indeed (had I wisely done) observed that precept of the poet,

> ———*nonumque prematur in annum,*[3]

And have taken more care: Or as *Alexander* the physician would have done by *Lapis Lazuli,* fifty times washed before it be used, I should have revised, corrected and amended this tract; but I had not as (I said) that happy leasure, no *Amanuenses* or assistants. *Pancrates* in *Lucian,* wanting a servant as he went from *Memphis* to *Coptus* in *Egypt,* took a door bar, and after some superstitious words pronounced (*Eucrates* the relator was then present) made it stand up like a serving-man, fetch him water, turn the spit, serve in supper, and what work he would besides; and when he had done that service he desired, turn'd his man to a stick again. I have no such skil to make new men at my pleasure, or means to hire them, no whistle to call like the master of a ship, and bid them run, &c. I have no such authority, no such benefactors, as that noble *Ambrosius* was to *Origen,* allowing him six or seven *Amanuenses* to write out his dictats, I must for that cause do my businesse my self, And was therefore enforced, as a Bear doth her whelps, to bring forth this confused lump, I had not time to lick it into form, as she doth her yong ones, but even

---

[1] And what is most serious.
[2] My years and opinions have changed.
[3] Suppress your book for nine years.

so to publish it, as it was first written, *quicquid in buccam venit,*[4] in an extemporean stile, as I do commonly all other exercises, *effudi quicquid dictavit genius meus,*[5] out of a confused company of notes, and writ with as small deliberation as I do ordinarily speak, without all affectation of big words, fustian⁵ phrases, jingling terms, tropes, strong⁵ lines, that like *Acestes* arrows caught fire as they flew, strains of wit, brave heats, elogies, hyperbolical exornations,⁵ elegancies, &c. which many so much affect. I am *aquæ potor,*[6] drink no wine at all, which so much improves our modern wits, a loose, plain, rude writer, *ficum voco ficum, & ligonem ligonem,*[7] and as free, as loose, *idem calamo quod in mente,*[8] I call a spade a spade, *animis hæc scribo, non auribus,*[9] I respect matter, not words; remembring that of *Cardan, verba propter res, non res propter verba:*[1] and seeking with *Seneca, quid scribam, non quemadmodum,* rather what, then how to write. For as *Philo* thinks, *He that is conversant about matter, neglects words, and those that excell in this art of speaking, have no profound learning,*

> *Verba nitent phaleris, at nullas verba medullas*
> *Intus habent*————[2]

Besides, it was the observation of that wise *Seneca, when you see a fellow carefull about his words, and neat in his speech, know this for a certaintie, that mans mind is busied about toyes, there's no soliditie in him. Non est ornamentum virile concinnitas;*[3] as he said of a nightingale,

> ————*vox es, præterea nihil, &c.*[4]

I am therefore in this point a professed disciple of *Apollonius,* a scholar of *Socrates,* I neglect phrases, and labor wholly to inform my readers understanding, not to please his ear; 'tis not my study or intent to compose neatly, which an Orator requires, but to ex-

4 Whatever came out first.
5 I poured out whatever my talent dictated.
6 A water drinker.
7 I call a fig a fig, and a spade a spade.
8 What's in my mind I write with my pen.
9 I write for minds, not for ears.
1 Words because of matter, not matter because of words.
2 The words glitter brilliantly, but they are empty at the core.
3 Elegance of style is not a manly adornment.
4 You are a voice, and nothing more.

press my self readily & plainly as it happens. So that as a River runs sometimes precipitate and swift, then dull and slow; now direct, then *per ambages;*[5] now deep, then shallow; now muddy, then clear; now broad, then narrow; doth my stile flow: now serious, then light; now comical, then satyrical; now more elaborate,[§] then remisse,[§] as the present subject required, or as at that time I was affected. And if thou vouchsafe to reade this treatise, it shall seem no otherwise to thee, then the way to an ordinary Traveller, sometimes fair, sometimes foul; here champion,[§] there inclosed; barren in one place, better soyl in another: by woods, groves, hils, dales, plains, &c. I shall lead thee *per ardua montium, & lubrica vallium, & rescida cespitum, & glebosa camporum,*[6] through variety of objects, that which thou shalt like and surely dislike.

For that matter it self or method, if it be faulty, consider I pray you that of *Columella, Nihil perfectum, aut à singulari consummatum industriâ,*[7] no man can observe all, much is defective no doubt, may be justly taxed, altered, and avoided[§] in *Galen, Aristotle,* those great Masters. *Boni venatoris* (one holds) *plures feras capere, non omnes;* He is a good Huntsman can catch some, not all: I have done my endeavor. Besides, I dwell not in this study, *Non hic sulcos ducimus, non hoc pulvere desudamus,*[8] I am but a smatterer, I confesse, a stranger, here and there I pull a flower; I do easily grant, if a rigid censurer should criticize on this which I have writ, he should not finde three sole faults, as *Scaliger* in *Terence,* but 300. so many as he hath done in *Cardans* subtleties, as many notable errors as *Gul. Laurembergius,* a late professor of *Rostocke,* discovers in that anatomie of *Laurentius,* or *Barocius* the *Venetian* in *Sacroboscus.* And although this be a sixth Edition, in which I should have been more accurate, corrected all those former escapes,[§] yet it was *magni laboris opus,*[9] so difficult and tedious, that as Carpenters do finde out of experience, tis much better build anew sometimes; then repair an old house; I could as soon write as much more, as alter that which is written.

5 In a roundabout way.
6 Over steep mountains, through slippery valleys, wet meadows, and lumpy fields.
7 Nothing can be perfected or completed by the industry of one person.
8 I don't make furrows here; I don't sweat in this field.
9 A work of great labor.

If ought therefore be amisse, (as I grant there is) I require a friendly admonition, no bitter invective,

Sint musis socii Charites, Furia omnis abesto,[1]

Otherwise as in ordinarie controversies, *funem contentionis nectamus, sed cui bono?* We may contend, and likely misuse each other, but to what purpose? We are both scholars, say,

——*Arcades ambo,*
Et cantare pares, & respondere parati.[2]

If we do wrangle, what shal we get by it? Trouble and wrong our selvs, make sport to others. If I be convict of an error, I wil yield, I wil amend. *Si quid bonis moribus, si quid veritati dissentaneum, in sacris vel humanis literis a me dictum sit, id nec dictum esto.*[3] In the mean time I require a favorable censure[§] of all faults omitted, harsh compositions, pleonasmes of words, tautological repetitions (though *Seneca* bear me out, *nunquam nimis dicitur, quod nunquam satis dicitur*[4]) perturbations of tenses, numbers, printers faults, &c. My translations are sometimes rather paraphrases, then interpretations, *non ad verbum,*[5] but as an author, I use more liberty, and that's only taken, which was to my purpose: Quotations are often inserted in the Text, which make the stile more harsh, or in the margent as it hapned. *Greek* authors, *Plato, Plutarch, Athenæus,* &c. I have cited out of their interpreters, because the original was not so readie. I have mingled *sacra prophanis,*[6] but I hope not prophaned, and in repetition of authors names, ranked them *per accidens,*[7] not according to Chronologie; sometimes Neotericks before Ancients, as my memory suggested. Some things are here altered, expunged in this sixth Edition, others amended, much added, because many good authors in all kinds are come to my hands since, and tis no prejudice, no such *indecorum,* or oversight.

1 Let the Graces be friendly to the Muses, but let the Furies stay away.
2 Arcadians both, and prepared both to sing together and to answer each other in song.
3 If I have said anything contrary to good morals or to the truth in sacred or humane writing, let it be regarded as unsaid.
4 That cannot be repeated too often which cannot be said often enough.
5 Not word for word.
6 Sacred with profane.
7 Haphazardly.

Nunquam ita quicquam bene subductâ ratione ad vitam fuit,
Quin res, ætas, usus, semper aliquid apportent novi,
Aliquid moneant, ut illa quæ scire te credas, nescias,
Et quæ tibi putâris prima, in exercendo ut repudias.
Ne're was ought yet at first contriv'd so fit,
But use, age, or something would alter it;
Advise thee better, and, upon peruse,
Make thee not say, and what thou tak'st, refuse.

But I am now resolved never to put this treatise out again, *Ne quid nimis*,[8] I wil not hereafter add, alter, or retract, I have done. The last and greatest exception is, that I being a divine have medled with physick,

> ———*tantumne est ab re tuâ otii tibi,*
> *Aliena ut cures, eaque nihil quæ ad te attinent?*[9]

Which *Menedemus* objected to *Chremes;* have I so much leasure, or little businesse of mine own, as to look after other mens matters which concern me not? What have I to do with physick? *quod medicorum est promittant medici.*[1] The *Lacedemonians* were once in counsel about state-matters, a deboshed fellow spake excellent wel, and to the purpose, his speech was generally approved: A grave Senator steps up, and by all means would have it repealed, though good, because *dehonestabatur pessimo authore,* it had no better an author; let some good man relate the same, and then it should pass. This counsel was embraced, *factum est,* and it was registred forthwith, *Et sic bona sententia mansit, malus author mutatus est.*[2] Thou saiest as much of me, *stomachosus*[3] as thou art, & grantest peradventure this which I have written in physick, not to be amiss, had another done it, a professed physician, or so; but why should I meddle with this tract? Hear me speak: There be many other subjects, I do easily grant, both in humanity and divinity, fit to be treated of, of which had I written *ad ostentationem* only, to shew my self, I should have rather chosen, and in which I have been more conversant, I could have more willingly luxuriated, and better satisfied my self

8 Nothing to excess.
9 Do you have so much spare time that you can pay attention to strange things that are none of your business?
1 Let the doctors attend to the business of doctors.
2 And so the good plan prevailed, its bad author was changed.
3 Peevish.

and others; but that at this time I was fatally driven upon this rock of melancholy, and carried away by this by-stream, which as a rillet, is deducted§ from the main chanel of my studies, in which I have pleased and busied my self at idle hours, as a subject most necessary and commodious. Not that I prefer it before Divinity, which I do acknowledge to be the Queen of professions, and to which all the rest are as handmaids, but that in Divinity I saw no such great need. For had I written positively, there be so many books in that kinde, so many commentators, treatises, pamphlets, expositions, sermons, that whole teemes of oxen cannot draw them; and had I been as forward and ambitious as some others, I might have haply printed a sermon at *Pauls-Cross*, a sermon in St. *Maries Oxon*, a sermon in *Christ-Church*, or a sermon before the right honorable, right reverend, a sermon before the right worshipful, a sermon in latine, in english, a sermon with a name, a sermon without, a sermon, a sermon, &c. But I have been ever as desirous to suppresse my labours in this kinde, as others have been to presse and publish theirs. To have written in controversie, had been to cut off an *Hydra's* head, *lis litem generat,*[4] one begets another, so many duplications, triplications, & swarms of questions, *In sacro bello hoc quod stili mucrone agitur,*[5] that having once begun, I should never make an end. One had much better, as *Alexander* the sixth Pope, long since observed, provoke a great prince than a beging friar, a Jesuit, or a seminary priest, I will add, for *inexpugnabile genus hoc hominum,* they are an irrefragable society, they must and wil have the last word; and that with such eagernesse, impudence, abominable lying, falsifying, and bitterness in their questions they proceed, that as he [Horace] said, *furone cæcus, an rapit vis acrior, an culpa? responsum date.* Blinde fury, or error, or rashnesse, or what it is that eggs them, I know not, I am sure many times, which *Austin*§ perceived long since, *tempestate contentionis, serenitas charitatis obnubilatur,* with this tempest of contention, the serenity of charity is over-clouded, and there be too many spirits conjured up already in this kinde in all sciences, and more than we can tel how to lay, which do so furiously rage, and keep such a racket, that as *Fabius* said, *It had been much*

---

4 One dispute gives rise to another.
5 In this crusade which is fought at penpoint.

*better for some of them to have been born dumb, and altogether
illiterate, then so far to dote to their own destruction.*

> *At melius fuerat non scribere, namque tacere*
> *Tutum semper erit, ——*[6]

Tis a generall fault, so *Severinus* the *Dane* complains in physick,
*unhappy men as we are, we spend our daies in unprofitable
questions and disputations,* intricate subtilties, *de lanâ caprinâ,*[7]
about moonshine in the water, *leaving in the mean time those
chiefest treasures of nature untouched, wherein the best medicines for all manner of diseases are to be found, and do not only
neglect them our selves, but hinder, condemn, forbid and scoffe
at others, that are willing to enquire after them.* These motives
at this present have induced me to make choice of this medicinal
subject.

If any physitian in the mean time shall infer, *Ne sutor ultra
crepidam,*[8] and finde himself grieved that I have intruded into
his profession, I will tell him in brief, I do not otherwise by them,
than they do by us. If it be for their advantage, I know many of
their sect which have taken orders, in hope of a benefice, tis a
common transition, and why may not a melancholy divine, that
can get nothing but by simonie, professe physick? *Drusianus* an
Italian (*Crusianus,* but corruptly, *Trithemius* cals him) *because
he was not fortunate in his practice, forsook his profession, and
writ afterwards in Divinity. Marcilius Ficinus* was *semel & simul,*
a priest and a physician at once, and *T. Linacer* in his old age
took orders. The *Jesuits* professe both at this time, divers of them
permissu superiorum,[9] Chirurgions, panders, bawds, and mid-
wives, &c. Many poor countrey-vicars for want of other means,
are driven to their shifts; to turn mountebanks, quacksalvers,
empiricks, and if our greedy patrons hold us to such hard conditions, as commonly they do, they will make most of us work at
some trade, as *Paul* did, at last turn taskers,[§] maltsters, coster-
mongers, grasiers, sel ale as some have done, or worse. Howsoever in undertaking this task, I hope I shall commit no great

---

[6] It would have been better not to write, for silence is always safe.
[7] About goat's wool (trifles).
[8] Let no shoemaker go beyond a shoe.
[9] With the permission of superiors.

error or *indecorum,* if all be considered aright, I can vindicate my self with *Georgius Braunus,* and *Hieronymus Hemingius,* those two learned Divines; who (to borrow a line or two of mine elder brother) drawn by a *natural love, the one of pictures and maps, prospectives*§ *and corographical*§ *delights, writ that ample theatre*§ *of cities; the other to the studie of genealogies, penned* theatrum genealogicum.[1] Or else I can excuse my studies with *Lessius* the *Jesuit* in like case, It is a disease of the soul, on which I am to treat, and as much appertaining to a Divine as to a physician; and who knows not what an agreement there is betwixt these two professions? A good Divine either is or ought to be a good physician, a spiritual physician at least, as our Saviour cals himself, and was indeed, *Mat.* 4.23. *Luke* 5.18. *Luke* 7.8. They differ but in object, the one of the body, the other of the soul, and use divers medicines to cure: one amends *animam per corpus,*[2] the other *corpus per animam,*[3] as our Regius Professor of physick well informed us in a learned lecture of his not long since. One helps the vices and passions of the soul, anger, lust, desperation, pride, presumption, &c. by applying that spiritual physick; as the other use proper remedies in bodily diseases. Now this being a common infirmity of body and soul, and such a one that hath as much need of spiritual as a corporal cure, I could not finde a fitter task to busie my self about, a more apposite theam, so necessary, so commodious, and generally concerning all sorts of men, that should so equally participate of both, and require a whole physician. A divine in this compound mixt maladie, can do little alone, a physician in some kinds of melancholy much lesse, both make an absolute cure.

Alterius sic altera poscit opem.[4]

And tis proper to them both, and I hope not unbeseeming me, who am by my profession a Divine, and by mine inclination a physician. I had *Jupiter* in my fixt house; I say with *Beroaldus, Non sum medicus, nec medicinæ prorsus expers,*[5] in the theorick of physick I have taken some pains, not with an intent to prac-

1 *The Theater of Genealogies.*
2 The soul through the body.
3 The body through the soul.
4 So the skill of one requires the skill of the other.
5 I am not a doctor, but I am not entirely ignorant of medicine.

tise, but to satisfie my self, which was a cause likewise of the first undertaking of this subject.

If these reasons do not satisfie thee good Reader, as *Alexander Munificus* that bountiful prelate, sometimes bishop of *Lincoln,* when he had built six castles, *ad invidiam operis eluendam,* saith Mr. *Camden,* to take away the envy of his work (which very words *Nubrigensis* hath of *Roger* the rich bishop of *Salisbury,* who in King *Stephens* time, built *Shirburn* castle, and that of *Devises*) to divert the scandal or imputation, which might be thence inferred, built so many religious houses: If this my discourse be over medicinal, or savor too much of humanitie, I promise thee, that I wil hereafter make thee amends in some treatise of divinity. But this I hope shal suffice, when you have more fully considered of the matter of this my subject, *rem substratam,*[6] melancholy, madness, and of the reasons following, which were my chief motives: the generality of the disease, the necessity of the cure, and the commodity or common good that will arise to all men by the knowledg of it, as shal at large appear in the ensuing preface. And I doubt not but that in the end you will say with me, that to anatomize this humor aright, through all the members of this our *Microcosmus,* is as great a task, as to reconcile those Chronologicall errors in the Assyrian monarchie, finde out the *quadrature* of a circle, the creeks and sounds of the north-east, or north-west passages, & all out as good a discovery as that hungry *Spaniards* [Pedro Fernandez Queiros] of *Terra Australis Incognita,*[7] as great trouble as to perfect the motion of *Mars* and *Mercury,* which so crucifies our Astronomers, or to rectifie the *Gregorian* Kalender. I am so affected for my part, and hope as *Theophrastus* did by his characters, *That our posterity, O friend* Policles, *shall be the better for this which we have written, by correcting and rectifying what is amiss in themselves by our examples, and applying our precepts and cautions to their own use.* And as that great captain *Zisca* would have a drum made of his skin when he was dead, because he thought the very noise of it would put his enemies to flight, I doubt not but that these following lines, when they shall be recited, or hereafter read, wil drive away melancholy (though I be gone) as

6 The underlying idea.
7 The unknown southern land.

much as *Ziscaes* drum could terrifie his foes. Yet one caution let me give by the way to my present, or future Reader, who is actually melancholy, that he reade not the symptomes or prognosticks in this following tract, lest by applying that which he reads to himself, aggravating, appropriating things generally spoken, to his own person (as melancholy men for the most part do) he trouble or hurt himself, and get in conclusion more harm then good. I advise them therefore warily to peruse that tract, *Lapides loquitur* (so said *Agrippa de occ. Phil.*) *& caveant lectores ne cerebrum iis excutiat.*[8] The rest I doubt not they may securely reade, and to their benefit. But I am over-tedious, I proceed.

Of the necessity and generality of this which I have said, if any man doubt, I shall desire him to make a brief survey of the world, as *Cyprian* adviseth *Donat, supposing himself to be transported to the top of some high mountain, and thence to behold the tumults and chances of this wavering world, he cannot chuse but either laugh at, or pity it.* S. *Hierom* out of a strong imagination, being in the wilderness, conceived with himself, that he then saw them dancing in *Rome;* and if thou shalt either conceive, or clime to see, thou shalt soon perceive that all the world is mad, that it is melancholy, dotes: that it is (which *Epichthonius Cosmopolites* expressed not many years since in a map) made like a fools head (with that Motto, *Caput helleboro dignum*[9]) a crased head, *cavea stultorum*, a fools paradise, or as *Apollonius*, a common prison of guls, cheaters, flatterers, &c. and needs to be reformed. *Strabo* in the ninth book of his geographie, compares *Greece* to the picture of a man, which comparison of his, *Nic. Gerbelius* in his exposition of *Sophianus* map, approves; The breast lies open from those *Acroceraunian* hils in *Epirus,* to the *Sunian* promontory in *Attica; Pagæ* and *Magæra* are the two shoulders; that *Istmos* of *Corinth* the neck; and *Peloponnesus* the head. If this allusion hold, tis sure a mad head; *Morea*[1] may be *Moria;*[2] and to speak what I think, the inhabitants of moderne *Greece,* swerve as much from reason, & true religion at this day,

8 He speaks about stones, and his readers must watch out lest he break their heads (Agrippa, *Occult Philosophy*).
9 A head that needs hellebore.
1 Alternative name for Peloponnesus.
2 Folly.

as that *Morea* doth from the picture of a man. Examine the rest in like sort, and you shall finde that Kingdoms and Provinces are melancholy, cities and families, all creatures, vegetal, sensible, and rational, that all sorts, sects, ages, conditions, are out of tune, as in *Cebes* table,[3] *omnes errorem bibunt,* before they come into the world, they are intoxicated by errors cup, from the highest to the lowest, have need of Physick, and those particular actions in *Seneca,* where father & son prove one another mad, may be general; *Porcius Latro* shall plead against us all. For indeed who is not a fool, melancholy, mad?—*Qui nil molitur inepte,*[4] who is not brain-sick? Folly, melancholy, madnes, are but one disease, *Delirium* is a common name to all. *Alexander, Gordonius, Jason Pratensis, Savanarola, Guianerius, Montaltus,* confound them as differing *secundum magis & minus;*[5] so doth *David, Psal.* 75.4. *I said unto the fools, deal not so madly,* & twas an old *Stoicall* Paradox, *omnes stultos insanire,* all fools are mad, though some madder then others. And who is not a fool, who is free from melancholy? Who is not touched more or lesse in habit or disposition? If in disposition, *ill dispositions beget habits, if they persevere,* saith *Plutarch,* habits either are, or turn to diseases. Tis the same which *Tully* maintains in the second of his *Tusculanes,*[6] *omnium insipientum animi in morbo sunt, & perturbatorum,* Fools are sick, and all that are troubled in minde: for what is sickness, but as *Gregorie Tholosanus* defines it, *A dissolution or perturbation of the bodily league, which health combines:* And who is not sick, or ill disposed? in whom doth not passion, anger, envy, discontent, fear and sorrow raign? Who labours not of this disease? Give me but a little leave, & you shall see by what testimonies, confessions, arguments I wil evince it, that most men are mad, that they had as much need to go a pilgrimage to the *Anticyræ*[§] (as in *Strabo's* time they did) as in our daies they run to *Compostella,* our Lady of *Sichem,* or *Lauretta,*[§] to seek for help; that it is like to be as prosperous a voyage as that of *Guiana,* and that there is much more need of *Hellebor* then of *Tobacco.*

That men are so misaffected, melancholy, mad, giddy-headed,

---

3 *The Table,* or, *The Picture,* a book on the human condition.
4 Who doesn't busy himself with silly things?
5 In degree.
6 *Tusculan Disputations.*

hear the testimony of *Solomon, Eccl.* 2.12. *And I turned to behold wisdom, madness and folly, &c.* And *ver.* 23. *All his dayes are sorrow, his travel grief, and his heart taketh no rest in the night.* So that take melancholy in what sense you will, properly or improperly, in disposition or habit, for pleasure or for pain, dotage, discontent, fear, sorrow, madness, for part, or all, truly, or metaphorically, tis all one. Laughter it self is madness according to *Solomon,* and as S. *Paul* hath it, *worldly sorrow brings death. The hearts of the sons of men are evil, and madness is in their hearts while they live, Eccl.* 9.3. *Wise men themselves are no better, Ecc.* 1.18. *In the multitude of wisdom is much grief, and he that increaseth wisdom increaseth sorrow, Cap.*[7] 2.17. He [Ecclesiastes] hated life it self, nothing pleased him; he hated his labor, all, as he concludes, is *sorrow, grief, vanity, vexation of spirit.* And though he were the wisest man in the world, *sanctuarium sapientiæ,*[8] and had wisdom in abundance, he wil not vindicate himself, or justifie his own actions. *Surely I am more foolish then any man, and have not the understanding of a man in me, Pro.* 30.2. Be they *Solomons* words, or the words of *Agur* the son of *Jakeh,* they are canonicall. *David* a man after Gods own heart, confesseth as much of himself, *Psal.* 73.21, 22. *So foolish was I and ignorant, I was even as a beast before thee.* And condemns all for fools, *Ps.* 53. & 32.9. & 49.20. He compares them to *beasts, horses, and mules, in which there is no understanding.* The Apostle *Paul* accuseth himself in like sort, 2 *Cor.* 11.21. I *would you would suffer a little my foolishness, I speak foolishly. The whole head is sick* saith *Esay, and the heart is heavy, Cap.* 1.5. And makes lighter of them *then of Oxen and Asses, The Ox knows his owner, &c.* reade *Deut.* 32.6. *Jer.* 4. *Amos* 3.1. *Ephes.* 5.6. *Be not mad, be not deceived, foolish Galatians, who hath bewitched you?* How often are they branded with this Epithet of madnesse and folly? No word so frequent amongst the fathers of the Church and Divines; you may see what an opinion they had of the world, and how they valued mens actions.

I know that we think far otherwise, and hold them most part wise men that are in authority, princes, magistrates, rich men, they are wise men born, all Politicians and States-men must

7 Chapter.
8 The shrine of wisdom.

needs be so, for who dare speak against them? And on the other, so corrupt is our judgment, we esteem wise and honest men fools. Which *Democritus* wel signified in an *Epistle* of his to *Hyppocrates:* The *Abderites account vertue madnesse,* and so do most men living. Shall I tell you the reason of it? *Fortune* and *Vertue, Wisdom* and *Folly,* their seconds, upon a time contended in the *Olympicks;* Every man thought that *fortune* and *folly* would have the worst, and pitied their cases. But it fell out otherwise. *Fortune* was blind and cared not where she stroke, nor whom, without laws, *Andabatarum instar,*[9] &c. *Folly* rash and inconsiderate, esteemed as little what she said or did. *Vertue* and *Wisdom* gave[8] place, were hissed out, and exploded by the common people; *folly* and *fortune* admired, and so are all their followers ever since: knaves and fools commonly fare and deserve best in worldlings eyes & opinions. Many good men have no better fate in their ages: *Achish,* 1 *Sam.* 21.14. held *David* for a mad-man. *Elisha* & the rest were no otherwise esteemed. *David* was derided of the common people, *Psa.* 71.7. *I am become a monster to many.* And generally we are accounted fools for Christ, 1 *Cor.* 4. *We fools thought his life madnesse, and his end without honour, Wisd.* 5.4. Christ and his Apostles were censured in like sort, *John* 10. *Mark* 3. *Acts* 26. And so were all christians in *Pliny's* time, *fuerunt & alii similis dementiæ,* &c.[1] And called not long after, *Vesaniæ sectatores, eversores hominum, polluti novatores, fanatici, canes, malefici, venefici, Galilæi homunciones,* &c.[2] Tis an ordinary thing with us, to account honest, devout, orthodox, divine, religious, plain-dealing-men, idiots, asses, that cannot, or will not ly and dissemble, shift, flatter, *accommodare se ad eum locum ubi nati sunt,*[3] make good bargains, supplant, thrive, *patronis inservire; solennes ascendendi modos apprehendere, leges, mores, consuetudines rectè observare, candidè laudare, fortiter defendere, sententias amplecti, dubitare de nullis, credere omnia, accipere omnia, nihil reprehendere, cæteraque quæ promotionem ferunt & securitatem, quæ sine ambage fœlicem reddunt hominem, & verè sapientem*

---

9 Like blindfolded gladiators.
1 And there were others of a similar madness.
2 Devotees of madness, subversives, blasphemous innovators, fanatics, dogs, criminals, sorcerers, Galilean manikins.
3 Adapt themselves to the station in which they were born.

apud nos;[4] That cannot temporize as other men do, hand and take bribes, &c. but fear God, and make a conscience of their doings. But the holy Ghost that knowes better how to judge, he cals them fools. *The fool hath said in his heart, Psal.* 53.1. *And their wayes utter their folly, Psal.* 49.14. *For what can be more mad, than for a little worldly pleasure to procure unto themselves eternall punishment?* As *Gregorie* and others inculcate unto us.

Yea even all those great Philosophers, the world hath ever had in admiration, whose works we do so much esteem, that gave precepts of wisdom to others, inventers of Arts and Sciences, *Socrates* the wisest man of his time by the Oracle of *Apollo*, whom his two Scholars *Plato* and *Xenophon* so much extol and magnifie with those honourable titles, *best and wisest of all mortal men, the happiest, and most just;* and as *Alcibiades* incomparably commends him; *Achilles* was a worthy man, but *Bracides* and others were as worthy as himself; *Antenor* and *Nestor* were as good as *Pericles*, and so of the rest, but none present, before, or after *Socrates, nemo veterum neque eorum qui nunc sunt,*[5] were ever such, will match, or come neer him. Those seven wise men of *Greece*, those *Britain Druides, Indian Brachmanni, Æthiopian Gymnosophists, Magi* of the *Persians, Apollonius,* of whom *Philostratus, Non doctus sed natus sapiens,*[6] wise from his cradle, *Epicurus* so much admired by his Scholar *Lucretius;*

> *Qui genus humanum ingenio superavit, & omnes*
> *Perstrinxit Stellas exortus ut ætherius Sol.*
> Whose wit excel'd the wits of men as far,
> As the Sun rising doth obscure a Star.

Or that so much renowned *Empedocles,*

> *Ut vix humana videatur stirpe creatus.*[7]

All those, of whom we read such *Hyperbolicall elogiums;* as of *Aristotle*, that he was wisdom it self in the abstract, a Miracle

---

[4] Fawn upon their patrons, learn the usual methods of getting ahead, follow laws, manners, customs to the letter, praise glowingly, defend staunchly, embrace others' opinions, doubt nothing, believe everything, endure everything, find fault with nothing, and do all the other things which lead to promotion and security, which directly make a man happy and truly wise among us.
[5] None of the ancients or of those now alive.
[6] Not made, but born, wise.
[7] That he hardly seems to have been begotten of human stock.

of nature, breathing liberaries, as *Eunapius* of *Longinus*, lights of nature, gyants for wit, quintessence of wit, divine spirits, eagles in the clouds, fallen from heaven, gods, spirits, lamps of the world, dictators,

Nulla ferant talem secla futura virum:[8]

Monarchs, miracles, superintendents of wit and learning, *Oceanus, Phœnix, Atlas, Monstrum, portentum hominis, orbis universi musæum, ultimus humanæ naturae conatus, naturæ maritus,*[9]

———*meritò cui doctior orbis*
Submissis defert fascibus imperium.[1]

As *Ælian* writ of *Protagoras* and *Gorgias*, we may say of them all, *tantum à sapientibus abfuerunt, quantum à viris pueri,*[2] they were children in respect, infants, not eagles but kites; novices, illiterate, *Eunuchi sapientiæ.*[3] And although they were the wisest, and most admired in their age, as he censured *Alexander*, I do them, there were 10,000 in his army as worthy Captains (had they been in place of command) as valiant as himself; there were Myriades of men wiser in those dayes, & yet all short of what they ought to be. *Lactantius* in his book of wisdom, proves them to be dizards, fools, asses, mad-men, so full of absurd and ridiculous tenents, and brain-sick positions, that to his thinking never any old woman or sick person doted worse. *Democritus* took all from *Leucippus,* and left, saith he, *the inheritance of his folly to* Epicurus, *insanientis dum sapientiæ,* &c. The like he holds of *Plato, Aristippus,* and the rest, making no difference *betwixt them and beasts, saving that they could speak. Theodoret* in his tract *De cur. grec. affect.*[4] manifestly evinces as much of *Socrates,* whom though that Oracle of *Apollo* confirmed to be the wisest man then living, and saved him from the plague, whom 2,000 years have admired, of whom

---

8 No future generations will produce such a man.
9 A prodigy, a marvel of a man, the seat of learning of the whole world, the supreme product of human nature, the husband of Nature.
1 The deserving man to whom the learned world pays homage.
2 They were as different from wise men as boys are from men.
3 Eunuchs of wisdom.
4 *Remedy for the Diseases of the Greeks.*

some will as soon speak evil as of *Christ,* yet *re vera,*[5] he was
an illiterate idiot, as *Aristophanes* cals him, *irrisor & ambi-
tiosus,*[6] as his Master *Aristotle* terms him, *scurra Atticus,*[7] as
Zeno, an enemy to all arts & sciences, as *Athæneus,* to Philosophers & Travellers, an opinative[s] asse, a caviller, a kinde of
Pedant; for his manners, as *Theod. Cyrensis* describes him, a
Sodomite, an *Athiest,* (so convict[s] by *Anytus*) *iracundus & ebrius,
dicax,*[8] *&c.* a pot-companion, by *Plato's* own confession, a sturdy
drinker; and that of all others he was most sottish, a very mad-
man in his actions and opinions. *Pythagoras* was part philosopher, part magician, or part witch. If you desire to hear more
of *Apollonius* a great wise man, sometime parallel'd by *Julian*
the apostate to Christ, I refer you to that learned tract of *Euse-
bius* against *Hyerocles,* and for them al to *Lucians Piscator,
Icaromenippus, Necyomantia:*[9] their actions, opinions in general
were so prodigious, absurd, ridiculous, which they broached
and maintained, their books and elaborate Treatises were full
of dotage, which *Tully ad Atticum,*[1] long since observed, *delirant
plerumque scriptores in libris suis,*[2] their lives being opposite
to their words, they commended poverty to others, and were
most covetous themselves, extolled love and peace, and yet persecuted one another with virulent hate and malice. They could
give precepts for verse and prose, but not a man of them (as
Seneca tels them home) could moderate his affections. Their
musick did shew us *flebiles modos,*[3] *&c.* how to rise and fall,
but they could not so contain themselves as in adversity not to
make a lamentable tone. They will measure ground by Geom-
etrie, set down limits, divide and subdivide, but cannot yet
prescribe *quantum homini satis,*[4] or keep within compasse of
reason and discretion. They can square circles, but understand
not the state of their own souls, describe right lines, and crooked,

5 In reality.
6 A scoffer, and eager for favor.
7 An Attic buffoon.
8 Hot-tempered, drunk, sarcastic.
9 *The Fisherman, The Sky-Man, Menippus* (or, *Necromancy*).
1 *To Atticus.*
2 Writers usually rave in their books.
3 Doleful measures.
4 How much is enough for a man.

&c. but know not what is right in this life, *quid in vitâ rectum sit, ignorant;* so that as he said,

Nescio an Anticyram ratio illis destinet omnem.

I think all the *Anticyræ* will not restore them to their wits, if these men now, that held *Xenodotus* heart, *Crates* liver, *Epictetus* lanthorn, were so sottish, and had no more brains then so many beetles, what shall we think of the commonalty? what of the rest?

Yea, but will you infer, that is true of *heathens,* if they be conferred[§] with Christians, 1 *Cor.* 3.19. *The wisdom of this world is foolishnesse with God, earthly and devillish,* as *James* cals it, 3.15. *They were vain in their imaginations, and their foolish heart was full of darknesse, Rom.* 1.21, 22. *When they professed themselves wise, became fools.* Their witty works are admired here on earth, whilest their souls are tormented in hell fire. In some sense, *Christiani Crassiani,* Christians are Crassians,[§] & if compared to that wisdom, no better then fools. *Quis est sapiens?* [5] *Solus Deus, Pythagoras* replies, *God is only wise, Rom.* 16. *Paul* determines *only good,* as *Austine* well contends, *and no man living can be justified in his sight. God looked down from heaven upon the children of men, to see if any did understand, Psalm* 53.2, 3. but all are corrupt, erre. *Rom.* 3.12. *None doth good, no not one. Job* aggravates[§] this, 4.18. *Behold he found no stedfastnesse in his servants, and laid folly upon his angels,* 19. *How much more on them that dwell in houses of clay?* In this sense we are all as fools, and the Scripture alone is *arx Minervæ,*[6] we and our writings are shallow and unperfect. But I do not so mean; even in our ordinary dealings, we are no better then fools. All our actions, as *Pliny* told *Trajan, upbraid us of folly,* our whole course of life is but matter of laughter: we are not soberly wise; and the world it self, which ought at least to be wise by reason of his[§] antiquity, as *Hugo de Prato Florido* will have it, *semper stultizat, is every day more foolish then other; the more it is whipped, the worse it is, and as a child, will still be crowned with roses and flowers.* We are apish

[5] Who is wise?
[6] The fortress of Minerva.

in it, *asini bipedes*,[7] and every place is full *inversorum Apuleio-rum*,[8] of metamorphosed and two-legged asses, *inversorum Silenorum*,[9] childish, *pueri instar bimuli, tremulâ patris dormien-tis in ulnâ.*[1] *Jovianus Pontanus, Antonio Dial.*,[2] brings in some laughing at an old man, that by reason of his age was a little fond,[§] but as he admonisheth there, *Ne mireris mî hospes de hoc sene*,[3] marvel not at him only, for *tota hæc civitas delirium,* all our Town dotes in like sort, we are a company of fools. Ask not with him in the Poet, *Larvæ hunc intemperiæ insaniæque agitant senem?* What madnesse ghosts this old man, but what madnesse ghosts us all? For we are *ad unum omnes,* all mad, *semel insanivimus omnes,* not once; but alway so, *& semel, & simul, & semper,* ever and altogether as bad as he; and not *senex bis puer, delira anus,*[4] but say it of us all, *semper pueri,* yong and old, all dote, as *Lactantius* proves out of *Seneca;* and no difference betwixt us and children, saving that, *majora ludimus, & grandioribus pupis,* they play with babies[§] of clouts[§] & such toyes, we sport with greater bables.[§] We cannot ac-cuse or condemn one another, being faulty our selves, *delira-menta loqueris,* you talk idly, or as *Mitio* upbraided *Demea,* *insanis, aufer te,*[5] for we are as mad our own selves, and it is hard to say which is the worst. Nay tis universally so,

Vitam regit fortuna, non sapientia.[6]

When *Socrates* had taken great pains to finde out a wise man, and to that purpose had consulted with philosophers, poets, artificers, he concludes all men were fools; and though it pro-cured him both anger and much envy, yet in all companies he would openly professe it. When *Supputius* in *Pontanus* had travelled all over *Europe* to conferre with a wise man, he re-turned at last without his errand,[§] and could finde none. *Cardan*

---

7 Two-legged asses.
8 Metamorphosed Apuleiuses.
9 Metamorphosed Silenuses.
1 Like a two year old child, rocked asleep in its father's arms.
2 In *The Dialogue Entitled Antonio.*
3 Do not marvel, my friends, at this old man.
4 An old man is in his second childhood, an old woman is mad.
5 You are mad; go away.
6 Chance rules our lives, not wisdom.

concurs with him, *Few there are (for ought I can perceive) well in their wits.* So doth *Tully, I see every thing to be done foolishly and unadvisedly.*

> *Ille sinistrorsum, hic dextrorsum, unus utrique*
> *Error, sed variis illudit partibus omnes.*
> One reels to this, another to that wall.
> Tis the same error that deludes them all.

They dote all, but not alike, Μανία γὰρ οὐ πᾶσιν ὁμοία, not in the same kinde, *One is covetous, a second lascivious, a third ambitious, a fourth envious,* &c. as *Damisippus* the *Stoick* hath well illustrated in the poet [Horace],

> *Desipiunt omnes æquè ac tu.*[7]

Tis an inbred maladie in every one of us, there is *seminarium stultitiæ,* a seminarie of folly, *which if it be stirred up, or get a head, will run* in infinitum, *& infinitely varies, as we our selves are severally addicted,* saith *Balthazar Castilio:* and cannot so easily be rooted out, it takes such fast hold, as *Tully* holds, *altæ radices stultitiæ,*[8] so we are bred, and so we continue. Some say there be two main defects of wit, error and ignorance, to which all others are reduced; by ignorance we know not things necessary, by error we know them falsly. Ignorance is a privation, error a positive act. From ignorance comes vice, from error heresie, &c. But make how many kinds you will, divide and subdivide, few men are free, or that do not impinge on some one kinde or other. *Sic plerumque agitat stultos inscitia,*[9] as he that examines his own and other mens actions, shall finde.

Charon in *Lucian,* as he wittily faigns, was conducted by *Mercury* to such a place, where he might see all the world at once; after he had sufficiently viewed, and looked about, *Mercury* would needs know of him what he had observed: He told him, that he saw a vast multitude, and a promiscuous,[§] their habitations like mole-hils, the men as emmets, *he could discern cities like so many hives of Bees, wherein every Bee had a sting, and they did nought else but sting one another, some domineer-*

---

[7] All act just as foolishly as you do.
[8] Deep are the roots of folly.
[9] So ignorance commonly dominates foolish people.

*ing like Hornets, bigger then the rest, some like filching Wasps,
others as drones.* Over their heads were hovering a confused
companie of perturbations, hope, fear, anger, avarice, ignorance,
&c. and a multitude of diseases hanging, which they still pulled
on their pates. Some were Brawling, some fighting, riding, running, *sollicitè ambientes, callidè litigantes,*[1] for toyes, and trifles,
and such momentanie things. Their Towns and Provinces meer
factions, rich against poor, poor against rich, nobles against
artificers, they against nobles, and so the rest. In conclusion,
he condemned them all for mad-men, fools, idiots, asses, *O
stulti, quænam hæc est amentia?* [2] O fools, O mad-men he ex-
claims, *insana studia, insani labores, &c.* Mad endeavors, mad
actions, mad, mad, mad, *O seclum insipiens & infacetum,* a giddy-headed age. *Heraclitus* the Philosopher, out of a serious meditation of mens lives, fell a weeping, and with continual tears
bewailed their misery, madnes, and folly. *Democritus* on the
other side burst out a laughing, their whole life seemed to him
so ridiculous, & he was so far carried with this ironical passion,
that the Citizens of *Abdera* took him to be mad, and sent therefore Embassadors to *Hyppocrates* the Physitian, that he would
exercise his skill upon him. But the story is set down at large
by *Hyppocrates,* in his epistle to *Damagetus,* which because it
is not impertinent to this discourse, I wil insert *verbatim* almost, as it is delivered by *Hyppocrates* himself, with all the
circumstances belonging unto it.

When *Hyppocrates* was now come to *Abdera,* the people of
the City came flocking about him, some weeping, some intreating of him, that he would do his best. After some little repast,
he went to see *Democritus,* the people following him, whom he
found (as before) in his garden in the suburbs all alone, *sitting
upon a stone under a plane tree, without hose or shoes, with
a book on his knees, cutting up severall beasts, and busie at his
study.* The multitude stood gazing round about to see the con-
gresse.[§] *Hyppocrates* after a little pause, saluted him by his name,
whom he resaluted, ashamed almost that he could not call him
likewise by his, or that he had forgot it. *Hyppocrates* demanded
of him what he was doing: He told him that he was *busie in cut-*

1 Earnestly soliciting (votes), cunningly pursuing lawsuits.
2 O fools, what in the world is this folly?

ting up several beasts, to finde out the cause of madness and mel-
ancholy. *Hyppocrates* commended his work, admiring his happinesse and leasure. And why, quoth *Democritus*, have not you
that leasure? Because, replied *Hyppocrates*, domestical affairs
hinder, necessary to be done, for our selves, neighbors, friends;
expenses, diseases, frailties and mortalities which happen; wife,
children, servants, and such businesses which deprive us of our
time. At this speech *Democritus* profusely laughed, (his friends
and the people standing by, weeping in the mean time, and
lamenting his madness.) *Hyppocrates* asked the reason why he
laughed. He told him, at the vanities and fopperies of the time,
to see men so empty of all vertuous actions, to hunt so far after
gold, having no end of ambition; to take such infinite pains for
a little glory, and to be favored of men; to make such deep
mines into the earth for gold, and many times to finde nothing,
with losse of their lives and fortunes. Some to love dogs, others
horses, some to desire to be obeyed in many Provinces, and yet
themselves will know no obedience. Some to love their wives
dearly at first, and after a while to forsake & hate them, begetting children, with much care and cost for their education,
yet when they grow to mans estate, to despise, neglect, and leave
them naked to the worlds mercy. Do not these behaviours expresse their intollerable folly? When men live in peace, they
covet war, detesting quietness, deposing Kings, and advancing
others in their stead, murdering some men to beget children of
ther wives. How many strange humors are in men? When they
are poor and needy, they seek riches, and when they have them,
they do not enjoy them, but hide them under ground, or else
wastfully spend them. O wise *Hyppocrates*, I laugh at such
things being done, but much more when no good comes of
them, and when they are done to so ill purpose. There is no
truth or justice found amongst them, for they daily plead one
against another, the son against the father and the mother,
brother against brother, kinred[§] & friends of the same quality;
and all this for riches, whereof after death they cannot be
possessors. And yet notwithstanding they wil defame & kil one
another, commit all unlawfull actions, contemning God and
men, friends and countrey. They make great account of many
senslesse things, esteeming them as a great part of their treas-

ure, statues, pictures, and such like moveables, dear bought, & so cunningly wrought, as nothing but speech wanteth in them, and yet they hate living persons speaking to them. Others affect difficult things; if they dwel on firm Land, they wil remove to an Iland, and thence to land again, being no way constant to their desires. They commend courage & strength in wars, & let themselves be conquered by lust & avarice; they are in brief, as disordered in their minds, as *Thersites* was in his body. And now me thinks, O most worthy *Hyppocrates,* you should not reprehend my laughing, perceiving so many fooleries in men; for no man will mock his own folly, but that which he seeth in a second, and so they justly mock one another. The drunkard cals him a glutton, whom he knows to be sober. Many men love the sea, others husbandry; briefly, they cannot agree in their own trades and professions, much lesse in their lives and actions.

When *Hyppocrates* heard these words so readily uttered, without premeditation, to declare the worlds vanity, full of ridiculous contrariety, he made answer, That necessity compelled men to many such actions, & divers wils ensuing from divine permission, that we might not be idle, being nothing is so odious to them as sloth and negligence. Besides, men cannot foresee future events, in this uncertainty of humane affairs; they would not so marry, if they could foretell the causes of their dislike and separation; or parents, if they knew the hour of their childrens death, so tenderly provide for them; or an husbandman sowe, if he thought there would be no increase; or a merchant adventure to sea, if he foresaw shipwrack; or be a Magistrate, if presently to be deposed. Alas, worthy *Democritus,* every man hopes the best, and to that end he doth it, and therefore no such cause, or ridiculous occasion of laughter.

Democritus hearing this poor excuse, laughed again aloud, perceiving he wholly mistook him, and did not well understand what he had said concerning perturbations, and tranquility of the minde. Insomuch, that if men would govern their actions by discretion and providence, they would not declare themselves fools, as now they do, and he should have no cause of laughter; but (quoth he) they swell in this life, as if they were immortal, and demi-gods, for want of understanding. It were enough to make them wise, if they would but consider the mutability of this world, and how it wheels about, nothing being firm and sure. He that is now above, to morrow is beneath; he that sate on this side to day, to morrow is hurled on the other: and not considering these matters, they fall into many inconveniences and troubles, coveting things of no profit, and thirsting after them, tumbling headlong into many calamities. So that if men would attempt no more then what they can bear, they should lead contented lives, and learning to know themselves, would limit their ambition, they would perceive then that Nature hath enough without seeking such superfluities, & unprofitable things, which bring nothing with them but grief and molestation. As a fat body is more subject to diseases, so are rich men to absurdities and fooleries, to many casualties and cross inconveniences. There are many that take no heed what happeneth to others by bad conversation,§ and therefore overthrow themselves in the same manner through their own fault, not foreseeing dangers manifest. These are things (O more then mad, quoth he) that give me matter of laughter, by suffering the pains of your impieties, as your avarice, envy, malice, enormous villanies, mutinies, unsatiable desires, conspiracies, and other incurable vices; besides, your dissimulation and hypocrisie, bearing deadly hatred one to the other, and yet shadowing it with a good face, flying out into all filthy lusts, and transgressions of all laws, both of nature and civility. Many things which they have left off, after a while they fall to again, husbandry, navigation; and leave again, fickle and unconstant as they are. When they are yong, they would be old, and old, yong. Princes commend a private life, private men itch after honour: a Magistrate commends a quiet life, a quiet man would be in his office, and obeyed as he is: and what is the cause of all this, but that they know not themselves. Some delight to destroy, one to build, another to spoil one countrey to enrich another and himself. In all these things they are like children, in whom is no judgment or councel, and resemble beasts, saving that beasts are better then they, as being contented with nature. When shall you see a Lion hide gold in the ground, or a Bul contend for a better pasture? when a Boar is thirsty, he drinks what will serve him, and no more; and when his belly is ful, he ceaseth to eat: But men are immoderate in both; as in lust, they covet carnal

copulation at set times; men always, ruinating thereby the
health of their bodies. And doth it not deserve laughter, to see
an amorous fool torment himself for a wench; weep, howl for
a mis-shapen slut, a dowdy, sometimes that might have his
choice of the finest beauties? Is there any remedy for this in
physick? I do anatomize and cut up these poor beasts, to see
these distempers, vanities, and follies, yet such proof were better
made on mans body, if my kinde nature would indure it: Who
from the hour of his birth is most miserable, weak and sickly;
when he sucks he is guided by others, when he is grown great
practiseth unhappinesse, and is sturdy, and when old, a childe
again, and repenteth him of his life past. And here being interrupted by one that brought books, he fell to it again, that all
were mad, carelesse, stupid. To prove my former speeches, look
into courts, or private houses. Judges give judgement according
to their own advantage, doing manifest wrong to poor innocents,
to please others. Notaries alter sentences, and for money lose
their Deeds. Some make false moneys, others counterfeit false
weights. Some abuse their parents, yea corrupt their own sisters,
others make long libels and pasquils, defaming men of good
life, and extol such as are lewd and vicious. Some rob one, some
another; Magistrates make laws against theeves, and are the
veriest theeves themselves. Some kill themselves, others despair,
not obtaining their desires. Some dance, sing, laugh, feast and
banquet, whilest others sigh, languish, mourn and lament, having neither meat, drink, nor clothes. Some prank up their bodies,
and have their mindes full of execrable vices. Some trot about
to bear false witnesse, and say any thing for money; and though
Judges know of it, yet for a bribe they wink at it, and suffer
false Contracts to prevail against Equity. Women are all day
a dressing, to pleasure other men abroad, and go like sluts at
home, not caring to please their own husbands whom they
should. Seeing men are so fickle, so sottish, so intemperate,
why should not I laugh at those, to whom folly seems wisdom,
will not be cured, and perceive it not?

It grew late, *Hyppocrates* left him, and no sooner was he come
away, but all the Citizens came about flocking, to know how he
liked him. He told them in brief, that notwithstanding those
small neglects of his attire, body, diet, the world had not a wiser,

a more learned, a more honest man, and they were much deceived to say that he was mad.

Thus *Democritus* esteemed of the World in his time, and this
was the cause of his laughter: and good cause he had.

> *Olim jure quidem, nunc plus Democrite ride;*
> *Quin rides? vita hæc nunc magè ridicula est.*
> *Democritus* did well to laugh of old,
> Good cause he had, but now much more,
> This life of ours is more ridiculous
> Then that of his, or long before.

Never so much cause of laughter, as now, never so many
fools and mad men. Tis not one *Democritus* wil serve turn to
laugh in these days, we have now need of a *Democritus to
laugh at Democritus*, one Jester to flout at another, one fool
to flear at another. A great *Stentorian Democritus*, as big as
that *Rhodian Colossus*. For now, as *Sarisburiensis* said in his
time, *totus mundus histrionem agit*, the whole world playes the
fool; we have a new theatre, a new scene, a new comedie of
errors, a new company of personate actors, *volupiæ sacra*[3] (as
Calcagninus wittily feigns[5] in his Apologs) are celebrated all the
world over, where all the actors were mad men and fools, and
every hour changed habits, or took that which came next. He
that was a Marriner to day, is an Apothecary to morrow; a
smith one while, a philosopher another, *in his volupiæ ludis*;[4]
a king now with his crown, robes, scepter, attendants, by and
by drove a loaded asse before him like a carter, &c. If *Democritus* were alive now, he should see strange alterations, a new
company of counterfeit vizards, whiflers,[§] *Cumane* asses, mask-
ers, mummers, painted Puppets, outsides, phantastick shadows,
guls, monsters, giddy-heads, butter-flies. And so many of them
are indeed (if all be true that I have read) For when *Jupiter* &
Juno's wedding was solemnized of old, the gods were all invited
to the feast, and many noble men besides: Amongst the rest
came *Crysalus* a *Persian* prince, bravely attended, rich in golden
attires, in gay robes, with a majestical presence, but otherwise
an asse. The gods seeing him come in such pomp and state,

[3] The rites of the Goddess of Pleasure.
[4] In these celebrations of the Goddess of Pleasure.

rose up to give him place, *ex habitu hominem metientes;*[5] but *Jupiter* perceiving what he was, a light, phantastick, idle fellow, turned him and his proud followers into butter-flies: and so they continue still (for ought I know to the contrary) roving about in pied-coats, and are called *Chrysalides* by the wiser sort of men: that is, golden outsides, drones, flies, and things of no worth. Multitudes of such, &c.

> ——*ubique invenies*
> *Stultos avaros, sycophantas prodigos.*[6]

Many additions, much increase of madnesse, folly, vanity, should *Democritus* observe, were he now to travel, or could get leave of *Pluto* to come see fashions, as *Charon* did in *Lucian* to visit our cities of *Moronia Pia,* and *Moronia Fœlix,*[7] sure I think he would break the rim of his belly with laughing.

> *Si foret in terris rideret Democritus, seu, &c.*[8]

A satyrical *Roman* in his time, thought all vice, folly, and madnesse were all at full sea,

> *Omne in præcipiti vitium stetit.*——

Josephus the historian taxeth his countrey-men *Jews* for bragging of their vices, publishing their follies, and that they did contend amongst themselves, who should be most notorious in villanies; but we flow higher in madnesse, far beyond them,

> *Mox daturi progeniem vitiosiorem,*[9]

and the latter end (you know whose oracle it is) is like to be worst. 'Tis not to be denied, the world alters every day, *Ruunt urbes, regna transferuntur, &c. variantur habitus, leges innovantur,*[1] as *Petrarch* observes, we change language, habits, laws, customs, manners, but not vices, not diseases, not the symptoms of folly and madnesse, they are still the same. And as a River we see, keeps the like name and place, but not water, and yet ever runs,

5 Judging the man by his clothes.
6 You will find greedy fools and spendthrift sycophants everywhere.
7 Religious Imbecility and Happy Imbecility.
8 If Democritus were alive, how he would laugh.
9 Soon we'll produce more wicked offspring.
1 Cities fall, kingdoms change hands, fashions change, laws are altered.

Labitur & labetur in omne volubilis ævum;

Our times and persons alter, vices are the same, and ever will be; look how Nightingals sang of old, Cocks crowed, Kine lowed, Sheep bleated, Sparrows chirped, Dogs barked, so they do still; we keep our madnesse still, play the fools still, *nec dum finitus Orestes,*[2] we are of the same humors and inclinations as our predecessors were, you shall finde us all alike, much at one, we and our sons,

Et nati natorum, & qui nascuntur ab illis,

And so shall our posterity continue to the last. But to speak of times present.

If *Democritus* were alive now, and should but see the superstition of our age, our religious madnesse, as *Meteran* cals it, *Religiosam insaniam,* so many professed Christians, yet so few imitators of *Christ,* so much talk of religion, so much science, so little conscience, so much knowledge, so many preachers, so little practice; such variety of sects, such have and hold of all sides,

——obvia signis Signa, &c.[3]

such absurd and ridiculous traditions and ceremonies: If he should meet a *Capuchin,* a *Franciscan,* a *Pharesaical Jesuite,* a man-serpent, a shave-crowned *Monk* in his robes, a begging Frier, or see their three crown'd Soveraign Lord the Pope, poor *Peters* successor, *servus servorum Dei,*[4] to depose Kings with his foot, to tread on Emperors necks, make them stand bare foot and bare-legg'd at his gates, hold his bridle and stirrup, &c. (O that *Peter* and *Paul* were alive to see this!) If he should observe a Prince creep so devoutly to kiss his toe, and those Red-cap Cardinals, poor parish priests of old, now Princes companions; what would he say? *Cælum ipsum petitur stultitia.*[5] Had he met some of our devout pilgrims going barefoot to *Jerusalem,* our lady of *Lauretto, Rome,* S. *Iago,* S. *Thomas Shrine,* to creep to those counterfeit & Maggot-eaten Reliques. Had he

2 And the play is not yet finished.
3 Banners opposing banners.
4 The servant of the servants of God.
5 Heaven itself is sought by folly.

been present at a Masse, and seen such kissing of Paxes, cruci-
fixes, cringes,§ duckings, their several attires and ceremonies,
pictures of saints, indulgences, pardons, vigils, fasting, feasts,
crossing, knocking, kneeling at *Ave-Maries*, bels, with many
such;

>——*jucunda rudi spectacula plebi,*6

praying in Gibberish, and mumbling of beads. Had he heard
an old woman say her prayers in latine, their sprinkling of
holy water, and going a Procession,

>——*incedunt monachorum agmina mille;*
>*Quid memorem vexilla, cruces, idolaque culta, &c.*7

Their Breviaries, buls, hallowed beans, exorcisms, pictures, curious crosses, fables, and bables. Had he read the *Golden Legend*,
the *Turks Alcoran*, or *Jews Talmud*, the *Rabbins Comments*,
what would he have thought? How doest thou think he might
have been affected? Had he more particularly examined a *Jesuits*
life amongst the rest, he should have seen an hypocrite professe
povertie, and yet possess more goods & lands then many princes,
to have infinite treasures and revenues; teach others to fast, and
play the gluttons themselves; like watermen, that rowe one way,
and look another. Vow virginity, talk of holinesse, and yet indeed a notorious Bawd, and famous fornicator, *lascivum pecus*,8
a very goat. Monks by profession, such as give over the world,
and the vanities of it, and yet a *Machivilian* rout interested in
all maner of state: holy men, peace-makers, and yet composed
of envy, lust, ambition, hatred and malice, fire-brands, *adulta
patriæ pestis*,9 traitors, assasinats, *hâc itur ad astra*,1 and this is
to supererogate, and merit heaven for themselvs and others.
Had he seen on the adverse side, some of our nice & curious
schismaticks in another extream, abhor all ceremonies, and
rather lose their lives and livings, then do or admit any thing
Papists have formerly used, though in things indifferent (they
alone are the true Church, *sal terræ, cum sint omnium insul-*

6 Shows to please the mob.
7 A thousand columns of monks march along, to say nothing of banners,
crosses, images.
8 A lascivious animal.
9 A full-grown plague of their country.
1 In this way do men get to heaven.

sissimi.[2]) Formalists, out of fear and base flattery, like so many weather-cocks turn round, a rout of temporisers, ready to embrace and maintain all that is, or shall be proposed in hope of preferment: Another Epicurean company, lying at lurch as so many vultures, watching for a prey of Church goods, and ready to rise by the down fall of any: as *Lucian* said in like case, what dost thou think *Democritus* would have done, had he been spectator of these things?

Or had he but observed the common people follow like so many sheep one of their fellows drawn by the horns over a gap, some for zeal, some for fear, *quò se cunque rapit tempestas,*[3] to credit all, examine nothing, and yet ready to dye before they will abjure any of those ceremonies, to which they have been accustomed; others out of hypocrisie frequent sermons, knock their brests, turn up their eyes, pretend zeal, desire reformation, and yet professed userers, gripers,[5] monsters of men, harpies, devils, in their lives to expresse nothing lesse.

What would he have said to see, hear, and reade so many bloudy battels, so many thousands slain at once, such streams of blood able to turn Mils: *unius ob noxam furiasque,*[4] or to make sport for princes, without any just cause, *for vain titles* (saith *Austin*) *precedency, some wench, or such like toy, or out of desire of domineering, vain-glory, malice, revenge, folly, madness,* (goodly causes all, *ob quas universus orbis bellis & cædibus misceatur*[5]) whilst Statesmen themselves in the mean time are secure at home, pampered with all delights & pleasures, take their ease, and follow their lusts, not considering what intolerable misery poor soldiers endure, their often wounds, hunger, thirst, &c. the lamentable cares, torments, calamities & oppressions that accompany such proceedings, they feel not, take no notice of it. *So wars are begun, by the perswasion of a few deboshed, hairbrain, poor, dissolute, hungry captains, parasitical fawners, unquiet hotspurs, restless innovators, green heads, to satisfie one mans private spleen, lust, ambition, avarice, &c. tales rapiunt scelerata in prœlia causæ.*[6] *Flos homi-*

2 The salt of the earth, though they are the most insipid of all.
3 Wherever the storm drives them.
4 Because of the violent crime of one person.
5 For which the whole world should be embroiled in war and slaughter.
6 Such causes drive men to the atrocities of war.

num,[7] Proper men, well proportioned, carefully brought up, able
both in body and minde, found, led like so many beasts to the
slaughter in the flower of their years, pride, and full strength,
without all remorse and pity, sacrificed to *Pluto,* killed up as so
many sheep, for devils food, 40000 at once. At once, said I, that
were tollerable, but these wars last alwayes, and for many ages;
nothing so familiar as this hacking and hewing, massacres, murders, desolations.

———*ignoto cælum clangore remugit,*[8]

they care not what mischief they procure, so that they may
enrich themselves for the present; they will so long blow the
coals of contention, till all the world be consumed with fire.
The siege of *Troy* lasted ten years eight months, there died
870000 *Grecians,* 670000 *Trojans,* at the taking of the City,
and after were slain 276000 men, women, and children of all
sorts.[§] *Cæsar* killed a million, *Mahomet* the second *Turk* 300000
persons: *Sicinius Dentatus* fought in an hundred battels, eight
times in single combat he overcame, had forty wounds before,
was rewarded with 140 crowns, triumphed[§] nine times for his
good service. *M. Sergius* had 32 wounds; *Scæva* the Centurion
I know not how many; every nation hath their *Hectors, Scipio's,
Cæsars* and *Alexanders.* Our *Edward* the fourth was in 26 battels
afoot: and as they do all, he glories in it, tis related to his honor.
At the siege of *Hierusalem* 1100000 died with sword and famine. At the battel of *Cannæ,* 70000 men were slain, as *Polibius* records, and as many at Battle[§] *Abbye* with us; and tis
no news to fight from sun to sun, as they did, as *Constantine*
and *Licinius* &c. At the siege of *Ostend* (the devils Academie)
a poor town in respect, a small fort, but a great grave, 120000
men lost their lives, besides whole towns, dorpes,[§] and hospitals,
full of maimed souldiers; there were engines, fire-works, and
whatsoever the devil could invent to do mischief with 2500000
iron bullets shot of 40 pound weight, three or four millions of
gold consumed. *Who* (saith mine Author) *can be sufficiently
amazed at their flinty hearts, obstinacy, fury, blindness, who
without any likelyhood of good successe, hazard poor souldiers,*

[7] The flower of mankind.
[8] The sky re-echoes with a strange noise.

*and lead them without pitty to the slaughter, which may justly
be called the rage of furious beasts, that run without reason upon
their own deaths: quis malus genius, quæ furia, quæ pestis, &c.*
what plague, what fury brought so devillish, so brutish a thing
as war first into mens minds? Who made so soft and peaceable
a creature, born to love, mercy, meeknesse, so to rave, rage like
beasts, & run on to their own destruction? how may nature expostulate with mankinde, *Ego te divinum animal finxi, &c.* I
made thee an harmless, quiet, a divine creature: how may God
expostulate, and all good men? yet, *horum facta* (as one [Richard
Dinoth] condoles) *tantum admirantur, & heroum numero habent:*[9] these are the brave spirits, the gallants of the world, these
admired alone, triumph alone, have statues, crowns, piramids,
obelisks to their eternal fame, that immortall *Genius* attends on
them, *hâc itur ad astra.* When *Rhodes* was besieged, *fossæ urbis
cadaveribus repletæ sunt,* the ditches were full of dead carcases;
and as when the said *Solyman* great *Turk* belegred *Vienna,* they
lay level with the top of the wals. This they make a sport of,
and will do it to their friends and confederates, against oaths,
vows, promises, by trechery or otherwise.

> ———*dolus an virtus? quis in hoste requirat?* [1]

leagues and laws of arms, (*silent leges inter arma*[2]) for their
advantage, *omnia jura, divina, humana, proculcata plerumque
sunt;* Gods and mens laws are trampled under foot, the sword
alone determines all; to satisfie their lust and spleen, they care
not what they attempt, say, or do,

> *Rara fides, probitasque viris qui castra sequuntur,*[3]

Nothing so common as to have *father fight against the son,
brother against brother, kinsman against kinsman, kingdom
against kingdom, province against province, christians against
christians: à quibus nec unquam cogitatione fuerunt læsi,* of
whom they never had offence in thought, word or deed. Infinite
treasures consumed, towns burned, flourishing cities sacked

---

9 The deeds of these men are greatly admired, and they are considered heroes.
1 Guile or valor? Who asks when they are directed against an enemy?
2 Laws are silent amidst the clash of arms.
3 Faith and honor are rare in men who go to war.

and ruinated, *quodque animus meminisse horret,*[4] goodly countries depopulated and left desolate, old inhabitants expelled, trade and traffick decayed, maids defloured, *Virgines nondum thalamis jugatæ, Et comis nondum positis ephæbi,*[5] chast matrons cry out with *Andromache, Concubitum mox cogar pati ejus, qui interemit Hectorem,* they shall be compelled peradventure to ly with them that erst kil'd their husbands: to see rich, poor, sick, sound, Lords, servants, *eodem omnes incommodo macti,* consumed all or maimed, &c. *Et quicquid gaudens scelere animus audet, & perversa mens,*[6] saith *Cyprian,* and whatsoever torment, misery, mischief, hell it self, the devill, fury and rage can invent to their own ruin and destruction; so abominable thing is war, as *Gerbelius* concludes, *adeo fœda & abominanda res est bellum, ex quo hominum cædes, vastationes, &c.*[7] the scourge of God, cause, effect, fruit and punishment of sin, and not *tonsura humani generis,*[8] as *Tertullian* cals it, but *ruina.*[9] Had *Democritus* been present at the late civill wars in *France,* those abominable wars,

————bellaque matribus detestata,[1]

Where in lesse then ten years, ten hundred thousand men were consumed, saith *Collignius,* 20 thousand Churches overthrown; nay, the whole kingdom subverted (as *Richard Dinoth* adds.) So many myriades of the Commons were butchered up, with sword, famine, war, *tanto odio utrinque ut barbari ad abhorrendam lanienam obstupescerent,* with such ferall hatred, the world was amazed at it: or at our late *Pharsalian* fields in the time of *Henry* the sixt, betwixt the houses of *Lancaster* and *York,* an hundred thousand men slain, one writes, another, ten thousand families were rooted out, *that no man can but marvel,* saith *Comineus, at that barbarous immanitie,*[§] *ferall madness, committed betwixt men of the same nation, language and religion. Quis furor O cives? Why do the Gentiles so*

4 And what the mind shudders to remember.
5 Maidens not yet married and youths not yet come to manhood.
6 And whatever a criminal mind and perverted disposition joyfully hear.
7 So loathsome and abominable a thing is war, from which come slaughter and devastation.
8 The trimming of the human race.
9 Destruction.
1 Wars, hated by mothers.

furiously rage, saith the Prophet *David, Psal.* 2.1. But we may ask, why do the Christians so furiously rage?

Arma volunt, quare poscunt, rapiuntque juventus? [2]

Unfit for Gentiles, much lesse for us so to tyranize, as the *Spaniard* in the West *Indies,* that killed up in 42 years (if we may believe *Bartholomæus à Casa* their own bishop) 12 millions of men, with stupend[§] & exquisite[§] torments; neither should I ly (said he) if I said 50 millions. I omit those *French* Massacres, *Sicilian* Evensongs, the Duke of *Alvas* tyrannies, our gunpowder machinations, and that fourth fury, as one [Heinsius] cals it, the *Spanish* inquisition, which quite obscures those ten persecutions,

————*sævit toto Mars impius orbe,*[3]

Is not this *Mundus furiosus,* a mad world, as he [Jansenius Gallobelgicus] terms it, *insanum bellum?* [4] are not these mad men, as *Scaliger* concludes, *qui in prœlio acerbâ morte, insaniæ suæ memoriam pro perpetuo teste relinquunt posteritati;* which leave so frequent battels, as perpetual memorials of their madnesse to all succeeding ages? Would this, think you, have enforced our *Democritus* to laughter, or rather made him turn his tune, alter his tone, and weep with *Heraclitus,* or rather howl, roar, and tear his hair in commiseration, stand amazed; or as the Poets faign, that *Niobe* was for grief quite stupified, and turned to a stone? I have not yet said the worst, that which is more absurd and mad, In their tumults, seditions, civil & unjust wars, *quod stultè suscipitur, impiè geritur, miserè finitur,*[5] such wars I mean, for all are not to be condemned, as those phantastical *Anabaptists* vainly conceive. Our Christian Tacticks are all out as necessary as the *Roman Acies,*[6] or *Grecian* Phalanx; to be a souldier is a most noble and honorable profession (as the world is) not to be spared, they are our best wals and bulwarks, and I do therefore acknowledg that of *Tully* to be most true, *All our civil affairs, all our studies, all our pleading, in-*

2 Why do the young men want arms, demand arms, seize arms?
3 Impious war rages over the whole world.
4 Is not war insane?
5 Begun in folly, carried on in crime, ended in misery.
6 Battle line, column.

dustrie and commendation lies under the protection of warlike
vertues, and whensoever there is any suspition of tumult, all our
arts cease; wars are most behovefull, & *bellatores agricolis
civitati sunt utiliores,*[7] as *Tyrius* defends: and valor is much
to be commended in a wise man, but they mistake most part,
auferre, trucidare, rapere, falsis nominibus virtutem vocant, &c.
(Twas *Galgacus* observation in *Tacitus*) they term theft, murder,
and rapine, vertue, by a wrong name; rapes, slaughters, massacres, &c. *jocus & ludus,* are pretty pastimes, as *Ludovicus Vives*
notes. *They commonly call the most hair-brain blood-suckers,
strongest theeves, the most desperate villains, trecherous rogues,
inhumane murderers, rash, cruel and dissolute caitiffs, couragious and generous spirits, heroical and worthy Captains, brave
men at arms, valiant and renowned souldiers, possessed with
a brute perswasion of false honour,* as *Pontus Huter* in his
Burgundian historie complains. By means of which it comes to
passe that daily so many voluntaries[§] offer themselves, leaving
their sweet wives, children, friends, for six pence (if they can
get it) a day, prostitute their lives and limbs, desire to enter
upon breaches, ly sentinel, perdue,[§] give the first onset, stand in
the fore-front of the battell, marching bravely on, with a cheer-
ful noise of drums and trumpets, such vigor and alacrity, so
many banners streaming in the ayr, glittering armours, motions
of plumes, woods of pikes, and swords, variety of colours, cost
and magnificence, as if they went in triumph, now victors to the
Capitol, and with such pomp, as when *Darius* army marched
to meet *Alexander* at *Issus.* Void of all fear they run into eminent
dangers, *Canons* mouth, &c. *ut vulneribus suis ferrum hostium
hebetent,*[8] saith *Barletius,* to get a name of valour, honour and
applause, which lasts not neither, for it is but a meer flash this
fame, and like a rose, *intra diem unum extinguitur,* tis gone in
an instant. Of 15000 proletaries[§] slain in a battel, scarce fifteen
are recorded in history, or one alone, the General perhaps, and
after a while his and their names are likewise blotted out, the
whole battel it self is forgotten. Those *Græcian* Orators, *summa
vi ingenii & eloquentiæ,*[9] set out the renowned overthrows at

[7] Fighting men are more useful to a state than farmers.
[8] To blunt the sword of the enemy on their own wounded skins.
[9] With the greatest force of genius and of eloquence.

Thermopylæ, Salamina, Marathon, Micale, Mantinea, Cheronæa, Platæa: The *Romans* record their battel at *Cannæ,* and *Pharsalian* fields, but they do but record, and we scarce hear of them. And yet this supposed honor, popular applause, desire of immortality by this means, pride and vain-glory spurs them on many times rashly and unadvisedly, to make away themselves and multitudes of others. *Alexander* was sorry, because there were no more worlds for him to conquer, he is admired by some for it, *animosa vox videtur, & regia,* twas spoken like a Prince, but as wise *Seneca* censures him, twas *vox inquissima & stultissima,* twas spoken like a bedlam§ fool; and that sentence which the same *Seneca* appropriates to his father *Philip* and him, I apply to them all, *Non minores fuêre pestes mortalium quàm inundatio, quàm conflagratio, quibus, &c.* they did as much mischief to mortall men as fire and water, those mercilesse elements when they rage. Which is yet more to be lamented, they perswade them, this hellish course of life is holy, they promise heaven to such as venture their lives *bello sacro,*[1] and that by these bloody wars, as *Persians, Greeks,* and *Romans* of old, as modern *Turks* do now their Commons, to encourage them to fight, *ut cadant infeliciter,*[2] *If they dy in the field, they go directly to heaven, and shall be canonized for saints,* (O diabolical invention) put in the Chronicles, *in perpetuam rei memoriam,* to their eternal memorie: when as in truth, as some hold, it were much better (since wars are the scourge of God for sin, by which he punisheth mortal mens peevishnes§ and folly) such brutish stories were suppressed, because *ad morum institutionem nihil habent,* they conduce not at all to maners, or good life. But they will have it thus neverthelesse, & so they put a note of *divinity upon the most cruel, and pernicious plague of humane kinde,* adore such men with grand titles, degrees, statues, images, honor, applaud and highly reward them for their good service, no greater glory then to die in the field. So *Africanus* is extolled by *Ennius: Mars,* and *Hercules,* & I know not how many besides of old were deified, went this way to heaven, that were indeed bloody butchers, wicked de-

[1] In a sacred war.
[2] Should they unfortunately fall. (*Infeliciter* is probably correct; it points up the duplicity of the Turks.)

stroyers, and troublers of the world, prodigious monsters, hel-hounds, feral plagues, devourers, common executioners of human kinde, as *Lactantius* truely proves, & *Cyprian* to *Donat,* such as were desperate in wars, and precipitately made away themselves (like those *Celtes* in *Damascen,* with ridiculous valour, *ut dedecorosum putarent*[3] *muro ruenti se subducere,* a disgrace to run away for a rotten wall, now ready to fall on their heads) such as will not rush on a swords point, or seek to shun a canons shot, are base cowards, & no valiant men. By which means, *Madet orbis mutuo sanguine,* the earth wallows in her own blood, *Sævit amor ferri & scelerati insania belli,*[4] and for that, which if it be done in private, a man shall be rigorously executed, *and which is no less then murder it self, if the same fact*[5] *be done in publike in wars, it is called manhood, and the party is honored for it.*

———*prosperum & fœlix scelus*
Virtus vocatur[5]———

We measure all as *Turks* do, by the event,[5] and most part, as *Cyprian* notes, in all ages, countreys, places, *sævitiæ magnitudo impunitatem sceleris acquirit,* the foulnesse of the fact vindicates the offender. One is crowned for that which another is tormented:

Ille crucem sceleris precium tulit, hic diadema.

made a Knight, a Lord, an Earl, a great Duke, (as *Agrippa* notes) for which another should have hung in gibbets, as a terror to the rest,

& tamen alter,
Si fecisset idem, caderet sub judice morum.[6]

A poor sheep-stealer is hanged for stealing of victuals, compelled peradventure by necessity of that intollerable cold, hunger, and thirst, to save himself from starving: but a great man in office, may securely rob whole provinces, undo thousands,

---

3 So that they thought it utterly dishonorable.
4 Love of the sword is rampant, and the madness of accursed war.
5 A successful crime is called virtue.
6 And if another had done the same thing, he would have fallen into the hands of the censor.

pill and pole, oppresse *ad libitum,* flea,§ grinde, tyrannize, enrich himself by spoils of the Commons, be uncontroleable in his actions, and after all, be recompensed with turgent§ titles, honored for his good service, and no man dare finde fault, or mutter at it.

How would our *Democritus* have been affected, to see a wicked caitiffe, or *fool, a very idiot, a funge,§ a golden ass, a monster of men, to have many good men, wise men, learned men to attend upon him with all submission, as an appendix to his riches, for that respect alone, because he hath more wealth and money, and to honour him with divine titles, and bumbast§ Epithets,* to smother him with fumes§ and eulogies, whom they know to be a dizard, a fool, a covetous wretch, a beast, &c. *because he is rich?* To see *sub exuviis leonis onagrum,*⁷ a filthy lothsome carcasse, a *Gorgons* head puffed up by parasites, assume this unto himself, glorious titles, in worth an infant, a Cuman asse, a painted sepulchre, an *Egyptian* temple? To see a withered face, a diseased, deformed, canckred complexion, a rotten carcass, a viperous minde, and Epicurean soul set out with orient pearls, jewels, diadems, perfumes, curious elaborate works, as proud of his clothes, as a childe of his new coats; and a goodly person, of an angelike divine countenance, a saint, an humble minde, a meek spirit clothed in rags, beg, and now ready to be starved? To see a silly contemptible sloven in apparel, ragged in his coat, polite in speech, of a divine spirit, wise? another neat in clothes, spruce, full of curtesie, empty of grace, wit, talk non-sense?

To see so many lawyers, advocates, so many tribunals, so little Justice; so many Magistrates, so little care of common good; so many Laws, yet never more disorders; *Tribunal litium segetèm,* the Tribunal a Labyrinth, so many thousand suits in one court sometimes, so violently followed? To see *injustissimum sæpè juri præsidentem, impium religioni, imperitissimum eruditioni, otiosissimum labori, monstrosum humanitati?* ⁸ To see a lamb executed, a woolf pronounce sentence, *latro*⁹ ar-

---

⁷ An ass in a lion's skin.
⁸ To see often the most unjust man preside over justice; the most impious determine matters of religion; the most ignorant, questions of learning; the most idle, questions about work; the most monstrous, questions of humanity.
⁹ A robber.

raigned, and *fur*[1] sit on the bench, the Judge severely punish others, and do worse himself, *eundem furtum facere & punire, rapinam plectere, quum sit ipse raptor?* [2] Laws altered, misconstrued, interpreted *pro* and *con*, as the Judge is made by friends, bribed, or otherwise affected as a nose of wax, good to day, none to morrow; or firm§ in his§ opinion, cast§ in his? Sentence prolonged, changed, *ad arbitrium judicis*,[3] still the same case, *one thrust out of his inheritance, another falsly put in by favor, false forged deeds or wils. Incisæ leges negligantur,* laws are made and not kept; or if put in execution, they be some silly§ ones that are punished. As put case it be fornication, the father will dis-inherit or abdicate his child, quite casheer him, (out villain be gone, come no more in my sight) a poor man is miserably tormented with losse of his estate perhaps, goods, fortunes, good name, for ever disgraced, forsaken, and must do penance to the utmost; a mortal sin, and yet make the worst of it, *nunquid aliud fecit,* saith *Tranio* in the poet [Plautus], *nisi quod faciunt summis nati generibus?* he hath done no more then what Gentlemen usually do.

> *Neque novum, neque mirum, neque secus quam alii solent.*[4]

For in a great person, right worshipful Sir, a right honorable Grandy,§ tis not a venial sin, no not a *peccadillo*, tis no offence at all, a common and ordinary thing, no man takes notice of it; he justifies it in publike, and peradventure brags of it,

> *Nam quod turpe bonis, Titio, Seioque, decebat*
> *Crispinum*[5]———

Many poor men, yonger brothers, &c. by reason of bad policie, and idle education (for they are likely brought up in no calling) are compelled to beg or steal, and then hanged for theft; then which, what can be more ignominious, *non minus enim turpe principi multa supplicia, quàm medico multa funera,*[6] tis the

1 A thief.
2 The same man commit the theft and punish it, punish robbery when he is himself a robber.
3 At the judge's pleasure.
4 It's neither new, nor startling, nor different from what others usually do.
5 For what would be base in good men, in Titius and Seius, was proper for Crispinus.
6 For frequent death sentences are not less disgraceful to a governor than frequent funerals are to a doctor.

governours fault. *Libentiùs verberant quàm docent,* as School-masters do rather correct their pupils, then teach them when they do amisse. *They had more need provide there should be no more theeves and beggers, as they ought with good policy, and take away the occasions, then let them run on, as they do to their own destruction:* root out likewise those causes of wrangling, a multi-tude of lawyers, and compose controversies, *lites lustrales & secu-lares,*[7] by some more compendious means. Whereas now for every toy and trifle they go to law, *Mugit litibus insanum forum, & sævit invicem discordantium rabies,*[8] they are ready to pull out one anothers throats; and for commodity *to squieze blood,* saith *Hierom, out of their brothers heart,* defame, lie, disgrace, back-bite, rail, bear false witnesse, swear, forswear, fight and wrangle, spend their goods, lives, fortunes, friends, undo one another, to enrich an *Harpy* advocate, that preys upon them both, and cryes *Eia*[9] *Socrates, Eia Xantippe;* or some corrupt Judg, that like the Kite in *Æsop,* while the mouse & frog fought, carried both away. Generally they prey one upon another as so many ravenous birds, brute beasts, devouring fishes, no *medium, omnes hic aut captan-tur aut captant; aut cadavera quæ lacerantur, aut corvi qui lace-rant,* either deceive or be deceived; tear others, or be torn in pieces themselves; like so many buckets in a Well, as one riseth another falleth, one's emptie, another's full; his ruine is a ladder to the third; such are our ordinary proceedings. What's the market? A place according to *Anacharsis,* wherein they cozen one another, a trap; nay, what's the world it self? A vast *Chaos,* a confusion of maners, as fickle as the air, *domicilium insano-rum,*[1] a turbulent troop full of impurities, a mart of walking spirits, goblins, the theatre of hypocrisie, a shop of knavery, flattery, a nursery of villanie, the scene of babling, the school of giddinesse, the academie of vice; a warfare, *ubi velis nolis pug-nandum, aut vincas aut succumbas,*[2] in which kill or be killed;

[7] Litigation that has dragged on for years.
[8] Mad voices bellow in the courts, and the frenzy of one litigant exceeds that of another.
[9] Go to it!
[1] A madhouse.
[2] Where you must fight whether you want to or not, and either conquer or go under.

wherein every man is for himself, his private ends, and stands upon his own guard. No charity, love, friendship, fear of God, alliance, affinitie, consanguinitie, Christianitie can contain them, but if they be any ways offended, or that string of commodity be touched, they fall foul. Old friends become bitter enemies on a suddain, for toyes and small offences, and they that erst were willing to do all mutual offices of love and kindness, now revile, & persecute one another to death, with more then *Vatinian*§ hatred, & will not be reconciled. So long as they are behoveful, they love, or may bestead§ each other, but when there is no more good to be expected, as they do by an old dog, hang him up or casheer him: which *Cato* counts a great *indecorum,* to use men like old shoes or broken glasses, which are flung to the dunghil; he could not finde in his heart to fell an old Ox, much lesse to turn away an old servant: but they in stead of recompense, revile him, and when they have made him an instrument of their villany, as *Bajazet* the second Emperor of the *Turks,* did by *Acomethes Bassa,* make him away, or in stead of reward, hate him to death, as *Silius* was served by *Tiberius.* In a word, every man for his own ends. Our *summum bonum* is commodity, and the goddesse we adore *Dea moneta,* Queen money, to whom we daily offer sacrifice, which steers our hearts, hands, affections, all: that most powerful goddess, by whom we are reared, depressed, elevated, esteemed the sole commandresse of our actions, for which we pray, run, ride, go, come, labor, and contend as fishes do for a crum that falleth into the water. Its not worth, vertue, (that's *bonum theatrale*[3]) wisdom, valor, learning, honesty, religion, or any sufficiency for which we are respected, but money, greatnesse, office, honour, authority; honesty is accounted folly; knavery, policie; men admired out of opinion, not as they are, but as they seem to be: such shifting, lying, cogging,§ ploting, counterploting, temporizing, flattering, cozening, dissembling, *that of necessity one must highly offend God if he be conformable to the world,* Cretizare cum Crete,[4] *or else live in contempt, disgrace, and misery.* One takes upon him temperance, holinesse, another austeritie, a third an affected kinde of simplicity, when

---

3 A value in the theater.
4 In Crete, do as the Cretans do.

as indeed he, and he, and he, and the rest are *hypocrites, ambodexters,*§ out sides, so many turning pictures, a lyon on the one side, a lamb on the other. How would *Democritus* have been affected to see these things?

To see a man turn himself into all shapes like a Camelion, or as *Proteus, omnia transformans sese in miracula rerum,*5 to act twenty parts and persons at once, for his advantage, to temporize & vary like *Mercurie* the Planet, good with good, bad with bad; having a several§ face, garb, & character for every one he meets; of all religions, humors, inclinations; to fawn like a Spaniel, *mentitis & mimicis obsequiis,*6 rage like a lion, bark like a Cur, fight like a dragon, sting like a serpent, as meek as a lamb, & yet again grin like a tygre, weep like a crocodile, insult over some, & yet others domineer over him, here command, there crouch, tyrannize in one place, be bafled in another, a wise man at home, a fool abroad to make others merry.

To see so much difference betwixt words and deeds, so many parasanges betwixt tongue and heart, men like stage-players act variety of parts, give good precepts to others, sore aloft, whilest they themselves grovel on the ground.

To see a man protest friendship, kisse his hand, *quem mallet truncatum videre,*7 smile with an intent to do mischief, or cozen him whom he salutes, magnifie his friend unworthy with hyperbolical elogiums; his enemy albeit a good man, to vilifie and disgrace him, yea all his actions, with the utmost livor§ and malice can invent.

To see a servant able to buy out his Master, him that carries the mace more worth then the Magistrate, which *Plato lib.* 11, *de leg.*8 absolutely forbids, *Epictetus* abhors. An horse that tils the land fed with chaff, an idle jade have provender in abundance; him that makes shoes go barefoot himself, him that sels meat almost pined; a toiling drudge starve, a drone flourish.

To see men buy smoke for wares, castles built with fools heads, men like apes follow the fashions in tires,§ gestures, actions: if the King laugh, all laugh;

---

5 Transforming himself into every strange form.
6 With lying and hypocritical compliance.
7 Whom he would like to see dismembered.
8 *Laws*, Book XI.

Rides? majore chachinno
Concutitur, flet si lachrimas conspexit amici.[9]

Alexander stooped, so did his Courtiers; *Alphonsus* turned his head, and so did his parasites. *Sabina Poppea, Nero's* wife, wore amber-colour'd hair, so did all the *Roman* Ladies in an instant, her fashion was theirs.

To see men wholly led by affection, admired and censured out of opinion without judgement: an inconsiderate multitude, like so many dogs in a village, if one bark all bark without a cause: as fortunes fan turns, if a man be in favor, or commended by some great one, all the world applauds him; if in disgrace, in an instant al hate him, & as at the Sun when he is eclipsed, that erst took no notice, now gaze, and stare upon him.

To see a man were[§] his brains in his belly, his guts in his head, an hundred oaks on his back, to devour 100 oxen at a meal, nay more, to devour houses and towns, or as those *Anthropophagi,* to eat one another.

To see a man roll himself up like a snow ball, from base beggery to right worshipfull and right honourable titles, injustly to screw himself into honours and offices; another to starve his *genius,* damn his soul to gather wealth, which he shall not enjoy, which his prodigall son melts and consumes in an instant.

To see the κακοζηλίαν[1] of our times, a man bend all his forces, means, time, fortunes, to be a favorites, favorites, favorite, &c. a parasites, parasites, parasite, that may scorn the servile world as having enough already.

To see an hirsute beggars brat, that lately fed on scraps, crept and whin'd, crying to all, and for an old jerkin ran of errands, now ruffle[§] in silk and satten, bravely mounted, jovial and polite, now scorn his old friends and familiars, neglect his kindred, insult over his betters, domineer over all.

To see a scholar crouch and creep to an illiterate pesant for a meals meat; a scrivener better paid for an obligation; a faulkner[§] receive greater wages then a student: a lawyer get more in a day then a philosopher in a year, better reward for an hour, then a scholar for a twelve moneths studie; him that can paint *Thais,*

[9] Do you laugh? He shakes with louder laughter. He weeps, after he's seen the tears of a friend.
[1] Unhappy rivalry.

play on a fiddle, curl hair, &c. sooner get preferment then a philologer or a poet.

To see a fond mother like *Æsops* ape, hug her child to death, a wittal[§] wink at his wives honesty, and too perspicuous in all other affairs; one stumble at a straw, and leap over a block; rob *Peter,* and pay *Paul;* scrape unjust sums with one hand, purchase great Mannors by corruption, fraud and cozenage, and liberally to distribute to the poor with the other, give a remnant to pious uses, &c. Peny wise, pound foolish; Blind men judge of colours; wise men silent, fools talk; finde fault with others, and do worse themselves; denounce that in publike which he doth in secret; and which *Aurelius Victor* gives out of *Augustus,* severely censure that in a third, of which he is most guilty himself.

To see a poor fellow, or an hired servant venture his life for his new Master that will scarce give him his wages at years end; A country colone[§] toil and moil, till and drudg for a prodigal idle drone, that devours all the gain, or lasciviously consumes with phantastical expences; A noble man in a bravado to encounter death, and for a small flash of honor to cast away himself; A worldling tremble at an Executor, and yet not fear hel-fire; To wish and hope for immortality, desire to be happy, and yet by all means avoyd death, a necessary passage to bring him to it.

To see a fool-hardy fellow like those old *Danes, qui decollari malunt*[2] *quam verberari,* die rather then be punished, in a sottish humor imbrace death with alacrity, yet scorn to lament his own sins and miseries, or his dearest friends departures.

To see wise men degraded, fools preferred, one govern Towns and Cities, and yet a silly woman over-rules him at home; Command a Province, and yet his own servants or children prescribe laws to him, as *Themistocles* son did in *Greece; What I will* (said he) *my mother will, and what my mother will, my father doth.* To see horses ride in a Coach, men draw it; dogs devour their masters; towers build masons; children rule; old men go to school; women wear the breeches; sheep demolish towns, devour men, &c. And in a word, the world turned upside downward. *O viveret Democritus.*[3]

---

[2] Who prefer to. . . .
[3] O that Democritus were alive again.

To insist in every particular were one of *Hercules labors,* there's so many ridiculous instances, as motes in the Sun. *Quantum est in rebus inane?* [4] And who can speak of all? *Crimine ab uno disce omnes,*[5] take this for a taste.

But these are obvious to sense, trivial and well known, easie to be discerned. How would *Democritus* have been moved, had he seen the secrets of their hearts? If every man had a window in his brest, which *Momus* would have had in *Vulcans* man, or that which *Tully* so much wisht it were written in every mans forehead, *Quid quisque de republicâ sentiret,* what he thought; or that it could be effected in an instant, which *Mercurie* did by *Charon* in *Lucian,* by touching of his eyes, to make him discern *semel & simul rumores & susurros.*[6]

> *Spes hominum cæcas, morbos, votumque labores,*
> *Et passim toto volitantes æthere curas.*
> Blinde hopes and wishes, their thoughts and affairs,
> Whispers and rumors, and those flying cares.

That he could *cubiculorum obductas foras recludere, & secreta cordium penetrare,*[7] which *Cyprian* desired, open doors and locks, shoot bolts, as *Lucians Gallus* did with a feather of his tail: or *Gyges* invisible ring, or some rare perspective glasse, or *Otacousticon,* which would so multiply *species,*[8] that a man might hear and see all at once (as *Martianus Capella's Jupiter* did in a spear, which he held in his hand, which did present unto him all that was daily done upon the face of the earth), observe cuckolds horns, forgeries of alcumists, the philosophers stone, new projectors, &c. and all those works of darknesse, foolish vows, hopes, fears and wishes, what a deal of laughter would it have afforded? He should have seen Wind-mils in one mans head, an Hornets nest in another. Or had he bin present with *Icaromenippus* in *Lucian* at *Jupiters* whispering place, and heard one pray for rain, another for fair weather; one for his wives, another for his fathers death, &c. *to ask that at Gods hand which they are*

4 How much vanity there is in human affairs!
5 From one offense, learn all.
6 At once rumors and whispers.
7 Throw open the doors of bedrooms and discover inmost secrets.
8 Appearances.

abashed any man should hear: How would he have been confounded? Would he, think you, or any man else, say that these
men were well in their wits?

> *Hæc sani esse hominis quis sanus juret Orestes?* [9]

Can all the *Hellebor* in the *Anticyræ* cure these men? No, sure,
an acre of Hellebor will not do it.

That which is more to be lamented, they are mad like *Seneca's*
blind woman, and will not acknowledge, or seek for any cure of
it, for *pauci vident morbum suum, omnes amant,*[1] If our leg or
arm offend§ us, we covet by all means possible to redresse§ it; and
if we labor of a bodily disease, we send for a physician; but for
the diseases of the minde we take no notice of them: Lust har-
rows us on the one side, envy, anger, ambition on the other. We
are torn in pieces by our passions, as so many wilde horses, one
in disposition, another in habit; one is melancholy, another mad;
and which of us all seeks for help, doth acknowledge his error, or
knows he is sick? As that stupid fellow put out the Candle, because the biting fleas should not finde him; he shrouds himself
in an unknown habit, borrowed titles, because no body should discern him. Every man thinks with himself *Egomet videor mihi
sanus,*[2] I am well, I am wise, and laughs at others. And tis a
generall fault amongst them all, that which our forefathers have
approved, diet, apparel, opinions, humors, customs, manners, we
deride and reject in our time as absurd. Old men account Juniors
all fools, when they are meer dizards; and as to sailers

> ———*terræque urbesque recedunt*[3]

they move, the land stands still, the world hath much more wit,
they dote themselves. *Turks* deride us, we them; *Italians Frenchmen,* accounting them light headed fellows; the *French* scoffe
again at *Italians,* and at their several customs; *Greeks* have condemned all the world but themselves of *barbarism,* the world as
much vilifies them now; we account *Germans* heavy, dull fellows,
explode many of their fashions; they as contemptibly think of us;

---

[9] You say and do such things as mad Orestes himself would attribute to a mad-
man.
[1] Few see their own disease; all love it.
[2] I regard myself as sane.
[3] The lands and cities move back.

Spaniards laugh at all, and all again at them. So are we fools and ridiculous, absurd in our actions, carriages, dyet, apparel, customs and consultations; we scoffe and point one at another, when as in conclusion all are fools, *and they the veriest asses that hide their ears most.* A private man if he be resolved with himself, or set on an opinion, accounts all idiots and asses that are not affected as he is,

------*nil rectum, nisi quod placuit sibi, ducit,*[4]

that are not so minded, (*quodque volunt homines se bene velle putant*[5]) all fools that think not as he doth: he will not say with *Atticus, Suam quisque sponsam, mihi meam,* let every man enjoy his own spouse; but his alone is fair, *suus amor, &c.* and scorns all in respect of himself, wil imitate none, hear none but himself, as *Pliny* said, a law and example to himself. And that which *Hippocrates* in his epistle to *Dyonysius,* reprehended of old, is verified in our times, *Quisque in alio superfluum esse censet, ipse quod non habet nec curat,* that which he hath not himself or doth not esteem, he accounts superfluity, an idle quality, a meer foppery in another: like *Æsops* fox, when he had lost his tail, would have all his fellow foxes cut off theirs. The *Chinezes* say, that we *Europeans* have one eye, they themselves two, all the world else is blinde: (though *Scaliger* accounts them Brutes too, *merum pecus*[6]) so thou and thy sectaries are only wise, others indifferent, the rest beside themselves, meer idiots and asses. Thus not acknowledging our own errors, and imperfections, we securely deride others, as if we alone were free, and spectators of the rest, accounting it an excellent thing, as indeed it is, *Alienâ optimum frui insaniâ,* to make our selvs merry with other mens obliquities, whenas he himself is more faulty then the rest: *mutato nomine, de te fabula narratur.*[7] . . .

Kingdoms, Provinces, and politick bodies are likewise sensible and subject to this disease, as *Boterus* in his politicks hath proved at large. *As in humane bodies* (saith he) *there be divers*

[4] Nothing is right except what pleases him.
[5] What men wish, they think they wish wisely.
[6] Mere cattle.
[7] Change the name, and the tale is about you.

alterations proceeding from humors, so there be many diseases
in a common-wealth, which do as diversly happen from severall
distempers, as you may easily perceive by their particular symptomes. For where you shall see the people civil, obedient to God
and Princes, judicious, peaceable and quiet, rich, fortunate, and
flourish, to live in peace, in unity and concord, a Country well
tilled, many fair built and populous Cities, *ubi*[8] *incolæ nitent,* as
old *Cato* said, the people are neat, polite and terse,[§] *ubi bene,*
beateque vivunt,[9] which our Politicians make the chief end of a
Common-wealth; and which *Aristotle Polit. lib. 3. cap. 4.* cals
Commune bonum,[1] *Polibius lib. 6. optabilem & selectum statum,*[2]
That countrey is free from melancholy; As it was in *Italy* in the
time of *Augustus,* now in *China,* now in many other flourishing
kingdoms of *Europe.* But whereas you shall see many discontents, common grievances, complaints, poverty, barbarism, beggery, plagues, wars, rebellions, seditions, mutinies, contentions,
idlenesse, riot, epicurism, the land ly untilled, waste, full of bogs,
fens, desarts, &c. cities decayed, base and poor towns, villages
depopulated, the people squalid, ougly, uncivil; that kingdom,
that country, must needs be discontent, melancholy, hath a sick
body, and had need to be reformed.

. . . We had need of some general visitor in our age, that should
reform what is amiss; a just army of *Rosie*[§] crosse men, for they
wil amend all matters, (they say) religion, policy, maners, with
arts, sciences, &c. Another *Attila, Tamberlane, Hercules,* to strive
with *Achelous, Augeæ stabulum purgare,*[3] to subdue tyrants, as
he did *Diomedes* and *Busiris:* to expel theeves, as he did *Cacus*
and *Lacinius:* to vindicate poor captives, as he did *Hesione:* to
passe the Torrid Zone, the deserts of *Lybia,* and purge the world
of monsters and *Centaures:* Or another *Theban Crates* to reform
our maners, to compose quarrels and controversies, as in his time
he did, and was therefore adored for a god in *Athens. As Hercu-*
les purged the world of Monsters, & subdued them, so did he fight

8 Where.
9 Where they live well and happily.
1 The common weal.
2 An enviable and ideal condition.
3 To clean the Augean stables.

*against envy, lust, anger, avarice, &c. and al those feral vices and
monsters of the minde.* It were to be wished we had some such
visitor, or if wishing would serve, one had such a ring or rings,
as *Timolaus* desired in *Lucian,* by vertue of which he should be
as strong as 10000 men, or an army of gyants, go invisible, open
gates & castle doors, have what treasure he would, transport himself in an instant, to what place he desired, alter affections, cure
all maner of diseases, that he might range over the world, and reform all distressed states and persons, as he would himself. He
might reduce those wandring *Tartars* in order, that infest *China*
on the one side, *Muscovy, Poland* on the other; and tame the vag-
abond *Arabians* that rob and spoil those *Eastern* countries, that
they should never use more *Caravans,* or *Janisaries* to conduct
them. He might root out Barbarism out of *America,* and fully discover *Terra Australis Incognita,* find out the North-east, and
North-west passages, drean§ those mighty *Mæotian* fens, cut
down those vast *Hircinian* woods, irrigate those barren *Arabian*
deserts, &c. cure us of our Epidemical diseases, *Scorbutum, Plica,
morbus Neapolitanus,*[4] &c. end all our idle controversies, cut off
our tumultuous desires, inordinate lusts, root out athiesm, impiety, heresie, schism and superstition, which now so crucifie the
world, catechise grosse ignorance, purge *Italy* of luxury and riot;
Spain of superstition and jealousie, *Germany* of drunkennesse,
all our Northern country of gluttony and intemperance, castigate
our hard-hearted parents, masters, tutors; lash disobedient children, negligent servants, correct these spendthrifts and prodigall
sons, enforce idle persons to work, drive drunkards off the ale-
house, represse theeves, visit corrupt and tyrannizing magistrates, &c. But as *L. Licinius* taxed *Timolaus,* you may us. These
are vain, absurd and ridiculous wishes not to be hoped: all must
be as it is, *Bocchalinus* may cite Common-wealths to come before
Apollo, and seek to reform the world it self by Commissioners,
but there is no remedy, it may not be redressed, *desinent homines
tum demum stultescere quando esse desinent,*[5] so long as they
can wag their beards, they will play the knaves and fools.

Because therefore it is a thing so difficult, impossible, and far
beyond *Hercules* labours to be performed; let them be rude,

4 Scurvy, plica, syphilis.
5 Men will cease to be fools only when they cease to be men.

stupid, ignorant, incult,[§] *lapis super lapidem sedeat*,[6] and as the Apologist [Johann Valentin Andrea] will, *Resp. tussi, & graveolentia laboret, mundus vitio*,[7] let them be barbarous as they are, let them tyrannize, epicurize, oppresse, luxuriate,[§] consume themselves with factions, superstitions, law-suits, wars and contentions, live in riot, poverty, want, misery; rebel, wallow as so many swine in their own dung, with *Ulysses* companions, *stultos jubeo esse libentèr*.[8] I wil yet to satisfie and please my self, make an *Utopia* of mine own, a new *Atlantis*, a poetical Commonwealth of mine own, in which I will freely domineer, build cities, make laws, statutes, as I list my self. And why may I not?

—————*Pictoribus atque Poetis, &c.*[9]

You know what liberty Poets ever had, and besides, my predecessor *Democritus* was a Politician, a Recorder of *Abdera*, a lawmaker as some say; and why may not I presume so much as he did? Howsoever I will adventure. For the site, if you will needs urge me to it, I am not fully resolved, it may be in *Terra Australis Incognita*, there is room enough (for of my knowledge neither that hungry *Spaniard* [Pedro Fernandez Queiros], nor *Mercurius Britannicus* [Joseph Hall], have yet discovered half of it) or else one of those floting Islands in *Mare del Zur*,[§] which like the *Cyanian* Isles in the *Euxine* sea, alter their place, and are accessible only at set times, and to some few persons; or one of the Fortunate Isles, for who knows yet where, or which they are? there is room enough in the inner parts of *America*, and northern coasts of *Asia*. But I will chuse a site, whose latitude shall be 45 degrees (I respect not minutes) in the midst of the temperate Zone, or perhaps under the *Æquator*, that Paradise of the world, *ubi semper virens laurus, &c.*[1] where is a perpetual Spring: the longitude for some reasons I will conceal. Yet *be it known to all men by these presents*, that if any honest gentlemen will send in so much money, as *Cardan* allows an Astrologer for casting a Nativity, he shall be a sharer,[§] I will acquaint him with my project,

---

6 Let stone sit on stone.
7 Let the State suffer from coughing and shortness of breath, the world from vice.
8 I give them full permission to be fools.
9 Painters and poets (have always been allowed to do as they like).
1 Where the laurel is always green.

or if any worthy man will stand for any temporal or spiritual office or dignity, (for as he said of his Archbishoprick of *Utopia*, tis *sanctus ambitus*,[2] and not amisse to be sought after) it shall be freely given without all intercessions, bribes, letters, &c., his own worth shal be the best spokesman; & because we shal admit of no deputies or advousons, if he be sufficiently qualified, and as able as willing to execute the place himself, he shall have present possession. It shall be divided into 12 or 13 Provinces, and those by hils, rivers, rode-wayes, or some more eminent[§] limits exactly bounded. Each province shall have a *Metropolis*, which shall be so placed as a center almost in a circumference, and the rest at equal distances, some 12 *Italian* miles asunder, or thereabout, and in them shall be sold all things necessary for the use of man; *statis horis & diebus*,[3] no market towns, markets or fairs, for they do but beggar cities (no village shall stand above 6, 7, or 8 miles from a city) except those Emporiums which are by the sea side, generall Staples,[§] Marts, as *Antwerp, Venice, Bergen* of old, *London, &c.* Cities most part shal be situat upon navigable rivers or lakes, creeks, havens, and for their form, regular, round, square, or long square, with fair, broad, and strait streets, houses uniform, built of brick and stone, like *Bruges, Bruxels, Rhegium Lepidi, Berna* in *Switzerland, Millan, Mantua, Crema, Cambalu* in *Tartary* described by *M. Polus*, or that *Venetian Palma*. I wil admit very few or no suburbs, & those of baser building, wals only to keep out man & horse, except it be in some frontier towns, or by the sea side, and those to be fortified after the latest maner of fortification, and sited upon convenient havens, or opportune places. In every so built city, I will have convenient churches, and separate places to bury the dead in, not in churchyards; a *citadella* (in some, not all) to command it, prisons for offenders, opportune market places of all sorts, for corn, meat, cattel, fuel, fish, &c., commodious courts of Justice, publike hals for all societies, burses,[§] meeting places, armories, in which shall be kept engines for quenching of fire, artillery[§] gardens, publike walks, theaters, and spacious fields allotted for all gymnicks,[§] sports, and honest recreations, hospitals of all kindes, for children, orphans, old folks, sick men, mad men,

---

2 A holy ambition.
3 At stated hours and on stated days.

souldiers, pest-houses, &c., not built *precariò*,[4] or by gowty benefactors, who, when by fraud and rapin they have extorted all
their lives, oppressed whole provinces, societies, &c. give something to pious uses, build a satisfactory alms-house, school, or
bridge, &c. at their last end, or before perhaps, which is no otherwise then to steal a goose, and stick down a feather, rob a thousand to relieve ten: And those hospitals so built and maintained,
not by collections, benevolences, donaries,[§] for a set number, (as
in ours) just so many and no more at such a rate, but for all those
who stand in need, be they more or lesse, and that *ex publico æra-
rio*,[5] and so still maintained, *non nobis solùm nati sumus, &c.*[6] I
will have conduits of sweet and good water, aptly disposed in
each town, common granaries, as at *Dresden* in *Misnia*, *Stetein*
in *Pomerland*, *Noremberg*, *&c.* Colledges of mathematicians,
musicians, and actors, as of old at *Labedum* in *Ionia*, alcumists,
physicians, artists and philosophers; that all arts and sciences
may sooner be perfected & better learned; and publick historiographers, as amongst those ancient *Persians, qui in commen-
tarios referebant quæ memoratu digna gerebantur,* informed and
appointed by the state to register all famous acts, & not by each
insufficient scribler, partial or parasitical pedant, as in our times.
I will provide publike schools of all kinds, singing, dancing, fencing, &c. especially of Grammar & languages, not to be taught by
those tedious precepts ordinarily used, but by use, example, conversation, as travelers learn abroad, & nurses teach their children: as I wil have all such places, so will I ordain publike governors, fit officers to each place, Treasurers, Ædiles, Questors,
Overseers of pupils, widows goods, and all publike houses, &c.
and those once a year to make strict accounts of all receipts, expences, to avoid confusion, *& sic fiet ut non absumant* (as *Pliny*
to *Trajan*,) *quod pudeat dicere*.[7] They shall be subordinate to
those higher officers, and governors of each City, which shall not
be poor Tradesmen, and mean Artificers, but Noblemen and
Gentlemen, which shal be tied to residence in those towns they
dwel next, at such set times and seasons: for I see no reason
(which *Hippolitus* complains of) *that it should be more dis-*

---

4 In response to a plea for charity.
5 Out of the public treasury.
6 We are not born for ourselves alone.
7 And in this way, they will not waste money—which it's a shame to talk about.

honourable for Noblemen to govern the City, then the Country, *or*
unseemly to dwell there now, then of old. I will have no bogs,
fens, marishes,§ vast woods, desarts, heaths, commons, but all inclosed; (yet not depopulated, and therefore take heed you mistake me not) for that which is common, and every mans, is no
mans; the richest countries are still inclosed, as *Essex, Kent,*
with us, &c., *Spain, Italy;* and where inclosures are least in
quantity, they are best husbanded, as about *Florence* in *Italy,*
Demascus in *Syria,* &c. which are liker gardens then fields. I will
not have a barren acre in all my Territories, not so much as the
tops of mountains: where nature fails, it shall be supplied by art:
lakes and rivers shall not be left desolate. All common high-ways,
bridges, banks, corrivations§ of waters, aqueducts, chanels, publike works, building, &c. out of a common stock, curiously maintained and kept in repair; no depopulations, ingrossings,§ alterations of wood, arable,§ but by the consent of some supervisors
that shall be appointed for that purpose, to see what reformation
ought to be had in all places, what is amisse, how to help it.

Et quid quæque ferat regio, & quid quæque recuset,[8]

what ground is aptest for wood, what for corn, what for cattle,
gardens, orchards, fishponds, &c. with a charitable division in
every Village, (not one dominering house greedily to swallow up
all, which is too common with us) what for Lords, what for tenants: and because they shall be better incouraged to improve
such lands they hold, manure, plant trees, drean, fence, &c. they
shall have long leases, a known rent, and known fine§ to free
them from those intollerable exactions of tyranizing Landlords.
These supervisors shall likewise appoint what quantity of land in
each mannor is fit for the Lords Demesns, what for holding of
Tenants, how it ought to be husbanded,

Ut Magnetis equis, Minyæ gens cognita remis,[9]

how to be manured, tilled, rectified, *hic segetes veniunt, illic*
fœliciùs uvæ, Arborei fœtus alibi, atque injussa virescunt Gram-
ina,[1] and what proportion is fit for all callings, because private

8 And what each region will produce, and what it refuses to bear.
9 As the Magnesians are famous for their horses, the Argonauts for their ships.
1 Here corn, there grapes grow more profusely; elsewhere young trees shoot up,
and unexpected grass.

possessors are many times idiots, ill husbands, oppressors, covetous, and know not how to improve their own, or else wholly respect their own, and not publike good.

Utopian parity is a kinde of government, to be wished for,
rather then effected, *Respub. Christianopolitana, Campanella's*
city of the Sun, and that new *Atlantis,* witty fictions, but meer
Chimera's and *Platoes* community in many things is impious,
absurd and ridiculous, it takes away all splendor and magnificence. I will have several orders, degrees of nobility, and those
hereditary, not rejecting yonger brothers in the mean time, for
they shall be sufficiently provided for by pensions, or so qualified,§ brought up in some honest calling, they shal be able to live
of themselves. I wil have such a proportion of ground belonging
to every *Barony,* he that buyes the land, shall buy the *Barony,* he
that by riot consumes his patrimony, & ancient demeans,§
shall forfeit his honours. As some dignities shall be hereditary,
so some again by election, or by gift (besides free offices, pensions, annuities) like our *Bishopricks, Prebends,* the *Bassa's*§
palaces in *Turky,* the *Procurators* houses, & offices in *Venice,*
which like the golden Apple, shall be given to the worthiest, &
best deserving both in war and peace, as a reward of their worth
and good service, as so many goals for all to aim at, (*honos alit
artes*[2]) and encouragements to others. For I hate these severe,
unnatural, harsh, *German, French,* and *Venetian* Decrees, which
exclude Plebeians from honors, be they never so wise, rich, vertuous, valiant, and well qualified, they must not be *Patritians,* but
keep their own rank, this is *naturæ bellum inferre,*[3] odious to
God and men, I abhor it. My form of government shall be Mon-
archical.

> ——*nunquam libertas gratior extat,*
> *Quam sub Rege pio, &c.*[4]

few lawes, but those severely kept, plainly put down, and in the
mother tongue, that every man may understand. Every city shall
have a peculiar trade or priviledge, by which it shall be chiefly
maintained: and Parents shal teach their children, one of three

---

2 Honor nourishes the arts.
3 To make war on nature.
4 Liberty is never more pleasing than under a good king.

at least, bring up and instruct them in the mysteries of their own trade. In each town these several tradesmen shall be so aptly disposed, as they shall free the rest from danger or offence: Firetrades, as Smiths, Forge-men, Brewers, Bakers, Metal-men, &c. shall dwell apart by themselves: Dyars, Tanners, Fel-mongers,§ and such as use water in convenient places by themselves: noysom or fulsome for bad smels, as Butchers slaughter-houses, Chandlers, curriers, in remote places, & some back lanes. Fraternities and companies, I approve of, as Merchants Burses, Colledges of Druggers,§ Physicians, Musicians, &c. but all trades to be rated§ in the sale of wares, as our Clerks of the market do Bakers and Brewers; Corn it self, what scarcity soever shall come, not to exceed such a price. Of such wares as are transported or brought in, if they be necessary, commodious, and such as neerly concern mans life, as corn, wood, cole, &c. & such provision we cannot want, I will have little or no custom paid, no taxes; but for such things as are for pleasure, delight, or ornament, as wine, spice, tobacco, silk, velvet, cloth of gold, lace, jewels, &c. a greater impost. I will have certain ships sent out for new discoveries every year, & some discreet men appointed to travel into all neighbor kingdoms by land, which shall observe what artificial inventions, and good laws are in other Countries, customes, alterations, or ought else, concerning war or peace, which may tend to the common good. Ecclesiastical discipline, *penes Episcopos*,[5] subordinate as the other. No impropriations, no lay patrons of church livings, or one private man, but common societies, corporations, &c. and those Rectors of benefices to be chosen out of the Universities, examined and approved as the *literati* in *China*. No Parish to contain above a thousand Auditors. If it were possible, I would have such priests as should imitate *Christ*, charitable lawyers should love their neighbors as themselves, temperate and modest Physicians, Politicians contemn the world, Philosophers should know themselves, Noblemen live honestly, Tradesmen leave lying and cosening,§ Magistrates corruption, &c. but this is unpossible, I must get such as I may. I will therefore have of lawyers, judges, advocates, physicians, chirurgions, &c. a set number, and every man, if it be possible, to plead his own cause, to tell that tale to the judge, which

[5] In the hands of the bishops.

he doth to his advocate, as at *Fez* in *Africk, Bantam, Aleppo, Raguse, suam quisque causam dicere tenetur.*[6] Those Advocates, Chirurgions and Physicians, which are allowed, to be maintained out of the common treasure, no fees to be given or taken upon pain of losing their places; or if they do, very small fees, and when the cause is fully ended. He that sues any man shall put in a pledge, which if it be proved he hath wrongfully sued his adversary, rashly or maliciously, he shall forfeit, and lose. Or else before any suit begin, the plantiff shall have his complaint approved by a set delegacy to that purpose; if it be of moment he shall be suffered as before, to proceed, if otherwise they shall determine it. All causes shall be pleaded *suppresso nomine,* the parties names concealed, if some circumstances do not otherwise require. Judges and other officers shall be aptly disposed in each Province, Villages, Cities, as common arbitrators to hear causes, and end all controversies, and those not single, but three at least on the bench at once, to determine[§] or give sentence and those again to sit by turns or lots, and not to continue stil in the same office. No controversie to depend[§] above a year, but without all delays and further appeals to be speedily dispatched, and finally concluded in that time allotted. These and all other inferior Magistrates, to be chosen as the *Literati* in *China,* or by those exact suffrages of the *Venetians,* and such again not be eligible, or capable of magistracies, honours, offices, except they be sufficiently qualified for learning, maners, and that by the strict approbation of deputed examinators: first Scholars to take place, then Souldiers; for I am of *Vigetius* his opinion, a Scholar deserves better then a Souldier, because *Unius ætatis sunt quæ fortiter fiunt, quæ vero pro utilitate Reipub. scribuntur, æterna:* a Souldiers work lasts for an age, a Scholars for ever. If they misbehave themselves, they shal be deposed, and accordingly punished, & whether their offices be annual or otherwise, once a year they shall be called in question, and give an account; for men are partial and passionate, mercilesse, covetous, corrupt, subject to love, hate, fear, favor, &c. *omne sub regno graviore regnum:*[7] like *Solons Areopagites,* or those *Roman* Censors, some

6 Everyone is expected to plead his own cause.
7 All power is subject to a greater power.

shall visit others, and be visited *invicem*[8] themselves, they shall oversee that no proling[§] officer, under colour of authority shal insult over his inferiors, as so many wild beasts, oppresse, domineer, flea,[§] grinde, or trample on, be partial or corrupt, but that there be *æquabile jus,* justice equally done, live as friends & brethren together; and which *Sesellius* would have and so much desires in his kingdom of *France, a diapason and sweet harmony of Kings, Princes, Nobles, and Plebeians so mutualy tied and involved in love, as well as laws and authority, as that they never disagree, insult or incroach one upon another.* If any man deserve well in his office he shall be rewarded.

> ——*quis enim virtutem amplectitur ipsam,*
> *præmia si tollas?* [9]——

He that invents any thing for publike good in any Art or Science, writes a Treatise, or performs any noble exploit, at home or abroad, shall be accordingly enriched, honored, and preferred. I say with *Hannibal* in *Ennius, Hostem qui feriet erit mihi Carthaginensis,*[1] let him be of what condition he will, in all offices, actions, he that deserves best shall have best.

Tilianus in *Philonius* out of a charitable minde no doubt, wisht all his books were gold and silver, jewels and precious stones, to redeem captives, set free prisoners, and relieve all poor distressed souls that wanted means; religiously done, I deny not, but to what purpose? Suppose this were so well done, within a little after, though a man had *Crœsus* wealth to bestow, there would be as many more. Wherefore I will suffer no Beggers, Rogues, Vagabonds, or idle persons at all, that cannot give an account of their lives how they maintain themselves: If they be impotent, lame, blinde, and single, they shall be sufficiently maintained in several hospitals, built for that purpose; if married and infirm, past work, or by inevitable losse, or some such like misfortune cast behind, by distribution of corn, house-rent free, annual pensions or money, they shall be relieved, and highly rewarded for their good service they have formerly done; if able, they shall be

---

[8] In turn.
[9] For who will choose virtue for its own sake, if you take away the rewards?
[1] Whoever shall slay an enemy shall be a Carthaginian in my eyes.

enforced to work. *For I see no reason* (as he [Sir Thomas More] said) *why an Epicure or idle drone, a rich glutton, a usurer should live at ease, and do nothing, live in honor, in all manner of pleasures, and oppresse others, when as in the mean time a poor laborer, a smith, a carpenter, an husbandman that hath spent his time in continual labour, as an Asse to carry burdens, to do the Commonwealth good, and without whom we cannot live, shall be left in his old age to begge or starve, and lead a miserable life worse then a jument.*§ As all conditions§ shall be tied to their task, so none shall be overtired, but have their set times of recreations and holidaies, *indulgere genio,*[2] feasts & merry meetings, even to the meanest artificer, or basest servant, once a week to sing or dance, (though not al at once) or do whatsoever he shall please; like that *Saccarum festum,*[3] amongst the Persians, those *Saturnals* in *Rome,* as well as his master. If any be drunk, he shall drink no more wine or strong drink in a twelve moneth after. A bankrupt shall be *Catomidiatus in Ampitheatro,*[4] publikely shamed, and he that cannot pay his debts, if by riot or negligence he have been impoverished, shal be for a twelve-month imprisoned, if in that space his creditors be not satisfied, he shall be hanged. He that commits sacriledge shall lose his hands; he that bears false-witnesse, or is of perjury convict, shall have his tongue cut out, except he redeem it with his head. Murder, adultery shall be punished by death, but not theft, except it be some more grievous offence, or notorious offenders: otherwise they shal be condemned to the gallies, mines, be his slaves whom they offended, during their lives. I hate all hereditary slaves, and that *duram Persarum legem,*[5] as *Brisonius* cals it; or as *Ammianus, impendio formidatas & abominandas leges, per quas ob noxam unius, omnis propinquitas perit,* hard law that wife and children, friends and allies should suffer for the fathers offence.

No man shall marry until he be 25., no woman till she be 20. *nisi aliter dispensatum fuerit.*[6] If one die, the other party

2 To follow their own bent.
3 Festival of Sacaea; a Babylonian holiday, perhaps in celebration of the new year.
4 Flogged in the amphitheater.
5 Hard law of the Persians.
6 Without special dispensation.

shall not marry till six months after; and because many families
are compelled to live niggardly, exhaust and undone by great
dowers, none shal be given at all, or very little, and that by
supervisors rated, they that are foul[§] shal have a greater portion;
if fair, none at all, or very little: howsoever not to exceed such
a rate as those supervisors shal think fit. And when once they
come to those years, poverty shall hinder no man from marriage, or any other respect,[§] but all shall be rather inforced then
hindered, except they be dismembred, or grievously deformed,
infirm, or visited with some enormous hereditary disease, in
body or mind; in such cases upon a great pain, or mulct, man
or woman shall not marry, other order shall be taken for them
to their content. If people overabound, they shall be eased by
Colonies.

No man shall wear weapons in any City. The same attire
shall be kept, and that proper to several callings, by which they
shall be distinguished. *Luxus funerum*[7] shall be taken away,
that intempestive[§] expense moderated, and many others. Brok-
ers, takers of pawns, biting usurers, I will not admit; yet because *hic cum hominibus non cum diis agitur,* we converse here
with men, not with gods, and for the hardnesse of mens hearts
I will tollerate some kinde of usury. If we were honest, I confesse, *si probi essemus,* we should have no use of it, but being
as it is, we must necessarily admit it. Howsoever most Divines
contradict[§] it,

Dicimus inficias, sed vox ea sola reperta est.[8]

it must be winked at by Politicians. And yet some great Doctors
approve of it, *Calvin, Bucer, Zanchius, P. Martyr,* because by
so many grand lawyers, decrees of Emperors, Princes Statutes,
customs of Commonwealths, churches approbations it is permitted, &c. I wil therefore allow it. But to no private persons,
not to every man that wil, to orphans only, maids, widows, or
such as by reason of their age, sex, education, ignorance of
trading, know not otherwise how to employ it, and those so
approved, not to let it out apart, but to bring their money to a
common bank which shall be allowed in every city, as in *Genua,*

7 Display at funerals.
8 We say no, but it's just so much talk.

Geneva, Noremberg, Venice, at 5, 6, 7. not above 8 *per centum,* as the supervisors, or *ærarii præfecti*[9] shall think fit. And as it shall not be lawful for each man to be an Usurer that will, so shall it not be lawful for all to take[§] up money at use,[§] not to prodigals and spendthrifts, but to merchants, yong tradesmen, such as stand in need, or know honestly how to imploy it, whose necessity, cause and condition the said supervisors shall approve of.

I wil have no private monopolies, to enrich one man, and begger a multitude, multiplicity of offices, of supplying by deputies, weights and measures the same throughout, and those rectified by the *Primum mobile,* and Suns motion, threescore miles to a degree according to observation, 1000. Geometrical paces to a mile, five foot to a pace, twelve inches to a foot, &c. & from measures known it is an easie matter to rectifie weights &c. to cast up all, and resolve[§] bodies by Algebra, Stereometry.[§] I hate wars if they be not *ad populi salutem,*[1] upon urgent occasion,

> *Odimus accipitrem, quia semper vivit in armis.*[2]

offensive wars, except the cause be very just, I will not allow of. For I do highly magnifie that saying of *Hannibal* to *Scipio,* in *Livy, It had been a blessed thing for you and us, if God had given that minde to our predecessors, that you had been content with Italy, we with Africk. For neither Sicily, nor Sardinia are worth such cost and pains, so many fleets and armies, or so many famous Captains lives. Omnia prius tentanda,* fair means shall first be tried. *Peragit tranquilla potestas, Quod violenta nequit.*[3] I will have them proceed with all moderation: but hear you, *Fabius* my General, not *Minutius, nam qui Consilio nititur plus hostibus nocet, quam qui sine animi ratione, viribus:*[4] And in such wars to abstain as much as is possible from depopulations, burning of towns, massacring of infants, &c. For defensive wars, I will have forces still ready at a small warning, by

---

9 Managers of the treasury.
1 For the welfare of the people.
2 We hate the hawk because it is always in battle dress.
3 Quiet power accomplishes what violence cannot.
4 For he who relies on strategy hurts the enemy more than he who uses brute force.

land and sea, a prepared Navy, souldiers *in procinctu, & quam Bonfinius apud Hungaros suos vult, virgam ferream,*[5] and money which is *nervus belli,*[6] still in a readinesse, and a sufficient revenue, a third part as in old *Rome* and *Egypt,* reserved for the Common-wealth; to avoid those heavy taxes and impositions, as well to defray this charge of wars, as also all other publike defalcations,[§] expences, fees, pensions, reparations, chast sports, feasts, donaries, rewards, and entertainments. All things in this nature especially I will have maturely done, and with great deliberation: *ne quid temerè, ne quid remissè ac timide fiat;*[7] *Sed quò feror hospes?* [8] To prosecute the rest would require a volume. *Manum de tabella,*[9] I have been overtedious in this subject; I could have here willingly ranged, but these straits wherein I am included will not permit.

From Common-wealths and cities, I will descend to Families, which have as many corsives[§] & molestations, as frequent discontents as the rest. . . .

If any man shall ask in the mean time, who I am that so boldly censure others, *tu nullane habes vitia?* have I no faults? Yes more then thou hast, whatsoever thou art. *Nos numerus sumus,*[1] I confesse it again, I am as foolish, as mad as any one.

> *Insanus vobis videor, non deprecor ipse,*
> *Quo minus insanus,*[2]———

I do not deny it, *demens de populo dematur.*[3] My comfort is, I have more fellows, and those of excellent note. And though I be not so right, or so discreet as I should be, yet not so mad, so bad neither as thou perhaps takest me to be.

To conclude, this being granted, that all the world is melancholy, or mad, dotes, and every member of it, I have ended

[5] Ready for action, and, as Bonfinius wished for his Hungarians, an iron scourge.
[6] The sinews of war.
[7] So that nothing is done rashly or remissly or timidly.
[8] But where am I, a newcomer, rushing to?
[9] Stop writing!
[1] I am not different.
[2] I seem mad to you; I don't beg off.
[3] Let the madman be removed from society.

my task, and sufficiently illustrated that which I took upon me
to demonstrate at first. At this present I have no more to say;
His sanam mentem Democritus,[4] I can but wish my self, &
them a good Physician, and all of us a better minde.

And although for the abovenamed reasons, I had a just cause
to undertake this subject, to point at these particular species of
dotage, that so men might acknowledg their imperfections, and
seek to reform what is amiss; yet I have a more serious intent
at this time; and to omit al impertinent digressions, to say no
more of such as are improperly melancholy, or metaphorically
mad, lightly mad, or in disposition, as stupid, angry, drunken,
silly, sottish, sullen, proud, vain-glorious, ridiculous, beastly,
peevish, obstinate, impudent, extravagant, dry, doting, dull, desperate, harebrain, &c. mad, frantick, foolish, heteroclites, which
no new *Hospitall* can hold, no physick help: my purpose and
endeavor is, in the following discourse to anatomize this humor
of melancholy, through all his parts and species, as it is an habit,
or an ordinary disease, and that philosophically, medicinally, to
shew the causes, symptoms, and several cures of it, that it may
be the better avoyded. Moved thereunto for the generality of it,
and to do good, it being a disease so frequent, as *Mercurialis*
observes *in these our dayes; so often happening,* saith *Laurentius, in our miserable times,* as few there are that feel not the
smart of it. Of the same minde is *Ælian Montaltus, Melancton,*
and others; *Julius Cæsar Claudinus* cals it the *fountain of all
other diseases, and so common in this crased age of ours, that
scarce one of a thousand is free from it:* and that Splenetick
Hypocondriacal winde especially, which proceeds from the spleen
and short ribs. Being then it is a disease so grievous, so common, I know not wherein to do a more generall service, and
spend my time better, then to prescribe means how to prevent
and cure so universall a malady, an Epidemical disease, that so
often, so much crucifies the body and minde.

If I have overshot my self in this which hath been hitherto
said, or that it is, which I am sure some will object, too phantastical, *too light and comicall for a Divine, too satyrical for one
of my profession,* I will presume to answer with *Erasmus,* in
like case, Tis not I, but *Democritus, Democritus dixit:* you must

4 Democritus wishes them sanity.

consider what it is to speak in ones own or anothers person, an assumed habit and name; a difference betwixt him that affects or acts a Princes, a Philosophers, a Magistrates, a Fools part, and him that is so indeed; and what liberty those old Satyrists have had, it is a *Cento* collected from others, not I, but they that say it.

> *Dixero si quid fortè jocosius, hoc mihi juris*
> *Cum veniâ dabis*[5]——

Take heed you mistake me not. If I do a little forget my self, I hope you wil pardon it. And to say truth, why should any man be offended, or take exceptions at it?

> ——*Licuit, semperque licebit,*
> *Parcere personis, dicere de vitiis.*
> It lawful was of old, and still will be,
> To speak of vice, but let the name go free:

I hate their vices, not their persons. If any be displeased, or take ought unto himself, let him not expostulate or cavil with him that said it (so did *Erasmus* excuse himself to *Dorpius, si parva licet componere magnis*[6]) and so do I; *but let him be angry with himself, that so betrayed and opened his own faults in applying it to himself: If he be guilty and deserve it, let him amend who-ever he is, and not be angry. He that hateth correction is a fool, Prov.* 12.1. If he be not guilty, it concerns him not; it is not my freenesse of speech, but a guilty conscience, a gauled back of his own that makes him winch.[§]

> *Suspitione si quis errabit suâ,*
> *Et rapiet ad se, quod erit commune omnium,*
> *Stultè nudabit animi conscientiam.*[7]

I deny not this which I have said savors a little of *Democritus; Quamvis ridentem dicere verum quid vetat;* one may speak in jest, and yet speak truth. It is somewhat tart, I grant it; *acriora orexim excitant embammata,* as he said, sharp sauces increase appetite,

---

5 If I speak too lightly, pardon and indulge me.
6 If I may compare small things to great.
7 If any one is mistaken because he's suspicious and applies to himself what is common to all, his foolishness will reveal his guilty conscience.

Nec cibus ipse juvat morsu fraudatus aceti.[8]

Object then and cavil what thou wilt, I ward all with *Democritus* buckler, his medicine shall salve it; strike where thou wilt, and when: *Democritus dixit, Democritus* will answer it. It was written by an idle fellow, at idle times, about our *Saturnalian* or *Dyonisian* feasts, when as he said, *nullum libertati periculum est,*[9] servants in old *Rome* had liberty to say and do what them list. When our country men sacrificed to their goddess *Vacuna,* and sat tipling by their *Vacunall*[§] fires, I writ this, and published this. Οὖτις ἔλεγεν,[1] it is *neminis nihil.*[2] The time, place, persons, and all circumstances apologize for me, and why may I not then be idle with others? speak my minde freely? If you deny me this liberty, upon these presumptions I will take it: I say again, I will take it.

> *Si quis est qui dictum in se inclementius*
> *Existimavit esse, sic existimet.*[3]

If any man take exceptions, let him turn[§] the buckle of his girdle, I care not. I owe thee nothing (Reader) I look for no favor at thy hands, I am independent, I fear not.

No, I recant, I will not, I care, I fear, I confesse my fault, acknowledg a great offence,

> ———*motos præstat componere fluctus,*[4]

I have overshot my self, I have spoken foolishly, rashly, unadvisedly, absurdly, I have anatomized mine own folly. And now me thinks upon a sudden I am awaked as it were out of a dream, I have had a raving fit, a phantastical fit, ranged up and down, in and out, I have insulted over most kinde of men, abused some, offended others, wronged my self; and now being recovered, and perceiving mine error, cry with *Orlando, Solvite me,* pardon (*o boni*[5]) that which is past, and I will make you amends in that which is to come; I promise you a more sober discourse in my following Treatise.

[8] Food doesn't please without a dash of vinegar.
[9] Liberty is not endangered.
[1] No one has said it.
[2] It is nothing by nobody.
[3] If any one thinks that he's been spoken of too harshly, let him think so.
[4] It is better to calm the troubled waves.
[5] Good friends.

If through weaknesse, folly, passion, discontent, ignorance, I have said amisse, let it be forgotten and forgiven. I acknowledg that of *Tacitus* to be true, *Asperæ facetiæ ubi nimis ex vero traxere, acrem sui memoriam relinquunt*, a bitter jest leaves a sting behind it: and as an honorable man observes, *They fear a Satyrists wit, he their memories*. I may justly suspect the worst; and though I hope I have wronged no man, yet in *Medeas* words I will crave pardon,

> ——*Illudjam voce extrema peto,*
> *Ne si qua noster dubius effudit dolor,*
> *Maneant in animo verba, sed melior tibi*
> *Memoria nostri subeat, hæc iræ data*
> *Obliterentur——*
> And in my last words this I do desire,
> That what in passion I have said, or ire,
> May be forgotten, and a better minde
> Be had of us, hereafter as you finde.

I earnestly request every private man, as *Scaliger* did *Cardan*, not to take offence. I will conclude in his lines, *Si me cognitum haberes, non solum donares nobis has facetias nostras, sed etiam indignum duceres, tam humanum animum, lene ingenium, vel minimam suspitionem deprecari oportere.*[6] If thou knewest my modesty and simplicity, thou woulds easily pardon and forgive what is here amiss, or by thee misconceived. If hereafter anatomizing this surly humor, my hand slip, as an unskilful prentise I launce too deep, and cut through skin and al at unawares, make it smart, or cut awry, pardon a rude hand, an unskilfull knife, tis a most difficult thing to keep an even tone, a perpetual tenor, and not sometimes to lash out; *difficile est Satyram non scribere,*[7] there be so many objects to divert, inward perturbations to molest, and the very best may sometimes erre; *aliquando bonus dormitat Homerus,*[8] it is impossible not in so much to overshoot:

> ——*opere in longo fas est obrepere somnum.*[9]

---

6 If you knew me well, you would not only pardon these jests of mine but you would also consider it shameful that a man so humane in spirit and mild in nature should have to ward off even the slightest suspicion.
7 It's hard not to write satire.
8 Sometimes worthy Homer nods.
9 In a long work, there's reason to get sleepy.

But what needs all this? I hope there will no such cause of offence be given; if there be,

> *Nemo aliquid recognoscat, nos mentimur omnia.*[1]

Ile deny all (my last refuge), recant all, renounce all I have said, if any man except, and with as much facility excuse, as he can accuse; but I presume of thy good favor, and gratious acceptance (gentle reader). Out of an assured hope and confidence thereof, I will begin.

[1] Let no one take this seriously; it's all fiction.

III

Izaak Walton

THE
LIFE
OF
Dr. *JOHN DONNE,*
Late Dean of St. *Paul's* Church,
LONDON

THE INTRODUCTION.

If that great Master of Language and Art, Sir Henry Wotton, the late Provost of Eaton Colledge, had liv'd to see the Publication of these Sermons, he had presented the World with the Authors Life exactly written; And, 'twas pity he did not; for it was a work worthy his undertaking, and he fit to undertake it: betwixt whom, and the Author, there was so mutual a knowledge, and such a friendship contracted in their Youth, as nothing but death could force a separation. And, though their bodies were

divided, their affections were not: for, that learned Knight's love
followed his Friends fame beyond death and the forgetful grave;
which he testified by intreating me, whom he acquainted with
his design, to inquire of some particulars that concern'd it, not
doubting but my knowledge of the Author, and love to his mem-
ory, might make my diligence useful: I did most gladly under-
take the employment, and continued it with great content 'till
I had made my Collection ready to be augmented and compleated
by his matchless Pen: but then, Death prevented his intentions.

When I heard that sad news, and heard also that these Sermons *were to be printed, and want the* Authors Life, *which I*
thought to be very remarkable: Indignation or grief (indeed I
know not which) transported me so far, that I reviewed my
forsaken-Collections, and resolv'd the World should see the best
plain Picture of the Authors Life *that my artless Pensil, guided*
by the hand of truth, could present to it.

And, If I shall now be demanded as once Pompey's *poor*
bondman was,[1] *"(The grateful wretch had been left alone on*
"the Sea-shore, with the forsaken dead body of his once glorious
"lord and master: and, was then gathering the scatter'd pieces
"of an old broken boat to make a funeral pile to burn it, which
"was the custom of the Romans) who art thou that alone hast
the honour to bury the body of Pompey the great? *so,* who am
I that do thus officiously set the Authors memory on fire? *I hope*
the question will prove to have in it, more of wonder then
disdain; But wonder indeed the Reader may, that I who profess
my self artless should presume with my faint light to shew forth
his Life whose very name makes it illustrious! but be this to the
disadvantage of the person represented: Certain I am, it is to
the advantage of the beholder, who shall here see the Authors
Picture in a natural dress, which ought to beget faith in what
is spoken: for he that wants skill to deceive, may safely be
trusted.

And if the Authors glorious spirit, which now is in Heaven;
can have the leasure to look down and see me, the poorest, the
meanest of all his friends, in the midst of this officious[§] *duty,*
confident I am, that he will not disdain this well-meant sacrifice

1 *Plutark.

to his memory: for, whilest his Conversation made me and many others happy below, I know his Humility and Gentleness was then eminent; and, I have heard Divines say, those Vertues that were but sparks upon Earth, become great and glorious flames in Heaven.

Before I proceed further, I am to intreat the Reader to take notice, that when *Doctor Donn's* Sermons were first printed, this was then my excuse for daring to write his life; and, I dare not now appear without it.

THE LIFE.

Master *John Donne* was born in *London*, in the year 1573. of good and vertuous Parents: and, though his own Learning and other multiplyed merits may justly appear sufficient to dignifie both Himself and his Posterity: yet, the Reader may be pleased to know, that his Father was masculinely and lineally descended from a very antient Family in *Wales*, where many of his name now live, that deserve and have great reputation in that Countrey.

By his Mother he was descended of the Family of the famous and learned Sir *Thomas Moor*, sometime Lord *Chancellour* of *England*: as also, from that worthy and laborious§ *Judge Rastall*, who left Posterity the vast Statutes of the Law of this Nation most exactly abridged.

He had his first breeding§ in his Fathers house, where a private Tutor had the care of him, until the tenth year of his age; and, in his eleventh year, was sent to the University of *Oxford*; having at that time a good command both of the French and Latine Tongue. This and some other of his remarkable Abilities, made one then give this censure§ of him; *That this age had brought forth another* Picus Mirandula; *of whom Story says, That he was rather born, than made wise by study.*

There he remained for some years in *Hart-Hall*, having for the advancement of his studies Tutors of several Sciences§ to attend and instruct him, till time made him capable, and his learning expressed in publick exercises declared him worthy to receive his first degree in the Schools, which he forbore by ad-

vice from his friends, who being for their Religion of the Romish
perswasion, were *conscionably* averse to some parts of the Oath
that is alwaies tendered at those times; and, not to be refused
by those that expect the titulary honour of their studies.

About the fourteenth year of his age, he was transplanted
from *Oxford* to *Cambridge;* where, that he might receive nourishment from both Soils, he staied till his seventeenth year; all
which time he was a most laborious Student, often changing his
studies, but endeavouring to take no degree, for the reasons
formerly mentioned.

About the seventeenth year of his age, he was removed to
London, and then admitted into *Lincolns-Inne,* with an intent to
study the *Law;* where he gave great testimonies of his Wit, his
Learning, and of his Improvement in that profession: which
never served him for other use than an Ornament and Self-
satisfaction.

His Father died before his admission into this Society; and being a Merchant, left him his portion in money (it was 3000 l.).
His Mother and those to whose care he was committed, were
watchful to improve his knowledge, and to that end appointed
him Tutors both in the *Mathematicks,* and in all the other
Liberal Sciences, to attend him. But with these Arts they were
advised to instil into him particular Principles of the *Romish
Church;* of which those Tutors profest (though secretly) themselves to be members.

They had almost obliged him to their faith; having for their
advantage, besides many opportunities, the example of his dear
and pious Parents, which was a most powerful perswasion, and
did work much upon him, as he professeth in his Preface to his
Pseudo-Martyr; a Book of which the Reader shall have some
account in what follows.

He was now entered into the eighteenth year of his age; and
at that time had betrothed himself to no Religion that might
give him any other denomination than *a Christian.* And Reason,
and Piety had both perswaded him, that there could be no such
sin as *Schism,* if an adherence to some visible Church were not
necessary.

About the nineteenth year of his age: he, being then unresolv'd what Religion to adhere to, and, considering how much it concern'd his soul to choose the most Orthodox, did therefore (though his youth and health, promised him a long life) to rectifie all scruples that might concern that, presently lay aside all study of the Law: and, of all other Sciences that might give him a denomination; and, begun seriously to survey, and consider the Body of Divinity, as it was then controverted betwixt the *Reformed* and the *Roman Church.* And as *Gods blessed Spirit did then awaken him to the search, and in that industry did never forsake him,* (they be his own words[2]) *so he calls the same holy Spirit to witness this Protestation; that, in that disquisition and search, he proceeded with humility and diffidence in himself; and, by that which he took to be the safest way; namely, frequent Prayers, and an indifferent*[§] *affection to both parties;* and indeed, truth had too much light about her to be hid from so sharp an Inquirer; and, he had too much ingenuity,[§] not to acknowledge he had found her.

Being to undertake this search, he believed the *Cardinal Bellarmine* to be the best defender of the *Roman cause,* and therefore betook himself to the examination of his Reasons. The Cause was weighty: and wilful delays had been inexcusable both towards God and his own Conscience; he therefore proceeded in this search with all moderate haste, and about the twentieth year of his age, did shew the then *Dean* of *Gloucester* (whose name my memory hath now lost) all the Cardinals works marked with many weighty observations under his own hand; which works were bequeathed by him at his death as a Legacy to a most dear Friend.

About a year following he resolved to travel; and the Earl of *Essex* going first the *Cales,*[§] and after the *Island voyages,* the first *Anno* 1596. the second 1597. he took the advantage of those opportunities, waited[§] upon his Lordship, and was an eye-witness of those happy and unhappy employments.

But he returned not back into *England,* till he had staid some years first in *Italy,* and then in *Spain,* where he made many useful observations of those Countreys, their Laws and manner of Government, and returned perfect in their Languages.

2 *In his Preface to *Pseudo-Martyr.*

The time that he spent in *Spain* was at his first going into *Italy* designed for travelling to the *Holy Land,* and for viewing *Jerusalem* and the Sepulchre of our Saviour. But at his being in the furthest parts of *Italy,* the disappointment of Company, or of a safe Convoy, or the uncertainty of returns of Money into those remote parts, denied him that happiness: which he did often occasionally mention with a deploration.

Not long after his return into *England,* that exemplary Pattern of Gravity and Wisdom, the Lord *Elsemore,* then Keeper of the Great Seal, and *Lord Chancellour of England,* taking notice of his Learning, Languages, and other Abilities, and much affecting[§] his Person and Behaviour, took him to be his chief Secretary; supposing and intending it to be an Introduction to some more weighty Employment in the State; for which, his Lordship did often protest, he thought him very fit.

Nor did his Lordship in this time of Master *Donne's* attendance upon him, account him to be so much his Servant, as to forget he was his Friend; and to testifie it, did alwayes use him with much courtesie, appointing him a place at his own Table, to which he esteemed his Company and Discourse to be a great Ornament.

He continued that employment for the space of five years, being daily useful, and not mercenary to his Friends. During which time he (I dare not say unhappily) fell into such a liking, as (with her approbation) increased into a love with a young Gentlewoman that lived in that Family, who was Niece to the Lady *Elsemore,* and Daughter to Sir *George Moor,* then Chancellor of the Garter and Lieutenant of the Tower.

Sir *George* had some intimation of it, and knowing prevention[§] to be a great part of wisdom, did therefore remove her with much haste from that to his own house at *Lothesley,* in the County of *Surry;* but too late, by reason of some faithful promises which were so interchangeably passed, as never to be violated by either party.

These promises were only known to themselves: and, the friends of both parties used much diligence, and many arguments to kill or cool their affections to each other: but in vain; for, love is a flattering mischief, that hath denied aged and wise men a foresight of those evils that too often prove to be the children of that blind father, a passion! that carries us to commit *Errors* with as much ease as whirlwinds remove feathers, and begets in us an unwearied industry to the attainment of what we desire. And such an Industry did, notwithstanding much watchfulness against it, bring them secretly together (I forbear to tell the manner how) and at last to a marriage too, without the allowance of those friends, whose approbation always was, and ever will be necessary, to make even a vertuous love become lawful.

And that the knowledge of their marriage might not fall, like an unexpected tempest, on those that were unwilling to have it so: and, that preapprehensions might make it the less enormous,§ when it was known: it was purposely whispered into the ears of many that it was so, yet by none that could affirm it. But, to put a period to the jealousies of Sir *George* (Doubt often begetting more restless thoughts then the certain knowledge of what we fear) the news was in favour to Mr. *Donne,* and with his allowance, made known to Sir *George,* by his honourable friend and neighbour *Henry* Earl of *Northumberland:* but it was to Sir *George* so immeasurably unwelcome, and, so transported him; that as though his passion of anger and inconsideration, might exceed theirs of love and errour, he presently engaged his Sister the Lady *Elsemore,* to join with him to procure her Lord to discharge Mr. *Donne* of the place he held under his Lordship.—This request was followed with violence; and though Sir *George* were remembred, that Errors might be overpunished, and desired therefore to forbear till second considerations might clear some scruples: yet, he became restless until his suit was granted, and the punishment executed. And though the *Lord Chancellor* did not at Mr. *Donnes* dismission, give him such a Commendation as the great Emperour *Charles* the fifth, did of his Secretary *Eraso,* when he presented him to his Son and Successor *Philip* the Second, saying, *That in his* Eraso, *he gave to him a greater gift then all his Estate, and all the Kingdoms which he then resigned to him:* yet the Lord *Chancellor* said, *He parted with a Friend; and such a Secretary as was fitter to serve a King then a Subject.*

Immediately after his dismission from his service, he sent a
sad Letter to his Wife, to acquaint her with it: and, after the
subscription of his name, writ,

> *John Donne, Anne Donne, Un-done,*

and God knows it proved too true.

For this bitter Physick of Mr. *Donnes* dismission was not
strong enough to purge out all Sir *George's* choler; for, he was
not satisfied till Mr. *Donne* and his sometime Compupil in
Cambridge that married him; namely, *Samuel Brook* (who was
after Doctor in Divinity, and Master of Trinity Colledge) and
his brother Mr. *Christopher Brook,* sometime Mr. *Donnes* Chamber-fellow in *Lincolns-Inn,* who gave Mr. *Donne* his Wife, and
witnessed the marriage, were all committed, to three several
prisons.

Mr. *Donne* was first enlarged,§ who neither gave rest to his
body or brain, nor to any friend in whom he might hope to
have an interest, until he had procured an enlargement for his
two imprisoned friends.

He was now at liberty; but his days were still cloudy: and
being past these troubles, others did still multiply upon him;
for his wife was (to her extream sorrow) detained from him;
and, though with *Jacob* he endured not an hard service for her,
yet, he lost a good one, and, was forced to make good his title,
and to get possession of her by a long and restless suit in Law;
which proved troublesome and sadly-chargeable§ to him, whose
youth, and travel, and needless bounty, had brought his estate
into a narrow compass.

It is observed, and most truly, that silence and submission
are charming qualities, and work most upon passionate men;
and it proved so with Sir *George;* for these, and a general report
of Mr. *Donnes* merits, together with his winning behaviour
(which when it would intice, had a strange kind of elegant
irresistible art) these, and time had so dispassionated Sir *George,*
that as the world had approved his Daughters choice, so he also
could not but see a more then ordinary merit in his new son:
and this at last melted him into so much remorse (for Love
and Anger are so like Agues, as to have hot and cold fits; and
love in Parents, though it may be quenched, yet is easily re-

kindled, and expires not, till death denies mankind a natural heat) that he laboured his Sons restauration to his place; using to that end, both his own and his Sisters power to her Lord; but with no success; for his Answer was, *That though he was un-feignedly sorry for what he had done, yet it was inconsistent with his place and credit, to discharge and readmit servants at the request of passionate petitioners.*

Sir *Georges* endeavour for Mr. *Donnes* readmission, was by all means to be kept secret (for men do more naturally reluct[§] for errors, then submit to put on those blemishes that attend their visible acknowledgment.) But however it was not long before Sir *George* appeared to be so far reconciled, as to wish their happiness; and not to deny them his paternal blessing, but yet, refused to contribute any means that might conduce to their livelyhood.

Mr. *Donnes* estate was the greatest part spent in many and chargeable Travels, Books and dear-bought Experience: he out of all employment that might yield a support for himself and wife, who had been curiously[§] and plentifully educated; both their natures generous, and accustomed to confer, and not to receive Courtesies: These and other considerations, but chiefly that his wife was to bear a part in his sufferings, surrounded him with many sad thoughts, and some apparent apprehensions of want.

But his sorrows were lessened and his wants prevented by the seasonable courtesie of their noble kinsman *Sir Francis Wolly* of *Pirford* in *Surry,* who intreated them to a cohabitation with him; where they remained with much freedom to them-selves, and equal content to him for some years; and, as their charge encreased (she had yearly a child) so did his love and bounty.

It hath been observed by wise and considering men, that Wealth hath seldom been the Portion, and never the Mark to discover good People; but, that Almighty God, who disposeth all things wisely, hath of his abundant goodness denied it (he only knows why) to many, whose minds he hath enriched with the greater Blessings of *Knowledge* and *Vertue,* as the fairer Testimonies of his love to Mankind; and this was the present condition of this man of so excellent Erudition and Endow-

ments; whose necessary and daily expences were hardly reconcileable with his uncertain and narrow estate. Which I mention,
for that at this time there was a most generous offer made him
for the moderating of his worldly cares; the declaration of which
shall be the next employment of my Pen.

God hath been so good to his Church, as to afford it in every
age some such men to serve at his Altar as have been piously
ambitious of doing good to mankind; a disposition that is so like
to God himself, that it owes it self only to him who takes a
pleasure to behold it in his Creatures. These times[3] he did bless
with many such; some of which still live to be Patterns of Apos-
tolical Charity, and, of more than Humane Patience. I have said
this, because I have occasion to mention one of them in my
following discourse; namely, Dr. *Morton,* the most laborious
and learned Bishop of *Durham;* one, that God hath blessed with
perfect intellectuals, and a chearful heart at the age of 94
years (and is yet living:) one, that in his days of plenty had
so large a heart as to use his large Revenue to the encouragement of *Learning* and *Vertue,* and is now (be it spoken with
sorrow) reduced to a narrow estate, which he embraces without
repining; and still shews the beauty of his mind by so liberal
a hand, as if this were an age in which *to morrow were to care
for it self.* I have taken a pleasure in giving the Reader a short,
but true character of this good man, my friend, from whom I
received this following relation.—He sent to Mr. *Donne,* and
intreated to borrow an hour of his time for a Conference the
next day. After their meeting, there was not many minutes
passed before he spake to Mr. *Donne* to this purpose; 'Mr. *Donne,*
'The occasion of sending for you is to propose to you what I have
'often revolv'd in my own thought since I last saw you: which
'nevertheless, I will not declare but upon this condition, that
'you shall not return me a present answer, but forbear three
'days, and bestow some part of that time in Fasting and Prayer;
'and after a serious consideration of what I shall propose; then
'return to me with your answer. Deny me not, Mr. *Donne;* for,
'it is the effect of a true love, which I would gladly pay as a debt
'due for yours to me.

3 *1648.

This request being granted, the
Doctor exprest himself thus:

'Mr. *Donne*, I know your Education and Abilities; I know your
'expectation of a State-employment; and I know your fitness for
'it; and I know too, the many delays and contingencies that
'attend Court-promises; and let me tell you that, my love begot
'by our long friendship, and your merits, hath prompted me to
'such an inquisition§ after your present temporal estate, as makes
'me no stranger to your necessities; which I know to be such
'as your generous spirit could not bear, if it were not supported
'with a pious Patience: you know I have formerly perswaded
'you to wave§ your Court-hopes, and enter into holy Orders;
'which I now again perswade you to embrace, with this reason
'added to my former request: The King hath yesterday made
'me Dean of *Gloucester,* and I am also possessed of a Benefice,
'the profits of which are equal to those of my Deanry; I will
'think my Deanry enough for my maintenance (who am and
'resolve to dye a single man) and will quit my Benefice, and
'estate you in it, (which the Patron is willing I shall do) if God
'shall incline your heart to embrace this motion. *Remember*, Mr.
'*Donne,* no mans Education or Parts make him too good for
'this employment, *which is to be an Ambassadour for the God*
'*of glory, that God who by a vile death opened the gates of life*
'*to mankind.* Make me no present answer; but remember your
'promise, and return to me the third day with your Resolution.

At the hearing of this, Mr. *Donne*'s faint breath and perplext
countenance gave a visible testimony of an inward conflict; but
he performed his promise and departed without returning an
answer till the third day, and then his answer was to this effect;

'My most worthy and most dear friend, since I saw you, I have
'been faithful to my promise, and have also meditated much of
'your great kindness, which hath been such as would exceed
'even my gratitude; but that it cannot do; and more I cannot
'return you; and I do that with an heart full of Humility and
'Thanks, though I may not accept of your offer; but, Sir, my
'refusal is not for that I think my self too good for that calling,
'for which Kings, if they think so, are not good enough: nor, for
'that my Education and Learning, though not eminent, may

'not, being assisted with God's Grace and Humility, render me 'in some measure fit for it: but, I dare make so dear a friend as 'you are my Confessor; some irregularities of my life have been 'so visible to some men, that though I have, I thank God, made 'my peace with him by penitential resolutions against them, and 'by the assistance of his Grace banish'd them my affections; yet 'this, which God knows to be so, is not so visible to man, as to 'free me from their censures, and it may be that sacred calling 'from a dishonour. And besides; whereas it is determined by the 'best of *Casuists*, that *Gods Glory should be the first end, and a* '*maintenance the second motive to embrace that calling;* and 'though each man may propose to himself both together; yet 'the first may not be put last without a violation of Conscience, 'which he that searches the heart will judge. And truly my 'present condition is such, that if I ask my own Conscience, 'whether it be reconcileable to that rule, it is at this time so 'perplexed about it, that I can neither give my self nor you an 'answer. You know, Sir, who sayes, *Happy is that man whose* '*Conscience doth not accuse him for that thing which he does.* 'To these I might add other reasons that disswade me; but I 'crave your favour that I may forbear to express them, and, 'thankfully decline your offer.

This was his present resolution; but, the heart of man is not in his own keeping; and he was destined to this sacred service by an higher hand; a hand so powerful, as at last forced him to a compliance: of which I shall give the Reader an account before I shall give a rest to my Pen.

Mr. *Donne* and his wife continued with Sir *Francis Wolly* till his death: a little before which time, Sir *Francis* was so happy as to make a perfect reconciliation betwixt Sir *George* and his forsaken son and daughter; Sir *George* conditioning by bond, to pay to Mr. *Donne* 800 l. at a certain day, as a portion with his wife, or 20 l. quarterly for their maintenance: as the interest for it, till the said portion was paid.

Most of those years that he lived with Sir *Francis,* he studied the *Civil* and *Canon Laws;* in which he acquired such a perfection, as was judged to hold proportion with many who had made that study the employment of their whole life.

Sir *Francis* being dead, and that happy family dissolved, Mr.

Donne took for himself a house in *Micham* (near to *Croydon* in *Surrey*) a place noted for good air, and choice company: there his wife and children remained: and for himself he took lodgings in *London*, near to White-Hall, whither, his friends and occasions drew him very often, and where he was as often visited by many of the Nobility and others of this Nation, who used him in their Counsels of greatest consideration: and with some rewards for his better subsistence.

Nor, did our own Nobility only value and favour him, but his acquaintance and friendship was sought for by most Ambassadours of forraign Nations, and by many other strangers, whose learning or business occasioned their stay in this Nation.

He was much importuned by many friends to make his constant residence in *London*, but he still denied it, having setled his dear wife and children at *Micham*, and near some friends that were bountiful to them and him: for they, God knows, needed it: and that you may the better now judge of the then present Condition of his mind and fortune, I shall present you with an extract collected out of some few of his many Letters.

——*And the reason why I did not send an answer to your last weeks letter, was, because it then found me under too great a sadness; and at present 'tis thus with me: There is not one person, but my self, well of my family: I have already lost half a Child, and with that mischance of hers, my wife is fallen into such a discomposure, as would afflict her too extreamly, but that the sickness of all her other children stupifies her: of one of which, in good faith, I have not much hope: and these meet with a fortune so ill provided for Physick, and such relief, that if God should ease us with burials, I know not how to perform even that: but, I flatter my self with this hope, that I am dying too: for, I cannot waste faster then by such griefs. As for,——*

From my hospital
at *Micham*,

JOHN DONNE.

Aug. 10.

Thus he did bemoan himself: And thus in other letters.

——*For, we hardly discover a sin, when it is but an omission of some good, and no accusing act; with this or the former, I have often suspected my self to be overtaken; which is,* with an over earnest desire of the next life: *and though I know it is not meerly a weariness of this, because I had the same desire when I went with the tide, and injoyed fairer hopes then I now do: yet, I doubt*[§] *worldly troubles have increased it: 'tis now Spring, and all the pleasures of it displease me; every other tree blossoms, and I wither: I grow older and not better; my strength diminisheth and my load grows heavier; and yet, I would fain be or do something; but, that I cannot tell what, is no wonder in this time of my sadness; for, to chuse is to do; but, to be no part of any body, is as to be nothing; and so I am, and shall so judge my self, unless I could be so incorporated into a part of the world, as by business to contribute some sustentation to the whole. This I made account, I began early when I understood the study of our Laws: but was diverted by leaving that and imbracing the worst voluptuousness,* an hydroptique[§] immoderate desire of humane learning and languages: *Beautiful ornaments indeed to men of great fortunes; but mine was grown so low as to need an occupation: which I thought I entred well into, when I subjected my self to such a service as I thought might exercise my poor abilities: and there I stumbled, and fell too: and now I am become so little, or such a nothing, that I am not a subject good enough for one of my own letters;—Sir, I fear my present discontent does not proceed from a good root, that I am so well content to be nothing, that is, dead. But, Sir, though my fortune hath made me such, as that I am rather a Sickness or a Disease of the world, than any part of it, and therefore neither love it nor life; yet, I would gladly live to become some such thing as you should not repent loving me: Sir, your own Soul cannot be more zealous for your good then I am, and, God who loves that zeal in me, will not suffer you to doubt it: you would pity me now, if you saw me write, for my pain hath drawn my head so much awry, and holds it so, that my eye cannot follow my pen. I therefore receive you into my Prayers with mine own weary soul, and, Commend my self to yours. I doubt not but next week will bring you good news, for I have either mending or dying on my side: but, If I do continue longer thus, I shall have Comfort in this, That my blessed Saviour in exercising his Justice upon my two worldly parts,* my Fortune *and* my Body, *reserves all his Mercy for that which most needs it*, my Soul! *which is, I doubt, too like a Porter, that is very often near the gate, and yet goes not out. Sir, I profess to you truly, that my lothness to give over writing now, seems to my self a sign that I shall write no more—*

Your poor friend, *and*

Gods poor patient

J O H N   D O N N E .

Sept. 7.

By this you have seen, a part of the picture of his narrow fortune, and the perplexities of his generous mind; and, thus it continued with him for about two years; all which time his family remained constantly at *Micham;* and, to which place he often retir'd himself, and destined some days to a constant study of some points of Controversie betwixt the *English* and *Roman Church;* and especially those of *Supremacy* and *Allegiance:* and, to that place and such studies he could willingly have wedded himself during his life: but, the earnest perswasion of friends became at last to be so powerful, as to cause the removal of himself and family to *London,* where Sir *Robert Drewry,* a Gentleman of a very noble estate, and a more liberal mind, assigned him and his wife an useful apartment in his own large house in *Drewry lane,* and not only rent-free, but was also a cherisher of his studies, and such a friend as sympathized with him and his in all their joy and sorrows.

At this time of Mr. *Donne's,* and his wives living in Sir *Roberts* house, the Lord *Hay* was by King *James* sent upon a glorious Embassie to the then *French* King *Henry* the fourth, and, Sir *Robert* put on a suddain resolution to accompany him to the *French* Court, and, to be present at his audience there. And, Sir *Robert* put on as suddain a resolution, to solicit Mr. *Donne* to be his Companion in that Journey: And this desire was suddainly made known to his wife, who was then with Child, and otherways under so dangerous a habit of body, as to her health, that she profest an unwillingness to allow him any absence from her; saying, *her divining soul boded her some ill in his absence;* and therefore, desired him not to leave her. This made Mr. *Donne* lay aside all thoughts of the Journey, and, really to resolve against it. But Sir *Robert* became restless in his perswasions for it; and, Mr. *Donne* was so generous, as to think he had sold his liberty when he received so many Charitable kindnesses from him: and, told his wife so; who did therefore with an unwilling-willingness give a faint Consent to the Journey, which was proposed to be but for two months: for, about that time they determin'd§ their return.—Within a few days after this resolve, the *Embassador,* Sir *Robert,* and Mr. *Donne* left *London:* and, were the twelfth day got all safe to *Paris.*— two days after their arrival there, Mr. *Donne* was left alone, in that room in which Sir *Robert,* and he, and some other friends had din'd together. To this place Sir *Robert* return'd within half an hour; and, as he left, so he found Mr. *Donne* alone; but, in such an Extasie, and, so alter'd as to his looks, as amaz'd Sir *Robert* to behold him: insomuch that he earnestly desired Mr. *Donne* to declare what had befaln him in the short time of his absence? to which, Mr. *Donne* was not able to make a present answer: but, after a long and perplext pause, did at last say, *I have seen a dreadful Vision since I saw you: I have seen my dear wife pass twice by me through this room, with her hair hanging about her shoulders, and a dead child in her arms: this, I have seen since I saw you.* To which, Sir *Robert* reply'd; *Sure Sir, you have slept since I saw you; and, this is the result of some melancholy dream, which I desire you to forget, for, you are now awake.* To which Mr. *Donnes* reply was: *I cannot be surer that I now live, then that I have not slept since I saw you: and am, as sure, that at her second appearing, she stopt, and look'd me in the face, and vanisht.*——Rest and sleep, had not alter'd Mr. *Donne*'s opinion the next day: for, he then affirm'd this Vision with a more deliberate, and, so confirm'd a confidence, that he inclin'd Sir *Robert* to a faint belief that the Vision was true.——It is truly said, *that desire, and doubt, have no rest:* and it prov'd so with Sir *Robert,* for he immediately sent a servant to *Drewry* house with a charge to hasten back, and bring him word, whether Mrs. *Donne* were alive? and if alive, in what condition she was, as to her health?—The twelfth day the Messenger returned with this account—That he found and left Mrs. *Donne* very sad, and sick in her bed: and, that after a long and dangerous labor she had been deliver'd of a dead child.

And, upon examination, the abortion[3] prov'd to be the same day, and about the very hour that Mr. *Donne* affirm'd he saw her pass by him in his Chamber.

This is a relation that will beget some wonder: and, it well may; for, most of our world are at present possest with an opinion that *Visions* and *Miracles* are ceas'd. And, though 'tis most certain, that two Lutes, being both strung and tun'd to an equal pitch, and then, one plaid upon, the other, that is not totcht, being laid upon a Table at a fit distance, will (like an Eccho to a trumpet) warble a faint audible harmony, in answer to the same tune: yet many will not believe there is any such thing, as a *sympathy* of *souls;* and I am well pleas'd, that every Reader do injoy his own opinion: but, if the unbelieving will not allow the believing Reader of this story, a liberty to believe that it may be true; then, I wish him to consider, many Wise men have believed, that, the ghost of *Julius Cæsar* did appear to *Brutus,* and that both St. *Austin,* and *Monica* his mother, had Visions in order to his Conversion. And, though these and many others (too many to name) have but the authority of humane story, yet, the incredible Reader may find in the Sacred story,[4] that *Samuel* did appear to *Saul* even after his death (whether really or not? I undertake not to determine.) And, *Bildad* in the Book of *Job,* says these words,[5] *A spirit passed before my face, the hair of my head stood up, fear and trembling came upon me; and made all my bones to shake.* Upon which words I will make no Comment, but, leave them to be considered by the incredulous Reader; to whom, I will also commend this following consideration: That there be many pious and learned men, that believe our merciful God hath assign'd to every man a particular *guardian Angel,* to be his constant monitor; and, to attend him in all his dangers, both of body and soul. And the opinion that every man hath his particular *Angel,* may gain some authority, by the relation of St. *Peters* miraculous deliverance out of prison,[6] not by many, *but by one Angel.* And this belief may yet gain more credit, by the readers considering that when *Peter* after his inlargement knockt at the door of *Mary* the mother of

4 *1 Sam. 28.
5 *Job 4.
6 *Acts 12.

John; and *Rode* the maid servant being surpriz'd with joy that *Peter* was there, did not let him in, but ran in haste and told the Disciples (who were then, and there met together) that *Peter* was at the door: and, they not believing it, *said she was mad:* yet, when she again affirm'd it, though they then believed it not: yet, they concluded, and said: *It is his Angel.*

More observations of this nature, and inferences from them, might be made to gain the relation a firmer belief: but I forbear, least,[§] I that intended to be but a Relator, may be thought to be an ingag'd person for the proving what was related to me; and yet, I think my self bound to declare, that though it was not told me by Mr. *Donne* himself; it was told me (*now long since*) by a Person of Honour, and of such intimacy with him, that he knew more of the secrets of his soul, then any person then living: and I think they told me the truth; for, it was told with such circumstances, and such asseveration, that (to say nothing of my own thoughts) I verily believe he that told it me, did himself believe it to be true.

I forbear the Readers farther trouble, as to the relation, and what concerns it; and will conclude mine, with commending to his view a Copy of Verses given by Mr. *Donne* to his wife at the time that he then parted from her. And I beg leave to tell, that I have heard some Criticks, learned, both in Languages and Poetry, say, that none of the Greek or Latine Poets did ever equal them.

A Valediction, forbidding to Mourn.

As vertuous men pass mildly away,
And, whisper to their Souls to go,
Whilest, some of their sad Friends do say,
The breath goes now, and some say no:

So, let us melt, and make no noise;
No wind-sighs, or tear-flouds us move,
'Twere profanation of our joys,
To tell the Laity our love.

Movings of th' earth, cause harms, and fears;
Men reckon what they did or meant!

> But, trepidation of the Sphears,
> Though greater far, is innocent.

> Dull sublunary lovers love,
> (Whose soul is sense) cannot admit
> Absence: because, that doth remove
> Those things that Elemented it.

> But we, by a Soul so much refin'd,
> That our souls know not what it is,
> Inter-assured of the mind,
> Care not, hands, eyes, or lips to miss.

> Our two souls therefore, which are one:
> Though I must go, indure not yet
> A breach, but an expansion,
> Like gold, to aiery thinness beat.

> If we be two? we are two so
> As stiff twin-compasses are two:
> Thy soul, the fixt foot, makes no show
> To move, but does, if th'other do.

> And, though thine in the Center sit,
> Yet, when my other far does rome,
> Thine leans, and hearkens after it,
> And grows erect as mine comes home.

> Such thou must be to me, who must
> Like th'other foot, obliquely run:
> Thy firmness, makes my circle just,
> And me to end, where I begun.

I return from my account of the *Vision*, to tell the Reader, that both before Mr. *Donne's* going into *France*, at his being there, and after his return many of the Nobility, and others that were powerful at Court, were watchful and solicitous to the *King* for some Secular imployment for him. The *King* had formerly both known and put a value upon his Company: and had also given him some hopes of a State-imployment; being always much pleas'd when Mr. *Donne* attended him, especially at his meals, where there were usually many deep discourses

of general Learning: and very often friendly disputes or debates
of Religion betwixt his Majesty and those Divines, whose places
required their attendance on him at those times: particularly
the Dean of the Chappel; who then was Bishop *Montague* (the
publisher of the learned and eloquent Works of his Majesty)
and the most reverend Doctor *Andrews,* the late learned Bishop
of *Winchester,* who then was the Kings Almoner.

About this time, there grew many disputes that concerned
the *Oath of Supremacy* and *Allegiance,* in which the King had
appeared, and engaged himself by his publick writings now
extant: and, his Majesty discoursing with Mr. *Donne,* concerning many of the reasons which are usually urged against the
taking of those Oaths; apprehended, such a validity and clearness in his stating the Questions, and his Answers to them,
that his Majesty commanded him to bestow some time in drawing the Arguments into a method,§ and then to write his Answers to them: and, having done that, not to send, but be his
own messenger and bring them to him. To this he presently
and diligently applied himself, and, within six weeks brought
them to him under his own handwriting, as they be now printed;
the Book bearing the name of *Pseudo-martyr,* printed *anno* 1610.

When the King had read and considered that Book, he perswaded Mr. *Donne* to enter into the Ministery; to which at that
time he was, and appeared very unwilling, apprehending it
(such was his mistaking modesty) to be too weighty for his
Abilities; and though his Majesty had promised him a favour,
and many persons of worth mediated with his Majesty for some
secular employment for him (to which his Education had apted
him) and particularly the Earl of *Somerset,* when in his greatest
height of favour; who being then at *Theobalds* with the King,
where one of the Clerks of the Council died that night, the Earl
posted a messenger for Mr. *Donne* to come to him immediately,
and at Mr. *Donne*'s coming, said, Mr. *Donne, To testifie the
reality of my Affection, and my purpose to prefer§ you, Stay in
this Garden till I go up to the King, and bring you word that you
are Clark of the Council: doubt not my doing this, for I know the
King loves you, and know the King will not deny me.* But the
King gave a positive denial to all requests, and having a discerning spirit, replied, *I know Mr.* Donne *is a learned man, has the*

abilities of a learned Divine; and will prove a powerful Preacher, and my desire is to prefer him that way, and in that way, I will deny you nothing for him. After that time, as he professeth,[7] *The King descended to a perswasion, almost to a solicitation of him to enter into sacred Orders:* which though he then denied not, yet he deferred it for almost three years. All which time he applied himself to an incessant study of Textual Divinity, and to the attainment of a greater perfection in the learned Languages, *Greek* and *Hebrew.*

In the first and most blessed times of Christianity, when the Clergy were look'd upon with reverence, and deserved it, when they overcame their opposers by high examples of Vertue, by a blessed Patience and long Suffering: those only were then judged worthy the Ministry, whose quiet and meek spirits did make them look upon that sacred calling with an humble adoration and fear to undertake it; which indeed requires such great degrees of *humility,* and *labour,* and *care,* that none but such were then thought worthy of that celestial dignity. And such only were then sought out, and solicited to undertake it. This I have mentioned because forwardness and inconsideration, could not in Mr. *Donne,* as in many others, be an argument of insufficiency or unfitness; for he had considered long, and had many strifes within himself concerning the strictness of life and competency of learning required in such as enter into sacred Orders; and doubtless, considering his own demerits, did humbly ask God with St. *Paul, Lord, who is sufficient for these things?* and, with meek *Moses, Lord, who am I?* And sure, if he had consulted with flesh and blood, he had not for these reasons put his hand to that holy plough. But, God who is able to prevail, wrestled with him, as the *Angel* did with *Jacob, and marked him;* mark'd him for his own; mark'd him with a blessing; a blessing of obedience to the motions of his blessed Spirit. And then, as he had formerly asked God with *Moses, Who am I?* So now being inspired with an apprehension of Gods particular mercy to him, in the Kings and other solicitations of him, he came to ask *King Davids* thankful question, *Lord, who am I, that thou art so mindful of me?* So mindful of me,

7 *In his Book of Devotions.

as to lead me for more then forty years through this wilderness
of the many temptations, and various turnings of a dangerous
life: so merciful to me, as to move the learned'st of Kings, to
descend to move me to serve at the Altar! so merciful to me,
as at last, to move my heart to imbrace this holy motion: thy
motions I will and do imbrace: And, I now say with the blessed
Virgin, *Be it with thy servant as seemeth best in thy sight:* and
so, *blessed Jesus,* I do take the cup of Salvation, and will call
upon thy Name, and will preach thy Gospel.

Such strifes as these St. *Austine*⁵ had, when St. *Ambrose*
indeavoured his conversion to Christianity; with which he confesseth, he acquainted his friend *Alipius.* Our learned Author
(a man fit to write after no mean Copy) did the like. And declaring his intentions to his dear friend Dr. *King* then *Bishop*
of *London,* a man famous in his generation, and no stranger to
Mr. *Donne*'s abilities, (for he had been Chaplain to the Lord
Chancellor, at the time of Mr. *Donne*'s being his Lordships
Secretary) That Reverend man did receive the news with much
gladness; and, after some expressions of joy, and a perswasion
to be constant in his pious purpose, he proceeded with all convenient speed to ordain him first *Deacon,* and then *Priest* not
long after.

Now the *English Church* had gain'd a second St. *Austine,* for,
I think, none was so like him before his Conversion: none so
like St. *Ambrose* after it: and if his youth had the infirmities
of the one, his age had the excellencies of the other; the learning
and holiness of both.

And now all his studies which had been occasionally diffused,
were all concentred in Divinity. Now he had a new calling, new
thoughts, and a new imployment for his wit and eloquence:
Now, all his earthly affections were changed into divine love;
and all the faculties of his own soul, were ingaged in the Conversion of others: In preaching the glad tidings of Remission to
repenting Sinners, and peace to each troubled soul. To these
he applied himself with all care and diligence: and now, such
a change was wrought in him, that he could say with *David,*
Oh how amiable are thy Tabernacles, O Lord God of Hosts!
Now he declared openly, *that when he required a temporal, God
gave him a spiritual blessing.* And that, *he was now gladder to*

be a door-keeper in the house of God, then he could be to injoy
the noblest of all temporal imployments.

Presently after he entred into his holy profession, the King
sent for him, and made him his Chaplain in Ordinary; and
promised to take a particular care for his preferment.

And though his long familiarity with Scholars, and persons
of greatest quality, was such as might have given some men
boldness enough to have preached to any eminent Auditory; yet,
his modesty in this imployment was such, that he could not be
perswaded to it, but went usually accompanied with some one
friend, to preach privately in some village, not far from *London:*
his first Sermon being preached at *Paddington.* This he did, till
His Majesty sent and appointed him a day to preach to him at
White-hall, and, though much were expected from him, both
by His Majesty and others, yet he was so happy (which few
are) as to satisfie and exceed their expectations: preaching the
Word so, as shewed his own heart was possest with those very
thoughts and joys that he laboured to distill into others: A
Preacher in earnest; weeping sometimes for his Auditory, sometimes with them: always preaching to himself, like an Angel
from a cloud, but in none; carrying some, as St. *Paul* was, to
Heaven in holy raptures, and inticing others by a sacred Art
and Courtship[§] to amend their lives; here picturing a vice so as
to make it ugly to those that practised it; and a vertue so, as to
make it be beloved even by those that lov'd it not; and all this
with a most particular grace and an unexpressible addition of
comeliness.

There may be some that may incline to think (such indeed
as have not heard him) that my affection to my Friend, hath
transported me to an immoderate Commendation of his Preaching. If this meets with any such, Let me intreat, though I will
omit many, yet that they will receive a double witness for what
I say; it being attested by a Gentleman of worth (Mr. *Chidley,* a
frequent hearer of his Sermons) in part of a funeral Elogie writ
by him on Dr. *Donne;* and is a known truth, though it be in
Verse.

———— *Each Altar had his fire*————
He kept his love, but not his object: wit,
He did not banish, but transplanted it;

Taught it both time and place, and brought it home
To Piety, which it doth best become.
For say, had ever pleasure such a dress?
Have you seen crimes so shap't, or loveliness
Such as his lips did clothe Religion in?
Had not reproof a beauty, passing sin?
Corrupted nature sorrowed that she stood
So near the danger of becoming good.
And, when he preach't she wish't her ears exempt
From Piety, that had such pow'r to tempt.
How did his sacred flattery beguile
Men to amend?——

More of this, and more witnesses might be brought, but I forbear and return.

That Summer, in the very same month in which he entred into sacred Orders, and was made the *Kings Chaplain,* His Majesty then going his Progress,[§] was intreated to receive an entertainment in the University of *Cambridge.* And Mr. *Donne* attending his Majesty at that time, his Majesty was pleased to recommend him to the University, to be made *Doctor* in *Divinity; Doctor Harsnet* (after Archbishop of *York*) was then *Vice-Chancellor,* who knowing him to be the Author of that learned Book the *Pseudo-Martyr,* required no other proof of his Abilities, but proposed it to the *University,* who presently assented, and exprest a gladness, that they had such an occasion to intitle him to be theirs.

His Abilities and Industry in his Profession were so eminent, and he so known, and so beloved by Persons of Quality, that within the first year of his entring into sacred Orders, he had fourteen Advowsons of several Benefices presented to him: But they were in the Countrey, and he could not leave his beloved *London,* to which place he had a natural inclination, having received both his Birth and Education in it, and, there contracted a friendship with many, whose conversation multiplied the joys of his life: But, an imployment that might affix him to that place would be welcome; for he needed it.

Immediately after his return from *Cambridge,* his wife died; leaving him a man of a narrow unsetled estate, and (having buried five) the careful[§] father of seven children then living, to whom he gave a voluntary assurance, never to bring them under the subjection of a step-mother; which promise he kept most faithfully, burying with his tears, all his earthly joys in his most dear and deserving wives grave; and betook himself to a most retired and solitary life.

In this retiredness, which was often from the sight of his dearest friends, he became *crucified to the world,* and all those vanities, those imaginary pleasures that are daily acted on that restless stage; and, they were as perfectly crucified to him. Nor is it hard to think (being passions may be both changed, and heightned by accidents) but that that abundant affection which once was betwixt him and her, who had long been the delight of his eyes, and the Companion of his youth; her, with whom he had divided so many pleasant sorrows, and contented fears, as Common-people are not capable of; not hard to think but that she, being now removed by death, a commeasurable grief took as full a possession of him as joy had done; and so indeed it did: for, now his very soul was elemented of nothing but sadness; now, grief took so full a possession of his heart, as to leave no place for joy: If it did? It was a joy to be alone, where like a *Pelican in the wilderness,* he might bemoan himself without witness or restraint, and, pour forth his passions like *Job* in the days of his affliction, *Oh that I might have the desire of my heart! Oh that God would grant the thing that I long for!* For then, *as the grave is become her house,* so I would hasten to make it mine also; *that we two might there make our beds together in the dark.* Thus as the *Israelites* sate mourning by the rivers of *Babylon,* when they remembred *Sion;* so he gave some ease to his oppressed heart by thus venting his sorrows: Thus he began the day, and ended the night; ended the restless night and began the weary day in *Lamentations.* And, thus he continued till a consideration of his new ingagements to God, and St. *Pauls Wo is me, if I preach not the Gospel:* disper'st those sad clouds that had then benighted his hopes, and now forc'd him to behold the light.

His first motion from his house was to preach, where his beloved wife lay buried (in St. *Clements* Church, near Temple-Bar *London*) and his Text was a part of the Prophet *Jeremy's* Lamentation: *Lo, I am the man that have seen affliction.*

And indeed, his very words and looks testified him to be truly such a man; and they, with the addition of his sighs and tears, exprest in his Sermon, did so work upon the affections of his hearers, as melted and moulded them into a companionable sadness; and so they left the Congregation; but then their houses presented them with objects of diversion: and his, presented him with nothing but fresh objects of sorrow, in beholding many helpless children, a narrow fortune, and a consideration of the many cares and casualties that attend their education.

In this time of sadness he was importuned by the grave Benchers of *Lincolns Inne,* who were once the Companions and Friends of his youth, to accept of their Lecture,§ which by reason of Dr. *Gatakers* removal from thence was then void: of which he accepted; being most glad to renew his intermitted friendship with those whom he so much loved; and, where he had been a *Saul,* though not to persecute Christianity, or to deride it, yet in his irregular youth to neglect the visible practice of it: there to become a *Paul,* and preach salvation to his beloved brethren.

And now his life was as a *Shining light* among his old friends: now he gave an ocular testimony of the strictness and regularity of it; now he might say as St. *Paul* adviseth his *Corinthians, Be ye followers of me, as I follow Christ, and walk as ye have me for an example;* not the example of a busie-body; but, of a contemplative, a harmless, an humble and an holy life and conversation.

The love of that noble society was expressed to him many ways: for, besides fair lodgings that were set apart and newly furnished for him, with all necessaries, other courtesies were also daily added; indeed, so many, and so freely, as if they meant their gratitude should exceed his merits; and, in this love-strife of desert and liberality, they continued for the space of two years, he preaching faithfully and constantly to them, and they liberally requiting him. About which time the Emperour of *Germany* died, and the Palsgrave, who had lately married the Lady *Elizabeth* the Kings only daughter, was elected and crowned King of *Bohemia,* the unhappy beginning of many miseries in that Nation.

King *James*, whose Motto (*Beati pacifici*[8]) did truly speak the very thoughts of his heart, endeavoured first to prevent, and after to compose the discords of that discomposed§ State; and amongst other his endeavours did then send the Lord *Hay* Earl of *Doncaster* his Ambassadour to those unsetled Princes; and by a special command from his Majesty Dr. *Donne* was appointed to assist and attend that employment to the Princes of the Union: for which the Earl was most glad, who had always put a great value on him, and taken a great pleasure in his conversation and discourse: and his friends of *Lincolns Inne* were as glad; for, they feared that his immoderate study, and sadness for his wives death, would, as *Jacob* said, *make his days few,* and respecting his bodily health, *evil* too: and of this there were many visible signs.

At his going, he left his friends of *Lincolns Inne*, and they him with many reluctations: for, though he could not say as S. *Paul* to his *Ephesians, Behold you to whom I have preached the Kingdom of God, shall from henceforth see my face no more;* yet, he believing himself to be in a Consumption, questioned, and they feared it: all concluding that his troubled mind, with the help of his unintermitted studies, hastened the decays of his weak body: But God who is the God of all wisdom and goodness, turn'd it to the best; for this employment (to say nothing of the event§ of it) did not only divert him from those too serious studies, and sad thoughts; but seemed to give him a new life by a true occasion of joy, to be an eye-witness of the health of his most dear and most honoured Mistress the Queen of *Bohemia,* in a forraign Nation; and, to be a witness of that gladness which she expressed to see him: Who, having formerly known him a Courtier, was much joyed to see him in a Canonical habit, and more glad to be an ear-witness of his excellent and powerful Preaching.

About fourteen months after his departure out of *England,* he returned to his friends of *Lincolns-Inne* with his sorrows moderated, and his health improved; and there betook himself to his constant course of Preaching.

About a year after his return out of *Germany,* Dr. *Cary* was made Bishop of *Exeter,* and by his removal the Deanry of St.

8 Blessed are the peacemakers.

Pauls being vacant, the King sent to Dr. *Donne,* and appointed him to attend him at Dinner the next day. When his Majesty was sate down, before he had eat any meat,§ he said after his pleasant manner, Dr. *Donne, I have invited you to Dinner; and, though you sit not down with me, yet I will carve to you of a dish that I know you love well; for knowing you love* London, *I do therefore make you Dean of* Pauls; *and when I have dined, then do you take your beloved dish home to your study; say grace there to your self, and much good may it do you.*

Immediately after he came to his Deanry, he employed workmen to repair and beautifie the Chapel; suffering,§ as holy *David* once vowed, *his eyes and temples to take no rest, till he had first beautified the house of God.*

The next quarter following, when his Father-in-law Sir *George Moor* (whom Time had made a lover and admirer of him) came to pay to him the conditioned§ sum of twenty pounds; he refused to receive it, and said (as good *Jacob* did, when he heard his beloved son *Joseph* was alive, *It is enough*) You have been kind to me and mine: I know your present condition is such as not to abound: and I hope mine is or will be such as not to need it: I will therefore receive no more from you upon that contract; and in testimony of it freely gave him up his bond.

Immediately after his admission into his Deanry, the Vicarage of St. *Dunstan* in the West, *London,* fell to him by the death of Dr. *White,* the Advowson of it having been given to him long before by his honourable friend, *Richard* Earl of *Dorset,* then the Patron, and confirmed by his brother the late deceased *Edward,* both of them men of much honour.

By these and another Ecclesiastical endowment which fell to him about the same time, given to him formerly by the Earl of *Kent,* he was enabled to become charitable to the poor, and kind to his friends, and to make such provision for his children, that they were not left scandalous,§ as relating to their or his Profession and Quality.§

The next *Parliament,* which was within that present year, he was chosen *Prolocutor* to the *Convocation;* and about that time was appointed by his Majesty, his most gracious Master, to preach very many occasional Sermons, as at St. *Paul's* Cross, and other places. All which employments he performed to the admiration of the Representative Body of the whole Clergy of this Nation.

He was once, and but once, clouded with the Kings displeasure; and, it was about this time; which was occasioned by some malicious whisperer, who had told his Majesty that Dr. *Donne* had put on the general humor of the Pulpits, and was become busie in insinuating a fear of the Kings inclining to *Popery*, and a dislike of his Government: and particularly, for the Kings then turning the Evening Lectures into *Catechising*, and expounding the *Prayer* of our *Lord*, and of the *Belief*, and *Commandments*. His Majesty was the more inclineable to believe this, for that a Person of Nobility and great note, betwixt whom and Dr. *Donne*, there had been a great friendship, was at this very time discarded the Court (I shall forbear his name, unless I had a fairer occasion) and justly committed to prison; which begot many rumors in the common people, who in this Nation think they are not wise, unless they be busie about what they understand not: and especially about Religion.

The King received this news with so much discontent and restlesness, that he would not suffer the Sun to set and leave him under this doubt; but sent for Dr. *Donne*, and required his answer to the Accusation; which was so clear and satisfactory, that the King said *he was right glad he rested no longer under the suspicion.* When the King had said this, Doctor *Donne* kneeled down and thanked his Majesty, and protested his answer was faithful and free from all collusion, and therefore *desired that he might not rise, till, as in like cases he always had from God, so he might have from his Majesty, some assurance that he stood clear and fair in his opinion.* At which the King raised him from his knees with his own *hands,* and *protested he believ'd him: and that he knew he was an honest man, and doubted not but that he loved him truly.* And, having thus dismissed him, he called some Lords of his Council into his Chamber, and said with much earnestness, *My Doctor is an honest man: and my Lords, I was never better satisfied with an answer then he hath now made me: and I always rejoice when I think that by my means he became a Divine.*

He was made Dean the fiftieth year of his age; and in his fifty fourth year, a dangerous sickness seized him, which inclined him to a Consumption. But God, as *Job* thankfully acknowledged, *preserved his spirit,* and kept his intellectuals as clear and perfect, as when that sickness first seized his body: but it continued long and threatned him with death; which he dreaded not.

In this distemper of body, his dear friend Doctor *Henry King* (then chief Residenciary of that Church, and late Bishop of *Chichester*) a man generally known by the Clergy of this Nation, and as generally noted for his obliging nature, visited him daily; and observing that his sickness rendred his recovery doubtful, he chose a seasonable time to speak to him, to this purpose.

'Mr. *Dean,* I am by your favour no stranger to your temporal 'estate, and you are no stranger to the Offer lately made us, for 'the renewing a Lease of the best Prebends§ Corps belonging to 'our Church; and you know, 'twas denied, for that our Tenant 'being very rich, offered to fine§ at so low a rate as held not pro- 'portion with his advantages: but I will either raise him to an 'higher sum, or procure that the other Residenciaries shall join to 'accept of what was offered: one of these I can and will by your 'favour do without delay, and without any trouble either to your 'body or mind; I beseech you to accept of my offer, for I know it 'will be a considerable addition to your present estate, which I 'know needs it.

To this, after a short pause, and raising himself upon his bed, he made this reply.

'My most dear friend, I most humbly thank you for your many 'favours, and this in particular: But, in my present condition, I 'shall not accept of your proposal; for doubtless there is such a 'Sin as *Sacriledge;* if there were not, it could not have a name in 'Scripture: And the Primitive Clergy were watchful against all 'appearances of that evil; and indeed then all Christians lookt 'upon it with horror and detestation: Judging it to be even an '*open defiance of the Power and Providence of Almighty God,* '*and a sad presage of a declining Religion.* But in stead of such 'Christians, who had selected times set apart to fast and pray to 'God, for a pious Clergy which they then did obey; Our times 'abound with men that are busie and litigious about trifles and 'Church-Ceremonies; and yet so far from scrupling *Sacriledge,* 'that they make not so much as a *quære* what it is: But, I thank 'God I have; and, dare not now upon my sick-bed, when Almighty

'God hath made me useless to the service of the Church, make
'any advantages out of it. But, if he shall again restore me to such
'a degree of health, as again to serve at his *Altar;* I shall then
'gladly take the reward which the bountiful Benefactors of this
'Church have designed me; for God knows my Children and Re-
'lations will need it. In which number my Mother (whose Credu-
'lity and Charity has contracted a very plentiful, to a very nar-
'row estate) must not be forgotten: But Doctor *King,* if I recover
'not, that little worldly estate that I shall leave behind me (that
'very little, when divided into eight parts) must, if you deny me
'not so Charitable a favour, fall into your hands as my most *faith-
'ful friend* and Executor; of whose Care and Justice, I make no
'more doubt then of Gods blessing on that which I have con-
'scientiously collected for them; but it shall not be augmented on
'my sick-bed; and, this I declare to be my unalterable resolution.

The reply to this was only a promise to observe his request.

Within a few days his distempers abated; and as his strength
increased, so did his thankfulness to Almighty God, testified in
his most excellent Book of *Devotions,* which he published at his
Recovery. In which the Reader may see, the most secret thoughts
that then possess his Soul, Paraphrased and made publick: a
book, that may not unfitly be called a *Sacred picture of Spiritual
Extasies,* occasioned and appliable to the emergencies of that
sickness; which book, being a composition of *Meditations, Dis-
quisitions* and *Prayers,* he writ on his sick-bed; herein imitating
the Holy Patriarchs, who were wont to build their Altars in that
place, where they had received their blessings.

This sickness brought him so near to the gates of death, and
he saw the grave so ready to devour him, that he would often say,
his recovery was supernatural: But that God that then restored
his health continued it to him, till the fifty-ninth year of his life.
And then in *August* 1630. being with his eldest Daughter Mrs.
Harvy at Abury hatch in *Essex,* he there fell into a Fever, which
with the help of his constant infirmity (vapours from the spleen)
hastened him into so visible a Consumption,§ that his beholders
might say, as St. *Paul* of himself, *He dyes daily;* and he might say
with *Job, My welfare passeth away as a cloud, the days of my
affliction have taken hold of me, and weary nights are appointed
for me.*

Reader, This sickness continued long, not only weakning but
wearying him so much, that my desire is, he may now take some
rest: and that before I speak of his death, thou wilt not think it an
impertinent digression to look back with me, upon some observa-
tions of his life, which, whilest a gentle slumber gives rest to his
spirits, may, I hope, not unfitly exercise thy consideration.

His marriage was the remarkable error of his life; an error
which though he had a wit able and very apt to maintain Paradoxes, yet, he was very far from justifying it: and though his
wives Competent years, and other reasons might be justly urged
to moderate severe Censures; yet, he would occasionally condemn himself for it: and doubtless it had been attended with an
heavy Repentance, if God had not blest them with so mutual
and cordial affections, as in the midst of their sufferings made
their bread of sorrow taste more pleasantly then the banquets of
dull and low-spirited people.

The Recreations of his youth were *Poetry,* in which he was so
happy, as if nature and all her varieties had been made only to
exercise his sharp wit, and high fancy; and in those pieces which
were facetiously[§] Composed and carelesly scattered (most of
them being written before the twentieth year of his age) it may
appear by his choice Metaphors, that both *Nature* and all the
Arts joyned to assist him with their utmost skill.

It is a truth, that in his penitential years, viewing some of
those pieces that had been loosely (God knows too loosely) scattered in his youth, he wish't they had been abortive, or, so short
liv'd that his own eyes had witnessed their funerals: But, though
he was no friend to them, he was not so fallen out with heavenly
Poetry as to forsake that: no not in his declining age; witnessed
then by many Divine Sonnets, and other high, holy, and harmonious Composures. Yea, even on his former sick-bed he wrote
this heavenly *Hymn,* expressing the great joy that then possest
his soul in the Assurance of Gods favour to him when he Composed it.

An Hymn to God the Father.

Wilt thou forgive that sin where I begun,
Which was my sin, though it were done before;

Wilt thou forgive that sin through which I run,
    And do run still though still I do deplore?
When thou hast done, thou hast not done,
        For I have more.

Wilt thou forgive that sin, which I have won
    Others to sin, and made my sin their door?
Wilt thou forgive that sin which I did shun
    A year or two, but wallowed in a score?
When thou hast done, thou hast not done,
        For I have more.

I have a sin of fear, that when I've spun
    My last thread, I shall perish on the shore:
But swear by thy self, that at my death thy Son
    Shall shine as he shines now, and heretofore;
And having done that, thou hast done,
        I fear no more.

I have the rather mentioned this *Hymn,* for that he caus'd it to be set to a most grave and solemn Tune, and to be often sung to the *Organ* by the *Choristers* of St. *Pauls* Church, in his own hearing; especially at the Evening Service, and at his return from his Customary Devotions in that place, did occasionally say to a friend, *The words of this* Hymn *have restored to me the same thoughts of joy that possest my Soul in my sickness when I composed it. And, O the power of Church-musick! that Harmony added to this Hymn has raised the Affections of my heart, and quickned my graces of zeal and gratitude;* and I observe, *that I always return from paying this publick duty of* Prayer *and* Praise *to God, with an unexpressible tranquillity of mind,* and a willingness *to leave the world.*

After this manner did the Disciples of our Saviour, and the best of Christians in those Ages of the Church nearest to his time, offer their praises to Almighty God. And the reader of St. *Augustines* life may there find, that towards his dissolution he wept abundantly, that the enemies of Christianity had broke in upon them, and prophaned and ruined their *Sanctuaries;* and, because their *Publick Hymns* and Lauds were lost out of their Churches. And after this manner have many devout Souls lifted up their

hands and offered acceptable Sacrifices unto Almighty God where
Dr. *Donne* offered his, and now lyes buried.

> But now, oh Lord, how is that place
> become desolate. } 1656.

Before I proceed further, I think fit to inform the Reader, that
not long before his death he caused to be drawn a figure of the
Body of Christ extended upon an Anchor, like those which Painters draw when they would present us with the picture of Christ
crucified on the Cross: his, varying no otherwise then to affix him
not to a Cross but to an Anchor (the Emblem of hope) this he
caused to be drawn in little, and then many of those figures thus
drawn to be ingraven very small in *Helitropian* Stones, and set
in gold, and of these he sent to many of his dearest friends to be
used as *Seals,* or *Rings,* and kept as memorials of him, and of his
affection to them.

His dear friends and benefactors, Sir *Henry Goodier,* and Sir
Robert Drewry, could not be of that number; Nor could the
Lady *Magdalen Herbert,* the mother of *George Herbert,* for they
had put off mortality, and taken possession of the grave before
him: But Sir *Henry Wotton,* and Dr. *Hall* the then late deceased
Bishop of *Norwich* were; and, so were Dr. *Duppa,* Bishop of
Salisbury, and Dr. *Henry King* Bishop of *Chichester* (lately deceased) men, in whom there was such a Commixture of general
Learning, of natural *Eloquence,* and Christian *Humility,* that
they deserve a Commemoration by a pen equal to their own,
which none have exceeded.

And in this enumeration of his friends, though many must be
omitted, yet that man of primitive piety, Mr. *George Herbert* may
not; I mean that *George Herbert,* who was the Author of the
Temple, or *Sacred Poems and Ejaculations.* A Book, in which by
declaring his own spiritual Conflicts, he hath Comforted and
raised many a dejected and discomposed Soul, and charmed
them into sweet and quiet thoughts: A Book, by the frequent
reading whereof, and the assistance of that Spirit that seemed to
inspire the Author, the Reader may attain habits of *Peace* and
Piety, and all the gifts of the *Holy Ghost* and *Heaven:* and may
by still reading, still keep those sacred fires burning upon the
Altar of so pure a heart, as shall free it from the anxieties of this

world, and keep it fixt upon things that are above; betwixt this *George Herbert* and Dr. *Donne* there was a long and dear friendship, made up by such a Sympathy of inclinations, that they coveted and joyed to be in each others Company; and this happy friendship, was still maintained by many sacred indearments; of which, that which followeth may be some Testimony.

To Mr. *George Herbert;* sent him with one of my Seals of the *Anchor* and *Christ.* (A sheaf of Snakes used heretofore to be my Seal, which is the Crest of our poor Family.)

> *Qui prius assuetus serpentum fasce tabellas*
> *Signare, hæc nostræ Symbola parva domus*
> *Adscitus domui domini.——*9
>
> *Adopted in Gods family, and so*
> *My old Coat lost into new Arms I go.*
> *The* Cross *my seal in Baptism spread below,*
> *Does by that form into an Anchor grow.*
> *Crosses grow Anchors, bear as thou should'st do*
> *Thy Cross, and that Cross grows an Anchor too.*
> *But he that makes our Crosses Anchors thus,*
> *Is* Christ; *who there is crucified for us.*
> *Yet with this I may my first Serpents hold:*
> *(God gives new blessings, and yet leaves the old)*
> *The Serpent may as wise my pattern be;*
> *My poison, as he feeds on dust, that's me.*
> *And, as he rounds the earth to murder, sure*
> *He is my death; but on the Cross my cure.*
> *Crucifie nature then; and then implore*
> *All grace from him, crucify'd there before.*
> *When all is* Cross, *and that* Cross *Anchor grown,*
> *This seals a Catechism, not a seal alone.*
> *Under that little seal great gifts I send,*
> *Both works and prayers, pawns & fruits of a friend;*
> *Oh may that Saint that rides on our great Seal,*
> *To you that bear his name large bounty deal.*

John Donne.

9 Walton quotes the first two and a half lines of Donne's Latin poem and the verse translation which appeared with it in Donne's *Poems*, 1650. Perhaps because he was misled by the form in which the poem and its translation were printed, he made a prose sentence of the first two lines of the translation, interpolating the words "which is,' and placed his version in the parenthesis which precedes the Latin lines.

In Sacram Anchoram Piscatoris[1]
GEORGE HERBERT.

Quod Crux nequibat fixa clavique additi,
Tenere Christum scilicet ne ascenderet
Tuive Christum——[2]

Although the Cross could not Christ here detain,
When nail'd unto't, but he ascends again:
Nor yet thy eloquence here keep him still,
But only whilest thou speak'st; this Anchor will:
Nor canst thou be content, unless thou to
This certain Anchor add a seal, and so
The water *and the* earth, *both unto thee*
Do owe the Symbole of their certainty.
Let the world reel, we and all ours stand sure,
This Holy Cable's from all storms secure.

George Herbert.

I return to tell the Reader, that besides these verses to his dear
Mr. *Herbert,* and that *Hymn* that I mentioned to be sung in the
Quire of St. *Pauls Church;* he did also shorten and beguile many
sad hours by composing other sacred Ditties; and he writ an
Hymn on his death-bed, which bears this title.

An Hymn to God, my God, in my sickness,
March 23. 1630.

Since I am coming to that holy room,
Where, with thy Quire of Saints for evermore
I shall be made thy musique, as I come
I tune my Instrument here at the dore,
And, what I must do then, think here before.

Since my Physitians by their loves are grown
Cosmographers! and I their map, who lye
Flat on this bed——

---

1 On the Holy Anchor of a Fisher (of Souls).
2 Translated immediately below.

So, in his purple wrapt, receive me, Lord!
By these, his thorns, *give me his other* Crown:
And, as to other souls I preach'd thy Word,
Be this my Text: my Sermon to mine own.
That, he may raise; therefore, the Lord throws down.

If these fall under the censure of a soul, whose too much mixture with earth makes it unfit to judge of these high raptures and illuminations; let him know that many holy and devout men have thought the Soul of *Prudentius* to be most refined, when not many days before his death *he charged it to present his God each morning and evening with a new and spiritual song;* justified, by the example of King *David* and the good King *Hezekias,* who upon the renovation of his years paid his thankful vows to Almighty God in a *royal Hymn,* which he concludes in these words, *The Lord was ready to save, therefore I will sing my songs to the stringed instruments all the days of my life in the temple of my God.*

The latter part of his life may be said to be a continued study; for as he usually preached once a week, if not oftner, so after his Sermon he never gave his eyes rest, till he had chosen out a new Text, and that night cast his Sermon into a form, and his Text into divisions; and the next day betook himself to consult the Fathers, and so commit his meditations to his memory, which was excellent. But upon Saturday he usually gave himself and his mind a rest from the weary burthen of his weeks meditations, and usually spent that day in visitation of friends, or some other diversions of his thoughts; and would say, that *he gave both his body and mind that refreshment, that he might be enabled to do the work of the day following, not faintly, but with courage and chearfulness.*

Nor was his age only so industrious, but in the most unsetled days of his youth, his bed was not able to detain him beyond the hour of four in a morning: and it was no common business that drew him out of his chamber till past ten. All which time was employed in study; though he took great liberty after it; and if this seem strange, it may gain a belief by the visible fruits of his labours: some of which remain as testimonies of what is here written: for he left the resultance of 1400. Authors, most of them abridged and analysed with his own hand; he left also sixscore of his Sermons, all written with his own hand; also an exact and laborious Treatise concerning *Self-murther,* called *Biathanatos;* wherein all the Laws violated by that Act are diligently surveyed and judiciously censured: a Treatise written in his younger days, which alone might declare him then not only perfect in the *Civil* and *Canon Law,* but in many other such studies and arguments, as enter not into the consideration of many that labour to be thought great Clerks, and pretend to know all things.

Nor were these only found in his study, but all businesses that past of any publick consequence, either in this, or any of our neighbour-nations, he abbreviated either in Latine, or in the Language of that Nation, and kept them by him for useful memorials. So he did the Copies of divers Letters and cases of Conscience that had concerned his friends, with his observations and solutions of them; and, divers other businesses of importance; all particularly and methodically digested by himself.

He did prepare to leave the world before life left him; making his Will when no faculty of his soul was damp'd or made defective by pain or sickness, or he surprized by a sudden apprehension of death: but it was made with mature deliberation, expressing himself an impartial father by making his childrens portions equal; and a lover of his friends, whom he remembred with Legacies fitly and discreetly chosen and bequeathed. I cannot forbear a nomination of some of them; for, methinks they be persons that seem to challenge a recordation in this place; as namely, to his Brother-in-law Sir *Thomas Grimes,* he gave that striking Clock which he had long worn in his pocket—— to his dear friend and Executor Dr. *King* (late Bishop of *Chichester*) that model of gold of the Synod of *Dort,* with which the States presented him at his last being at the *Hague*—— and the two Pictures of *Padre Paulo* and *Fulgentio,* men of his acquaintance when he travelled *Italy,* and of great note in that Nation for their remarkable learning.—— To his antient friend Dr. *Brook* (that married him) Master of *Trinity Colledge* in *Cambridge,* he gave the Picture of the blessed Virgin and *Joseph.*—— To Dr. *Winniff* (who succeeded him in the Deanry) he gave a Picture called the *Sceleton.*—— To the succeeding Dean, who was not then known, he gave many necessaries of worth, and useful for his house; and also several Pictures and Ornaments for the

Chappel, with a desire that they might be registered, and remain as a Legacy to his Successors.—— To the Earls of *Dorset* and *Carlile*, he gave several Pictures; and so he did to many other friends; Legacies, given rather to express his affection, than to make any addition to their Estates: but unto the Poor he was full of Charity, and unto many others, who by his constant and long continued bounty might intitle themselves to be his Almspeople; for all these, he made provision; and so largely, as having then six children living, might to some appear more than proportionable to his Estate. I forbear to mention any more, lest the Reader may think I trespass upon his patience: but I will beg his favour to present him with the beginning and end of his Will.

In the Name of the blessed and glorious Trinity, Amen. I John Donne, *by the mercy of* Christ Jesus, *and by the calling of the Church of* England Priest, *being at this time in good health and perfect understanding (praised be God therefore) do hereby make my last Will and Testament in manner and form following:*

First, I give my gracious God an intire sacrifice of body and soul, with my most humble thanks for that assurance which his blessed Spirit imprints in me now of the salvation of the one, and the Resurrection of the other; and for that constant and chearful resolution which the same Spirit hath establisht in me to live and dye in the Religion now professed in the Church of England. *In expectation of that Resurrection, I desire my body may be buried (in the most private manner that may be) in that place of* St. Pauls *Church* London, *that the now Residentiaries have at my request designed for that purpose,* &c.—— *And this my last Will and Testament, made in the fear of God (whose mercy I humbly beg, and constantly rely upon in Jesus Christ) and in perfect love and charity with all the world (whose pardon I ask, from the lowest of my servants, to the highest of my Superiors) written all with my own hand, and my name subscribed to every page, of which there are five in number.*

Sealed *Decemb.* 13. 1630.

Nor was this blessed sacrifice of Charity expressed only at his death, but in his life also, by a chearful and frequent visitation of any friend whose mind was dejected, or his fortune necessitous; he was inquisitive after the wants of Prisoners, and redeemed many from thence that lay for their Fees or small Debts; he was a continual Giver to poor Scholars, both of this and forraign Nations. Besides what he gave with his own hand, he usually sent a Servant, or a discreet and trusty Friend, to distribute his Charity to all the Prisons in *London* at all the Festival times of the year, especially at the *Birth* and *Resurrection* of our Saviour. He gave an hundred pounds at one time to an old Friend, whom he had known live plentifully, and by a too liberal heart and carelesness, became decayed in his Estate: and, when the receiving of it was denied, by the Gentlemans saying, *He wanted not;* for the Reader may note, that as there be some spirits so generous as to labour to conceal, and endure a sad poverty, rather than expose themselves to those blushes that attend the confession of it; so there be others to whom Nature and Grace have afforded such sweet and compassionate souls, as to pity and prevent the Distresses of Mankind; which I have mentioned because of Dr. *Donne's* Reply, whose Answer was, *I know you want not what will sustain nature, for a little will do that; but my desire is, that you who in the days of your plenty have cheared and raised the hearts of so many of your dejected friends, would now receive this from me, and use it as a cordial for the chearing of your own:* and upon these terms it was received. He was an happy reconciler of many differences in the Families of his Friends, and Kindred, (which he never undertook faintly; for such undertakings have usually faint effects) and they had such a faith in his judgment and impartiality, that he never advised them to any thing in vain. He was even to her death a most dutiful Son to his Mother, careful to provide for her supportation, of which she had been destitute, but that God raised him up to prevent her necessities; who having sucked in the Religion of the *Roman Church* with her Mothers Milk, spent her Estate in forraign Countreys, to enjoy a liberty in it, and died in his house but three Moneths before him.

And to the end it may appear how just a Steward he was of his Lord and Masters Revenue, I have thought fit to let the Reader know, that after his entrance into his Deanery, as he numbered his years, he (at the foot of a private account to which God and his Angels were only witnesses with him) computed first his Revenue, then what was given to the Poor, and other Pious Uses: and lastly, what rested for him and his; and, having done that, he then blest each years poor remainder with a thankful Prayer; which, for that they discover a more than common Devotion, the Reader shall partake some of them in his own words:

So all is that remains }
this year }

Deo Opt. Max. benigno
Largitori, à me, & ab iis
Quibus hæc à me reservantur,
Gloria & gratia in æternum.
Amen.

So, that this year, God hath }
blessed me and mine with }

Multiplicatæ sunt super
Nos misericordiæ tuæ
Domine.————

Da Domine, ut quæ ex immensâ
Bonitate tuâ nobis elargiri
Dignatus sis, in quorumcunque
Manus devenerint, in tuam
Semper cedant gloriam.
Amen.

In fine horum sex Annorum manet————

Quid habeo quod non accepi à Domino?
Largitur etiam ut quæ largitus est
Sua iterum fiant, bono eorum usu; ut
Quemadmodum nec officiis huius mundi,
Nec loci in quo me posuit; dignitati, nec
Servis, nec egenis, in toto huius anni
Curriculo mihi conscius sum me defuisse;
Ita & liberi, quibus quæ supersunt,

Supersunt, grato animo ea accipiant,
Et beneficum authorem recognoscant.

Amen.[3]

But I return from my long Digression.

We left the Author sick in *Essex,* where he was forced to spend much of that Winter, by reason of his disability to remove from that place: And having never for almost twenty years omitted his personal attendance on His Majesty in that month in which he was to attend and preach to him; nor, having ever been left out of the Roll and number of Lent-Preachers, and there being then (in *January* 1630.) a report brought to *London,* or raised there, that Dr. *Donne* was dead: That report gave him occasion to write this following Letter to a dear friend.

Sir,

'This advantage you and my other friends have by my frequent 'Fevers, that I am so much the oftner at the gates of Heaven; 'and this advantage by the solitude and close imprisonment that 'they reduce me to after, that I am so much the oftner at my 'prayers, in which I shall never leave out your happiness; and 'I doubt not among his other blessings, God will add some one to 'you for my prayers. A man would almost be content to dye (if 'there were no other benefit in death) to hear of so much sorrow, 'and so much good testimony from good men as I (God be blessed 'for it) did upon the report of my death; yet I perceive it went 'not through all; for, one writ to me that some (and he said of 'my friends) conceived I was not so ill as I pretended, but with-'drew my self to live at ease, discharged of preaching. It is an un-'friendly, and God knows an ill-grounded interpretation; for I

---

[3] To God the Best and Greatest, the benevolent Giver, from me, and from those for whom these things are set aside by me, be glory and grace forever. Amen. . . . Thy mercies are multiplied upon us, O Lord.—Grant, Lord, that the things which Thou hast deigned to bestow upon us out of boundless kindness, into the hands of whomever they may come, may always be used to Thy glory. Amen. . . . At the end of these six years there remains—What do I have which I have not received from the Lord? He also bestows the things he does bestow so that they may become his own again, through good use of them. As I am not conscious of having failed in anything during the whole course of this year in the services of this world or in the dignity of the position in which He has placed me, or in my obligations to my servants or to the needy; so let my children, to whom what is left remains, receive it gratefully and acknowledge the beneficent Giver. Amen.

'have always been sorrier when I could not preach, than any
'could be they could not hear me. It hath been my desire, and
'God may be pleased to grant it, that I might dye in the Pulpit; if
'not that, yet, that I might take my death in the Pulpit, that is,
'dye the sooner by occasion of those labours. Sir, I hope to see
'you presently after *Candlemas*, about which time will fall my
'*Lent-Sermon at Court*, except my *Lord Chamberlain* believe me
'to be dead, and so leave me out of the Roll; but as long as I live,
'and am not speechless, I would not willingly decline that service.
'I have better leisure to write, than you to read; yet I would not
'willingly oppress you with too much Letter. God so bless you
'and your Son as I wish, to

> *Your poor friend and servant*
> *in Christ Jesus,*
> J. Donne.

Before that month ended, he was appointed to preach upon his
old constant day, the first *Friday* in *Lent;* he had notice of it, and
had in his sickness so prepared for that imployment, that as he
had long thirsted for it: so he resolved his weakness should not
hinder his journey; he came therefore to *London,* some few days
before his appointed day of preaching. At his coming thither,
many of his friends (who with sorrow saw his sickness had left
him but so much flesh as did only cover his bones) doubted his
strength to perform that task; and, did therefore disswade him
from undertaking it, assuring him however, it was like to shorten
his life; but, he passionately denied their requests; saying, *he
would not doubt that that God who in so many weaknesses had
assisted him with an unexpected strength, would now withdraw
it in his last employment; professing an holy ambition to perform that sacred work.* And, when to the amazement of some
beholders he appeared in the Pulpit, many of them thought he
presented himself not to preach mortification by a living voice:
but, mortality by a decayed body and a dying face. And doubtless, many did secretly ask that question in *Ezekiel;*[4] *Do these
bones live? or, can that soul organize that tongue, to speak so
long time as the sand in that glass will move towards its centre,
and measure out an hour of this dying mans unspent life?* Doubt-

4 *Ezek. 37. 3.

less it cannot; and yet, after some faint pauses in his zealous prayer, his strong desires enabled his weak body to discharge his memory of his preconceived meditations, which were of dying: the Text being, *To God the Lord belong the issues from death.* Many that then saw his tears, and heard his faint and hollow voice, professing they thought the Text prophetically chosen, and that Dr. Donne *had preach't his own Funeral Sermon.*

Being full of joy that God had enabled him to perform this desired duty, he hastened to his house; out of which he never moved, till like St. *Stephen, he was carried by devout men to his Grave.*

The next day after his Sermon, his strength being much wasted, and his spirits so spent, as indisposed him to business, or to talk: A friend that had often been a witness of his free and facetious discourse, asked him, *Why are you sad?* To whom he replied with a coutenance so full of chearful gravity, as gave testimony of an inward tranquillity of mind, and of a soul willing to take a farewell of this world; And said,

'I am not sad, but most of the night past I have entertained 'my self with many thoughts of several friends that have left me 'here, *and are gone to that place from which they shall not re-*'turn; And, that within a few days *I also shall go hence, and be* 'no more seen. And, my preparation for this change is become my 'nightly meditation upon my bed, which my infirmities have now 'made restless to me. But, at this present time, I was in a serious 'contemplation of the providence and goodness of God to me: to 'me *who am less than the least of his mercies;* and looking back 'upon my life past, I now plainly see it was his hand that pre-'vented me from all temporal employment; and, that it was his 'Will I should never settle nor thrive till I entred into the Minis-'try; in which, I have now liv'd almost twenty years (I hope to his 'glory) and by which I most humbly thank him, I have been en-'abled to requite most of those friends which shewed me kind-'ness when my fortune was very low, as God knows it was: and '(as it hath occasioned the expression of my gratitude) I thank 'God most of them have stood in need of my requital. I have liv'd 'to be useful and comfortable to my good Father-in-law Sir *George* '*Moore,* whose patience God hath been pleased to exercise with

'many temporal Crosses; I have maintained my own Mother,
'whom it hath pleased God after a plentiful fortune in her
'younger days, to bring to a great decay in her very old age. I
'have quieted the Consciences of many that have groaned under
'the burthen of a wounded spirit, whose prayers I hope are avail-
'able for me: I cannot plead innocency of life, especially of my
'youth: But, I am to be judged by a merciful God, *who is not will-*
'*ing to see what I have done amiss.* And, though of my self I have
'nothing to present to him but sins and misery; yet, I know he
'looks not upon me now as I am of my self, but as I am in my
'Saviour, and hath given me even at this present time some testi-
'monies by his Holy Spirit, that I am of the number of his Elect:
'*I am therefore full of unexpressible joy, and shall dye in peace.*

I must here look so far back, as to tell the Reader, that at his
first return out of *Essex* to preach his last Sermon, his old Friend
and Physitian, Dr. *Fox*, a man of great worth, came to him to
consult his health; and that after a sight of him, and some queries concerning his distempers, he told him, *That by Cordials, and
drinking milk twenty days together, there was a probability of his
restauration to health;* but he passionately denied to drink it.
Nevertheless, Dr. *Fox*, who loved him most intirely, wearied him
with sollicitations, till he yielded to take it for ten days; at the
end of which time, he told Dr. *Fox, he had drunk it more to satisfie him, than to recover his health; and, that he would not drink
it ten days longer upon the best moral assurance of having
twenty years added to his life: for he loved it not; and, was so far
from fearing death, which to others is the King of terrors: that
he long'd for the day of his dissolution.*

It is observed, that a desire of glory or commendation is
rooted in the very nature of man; and that those of the severest
and most mortified lives, though they may become so humble
as to banish self-flattery, and such weeds as naturally grow
there: yet, they have not been able to kill this desire of glory,
but that, like our radical heat, it will both live and dye with
us; and, many think it should do so; and, we want not sacred
examples to justifie the desire of having our memory to out-live
our lives: which I mention, because Dr. *Donne*, by the perswasion of Dr. *Fox*, easily yielded at this very time to have a

Monument made for him; but Dr. *Fox* undertook not to perswade him how, or what Monument it should be; that was left
to Dr. *Donne* himself.

A Monument being resolved upon, Dr. *Donne* sent for a
Carver to make for him in wood the figure of an *Urn,* giving
him directions for the compass and height of it; and, to bring
with it a board of the just height of his body. 'These being got:
'then, without delay a choice Painter was got to be in a readiness
'to draw his Picture, which was taken as followeth.—— Several
'Charcole-fires being first made in his large Study, he brought
'with him into that place his winding-sheet in his hand, and,
'having put off all his cloaths, had this sheet put on him, and so
'tyed with knots at his head and feet, and his hands so placed,
'as dead bodies are usually fitted to be shrowded and put into
'their Coffin, or grave. Upon this *Urn* he thus stood with his eyes
'shut, and with so much of the sheet turned aside as might
'shew his lean, pale, and death-like face, which was purposely
'turned toward the East, from whence he expected the second
'coming of his and our Saviour Jesus. In this posture he was
drawn at his just height; and when the Picture was fully finished, he caused it to be set by his bed-side, where it continued,
and became his hourly object till his death: and, was then given
to his dearest friend and Executor Doctor *Henry King,* then chief
Residentiary of St. *Pauls,* who caused him to be thus carved in
one entire piece of white Marble, as it now stands in that
Church; and by Doctor *Donne*'s own appointment, these words
were to be affixed to it as his Epitaph:

JOHANNES DONNE

Sac. Theol. Profess.

*Post varia Studia quibus ab annis tenerrimis fi-
deliter, nec infeliciter incubuit;
Instinctu & impulsu Sp. Sancti, Monitu
& Hortatu*

*REGIS JACOBI, Ordines Sacros am-
plexus Anno sui Jesu, 1614. & suæ ætatis 42.
Decanatu huius Ecclesiæ indutus 27. Novem-
bris 1 6 2 1.*

Exutus morte ultimo Die Martii 1631.
Hic licet in Occiduo Cinere Aspicit Eum
Cuius nomen est Oriens.[5]

And now, having brought him through the many labyrinths and perplexities of a various life: even to the gates of death and the grave; my desire is, he may rest till I have told my Reader, that I have seen many Pictures of him, in several habits, and at several ages, and in several postures: And, I now mention this, because I have seen one Picture of him, drawn by a curious[s] hand at his age of eighteen; with his sword and what other adornments might then suit with the present fashions of youth, and the giddy gayeties of that age: and his Motto then was,

> *How much shall I be chang'd,*
> *Before I am chang'd.*

And if that young, and his now dying Picture, were at this time set together, every beholder might say, *Lord! How much is Dr.* Donne *already chang'd, before he is chang'd?* And, the view of them might give my Reader occasion, to ask himself with some amazement, *Lord! How much may I also, that am now in health be chang'd, before I am chang'd? before this vile, this changeable body shall put off mortality?* and therefore to prepare for it.—— But this is not writ so much for my Readers *Memento*, as to tell him, that Dr. *Donne* would often in his private discourses, and often publickly in his Sermons, mention the many changes both of his body and mind: especially of his mind from a vertiginous giddiness; and would as often say, *His great and most blessed change was from a temporal, to a spiritual imployment:* in which he was so happy, that he accounted the former part of his life to be lost. And, the beginning of it to be, from his first entring into *sacred Orders;* and, serving his most merciful God, at his Altar.

Upon *Monday* after the drawing this Picture, he took his last leave of his beloved Study; and, being sensible of his hourly

5 John Donne, Doctor of Divinity, after various studies which he pursued faithfully and not unsuccessfully from his earliest years, embraced Holy Orders, under the influence and impulse of the Divine Spirit and by the advice and exhortation of King James, in the year of his Saviour 1614, and of his own age 42. Invested with the Deanery of this Church 27 November 1621, he was stripped of it by death on the last day of March 1631. Though his life falls here in dust, he beholds Him Whose name is the Rising.

decay, retired himself to his bed-chamber: and, that week sent
at several times for many of his most considerable friends, with
whom he took a solemn and deliberate farewell; commending
to their considerations some sentences useful for the regulation
of their lives, and then dismist them, as good *Jacob* did his sons,
with a spiritual benediction. The *Sunday* following he appointed
his servants, that if there were any business yet undone that
concerned him or themselves, it should be prepared against
Saturday next; for, after that day he would not mix his thoughts
with any thing that concerned this world; nor ever did: But, as
Job, so he *waited for the appointed day of his dissolution.*

And now he was so happy as to have nothing to do but to
dye; to do which, he stood in need of no longer time, for he had
studied it long; and to so happy a perfection, that in a former
sickness he called God to witness[6] *he was that minute ready to
deliver his soul into his hands, if that minute God would determine his dissolution.* In that sickness he beg'd of God the constancy to be preserved in that estate for ever; and his patient
expectation to have his immortal soul disrob'd from her garment
of mortality, makes me confident he now had a modest assurance
that his Prayers were then heard, and his Petition granted. He
lay fifteen days earnestly expecting his hourly change; and, in
the last hour of his last day, as his body melted away and va-
poured into spirit, his soul having, I verily believe, some Revelation of the Beatifical Vision, he said, *I were miserable if I might
not dye;* and after those words, closed many periods of his faint
breath, by saying often, *Thy Kingdom come, Thy Will be done.*
His speech, which had long been his ready and faithful servant,
left him not till the last minute of his life, and then forsook him
not to serve another Master (for who speaks like him) but dyed
before him, for that it was then become useless to him that now
conversed with God on earth, as Angels are said to do in heaven,
only by thoughts and looks. Being speechless, and, seeing heaven
by that illumination by which he saw it; he did, as St. *Stephen,
look stedfastly into it, till he saw the Son of man, standing at
the right hand of God his Father;* and, being satisfied with this
blessed sight, as his soul ascended, and his last breath departed
from him, he closed his own eyes; and then, disposed his hands

6 *In his Book of Devotions written then.

and body into such a posture as required not the least alteration by those that came to shroud him.

Thus *variable,* thus *vertuous* was the Life; thus *excellent,* thus *exemplary* was the Death of this memorable man.

He was buried in that place of St. *Pauls* Church which he had appointed for that use some years before his death; and, by which he passed daily to pay his publick devotions to Almighty God (who was then served twice a day by a publick form of Prayer and Praises in that place) but, he was not buried privately, though he desired it; for, beside an unnumbred number of others, many persons of Nobility, and of eminency for Learning, who did love and honour him in his life, did shew it at his death, by a voluntary and sad attendance of his body to the grave, where nothing was so remarkable as a publick sorrow.

To which place of his Burial some mournful Friend repaired, and, as *Alexander the Great* did to the grave of the famous *Achilles,* so they strewed his with an abundance of curious and costly Flowers, which course they (who were never yet known) continued morning and evening for many days; not ceasing, till the stones that were taken up in that Church to give his body admission into the cold earth (now his bed of rest) were again by the Masons art so levelled and firm'd, as they had been formerly; and, his place of Burial undistinguishable to common view.

The next day after his Burial, some unknown friend, some one, of the many lovers and admirers of his vertue and learning; writ this *Epitaph* with a cole on the wall, over his grave.

> *Reader! I am to let thee know,*
> *Donne's Body only, lyes below:*
> *For, could the grave his Soul comprize,*
> *Earth would be richer then the skies.*

Nor was this all the Honor done to his reverend Ashes; for, as there be some persons that will not receive a reward for that for which God accounts himself a Debtor: persons, that dare trust God with their Charity, and without a witness; so there was by some grateful unknown Friend, that thought Dr. *Donne's* memory ought to be perpetuated, an hundred Marks sent to his two faithful Friends[7] and Executors, towards the making of his

7 *Dr. *King* and Dr. *Monfort.*

Monument. It was not for many years known by whom; but,
after the death of Dr. *Fox,* it was known that 'twas he that sent
it; and he lived to see as lively a representation of his dead
Friend, as Marble can express; a Statue indeed so like Dr. *Donne,*
that (as his Friend Sir *Henry Wotton* hath expressed himself)
*it seems to breath faintly; and, Posterity shall look upon it as a
kind of artificial Miracle.*

*He was of Stature moderately tall, of a strait and equally-
proportioned body, to which all his words and actions gave an
unexpressible addition of Comeliness.*

*The melancholy and pleasant humor, were in him so con-
tempered, that each gave advantage to the other, and made his
Company one of the delights of Mankind.*

His fancy *was unimitably high, equalled only by his great
wit; both being made useful by a commanding judgment.*

His aspect *was chearful, and such, as gave a silent testimony
of a clear knowing soul, and, of a Conscience at peace with it
self.*

His melting eye, *shewed that he had a soft heart, full of noble
compassion; of too brave a soul to offer injuries, and too much
a Christian not to pardon them in others.*

*He did much contemplate (especially after he entred into his
Sacred Calling) the* mercies *of Almighty God, the* immortality
of the Soul, *and the* joyes *of Heaven; and would often say, in
a kind of sacred extasie*—Blessed be God that he is God, only
and divinely like himself.

*He was by nature highly passionate, but more apt to reluct
at the excesses of it. A great lover of the offices[s] of humanity,
and of so merciful a spirit, that* he never beheld the miseries of
Mankind without pity and relief.

*He was earnest and unwearied in the search of knowledge;
with which, his vigorous soul is now satisfied, and employed in
a continual praise of that God that first breathed it into his
active body; that body, which once was a* Temple of the Holy
Ghost, *and is now become a small quantity of* Christian dust:
But I shall see it reanimated.

I. W.

Feb. 15. 1639.

IV

Sir Thomas Browne

HYDRIOTAPHIA,
URNE-BURIALL,

OR,

A Discourse of the Sepulchrall
Urnes lately found in
NORFOLK

[THE EPISTLE DEDICATORY]
TO MY WORTHY AND HONOURED FRIEND
THOMAS LE GROS OF CROSTWICK ESQUIRE

When the Funerall pyre was out, and the last valediction over,
men took a lasting adieu of their interred Friends, little expecting the curiosity of future ages should comment upon their
ashes, and having no old experience of the duration of their
Reliques, held no opinion of such after-considerations.

But who knows the fate of his bones, or how often he is to be
buried? who hath the Oracle of his ashes, or whether they are

to be scattered? The Reliques of many lie like the ruines of *Pompeys,* in all parts of the earth; And when they arrive at your hands, these may seem to have wandred far, who in a direct[1] and *Meridian* Travell, have but few miles of known Earth between your self and the Pole.

That the bones of *Theseus* should be seen again in *Athens,* was not beyond conjecture, and hopeful expectation; but that these should arise so opportunely to serve your self, was an hit of fate and honour beyond prediction.

We cannot but wish these Urnes might have the effect of Theatrical vessels, and great *Hippodrome* Urnes in *Rome;*[2] to resound the acclamations and honour due unto you. But these are sad and sepulchral Pitchers, which have no joyful voices; silently expressing old mortality, the ruines of forgotten times, and can only speak with life, how long in this corruptible frame, some parts may be uncorrupted; yet able to out-last bones long unborn, and noblest pyle among us.

We present not these as any strange sight or spectacle unknown to your eyes who have beheld the best of Urnes, and noblest variety of Ashes; Who are your self no slender master of Antiquities, and can daily command the view of so many Imperiall faces; Which raiseth your thoughts unto old things, and consideration of times before you, when even living men were Antiquities; when the living might exceed the dead, and to depart this world, could not be properly said, to go unto the greater number. And so run up your thoughts upon the ancient of dayes, the Antiquaries truest object, unto whom the eldest parcels are young, and earth it self an Infant; and without Ægyptian account[3] makes but small noise in thousands.

We were hinted by the occasion, not catched the opportunity to write of old things, or intrude upon the Antiquary. We are coldly drawn unto discourses of Antiquities, who have scarce time before us to comprehend new things, or make out learned Novelties. But seeing they arose as they lay, almost in silence among us, at least in short account suddenly passed over; we

---

1 *Little directly, but Sea between your house and *Greenland.*
2 *The great Urnes in the *Hippodrome* at *Rome* conceived to resound the voices of people at their shows.
3 *Which makes the world so many years old.

were very unwilling they should die again, and be buried twice among us.

Beside, to preserve the living, and make the dead to live, to keep men out of their Urnes, and discourse of humane fragments in them, is not impertinent[§] unto our profession; whose study is life and death, who daily behold examples of mortality, and of all men least need artificial *memento's,* or coffins by our bed side, to minde[§] us of our graves.

'Tis time to observe Occurrences, and let nothing remarkable escape us; The Supinity of elder dayes hath left so much in silence, or time hath so martyred the Records, that the most industrious heads do finde no easie work to erect a new *Britannia.*

'Tis opportune to look back upon old times, and contemplate our Forefathers. Great examples grow thin, and to be fetched from the passed world. Simplicity flies away, and iniquity[§] comes at long strides upon us. We have enough to do to make up our selves from present and passed times, and the whole stage of things scarce serveth for our instruction. A compleat peece of vertue must be made up from the *Centos* of all ages, as all the beauties of *Greece* could make but one handsome *Venus.*

When the bones of King *Arthur* were digged up,[4] the old Race might think, they beheld therein some Originals of themselves; Unto these of our Urnes none here can pretend relation, and can only behold the Reliques of those persons, who in their life giving the Law unto their predecessors, after long obscurity, now lye at their mercies. But remembring the early civility they brought upon these Countreys, and forgetting long passed mischiefs; We mercifully preserve their bones, and pisse not upon their ashes.

In the offer of these Antiquities we drive[§] not at ancient Families, so long out-lasted by them; We are farre from erecting your worth upon the pillars of your Fore-fathers, whose merits you illustrate. We honour your old Virtues, conformable unto times before you, which are the Noblest Armoury. And having long experience of your friendly conversation, void of empty Formality, full of freedome, constant and Generous Honesty. I look

4 *In the time of *Henry* the second, *Cambden.*

upon you as a Gemme of the Old Rock; and must professe my self
even to Urne and Ashes,

Norwich
May 1.

Your ever faithfull Friend,
and Servant,
Thomas Browne.

CHAPTER I

In the deep discovery of the Subterranean world, a shallow part
would satisfie some enquirers; who, if two or three yards were
open about the surface, would not care to rake the bowels of
Potosi[5] and regions towards the Centre. Nature hath furnished
one part of the Earth, and man another. The treasures of time
lie high, in Urnes, Coynes, and Monuments, scarce below the
roots of some vegetables. Time hath endlesse rarities, and shows
of all varieties; which reveals old things in heaven, makes new
discoveries in earth, and even earth it self a discovery. That
great Antiquity *America* lay buried for thousands of years; and
a large part of the earth is still in the Urne unto us.

Though if *Adam* were made out of an extract of the Earth,
all parts might challenge a restitution, yet few have returned
their bones farre lower then they might receive them; not affecting the graves of Giants, under hilly and heavy coverings, but
content with lesse then their owne depth, have wished their
bones might lie soft, and the earth be light upon them; Even
such as hope to rise again, would not be content with centrall
interrment, or so desperately to place their reliques as to lie
beyond discovery, and in no way to be seen again; which happy
contrivance hath made communication with our forefathers,
and left unto our view some parts, which they never beheld
themselves.

Though earth hath engrossed the name yet water hath proved
the smartest grave; which in forty dayes swallowed almost mankinde, and the living creation; Fishes not wholly escaping, except the Salt Ocean were handsomely contempered by admixture
of the fresh Element.

5 *The rich Mountain of *Peru*.

Many have taken voluminous pains to determine the state of the soul upon disunion; but men have been most phantasticall in the singular contrivances of their corporall dissolution: whilest the sobrest Nations have rested in two wayes, of simple inhumation and burning.

That carnall interment or burying, was of the elder date, the old examples of *Abraham* and the Patriarchs are sufficient to illustrate; And were without competition, if it could be made out, that *Adam* was buried near *Damascus,* or Mount *Calvary,* according to some Tradition. God himself, that buried but one, was pleased to make choice of this way, collectible from Scripture-expression, and the hot contest between Satan and the Arch-Angel, about discovering⁵ the body of *Moses.* But the practice of Burning was also of great Antiquity, and of no slender extent. For (not to derive the same from *Hercules*) noble descriptions there are hereof in the Grecian Funerals of *Homer,* In the formall Obsequies of *Patroclus,* and *Achilles;* and somewhat elder in the *Theban* warre, and solemn combustion of *Meneceus,* and *Archemorus,* contemporary unto *Jair* the Eighth Judge of *Israel.* Confirmable also among the *Trojans,* from the Funerall Pyre of *Hector,* burnt before the gates of *Troy,* And the burning of *Penthisilea* the *Amazonean Queen:* and long continuance of that practice, in the inward Countries of *Asia;* while as low⁵ as the Reign of *Julian,* we finde that the King of *Chionia* burnt the body of his Son, and interred the ashes in a Silver Urne.

The same practice extended also farre West, and besides *Herulians, Getes,* and *Thracians,* was in use with most of the *Celtæ, Sarmatians, Germans, Gauls, Danes, Swedes, Norwegians;* not to omit some use thereof among *Carthaginians* and *Americans:* Of greater Antiquity among the *Romans* then most opinion, or *Pliny* seems to allow. For (beside the old Table⁵ Laws of burning or burying within the City, of making the Funerall fire with plained wood, or quenching the fire with wine.) *Manlius* the Consul burnt the body of his Son: *Numa* by speciall clause of his Will, was not burnt but buried; And *Remus* was solemnly burned, according to the description of *Ovid.*

Cornelius Sylla was not the first whose body was burned in *Rome,* but of the *Cornelian* Family, which being indifferently, not frequently used before; from that time spread, and became the prevalent practice. Not totally pursued in the highest runne[s] of Cremation; For when even Crows were funerally burnt, *Poppæa* the Wife of *Nero* found a peculiar grave enterment. Now as all customes were founded upon some bottome of Reason, so there wanted not grounds for this; according to severall apprehensions of the most rationall dissolution. Some being of the opinion of *Thales*, that water was the originall of all things, thought it most equall to submit unto the principle of putrefaction, and conclude in a moist relentment.[§] Others conceived it most natural to end in fire, as due unto the master principle in the composition, according to the doctrine of *Heraclitus*. And therefore heaped up large piles, more actively to waft them toward that Element, whereby they also declined[§] a visible degeneration into worms, and left a lasting parcell of their composition.

Some apprehended a purifying virtue in fire, refining the grosser commixture, and firing out the Æthereall particles so deeply immersed in it. And such as by tradition or rationall conjecture held any hint of the finall pyre of all things; or that this Element at last must be too hard for all the rest; might conceive most naturally of the fiery dissolution. Others pretending no natural grounds, politickly declined the malice of enemies upon their buried bodies. Which consideration led *Sylla* unto this practise; who having thus served the body of *Marius*, could not but fear a retaliation upon his own; entertained after in the Civill wars, and revengeful contentions of *Rome*.

But as many Nations embraced, and many left it indifferent, so others too much affected, or strictly declined this practice. The *Indian Brachmans* seemed too great friends unto fire, who burnt themselves alive, and thought it the noblest way to end their dayes in fire; according to the expression of the Indian, burning himself at *Athens,* in his last words upon the pyre unto the amazed spectators, *Thus I make my selfe Immortall.*

But the *Chaldeans* the great Idolaters of fire, abhorred the burning of their carcasses, as a pollution of that Deity. The *Persian Magi* declined it upon the like scruple, and being only sollicitous about their bones, exposed their flesh to the prey of Birds and Dogges. And the *Persees* now in *India,* which expose their bodies unto Vultures, and endure not so much as *feretra* or Beers of Wood, the proper Fuell of fire, are led on with such niceties. But whether the ancient *Germans* who burned their dead, held any such fear to pollute their Deity of *Herthus,* or the earth, we have no Authentick conjecture.

The Ægyptians were afraid of fire, not as a Deity, but a devouring Element, mercilesly consuming their bodies, and leaving too little of them; and therefore by precious Embalments, depositure in dry earths, or handsome inclosure in glasses, contrived the notablest wayes of integrall conservation. And from such Ægyptian scruples imbibed by *Pythagoras,* it may be conjectured that *Numa* and the Pythagoricall Sect first waved[§] the fiery solution.

The *Scythians* who swore by winde and sword, that is, by life and death, were so farre from burning their bodies, that they declined all interrment, and made their graves in the ayr: And the *Ichthyophagi* or fish-eating Nations about Ægypt, affected the Sea for their grave: Thereby declining visible corruption, and restoring the debt of their bodies. Whereas the old Heroes in *Homer,* dreaded nothing more than water or drowning; probably upon the old opinion of the fiery substance of the soul, only extinguishable by that Element; And therefore the Poet emphatically implieth the totall destruction in this kinde of death, which happened to *Ajax Oileus.*

The old *Balearians* had a peculiar mode, for they used great Urnes and much wood, but no fire in their burials, while they bruised the flesh and bones of the dead, crowded them into Urnes, and laid heapes of wood upon them. And the *Chinois* without cremation or urnall interrment of their bodies, make use of trees and much burning, while they plant a Pine-tree by their grave, and burn great numbers of printed draughts[§] of slaves and horses over it, civilly content with their companies in effigie, which barbarous Nations exact unto reality.

Christians abhorred this way of obsequies, and though they stickt[§] not to give their bodies to be burnt in their lives, detested that mode after death; affecting rather a depositure than absumption, and properly submitting unto the sentence[§] of God, to return not unto ashes but unto dust againe, conformable unto the practice of the Patriarchs, the interrment of our Saviour, of *Peter, Paul* and the ancient Martyrs. And so farre at last declining promiscuous[§] enterrment with Pagans, that some have suffered Ecclesiastical censures, for making no scruple thereof.

The *Musselman* beleevers will never admit this fiery resolution. For they hold a present trial from their black and white Angels in the grave; which they must have made so hollow, that they may rise upon their knees.

The Jewish Nation, though they entertained the old way of inhumation, yet sometimes admitted this practice. For the men of *Jabesh* burnt the body of *Saul.* And by no prohibited practice to avoid contagion or pollution, in time of pestilence, burnt the bodies of their friends. And when they burnt not their dead bodies yet sometimes used great burnings neare and about them, deducible from the expressions concerning *Jehoram, Sedechias,* and the sumptuous pyre of *Asa:* And were so little averse from Pagan burning, that the Jews lamenting the death of *Cæsar* their friend, and revenger on *Pompey,* frequented the place where his body was burnt for many nights together. And as they raised noble Monuments and *Mausolæums* for their own Nation, so they were not scrupulous in erecting some for others, according to the practice of *Daniel,* who left that lasting sepulchrall pyle in *Echbatana,* for the *Medean* and *Persian* Kings.

But even in times of subjection and hottest[§] use,[§] they conformed not unto the *Romane* practice of burning; whereby the Prophecy was secured concerning the body of Christ, that it should not see corruption, or a bone should not be broken; which we beleeve was also providentially prevented, from the Souldiers spear and nails that past by the little bones both in his hands and feet: Nor of ordinary contrivance, that it should not corrupt on the Crosse, according to the Laws of *Romane* Crucifixion, or an hair of his head perish, though observable in Jewish customes, to cut the hairs of Malefactors.

Nor in their long co-habitation with Ægyptians, crept into a custome of their exact embalming, wherein deeply slashing the muscles, and taking out the brains and entrails, they had broken the subject[§] of so entire a Resurrection, nor fully answered the types of *Enoch, Eliah,* or *Jonah,* which yet to prevent or restore,

was of equall facility unto that rising power, able to break the
fasciations and bands of death, to get clear out of the Cerecloth, and an hundred pounds of oyntment, and out of the
Sepulchre before the stone was rolled from it.

But though they embraced not this practice of burning, yet
entertained they many ceremonies agreeable unto *Greeke* and
Romane obsequies. And he that observeth their funerall Feasts,
their Lamentations at the grave, their musick, and weeping
mourners; how they closed the eyes of their friends, how they
washed, anointed, and kissed the dead; may easily conclude
these were not meere Pagan-Civilities. But whether that mourn-
full burthen, and treble calling out after *Absalom,* had any
reference unto the last conclamation, and triple valediction,
used by other Nations, we hold but a wavering conjecture.

Civilians§ make sepulture§ but of the Law of Nations, others
doe naturally§ found§ it and discover it also in animals. They
that are so thick skinned as still to credit the story of the *Phœnix,* may say something for animall burning: More serious
conjectures finde some examples of sepulture in Elephants,
Cranes, the Sepulchrall Cells of Pismires and practice of Bees;
which civill society carrieth out their dead, and hath exequies,
if not interrments.

CHAPTER II

The Solemnities, Ceremonies, Rites of their Cremation or enterrment, so solemnly delivered by Authours, we shall not disparage§
our Reader to repeat. Only the last and lasting part in their
Urns, collected bones and Ashes, we cannot wholly omit, or
decline that Subject, which occasion lately presented, in some
discovered among us.

In a Field of old *Walsingham,* not many moneths past, were
digged up between fourty and fifty Urnes, deposited in a dry
and sandy soile, not a yard deep, nor farre from one another: Not
all strictly of one figure, but most answering§ these described:
Some containing two pounds of bones, distinguishable in skulls,
ribs, jawes, thigh-bones, and teeth, with fresh impressions of
their combustion. Besides the extraneous substances, like peeces

of small boxes, or combes handsomely wrought, handles of small brasse instruments, brazen nippers, and in one some kinde of *Opale*.

Near the same plot of ground, for about six yards compasse were digged up coals and incinerated substances, which begat conjecture that this was the *Ustrina* or place of burning their bodies, or some sacrificing place unto the *Manes*,[6] which was properly below the surface of the ground, as the *Aræ* and Altars unto the gods and *Heroes* above it.

That these were the Urnes of *Romanes* from the common custome and place where they were found, is no obscure conjecture, not farre from a *Romane* Garrison, and but five Miles from *Brancaster*, set down by ancient Record under the name of *Brannodunum*. And where the adjoyning Towne, containing seven Parishes, in no very different sound, but Saxon Termination, still retains the Name of *Burnham*, which being an early station, it is not improbable the neighbour parts were filled with habitations, either of *Romanes* themselves, or *Brittains Romanised,* which observed the *Romane* customes.

Nor is it improbable that the *Romanes* early possessed this Countrey; for though we meet not with such strict particulars of these parts, before the new Institution of *Constantine,* and military charge of the Count of the *Saxon* shore, and that about the *Saxon* Invasions, the *Dalmatian* Horsemen were in the Garrison of *Brancaster:* Yet in the time of *Claudius, Vespasian,* and *Severus,* we finde no lesse then three Legions dispersed through the Province of *Brittain.* And as high[§] as the Reign of *Claudius* a great overthrow was given unto the *Iceni,* by the *Romane* Lieutenant *Ostorius.* Not long after the Countrey was so molested, that in hope of a better state, *Prasutagus* bequeathed his Kingdome unto *Nero* and his Daughters; and *Boadicea* his Queen fought the last decisive Battle with *Paulinus.* After which time and Conquest of *Agricola* the Lieutenant of *Vespasian,* probable it is they wholly possessed this Countrey, ordering it into Garrisons or Habitations, best suitable with their securities. And so some *Romane* Habitations, not improbable in these parts, as high as the time of *Vespasian,* where the *Saxons* after seated, in whose thin-fill'd Mappes we yet finde

6 *The spirits of the dead and the gods of the lower world.

the Name of *Walsingham*. Now if the *Iceni* were but *Gamma-dims, Anconians*, or men that lived in an Angle wedge or Elbow of *Brittain*, according to the Originall Etymologie, this countrey will challenge the Emphaticall appellation, as most properly making the Elbow or Iken of *Icenia*.

That *Britain* was notably populous is undeniable, from that expression of *Cæsar*.[7] That the *Romans* themselves were early in no small Numbers, Seventy Thousand with their associats slain by *Boadicea*, affords a sure account. And though many *Roman* habitations are now unknowne, yet some by old works, Rampiers,[§] Coynes, and Urnes doe testifie their Possessions. Some Urnes have been found at *Castor*, some also about *South-creake*, and not many years past, no lesse then ten in a Field at *Buxton*, not near any recorded Garison. Nor is it strange to finde *Romane* Coynes of Copper and Silver among us; of *Ves-pasian, Trajan, Adrian, Commodus, Antoninus, Severus*, &c. But the greater number of *Dioclesian, Constantine, Constans, Valens*, with many of *Victorinus, Posthumius, Tetricus*, and the thirty Tyrants in the Reigne of *Gallienus;* and some as high as *Adrianus* have been found about *Thetford*, or *Sitomagus*, men-tioned in the itinerary of *Antoninus*, as the way from *Venta* or *Castor* unto *London*. But the most frequent discovery is made at the two *Casters* by *Norwich* and *Yarmouth*, at *Burghcastle* and *Brancaster*.

Besides, the *Norman, Saxon* and *Danish* peeces of *Cuthred, Canutus, William, Matilda*, and others, som Brittish Coynes of gold have been dispersedly found; And no small number of silver peeces near *Norwich;* with a rude head upon the obverse, and an ill formed horse on the reverse, with Inscriptions *Ic. Duro. T.* whether implying *Iceni, Durotriges, Tascia*, or *Trino-bantes*, we leave to higher conjecture. Vulgar Chronology will have *Norwich* Castle as old as *Julius Cæsar;* but his distance from these parts, and its *Gothick* form of structure, abridgeth such Antiquity. The *British* Coyns afford conjecture of early habitation in these parts, though the City of *Norwich* arose from the ruines of *Venta*, and though perhaps not without some

---

7 *Hominum infinita multitudo est, creberrimaque ædificia ferè Gallicis con-similia.* Cæs. *de bello Gal.* l. 5 [There is an infinite multitude of men, and the buildings are very numerous, just like those of the Gauls. Caesar, *Gallic War*, Book 5.]

habitation before, was enlarged, builded, and nominated by the *Saxons*. In what bulk or populosity it stood in the old East-angle Monarchy, tradition and history are silent. Considerable it was in the *Danish* Eruptions, when *Sueno* burnt *Thetford* and *Norwich,* and *Ulfketel* the Governour thereof, was able to make some resistance, and after endeavoured to burn the *Danish* Navy.

How the *Romanes* left so many Coynes in Countreys of their Conquests, seems of hard resolution,§ except we consider how they buried them under ground, when upon barbarous invasions they were fain to desert their habitations in most part of their Empire; and the strictnesse of their laws forbidding to transfer them to any other uses; Wherein the *Spartans* were singular, who to make their Copper money uselesse, contempered it with vinegar. That the *Brittains* left any, some wonder; since their money was iron, and Iron rings before *Cæsar;* and those of after stamp by permission, and but small in bulk and bignesse. That so few of the *Saxons* remain, because overcome by succeeding Conquerours upon the place, their Coynes by degrees passed into other stamps, and the marks of after ages.

Then the time of these Urnes deposited, or precise Antiquity of these Reliques, nothing of more uncertainty. For since the Lieutenant of *Claudius* seems to have made the first progresse into these parts, since *Boadicea* was overthrown by the Forces of *Nero,* and *Agricola* put a full end to these Conquests; it is not probable the Countrey was fully garrison'd or planted before; and therefore however these Urnes might be of later date, not likely of higher Antiquity.

And the succeeding Emperours desisted not from their Conquests in these and other parts; as testified by history and medall inscription yet extant. The Province of *Brittain* in so divided a distance from *Rome,* beholding the faces of many Imperiall persons, and in large account no fewer then *Cæsar, Claudius, Britannicus, Vespasian, Titus, Adrian, Severus, Commodus, Geta,* and *Caracalla.*

A great obscurity herein, because no medall or Emperours Coyne enclosed, which might denote the date of their enterrments. observable in many Urnes, and found in those of *Spittle* Fields by *London,* which contained the Coynes of *Claudius,*

Vespasian, Commodus, Antoninus, attended with Lacrymatories,[§] Lamps, Bottles of Liquor, and other appurtenances of affectionate superstition, which in these rurall interrements were wanting.

Some uncertainty there is from the period[§] or term[§] of burning, or the cessation of that practise. *Macrobius* affirmeth it was disused in his dayes. But most agree, though without authentick record, that it ceased with the *Antonini.* Most safely to be understood after the Reigne of those Emperours, which assumed the name of *Antoninus,* extending unto *Heliogabalus.* Not strictly after *Marcus;* For about fifty years later we finde the magnificent burning, and consecration of *Severus;* and if we so fix this period or cessation, these Urnes will challenge above thirteen hundred years.

But whether this practise was onely then left by Emperours and great persons, or generally about *Rome,* and not in other Provinces, we hold no authentick account. For after *Tertullian,* in the dayes of *Minucius* it was obviously objected upon Christians, that they condemned the practise of burning. And we finde a passage in *Sidonius,* which asserteth that practise in *France* unto a lower account. And perhaps not fully disused till Christianity fully established, which gave the finall extinction to these sepulchrall Bonefires.

Whether they were the bones of men or women or children, no authentick decision from ancient custome in distinct places of buriall. Although not improbably conjectured, that the double Sepulture or burying place of *Abraham,* had in it such intension. But from exility[§] of bones, thinnesse of skulls, smallnesse of teeth, ribbes, and thigh-bones; not improbable that many thereof were persons of *minor* age, or women. Confirmable also from things contained in them: In most were found substances resembling Combes, Plates like Boxes, fastened with Iron pins, and handsomely overwrought like the necks or Bridges of Musicall Instruments, long brasse plates overwrought like the handles of neat implements, brazen nippers to pull away hair, and in one a kind of *Opale* yet maintaining a blewish colour.

Now that they accustomed to burn or bury with them, things wherein they excelled, delighted, or which were dear unto them, either as farewells unto all pleasure, or vain apprehension that they might use them in the other world, is testified by all Antiquity. Observable from the Gemme or Berill Ring upon the finger of *Cynthia,* the Mistresse of *Propertius,* when after her Funerall Pyre her Ghost appeared unto him. And notably illustrated from the Contents of that *Romane* Urne preserved by Cardinall *Farnese,* wherein besides great number of Gemmes with heads of Gods and Goddesses, were found an Ape of *Agath,* a Grashopper, an Elephant of Ambre, a Crystall Ball, three glasses, two Spoones, and six Nuts of Crystall. And beyond the content of Urnes, in the Monument of *Childerick* the first, and fourth King from *Pharamond,* casually discovered three years past at *Tournay,* restoring unto the world much gold richly adorning his Sword, two hundred Rubies, many hundred Imperial Coyns, three hundred golden Bees, the bones and horseshoe of his horse enterred with him, according to the barbarous magnificence of those days in their sepulchral Obsequies. Although if we steer by the conjecture of many and Septuagint expression; some trace thereof may be found even with the ancient Hebrews, not only from the Sepulcrall treasure of *David,* but the circumcision knives which *Josuah* also buried.

Some men considering the contents of these Urnes, lasting peeces and toyes included in them, and the custome of burning with many other Nations, might somewhat doubt whether all Urnes found among us, were properly *Romane* Reliques, or some not belonging unto our *Brittish, Saxon,* or *Danish* Forefathers.

In the form of Buriall among the ancient *Brittains,* the large Discourses of *Cæsar, Tacitus,* and *Strabo* are silent: For the discovery whereof, with other particulars, we much deplore the losse of that Letter which *Cicero* expected or received from his Brother *Quintus,* as a resolution of *Brittish* customes; or the account which might have been made by *Scribonius Largus* the Physician, accompanying the Emperour *Claudius,* who might have also discovered that frugall Bit of the Old *Brittains,* which in the bignesse of a Bean could satisfie their thirst and hunger.

But that the *Druids* and ruling Priests used to burn and bury, is expressed by *Pomponius;* That *Bellinus* the Brother of *Brennus,* and King of *Brittains* was burnt, is acknowledged by *Polydorus.* That they held that practise in *Gallia, Cæsar* expresly delivereth. Whether the *Brittains* (probably descended from

them, of like Religion, Language and Manners) did not sometimes make use of burning; or whether at least such as were
after civilized unto the *Romane* life and manners, conformed
not unto this practise, we have no historical assertion or deniall.
But since from the account of *Tacitus* the *Romanes* early
wrought so much civility upon the *Brittish* stock, that they
brought them to build Temples, to wear the Gowne, and study
the *Romane* Laws and language, that they conformed also unto
their religious rites and customes in burials, seems no improbable conjecture.

That burning the dead was used in *Sarmatia*, is affirmed by
Gaguinus, that the *Sueons* and *Gothlanders* used to burne their
Princes and great persons, is delivered by *Saxo* and *Olaus;* that
this was the old *Germane* practise, is also asserted by *Tacitus.*
And though we are bare in historicall particulars of such obsequies in this Island, or that the *Saxons, Jutes,* and *Angles*
burnt their dead, yet came they from parts where 'twas of
ancient practise; the *Germanes* using it, from whom they were
descended. And even in *Jutland* and *Sleswick* in *Anglia Cym-
brica,* Urnes with bones were found not many years before us.

But the *Danish* and Northern Nations have raised an *Æra* or
point of compute from their Custome of burning their dead:
Some deriving it from *Unguinus*, some from *Frotho* the great;
who ordained by Law, that Princes and Chief Commanders
should be committed unto the fire, though the common sort
had the common grave enterrment. So *Starkatterus* that old
Heroe was burnt, and *Ringo* royally burnt the body of *Harald*
the King slain by him.

What time this custome generally expired in that Nation, we
discern no assured period; whether it ceased before Christianity,
or upon their Conversion, by *Ansgarius* the Gaul in the time of
Ludovicus Pius the Sonne of *Charles* the great, according to
good computes; or whether it might not be used by some persons,
while for a hundred and eighty years Paganisme and Christianity
were promiscuously embraced among them, there is no assured
conclusion. About which times the *Danes* were busie in *England*,
and particularly infested this Countrey: Where many Castles
and strong holds, were built by them, or against them, and great
number of names and Families still derived from them. But since

this custome was probably disused before their Invasion or Conquest, and the *Romanes* confessedly practised the same, since their possession of this Island, the most assured account will fall upon the *Romanes,* or *Brittains Romanized.*

However certain it is, that Urnes conceived of no *Romane* Originall, are often digged up both in *Norway,* and *Denmark,* handsomely described, and graphically represented by the Learned Physician *Wormius,* And in some parts of *Denmark* in no ordinary number, as stands delivered by Authours exactly describing those Countreys. And they contained not only bones, but many other substances in them, as Knives, peeces of Iron, Brasse and Wood, and one of *Norwaye* a brasse guilded Jewesharp.

Nor were they confused or carelesse in disposing the noblest sort, while they placed large stones in circle about the Urnes, or bodies which they interred: Somewhat answerable unto the Monument of *Rollrich* stones in *England,* or sepulcrall Monument probably erected by *Rollo,* who after conquered *Normandy.* Where 'tis not improbable somewhat might be discovered. Mean while to what Nation or person belonged that large Urne found at *Ashburie,* containing mighty bones, and a Buckler; What those large Urnes found at little *Massingham,* or why the *Anglesea* Urnes are placed with their mouths downward, remains yet undiscovered.

CHAPTER III

Playstered[§] and whited[§] Sepulchres, were anciently affected[§] in cadaverous, and corruptive Burials; And the rigid Jews were wont to garnish the Sepulchres of the righteous; *Ulysses* in *Hecuba*[8] cared not how meanly he lived, so he might finde a noble Tomb after death. Great persons affected great Monuments, And the fair and larger Urnes contained no vulgar ashes, which makes that disparity in those which time discovereth among us. The present Urnes were not of one capacity, the largest containing above a gallon, Some not much above half that measure; nor all of one figure,[§] wherein there is no strict conformity, in the same or different Countreys; Observable from

8 *Euripides.*

those represented by *Casalius, Bosio,* and others, though all
found in *Italy:* While many have handles, ears, and long necks,
but most imitate a circular figure, in a sphericall and round
composure; whether from any mystery, best duration or capacity, were but a conjecture. But the common form with necks
was a proper figure, making our last bed like our first; nor much
unlike the Urnes of our Nativity, while we lay in the nether
part of the Earth, and inward vault of our Microcosme. Many
Urnes are red, these but of a black colour, somewhat smooth,
and dully sounding, which begat some doubt, whether they were
burnt, or only baked in Oven or Sunne: According to the ancient
way, in many bricks, tiles, pots, and testaceous works; and as
the word *testa* is properly to be taken, when occurring without
addition: And chiefly intended by *Pliny,* when he commendeth
bricks and tiles of two years old, and to make them in the
spring. Nor only these concealed peeces, but the open magnificence of Antiquity, ran much in the Artifice of Clay. Hereof the
house of *Mausolus* was built, thus old *Jupiter* stood in the Capi-
toll, and the *Statua* of *Hercules* made in the Reign of *Tarquinius
Priscus,* was extant in *Plinies* dayes. And such as declined burning or Funerall Urnes, affected Coffins of Clay, according to the
mode of *Pythagoras,* and way preferred by *Varro.* But the spirit
of great ones was above these circumscriptions, affecting copper,
silver, gold, and *Porphyrie* Urnes, wherein *Severus* lay, after a
serious view and sentence on that which should contain him.[9]
Some of these Urnes were thought to have been silvered over,
from sparklings in several pots, with small Tinsell parcels[s];
uncertain whether from the earth, or the first mixture in them.

Among these Urnes we could obtain no good account of their
coverings; Only one seemed arched over with some kinde of
brickwork. Of those found at *Buxton* some were covered with
flints, some in other parts with tiles, those at *Yarmouth Caster,*
were closed with *Romane* bricks. And some have proper earthen
covers adapted and fitted to them. But in the *Homericall* Urne
of *Patroclus,* whatever was the solid Tegument, we finde the
immediate covering to be a purple peece of silk: And such as
had no covers might have the earth closely pressed into them,

9 * Χωρήσεις τὸν ἄνθρωπον, ὃν ἡ οἰκουμένη οὐκ ἠχώρησεν. *Dion.* [Thou shalt hold a
man that the world could not hold. *Cassius Dio.*]

after which disposure were probably some of these, wherein we found the bones and ashes half mortered unto the sand and sides of the Urne; and some long roots of Quich,§ or Dogs-grass wreathed about the bones.

No Lamps, included Liquors, Lachrymatories, or Tear-bottles attended these rurall Urnes, either as sacred unto the *Manes,* or passionate expressions of their surviving friends. While with rich flames, and hired tears they solemnized their Obsequies, and in the most lamented Monuments made one part of their Inscriptions. Some finde sepulchrall Vessels containing liquors, which time hath incrassated into gellies. For beside these Lachrymatories, notable Lamps, with Vessels of Oyles and Aromaticall Liquors attended noble Ossuaries. And some yet retaining a Vinosity and spirit in them, which if any have tasted they have farre exceeded the Palats of Antiquity. Liquors not to be computed by years of annuall Magistrates, but by great conjunctions and the fatall periods of Kingdomes.[1] The draughts of Consulary date, were but crude unto these, and *Opimian* Wine but in the must unto them.

In sundry Graves and Sepulchres, we meet with Rings, Coynes, and Chalices; Ancient frugality was so severe, that they allowed no gold to attend the Corps, but only that which served to fasten their teeth. Whether the *Opaline* stone in this Urne were burnt upon the finger of the dead, or cast into the fire by some affectionate friend, it will consist with either custome. But other incinerable substances were found so fresh, that they could feel no sindge from fire. These upon view were judged to be wood, but sinking in water and tried by the fire, we found them to be bone or Ivory. In their hardnesse and yellow colour they most resembled Box,§ which in old expressions found the Epithete of Eternall, and perhaps in such conservatories§ might have passed uncorrupted.

That Bay-leaves were found green in the Tomb of S. *Humbert,* after an hundred and fifty years, was looked upon as miraculous. Remarkable it was unto old Spectators, that the Cypresse of the Temple of *Diana,* lasted so many hundred years: The wood of the Ark and Olive Rod of *Aaron* were older at the Captivity. But the Cypresse of the Ark of *Noah,* was the greatest vegetable An-

[1] *About five hundred years. *Plato.*

tiquity, if *Josephus* were not deceived, by some fragments of it in his dayes. To omit the Moore-logs, and Firre-trees found under-ground in many parts of *England;* the undated ruines of windes, flouds or earthquakes; and which in *Flanders* still shew from what quarter they fell, as generally lying in a North-East position.

But though we found not these peeces to be Wood, according to first apprehension, yet we missed not altogether of some woody substance; For the bones were not so clearly pickt, but some coals were found amongst them; A way to make wood perpetuall, and a fit associat for mentall, whereon was laid the foundation of the great *Ephesian* Temple, and which were made the lasting tests of old boundaries and Landmarks; Whilest we look on these, we admire not Observations of Coals found fresh, after four hundred years. In a long deserted habitation, even Egge-shels have been found fresh, not tending to corruption.

In the Monument of King *Childerick,* the Iron Reliques were found all rusty and crumbling into peeces. But our little Iron pins which fastened the Ivory works, held well together, and lost not their Magneticall quality, though wanting a tenacious moisture for the firmer union of parts, although it be hardly drawn into fusion, yet that metall soon submitteth unto rust and dissolution. In the brazen peeces we admired[§] not the dura-tion but the freedome from rust, and ill savour, upon the hardest attrition; but now exposed unto the piercing Atomes of ayre, in the space of a few moneths, they begin to spot and betray their green entrals.[§] We conceive not these Urnes to have descended thus naked as they appear, or to have entred their graves with-out the old habit of flowers. The Urne of *Philopæmen* was so laden with flowers and ribbons, that it afforded no sight of it self. The rigid *Lycurgus* allowed Olive and Myrtle. The *Athenians* might fairly except against the practise of *Democritus* to be buried up in honey; as fearing to embezzle a great commodity of their Countrey, and the best of that kinde in *Europe.* But *Plato* seemed too frugally politick, who allowed no larger Monu-ment then would contain four Heroick Verses, and designed the most barren ground for sepulture: Though we cannot commend the goodnesse of that sepulchrall ground, which was set at no higher rate then the mean salary of *Judas.* Though the earth

had confounded the ashes of these Ossuaries, yet the bones
were so smartly⁵ burnt, that some thin plates of brasse were
found half melted among them: whereby we apprehend they
were not of the meanest carcasses, perfunctorily fired as sometimes in military, and commonly in pestilence, burnings; or after
the manner of abject corps, hudled forth and carelesly burnt,
without⁵ the Esquiline Port at *Rome;* which was an affront contrived upon *Tiberius,* while they but half burnt his body, and in
the Amphitheatre, according to the custome in notable Malefactors; whereas *Nero* seemed not so much to feare his death,
as that his head should be cut off, and his body not burnt entire.

Some finding many fragments of sculs in these Urnes, suspected a mixture of bones; In none we searched was there cause
of such conjecture, though sometimes they declined not that
practise; The ashes of *Domitian* were mingled with those of
Julia, of *Achilles* with those of *Patroclus:* All Urnes contained
not single ashes; Without confused burnings they affectionately
compounded their bones; passionately endeavouring to continue
their living Unions. And when distance of death denied such
conjunctions, unsatisfied affections, conceived some satisfaction
to be neighbours in the grave, to lye Urne by Urne, and touch
but in their names. And many were so curious⁵ to continue their
living relations, that they contrived large, and family Urnes,
wherein the Ashes of their nearest friends and kindred might
successively be received, at least some parcels thereof, while
their collaterall memorials lay in *minor* vessels about them.

Antiquity held too light thoughts from Objects of mortality,
while some drew provocatives of mirth from Anatomies,[2] and
Juglers shewed tricks with Skeletons. When Fidlers made not
so pleasant mirth as Fencers, and men could sit with quiet
stomacks while hanging was plaied [3] before them. Old considerations made few *memento's* by sculs and bones upon their monuments. In the Ægyptian Obelisks and Hieroglyphicall figures, it
is not easie to meet with bones. The sepulchrall Lamps speak

[2] *Sic erimus cuncti, &c. Ergo dum vivimus vivamus.* [So, all of us will come to
this. Therefore, let us sport us while we may.]
[3] *Ἀγχόνην παίζειν.* [The hanging game.] A barbarous pastime at Feasts,
when men stood upon a rolling Globe, with their necks in a Rope fastned to a
beame, and a knife in their hands, ready to cut it when the stone was rolled
away, wherein if they failed, they lost their lives to the laughter of their spectators. *Athenæus.*

nothing lesse then sepulture; and in their literall draughts prove often obscene and antick peeces: Where we finde *D. M.*[4] it is obvious to meet with sacrificing *patera's*, and vessels of libation, upon old sepulchrall Monuments. In the Jewish *Hypogæum* and subterranean Cell at *Rome*, was little observable beside the variety of Lamps, and frequent draughts of the holy Candlestick. In authentick draughts of *Anthony* and *Jerome*, we meet with thigh-bones and deaths heads; but the cemiteriall Cels of ancient Christians and Martyrs, were filled with draughts of Scripture Stories; not declining the flourishes of Cypresse, Palmes, and Olive; and the mysticall Figures of Peacocks, Doves and Cocks. But iterately affecting[s] the pourtraits of *Enoch, Lazarus, Jonas,* and the Vision of *Ezechiel,* as hopefull draughts, and hinting imagery of the Resurrection; which is the life of the grave, and sweetens our habitations in the Land of Moles and Pismires.

Gentile Inscriptions precisely delivered[s] the extent of mens lives, seldome the manner of their deaths, which history it self so often leaves obscure in the records of memorable persons. There is scarce any Philosopher but dies twice or thrice in *Laertius;* Nor almost any life without two or three deaths in *Plutarch;* which makes the tragicall ends of noble persons more favourably resented[s] by compassionate Readers, who finde some relief in the Election of such differences.

The certainty of death is attended with uncertainties, in time, manner, places. The variety of Monuments hath often obscured true graves: and *Cenotaphs* confounded Sepulchres. For beside their reall Tombs, many have found honorary and empty Sepulchres. The variety of *Homers* Monuments made him of various Countreys. *Euripides* had his Tomb in *Attica,* but his sepulture in *Macedonia.* And *Severus* found his real Sepulchre in *Rome,* but his empty grave in *Gallia.*

He that lay in a golden Urne[5] eminently above the Earth, was not like to finde the quiet of these bones. Many of these Urnes were broke by a vulgar discoverer in hope of inclosed treasure. The ashes of *Marcellus* were lost above ground, upon the like account. Where profit hath prompted, no age hath wanted such

4 **Diis manibus.* [For the deified souls of the dead or the gods of the Lower World.]
5 *Trajanus. *Dion.*

miners. For which the most barbarous Expilators[§] found the most civill Rhetorick. Gold once out of the earth is no more due unto it; What was unreasonably committed to the ground is reasonably resumed[§] from it: Let Monuments and rich Fabricks, not Riches adorn mens ashes. The commerce of the living is not to be transferred unto the dead: It is no injustice to take that which none complains to lose, and no man is wronged where no man is possessor.

What virtue[§] yet sleeps in this *terra damnata*[6] and aged cinders, were petty magick to experiment; These crumbling reliques and long-fired particles superannate[§] such expectations: Bones, hairs, nails, and teeth of the dead, were the treasures of old Sorcerers. In vain we revive such practices; Present superstition too visibly perpetuates the folly of our Fore-fathers, wherein unto old Observation this Island was so compleat, that it might have instructed *Persia.*

Plato's historian of the other world, lies twelve dayes incorrupted, while his soul was viewing the large stations of the dead. How to keep the corps seven dayes from corruption by anointing and washing, without exenteration,[§] were an hazardable peece of art, in our choisest practise. How they made distinct separation of bones and ashes from fiery admixture, hath found no historicall solution. Though they seemed to make a distinct collection, and overlooked not *Pyrrhus* his toe.[7] Some provision they might make by fictile Vessels, Coverings, Tiles, or flat stones, upon and about the body. And in the same Field, not farre from these Urnes, many stones were found under ground, as also by carefull separation of extraneous matter, composing and raking up the burnt bones with forks, observable in that notable lamp of *Galvanus. Marlianus,* who had the sight of the *Vas Ustrinum,* or vessell wherein they burnt the dead, found in the Esquiline Field at *Rome,* might have afforded clearer solution. But their insatisfaction herein begat that remarkable invention in the Funerall Pyres of some Princes, by incombustible sheets made with a texture of *Asbestos,* incremable[§] flax, or Salamanders[§] wool, which preserved their bones and ashes incommixed.[§]

---

6 Literally, "condemned earth." In alchemy, the residue remaining after sublimation or calcination, sometimes called "caput mortuum" (death's-head).
7 *Which could not be burnt.

How the bulk of a man should sink into so few pounds of bones and ashes, may seem strange unto any who considers not its constitution, and how slender a masse will remain upon an open and urging fire of the carnall composition. Even bones themselves reduced into ashes, do abate a notable proportion. And consisting much of a volatile salt, when that is fired out, make a light kind of cinders. Although their bulk be disproportionable to their weight, when the heavy principle of Salt is fired out, and the Earth almost only remaineth; Observable in sallow,[§] which makes more Ashes then Oake; and discovers the common fraud of selling Ashes by measure, and not by ponderation.[§]

Some bones make best Skeletons,[8] some bodies quick and speediest ashes: Who would expect a quick flame from Hydropicall *Heraclitus?* The poysoned Souldier when his Belly brake, put out two pyres in *Plutarch.* But in the plague of *Athens,* one private pyre served two or three Intruders; and the *Saracens* burnt in large heaps, by the King of *Castile,* shewed how little Fuell sufficeth. Though the Funerall pyre of *Patroclus* took up an hundred foot, a peece of an old boat burnt *Pompey;* And if the burthen of *Isaac* were sufficient for an holocaust, a man may carry his owne pyre.

From animals are drawn good burning lights, and good medicines against burning; Though the seminall humour seems of a contrary nature to fire, yet the body compleated proves a combustible lump, wherein fire findes flame even from bones, and some fuell almost from all parts. Though the Metropolis of humidity[9] seems least disposed unto it, which might render the sculls of these Urnes lesse burned then other bones. But all flies or sinks before fire almost in all bodies: When the common ligament is dissolved, the attenuable[§] parts ascend, the rest subside in coal, calx or ashes.

To burn the bones of the King of *Edom* for Lyme, seems no irrationall ferity[§]; But to drink of the ashes of dead relations, a passionate prodigality. He that hath the ashes of his friend, hath an everlasting treasure: where fire taketh leave, corruption

8 *Old bones according to *Lyserus.* Those of young persons not tall nor fat according to *Columbus.*
9 *The brain. *Hippocrates.*

slowly enters; In bones well burnt, fire makes a wall against it self; experimented in copels,§ and tests§ of metals, which consist of such ingredients. What the Sun compoundeth,§ fire analyseth,§ not transmuteth. That devouring agent leaves almost allwayes a morsell for the Earth, whereof all things are but a colonie; and which, if time permits, the mother Element will have in their primitive masse again.

He that looks for Urnes and old sepulchrall reliques, must not seek them in the ruines of Temples: where no Religion anciently placed them. These were found in a Field, according to ancient custome, in noble or private buriall; the old practise of the *Canaanites*, the Family of *Abraham*, and the burying place of *Josua*, in the borders of his possessions; and also agreeable unto *Roman* practice to bury by high-wayes, whereby their Monuments were under eye: Memorials of themselves, and *memento's* of mortality into living passengers; whom the Epitaphs of great ones were fain to beg to stay and look upon them. A language though sometimes used, not so proper in Church-Inscriptions.[1] The sensible Rhetorick of the dead, to exemplarity of good life, first admitted the bones of pious men, and Martyrs within Church-wals; which in succeeding ages crept into promiscuous practise. While *Constantine* was peculiarly favoured to be admitted unto the Church Porch; and the first thus buried in *England* was in the dayes of *Cuthred*.

Christians dispute how their bodies should lye in the grave. In urnall enterrment they clearly escaped this Controversie: Though we decline the Religious consideration, yet in cemiteriall and narrower burying places, to avoid confusion and crosse position, a certain posture were to be admitted; Which even Pagan civility observed, The *Persians* lay North and South, The *Megarians* and *Phœnicians* placed their heads to the East: the *Athenians*, some think, towards the West, which Christians still retain. And *Beda* will have it to be the posture of our Saviour. That he was crucified with his face towards the West, we will not contend with tradition and probable account; But we applaud not the hand of the Painter, in exalting his Crosse so high above those on either side; since hereof we finde no authentick account in

1 *Siste viator.* [Stay, traveller.]

history, and even the crosses found by *Helena* pretend no such
distinction from longitude or dimension.

To be gnaw'd out of our graves, to have our sculs made drink-
ing-bowls, and our bones turned into Pipes, to delight and sport
our Enemies, are Tragicall abominations, escaped in burning
Burials.

Urnall enterrments, and burnt Reliques lye not in fear of
worms, or to be an heritage for Serpents; In carnall sepulture,
corruptions seem peculiar unto parts, and some speak of snakes
out of the spinall marrow. But while we suppose common
wormes in graves, 'tis not easie to finde any there; few in
Church-yards above 'a foot deep, fewer or none in Churches,
though in fresh decayed bodies. Teeth, bones, and hair, give
the most lasting defiance to corruption. In an Hydropicall body
ten years buried in a Church-yard, we met with a fat concretion,
where the nitre of the Earth, and the salt and lixivious[§] liquor
of the body, had coagulated large lumps of fat, into the consistence of the hardest castle-soap[§]; whereof part remaineth
with us. After a battle with the *Persians* the *Roman* Corps
decayed in few dayes, while the *Persian* bodies remained dry
and uncorrupted. Bodies in the same ground do not uniformly
dissolve, nor bones equally moulder; whereof in the opprobrious[§]
disease we expect no long duration. The body of the Marquesse
of *Dorset* seemed sound and handsomely cereclothed, that after
seventy eight years was found uncorrupted.[2] Common Tombs
preserve not beyond powder: A firmer consistence and compage[§] of parts might be expected from Arefaction,[§] deep buriall
or charcoal. The greatest Antiquities of mortall bodies may remain in petrified bones, whereof, though we take[§] not in the
pillar of *Lots* wife, or Metamorphosis of *Ortelius*, some may be
older then Pyramids, in the petrified Reliques of the generall
inundation. When *Alexander* opened the Tomb of *Cyrus*, the
remaining bones discovered his proportion, whereof urnall fragments afford but a bad conjecture, and have this disadvantage of
grave enterrments, that they leave us ignorant of most personall
discoveries. For since bones afford not only rectitude and sta-

2 *Of *Thomas* Marquesse of *Dorset*, whose body being buried 1530 was 1608
upon the cutting open of the Cerecloth found perfect and nothing corrupted, the
flesh not hardened, but in colour, proportion, and softnesse like an ordinary
corps newly to be interred. *Burtons* descript. of *Leicestershire*.

bility, but figure unto the body; It is no impossible Physiognomy
to conjecture at fleshy appendencies; and after what shape the
muscles and carnous parts might hang in their full consistences.
A full spread *Cariola*[3] shews a well-shaped horse behinde, handsome formed sculls, give some analogie of fleshy resemblance.
A criticall view of bones makes a good distinction of sexes. Even
colour is not beyond conjecture; since it is hard to be deceived in
the distinction of *Negro*'s sculls.[4] *Dantes* Characters are to be
found in sculls as well as faces.[5] *Hercules* is not onely known by
his foot. Other parts make out their comproportions, and inferences upon whole or parts. And since the dimensions of the head
measure the whole body, and the figure thereof gives conjecture
of the principall faculties; Physiognomy outlives our selves, and
ends not in our graves.

Severe[s] contemplators observing these lasting reliques, may
think them good monuments of persons past, little advantage to
future beings. And considering that power which subdueth all
things unto it self, that can resume[s] the scattered Atomes, or
identifie out of any thing, conceive it superfluous to expect a resurrection out of Reliques. But the soul subsisting, other matter
clothed with due accidents, may salve[s] the individuality: Yet the
Saints we observe arose from graves and monuments, about the
holy City. Some think the ancient Patriarchs so earnestly desired
to lay their bones in *Canaan*, as hoping to make a part of that
Resurrection, and though thirty miles from Mount *Calvary*, at
least to lie in that Region, which should produce the first-fruits of
the dead. And if according to learned conjecture, the bodies of
men shall rise where their greatest Reliques remain, many are
not like to erre in the Topography of their Resurrection, though
their bones or bodies be after translated by Angels into the field
of *Ezechiels* vision, or as some will order it, into the Valley of
Judgement, or *Jehosaphat*.

3 *That part in the Skeleton of an Horse, which is made by the hanch-bones.
4 *For their extraordinary thicknesse.
5 *The Poet *Dante* in his view of Purgatory, found gluttons so meagre, and ex-
tenuated, that he conceited them to have been in the Siege of *Jerusalem*, and
that it was easie to have discovered *Hômo* or *Omo* in their faces: M being
made by the two lines of their cheeks, arching over the Eye brows to the nose,
and their sunk eyes making O O which makes up *Omo*. *Parean l'occhiaie anella
senza gemme / che nel viso de gli huomini legge huomo / Ben'hauria quiui con-
osciuto l'emme.* [Their sockets were like rings without the gems; / Whoever in
the face of men reads *omo* / Might well in these have recognized the *m*.]

CHAPTER IV

Christians have handsomely glossed the deformity of death, by careful consideration of the body, and civil rites which take⁵ of brutall terminations. And though they conceived all reparable by a resurrection, cast not off all care of enterrment. For since the ashes of Sacrifices burnt upon the Altar of God, were carefully carried out by the Priests, and deposed⁵ in a clean field; since they acknowledged their bodies to be the lodging of Christ, and temples of the holy Ghost, they devolved⁵ not all upon the sufficiency of soul existence; and therefore with long services and full solemnities concluded their last Exequies, wherein to all distinctions the Greek devotion seems most pathetically ceremonious.

Christian invention hath chiefly driven at Rites, which speak hopes of another life, and hints of a Resurrection. And if the ancient Gentiles held not the immortality of their better part, and some subsistence after death; in severall rites, customes, actions and expressions, they contradicted their own opinions: wherein *Democritus* went high, even to the thought of a resurrection, as scoffingly recorded by *Pliny*.⁶ What can be more expresse⁵ than the expression of *Phocyllides*?⁷ Or who would expect from *Lucretius*⁸ a sentence of *Ecclesiastes*? Before *Plato* could speak, the soul had wings in *Homer*, which fell not, but flew out of the body into the mansions of the dead; who also observed that handsome distinction of *Demas* and *Soma*, for the body conjoyned to the soul and body separated from it. *Lucian* spoke much truth in jest, when he said, that part of *Hercules* which proceeded from *Alchmena* perished, that from *Jupiter* remained immortall. Thus *Socrates* was content that his friends should bury his body, so they would not think they buried *Socrates*, and regarding only his immortall part, was indifferent to be burnt or buried. From such

---

6 *Similis reviviscendi promissa Democrito vanitas, qui non revixit ipse. Quæ, malùm, ista dementia est; iterari vitam morte.* Plin. l. 7. c. 55. [A similar vanity of coming to life again was promised by Democritus, who did not come to life again himself. Plague take it, what is this mad idea that life is renewed by death? Pliny, Book 7, section 55.]

7 *Καὶ τάχα δ' ἐκ γαίης ἐλπίζομεν ἐς φάον ἐλθεῖν / λείψαν' ἀποιχομένων. & deinceps.* [We, left behind by the dead, hope to go soon from earth to the light, etc.]

8 *Cedit enim retro de terrâ quod fuit ante In terram*, &c. Lucret. [For what came from the earth returns again to the earth (Then shall the dust return to the earth as it was).]

Considerations *Diogenes* might contemn Sepulture. And being
satisfied that the soul could not perish, grow carelesse of corporall enterrment. The *Stoicks* who thought the souls of wise men
had their habitation about the *moon,* might make slight account
of subterraneous deposition;§ whereas the *Pythagorians* and
transcorporating§ Philosophers, who were to be often buried, held
great care of their enterrment. And the Platonicks rejected not a
due care of the grave, though they put their ashes to unreasonable expectations, in their tedious term of return and long set
revolution.

Men have lost their reason in nothing so much as their religion, wherein stones and clouts make Martyrs; and since the
religion of one seems madnesse unto another, to afford an account or rationall of old Rites, requires no rigid§ Reader; That
they kindled the pyre aversly, or turning their face from it, was
an handsome Symbole of unwilling ministration; That they
washed their bones with wine and milk, that the mother wrapt
them in Linnen, and dryed them in her bosome, the first foster-
ing part, and place of their nourishment; That they opened their
eyes towards heaven, before they kindled the fire, as the place of
their hopes or originall, were no improper Ceremonies. Their last
valediction[9] thrice uttered by the attendants was also very
solemn, and somewhat answered§ by Christians, who thought it
too little, if they threw not the earth thrice upon the enterred
body. That in strewing their Tombs the *Romans* affected the
Rose, the Greeks *Amaranthus* and myrtle; that the Funerall
pyre consisted of sweet fuell, Cypresse, Firre, Larix,§ Yewe, and
Trees perpetually verdant, lay silent expressions of their surviv-
ing§ hopes: Wherein Christians which deck their Coffins with
Bays have found a more elegant Embleme. For that tree seeming
dead, will restore it self from the root, and its dry and exuccous§
leaves resume their verdure again; which if we mistake not, we
have also observed in furze. Whether the planting of yewe in
Churchyards, hold not its originall from ancient Funerall rites, or
as an Embleme of Resurrection from its perpetual verdure, may
also admit conjecture.

They made use of Musick to excite or quiet the affections§ of

9 *Vale, vale, nos te ordi[ne] quo natura permittet sequemur.* [Farewell, farewell, we shall follow you in the order which nature will allow.]

their friends, according to different harmonies. But the secret and symbolicall hint was the harmonical nature of the soul; which delivered from the body, went again to enjoy the primitive harmony of heaven, from whence it first descended; which according to its progresse traced by antiquity, came down by *Cancer,* and ascended by *Capricornus.*

They burnt not children before their teeth appeared as apprehending their bodies too tender a morsell for fire, and that their gristly bones would scarce leave separable reliques after the pyrall combustion. That they kindled not fire in their houses for some dayes after, was a strict memoriall of the late afflicting fire. And mourning without hope, they had an happy fraud against excessive lamentation, by a common opinion that deep sorrows disturbed their ghosts.

That they buried their dead on their backs, or in a supine position, seems agreeable unto profound sleep, and common posture of dying; contrary to the most naturall way of birth; Nor like our pendulous posture, in the doubtfull§ state of the womb. *Diogenes* was singular, who preferred a prone situation in the grave, and some Christians[1] like neither, who decline the figure of rest, and make choice of an erect posture.

That they carried them out of the world with their feet forward, not inconsonant unto reason: As contrary unto the native posture of man, and his production§ first into it. And also agreeable unto their opinions, while they bid adieu unto the world, not to look again upon it; whereas *Mahometans* who think to return to a delightfull life again, are carried forth with their heads forward, and looking toward their houses.

They closed their eyes as parts which first die or first discover the sad effects of death. But their iterated clamations to excitate their dying or dead friends, or revoke§ them unto life again, was a vanity of affection; as not presumably ignorant of the criticall tests of death, by apposition of feathers, glasses, and reflexion of figures, which dead eyes represent not; which however not strictly verifiable in fresh and warm *cadavers,* could hardly elude the test, in corps of four or five dayes.

That they suck'd in the last breath of their expiring friends, was surely a practice of no medicall institution, but a loose opin-

1 **Russians,* &c.

ion that the soul passed out that way, and a fondnesse[s] of affection from some *Pythagoricall* foundation, that the spirit of one body passed into another; which they wished might be their own.

That they powred oyle upon the pyre, was a tolerable practise, while the intention rested in facilitating the accension; But to place good *Omens* in the quick and speedy burning, to sacrifice unto the windes for a dispatch in this office, was a low form of superstition.

The *Archimime* or *Jester* attending the Funerall train, and imitating the speeches, gesture, and manners of the deceased, was too light for such solemnities, contradicting their Funerall Orations, and dolefull rites of the grave.

That they buried a peece of money with them as a Fee of the *Elysian Ferriman,* was a practise full of folly. But the ancient custome of placing coynes in considerable Urnes, and the present practise of burying medals in the Noble Foundations of *Europe*, are laudable wayes of historicall discoveries, in actions, persons, Chronologies; and posterity will applaud them.

We examine not the old Laws of Sepulture, exempting certain persons from buriall or burning. But hereby we apprehend that these were not the bones of persons Planet-struck or burnt with fire from Heaven: No Reliques of Traitors to their Countrey, Self-killers, or Sacrilegious Malefactors; Persons in old apprehension unworthy of the *earth;* condemned unto the *Tartara's*[2] of Hell, and bottomlesse pit of *Pluto,* from whence there was no redemption.

Nor were only many customes questionable in order to their Obsequies, but also sundry practises, fictions, and conceptions, discordant or obscure, of their state and future beings; whether unto eight or ten bodies of men to adde one of a woman, as being more inflammable, and unctuously constituted for the better pyrall combustion, were any rationall practise: Or whether the complaint of *Perianders* Wife be tolerable, that wanting her Funerall burning she suffered intolerable cold in Hell, according to the constitution of the infernall house of *Pluto,* wherein cold makes a great part of their tortures; it cannot passe without some question.

Why the Female Ghosts appear unto *Ulysses,* before the *Heroes*

2 The infernal regions.

and masculine spirits? Why the *Psyche* or soul of *Tiresias* is of the masculine gender; who being blinde on earth sees more then all the rest in hell; Why the Funerall Suppers consisted of Egges, Beans, Smallage,§ and Lettuce, since the dead are made to eat *Asphodels* about the *Elyzian* medows? Why since there is no Sacrifice acceptable, nor any propitiation for the Covenant of the grave; men set up the Deity of *Morta,* and fruitlesly adored Divinities without ears? it cannot escape some doubt.

The dead seem all alive in the humane *Hades* of *Homer,* yet cannot well speak, prophesie, or know the living, except they drink bloud, wherein is the life of man. And therefore the souls of *Penelope*'s Paramours conducted by *Mercury* chirped like bats, and those which followed *Hercules* made a noise but like a flock of birds.

The departed spirits know things past and to come, yet are ignorant of things present. *Agamemnon* foretels what should happen unto *Ulysses,* yet ignorantly enquires what is become of his own Son. The Ghosts are afraid of swords in *Homer,* yet *Sybilla* tels *Æneas* in *Virgil,* the thin habit of spirits was beyond the force of weapons. The spirits put off their malice with their bodies, and *Cæsar* and *Pompey* accord in Latine Hell, yet *Ajax* in *Homer* endures not a conference with *Ulysses:* And *Deiphobus* appears all mangled in *Virgils* Ghosts, yet we meet with perfect shadows among the wounded ghosts of *Homer.*

Since *Charon* in *Lucian* applauds his condition among the dead, whether§ it be handsomely said of *Achilles,* that living contemner of death, that he had rather be a Plowmans servant then Emperour of the dead? How *Hercules* his soul is in hell, and yet in heaven, and *Julius* his soul in a Starre, yet seen by *Æneas* in hell, except the Ghosts were but Images and shadows of the soul, received in higher mansions, according to the ancient division of body, soul, and image or *simulachrum* of them both. The particulars of future beings must needs be dark unto ancient Theories, which Christian Philosophy yet determines but in a Cloud of opinions. A Dialogue between two Infants in the womb concerning the state of this world, might handsomely illustrate our ignorance of the next, whereof methinks we yet discourse in *Platoes* denne, and are but *Embryon* Philosophers.

Pythagoras escapes§ in the fabulous hell of *Dante,* among that swarm of Philosophers, wherein whilest we meet with *Plato* and *Socrates, Cato* is to be found in no lower place then Purgatory. Among all the set, *Epicurus* is most considerable, whom men make honest without an *Elyzium,* who contemned life without encouragement of immortality, and making nothing after death, yet made nothing of the King of terrours.

Were the happinesse of the next world as closely apprehended as the felicities of this, it were a martyrdome to live; and unto such as consider none hereafter, it must be more then death to dye, which makes us amazed at those audacities,[§] that durst be nothing, and return into their *Chaos* again. Certainly such spirits as could contemn death, when they expected no better being after, would have scorned to live had they known any. And therefore we applaud not the judgment of *Machiavel,* that Christianity makes men cowards, or that with the confidence of but half dying, the despised virtues of patience and humility, have abased the spirits of men, which Pagan principles exalted, but rather regulated the wildenesse of audacities, in the attempts, grounds, and eternall sequels of death; wherein men of the boldest spirits are often prodigiously temerarious. Nor can we extenuate[§] the valour of ancient Martyrs, who contemned death in the uncomfortable scene of their lives, and in their decrepit Martyrdomes did probably lose not many moneths of their dayes, or parted with life when it was scarce worth the living. For (beside that long time past holds no consideration unto a slender time to come) they had no small disadvantage from the constitution of old age, which naturally makes men fearfull; complexionally superannuated from the bold and couragious thoughts of youth and fervent years. But the contempt of death from corporall animosity, promoteth not our felicity. They may set in the *Orchestra,* and noblest Seats of Heaven, who have held up shaking hands in the fire, and humanely contended for glory.

Mean while *Epicurus* lyes deep in *Dante*'s hell, wherein we meet with Tombs enclosing souls which denied their immortalities. But whether the virtuous heathen, who lived better then he spake, or erring in the principles of himself, yet lived above Philosophers of more specious Maximes, lye so deep as he is placed; at least so low as not to rise against[§] Christians, who beleeving or knowing that truth, have lastingly denied it in their practise and conversation,[§] were a quæry too sad to insist on.

But all or most apprehensions rested in Opinions of some future being, which ignorantly or coldly[§] beleeved, begat those perverted conceptions, Ceremonies, Sayings, which Christians pity or laugh at. Happy are they, which live not in that disadvantage of time, when men could say little for futurity, but from reason. Whereby the noblest mindes fell often upon doubtfull deaths, and melancholly Dissolutions; With these hopes *Socrates* warmed his doubtfull spirits, against that cold potion, and *Cato* before he durst give the fatall stroak spent part of the night in reading the immortality of *Plato,* thereby confirming his wavering hand unto the animosity of that attempt.

It is the heaviest stone that melancholy can throw at a man, to tell him he is at the end of his nature; or that there is no further state to come, unto which this seemes progressionall, and otherwise made in vaine; Without this accomplishment the naturall expectation and desire of such a state, were but a fallacy in nature; unsatisfied Considerators would quarrell the justice of their constitutions, and rest content that *Adam* had fallen lower, whereby by knowing no other Originall, and deeper ignorance of themselves, they might have enjoyed the happinesse of inferiour Creatures; who in tranquility possesse their Constitutions, as having not the apprehension to deplore their own natures. And being framed below the circumference of these hopes, or cognition of better being, the wisedom of God hath necessitated their Contentment: But the superiour ingredient and obscured part of our selves, whereto all present felicities afford no resting contentment, will be able at last to tell us we are more then our present selves; and evacuate[§] such hopes in the fruition of their own accomplishments.

CHAPTER V

Now since these dead bones have already out-lasted the living ones of *Methuselah,* and in a yard under ground, and thin walls of clay, out-worn all the strong and specious[§] buildings above it; and quietly rested under the drums and tramplings of three con-

quests; What Prince can promise such diuturnity§ unto his Reliques, or might not gladly say,

Sic ego componi versus in ossa velim.[3]

Time which antiquates Antiquities, and hath an art to make dust
of all things, hath yet spared these *minor* Monuments. In vain we
hope to be known by open and visible conservatories, when to be
unknown was the means of their continuation and obscurity their
protection: If they dyed by violent hands, and were thrust into
their Urnes, these bones become considerable, and some old Philosophers would honour them, whose souls they conceived most
pure, which were thus snatched from their bodies; and to retain a
stronger propension§ unto them: whereas they weariedly left a
languishing corps, and with faint desires of re-union. If they fell
by long and aged decay, yet wrapt up in the bundle of time, they
fall into indistinction, and make but one blot with Infants. If we
begin to die when we live, and long life be but a prolongation of
death; our life is a sad composition; We live with death, and die
not in a moment. How many pulses made up the life of *Methuselah,* were work for *Archimedes:* Common Counters summe up
the life of *Moses* his man. Our dayes become considerable like
petty sums by minute accumulations; where numerous fractions
make up but small round numbers; and our dayes of a span§ long
make not one little finger.[4]

If the nearnesse of our last necessity, brought a nearer conformity unto it, there were a happinesse in hoary hairs, and no
calamity in half senses. But the long habit of living indisposeth
us for dying; When Avarice makes us the sport of death; When
even *David* grew politickly cruell; and *Solomon* could hardly be
said to be the wisest of men. But many are too early old, and before the date of age. Adversity stretcheth our dayes, misery
makes *Alcmenas* nights,[5] and time hath no wings unto it. But the
most tedious§ being is that which can unwish it self, content to
be nothing, or never to have been, which was beyond the *male-
content§* of *Job,* who cursed not the day of his life, but his Nativity: Content to have so farre been, as to have a Title to future

---

3 Thus would I wish to be gathered together when turned into bones.
4 *According to the ancient Arithmetick of the hand wherein the little finger of
the right hand contracted, signified an hundred. *Pierius in Hieroglyph.*
5 *One night as long as three.

being; Although he had lived here but in an hidden state of life, and as it were an abortion.

What Song the *Syrens* sang, or what name *Achilles* assumed when he hid himself among women, though puzling Questions are not beyond all conjecture. What time the persons of these Ossuaries entred the famous Nations of the dead, and slept with Princes and Counsellours, might admit a wide solution. But who were the proprietaries of these bones, or what bodies these ashes made up, were a question above Antiquarism. Not to be resolved by man, nor easily perhaps by spirits, except we consult the Provinciall Guardians, or tutellary Observators. Had they made as good provision for their names, as they have done for their Reliques, they had not so grosly erred in the art of perpetuation. But to subsist in bones, and be but Pyramidally extant, is a fallacy in duration. Vain ashes, which in the oblivion of names, persons, times, and sexes, have found unto themselves, a fruitlesse continuation, and only arise unto late posterity, as Emblemes of mortall vanities; Antidotes against pride, vain-glory, and madding vices. Pagan vain-glories which thought the world might last for ever, had encouragement for ambition, and finding no *Atropos* unto the immortality of their Names, were never dampt with the necessity§ of oblivion. Even old ambitions had the advantage of ours, in the attempts of their vain-glories, who acting early, and before the probable Meridian§ of time, have by this time found great accomplishment of their designes, whereby the ancient *Heroes* have already out-lasted their Monuments, and Mechanicall preservations. But in this latter Scene of time we cannot expect such Mummies unto our memories, when ambition may fear the Prophecy of *Elias*,[6] and *Charles* the fifth can never hope to live within two *Methusela's* of *Hector*.[7]

And therefore restlesse inquietude for the diuturnity of our memories unto present considerations, seems a vanity almost out of date, and superanuated peece of folly. We cannot hope to live so long in our names, as some have done in their persons, one face of *Janus* holds no proportion unto the other. 'Tis too late to be ambitious. The great mutations of the world are acted, or

[6] *That the world may last but six thousand years.
[7] *Hectors fame lasting above two lives of *Methuselah*, before that famous Prince was extant.

time may be too short for our designes. To extend our memories by Monuments, whose death we dayly pray for, and whose duration we cannot hope, without injury to our expectations, in the advent of the last day, were a contradiction to our beliefs. We whose generations are ordained in this setting part of time, are providentially taken off from such imaginations. And being necessitated to eye the remaining particle of futurity, are naturally constituted unto thoughts of the next world, and cannot excusably decline the consideration of that duration, which maketh Pyramids pillars of snow, and all that's past a moment.

Circles and right§ lines limit and close all bodies, and the mortall right-lined circle,[8] must conclude and shut up all. There is no antidote against the *Opium* of time, which temporally considereth all things; Our Fathers finde their graves in our short memories, and sadly tell us how we may be buried in our Survivors. Gravestones tell truth scarce fourty years:[9] Generations passe while some trees stand, and old Families last not three Oaks. To be read by bare Inscriptions like many in *Gruter*, to hope for Eternity by Ænigmaticall Epithetes, or first letters of our names, to be studied by Antiquaries, who we were, and have new Names given us like many of the Mummies,[1] are cold consolations unto the Students of perpetuity, even by everlasting Languages.

To be content that times to come should only know there was such a man, not caring whether they knew more of him, was a frigid ambition in *Cardan:* disparaging his horoscopal inclination and judgement of himself. Who cares to subsist like *Hippocrates* Patients, or *Achilles* horses in *Homer*, under naked nominations, without deserts and noble acts, which are the balsame of our memories, the *Entelechia*[2] and soul of our subsistences? To be namelesse in worthy deeds exceeds an infamous history. The *Canaanitish* woman lives more happily without a name, then *Herodias* with one. And who had not rather have been the good theef, then *Pilate*?

But the iniquity of oblivion blindely scattereth her poppy, and

---

8 *$_θ$ The Character§ of death.
9 *Old ones being taken up, and other bodies laid under them.
1 *Which men show in several Countries, giving them what Names they please; and unto some the Names of the old Ægyptian Kings out of *Herodotus*.
2 That which gives form or perfection to anything.

deals with the memory of men without distinction to merit of perpetuity. Who can but pity the founder of the Pyramids? *Herostratus* lives that burnt the Temple of *Diana,* he is almost lost that built it; Time hath spared the Epitaph of *Adrians* horse, confounded[§] that of himself. In vain we compute our felicities by the advantage of our good names, since bad have equall durations; and *Thersites* is like to live as long as *Agamemnon.* Who knows whether the best of men be known? or whether there be not more remarkable persons forgot, then any that stand remembred in the known account of time? without the favour of the everlasting Register the first man had been as unknown as the last, and *Methuselahs* long life had been his only Chronicle.

Oblivion is not to be hired: The greater part must be content to be as though they had not been, to be found in the Register of God, not in the record of man. Twenty seven Names make up the first story,[3] and the recorded names ever since contain not one living Century. The number of the dead long exceedeth all that shall live. The night of time far surpasseth the day, and who knows when was the Æquinox[§]? Every houre addes unto that current Arithmetique, which scarce stands one moment. And since death must be the *Lucina*[§] of life, and even Pagans could doubt whether thus to live, were to dye. Since our longest Sunne sets at right[§] descensions, and makes but winter arches,[§] and therefore it cannot be long before we lie down in darknesse, and have our light in ashes.[4] Since the brother of death daily haunts us with dying *memento*'s, and time that grows old it self, bids us hope no long duration: Diuturnity is a dream and folly of expectation.

Darknesse and light divide the course of time, and oblivion shares with memory, a great part even of our living beings; we slightly remember our felicities, and the smartest stroaks of affliction leave but short smart upon us. Sense endureth no extremities, and sorrows destroy us or themselves. To weep into stones are fables. Afflictions induce callosities, miseries are slippery, or fall like snow upon us, which notwithstanding is no unhappy stupidity. To be ignorant of evils to come, and forgetfull of

3 *Before the flood.
4 *According to the custome of the Jewes, who placed a lighted wax-candle in a pot of ashes by the Corps. *Leo.*

evils past, is a mercifull provision in nature, whereby we digest the mixture of our few and evil dayes, and our delivered senses not relapsing into cutting remembrances, our sorrows are not kept raw by the edge of repetitions. A great part of Antiquity contented their hopes of subsistency with a transmigration of their souls. A good way to continue their memories, while having the advantage of plurall successions, they could not but act something remarkable in such variety of beings, and enjoying the fame of their passed selves, make accumulation of glory unto their last durations. Others rather then be lost in the uncomfortable night of nothing, were content to recede into the common being, and make one particle of the publick soul of all things, which was no more then to return into their unknown and divine Originall again. Ægyptian ingenuity was more unsatisfied, contriving their bodies in sweet consistences, to attend§ the return of their souls. But all was vanity, feeding the winde, and folly. The Ægyptian Mummies, which *Cambyses* or time hath spared, avarice now consumeth. Mummie§ is become Merchandise, *Mizraim*§ cures wounds, and *Pharaoh* is sold for balsoms.

In vain do individuals hope for Immortality, or any patent§ from oblivion, in preservations below the Moon: Men have been deceived even in their flatteries above the Sun, and studied conceits§ to perpetuate their names in heaven. The various Cosmography of that part hath already varied the names of contrived constellations; *Nimrod* is lost in *Orion*, and *Osyris* in the Doggestarre. While we look for incorruption in the heavens, we finde they are but like the Earth; Durable in their main bodies, alterable in their parts: whereof beside Comets and new Stars, perspectives§ begin to tell tales. And the spots that wander about the Sun, with *Phaetons* favour, would make clear conviction.

There is nothing strictly immortall, but immortality; whatever hath no beginning may be confident of no end. All others have a dependent being, and within the reach of destruction,§ which is the peculiar of that necessary essence that cannot destroy it self; And the highest strain of omnipotency to be so powerfully constituted, as not to suffer even from the power of it self. But the sufficiency of Christian Immortality frustrates all earthly glory, and the quality of either state after death, makes a folly of posthumous memory. God who can only destroy our souls, and hath assured our resurrection, either of our bodies or names hath directly promised no duration. Wherein there is so much of chance that the boldest Expectants have found unhappy frustration; and to hold long subsistence, seems but a scape[§] in[§] oblivion. But man is a Noble Animal, splendid in ashes, and pompous in the grave, solemnizing Nativities and Deaths with equall lustre, nor omitting Ceremonies of bravery,[§] in the infamy of his nature.

Life is a pure flame, and we live by an invisible Sun within us. A small fire sufficeth for life, great flames seemed too little after death, while men vainly affected precious pyres, and to burn like *Sardanapalus,* but the wisedom of funerall Laws found the folly of prodigall blazes, and reduced undoing[§] fires, unto the rule of sober obsequies, wherein few could be so mean as not to provide wood, pitch, a mourner, and an Urne.[5]

Five Languages secured not the Epitaph of *Gordianus;*[6] The man of God lives longer without a Tomb then any by one, invisibly interred by Angels, and adjudged to obscurity, though not without some marks directing humane discovery. *Enoch* and *Elias* without either tomb or buriall, in an anomalous state of being, are the great Examples of perpetuity, in their long and living memory, in strict account being still on this side death, and having a late part yet to act upon this stage of earth. If in the decretory[§] term of the world we shall not all dye but be changed, according to received translation; the last day will make but few graves; at least quick Resurrections will anticipate lasting Sepultures; Some Graves will be opened before they be quite closed, and *Lazarus* be no wonder. When many that feared to dye shall groane that they can dye but once, the dismall state is the second

---

5 *According to the Epitaph of *Rufus* and *Beronica* in *Gruterus,*

—Nec ex
Eorum bonis plus inventum est, quam
Quod sufficeret ad emendam pyram
Et picem quibus corpora cremarentur,
Et præfica conducta & olla empta.

[Nor did they possess more than what sufficed to buy a pyre and pitch, with which their bodies might be burned, and to hire a mourner and purchase an urn.]

6 *In Greek, Latine, Hebrew, Ægyptian, Arabick, defaced by *Licinius* the Emperour.

and living death, when life puts despair on the damned; when
men shall wish the coverings of Mountaines, not of Monuments,
and annihilation shall be courted.

While some have studied[§] Monuments, others have studiously
declined them: and some have been so vainly boisterous, that
they durst not acknowledge their Graves; wherein *Alaricus* seems
most subtle, who had a River turned to hide his bones at the bottome. Even *Sylla* that thought himself safe in his Urne, could not
prevent revenging tongues, and stones thrown at his Monument.
Happy are they whom privacy makes innocent, who deal so with
men in this world, that they are not afraid to meet them in the
next, who when they dye, make no commotion among the dead,
and are not toucht with that poeticall taunt of *Isaiah*.

Pyramids, Arches, Obelisks, were but the irregularities of vain-
glory, and wilde enormities of ancient magnanimity.[§] But the
most magnanimous resolution rests in the Christian Religion,
which trampleth upon pride, and sets on the neck of ambition,
humbly pursuing that infallible perpetuity, unto which all others
must diminish their diameters, and be poorly seen in Angles of
contingency.[7]

Pious spirits who passed their dayes in raptures of futurity,
made little more of this world, then the world that was before it,
while they lay obscure in the Chaos of pre-ordination, and night
of their fore-beings. And if any have been so happy as truly to
understand Christian annihilation, extasis,[§] exolution,[§] liquefac-
tion, transformation, the kisse of the Spouse, gustation of God,
and ingression into the divine shadow, they have already had an
handsome anticipation of heaven; the glory of the world is surely
over, and the earth in ashes unto them.

To subsist in lasting Monuments, to live in their productions,
to exist in their names, and prædicament of *Chymera*'s, was large
satisfaction unto old expectations, and made one part of their
Elyziums. But all this is nothing in the Metaphysicks of true belief. To live indeed is to be again our selves, which being not only
an hope but an evidence in noble beleevers; 'Tis all one to lye in
S. *Innocents* Church-yard,[8] as in the Sands of *Ægypt:* Ready to

7 **Angulus contingentiæ*, the least of Angles.
8 *In *Paris* where bodies soon consume.

be any thing, in the extasie of being ever, and as content with six foot as the Moles of *Adrianus*.[9]

Lucan
——*Tabesne cadavera solvat*
An rogus haud refert.——[1]

[9] *A stately *Mausoleum* or sepulchral pyle built by *Adrianus* in *Rome*, where now standeth the Castle of S. *Angelo*.
[1] It makes little difference whether gradual decay or the funeral fire consumes the corpses.

V

John Bunyan

FROM

*Grace Abounding
to the chief of Sinners:*

OR, A BRIEF AND FAITHFUL RELATION
OF THE EXCEEDING MERCY OF GOD IN
CHRIST, TO HIS POOR SERVANT
JOHN BUNYAN

A PREFACE:

Or brief Account of the publishing of this Work:

Written by the Author thereof,
and dedicated to those whom
God hath counted him wor-
thy to beget to Faith, by his
Ministry in the Word.

*Children, Grace be with you, Amen. I being taken from you in
presence, and so tied up, that I cannot perform that duty that
from God doth lie upon me, to you-ward, for your further edify-*

ing and building up in Faith and Holiness, &c., *yet that you may see my Soul hath fatherly care and desire after your spiritual and everlasting welfare; I now once again, as before from the top of* Shenir *and* Hermon, *so now from* the Lions Dens, and from the Mountains of the Leopards (*Song* 4. 8), *do look yet after you all, greatly longing to see your safe arrival into* THE *desired haven.*

I thank God upon every Remembrance of you, and rejoyce even while I stick between the Teeth of the Lions in the Wilderness, at the grace, and mercy, and knowledge of Christ our Saviour, which God hath bestowed upon you, with abundance of Faith and Love. Your hungerings and thirstings also after further acquaintance with the Father, in his Son; your tenderness of Heart, your trembling at sin, your sober and holy department also, before both God and men, is great refreshment to me: For you are my glory and joy, (I *Thes.* 2. 20).

I have sent you here enclosed a drop of that honey, that I have taken out of the Carcase of a Lyon (*Judg.* 14. 5, 6, 7, 8). *I have eaten thereof my self also, and am much refreshed thereby.* (*Temptations when we meet them at first, are as the* Lyon *that roared upon* Sampson; *but if we overcome them, the next time we see them, we shall finde a Nest of Honey within them.*) *The* Philistians *understand me not. It is a Relation of the work of God upon my own Soul, even from the very first, till now; wherein you may perceive my castings down, and raisings up; for he woundeth, and his hands make whole. It is written in the Scripture* (*Isai.* 38. 19), The father to the children shall make known the truth of God. *Yea, it was for this reason I lay so long at* Sinai⁵ (*Deut.* 4. 10, 11), *to see the fire, and the cloud, and the darkness,* that I might fear the Lord all the days of my life upon earth, and tell of his wondrous works to my children, *Psal.* 78. 3, 4, 5.

Moses (*Numb.* 33. 1, 2) *writ of the Journeyings of the children of* Israel, *from* Egypt *to the Land of* Canaan; *and commanded also, that they did remember their forty years travel in the wilderness.* Thou shalt remember all the way which the Lord thy God led thee these forty years in the wilderness, to humble thee, and to prove thee, to know what was in thine heart, whether thou wouldst keep his commandments, or no, *Deut.* 8. 2, 3. *Wherefore this I have endeavoured to do; and not onely so, but to publish it also; that, if God will, others may be put in re-*

membrance of what he kath done for their Souls, by reading his work upon me.

It is profitable for Christians to be often calling to mind the very beginnings of Grace with their Souls. It is a night to be much observed to the Lord, for bringing them out from the land of *Egypt.* This is that night of the Lord to be observed of all the children of *Israel* in their generations, *Exod.* 12. 42. My God, *saith David,* Psal. 42. 6. my soul is cast down within me; but I will remember thee from the land of Jordan, and of the Hermonites, from the hill Mizar. *He remembred also the Lyon and the Bear, when he went to fight with the Giant of Gath,* I Sam. 17. 36, 37.

It was Pauls *accustomed manner,* Acts 22. *and that when tried for his life,* Acts 24. *even to open before his Judges, the manner of his Conversion: He would think of that day and that hour, in the which he first did meet with Grace: for he found it support unto him. When God had brought the children of* Israel *thorow⁵ the* Red Sea, *far into the wilderness; yet they must turn quite about thither again, to remember the drowning of their enemies there,* Num. 14. 25. *for though they sang his praise before, yet they soon forgat his works,* Psal. 106. 12, 13.

In this Discourse of mine, you may see much; much, I say, of the Grace of God towards me: I thank God *I can count it much; for it was above my sins, and* Satans *temptations too. I can remember my fears, and doubts, and sad moneths, with comfort; they are as the head of* Goliah *in my hand. There was nothing to* David *like* Goliahs *sword, even that sword that should have been sheathed in his bowels; for the very sight and remembrance of that, did preach forth* Gods *Deliverance to him. O the remembrance of my great sins, of my great temptations, and of my great fears of perishing for ever! They bring fresh into my mind the remembrance of my great help, my great support from* Heaven, *and the great grace that* God *extended to such a Wretch as I.*

My dear Children, call to mind the former days, the years of ancient times; remember also your songs in the night, and commune with your own heart, Psal. 77. 5, 6, 7, 8, 9, 10, 11, 12. *Yea, look diligently, and leave no corner therein unsearched, for there is treasure hid, even the treasure of your first and second experi-*

ence of the grace of God *toward you. Remember, I say, the Word
that first laid hold upon you; remember your terrours of conscience, and fear of death and hell: remember also your tears
and prayers to* God; *yea, how you sighed under every hedge for
mercy. Have you never a Hill Mizar to remember? Have you forgot the Close,§ the Milk-house, the Stable, the Barn, and the like,
where* God *did visit your Soul? Remember also the Word, the
Word, I say, upon which the Lord hath caused you to hope: If
you have sinned against light, if you are tempted to blaspheme,
if you are down in despair, if you think* God *fights against you,
or if heaven is hid from your eyes; remember 'twas thus with
your father,* but out of them all the Lord delivered me.

*I could have enlarged much in this my discourse of my temp-
tations and troubles for sin, as also of the merciful kindness and
working of* God *with my Soul: I could also have stepped into a
stile much higher then this in which I have here discoursed,
and could have adorned all things more then here I have seemed
to do: but I dare not:* God *did not play in convincing of me; the*
Devil *did not play in tempting of me; neither did I play when I
sunk as into a bottomless pit, when* the pangs of hell caught hold
upon me: *wherefore I may not play in my relating of them, but
be plain and simple, and lay down the thing as it was: He that
liketh it, let him receive* it; *and he that does not, let him produce
a better.* Farewel.

My dear Children,

The Milk and Honey is beyond this Wilderness: God be merciful to you, and grant that you be not slothful to go in to possess
the Land.

Jo. Bunyan.

1. IN this my relation of the merciful working of God upon my
Soul, it will not be amiss, if in the first place, I do, in a few
words, give you a hint of my pedegree, and manner of bringing
up; that thereby the goodness and bounty of God towards me,
may be the more advanced and magnified before the sons of
men.

2. For my descent then, it was, as is well known by many, of a low and inconsiderable generation; my fathers house being of that rank that is meanest, and most despised§ of all the families in the Land. Wherefore I have not here, as others, to boast of Noble blood, or of a High-born state according to the flesh; though all things considered, I magnifie the Heavenly Majesty, for that by this door he brought me into this world, to partake of the Grace and Life that is in Christ by the Gospel.

3. But yet notwithstanding the meanness and inconsiderableness of my Parents, it pleased God to put it into their heart, to put me to School, to learn both to Read and Write; the which I also attained, according to the rate of other poor mens children, though to my shame I confess, I did soon loose§ that little I learned, even almost utterly, and that long before the Lord did work his gracious work of conversion upon my Soul.

4. As for my own natural life, for the time that I was without God in the world, it was indeed according to the course of this world, and the spirit that now worketh in the children of disobedience: Eph. 2. 2, 3. it was my delight to be taken captive by the Devil *at his will*, 2 Tim. 2. 26. being filled with all unrighteousness; the which did also so strongly work, and put forth itself, both in my heart and life, and that from a childe, that I had but few Equals, (especially considering my years, which were tender, being few) both for cursing, swearing, lying and blaspheming the holy Name of God.

5. Yea, so setled and rooted was I in these things, that they became as a second Nature to me; the which, as I also have with soberness considered since, did so offend the Lord, that even in my childhood he did scare and affright me with fearful dreams, and did terrifie me with dreadful visions. For often, after I had spent this and the other day in sin, I have in my bed been greatly afflicted, while asleep, with the apprehensions of Devils, and wicked spirits, who still, as I then thought, laboured to draw me away with them; of which I could never be rid.

6. Also I should at these years be greatly afflicted and troubled with the thoughts of the day of Judgment, and that both night and day, and should tremble at the thoughts of the fearful torments of Hell-fire; still fearing that it would be my lot to be found

at last amongst those Devils and Hellish Fiends, who are there bound down with the chains and bonds of eternal darkness.

7. These things, I say, when I was but a childe, about nine or ten years old, did so distress my Soul, that then in the midst of my many sports and childish vanities, amidst my vain companions, I was often much cast down and afflicted in my mind therewith, yet could I not let go my sins: yea, I was so overcome with despair of Life and Heaven, that then I should often wish, either that there had been no Hell, or that I had been a Devil; supposing they were onely tormentors; that if it must needs be, that I indeed went thither, I might be rather a tormentor, then tormented my self.

8. A while after, these terrible dreams did leave me, which also I soon forgot; for my pleasures did quickly cut off the remembrance of them, as if they had never been: wherefore, with more greediness, according to the strength of Nature, I did still let loose the reins to my lusts, and delighted in all transgression against the Law of God: so that until I came to the state of marriage, I was the very ringleader of all the Youth that kept me company, into all manner of vice and ungodliness.

9. Yea, such prevalency had the lusts and fruits of the flesh, in this poor Soul of mine, that had not a miracle of precious grace prevented, I had not onely perished by the stroke of eternal Justice, but had also laid my self open, even to the stroke of those Laws, which bring some to disgrace and open shame before the face of the world.

10. In these days, the thoughts of Religion was very grievous to me; I could neither endure it my self, nor that any other should; so that when I have but seen some read in those books that concerned Christian piety, it would be as it were a prison to me. *Then I said unto God, Depart from me, for I desire not the knowledge of thy ways*, Job. 21. 14, 15. I was now void of all good consideration; Heaven and Hell were both out of sight and minde; and as for Saving and Damning, they were least in my thoughts. *O Lord, thou knowest my life, and my ways were not hid from thee.*

11. Yet this I well remember, that though I could my self sin with the greatest delight and ease, and also take pleasure in the

vileness of my companions; yet even then, if I have at any time seen wicked things by those who professed goodness, it would make my spirit tremble. As once above all the rest, when I was in my heighth of vanity, yet hearing one to swear that was reckoned for a religious man, it had so great a stroke upon my spirit, as it made my heart to ake.

12. But God did not utterly leave me, but followed me still, not now with convictions, but Judgements, yet such as were mixed with mercy. For once I fell into a crick of the Sea, and hardly escaped drowning: another time I fell out of a Boat into *Bedford-*River, but mercy yet preserved me alive: Besides, another time being in the field, with one of my companions, it chanced that an Adder passed over the High way, so I having a stick in mine hand, struck her over the back; and having stounded§ her, I forced open her mouth with my stick, and plucked her sting out with my fingers, by which act had not God been mercifull to me, I might by my desperateness§ have brought myself to mine end.

13. This also have I taken notice of with thanksgiving; when I was a Souldier, I with others were drawn out to go to such a place to besiege it; but when I was just ready to go, one of the company desired to go in my room, to which, when I had consented he took my place; and coming to the siege, as he stood Sentinel, he was shot into the head with a Musket bullet and died.

14. Here, as I said, were Judgements and Mercy, but neither of them did awaken my soul to Righteousness, wherefore I sinned still, and grew more and more rebellious against God, and careless of mine own Salvation.

15. Presently after this, I changed my condition into a married state, and my mercy was, to light upon a Wife whose Father was counted godly: this Woman and I, though we came together as poor as poor might be, (not having so much houshold-stuff as a Dish or Spoon betwixt us both), yet this she had for her part, *The Plain Mans Path-way to Heaven,* and *The Practice of Piety,* which her Father had left her when he died. In these two Books I should sometimes read with her, wherein I also found some things that were somewhat pleasing to me: (but all this while I met with no conviction.) She also would be often telling of me what a godly man her Father was, and how he would reprove and

correct Vice, both in his house, and amongst his neighbours; what a strict and holy life he lived in his day, both in word and deed.

16. Wherefore these books, with this relation, though they did not reach my heart to awaken it about my sad and sinful state, yet they did beget within me some desires to Religion: so that, because I knew no better, I fell in very eagerly with the Religion of the times, to wit, to go to Church twice a day, and that too with the foremost, and there should very devoutly both say and sing as others did; yet retaining my wicked life: but withal, I was so over-run with the spirit of superstition, that I adored, and that with great devotion, even all things, (both the High-place,§ Priest, Clerk, Vestments, Service, and what else) belonging to the Church; counting all things holy that were therein contained; and especially the Priest and Clerk most happy, and without doubt greatly blessed, because they were the Servants, as I then thought, of God, and were principal in the holy Temple, to do his work therein.

17. This conceit§ grew so strong in little time upon my spirit, that had I but seen a Priest, (though never so sordid and debauched in his life) I should find my spirit fall under him, reverence him, and knit unto him; yea, I thought for the love I did bear unto them, (supposing they were the Ministers of God) I could have layn down at their feet, and have been trampled upon by them; their Name, their Garb, and Work, did so intoxicate and bewitch me.

18. After I had been thus for some considerable time, another thought came into my mind, and that was, Whether we were of the *Israelites,* or no: for finding in the Scriptures that they were once the peculiar§ People of God, thought I, if I were one of this race, my Soul must needs be happy. Now again I found within me a great longing to be resolved about this question, but could not tell how I should: at last, I asked my father of it, who told me, *No, we were not:* wherefore then I fell in my spirit, as to the hopes of that, and so remained.

19. But all this while, I was not sensible of the danger and evil of sin; I was kept from considering that sin would damn me, what Religion soever I followed, unless I was found in Christ: nay, I never thought of him, nor whether there was one

or no. Thus man, while blind, doth wander, but wearieth himself with vanity: for he knoweth not the way to the City of God, *Eccles.* 10. 15.

20. But one day, (amongst all the Sermons our Parson made) his subject was, to treat of the Sabbath day, and of the evil of breaking that, either with labour, sports, or otherwise: (now I was, notwithstanding my Religion, one that took much delight in all manner of vice, and especially that was the Day that I did solace my self therewith.) Wherefore I fell in my conscience under his Sermon, thinking and believing that he made that Sermon on purpose to shew me my evil-doing; and at that time I felt what guilt was, though never before, that I can remember; but then I was for the present greatly loaden therewith, and so went home when the Sermon was ended, with a great burden upon my spirit.

21. This, for that instant, did benum the sinews of my best delights, and did imbitter my former pleasures to me: but behold, it lasted not; for before I had well dined, the trouble began to go off my minde, and my heart returned to its old course: but Oh how glad was I, that this trouble was gone from me, and that the fire was put out, that I might sin again without controul! Wherefore, when I had satisfied nature with my food, I shook the Sermon out of my mind, and to my old custom of sports and gaming I returned with great delight.

22. But the same day, as I was in the midst of a game at Cat,[§] and having struck it one blow from the hole; just as I was about to strike it the second time, a voice did suddenly dart from Heaven into my Soul, which said, *Wilt thou leave thy sins, and go to Heaven? or have thy sins, and go to Hell?* At this I was put to an exceeding maze; wherefore, leaving my Cat upon the ground, I looked up to Heaven, and was as if I had with the eyes of my understanding, seen the Lord Jesus looking down upon me, as being very hotly displeased with me, and as if he did severely threaten me with some grievous punishment for these, and other my ungodly practices.

23. I had no sooner thus conceived in my mind, but suddenly this conclusion was fastned on my spirit (for the former hint did set my sins again before my face) *That I had been a great and grievous Sinner, and that it was now too late for me to*

look after Heaven; for Christ would not forgive me, nor pardon my transgressions. Then I fell to musing upon this also; and while I was thinking on it, and fearing lest it should be so, I felt my heart sink in despair, concluding it was too late; and therefore I resolved in my mind I would go on in sin: for thought I, if the case be thus, my state is surely miserable; miserable if I leave my sins; and but miserable if I follow them: I can but be damned; and if I must be so, I had as good be damned for many sins, as be damned for few.

24. Thus I stood in the midst of my play, before all that then were present; but yet I told them nothing: but, I say, I having made this conclusion, I returned desperately to my sport again; and I well remember, that presently this kind of despair did so possess my Soul, that I was perswaded I could never attain to other comfort then what I should get in sin; for Heaven was gone already, so that on that I must not think: wherefore I found within me a great desire to take my fill of sin, still studdying what sin was set to be committed, that I might taste the sweetness of it; and I made as much haste as I could to fill my belly with its delicates, lest I should die before I had my desire; for that I feared greatly. In these things, I protest before *God,* I lye not, neither do I feign this sort of speech: these were really, strongly, and with all my heart, my desires; *the good Lord, whose mercy is unsearchable, forgive me my transgressions.*

25. (And I am very confident, that this temptation of the Devil is more than usual amongst poor creatures then many are aware of, even to over-run their spirits with a scurvie[§] and seared[§] frame of heart, and benumming of conscience: which frame, he stilly and slyly supplyeth with such despair, that though not much guilt attendeth the Soul, yet they continually have a secret conclusion within them, that there is no hopes for them; *for they have loved sins, therefor after them they will go,* Jer. 2. 25 & 18. 12.)

26. Now therefore I went on in sin with great greediness of mind, still grudging that I could not be so satisfied with it as I would: this did continue with me about a moneth, or more. But one day, as I was standing at a Neighbours Shop-window, and there cursing and swearing, and playing the Mad-man, after

my wonted manner, there sate within the woman of the house, and heard me; who, though she was a very loose and ungodly Wretch, yet protested that I swore and cursed at that most fearful rate, that she was made to tremble to hear me; And told me further, *That I was the ungodliest Fellow for swearing that ever she heard in all her life; and that I, by thus doing, was able to spoile all the Youth in a whole Town, if they came but in my company.*

27. At this reproof I was silenced, and put to secret shame; and that too, as I thought, before the God of Heaven: wherefore, while I stood there, and hanging down my head, I wished with all my heart that I might be a little childe again, that my Father might learn me to speak without this wicked way of swearing: for, thought I, I am so accustomed to it, that it is but in vain for me to think of a reformation, for I thought it could never be.

28. But how it came to pass I know not, I did from this time forward so leave my swearing, that it was a great wonder to my self to observe it; and whereas before I knew not how to speak unless I put an Oath before, and another behind, to make my words have authority, now, I could, without it, speak better, and with more pleasantness then ever I could before: all this while I knew not Jesus Christ, neither did I leave my sports and play.

29. But quickly after this, I fell in company with one poor man that made profession§ of Religion; who, as I then thought, did talk pleasantly of the Scriptures, and of the matters of Religion: wherefore falling into some love and liking to what he said, I betook me to my Bible, and began to take great pleasure in reading, but especially with the historical part thereof: for, as for *Pauls* Epistles, and Scriptures of that nature, I could not away§ with them, being as yet but ignorant either of the corruptions of my nature, or of the want and worth of Jesus Christ to save me.[1]

30. Wherefore I fell to some outward Reformation, both in my words and life, and did set the Commandments before me for my way to Heaven: which Commandments I also did strive to keep; and, as I thought, did keep them pretty well sometimes,

---

[1] He was ignorant of his own need to be saved by Christ and of Christ's role in his salvation.

and then I should have comfort; yet now and then should break one, and so afflict my Conscience; but then I should repent, and say I was sorry for it, and promise God to do better next time, and there get help again, for then I thought I pleased God as well as any man in *England*.

31. Thus I continued about a year, all which time our Neighbours did take me to be a very godly man, a new and religious man, and did marvel much to see such a great and famous alteration in my life and manners; and indeed so it was, though yet I knew not Christ, nor Grace, nor Faith, nor Hope; and truly as I have well seen since, had I then died, my state had been most fearful: well, this I say, continued about a twelve-month, or more.

32. But, I say, my Neighbours were amazed at this my great Conversion, from prodigious profaneness, to something like a moral life; and, truly, so they well might; for this my Conversion was as great, as for *Tom*^{s} of *Bethlem* to become a sober man. Now, therefore, they began to praise, to commend, and to speak well of me, both to my face, and behind my back. Now, I was, as they said, become godly; now, I was become a right honest man. But Oh! when I understood that these were their words and opinions of me, it pleased me mighty well: For though, as yet, I was nothing but a poor painted Hypocrite, yet I love to be talked of as one that was truly Godly. I was proud of my Godliness; and, I did all I did, either to be seen of, or to be well spoken of, by men: well, this I say, continued for about a twelve-month or more.

33. Now you must know, that before this I had taken much delight in ringing, but my Conscience beginning to be tender, I thought that such a practice was but vain, and therefore forced my self to leave it, yet my mind hanckered, wherefore I should go to the Steeple^s house, and look on: though I durst not ring. But I thought this did not become Religion neither, yet I forced my self and would look on still; but quickly after, I began to think, How, if one of the Bells should fall: then I chose to stand under a main Beam that lay over thwart the Steeple from side to side, thinking there I might stand sure: But then I should think again, Should the Bell fall with a swing, it might first hit the Wall, and then rebounding upon me, might kill me for all

this Beam; this made me stand in the Steeple door, and now thought I, I am safe enough, for if a Bell should then fall, I can slip out behind these thick Walls, and so be preserved notwithstanding.

34. So after this, I would yet go to see them ring, but would not go further than the Steeple door; but then it came into my head, how if the Steeple it self should fall, and this thought, (it may fall for ought I know) would when I stood and looked on, continually so shake my mind, that I durst not stand at the Steeple door any longer, but was forced to fly, for fear it should fall upon my head.

35. Another thing was my dancing, I was a full year before I could quite leave it; but all this while, when I thought I kept this or that Commandment, or did by word or deed any thing that I thought were good, I had great peace in my Conscience, and should think with my self, God cannot chuse but be now pleased with me, yea, to relate it in mine own way, I thought no man in *England* could please God better than I.

36. But poor Wretch as I was, I was all this while ignorant of Jesus Christ, and going about to establish my own righteousness, had perished therein, had not God in mercy shewed me more of my state by nature.

37. But upon a day, the good providence of God did cast me to *Bedford,* to work on my calling;§ 2 and in one of the streets of that town, I came where there was three or four poor women sitting at a door in the Sun, and talking about the things of God; and being now willing to hear them discourse, I drew near to hear what they said; for I was now a brisk talker also my self in the matters of Religion: but now I may say, *I heard, but I understood not;* for they were far above out of my reach, for their talk was about a new birth, the work of God on their hearts, also how they were convinced of their miserable state by nature: they talked how God had visited their souls with his love in the Lord Jesus, and with what words and promises they had been refreshed, comforted, and supported against the temptations of the Devil; moreover, they reasoned of the suggestions and temptations of Satan in particular, and told to each other by which they had been afflicted, and how they were borne up under his

2 Bunyan was an itinerant tinker.

assaults: they also discoursed of their own wretchedness of heart, of their unbelief, and did contemn, slight, and abhor their own righteousness, as filthy, and insufficient to do them any good.

38. And me thought they spake as if joy did make them speak: they spake with such pleasantness of Scripture language, and with such appearance of grace in all they said, that they were to me as if they had found a new world, as if they were people that dwelt alone, and were not to be reckoned among their Neighbours, Num. 23. 9.

39. At this I felt my own heart began to shake, as mistrusting my condition to be naught; for I saw that in all my thoughts about Religion and Salvation, the New birth did never enter into my mind, neither knew I the comfort of the Word and Promise, nor the deceitfulness and treachery of my own wicked heart. As for secret thoughts, I took no notice of them; neither did I understand what Satans temptations were, nor how they were to be withstood and resisted, &c.

40. Thus therefore when I had heard and considered what they said, I left them, and went about my employment again: but their talk and discourse went with me, also my heart would tarry with them, for I was greatly affected with their words, both because by them I was convinced that I wanted the true tokens of a truly godly man, and also because by them I was convinced of the happy and blessed condition of him that was such a one.

41. Therefore I should often make it my business to be going again and again into the company of these poor people; for I could not stay away; and the more I went amongst them, the more I did question my condition; and as still I do remember, presently I found two things within me, at which I did sometimes marvel, (especially considering what a blind, ignorant, sordid, and ungodly Wretch but just before I was) the one was, a very great softness and tenderness of heart, which caused me to fall under the conviction of what by Scripture they asserted; and the other was, a great bending in my mind to a continual meditating on them, and on all other good things which at any time I heard or read of.

42. By these things my mind was now so turned, that it lay

like a Horseleach at the vein, still crying out, *Give, give*, Prov.
30. 15. Yea, it was so fixed on Eternity, and on the things about
the Kingdome of Heaven, that is, so far as I knew, though as yet
God knows, I knew but little, that neither pleasures nor profits,
nor perswasions, nor threats, could loosen it, or make it let go
its hold; and though I may speak it with shame, yet it is in very
deed a certain truth, it would then have been as difficult for
me to have taken my mind from heaven to earth, as I have
found it often since to get it again from earth to heaven.

43. One thing I may not omit, there was a young man in
our Town, to whom my heart before was knit more than to any
other, but he being a most wicked Creature for cursing and
swearing, and whoring, I shook him off and forsook his company; but about a quarter of a year after I had left him, I met
him in a certain Lane, and asked him how he did; he after his
old swearing and mad way, answered, he was well. *But* Harry,
said I, *why do you swear and curse thus? what will become of
you if you die in this condition?* He answered me in a great
chafe, *What would the Devil do for company if it were not for
such as I am?*

44. About this time I met with some *Ranters*§ books, that
were put forth by some of our Country men; which Books were
also highly in esteem by several old Professors;§ some of these
I read, but was not able to make a Judgement about them;
wherefore, as I read in them, and thought upon them, feeling
myself unable to judge, I should betake myself to hearty prayer,
in this manner; *O Lord, I am a fool, and not able to know the
Truth from Errour; Lord leave me not to my own blindness,
either to approve of, or condemn this Doctrine; If it be of God,
let me not despise it; if it be of the Devil, let me not embrace it.
Lord, I lay my Soul, in this matter, only at thy foot, let me not
be deceived, I humbly beseech thee.* I had one religious intimate
Companion all this while, and that was the poor man that I
spoke of before; but about this time he also turned a most
devilish *Ranter*, and gave himself up to all manner of filthiness,
especially Uncleanness; he would also deny that there was a
God, Angel, or Spirit, and would laugh at all exhortations to
sobriety. When I laboured to rebuke his wickedness, he would
laugh the more, and pretend that he had gone through all Reli-

gions, and could never light on the right till now, he told me also that in little time I should see all Professors turn to the ways of the Ranters: Wherefore abominating those cursed principles, I left his company forth with, and became to him as great a stranger as I had been before a familiar.

45. Neither was this man onely a temptation to me, but my Calling lying in the Countrey, I happened to light into several peoples company; who though strict in Religion formerly, yet were also swept away by these Ranters. These would also talk with me of their ways, and condemn me as legal§ and dark,§ pretending that they only had attained to perfection that could do what they would and not sin. O these temptations were suitable to my flesh, I being but a young man and my nature in its prime; but God, who had as I hope designed me for better things, kept me in the fear of his name, and did not suffer me to accept of such cursed principles. And blessed be God, who put it into my heart to cry to him to be kept and directed, still distrusting mine own Wisdom; for I have since seen even the effect of that prayer in his preserving me, not onely from *Ranting* Errors, but from those also that have sprung up since. The Bible was precious to me in those days.

46. And now, me thought, I began to look into the Bible with new eyes, and read as I never did before; and especially the Epistles of the Apostle S. *Paul* were sweet and pleasant to me: and indeed, I was then never out of the Bible, either by reading or meditation, still crying out to *God,* that I might know the truth, and way to Heaven and Glory.

47. And as I went on and read, I lighted on that passage, *To one is given by the Spirit the word of wisdome; to another the word of knowledge by the same Spirit, and to another Faith,* &c. I Cor. 12. And though, as I have since seen, that by this Scripture the holy Ghost intends, in special, things extraordinary, yet on me it did then fasten with conviction, that I did want things ordinary, even that understanding and wisdome that other Christians had. On this word I mused, and could not tell what to do, especially this word Faith put me to it, for I could not help it, but sometimes must question, whether I had any Faith or no; for I feared that it shut me out of all the blessings that other good people had given them of *God:* but I was loath to

conclude I had no Faith in my soul: for if I do so, thought I,
then I shall count my self a very Cast-away indeed.

48. No, said I with myself, though I am convinced that I
am an ignorant Sot,§ and that I want those blessed gifts of
knowledge and understanding that other good people have, yet
at a venture I will conclude I am not altogether faithless, though
I know not what Faith is. For it was shewed me, and that too
(as I have since seen) by Satan, That those who conclude themselves in a faithless state, have neither rest nor quiet in their
Souls; and I was loath to fall quite into despair.

49. Wherefore by this suggestion, I was for a while made
afraid to see my want of Faith; but God would not suffer§ me
thus to undo and destroy my *Soul,* but did continually, against
this my blinde and sad conclusion, create still within me such
suppositions, insomuch that I could not rest content until I did
now come to some certain knowledge whether I had Faith or
no; this always running in my minde, *But how if you want
Faith indeed? But how can you tell you have Faith?* And besides, I saw for certain, if I had not, I was sure to perish for ever.

50. So that though I endeavoured at the first to look over the
business of Faith, yet in a little time, I better considering the
matter, was willing to put myself upon the tryal, whether I had
Faith or no. But alas, poor Wretch! so ignorant and brutish was
I, that I knew to this day no more how to do it, than I know
how to begin and accomplish that rare and curious piece of Art,
which I never yet saw nor considered.

51. Wherefore while I was thus considering, and being put
to my plunge§ about it, (for you must know that as yet I had in
this matter broken§ my mind to no man, onely did hear and
consider) the Tempter came in with this delusion, That there
was no way for me to know I had Faith, but by trying to work
some miracle, urging those *Scriptures* that seem to look that way,
for the inforcing and strengthening his Temptation. Nay, one
day as I was betwixt *Elstow* and *Bedford,* the Temptation was
hot upon me to try if I had Faith by doing of some miracle;
which miracle at that time was this, I must say to the puddles
that were in the horse§ pads, *Be dry;* and to the dry places, *Be
you the puddles:* and truly, one time I was a going to say so
indeed; but just as I was about to speak, this thought came into

my minde, *But go under yonder Hedge, and pray first, that God would make you able:* but when I had concluded to pray, this came hot upon me, That if I prayed and came again and tried to do it, and yet did nothing notwithstanding, then besure I had no Faith, but was a Cast-away and lost: Nay, thought I, if it be so, I will never try yet, but will stay a little longer.

52. So I continued at a great loss; for I thought, if they onely had Faith, which could do such wonderful things, then I concluded that for the present I neither had it, nor yet for time to come were ever like to have it. Thus I was tossed betwixt the Devil and my own ignorance, and so perplexed, especially at some times, that I could not tell what to doe.

53. About this time, the state and happiness of these poor people at *Bedford* was thus, in a kind of Vision, presented to me: I saw as if they were set on the Sunny side of some high Mountain, there refreshing themselves with the pleasant beams of the Sun, while I was shivering and shrinking in the cold, afflicted with frost, snow, and dark clouds; methought also betwixt me and them I saw a wall that did compass about this Mountain; now, thorow this wall my Soul did greatly desire to pass, concluding that if I could, I would goe even into the very midst of them, and there also comfort myself with the heat of their Sun.

54. About this wall I thought myself to goe again and again, still prying as I went, to see if I could find some way or passage, by which I might enter therein, but none could I find for some time: at the last I saw as it were, a narrow gap, like a little door-way in the wall, thorow which I attempted to pass: but the passage being very straight, and narrow, I made many offers§ to get in, but all in vain, even untill I was well nigh quite beat out by striving to get in: at last, with great striving, me thought I at first did get in my head, and after that, by a side-ling striving, my shoulders, and my whole body; then I was exceeding glad, and went and sat down in the midst of them, and so was comforted with the light and heat of their Sun.

55. Now, this Mountain and Wall, &c., was thus made out to me; the Mountain signified the Church of the living God; the Sun that shone thereon, the comfortable shining of his mercifull face on them that were therein: the wall I thought was the

Word that did make separation between the Christians and the world: and the gap which was in this wall, I thought was Jesus Christ, who is the way to God the Father, *Job.* 14. 6. *Mat.* 7. 14. But for as much as the passage was wonderful narrow, even so narrow, that I could not but with great difficulty, enter in thereat; it shewed me, that none could enter into life but those that were in down-right earnest, and unless they left this wicked world behind them; for here was only roome for Body and Soul, but not for Body and Soul, and Sin.

56. This resemblance abode upon my spirit many dayes, all which time I saw myself in a forlorn and sad condition, but yet was provoked to a vehement hunger and desire to be one of that number that did sit in this Sun-shine: now also I should pray where ever I was, whether at home or abroad, in house or field, and should also often with lifting up of heart, sing that of the fifty first Psalm, *O Lord, consider my distress:* for as yet I knew not where I was.

89. In this condition I went a great while, but when comforting time was come, I heard one preach a sermon upon those words in the *Song*[3] (*Song* 4. 1), *Behold thou art fair, my Love; behold, thou art fair;* but at that time he made these two words, *My Love,* his chief and subject matter; from which after he had a little opened the text, he observed these several conclusions: 1. *That the Church, and so every saved Soul, is Christs Love, when loveless:* 2. *Christs Love without a cause:* 3. *Christs Love when hated of the world:* 4. *Christs Love when under temptation, and under dissertion.*[§] 5. *Christs Love from first to last.*

90. But I got nothing by what he said at present, only when he came to the application of the fourth particular, this was the word he said, *If it be so, that the saved soul is Christs love when under temptation and dissertion; then poor tempted Soul, when thou art assaulted and afflicted with temptation, and the hidings of Gods Face, yet think on these two words,* MY LOVE, *still.*

91. So as I was a going home, these words came again into my thoughts, and I well remember as they came in, I said thus in my heart, What shall I get by thinking on these two words? this thought had no sooner passed thorow my heart, but the

[3] Of Solomon.

words began thus to kindle in my Spirit, *Thou art my Love, thou
art my Love,* twenty times together; and still as they ran thus
in my minde, they waxed stronger and warmer, and began to
make me look up; but being as yet between hope and fear, I
still replied in my heart, *But is it true too? but is it true?* at
which, that sentence fell in upon me, *He wist not that it was
true which was done unto him of the angel,* Act. 12. 9.

92. Then I began to give place to the Word, which with
power, did over and over make this joyful sound within my
Soul, *Thou art my Love, thou art my Love; and nothing shall
separate thee from my love;* and with that *Rom.* 8. 39 came
into my minde. Now was my heart filled full of comfort and
hope, and now I could believe that my sins should be forgiven
me; yea, I was now so taken with the love and mercy of God,
that I remember I could not tell how to contain till I got home;
I thought I could have spoken of his Love, and of his mercy to
me, even to the very Crows that sat upon the plow'd lands before
me, had they been capable to have understood me, wherefore
I said in my Soul with much gladness, Well, I would I had a pen
and ink here, I would write this down before I go any further,
for surely I will not forget *this* forty years hence; but alas!
within less then forty days I began to question all again.

93. Yet still at times, I was helped to believe that it was a
true manifestation of Grace unto my Soul, though I had lost
much of the life and savour of it. Now about a week or fortnight
after this, I was much followed by this scripture, *Simon, Simon,
behold, Satan hath desired to have you,* Luk. 22. 31. And sometimes it would sound so loud within me, yea, and as it were call
so strongly after me, that once above all the rest, I turned my
head over my shoulder, thinking verily that some man had behind me called to me, being at a great distance, methought he
called so loud, it came as I have thought since to have stirred
me up to prayer and to watchfulness. It came to acquaint me
that a cloud and a storm was coming down upon me, but I understood it not.

94. Also as I remember, that time as it called to me so loud,
it was the last time that it sounded in mine ears, but methinks
I hear still with what a loud voice these words, *Simon, Simon,*
sounded in my ears. I thought verily, as I have told you, that

somebody had called after me that was half a mile behind me; and although that was not my name, yet it made me suddenly look behind me, believing that he that called so loud meant me.

95. But so foolish was I, and ignorant, that I knew not the reason for this sound, (which as I did both see and feel soon after, was sent from heaven as an alarm to awaken me to provide for what was coming;) onely it would make me muse, and wonder in my minde to think what should be the reason that this Scripture, and that at this rate, so often and so loud, should still be sounding and ratling in mine ears. But, as I said before, I soon after perceived the end of God therein.

96. For about the space of a month after, a very great storm came down upon me, which handled me twenty times worse then all I had met with before: it came stealing upon me, now by one piece, then by another; first all my comfort was taken from me, then darkness seized upon me; after which whole flouds of Blasphemies, both against God, Christ, and the Scriptures, was poured upon my spirit, to my great confusion and astonishment. These blasphemous thoughts were such as also stirred up questions in me, against the very *being* of God, and of his onely beloved Son; as whether there were in truth a God or Christ, or no? and whether the holy Scriptures were not rather a Fable and cunning Story, then the holy and pure Word of God?

97. The Tempter would also much assault me with this: How can you tell but that the Turks had as good Scriptures to prove their *Mahomet* the Saviour, as we have to prove our *Jesus* is; and could I think that so many ten thousands in so many Countreys and Kingdoms, should be without the knowledge of the right way to Heaven (if there were indeed a Heaven) and that we onely, who live but in a corner of the Earth, should alone be blessed therewith? Everyone doth think his own Religion rightest, both *Jews*, and *Moors*, and *Pagans;* and how if all our Faith, and Christ, and Scriptures, should be but a think-so too?

98. Sometime I have endeavoured to argue against these suggestions, and to set some of the Sentences of blessed *Paul* against them; but, alas! I quickly felt when I thus did, such arguings as these would return again upon me; Though we made so great a matter of *Paul,* and of his words, yet how could

I tell but that in very deed, he, being a subtle and cunning man, might give himself up to deceive with strong delusions, and also take both that pains and travel[3] to undo and destroy his fellows?

99. These suggestions (with many other which at this time I may not, nor dare not utter, neither by word nor pen) did make such a seizure upon my spirit, and did so over-weigh my heart, both with their number, continuance, and fiery force, that I felt as if there were nothing else but these from morning to night within me, and as though, indeed, there could be room for nothing else; and also concluded that God had in very wrath to my Soul given me up unto them, to be carried away with them, as with a mighty whirlwind.

100. Onely by the distaste that they gave unto my spirit, I felt there was something in me that refused to embrace them: but this consideration I then onely had, when God gave me leave to swallow my spittle,[4] otherwise the noise, and strength, and force of these temptations would drown and overflow, and as it were bury all such thoughts or the remembrance of any such thing. While I was in this temptation, I should often find my mind suddenly put upon it, to curse and swear, or to speak some grievous thing of *God,* or *Christ* his *Son,* and of the *Scriptures.*

101. Now I thought surely I am possessed of the Devil; at other times again I thought I should be bereft of my wits, for instead of lauding and magnifying of *God* the *Lord* with others, if I have but heard him spoken of, presently some most horrible blasphemous thought or other would bolt out of my heart against him. So that whether I did think that God was, or again did think there were no such thing; no love, nor peace, nor gracious disposition could I feel within me.

102. These things did sink me into very deep despair, for I concluded, that such things could not possibly be found amongst them that loved God. I often, when these temptations have been with force upon me, did compare my self in the case of such a Child, whom some Gypsie hath by force took up under her apron, and is carrying from Friend and Country; kick sometimes I did, and also scream and cry; but yet I was as bound in the wings of the temptation, and the wind would carry me away. I thought

4 Bunyan has Job vii. 17 in mind; distress makes swallowing difficult.

also of *Saul,* and of the evil spirit that did possess him; and did
greatly fear that my condition was the same with that of his,
1 Sam. 16. 14.

103. In these days, when I have heard others talk of what
was the sin against the Holy *Ghost,* then would the Tempter so
provoke me to desire to sin that sin, that I was as if I could not,
must not, neither should be quiet until I had committed that;
now no sin would serve but that: if it were to be committed
by speaking of such a word, then I have been as if my mouth
would have spoken that word whether I would or no; and in so
strong a measure was this temptation upon me, that often I
have been ready to clap my hand under my chin, to hold my
mouth from opening; and to that end also I have had thoughts
at other times to leap with my head downward, into some
Muckhil-hole or other, to keep my mouth from speaking.

104. Now again I blessed the condition of the Dogge and
Toad, and counted the estate of everything that *God* had made
far better then this dreadfull state of mine, and such as my
companions was: yea, gladly would I have been in the condition
of Dog or Horse, for I knew they had no Soul to perish under
the everlasting weights of Hell for sin, as mine was like to do:
Nay, and though I saw this, felt this, and was broken to pieces
with it, yet that which added to my sorrow, was, that I could
not finde that with all my Soul I did desire deliverance. That
Scripture did also tear and rend my soul in the midst of these
distractions. *The wicked are like the troubled Sea which cannot
rest, whose waters cast up mire and dirt: There is no peace to
the wicked, saith my God,* Isa. 57. 20, 21.

105. And now my heart was, at times, exceeding hard; if I
would have given a thousand pounds for a tear, I could not shed
one; no, nor sometimes scarce desire to shed one. I was much
dejected to think that this should be my lot. I saw some could
mourn and lament their sin; and others, again, could rejoyce,
and bless God for Christ; and others, again, could quietly talk
of, and with gladness remember, the Word of God; while I only
was in the storm or tempest. This much sunk me; I thought my
condition was alone. I should, therefore, much bewail my hard
hap;§ but get out of, or get rid of, these things, I could not.

128. Now had I an evidence, as I thought, of my salvation from Heaven, with many golden Seals thereon, all hanging in my sight; now could I remember this manifestation, and the other discovery of grace with comfort; and should often long and desire that the last day were come, that I might for ever be inflamed with the sight, and joy, and communion of him, whose Head was crowned with Thorns, whose Face was spit on, and Body broken, and Soul made an offering for my sins: for whereas before I lay continually trembling at the mouth of Hell; now me thought I was got so far therefrom, that I could not, when I looked back, scarce discern it; and O thought I, that I were fourscore years old now, that I might die quickly, that my soul might be gone to rest.

129. But before I had got thus far out of these my temptations, I did greatly long to see some ancient Godly man's Experience, who had writ some hundred of years before I was born; for, for those who had writ in our days, I thought (but I desire them now to pardon me) that they had Writ only that which others felt, or else had, thorow the strength of their Wits and Parts, studied to answer such Objections as they perceived others were perplexed with, without going down themselves into the deep. Well, after many such longings in my mind, the God in whose hands are all our days and ways, did cast into my hand, one day, a book of *Martin Luther*, his comment on the *Galathians*, so old that it was ready to fall piece from piece, if I did but turn it over. Now I was pleased much that such an old book had fallen into my hand; the which, when I had but a little way perused, I found my condition in his experience, so largely and profoundly handled, as if his Book had been written out of my heart; this made me marvel: for thus thought I, this man could not know anything of the state of Christians now, but must needs write and speak of the Experience of former days.

130. Besides, he doth most gravely also, in that book debate of the rise of these temptations, namely, Blasphemy, Desperation, and the like, shewing that the law of *Moses*, as well as the Devil, Death, and Hell, hath a very great hand therein; the which at first was very strange to me, but considering and

watching, I found it so indeed. But of Particulars here I intend nothing, only this methinks I must let fall before all men, I do prefer this book of Mr. *Luther* upon the *Galathians* (excepting the Holy Bible) before all the books that ever I have seen, as most fit for a wounded Conscience.

131. And now I found, as I thought, that I loved Christ dearly. O me thought my Soul cleaved unto him, my affections cleaved unto him. I felt love to him as hot as fire, and now, as Job said, I thought I should die in my nest; but I did quickly find, that my great love was but little, and that I, who had, as I thought, such burning love to Jesus Christ, could let him go again for a very trifle. God can tell how to abase us; and can hide pride from Man. Quickly after this my love was tried to purpose.

132. For after the Lord had in this manner thus graciously delivered me from this great and sore temptation, and had set me down so sweetly in the Faith of his holy gospel, and had given me such strong consolation and blessed evidence from heaven touching my interest in his love through Christ; the Tempter came upon me again, and that with a more grievous and dreadful temptation then before.

133. And that was to sell and part with this most blessed Christ, to exchange him for the things of this life; for any thing: the temptation lay upon me for the space of a year, and did follow me so continually, that I was not rid of it one day in a month, no not sometimes one hour in many dayes together, unless I was asleep.

134. And though, in my judgement, I was perswaded, that those who were once effectually[§] in Christ (as I hoped, through his grace, I had seen my self) could never lose him for ever, *For the land shall not be sold for ever, for the Land is mine*, saith *God*, Levit. 25. 23, yet it was a continual vexation to me, to think that I should have so much as one such thought within me against a Christ, a Jesus, that had done for me as he had done; and yet then I had almost none others, but such blasphemous ones.

135. But it was neither my dislike of the thought, nor yet any desire and endeavour to resist it, that in the least did shake or abate the continuation or force and strength thereof; for it did alwayes in almost whatever I thought, intermix itself there-

with, in such sort that I could neither eat my food, stoop for
a pin, chop a stick, or cast mine eye to look on this or that, but
still the temptation would come, *Sell Christ for this, or sell
Christ for that; sell him, sell him.*

136. Sometimes it would run in my thoughts not so little as
a hundred times together, Sell him, sell him, sell him; against
which, I may say, for whole hours together I have been forced
to stand as continually leaning and forcing my spirit against it,
lest haply before I were aware, some wicked thought might arise
in my heart that might consent thereto; and sometimes also the
Tempter would make me believe I had consented to it, then
should I be as tortured on a Rack for whole dayes together.

137. This temptation did put me to such scares lest I should
at sometimes, I say, consent thereto, and be overcome therewith,
that by the very force of my mind in labouring to gainsay and
resist this wickedness my very Body also would be put into action or motion, by way of pushing or thrusting with my hands
or elbows; still answering, as fast as the destroyer said, *Sell him;*
I will not, I will not, I will not, I will not, no not for thousands,
thousands, thousands of worlds; thus reckoning lest I should in
the midst of these assaults, set too low a vallue of him, even
until I scarce well knew where I was, or how to be composed
again.

138. At these seasons he would not let me eat my food at
quiet, but forsooth, when I was set at the Table at my meat, I
must go hence to pray, I must leave my food now, just now, so
counterfeit holy would this Divel be. When I was thus tempted,
I should say in myself, *Now I am at my meat, let me make an
end. No,* said he, *you must do it now, or you will displease God,
and despise Christ.* Wherefore I was much afflicted with these
things; and because of the sinfulness of my nature, (imagining
that these things were impulses from God) I should deny to
do it as if I denyed God; and then should I be as guilty because
I did not obey a temptation of the Devil, as if I had broken the
Law of God indeed.

139. But to be brief, one morning, as I did lie in my Bed, I
was, as at other times, most fiercely assaulted with this temptation, to *sell and part with Christ;* the wicked suggestion still
running in my mind, *Sell him, sell him, sell him, sell him,* as

fast as a man could speak; against which also in my mind, as at other times, I answered, No, no, not for thousands, thousands, thousands, at least twenty times together; but at last, after much striving, even until I was almost out of breath, I felt this thought pass through my heart, *Let him go if he will!* and I thought also that I felt my heart freely consent thereto. Oh, the diligence of Satan! Oh, the desperateness of man's heart!

140. Now was the battel won, and down I fell, as a Bird that is shot from the top of a Tree, into great guilt and fearful despair; thus getting out of my Bed, I went moping into the field; but God knows with as heavy a heart as mortal man, I think, could bear; where for the space of two hours, I was like a man bereft of life, and as now past all recovery, and bound over to eternal punishment.

141. And withal, that Scripture did seize upon my Soul, *Or profane person, as Esau, who for one morsel of meat sold his Birth-right; for you know how that afterwards when he would have inherited the blessing, he was rejected, for he found no place of repentance, though he sought it carefully with tears,* Heb. 12. 16, 17.

142. Now was I as one bound, I felt myself shut up unto the Judgment to come; nothing now for two years together would abide with me, but damnation, and an expectation of damnation: I say, nothing now would abide with me but this, save some few moments for relief, as in the sequel you will see.

143. These words were to my Soul like Fetters of Brass to my Legs, in the continual sound of which I went for several months together. But about ten or eleven a Clock one day, as I was walking under a Hedge, full of sorrow and guilt God knows, and bemoaning myself for this hard hap, that such a thought should arise within me, suddenly this sentence bolted in upon me, *The Blood of Christ remits all guilt;* at this I made a stand in my Spirit: with that, this word took hold upon me, *The blood of Jesus Christ his Son cleanseth us from all sin,* 1 John 1. 7.

144. Now I began to conceive peace in my Soul, and methought I saw as if the Tempter did lear⁵ and steal away from me, as being ashamed of what he had done. At the same time also I had my sin, and the Blood of Christ thus represented to

me, That my sin when compared to the Blood of Christ, was no
more to it, than this little clot§ or stone before me, is to this vast
and wide field that here I see: This gave me good encouragement for the space of two or three hours; in which time also,
me thought I saw by faith the Son of God as suffering for my
sins. But because it tarried not, I therefore sunk in my spirit
under exceeding guilt again.

145. But chiefly by the aforementioned Scripture, concerning
Esaus selling of his Birth-right; for that Scripture would lie all
day long, all the week long; yea, all the year long in my mind,
and hold me down, so that I could by no means lift up my self;
for when I would strive to turn me to this Scripture, or that for
relief, still that Sentence would be sounding in me, *For ye know,*
how that afterward, when he would have inherited the blessing
he found no place of repentance, though he sought it carefully
with tears.

146. Sometimes, indeed, I should have a touch from that in
Luk. 22. 31, *I have prayed for thee, that thy Faith fail not;*
but it would not abide upon me: neither could I indeed, when
I consider'd my state, find ground to conceive in the least, that
there should be the root of that Grace within me, having sinned
as I had done. Now was I tore and rent in heavy§ case, for many
days together.

147. Then began I with sad and careful§ heart, to consider of
the nature and largeness of my sin, and to search in the word
of God, if I could in any place espy a word of Promise, or any
encouraging Sentence by which I might take relief. Wherefore
I began to consider that third of *Mark, All manner of sins and*
blasphemies shall be forgiven unto the sons of men, wherewith
soever they shall blaspheme: Which place, me thought, at a
blush,§ did contain a large and glorious Promise for the pardon
of high offences; but considering the place more fully, I thought
it was rather to be understood, as relating more chiefly to those
who had, while in a natural state, committed such things as
there are mentioned, but not to me, who had not onely received
light and mercie but that had both after and also contrary to
that, so slighted Christ as I had done.

148. I feared therefore that this wicked sin of mine might
be that sin unpardonable, of which he there thus speaketh, *But*

he that shall blaspheme against the Holy Ghost, hath never for-
giveness, but is in danger of eternal damnation, Mar. 3: And
I did the rather give credit to this, because of that sentence in
the *Hebrews, For you know how that afterwards, when he*
would have inherited the blessing, he was rejected; for he found
no place of repentance, though he sought it carefully with tears.
For this stuck always with me.

149. And *now* was I both a burthen and a terror to myself,
nor did I ever so know, as *now,* what it was to be weary of my
life, and yet afraid to die. Oh, how gladly now would I have
been anybody but myself! Any thing but a man! and in any condition but mine own! for there was nothing did pass more frequently over my mind, than that it was impossible for me to be
forgiven my transgression, and to be saved from wrath to come.

150. And now began I to labour to call again time that was
past; wishing a thousand times twice told, that the day was yet
to come, when I should be tempted to such a sin; concluding
with great indignation, both against my heart and all assaults,
how I would rather have been torn in pieces, than found a con-
senter thereto: but alas! these thoughts and wishings, and
resolvings, were now too late to help me; the thought had
passed my heart, God hath let me go, and I am fallen: O,
thought I, *that it was with me as in months past, as in the days*
when God preserved me! Job 29. 2.

151. Then again, being loath and unwilling to perish, I began
to compare my sin with others, to see if I could find that any of
those that are saved had done as I had done. So I considered
David's Adultery and Murder, and found them most hainous
crimes, and those too committed after light and grace received:
but yet by considering, I perceived that his transgressions were
onely such as were against the Law of *Moses,* from which the
Lord Christ could, with the consent of his Word deliver him:
but mine was against the *Gospel,* yea, against the Mediator
thereof; I had sold my Saviour.

152. Now again should I be as if racked[§] upon the Wheel;
when I considered, that, besides the guilt that possessed me,
I should be *so* void of grace, *so* bewitched: What, thought I,
must it be no sin but this? Must it needs be the *great transgres-*

sion, Psal. 19. 13? Must *that* wicked one touch my Soul, 1 *Job.*
5. 18? O what stings did I find in all these Sentences!

153. What? thought I, is there but one sin that is unpardonable? But one sin that layeth the Soul without the reach of
Gods Mercy, and must I be guilty of that? Must it needs be that?
Is there but one sin among so many millions of sins, for which
there is no forgiveness, and must I commit this? Oh! unhappy
sin! Oh unhappy Man! These things would so break and confound my Spirit, that I could not tell what to do, I thought at
times they would have broke my wits, and still to aggravate my
misery, that would run in my mind, *You know how that afterwards when he would have inherited the blessing, he was rejected.* Oh! none knows the terrors of those days but my self.

154. After this I came to consider of *Peters* sin which he
committed in denying his Master; and indeed this came nighest
to mine, of any that I could find; for he had denied his Saviour
as I, and that after Light and Mercy received; yea, and that too,
after warning given him: I also considered that he did it both
once and twice; and that, after time to consider betwixt. But
though I put all these circumstances together, that if possible I
might find help, yet I considered again, that his was but *a denial
of his Master,* but mine was *a selling of my Saviour.* Wherefore
I thought with my self, that I came nearer to *Judas,* than either
to *David* or *Peter.*

155. Here again, my torment would flame out and afflict me;
yea, it would grind me as it were to powder, to discern the
preservation of God towards others, while I fell into the snare:
For in my thus considering of other mens sins, and comparing
of them with my own, I could evidently see how God preserved
them notwithstanding their wickedness, and would not let them,
as he had let me, to become a son of perdition.

156. But O how did my Soul at this time prize the preservation that God did set about his People! Ah how safely did I see
them walk, whom God had hedged in! they were within his care,
protection, and special providence: though they were full as bad
as I by nature, yet because he loved them, he would not suffer
them to fall without§ the range of Mercy: but as for me, I was
gone, I had done it; he would not preserve me, nor keep me, but

suffered me, because I was a Reprobate, to fall as I had done. Now did those blessed places,§ that spake of *Gods keeping his people*, shine like the Sun before me, though not to comfort me, but to shew me the blessed state and heritage of those whom the Lord had blessed.

157. Now I saw, that as God had his hand in all providences and dispensations that overtook his Elect, so he had his hand in all the temptations that they had to sin against him, not to animate them unto wickedness, but to chuse their temptations and troubles for them; and also to leave them, for a time, to such sins only as might not destroy, but humble them; as might not put them beyond, but lay them in the way of the renewing of his mercie. But Oh, what love, what care, what kindness and mercy did I now see, mixing itself with the most severe and dreadful of all God's ways to his people! He would let *David, Hezekiah, Solomon, Peter,* and others fall, but he would not let them fall into sin unpardonable, nor into hell for sin. Oh! thought I, these be the men that God hath loved; these be the men that God, though he chastizes them, keeps them in safety by him, and them whom he makes to abide under the shaddow of the Almighty. But all these thoughts added sorrow, grief, and horrour to me, as whatever I now thought on, it was killing to me. If I thought how God kept his own, that was killing to me; If I thought of how I was falling myself, that was killing to me. As all things wrought together for the best, and to do good to them that were the called,§ according to his purpose; so I thought that all things wrought for my dammage, and for my eternal overthrow.

158. Then again, I began to compare my sin with the sin of *Judas,* that if possible I might find that mine differed from that which in truth is unpardonable; and, O thought I, if it should differ from it, though but the breadth of an hair, what a happy condition is my Soul in! And, by considering, I found that *Judas* did his intentionally, but mine was against my prayer and strivings; besides, his was committed with much deliberation, but mine in a fearful hurry, on a sudden; all this while I was tossed to and fro, like the Locusts, and driven from trouble to sorrow; hearing always the sound of *Esau's* fall in mine ears, and of the dreadful consequences thereof.

159. Yet this consideration about *Judas,* his sin, was for a while some little relief unto me: for I saw I had not, as to the circumstances, transgressed so foully as he: but this was quickly gone again, for, I thought with my self, there might be more ways then one to commit the unpardonable sin; and that too, there might be degrees of that, as well as of other transgressions: wherefore, for ought I yet could perceive, this iniquity of mine might be such as might never be passed by.

160. I was often now ashamed, that I should be like such an ugly man as *Judas:* I thought also how loathsome I should be unto all the Saints at the Day of Judgment, insomuch that now I could scarce see a good Man, that I believed had a good Conscience, but I should feel my heart tremble at him, while I was in his presence. Oh! how I saw a glory in walking with God, and what a mercy it was to have a good Conscience before him.

290. In my preaching I have really been§ in pain, and have as it were travelled§ to bring forth Children to God; neither could I be satisfied unless some fruits did appear in my work: if I were fruitless it matter'd not who commended me; but if I were fruitful, I cared not who did condemn. I have thought of that, *He that winneth souls is wise,* Pro. 11. 30. and again, *Lo Children are an heritage of the Lord; and the fruit of the Womb is his Reward: as arrows in the hand of a mighty man, so are Children of the youth; happy is the man that hath filled his quiver with them, they shall not be ashamed, but they shall speak with the Enemies in the gate,* Psal. 127. 3, 4, 5.

291. It pleased me nothing to see people drink in Opinions if they seemed ignorant of Jesus Christ, and the worth of their own Salvation, sound conviction for Sin, especially for Unbelief, and an heart set on fire to be saved by Christ, with strong breathings after a truly sanctified Soul: that was it that delighted me; those were the souls I counted blessed.

292. But in this work, as in all other, I had my temptations attending me, and that of diverse kinds: as sometimes I should be assaulted with great discouragement, therein fearing that I should not be able to speak the Word at all to edification, nay, that I should not be able to speak sence unto the people; at

which times I should have such a strange faintness and strength-
lessness seiz upon my body that my legs have scarce been able
to carry me to the place of Exercise.[§]

293. Sometimes again, when I have been preaching, I
have been violently assaulted with thoughts of blasphemy, and
strongly tempted to speak them with my mouth before the Congregation. I have also at some times, even when I have begun to
speak the Word with much clearness, evidence, and liberty
of speech, yet been before the ending of that Opportunity so
blinded, and so estranged from the things I have been speaking,
and have also bin so straitned in my speech, as to utterance
before the people, that I have been as if I had not known or
remembred what I have been about, or as if my head had been
in a bag all the time of the *exercise*.

294. Again, When as sometimes I have been about to preach
upon some smart[§] and scorching portion of the *Word,* I have
found the tempter suggest, What! will you preach this? this
condemns your self; of this your own Soul is guilty; wherefore
preach not of it at all, or if you do, yet so mince it as to make
way for your own escape, lest instead of awakening others, you
lay that guilt upon your own soul, as you will never get from
under.

295. But I thank the Lord I have been kept from consenting
to these so horrid suggestions, and have rather, as *Sampson,*
bowed my self with all my might, to condemn sin and transgression where ever I found it, yea though therein also I did
bring guilt upon my own Conscience; *Let me die,* thought I,
with the Philistines, Judg. 16. 29, 30, rather than deal corruptly
with the blessed Word of God, *Thou that teachest another,
teachest thou not thyself?* it is far better that thou do judge
thy self, even by preaching plainly to others, then that thou,
to save thyself, imprison the truth in unrighteousness: Blessed
be God for his help also in this.

296. I have also, while found in this blessed work of Christ,
been often tempted to pride and liftings up of heart; and though
I dare not say, I have not been infected with this, yet truly the
Lord of his precious mercy hath so carried it towards me, that
for the most part I have had but small joy to give way to such a
thing: for it hath been my every-days portion to be let into the

evil of my own heart, and still made to see such a multitude of corruptions and infirmities therein, that it hath caused hanging down of the head under all my Gifts and Attainments: I have felt this thorn in the flesh (2 *Cor.* 12. 8, 9.) the very mercy of God to me.

297. I have had also together with this, some notable place or other of the Word presented before me, which word hath contained in it some sharp and piercing sentence concerning the perishing of the Soul, notwithstanding gifts and parts; as for instance, that hath been of great use unto me, *Though I speak with the tongue of men and of angels, and have not charity, I am become as sounding-brass, and a tinkling cymbal,* 1 Cor. 13. 1, 2.

298. A tinkling Cymbal is an instrument of Musick with which a skilful player can make such melodious and heart-inflaming Musick, that all who hear him play, can scarcely hold from dancing; and yet behold the Cymbal hath not life, neither comes the musick from it, but because of the art of him that playes therewith: so then the instrument at last may come to nought and perish, though in times past such musick hath been made upon it.

299. Just thus I saw it was and will be with them who have Gifts, but want saving-Grace; they are in the hand of Christ, as the Cymbal in the hand of *David;* and as *David* could, with the Cymbal make that mirth§ in the service of God, as to elevate the hearts of the Worshippers; so Christ can use these gifted men, as with them to affect the Souls of his People in his Church, yet when he hath done all hang them by as lifeless, though sounding *Cymbals.*

300. This consideration therefore, together with some others, were for the most part as a maul§ on the head of pride and desire of vain-glory: What, thought I, shall I be proud because I am a sounding Brass? is it so much to be a Fiddle? hath not the least creature that hath life, more of God in it than these? besides, I knew 'twas Love should never die, but these must cease and vanish: So I concluded, a little Grace, a little Love, a little of the true Fear of God, is better then all these Gifts: Yea, and I am fully convinced of it, that it is possible for a Soul that can scarce give a man an answer, but with great confusion

as to method, I say it is possible for them to have a thousand times more Grace, and so to be more in the love and favour of the Lord, then some who by vertue of the Gift of Knowledge, can deliver§ themselves like Angels.

301. Thus, therefore, I came to perceive, that though gifts in themselves were good to the thing for which they are designed, to wit, the Edification of others; yet empty and without power to save the Soul of him that hath them, if they be *alone:* Neither are they, as so, any sign of a mans state to be happy, being only a dispensation of God to some, of whose improvement, or non improvement, they must, when a little life more is over, give an account to him that is ready to judge the quick and the dead.

302. This shewed me, too, that gifts being alone, were dangerous, not in themselves, but because of those evils that attend them that have them, to wit, pride, desire of vain glory, self-conceit, &c., all of which were easily blown up at the applause, and commendation of every unadvised Christian, to the endangering of a poor Creature to fall into the condemnation of the Devil.

303. I saw therefore that he that hath Gifts had need be let into a sight of the nature of them, to wit, that they come short of making of him to be in a truly saved condition, lest he rest in them, and so fall short of the grace of God.

304. He hath also cause to walk humbly with God, and be little in his own Eyes, and to remember withall, that his Gifts are not his own, but the Churches; and that by them he is made a Servant to the Church, and that he must give at last an account of his Stewardship unto the Lord Jesus; and to give a good account, will be a blessed thing!

305. Let all men therefore prize a little with the fear of the Lord, (Gifts indeed are desirable) but yet great Grace and small Gifts are better then great Gifts and no Grace. It doth not say, the Lord gives Gifts and Glory, but the Lord gives Grace and Glory! and blessed is such an one to whom the Lord gives Grace, true Grace, for that is a certain forerunner of Glory.

306. But when Satan perceived that his thus tempting, and assaulting of me, would not answer his design, to wit, to overthrow my Ministry, and make it ineffectual as to the ends

thereof: then he tryed another way, which was to stir up the minds of the ignorant and malicious, to load me with slanders and reproaches; now therefore I may say, That what the Devil could devise, and his instruments invent, was whirled up and down the Countrey against me, thinking, as I said, that by that means they should make my ministry to be abandoned.

307. It began therefore to be rumored up and down among the People, that I was a Witch, a Jesuit, a Highway-man, and the like.

308. To all which, I shall only say, God knows that I am innocent. But as for mine accusers, let them provide themselves to meet me before the tribunal of the Son of God, there to answer for these things, (with all the rest of their Iniquities) unless God shall give them Repentance for them, for the which I pray with all my heart.

309. But that which was reported with the boldest confidence, was, that I had my *Misses,* my *Whores,* my *Bastards,* yea, *two wives at once,* and the like. Now these slanders (with the other) I glory in, because but slanders, foolish, or knavish lies, and falshoods cast upon me by the Devil and his Seed; and should I not be dealt with thus wickedly by the World, I should want one sign of a Saint, and Child of God. *Blessed are ye* (said the Lord Jesus) *when men shall revile you, and persecute you, and shall say all manner of evil against you falsely for my sake; rejoyce, and be exceeding glad, for great is your Reward in Heaven; for so persecuted they the Prophets which were before you,* Mat. 5. 11.

310. These things therefore upon mine own account trouble me not, no, though they were twenty times more then they are. I have a good Conscience, and whereas they speak evil of me, as an evil doer, they shall be ashamed that falsely accuse my good Conversation§ in Christ.

311. So then, what shall I say to those that have thus bespattered me? shall I threaten them? Shall I chide them? shall I flatter them? shall I intreat them to hold their tongues? no, not I: were it not for that these things make them ripe for damnation that are the authors and abettors, I would say unto them: *report it!* because 'twill increase my Glory.

312. Therefore I bind these lies and slanders to me as an

ornament, it belongs to my Christian Profession, to be villified, slandered, reproached and reviled: and since all this is nothing else, as my God and my Conscience do bear me witness: I rejoyce in reproaches for Christs sake.

313. I also calling all those fools, or knaves, that have thus made it anything of their business to affirm any of the things aforenamed of me, namely, that I have been naught[§] with other Women, or the like, when they have used to the utmost of their endeavours, and made the fullest enquiry that they can, to prove against me truly, that there is any woman in Heaven, or Earth, or Hell, that can say, I have at any time, in any place, by day or night, so much as attempted to be naught with them; and speak I thus, to beg mine Enemies into a good esteem of me? No, not I. I will in this beg relief of no man: believe, or disbelieve me in this, all is a case to me.

314. My Foes have mist their mark in this their shooting at me. I am not the man, I wish that they themselves be guiltless, if all the Fornicators and Adulterers in *England* were hang'd by the Neck till they be dead, *John Bunyan*, the object of their Envie, would be still alive and well. I know not whether there be such a thing as a woman breathing under the Copes[§] of the whole Heaven but by their apparel, their Children, or by common Fame, except my Wife.

315. And in this I admire the Wisdom of God, that he made me shie of women from my first Convertion until now. Those know, and can also bear me witness, with whom I have been most intimately concerned, that it is a rare thing to see me carry it pleasant towards a Woman; the common Salutation[§] of a woman I abhor, 'tis odious to me in whosoever I see it. Their Company alone, I cannot away[§] with. I seldom so much as touch a Womans Hand, for I think these things are not so becoming me. When I have seen good men Salute[§] those Women that they have visited, or that have visited them, I have at times made my objection against it, and when they have answered, that it was but a peice of Civilitie, I have told them, it is not a comely sight; some indeed have urged the holy kiss but then I have asked why they made baulks,[§] why they did salute the most hansom, and let the ill-favoured go; thus, how laudable

so ever such things have been in the Eyes of others, they have
been unseemly in my sight.

316. And now for a wind up in this matter, I call on not only
Men, but Angels, to prove me guilty of having carnally to do
with any Woman save my Wife, nor am I afraid to do it a second
time, knowing that I cannot offend the Lord in such a case, to
call God for a Record upon my Soul, that in these things I am
innocent. Not that I have been thus kept, because of any goodness in me more than any other, but God has been merciful to
me, and has kept me, to whom I pray that he will keep me still,
not only from this, but from every evil way and work, and preserve me to his Heavenly Kingdom. Amen.

317. Now as Sathan laboured by reproaches and slanders to
make me vile among my Countrymen, that, if possible, my
preaching might be made of none effect, so there was added
hereto a long and tedious Imprisonment, that thereby I might
be frighted from my Service for Christ, and the World terrified,
and made afraid to hear me Preach, of which I shall in the next
place give you a brief account.

A brief Account of the Authors Imprisonment

318. Having made profession of the glorious Gospel of Christ
a long time, and preached the same about five year; I was apprehended at a Meeting of good People in the Countrey, (amongst
whom, had they let me alone, I should have preached that day,
but they took me away from amongst them) and had me before
a Justice, who, after I had offered security for my appearing at
the next Sessions yet committed me, because my Sureties would
not consent to be bound that I should preach no more to the
people.

319. At the Sessions after, I was indicted for an Upholder
and Maintainer of unlawful Assemblies and Conventicles, and
for not conforming to the National Worship of the Church of
England; and after some conference there with the Justices, they
taking my plain dealing with them for a confession, as they
termed it, of the indictment, did sentence me to perpetual banishment, because I refused to Conform. So being again delivered

up to the Goalers⁵ hands, I was had home to Prison again, and there have lain now compleat twelve years, waiting to see what God would suffer these men to do with me.

320. In which condition I have continued with much content thorow Grace, but have met with many turnings and goings upon my heart both from the Lord, Satan, and my own corruptions; by all which, (glory be to Jesus Christ) I have also received, among many things, much conviction, instruction, and understanding, of which at large I shall not here discourse; onely give you, in a hint or two, a word that may stir up the Godly to bless God, and to pray for me; and also to take encouragement, should the case be their own, *Not to fear what men can do unto them.*

321. I never had in all my life so great an inlet into the Word of God as now; them Scriptures that I saw nothing in before, are made in this place and state to shine upon me; Jesus Christ also was never more real and apparent then now; here I have seen him and felt him indeed: O that word, *We have not preached unto you cunningly devised fables,* 2 Pet. 1. 16: and that, *God raised Christ from the dead, and gave him glory, that your faith and hope might be in God,* 1 Pet. 1. 21. were blessed words unto me in this my imprisoned condition.

322. These three or four Scriptures also have been great refreshment in this condition to me: *Job.* 14. 1, 2, 3, 4. *Job.* 16. 33. *Col.* 3. 3, 4. *Heb.* 12. 22, 23, 24. So that sometimes when I have been in the savour of them, I have been able to laugh at destruction, *and to fear neither the Horse nor his Rider.* I have had sweet sights of the forgiveness of my sins in this place, and of my being with Jesus in another world: *O the mount Zion, the heavenly Jerusalem, the innumerable company of Angels, and God the Judge of all, and the Spirits of just men made perfect, and Jesus,* have been sweet unto me in this place: I have seen that here, that I am perswaded I shall never, while in this world, be able to express; I have seen a truth in that scripture, *Whom having not seen, ye love; in whom, though now ye see him not, yet believing, ye rejoyce with joy unspeakable, and full of glory,* 1 Pet. 1. 8.

323. I never knew what it was for God to stand by me at all turns, and at every offer of Satan to afflict me, &c., as I have

found him since I came in hither; for look how fears have presented themselves, so have supports and encouragements; yea, when I have started, even as it were at nothing else but my shadow, yet God, as being very tender of me, hath not suffered me to be molested, but would with one Scripture and another strengthen me against all: insomuch that I have often said, *Were it lawful, I could pray for greater trouble, for the greater comforts sake*, Eccles. 7. 14; 2 Cor. 1. 5.

324. Before I came to Prison, I saw what was a coming, and had especially two Considerations warm upon my heart; the first was, How to be able to endure, should my imprisonment be long and tedious; the second was, How to be able to encounter death, should that be here my portion; for the first of these, that Scripture, *Col.* 1. 11, was great information to me, namely, to pray to God *to be strengthened with all might, according to his glorious power, unto all patience and long-suffering with joy-fulness:* I could seldom go to prayer before I was imprisoned, but for not so little as a year together, this Sentence, or sweet Petition, would as it were thrust it self into my mind, and perswade me that if ever I would go thorow long-suffering, I must have all patience, especially if I would endure it joyfully.

325. As to the second Consideration, that Saying, 2 Cor. 1. 9, was of great use to me, *But we had the sentence of death in our selves, that we might not trust in our selves, but in God that raiseth the dead:* by this Scripture I was made to see, that if ever I would suffer rightly, I must first pass a sentence of death upon everything that can properly be called a thing of this life, even to reckon my Self, my Wife, my Children, my health, my enjoyments, and all, as dead to me, and my self as dead to them. *He that loveth father or mother, son or daughter, more than me, is not worthy of me*, Matt. 10. 37.

326. The second was, to live upon God that is invisible; as *Paul* said in another place, The way not to faint, is *to look not at the things that are seen, but at the things that are not seen; for the things that are seen are temporal; but the things that are not seen, they are eternal*, 2 Cor. 4. 18. And thus I reasoned with myself; If I provide only for a prison, then the whip comes at unawares; and so does also the pillory; again, if I provide onely for these, then I am not fit for banishment; further, if I

conclude that banishment is the worst, then if death come, I am surprized; so that I see the best way to go thorow sufferings, is to trust in God thorow Christ, as touching the world to come; and as touching this world, to *count the grave my house, to make my bed in darkness, and to say to Corruption, Thou art my Father, and to the Worm, Thou art my Mother and Sister;* that is, to familiarize these things to me.

327. But notwithstanding these helps, I found myself a man, and compassed with infirmities; the parting with my Wife and poor Children hath oft been to me in this place as the pulling the flesh from my bones; and that not onely because I am somewhat too fond of these great mercies,§ but also because I should have often brought to my mind the many hardships, miseries and wants that my poor family was like to meet with, should I be taken from them, especially my poor blind Child, who lay nearer my heart than all I had besides; O the thoughts of the hardship I thought my blind one might go under, would break my heart to pieces.

328. Poor Child! thought I, what sorrow art thou like to have for thy portion in this world? Thou must be beaten, must beg, suffer hunger, cold, nakedness, and a thousand calamities, though I cannot now endure the wind should blow upon thee: but yet recalling my self, thought I, I must venture you all with God, though it goeth to the quick to leave you: O I saw in this condition I was as a man who was pulling down his house upon the head of his Wife and Children; yet thought I, I must do it, I must do it: and now I thought of those *two milch Kine that were to carry the Ark of God into another Country, and to leave their Calves behind them,* 1 Sam. 6. 10, 11, 12.

329. But that which helped me in this temptation was divers considerations, of which three in special here I will name; the first was the consideration of those two Scriptures, *Leave thy fatherless children, I will preserve them alive, and let thy widows trust in me:* and again, *The Lord said, Verily it shall be well with thy remnant, verily I will cause the enemy to entreat thee well in the time of evil,* &c. Jer. 49. 11. Chap. 15. 11.

330. I had also this consideration, that if I should now venture all for God, I engaged God to take care of my concernments; but if I forsook him and his ways, for fear of any trouble that should

come to me or mine, then I should not only falsifie my profession, but should count also that my concernments were not so sure if left at Gods feet, while I stood to and for his name, as they would be if they were under my own tuition,§ though with the denial of the way of God. This was a smarting consideration, and was as spurs unto my flesh: that Scripture also greatly helped it to fasten the more upon me, where Christ prays against *Judas*, that God would disappoint him in all his selfish thoughts, which moved him to sell his Master. Pray read it soberly, *Psal.* 109. 6, 7, 8, &c.

331. I had also another consideration, and that was, The dread of the torments of Hell, which I was sure they must partake of, that for fear of the Cross do shrink from their profession of Christ, his Word and Laws, before the sons of men: I thought also of the glory that he had prepared for those that, in faith, and love, and patience, stood to his ways before them. These things, I say, have helped me, when the thoughts of the misery that both my self and mine might, for the sake of my profession, be exposed to, hath lain pinching on my mind.

332. When I have indeed conceited that I might be banished for my Profession, then I have thought of that Scripture, *They were stoned, they were sawn asunder, were tempted, were slain with the sword, they wandered about in sheepskins and goatskins; being destitute, afflicted, tormented, of whom the world was not worthy*, Heb. 11. 37, 38, for all they thought they were too bad to dwell and abide amongst them. I have also thought of that saying, *The Holy Ghost witnesseth in every city, that bonds and afflictions abide me;* I have verily thought that my Soul and it have sometimes reasoned about the sore and sad estate of a banished and exiled condition, how they are exposed to hunger, to cold, to perils, to nakedness, to enemies, and a thousand calamities; and at last it may be to die in a ditch like a poor forlorn and desolate sheep. But I thank God, hitherto I have not been moved by these most delicate reasonings, but have rather by them more approved my heart to God.

333. I will tell you a pretty business: I was once above all the rest in a very sad and low condition for many weeks, at which time also I being but a young Prisoner, and not acquainted with the Laws, had this lay much upon my spirit, That my imprison-

ment might end at the Gallows for ought that I could tell; now, therefore, Satan laid hard at me to beat me out of heart, by suggesting thus unto me: But how if when you come indeed to die, you should be in this condition; that is, as not to savour the things of God, nor to have any evidence upon your soul for a better state hereafter? (for indeed at that time all the things of God were hid from my soul).

334. Wherefore when I at first began to think of this, it was a great trouble to me: for I thought with my self that in the condition I now was in, I was not fit to die, neither indeed did I think I could, if I should be called to it: besides, I thought with myself, if I should make a scrabling⁵ shift to clamber up the Ladder, yet I should either with quaking or other symptoms of faintings, give occasion to the enemy to reproach the way of God and his People, for their timerousness: this therefore lay with great trouble upon me, for methought I was ashamed to die with a pale face, and tottering knees, for such a Cause as this.

335. Wherefore I prayed to God that he would comfort me, and give me strength to do and suffer what he should call me to; yet no comfort appeared, but all continued hid: I was also at this time so really possessed with the thought of death, that oft I was as if I was on the Ladder, with the Rope about my neck; onely this was some encouragement to me, I thought I might now have an opportunity to speak my last words to a multitude which I thought would come to see me die; and, thought I, if it must be so, if God will but convert one Soul by my very last words, I shall not count my life thrown away, nor lost.

336. But yet all the things of God were kept out of my sight, and still the tempter followed me with, *But whither must you go when you die? what will become of you? where will you be found in another world? what evidence have you for heaven and glory, and an inheritance among them that are sanctified?* Thus was I tossed for manie weeks, and knew not what to do; at last this consideration fell with weight upon me, That it was for the Word and Way of God that I was in this condition, wherefore I was ingaged not to flinch a hair's breadth from it.

337. I thought also, that God might chuse whether he would give me comfort now, or at the hour of death; but I might not therefore chuse whether I would hold my profession or no: I

was bound, but he was free: yea, it was my dutie to stand to his
Word, whether he would ever look upon me or no, or save me
at the last: Wherefore, thought I, the point being thus, I am
for going on, and venturing my eternal state with Christ, whether
I have comfort here or no; if God doth not come in, thought I, I
will leap off the Ladder even blindfold into Eternitie, sink or
swim, come heaven, come hell; Lord Jesus, if thou wilt catch me,
do; if not, I will venture for thy Name.

338. I was no sooner fixed upon this resolution, but that word
dropped upon me, *Doth Job serve God for nought?* as if the
accuser had said, Lord, *Job* is no upright man, he serves thee
for by-respects,§ hast thou not made a hedge about him, &c.
But put forth now thy hand, and touch all that he hath, and he
will curse thee to thy face: How now, thought I, is this the
sign of an upright Soul, to desire to serve God when all is taken
from him? is he a godlie man that will serve God for nothing
rather then give§ out? blessed be God, then, I hope I have an
upright heart, for I am resolved, (God give me strength) never
to denie my profession, though I have nothing at all for my
pains; and as I was thus considering, that Scripture was set before me, Psa. 44. 12. &c.

339. Now was my heart full of comfort, for I hoped it was
sincere; I would not have been without this trial for much; I
am comforted everie time I think of it, and I hope I shall bless
God for ever for the teaching I have had by it. Many more of
the Dealings of God towards me I might relate, but these out of
the spoils won in Battel have I dedicated to maintain the house
of God, 1 Chron. 26. 27.

VI

Samuel Pepys

_____

FROM

The Diary

[August] 30th [1666]. Up and all the morning at the office, dined at home, and in the afternoon, and at night till two in the morning, framing my great letter to Mr. Hayes[1] about the victualling of the fleete, about which there has been so much ado and exceptions taken by the Generalls.[2]

31st. To bed at 2 or 3 in the morning and up again at 6 to go by appointment to my Lord Bellasses, but he out of town, which vexed me. So back and got Mr. Poynter[3] to enter into my book while I read from my last night's notes the letter, and that being done to writing§ it fair. At noon home to dinner, and then the boy and I to the office, and there he read while I writ it fair, which done I sent it to Sir W. Coventry[4] to peruse and send to

1 James Hayes: Secretary to Prince Rupert.
2 Prince Rupert and General George Monk, 1st Duke of Albemarle.
3 Formerly one of Pepys's clerks; now a clerk in the Comptroller's office.
4 Sir William Coventry: Secretary to James, Duke of York; a Commissioner of the Navy and a Privy Councillor.

the fleete by the first opportunity; and so pretty betimes to bed. Much pleased to-day with thoughts of gilding the backs of all my books alike in my new presses.[§]

September 1st. Up and at the office all the morning, and then dined at home. Got my new closet[§] made mighty clean against to-morrow. Sir W. Pen[5] and my wife and Mercer[6] and I to "Polichinelly," [7] but were there horribly frighted to see Young Killigrew[8] come in with a great many more young sparks; but we hid ourselves, so as we think they did not see us. By and by they went away, and then we were at rest again; and so, the play being done, we to Islington, and there eat and drank and mighty merry; and so home singing, and, after a letter or two at the office, to bed.

2nd (Lord's day). Some of our mayds sitting up late last night to get things ready against[§] our feast to-day, Jane[9] called us up about three in the morning, to tell us of a great fire they saw in the City. So I rose and slipped on my night-gowne,[§] and went to her window, and thought it to be on the back-side of Marke-lane at the farthest; but, being unused to such fires as followed, I thought it far enough off; and so went to bed again and to sleep. About seven rose again to dress myself, and there looked out at the window, and saw the fire not so much as it was and further off. So to my closett to set things to rights after yesterday's cleaning. By and by Jane comes and tells me that she hears that above 300 houses have been burned down to-night by the fire we saw, and that it is now burning down all Fish-street, by London Bridge. So I made myself ready presently, and walked to the Tower, and there got up upon one of the high places, Sir J. Robinson's little son going up with me; and there I did see the houses at that end of the bridge all on fire, and an infinite great fire on this and the other side the end of the bridge; which, among other people, did trouble me for poor

5 Sir William Penn: Comptroller of the Navy, father of the founder of Pennsylvania.

6 Mary Mercer: companion to Mrs. Pepys.

7 A farcical entertainment which Pepys had already seen on August 22 and 29 and which he saw several times afterwards. *Polichinelle* is the French equivalent of *Punchinello*, one of the characters of the old Italian pantomime.

8 "Young" Henry Killigrew: courtier and rake, son of Thomas Killigrew, the playwright.

9 Jane Birch: one in a long series of maids employed by Pepys.

little Michell [1] and our Sarah[2] on the bridge. So down, with my heart full of trouble, to the Lieutenant of the Tower, who tells me that it begun this morning in the King's baker's house in Pudding-lane, and that it hath burned St. Magnus's Church and most part of Fish-street already. So I down to the water-side, and there got a boat and through bridge, and there saw a lamentable fire. Poor Michell's house, as far as the Old Swan, already burned that way, and the fire running further, that in a very little time it got as far as the Steele-yard, while I was there. Everybody endeavouring to remove their goods, and flinging into the river or bringing them into lighters[§] that lay off; poor people staying in their houses as long as till the very fire touched them, and then running into boats, or clambering from one pair of stairs by the water-side to another. And among other things, the poor pigeons, I perceive, were loth to leave their houses, but hovered about the windows and balconys till they were, some of them burned, their wings, and fell down. Having staid, and in an hour's time seen the fire rage every way, and nobody, to my sight, endeavouring to quench it, but to remove their goods, and leave all to the fire, and having seen it get as far as the Steele-yard, and the wind mighty high and driving it into the City; and every thing, after so long a drought, proving combustible, even the very stones of churches, and among other things the poor steeple by which pretty Mrs. —— lives, and whereof my old schoolfellow Elborough is parson, taken fire in the very top, and there burned till it fell down: I to White Hall (with a gentleman with me who desired to go off from the Tower, to see the fire, in my boat); to White Hall, and there up to the King's closett in the Chappell, where people come about me, and I did give them an account dismayed them all, and word was carried in to the King. So I was called for, and did tell the King and Duke of Yorke what I saw, and that unless his Majesty did command houses to be pulled down nothing could stop the fire. They seemed much troubled, and the King commanded me to go to my Lord Mayor from him, and command him to spare no houses, but to pull down before the fire every way. The Duke

---

[1] Betty Howlett Michell: wife of the son of Pepys's bookseller; one in a long series of young ladies pursued by Pepys.
[2] Formerly a maid of the Pepyses.

of York bid me tell him that if he would have any more soldiers
he shall; and so did my Lord Arlington afterwards, as a great
secret. Here meeting with Captain Cocke,[3] I in his coach, which
he lent me, and Creed [4] with me to Paul's,[§] and there walked
along Watling-street, as well as I could, every creature coming
away loaden with goods to save, and here and there sicke people
carried away in beds. Extraordinary good goods carried in carts
and on backs. At last met my Lord Mayor in Canning-street,
like a man spent, with a handkercher about his neck. To the
King's message he cried, like a fainting woman, "Lord! what can
I do? I am spent: people will not obey me. I have been pulling
down houses; but the fire overtakes us faster than we can do it."
That he needed no more soldiers; and that, for himself, he must
go and refresh himself, having been up all night. So he left me,
and I him, and walked home, seeing people all almost distracted,
and no manner of means used to quench the fire. The houses,
too, so very thick thereabouts, and full of matter for burning,
as pitch and tarr, in Thames-street; and warehouses of oyle, and
wines, and brandy, and other things. Here I saw Mr. Isaake
Houblon, the handsome man, prettily dressed and dirty, at his
door at Dow-gate, receiving some of his brothers' things, whose
houses were on fire; and, as he says, have been removed twice
already; and he doubts (as it soon proved) that they must be
in a little time removed from his house also, which was a sad
consideration. And to see the churches all filling with goods by
people who themselves should have been quietly there at this
time. By this time it was about twelve o'clock; and so home, and
there find my guests, which was Mr. Wood and his wife Barbary
Sheldon, and also Mr. Moone: she mighty fine, and her husband,
for aught I see, a likely man. But Mr. Moone's design and mine,
which was to look over my closett and please him with the sight
thereof, which he hath long desired, was wholly disappointed;
for we were in great trouble and disturbance at this fire, not
knowing what to think of it. However, we had an extraordinary
good dinner, and as merry as at this time we could be. While at

3 Captain George Cocke: Hemp-merchant; the Navy's "Receiver" or treasurer
for the sick and wounded and for prisoners.
4 John Creed: Deputy Treasurer of the Fleet and a member (as was Pepys) of
the Tangier Commission. (Tangier, in northwest Africa, was ceded to England
by Portugal in 1662.)

dinner Mrs. Batelier come to enquire after Mr. Woolfe and Stanes
(who, it seems, are related to them), whose houses in Fish-street
are all burned, and they in a sad condition. She would not stay
in the fright. Soon as dined, I and Moone away, and walked
through the City, the streets full of nothing but people and horses
and carts loaden with goods, ready to run over one another, and
removing goods from one burned house to another. They now
removing out of Canning-streete (which received goods in the
morning) into Lumbard-streete, and further; and among others
I now saw my little goldsmith, Stokes, receiving some friend's
goods, whose house itself was burned the day after. We parted
at Paul's; he home, and I to Paul's Wharf, where I had appointed
a boat to attend me, and took in Mr. Carcasse and his brother,
whom I met in the streete, and carried them below and above
bridge to and again to see the fire, which was now got further,
both below and above, and no likelihood of stopping it. Met
with the King and Duke of York in their barge, and with them
to Queenhithe, and there called Sir Richard Browne to them.
Their order was only to pull down houses apace, and so below
bridge at the water-side; but little was or could be done, the fire
coming upon them so fast. Good hopes there was of stopping it
at the Three Cranes above, and at Buttolph's Wharf below
bridge, if care be used; but the wind carries it into the City, so
as we know not by the water-side what it do there. River full of
lighters and boats taking in goods, and good goods swimming in
the water, and only I observed that hardly one lighter or boat in
three that had the goods of a house in, but there was a pair of
Virginalls§ in it. Having seen as much as I could now, I away
to White Hall by appointment, and there walked to St. James's
Parke, and there met my wife and Creed and Wood and his wife,
and walked to my boat; and there upon the water again, and to
the fire up and down, it still encreasing, and the wind great.
So near the fire as we could for smoke; and all over the Thames,
with one's face in the wind, you were almost burned with a
shower of fire-drops. This is very true; so as houses were burned
by these drops and flakes of fire, three or four, nay, five or six
houses, one from another. When we could endure no more upon
the water, we to a little ale-house on the Bankside, over against
the Three Cranes, and there staid till it was dark almost, and

saw the fire grow; and, as it grew darker, appeared more and more, and in corners and upon steeples, and between churches and houses, as far as we could see up the hill of the City, in a most horrid malicious bloody flame, not like the fine flame of an ordinary fire. Barbary and her husband away before us. We staid till, it being darkish, we saw the fire as only one entire arch of fire from this to the other side the bridge, and in a bow up the hill for an arch of above a mile long: it made me weep to see it. The churches, houses, and all on fire and flaming at once; and a horrid noise the flames made, and the cracking of houses at their ruine. So home with a sad heart, and there find every body discoursing and lamenting the fire; and poor Tom Hater[5] come with some few of his goods saved out of his house, which is burned upon Fish-streete Hill. I invited him to lie at my house, and did receive his goods, but was deceived in his lying there, the newes coming every moment of the growth of the fire; so as we were forced to begin to pack up our owne goods, and prepare for their removal; and did by moonshine (it being brave dry, and moonshine, and warm weather) carry much of my goods into the garden, and Mr. Hater and I did remove my money and iron chests into my cellar, as thinking that the safest place. And got my bags of gold into my office, ready to carry away, and my chief papers of accounts also there, and my tallys into a box by themselves. So great was our fear, as Sir W. Batten[6] hath carts come out of the country to fetch away his goods this night. We did put Mr. Hater, poor man, to bed a little; but he got but very little rest, so much noise being in my house, taking down of goods.

3rd. About four o'clock in the morning, my Lady Batten sent me a cart to carry away all my money, and plate, and best things, to Sir W. Rider's[7] at Bednall-greene. Which I did, riding myself in my night-gowne in the cart; and, Lord! to see how the streets and the highways are crowded with people running and riding, and getting of carts at any rate to fetch away things. I find Sir W. Rider tired with being called up all night, and receiving things from several friends. His house full of goods, and

---

5 Thomas Hayter: Pepys's chief clerk.
6 Sir William Batten: Surveyor of the Navy.
7 Sir William Rider: Member of the Tangier Commission.

much of Sir W. Batten's and Sir W. Pen's. I am eased at my
heart to have my treasure so well secured. Then home, with
much ado to find a way, nor any sleep all this night to me nor
my poor wife. But then and all this day she and I, and all my people labouring to get away the rest of our things, and did get Mr.
Tooker[8] to get me a lighter to take them in, and we did carry
them (myself some) over Tower Hill, which was by this time
full of people's goods, bringing their goods thither; and down
to the lighter, which lay at the next quay, above the Tower
Docke. And here was my neighbour's wife, Mrs. ——, with her
pretty child, and some few of her things, which I did willingly
give way to be saved with mine; but there was no passing with any
thing through the postern, the crowd was so great. The Duke of
Yorke come this day by the office, and spoke to us, and did ride
with his guard up and down the City to keep all quiet (he being
now Generall, and having the care of all). This day, Mercer
being not at home, but against her mistress's order gone to her
mother's, and my wife going thither to speak with W. Hewer,[9]
met her there, and was angry; and her mother saying that she
was not a 'prentice girl, to ask leave every time she goes abroad,
my wife with good reason was angry, and, when she came home,
bid her be gone again. And so she went away, which troubled
me, but yet less than it would, because of the condition we are
in, fear of coming into in a little time of being less able to
keepe one in her quality. At night lay down a little upon a quilt
of W. Hewer's in the office, all my owne things being packed up
or gone; and after me my poor wife did the like, we having
fed upon the remains of yesterday's dinner, having no fire nor
dishes, nor any opportunity of dressing[§] any thing.

4th. Up by break of day to get away the remainder of my
things; which I did by a lighter at the Iron gate: and my hands
so few, that it was the afternoon before we could get them all
away. Sir W. Pen and I to Tower-streete, and there met the
fire burning three or four doors beyond Mr. Howell's, whose
goods, poor man, his trayes, and dishes, shovells, &c., were
flung all along Tower-street in the kennels,[§] and people working
therewith from one end to the other; the fire coming on in that

8 John Tooker: Navy Office messenger.
9 William Hewer: Pepys's clerk and personal attendant since 1660.

narrow streete, on both sides, with infinite fury. Sir W. Batten
not knowing how to remove his wine, did dig a pit in the garden,
and laid it in there; and I took the opportunity of laying all the
papers of my office that I could not otherwise dispose of. And in
the evening Sir W. Pen and I did dig another, and put our wine
in it; and I my Parmazan cheese, as well as my wine and some
other things. The Duke of Yorke was at the office this day, at
Sir W. Pen's; but I happened not to be within. This afternoon,
sitting melancholy with Sir W. Pen in our garden, and thinking
of the certain burning of this office, without extraordinary
means, I did propose for the sending up of all our workmen
from Woolwich and Deptford yards (none whereof yet appeared), and to write to Sir W. Coventry to have the Duke of
Yorke's permission to pull down houses, rather than lose this
office, which would much hinder the King's business. So Sir
W. Pen he went down this night, in order to the sending them
up to-morrow morning; and I wrote to Sir W. Coventry about the
business, but received no answer. This night Mrs. Turner (who,
poor woman, was removing her goods all this day, good goods
into the garden, and knows not how to dispose of them), and
her husband supped with my wife and I at night, in the office,
upon a shoulder of mutton from the cook's, without any napkin
or any thing, in a sad manner, but were merry. Only now and
then walking into the garden, and saw how horridly the sky
looks, all on a fire in the night, was enough to put us out of our
wits; and, indeed, it was extremely dreadful, for it looks just as
if it was at us, and the whole heaven on fire. I after supper
walked in the darke down to Tower-streete, and there saw it all
on fire, at the Trinity House on that side, and the Dolphin
Taverne on this side, which was very near us; and the fire with
extraordinary vehemence. Now begins the practice of blowing
up of houses in Tower-streete, those next the Tower, which at
first did frighten people more than any thing; but it stopped
the fire where is was done, it bringing down the houses to the
ground in the same places they stood, and then it was easy to
quench what little fire was in it, though it kindled nothing almost. W. Hewer this day went to see how his mother did, and
comes late home, telling us how he hath been forced to remove
her to Islington, her house in Pye-corner being burned; so that

the fire is got so far that way, and all the Old Bayly, and was running down to Fleete-streete; and Paul's is burned, and all Cheapside. I wrote to my father this night, but the post-house being burned, the letter could not go.

5th. I lay down in the office again upon W. Hewer's quilt, being mighty weary, and sore in my feet with going till I was hardly able to stand. About two in the morning my wife calls me up and tells me of new cryes of fire, it being come to Barke-ing Church, which is the bottom of our lane. I up, and finding it so, resolved presently to take her away, and did, and took my gold, which was about £2,350, W. Hewer, and Jane, down by Proundy's boat to Woolwich; but, Lord! what a sad sight it was by moone-light to see the whole City almost on fire, that you might see it plain at Woolwich, as if you were by it. There, when I come, I find the gates shut, but no guard kept at all, which troubled me, because of discourse now begun, that there is plot in it, and that the French had done it. I got the gates open, and to Mr. Shelden's,[1] where I locked up my gold, and charged my wife and W. Hewer never to leave the room without one of them in it, night or day. So back again, by the way seeing my goods well in the lighters at Deptford, and watched well by people. Home, and whereas I expected to have seen our house on fire, it being now about seven o'clock, it was not. But to the fyre, and there find greater hopes than I expected; for my con-fidence of finding our Office on fire was such, that I durst not ask any body how it was with us, till I come and saw it not burned. But going to the fire, I find by the blowing up of houses, and the great helpe given by the workmen out of the King's yards, sent up by Sir W. Pen, there is a good stop given to it, as well as at Marke-lane end as ours; it having only burned the dyall of Barking Church, and part of the porch, and was there quenched. I up to the top of Barking steeple, and there saw the saddest sight of desolation that I ever saw; every where great fires, oyle-cellars, and brimstone, and other things burning. I became afeard to stay there long, and therefore down again as fast as I could, the fire being spread as far as I could see it; and to Sir W. Pen's, and there eat a piece of cold meat, having eaten

---

[1] William Sheldon: an officer (Clerk of the Cheque) in the royal dockyard at Woolwich.

nothing since Sunday, but the remains of Sunday's dinner. Here
I met with Mr. Young and Whistler; and having removed all my
things, and received good hopes that the fire at our end is
stopped, they and I walked into the town, and find Fanchurch-
streete, Gracious-streete, and Lumbard-streete all in dust. The
Exchange a sad sight, nothing standing there, of all the statues
or pillars, but Sir Thomas Gresham's picture⁵ in the corner.
Walked into Moorefields (our feet ready to burn, walking through
the towne among the hot coles), and find that full of people, and
poor wretches carrying their goods there, and every body keeping
his goods together by themselves (and a great blessing it is to
them that it is fair weather for them to keep abroad night and
day); drank there, and paid twopence for a plain penny loaf.
Thence homeward, having passed through Cheapside and New-
gate Market, all burned, and seen Anthony Joyce's² house in
fire. And took up (which I keep by me) a piece of glasse of
Mercers' Chappell in the streete, where much more was, so
melted and buckled with the heat of the fire like parchment. I
also did see a poor cat taken out of a hole in the chimney, joyn-
ing to the wall of the Exchange, with the hair all burned off the
body, and yet alive. So home at night, and find there good hopes
of saving our office; but great endeavours of watching all night,
and having men ready; and so we lodged them in the office,
and had drink and bread and cheese for them. And I lay down
and slept a good night about midnight, though when I rose I
heard that there had been a great alarme of French and Dutch
being risen, which proved nothing. But it is a strange thing to
see how long this time did look since Sunday, having been always full of variety of actions, and little sleep, that it looked
like a week or more, and I had forgot almost the day of the week.

6th. Up about five o'clock, and there met Mr. Gawden at
the gate of the office (I intending to go out, as I used, every now
and then to-day, to see how the fire is) to call our men to
Bishop's-gate, where no fire had yet been near, and there is now
one broke out: which did give great grounds to people, and to
me too, to think that there is some kind of plot in this (on which
many by this time have been taken, and it hath been dangerous
for any stranger to walk in the streets), but I went with the men,

2 A cousin, in the tallow trade, whom Pepys disliked.

and we did put it out in a little time; so that that was well again. It was pretty to see how hard the women did work in the cannells, sweeping of water; but then they would scold for drink, and be as drunk as devils. I saw good butts of sugar broke open in the street, and people go and take handsfull out, and put into beer, and drink it. And now all being pretty well, I took boat, and over to Southwarke, and took boat on the other side the bridge, and so to Westminster, thinking to shift§ myself, being all in dirt from top to bottom; but could not there find any place to buy a shirt or pair of gloves, Westminster Hall being full of people's goods, those in Westminster having removed all their goods, and the Exchequer money put into vessels to carry to Nonsuch; but to the Swan, and there was trimmed;§ and then to White Hall, but saw nobody; and so home. A sad sight to see how the River looks: no houses nor church near it, to the Temple, where it stopped. At home, did go with Sir W. Batten, and our neighbour, Knightly (who, with one more, was the only man of any fashion left in all the neighbourhood thereabouts, they all removing their goods and leaving their houses to the mercy of the fire), to Sir R. Ford's, and there dined in an earthen platter—a fried breast of mutton; a great many of us, but very merry, and indeed as good a meal, though as ugly a one, as ever I had in my life. Thence down to Deptford, and there with great satisfaction landed all my goods at Sir G. Carteret's[3] safe,§ and nothing missed I could see, or hurt. This being done to my great content, I home, and to Sir W. Batten's, and there with Sir R. Ford, Mr. Knightly, and one Withers, a professed lying rogue, supped well, and mighty merry, and our fears over. From them to the office, and there slept with the office full of labourers, who talked, and slept, and walked all night long there. But strange it was to see Cloathworkers' Hall on fire these three days and nights in one body of flame, it being the cellar full of oyle.

7th. Up by five o'clock; and, blessed be God! find all well; and by water to Paul's Wharfe. Walked thence, and saw all the towne burned, and a miserable sight of Paul's church, with all the roofs fallen, and the body of the quire fallen into St. Fayth's; Paul's school also, Ludgate, and Fleet-street, my father's house,

---

[3] Sir George Carteret: Treasurer of the Navy and Vice-chamberlain to the King.

and the church, and a good part of the Temple the like. So to Creed's lodging, near the New Exchange, and there find him laid down upon a bed; the house all unfurnished, there being fears of the fire's coming to them. There borrowed a shirt of him, and washed. To Sir W. Coventry, at St. James's, who lay without curtains, having removed all his goods; as the King at White Hall, and every body had done, and was doing. He hopes we shall have no publique distractions upon this fire, which is what every body fears, because of the talke of the French having a hand in it. And it is a proper time for discontents; but all men's minds are full of care to protect themselves, and save their goods: the militia is in armes every where. Our fleetes, he tells me, have been in sight one of another, and most un-happily by fowle weather were parted, to our great losse, as in reason they do conclude; the Dutch being come out only to make a shew, and please their people; but in very bad condition as to stores, victuals, and men. They are at Bullen,§ and our fleete come to St. Ellen's.§ We have got nothing, but have lost one ship, but he knows not what. Thence to the Swan, and there drank: and so home, and find all well. My Lord Bruncker,[4] at Sir W. Batten's, and tells us the Generall [5] is sent for up, to come to advise with the King about business at this juncture, and to keep all quiet; which is great honour to him, but I am sure is but a piece of dissimulation. So home, and did give orders for my house to be made clean; and then down to Woolwich, and there find all well. Dined, and Mrs. Markham come to see my wife. So I up again, and calling at Deptford for some things of W. Hewer's, he being with me, and then home and spent the eve-ning with Sir R. Ford, Mr. Knightly, and Sir W. Pen at Sir W. Batten's. This day our Merchants first met at Gresham College, which, by proclamation, is to be their Exchange. Strange to hear what is bid for houses all up and down here; a friend of Sir W. Rider's having £150 for what he used to let for £40 per annum. Much dispute where the Custome-house shall be; thereby the growth of the City again to be foreseen. My Lord Treasurer, they say, and others, would have it at the other end of the towne.

---

4 William, 2nd Viscount Brouncker: a Commissioner of the Navy, and the first president of the Royal Society.
5 The Duke of Albemarle.

I home late to Sir W. Pen's, who did give me a bed; but without
curtains or hangings, all being down. So here I went the first
time into a naked bed, only my drawers on; and did sleep
pretty well: but still both sleeping and waking had a fear of
fire in my heart, that I took little rest. People do all the world
over cry out of the simplicity of my Lord Mayor in generall; and
more particularly in this business of the fire, laying it all upon
him. A proclamation is come out for markets to be kept at
Leadenhall and Mile-end-greene, and several other places about
the towne; and Tower-hill, and all churches to be set open to
receive poor people.

8th. Up and with Sir W. Batten and Sir W. Pen by water
to White Hall and they to St. James's. I stopped with Sir G. Carteret to desire him to go with us, and to enquire after money.
But the first he cannot do, and the other as little, or says,
"when we can get any, or what shall we do for it?" He, it seems,
is employed in the correspondence between the City and the King
every day, in settling of things. I find him full of trouble, to
think how things will go. I left him, and to St. James's, where
we met first at Sir W. Coventry's chamber, and there did what
business we can, without any books. Our discourse, as every
thing else, was confused. The fleete is at Portsmouth, there staying a wind to carry them to the Downes, or towards Bullen,
where they say the Dutch fleete is gone, and stays. We concluded upon private meetings for a while, not having any money
to satisfy any people that may come to us. I bought two eeles
upon the Thames, cost me six shillings. Thence with Sir W.
Batten to the Cock-pit,[6] whither the Duke of Albemarle is come.
It seems the King holds him so necessary at this time, that he
hath sent for him, and will keep him here. Indeed, his interest
in the City, being acquainted, and his care in keeping things
quiet, is reckoned that wherein he will be very serviceable. We
to him; he is courted in appearance by every body. He very kind
to us; I perceive he lays by all business of the fleete at present,
and minds the City, and is now hastening to Gresham College,
to discourse with the Aldermen. Sir W. Batten and I home
(where met by my brother John, come to town to see how things
are with us), and then presently he with me to Gresham College;

6 The lodgings of Albemarle, in Whitehall.

where infinity of people, partly through novelty to see the new
place, and partly to find out and hear what is become one man
or another. I met with many people undone, and more that have
extraordinary great losses. People speaking their thoughts variously about the beginning of the fire, and the rebuilding of the
City. Then to Sir W. Batten's, and took my brother with me, and
there dined with a great company of neighbours, and much
good discourse; among others, of the low spirits of some rich
men in the City, in sparing any encouragement to the poor
people that wrought for the saving their houses. Among others,
Alderman Starling, a very rich man, without children, the fire
at next door to him in our lane, after our men had saved his
house, did give 2s. 6d. among thirty of them, and did quarrel
with some that would remove the rubbish out of the way of the
fire, saying that they come to steal. Sir W. Coventry told me of
another this morning in Holborne, which he shewed the King:
that when it was offered to stop the fire near his house for such
a reward that came but to 2s. 6d. a man among the neighbours
he would give but 18d. Thence to Bednall Green by coach, my
brother with me, and saw all well there, and fetched away my
journall-book to enter for five days past, and then back to the
office, where I find Bagwell's[7] wife, and her husband come home.
Agreed to come to their house to-morrow, I sending him away
to his ship to-day. To the office and late writing letters, and then
to Sir W. Pen's, my brother lying with me, and Sir W. Pen gone
down to rest himself at Woolwich. But I was much frighted and
kept awake in my bed, by some noise I heard a great while
below stairs; and the boys not coming up to me when I knocked.
It was by their discovery of people stealing of some neighbours'
wine that lay in vessels in the streets. So to sleep; and all well
all night.

9th (Sunday). Up; and was trimmed, and sent my brother
to Woolwich to my wife, to dine with her. I to church, where
our parson made a melancholy but good sermon; and many and
most in the church cried, specially the women. The church
mighty full; but few of fashion, and most strangers. I walked
to Bednall Green, and there dined well, but a bad venison pasty

---

7 William Bagwell: a carpenter, in the Naval Yard at Deptford, whose wife was
accommodating to Pepys.

at Sir W. Rider's. Good people they are, and good discourse; and
his daughter, Middleton, a fine woman, discreet. Thence home,
and to church again, and there preached Dean Harding; but,
methinks, a bad, poor sermon, though proper for the time; nor
eloquent, in saying at this time that the City is reduced from
a large folio to a decimo-tertio. So to my office, there to write
down my journall, and take leave of my brother, whom I sent
back this afternoon, though rainy; which it hath not done a good
while before. But I had no room or convenience for him here till
my house is fitted; but I was very kind to him, and do take very
well of him his journey. I did give him 40s. for his pocket, and
so, he being gone, and, it presently rayning, I was troubled for
him, though it is good for the fyre. Anon to Sir W. Pen's to bed,
and made my boy Tom to read me asleep.

10th. All the morning clearing our cellars, and breaking in
pieces all my old lumber, to make room, and to prevent fire.
And then to Sir W. Batten's, and dined; and there hear that Sir
W. Rider says that the towne is full of the report of the wealth
that is in his house, and would be glad that his friends would
provide for the safety of their goods there. This made me get a
cart; and thither, and there brought my money all away. Took
a hackney-coach myself (the hackney-coaches now standing at
Allgate). Much wealth indeed there is at his house. Blessed be
God, I got all mine well thence, and lodged it in my office; but
vexed to have all the world see it. And with Sir W. Batten, who
would have taken away my hands before they were stowed. But
by and by comes brother Balty[8] from sea, which I was glad of;
and so got him, and Mr. Tooker, and the boy, to watch with
them all in the office all night, while I upon Jane's coming went
down to my wife, calling at Deptford, intending to see Bagwell,
but did not ouvrir la porte comme je[9] did expect. So down late
to Woolwich, and there find my wife out of humour and indifferent, as she uses[s] upon her having much liberty abroad.

11th. Lay there, and up betimes, and by water with my gold,
and laid it with the rest in my office, where I find all well and
safe. So with Sir W. Batten to the New Exchange by water and

---

8 Balthazar St. Michel: brother of Mrs. Pepys, for whom Pepys had recently
secured the position of muster-master with one of the squadrons of the fleet.
9 . . . open the door as I. . . .

to my Lord Bruncker's house, where Sir W. Coventry and Sir G.
Carteret met. Little business before us but want of money. Broke
up, and I home by coach round the town. Dined at home, Balty
and myself putting up my papers in my closet in the office. He
away, I down to Deptford and there spoke with Bagwell and
agreed upon to-morrow, and come home in the rain by water.
In the evening at Sir W. Pen's, with my wife, at supper: he in a
mad, ridiculous, drunken humour; and it seems there have been
some late distances between his lady and him, as my [wife] tells
me. After supper, I home, and with Mr. Hater, Gibson, and Tom
alone, got all my chests and money into the further cellar with
much pains, but great content to me when done. So very late
and weary to bed.

12th. Up, and with Sir W. Batten and Sir W. Pen to St.
James's by water, and there did our usual business with the
Duke of Yorke. Thence I to Westminster, and there spoke with
Michell and Howlett, who tell me how their poor young ones
are going to Shadwell's. The latter told me of the unkindness of
the young man to his wife, which is now over, and I have promised to appear a counsellor to him. I am glad she is like to be
so near us again. Thence to Martin,[1] and there did tout ce que
je voudrais avec[2] her, and drank, and away by water home and
to dinner, Balty and his wife there. After dinner I took him
down with me to Deptford, and there the Bezan[3] loaded
above half my goods and sent them away. So we back home,
and then I found occasion to return in the dark and to Bagwell,
and there . . . did do all that I desired, but though I did intend
pour avoir demeurais con elle to-day last night, yet when I had
done ce que je voudrais I did hate both elle and la cose, and
taking occasion from the occasion of su marido's return . . .
did me lever,[4] and so away home late to Sir W. Pen's (Balty and
his wife lying at my house), and there in the same simple humour I found Sir W. Pen, and so late to bed.

13th. Up, and down to Tower Wharfe; and there, with Balty
and labourers from Deptford, did get my goods housed well at

1 Mrs. Betty Lane Martin, whom Pepys had known even before her marriage.
2 . . . everything I wanted with. . . .
3 The name of the yacht used by members of the Navy Office.
4 . . . to have stayed with her . . . what I wanted . . . her and the whole
thing . . . her husband's . . . get up. . . .

home. So down to Deptford again to fetch the rest, and there eat a bit of dinner at the Globe, with the master of the Bezan with me, while the labourers went to dinner. Here I hear that this poor towne do bury still of the plague seven or eight in a day. So to Sir G. Carteret's to work, and there did to my content ship off into the Bezan all the rest of my goods, saving my pictures and fine things, that I will bring home in wherrys when the house is fit to receive them: and so home, and unload them by carts and hands before night, to my exceeding satisfaction: and so after supper to bed in my house, the first time I have lain there; and lay with my wife in my old closett upon the ground, and Balty and his wife in the best chamber, upon the ground also.

14th. Up, and to work, having carpenters come to helpe in setting up bedsteads and hangings; and at that trade my people and I all the morning, till pressed by publique business to leave them against my will in the afternoon: and yet I was troubled in being at home, to see all my goods lie up and down the house in a bad condition, and strange workmen going to and fro might take what they would almost. All the afternoon busy; and Sir W. Coventry come to me, and found me, as God would have it, in my office, and people about me setting my papers to rights; and there discoursed about getting an account ready against the Parliament, and thereby did create me infinite of business, and to be done on a sudden; which troubled me: but, however, he being gone, I about it late, and to good purpose. And so home, having this day also got my wine out of the ground again, and set in my cellar; but with great pain to keep the porters that carried it in from observing the money-chests there. So to bed as last night, only my wife and I upon a bedstead with curtains in that which was Mercer's chamber, and Balty and his wife (who are here and do us good service), where we lay last night. This day, poor Tom Pepys,[5] the turner, was with me, and Kate Joyce,[6] to bespeake places; one for himself, the other for her husband. She tells me he hath lost £140 per annum, but have seven houses left.

15th. All the morning at the office, Harman being come to my

5 Pepys's cousin, a wood fashioner or lathe-worker.
6 Wife of Anthony, whose house had burned on the 5th.

great satisfaction to put up my beds and hangings, so I am at rest, and followed my business all day. Dined with Sir W. Batten, mighty busy about this account, and while my people were busy, wrote near thirty letters and orders with my owne hand. At it till eleven at night; and it is strange to see how clear my head was, being eased of all the matter of all these letters; whereas one would think that I should have been dazed. I never did observe so much of myself in my life. In the evening there comes to me Captain Cocke, and walked a good while in the garden. He says he hath computed that the rents of houses lost by this fire in the City comes to £600,000 per annum; that this will make the Parliament more quiet than otherwise they would have been, and give the King a more ready supply; that the supply must be by excise, as it is in Holland; that the Parliament will see it necessary to carry on the warr; that the late storm hindered our beating the Dutch fleete, who were gone out only to satisfy the people, having no business to do but to avoid us; that the French, as late in the yeare as it is, are coming; that the Dutch are really in bad condition, but that this unhappinesse of ours do give them heart; that there was a late difference between my Lord Arlington and Sir W. Coventry about neglect in the last to send away an express⁸ of the other's in time; that it come before the King, and the Duke of Yorke concerned himself in it; but this fire hath stopped it. The Dutch fleete is not gone home, but rather to the North, and so dangerous to our Gottenburgh fleete. That the Parliament is likely to fall foul upon some persons; and, among others, on the Vice-chamberlaine, though we both believe with little ground. That certainly never so great a loss as this was borne so well by citizens in the world; he believing that not one merchant upon the 'Change will break upon it. That he do not apprehend there will be any disturbances in State upon it; for that all men are busy in looking after their owne business to save themselves. He gone, I to finish my letters, and home to bed; and find to my infinite joy many rooms clean; and myself and wife lie in our own chamber again. But much terrified in the nights now-a-days with dreams of fire, and falling down of houses.

VII

Essays

John Donne

THAT ONLY COWARDS DARE DYE

Extreames are equally remooved from the *meane;* so that head-long *desperatenesse* asmuch offends true *valour,* as backward *Cowardice:* of which sort I reckon justly all *un-inforced deaths.* When will your *valiant* man dye of necessity? so *Cowards* suffer what cannot be avoided: and to runne into *death unimportun'd,* is to runne into the first condemned desperatenesse.[1] Will he dye when hee is *rich* and *happy?* then by living hee may doe more good: and in *Afflictions* and *miseries, death* is the chosen refuge of *Cowards.*

Fortiter ille facit, qui miser esse potest.[2]

But it is taught and practised among our *Gallants,* that rather than our reputations suffer any *maime,* or wee any *misery,* wee shall offer our *brests* to the *Cannons* mouth, yea to our swords points: And this seemes a very *brave* and a very *climbing* (which is a *Cowardly,* earthly, and indeed a very *groveling*) *spirit.* Why

[1] Cain's killing Abel.
[2] He acts bravely who can endure misery.

doe they *chaine* these slaves to the *Gallyes,* but that they thrust[§] their *deaths,* & would at every loose[§] leape into the *sea?* Why doe they take weapons from *condemned* men, but to barre them of that ease which *Cowards* affect, *a speedy death.* Truly this *life* is a *Tempest* and a *warfare,* and he which *dares dye,* to escape the *Anguish* of it, seemes to me, but so *valiant,* as he which dares *hang* himselfe, lest he bee *prest*[§] to the *wars.* I have seene one in that extremity of *Melancholy,* which was then become *Madnesse,* to make his owne *breath* an *Instrument* to stay his breath, and labour to choake himselfe; but alas, hee was *mad.* And we knew another that languished under the *oppression* of a poore *disgrace* so much, that he tooke more *paines* to *dye,* than would have served to have nourished *life* and *spirit* enough to have out-lived his *disgrace.* What *Foole* will call this *Cowardlinesse, Valour?* Or this *Basenesse, Humility?* And lastly, of these men which dye the *Allegoricall death* of entring into *Religion,* how few are found fit for any shew of valiancy? but onely a *soft* and *supple metall,*[§] made onely for *Cowardly* solitarinesse.

Sir William Cornwallis

OF ADVERSITIE

It is true that when wee are become of the world, we are throwne into a troublesome Inne, where respect goeth upon the leggs of riches, but this is our delicacie.[§] Nature for her part is not to bee blamed, for shee gave us leave to chuse our owne occupation;[§] it is custome and the softnesse of our mettalls,[§] and opinion is not an accessary, but a principall in the stealing the hearts of men, for ever since necessities banishment, there is a new account, & he that hath most, too much is honoured. Can there be a marvaile stranger, then that wee professing reason, doe best when compelled? He that is borne a beggar, playes the Philosopher, he that from rich becomes poore, the woman:[§] they are now in one state, why not in one continuance? Forsooth because once in abundance: who shold lament his corrupter thus? It is too pittiful, to spend teares on so trecherous an enemie. The Historiographers disputing about the easinesse of the Easterne Conquests, attribute it to the effeminatenesse of the men, their effeminatenesse to the climate: mee thinkes, and I am sure, that wealth hath the same operation: for her possessors grow weakelings. It is prooved often amongst us: for from industrious parents comes a slothfull and degenerate issue, and this I hold not Natures fault, but the heate of their aboundant fiers, their affections, which chokes their reason, and consumes their bodies. How many thousand of thinges have we intituled precious, that in themselves are meritlesse? and how many more dispised, to which estimation is due from our trouble? for had Judgement the survey[s] of our desires, we should go more bravely to worke, and if weepe, weepe for shame. For what a madnesse is it, to give the rule of our thoughts to our sicke appetites, to have our countenances governed by the Orbe of Vanity, and which is worse to binde our reason prentise to these transitory things. They that thinke thus, feele no Adversitie: it was onely ordained to punish the disciples of Fortune, who will needes sell the perfections of the minde, for the Jewels of Opinion; for the other, they looke not so lowe, but as their countenance is upward so their intentions, *Os homini sublime dedit cælumque tueri*.[3] This is to be a man; the other have but the shape, since we are made to no other purpose, but to witnesse the incomprehensible power of the Divine essence. It is besides the rest, even dishonest not to pay for our making; if it bee his pleasure I should serve him in a meane place, I will: if he like to try me with alterations, be it so. He hath done mee no wrong, for he hath given mee reason and patience, qualities able both to performe his pleasure, and comfort my travailes; he that carryes this about him, is safe: and now hee may (if other thinges fitte) come out of his study into the world: hee is armed, if not to resist, to suffer: it is no matter how often he bee hit, since hee feeles it not. If he findes opposition, he resists it; if it overcomes, not him but his Fortune: the man is safe, for his reckning is inward. How many revolutions, turnings, and reformings, have wee read, heard and seene? Empires, Kingdomes, States, nay

---

[3] He gave man eyes to gaze upon the sublime heavens.

even the whole world hath endured alterations of all kindes: wee
turne[§] not over this without great pleasure, and if we would take
pleasure in our profit, we should arme our selves with these examples, and indure our fortunes without grutching,[§] since wee
cannot doubt of his wisedome which governes, nor that our weaknes ought to glory in any thing more then obedience. What is it
now, that melts us into teares, or throws us into exclamations?
The false fier of opinion? Stand up man; it cannot hurte thee, if
thou beest a man. Wherefore let none complaine of Adversitie,
but those that will confesse themselves slaves to her glittering
contrary.

Owen Felltham

A RULE IN READING AUTHORS

Some men read Authors as our Gentlemen use flowers, onely for
delight and smell; to please their fancy, and refine their tongue.
Others like the Bee, extract onely the hony, the wholesome precepts, and this alone they beare away, leaving the rest, as little
worth, of small value. In reading I will care for both; though for
the last, most: the one serves to instruct the mind; the other fits
her to tell what she hath learned: pitty it is, they should be de-
vided: he that hath worth in him, and cannot expresse it, is a
chest keeping a rich Jewell, and the key lost. Concealing goodnesse, is vice; vertue is better by being communicated. A good
stile, with wholesome matter, is a faire woman with a vertuous
soule, which attracts the eyes of all; The good man thinkes
chastly, and loves her beauty, for her vertue; which hee still
thinks more faire, for dwelling in so faire an outside. The vicious
man hath lustfull thoughts; and he would for her beauty, faine
destroy her vertue: but comming to sollicite his purpose, findes
such divine lectures, from her Angels tongue, and those deliver'd
with so sweet a pleasing modesty, that he thinks vertue is dis-

secting her soule to him, to ravish man with a beauty which he dream'd not of. So hee could now curse himselfe, for desiring that lewdly, which he hath learn'd since, onely to admire, and reverence: Thus he goes away better, that came with an intent to bee worse. Quaint[§] phrases on a good subject, are baits to make an ill man vertuous: how many vile men seeking these, have found themselves Convertites? I may refine my speech without harme: but I will endevour more to reforme my life. 'Tis a good grace both of Oratory, or the Pen, to speake, or write proper: but that is the best work, where the Graces, and the Muses meet.

OF PURITANS

I finde many that are called *Puritans;* yet few, or none that will owne the *name.* Whereof the reason sure is this; that 'tis for the most part held a *name of Infamie;* and is so new, that it hath scarcely yet obtain'd a *definition:* nor is it an *appellation* derived from one *mans* name, whose *Tenents*[§] we may finde, digested into a *Volume:* whereby we doe much erre in the *application.* It imports a kinde of *excellencie* above another; which *man* (being conscious of his own fraile bendings) is ashamed to assume to himselfe. So that I beleeve there are men which *would be Puritans:* but indeed not any that *are.* One will have him one that lives religiously, and will not revell it in a shorelesse[§] excesse. Another, him that separates from our *Divine Assemblies.* Another, him that in some *tenents* onely is *peculiar.* Another, him that will not *sweare.* Absolutely to define him, is a worke, I thinke, of *Difficulty;* some I know that rejoice in the *name;* but sure they be such, as least *understand* it. As he is more generally in these times taken, I suppose we may call him *a Church-Rebell,* or one that would exclude *order,* that his *braine* might rule. To *decline offences;* to bee carefull and conscionable in our severall *actions,* is a *Puritie,* that every man ought to labour for, which we may well doe, without a sullen *segregation* from all *societie.* If there be any *Priviledges,* they are surely granted to the Children of the *King;* which are those that are the Children of *Heaven.* If *mirth* and *recreations* bee lawfull, sure such a one may lawfully use it. If *Wine* were given to cheere the *heart,* why should I feare to use it for that end? Surely, the *merry soule* is

freer from intended *mischiefe* then the *thoughtfull man*. A
bounded *mirth*, is a *Pattent* adding time and happines to the
crazed life of *Man*. Yet if *Laertius* reports him rightly, *Plato* deserves a *Censure*, for allowing *drunkennesse* at *Festivals;* because, saies he, as then, the *Gods* themselves reach *Wines* to
present *Men*. *God* delights in nothing more, then in a *cheerefull
heart*, carefull to performe him service. What *Parent* is it, that
rejoyceth not to see his *Child* pleasant, in the limits of a *filiall
duty?* I know wee reade of *Christs weeping*, not of his *laughter:*
yet wee see, hee graceth a *Feast* with his *first Miracle;* and that *a
Feast of joy:* And can we thinke that such a *meeting* could passe
without the noise of *laughter?* What a lumpe of *quickened care*
is the *melancholike man?* Change *anger* into *mirth*, and the Precept will hold good still: *Bee merry, but sinne not*. As there bee
many, that in their life assume too great a *Libertie;* so I beleeve
there are some, that abridge themselves of what they might lawfully use. *Ignorance* is an ill *Steward*, to provide for either *soule*,
or *Body*. A man that submits to reverent *Order*, that sometimes
unbends himselfe in a moderate *relaxation;* and in all, labours
to approve himselfe, in the serenenesse of a healthful *Conscience:* such a *Puritane* I will love immutably. But when a man,
in things but *ceremoniall*, shall spurne at the grave Authoritie
of the *Church*, and out of a needlesse *nicetie*, be a Thiefe to himselfe, of those benefits which God hath allowed him: or out of a
blinde and uncharitable *Pride*, censure, and scorne others, as
reprobates: or out of obstinacy, fill the World with *brawles*,
about *undeterminable Tenents*, I shall thinke him one of those,
whose *opinion* hath fevered his *zeale* to *madnesse* and *distraction*. I have more faith in one *Salomon*, then in a thousand
Dutch Parlours§ of such *Opinionists*. Behold then; what I have
seene good! That it is comely to eate, and to drinke, and to take
pleasure in all his labour wherein he travalleth§ under the *Sunne*,
the whole number of the dayes of his life, which God giveth him.
For, this is his *Portion*. Nay, *there is no profit to Man, but that
hee eate, and drinke, and delight his soule with the profit of his
labour*. For, he that saw other things but *vanitie*, saw this also,
that it was the *hand of God*. Me thinkes the reading of *Ecclesiastes*, should make a *Puritane* undresse his braine, and lay off all
those *Phanatique toyes* that gingle about his *understanding*. For

my owne part, I thinke the World hath not better men, then some, that suffer under that name: nor withall, more *Scelestique*[§] *Villaines*. For, when they are once *elated* with that *pride*, they so *contemne* others, that they infringe the Lawes of all *humane societie*.

OF THE WORSHIP OF ADMIRATION

Whatsoever is *rare*, and *passionate*,[§] carries the *soule* to the thought of *Eternitie*. And, by *contemplation*, gives it some *glympses* of more absolute *perfection*, then here 'tis *capable* of. When I see the *Royaltie* of a *State-show*, at some unwonted *solemnity*, my thoughts *present* me something, more *royall* then this. When I see the most *inchanting* beauties, that *Earth* can shew mee; I yet thinke, there is something farre more *glorious*: mee thinkes I see a kind of higher *perfection*, peeping through the *frailty* of a *face*. When I heare the *ravishing* straines, of a *sweet-tuned voyce*, married to the *warbles*, of the *Artfull* Instrument; I apprehend by this, a higher *Diapason*: and doe almost beleeve, I hear a little *Deity* whispering, through the *pory*[§] substance of the *tongue*. But, this I can but *grope* after. I can neither *finde*, nor *say*, what it is. When I reade a *rarely sententious*[§] *man*, I admire him, to[§] my owne *impatiency*.[§] I cannot reade some parts of *Seneca*, above two Leaves together. He raises my *soule* to a *contemplation*, which sets me a *thinking*, on more, then I can *imagine*. So I am forced to cast him by, and *subside* to an *admiration*. Such *effects* workes *Poetry*, when it lookes to towring *Vertues*. It gives up a man to *raptures;* and *inradiates* the *soule*, with such high *apprehensions*: that all the *Glories*, which this *World* hath, hereby appeare, *contemptible*. Of which the soft-soul'd *Ovid* gives a touch, when he complaines the *want*.

> *Impetus ille Sacer, qui vatum Pectora nutrit,*
> *Qui prius in nobis esse solebat, abest.*

> That Sacred vigor, which had wont, alone,
> To flame the *Poets* noble brest, is gone.

But this is, when these *excellencies* incline to *gravity*, and *seriousnesse*. For otherwise, light *aires* turne us into *sprightfull*

actions; which breathe away in a loose *laughter,* not leaving halfe
that *impression* behind them, which serious *considerations* doe.
As if *Mirth* were the *excellency* for the *body,* and *meditation* for
the *soule.* As if one were, for the *contentment* of this *life;* and
the other, *eying* to that of the *life to come.* All *Indevours* aspire
to *Eminency;* All *Eminencies* doe beget an *Admiration.* And, this
makes mee beleeve, that *contemplative admiration,* is a large part
of the *worship* of the *Deity.* 'Tis an *adoration,* purely, of the
Spirit; a more *sublime* bowing of the *soule* to the *Godhead.* And
this is it, which that *Homer* of *Philosophers*[4] avowed, could bring
a man to *perfect happinesse,* if to his *Contemplation,* he joyned
a constant *Imitation* of *God,* in *Justice, Wisedome, Holinesse.*
Nothing can carry us so neere to *God,* and *Heaven,* as this. The
mind can walke, beyond the *sight* of the *eye;* and (though in a
cloud) can lift us into *Heaven,* while wee live. *Meditation* is the
soules Perspective[§] *glasse:* whereby, in her long *remove,* shee dis-
cerneth *God,* as if hee were neerer hand. I perswade no man to
make it his whole *life's* businesse. Wee have *bodies,* as well as
soules. And even this *World,* while we are in it, ought somewhat
to be cared for. As those *States* are likely to *flourish,* where *execution* followes sound *advisements:* So is *Man,* when *contemplation* is seconded by *action. Contemplation* generates; *Action*
propagates. Without the first, the latter is *defective.* Without the
last, the first is but *abortive,* and *embrious.*[§] Saint *Bernard* compares *contemplation* to *Rachel,* which was the more *faire:* but
action to *Leah,* which was the more *fruitfull.* I will neither alwayes be *busie,* and *doing:* nor ever *shut up* in nothing but
thoughts. Yet, that which some would call *Idlenesse,* I will call
the *sweetest part* of my *life:* and that is, my *Thinking.* Surely,
God made so many *varieties* in his *Creatures,* as well for the *inward soul,* as the *outward senses;* though he made them *primarily,* for his owne *Free-will,* and *Glory.* He was a *Monke* of an
honester *age,* that being asked how he could indure that *life,*
without the *pleasure of bookes,* answered: The *Nature* of the
Creatures was his *Library:* wherein, when hee pleased, he could
muse upon *Gods deepe Oracles.*

4 Plato.

Ben Jonson

DE STYLO, ET OPTIMO SCRIBENDI GENERE[5]

For a man to write well, there are required three Necessaries. To reade the best Authors, observe the best Speakers: and much exercise of his owne style. In style to consider, what ought to be written; and after what manner; Hee must first thinke, and excogitate his matter; then choose his words, and examine the weight[§] of either. Then take care in placing, and ranking[§] both matter, and words, that the composition be comely;[§] and to doe this with diligence, and often. No matter how slow the style be at first, so it be labour'd,[§] and accurate; seeke the best, and be not glad of the forward conceipts,[§] or first words, that offer themselves to us, but judge of what wee invent; and order what wee approve. Repeat often, what wee have formerly written; which beside, that it helpes the consequence,[§] and makes the juncture[§] better, it quickens the heate of imagination, that often cooles in the time of setting downe, and gives it new strength, as if it grew lustier, by the going back. As wee see in the contention of leaping, they jumpe farthest, that fetch their race largest: or, as in throwing a Dart, or Javelin, wee force back our armes, to make our loose[§] the stronger. Yet, if we have a faire gale of wind, I forbid not the steering[§] out of our sayle, so the favour of the gale deceive us not. For all that wee invent doth please us in the conception, or birth; else we would never set it downe. But the safest is to returne to our Judgement, and handle over againe those things, the easinesse of which might make them justly suspected. So did the best Writers in their beginnings; they impos'd upon themselves care, and industry. They did nothing rashly. They obtain'd first to write well, and then custome made it easie, and a habit. By little and little, their matter shew'd it selfe to 'hem more plentifully; their words answer'd, their composition followed; and all, as in a well-order'd family, presented

[5] *On Style, and the Best Kind of Writing.*

it selfe in the place. So that the summe of all is: Ready[§] writing
makes not good writing; but good writing brings on ready writing: Yet when wee thinke wee have got the faculty,[§] it is even
then good to resist it: as to give a Horse a check sometimes with
[a] bit, which doth not so much stop his course, as stirre his mettle. Againe, whether[§] a mans *Genius* is best able to reach, thither
it should more and more contend, lift and dilate[§] it selfe, as men
of low stature, raise themselves on their toes; and so oft times
get even, if not eminent. Besides, as it is fit for grown and able
Writers to stand of themselves, and worke with their owne
strength, to trust and endeavour by their owne faculties: so it is
fit for the beginner, and learner, to study others, and the best.
For the mind, and memory are more sharpely exercis'd in comprehending an other mans things, then our owne; and such as
accustome themselves, and are familiar with the best Authors,
shall ever and anon find somewhat of them in themselves, and
in the expression of their minds, even when they feele it not, be
able to utter something like theirs, which hath an Authority
above their owne. Nay, sometimes it is the reward of a mans
study, the praise of quoting an other man fitly: And though a
man be more prone, and able for one kind of writing, then another, yet hee must exercise all. For as in an Instrument, so in
style, there must be a Harmonie, and consent[§] of parts.

PRÆCIPIENDI MODI[6]

I take this labour in teaching others, that they should not be alwayes to bee taught; and I would bring my Precepts into practise.
For rules are ever of lesse force, and valew, then experiments.
Yet with this purpose, rather to shew the right way to those that
come after, then to detect any that have slipt before by errour,
and I hope it will bee more profitable. For men doe more willingly listen, and with more favour, to precept, then reprehension.
Among diverse opinions of an Art, and most of them contrary in
themselves, it is hard to make election; and therefore, though a
man cannot invent new things after so many, he may doe a welcome worke yet to helpe posterity to judge rightly of the old. But
Arts and Precepts availe nothing, except nature by beneficiall,

6 *Methods of Teaching.*

and ayding. And therefore these things are no more written to a
dull disposition, then rules of husbandry to a barren Soyle. No
precepts will profit a Foole; no more then beauty will the blind, or
musicke the deafe. As wee should take care, that our style in
writing, be neither dry, nor empty: wee should looke againe it be
not winding, or wanton with far-fetcht-descriptions; Either is a
vice. But that is worse which proceeds out of want, then that
which riots out of plenty. The remedy of fruitfulnesse is easie,
but no labour will helpe the contrary: I will like, and praise some
things in a young Writer; which yet if hee continue in, I cannot
but justly hate him for the same. There is a time to bee given all
things for maturity; and that even your Countrey-husband-man
can teach; who to a young plant will not put the proyning§ knife,
because it seemes to feare the iron, as not able to admit the scarre.
No more would I tell a greene Writer all his faults, lest I should
make him grieve and faint,§ and at last despaire. For nothing
doth more hurt, then to make him so afraid of all things, as hee
can endeavour nothing. Therefore youth ought to be instructed
betimes, and in the best things: for we hold those longest, wee
take soonest. As the first sent§ of a Vessell§ lasts: and that tinct§
the wooll first receives. Therefore a Master should temper his
owne powers, and descend to the others infirmity. If you powre
a glut of water upon a Bottle, it receives little of it; but with a
Funnell, and by degrees, you shall fill many of them, and spill
little of your owne; to their capacity they will all receive, and be
full. And as it is fit to reade the best Authors to youth first, so let
them be of the openest, and clearest. As *Livy* before *Salust, Syd-
ney* before *Donne:* and beware of letting them taste *Gower,* or
Chaucer at first, lest falling too much in love with Antiquity, and
not apprehending the weight, they grow rough and barren in
language onely. When their judgements are firme, and out of
danger, let them reade both, the old and the new: but no lesse
take heed, that their new flowers, and sweetnesse doe not as
much corrupt, as the others drinesse, and squallor,§ if they
choose not carefully. *Spencer,* in affecting§ the Ancients, writ no
Language: Yet I would have him read for his matter; but as
Virgil read *Ennius.* The reading of *Homer* and *Virgil* is counsell'd
by *Quintilian,* as the best way of informing youth, and confirming man. For besides that the mind is rais'd with the height, and

sublimity of such a verse, it takes spirit from the greatnesse of the matter, and is tincted with the best things. *Tragicke,* and *Liricke* Poetry is good too: and *Comicke* with the best, if the manners of the Reader be once in safety. In the *Greeke* Poets, as also in *Plautus,* wee shall see the Oeconomy, and disposition of *Poems,* better observed then in *Terence,* and the later: who thought the sole grace, and vertue of their Fable, the sticking in of sentences,§ as ours doe the forcing in of jests.

Thomas Fuller

OF BOOKS

Solomon saith truly, *Of making many Books there is no end,* so insatiable is the thirst of men therein: as also endles is the desire of many in buying and reading them. But we come to our Rules.[7]

It is a vanity to perswade the world one hath much learning by getting a great library. As soon shall I believe every one is valiant that hath a well furnish'd armoury. I guesse good house-keeping by the smoking, not the number of the tunnels,§ as knowing that many of them (built merely for uniformity) are without chimnies, and more without fires. Once a dunce, void of learning but full of Books, flouted a library-lesse Scholar with these words, *Salve Doctor sine libris:*[8] But the next day the Scholar coming into this jeerers study crowded with Books, *Salvete libri* (saith he) *sine Doctore.*[9]

Few Books well selected are best. Yet as a certain Fool bought all the pictures that came out, because he might have his choice; such is the vain humour of many men in gathering of Books: yet when they have done all, they misse their end, it being in the Editions of Authours as in the fashions of clothes, when a man

[7] Fuller's rules are the italicized first sentences in the paragraphs which follow; in his marginal notes he calls them *maxims* and numbers them.
[8] Hail, doctor without books.
[9] Hail, books without doctor.

thinks he hath gotten the latest and newest, presently another
newer comes out.

Some Books are onely cursorily to be tasted of. Namely first
Voluminous Books, the task of a mans life to reade them over;
secondly, Auxiliary Books, onely to be repair'd§ to on occasions;
thirdly, such as are mere pieces of Formality, so that if you look
on them you look thorow§ them; and he that peeps thorow the
casement of the Index sees as much as if he were in the house.
But the lazinesse of those cannot be excused who perfunctorily
passe over Authours of consequence, and onely trade in their
Tables and Contents. These like City-Cheaters having gotten the
names of all countrey Gentlemen, make silly people believe they
have long lived in those places where they never were, and flourish with skill in those Authours they never seriously studied.

*The Genius of the Authour is commonly discovered in the Ded-
icatory epistle.* Many place the purest grain in the mouth of the
sack for chapmen to handle or buy: And from the dedication one
may probably guesse at the Work, saving some rare and peculiar
exceptions. Thus when once a Gentleman admired how so pithy,
learned, and witty a dedication was match'd to a flat, dull, foolish
book; *In truth,* said another, *they may be well match'd together,
for I professe they are nothing a kinne.*

*Proportion an houres meditation to an houres reading of a
staple Authour.* This makes a man master of his learning, and
dispirits§ the book into the Scholar. The King of Sweden never
filed his men above six deep in one company, because he would
not have them lie in useless clusters in his Army, but so that
every particular Souldier might be drawn out into service. Books
that stand thinne on the shelves, yet so as the owner of them can
bring forth every one of them into use, are better then farre
greater libraries.

*Learning hath gained most by those books by which the
Printers have lost.* Arius Montanus in printing the Hebrew Bible
(commonly called the Bible of the King of Spain) much wasted
himself, and was accused in the Court of Rome for his good deed,
and being cited thither, *Pro tantorum laborum præmio vix
veniam impetravit.*[1] Likewise Christopher Plantin by printing of
his curious§ interlineary Bible in Antwerp, through the unsea-

[1] Instead of a reward for such great labors, he barely got a pardon.

sonable exactions of the Kings Officers, sunk and almost ruin'd his estate. And our worthy English Knight, who set forth the golden-mouth'd Father in a silver print,[2] was a looser by it.

Whereas foolish Pamphlets prove most beneficiall to the Printers. When a French Printer complain'd that he was utterly undone by Printing a solid serious book of Rablais concerning Physick, Rablais to make him recompence made that his jesting scurrilous Work which repair'd the Printers losse with advantage. Such books the world swarms too much with. When one had set out a witlesse Pamphlet, writing *Finis* at the end thereof, another wittily wrote beneath it,

> ——*Nay there thou li'st, my friend,*
> *In writing foolish books there is no end.*

And surely such scurrilous scandalous papers do more then conceivable mischief. First their lusciousnesse puts many palats out of taste, that they can never after rellish any solid and wholsome Writers: secondly, they cast dirt on the faces of many innocent persons, which dryed on by continuance of time can never after be washed off: thirdly, the Pamphlets of this age may passe for Records with the next (because publickly uncontrolled) and what we laugh at, our children may believe: fourthly, grant the things true they jeer at, yet this musick is unlawfull in any Christian Church, to play upon the sinnes and miseries of others, the fitter object of the Elegies then the Satyrs of all truly religious.

But what do I speaking against multiplicity of books in this age, who trespasse in this nature my self? What was a learned mans complement may serve for my confession and conclusion, *Multi mei similes hoc morbo laborant, ut cum scribere nesciant tamen à scribendo temperare non possint.*[3]

2 Sir Henry Savile's edition of the works of St. Chrysostom (8 vols., 1610-13) was beautifully printed.
3 Many men suffer from a disease like mine; though they don't know how to write, they can't restrain themselves from writing. Erasmus.

Abraham Cowley

OF SOLITUDE

Nunquam minus solus, quam cum solus,[4] is now become a very
vulgar[§] saying. Every Man and almost every Boy for these seventeen hundred years, has had it in his mouth. But it was at first
spoken by the Excellent *Scipio,* who was without question a most
Eloquent and Witty person, as well as the most Wise, most
Worthy, most Happy, and the Greatest of all Mankind. His meaning no doubt was this, That he found more satisfaction to his
mind, and more improvement of it by Solitude then by Company,
and to shew that he spoke not this loosly or out of vanity, after
he had made *Rome,* Mistriss of almost the whole World, he retired himself from it by a voluntary exile, and at a private house
in the middle of a wood neer *Linternum,* passed the remainder of
his Glorious life no less Gloriously. This House *Seneca* went to
see so long after with great veneration, and among other things
describes his Baths to have been of so mean a structure, that
now, says he, the basest of the people would despise them, and
cry out, poor *Scipio* understood not how to live. What an Authority is here for the credit of Retreat? and happy had it been for
Hannibal, if Adversity could have taught him as much Wisdom
as was learnt by *Scipio* from the highest Prosperities. This would
be no wonder if it were as truly as it is colourably[§] and wittily
said by Monsieur *de Montagne.* That Ambition it self might
teach us to love Solitude; there's nothing does so much hate to
have Companions. 'Tis true, it loves to have its Elbows free, it
detests to have Company on either side, but it delights above all
things in a Train behind, I,[§] and Ushers too before it. But the
greatest part of men are so far from the opinion of that noble
Roman, that if they chance at any time to be without company,
they'r like a becalmed Ship, they never move but by the wind of
other mens breath, and have no Oars of their own to steer withal.

4 Never less alone than when alone.

It is very fantastical and contradictory in humane Nature, that
Men should love themselves above all the rest of the world, and
yet never endure to be with themselves. When they are in love
with a Mistriss, all other persons are importunate⁵ and burden-
some to them. *Tecum vivere amem, tecum obeam Lubens,* They
would live and dye with her alone.

> *Sic ego secretis possum bené vivere silvis*
> *Quà nulla humano sit via trita pedé,*
> *Tu mihi curarum requies, tu nocte vel atrâ*
> *Lumen, & in solis tu mihi turba locis.*

> With thee for ever I in woods could rest,
> Where never humane foot the ground has prest,
> Thou from all shades the darkness canst exclude,
> And from a Desart banish Solitude.

And yet our Dear Self is so wearisome to us, that we can
scarcely support its conversation for an hour together. This is
such an odd temper of mind as *Catullus* expresses towards one
of his Mistresses, whom we may suppose to have been of a very
unsociable humour.

> *Odi & Amo, quanám id faciam ratione requiris?*
> *Nescio, sed fieri sentio, & excrucior.*

> I Hate, and yet I Love thee too;
> How can that be? I know not how;
> Only that so it is I know,
> And feel with Torment that 'tis so.

It is a deplorable condition, this, and drives a man sometimes
to pittiful shifts in seeking how to avoid Himself.

The truth of the matter is, that neither he who is a Fop in the
world, is a fit man to be alone; nor he who has set his heart much
upon the world, though he have never so much understanding; so
that Solitude can be well fitted and set right, but upon a very
few persons. They must have enough knowledge of the World to
see the vanity of it, and enough Virtue to despise all Vanity; if
the Mind be possest with any Lust⁵ or Passions, a man had better
be in a Faire, then in a Wood alone. They may like petty Thieves
cheat us perhaps, and pick our pockets in the midst of company,

but like Robbers they use to strip and bind, or murder us when they catch us alone. This is but to retreat from Men, and fall into the hands of Devils. 'Tis like the punishment of Parricides among the *Romans,* to be sow'd into a Bag with an Ape, a Dog, and a Serpent. The first work therefore that a man must do to make himself capable of the good of Solitude, is, the very Eradication of all Lusts, for how is it possible for a Man to enjoy himself while his Affections are tyed to things without Himself? In the second place, he must learn the Art and get the Habit of Thinking; for this too, no less than well speaking, depends upon much practice, and Cogitation is the thing which distinguishes the Solitude of a God from a wild Beast. Now because the soul of Man is not by its own Nature or observation furnisht with sufficient Materials to work upon; it is necessary for it to have continual recourse to Learning and Books for fresh supplies, so that the solitary Life will grow indigent, and be ready to starve without them; but if once we be throughly engaged in the Love of Letters, instead of being wearied with the length of any day, we shall only complain of the shortness of our whole Life.

> *O vita, stulto longa, sapienti brevis!*
> O Life, long to the Fool, short to the Wise!

The first Minister of State has not so much business in publique, as a wise man has in private; if the one have little leisure to be alone, the other has less leisure to be in company; the one has but part of the affairs of one Nation, the other all the works of God and Nature under his consideration. There is no saying shocks me so much as that which I hear very often, That a man does not know how to pass his Time. 'Twould have been but ill spoken by *Methusalem* in the Nine hundred sixty ninth year of his Life, so far it is from us, who have not time enough to attain to the utmost perfection of any part of any Science, to have cause to complain that we are forced to be idle for want of work. But this you'l say is work only for the Learned, others are not capable either of the employments or divertisements that arrive from Letters. I know they are not; and therefore cannot much recommend Solitude to a man totally illiterate. But if any man be so unlearned as to want entertainment of the little Intervals of accidental Solitude, which frequently occurr in almost all condi-

tions (except the very meanest of the people, who have business
enough in the necessary provisions for Life) it is truly a great
shame both to his Parents and Himself, for a very small portion
of any Ingenious Art will stop up all those gaps of our Time,
either Musique, or Painting, or Designing, or Chymistry, or History, or Gardening, or twenty other things will do it usefully and
pleasantly; and if he happen to set his affections upon Poetry
(which I do not advise him too immoderately) that will over do
it; no wood will be thick enough to hide him from the impor-
tunities of company or business, which would abstract him from
his Beloved.

> ——*O quis me gelidis sub montibus Æmi*
> *Sistat, & ingenti ramorum protegat umbrâ?*[5]

1

Hail, old *Patrician* Trees, so great and good!
Hail ye *Plebeian* under wood!
Where the Poetique Birds rejoyce,
And for their quiet Nests and plentious Food,
Pay with their grateful voice.

2

Hail, the poor Muses richest Mannor Seat!
Ye Countrey Houses and Retreat,
Which all the happy Gods so love,
That for you oft they quit their Bright and Great
Metropolis above.

3

Here Nature does a House for me erect,
Nature the wisest Architect,
Who those fond Artists does despise
That can the fair and living Trees neglect;
Yet the Dead Timber prize.

4

Here let me careless and unthoughtful lying,
Hear the soft winds above me flying,
With all their wanton Boughs dispute,

[5] O that some one would place me in the shadow of the cold mountains of
Haemus, and shield me under the widespread shade of the branches.

And the more tuneful Birds to both replying
Nor be my self too Mute.

5

A Silver stream shall roul his waters neer,
    Guilt§ with the Sun-beams here and there
    On whose enamel'd Bank I'll walk,
And see how prettily they Smile, and hear
    How prettily they Talk.

6

Ah wretched, and too Solitary Hee
    Who loves not his own Company!
    He'l feel the weight of't many a day
Unless he call in Sin or Vanity
    To help to bear't away.

7

Oh Solitude, first state of Human-kind!
    Which blest remain'd till man did find
    Even his own helpers Company.
As soon as two (alas!) together joyn'd,
    The Serpent made up Three.

8

Though God himself, through countless Ages Thee
    His sole Companion chose to be,
    Thee, Sacred Solitude alone,
Before the Branchy head of Numbers Tree
    Sprang from the Trunk of One.

9

Thou (though men think thine an unactive part)
    Dost break and tame th'unruly heart,
    Which else would know no setled pace
Making it move, well mannag'd by thy Art,
    With Swiftness and with Grace.

10

Thou the faint beams of Reasons scatter'd Light,
    Dost like a Burning-glass unite,
    Dost multiply the feeble Heat,

And fortifie the strength, till thou dost bright
And noble Fires beget.

11

Whilst this hard Truth I teach, methinks, I see
The Monster *London* laugh at me,
I should at thee too, foolish City,
If it were fit to laugh at Misery,
But thy Estate I pity.

12

Let but thy wicked men from out thee go,
And all the Fools that crowd thee so,
Even thou who dost thy Millions boast,
A Village less than *Islington* wilt grow,
A Solitude almost.

OF MY SELF

It is a hard and nice Subject for a man to write of himself, it grates his own heart to say any thing of disparagement, and the Readers Eares to hear any thing of praise from him. There is no danger from me of offending him in this kind; neither my Mind, nor my Body, nor my Fortune, allow me any materials for that Vanity. It is sufficient, for my own contentment, that they have preserved me from being scandalous,[§] or remarkable on the defective side. But besides that, I shall here speak of myself, only in relation to the subject of these precedent discourses, and shall be likelier thereby to fall into the contempt, then rise up to the estimation of most people. As far as my Memory can return back into my past Life, before I knew, or was capable of guessing what the world, or glories, or business of it were, the natural affections of my soul gave me a secret bent of aversion from them, as some Plants are said to turn away from others, by an Antipathy imperceptible to themselves, and inscrutable to mans understanding. Even when I was a very young Boy at School, instead of running about on Holy-daies and playing with my fellows; I was wont to steal from them, and walk into the fields, either alone with a Book, or with some one Companion, if I could find any of the same temper. I was then too, so much an Enemy to all constraint, that my Masters could never prevail on me, by any perswasions or encouragements, to learn without Book the common rules of Grammar, in which they dispensed§ with me alone, because they found I made a shift§ to do the usual exercise out of my own reading and observation. That I was then of the same mind as I am now (which I confess, I wonder at my self) may appear by the latter end of an Ode, which I made when I was but thirteen years old, and which was then printed with many other Verses. The Beginning of it is Boyish, but of this part which I here set down (if a very little were corrected) I should hardly now be much ashamed.

9

This only grant me, that my means may lye
Too low for Envy, for Contempt too high.
   Some Honor I would have
Not from great deeds, but good alone.
The unknown are better than ill known.
   Rumour can ope' the Grave,
Acquaintance I would have, but when 't depends
Not on the number, but the choice of Friends.

10

Books should, not business entertain the Light,
And sleep, as undisturb'd as Death, the Night.
   My House a Cottage, more
Then Palace, and should fitting be
For all my Use, no Luxury.
   My Garden painted o're
With Natures hand, not Arts; and pleasures yeild,
Horace might envy in his Sabine field.

11

Thus would I double my Lifes fading space,
For he that runs it well, twice runs his race.
   And in this true delight,
These unbought sports, this happy State,
I would not fear nor wish my fate,
   But boldly say each night,
To morrow let my Sun his beams display,
Or in clouds hide them; I have liv'd to Day.

You may see by it, I was even then acquainted with the Poets
(for the Conclusion is taken out of *Horace;*) and perhaps it was
the immature and immoderate love of them which stampt first,
or rather engraved these Characters in me: They were like Letters cut into the Bark of a young Tree, which with the Tree still
grow proportionably. But, how this love came to be produced in
me so early, is a hard question: I believe I can tell the particular
little chance that filled my head first with such Chimes of Verse,
as have never since left ringing there: For I remember when I
began to read, and to take some pleasure in it, there was wont to
lie in my Mothers Parlour (I know not by what accident, for she
her self never in her life read any Book but of Devotion) but
there was wont to lie *Spencers* Works; this I happened to fall
upon, and was infinitely delighted with the Stories of the Knights,
and Giants, and Monsters, and brave Houses, which I found every
where there: (Though my understanding had little to do with all
this) and by degrees with the tinckling of the Rhyme and Dance
of the Numbers, so that I think I had read him all over before I
was twelve years old, and was thus made a Poet as immediately
as a Child is made an Eunuch. With these affections of mind,
and my heart wholly set upon Letters, I went to the University;
But was soon torn from thence by that violent Publick storm
which would suffer nothing to stand where it did, but rooted up
every Plant, even from the Princely Cedars to Me, the Hyssop.[§]
Yet I had as good fortune as could have befallen me in such a
Tempest; for I was cast by it into the Family of one of the best
Persons, and into the Court of one of the best Princesses of the
World. Now though I was here engaged in wayes most contrary
to the Original design of my life, that is, into much company,
and no small business, and into a daily sight of Greatness, both
Militant and Triumphant (for that was the state then of the
English and *French* Courts) yet all this was so far from altering
my Opinion, that it onely added the confirmation of Reason to
that which was before but Natural Inclination. I saw plainly all
the Paint of that kind of Life, the nearer I came to it; and that
Beauty which I did not fall in Love with, when, for ought I knew,
it was reall, was not like to bewitch, or intice me, when I saw
that it was Adulterate. I met with several great Persons, whom I
liked very well, but could not perceive that any part of their

Greatness was to be liked or desired, no more then I would be glad, or content to be in a Storm, though I saw many Ships which rid safely and bravely in it: A storm would not agree with my stomach, if it did with my Courage. Though I was in a croud of as good company as could be found any where, though I was in business of great and honourable trust, though I eate at the best Table, and enjoyed the best conveniences for present subsistance that ought to be desired by a man of my condition in banishment and publick distresses; yet I could not abstain from renewing my old School-boys Wish in a Copy of Verses to the same effect.

> Well then; I now do plainly see
> This busie World and I shall ne're agree, &c.

And I never then proposed to my self any other advantage from His Majesties Happy Restoration, but the getting into some moderately convenient Retreat in the Country, which I thought in that case I might easily have compassed, as well as some others, with no greater probabilities or pretences have arrived to extraordinary fortunes: But I had before written a shrewd Prophesie against my self, and I think *Apollo* inspired me in the Truth, though not in the Elegance of it.

> Thou, neither great at Court nor in the War,
> Nor at th' Exchange shal't be, nor at the wrangling Barr;
> Content thy self with the small barren praise
> Which neglected Verse does raise, &c.

However by the failing of the Forces which I had expected, I did not quit the Design which I had resolved on, I cast my self into it *A Corps Perdue,*§ without making capitulations, or taking counsel of Fortune. But God laughs at a Man, who sayes to his Soul, *Take thy ease:* I met presently not onely with many little encumbrances and impediments, but with so much sickness (a new misfortune to me) as would have spoiled the happiness of an Emperour as well as Mine: Yet I do neither repent nor alter my course. *Non ego perfidum Dixi Sacramentum;*6 Nothing shall separate me from a Mistress, which I have loved so long, and have now at last married; though she neither has brought me a rich Portion, nor lived yet so quietly with me as I hoped from Her.

6 I have not made a treacherous vow.

———*Nec vos, dulcissima mundi*
Nomina, vos Musæ, Libertas, Otia, Libri,
Hortique Sylvæque anima remanente relinquam.

Nor by me ere shall you,
You of all Names the sweetest, and the best,
You Muses, Books, and Liberty and Rest;
You Gardens, Fields, and Woods forsaken be,
As long as Life it self forsakes not Me.

But this is a very petty Ejaculation; because I have concluded all the other Chapters with a Copy of Verses,[7] I will maintain the Humour to the last.

[7] Each of Cowley's essays is followed by one or more poems, either his own or his translation (most frequently of Martial, Horace, and Virgil).

VIII

Characters

FROM

The Overburian Characters

AN AFFECTED TRAVELLER

Is a speaking fashion; he hath taken paines to bee ridiculous, and hath seen more then he hath perceived. His attire speakes *French* or *Italian*, and his *gate*§ cryes *Behold mee*. Hee censures all things by countenances,§ and shrugs, and speakes his owne language with shame and lisping: he will choake rather than confesse *Beere* good drinke: and his pick-tooth is a maine part of his behaviour. Hee chooseth rather to be counted a *Spie*, then not a *Polititian:* and maintaines his reputation by naming great men familiarly. He chooseth rather to tell lyes then not wonders, and talkes with men singly; his discourse sounds big but meanes nothing: and his boy is bound to admire him howsoever. He comes still from great personages, but goes with meane. He takes occasion to shew Jewells given him in regard of his vertue, that were bought in *S. Martins*, and not long after, having with a *Mountebancks* method, pronounced them worth thousands, empawneth them for a few shillings. Upon festivall daies he goes to Court, and salutes§ without re-saluting:§ at night in an Ordinarie§ hee confesseth the businesse in hand, and seemes as conversant with all intents and plots, as if he begot them. His extraordinary accompt of men is, first to tell them the ends of all matters of consequence, and then to borrow mony of them; hee offereth curtesies, to shew them, rather then himselfe humble. He disdaines all things above his reach, and preferreth all Countries before his owne. Hee imputeth his wants and provertie to the ignorance of the time, not his owne unworthines: and concludes his discourse with a halfe period,§ or a word, and leaves the rest to imagination. In a word, his religion is fashion, and both body and soule are governed by fame, he loves most voices above truth.

AN ELDER BROTHER

Is a creature borne to the best advantage of things without§ him; that hath the start at the beginning, but loyters it away before the ending. He lookes like his land, as heavily, and durtily, as stubbornely. He dares doe any thing but fight: and feares nothing but his Fathers life and minoritie. The first thing hee makes knowne is his estate; and the load-stone that drawes him is the upper end of the table. He wooeth by a particular,§ and his strongest argument is the joynture. His observation is all about the fashion, and he commends Partlets§ for a rare devise. Hee speakes no language, but smells of dogs or hawkes; and his ambition flies Justice§-hight. He loves to be commended, and hee will goe into the kitchin, but heele have it. He loves glory, but is so lazie as he is content with flatterie. He speakes most of the precedencie of age, and protests fortune the greatest vertue. He summoneth the old servants, and tells what strange acts hee will doe, when he raignes. Hee verily beleeves houskeepers§ the best common-wealths men; and therfore studies baking, brewing, greasing, and such, as the lyms of goodnesse. Hee judgeth it no small signe of wisdome to talke much, his tongue therefore goes continually his errand, but never speeds. If his understanding were not honester than his will, no man should keepe a good conceit by him; for hee thinkes it no theft, to sell all he can to opinion. His pedigree and his fathers seale-ring, are the stilts of his crazed disposition. He had rather keep companie with the dregs of men, than not to be the best man. His insinuation[§] is the inviting men to his house; and hee thinkes it a great modestie, to comprehend his cheere under a peece of mutton and a rabbet; if by this time he be not knowne, hee will goe home againe, for hee can no more abide to have himselfe concealed,[§] then his land; yet he is as you see good for nothing, except to make a stallion to maintaine the race.

A PURITANE

Is a diseas'd peece of Apocripha, bind him to the Bible and he corrupts the whole text; Ignorance, and fat feede, are his founders, his Nurses, Raylings, Rabbies, and round breeches; his life is but a borrowed blast of winde; for between two religions, as betweene two doores hee is ever whisling. Truely whose child he is, is yet unknowne; for willingly his Faith allowes no Father, onely thus far his pedigree is found, Bragger and he flourisht about a time first; his fierie zeale keepes him continuall Costive, which withers him into his own translation, and till hee eate a Schoolman hee is hide-bound; he ever prayes against *non*[§] *Residentes*, but is himselfe the greatest discontinuer, for he never keepes neere his text: any thing that the Law allowes: but marriage and March beare;[§] Hee murmures at: what it disallows and holds dangerous makes him a discipline. Where the gate stands open he is ever seeking a stile, and where his learning ought to clime, he creepes through; give him advice, you runne into traditions, and urge a modest course hee cries out, Councels. His greatest care is to contemne obedience, his last care to serve God handsomely and cleanely; hee is now become so crosse a kinde of teaching that should the Church enjoyne cleane shirts; hee were lousie: more sence then single prayers is not his, nor more in those then still the same petitions, from which he either feares a learned faith, or doubts[§] God understands not at first hearing. Shew him a Ring he runs back like a Beare; and hates square dealing as allied to Caps,[§] a paire of Organs blow him out o'th Parish, and are the only glister[§] pipes to coole him. Where the meate is best, there hee confutes most; for his arguing is but the efficacie of his eating; good bits he holds breeds good positions, and the Pope hee best concludes against in Plumbroth. He is often drunke, but not as we are, temporally, nor can his sleep then cure him, for the fumes of his ambition make his very soule reele, and that smal Beere that should alay him (silence) keeps him more surfeited, and makes his heate breake out in private houses: women and Lawyers are his best Disciples, the one next fruit, longs for forbidden Doctrine, the other to maintaine forbidden titles, both which hee sowes amongst them: honest hee dare not be for that loves order; yet if he can bee brought to Ceremonie, and made but master of it, he is converted.

A TINKER

Is a mooveable: for hee hath no abiding place; by his motion hee gathers heate, thence his cholericke nature. He seemes to be very devoute, for his life is a continuall Pilgrimage, and sometimes in humilitie goes barefoote, therein making necessitie a vertue. His house is as ancient as *Tubal-Caines*, and so is a runagate by antiquity: yet he proves himselfe a Gallant, for he carries all his wealth on his backe; or a Philosopher, for he beares all his substance about him. From his Art was Musicke first invented, and therefore is hee alwaies furnisht with a song; to which his hammer keeping tune, proves that he was the first founder of the Kettle-drumme. Note that where the best Ale is, there stands his musick most upon crotchets.§ The companion of his travels is some foule sunne-burnt queane,§ that since the terrible Statute recanted Gypsisme, and is turned Pedleresse. So marches he all over England with his bag and baggage. His conversation is unreprooveable; for he is ever mending. Hee observes truely the Statutes, and therefore hee had rather steale then begge, in which he is unremoveably constant in spight of whips or imprisonment: and so strong an enemie to idlenesse, that in mending one hole, he had rather make three then want worke; and when he hath done, he throwes the Wallet§ of his faults behinde him. Hee imbraceth naturally auncient customes, conversing in open fields, and lowly Cottages. If he visit Cities or Townes, tis but to deale upon the imperfections of our weaker vesselles. His tongue is very voluble, which with Canting§ prooves him a *Lin-*

guist. He is entertain'd in every place, but enters no further then the dore, to avoid suspicion. Some would take him to be a Coward; but beleeve it, he is a Ladde of mettle, his valour is commonly three or foure yards long, fastned to a pike in the end for flying off. He is very provident, for he will fight but with one at once, and then also he had rather submit then bee counted obstinate. To conclude, if he scape Tiburne and Banbury, he dyes a begger.

A FAYRE AND HAPPY MILKE-MAYD

Is a Countrey Wench, that is so farre from making her selfe beautifull by Art, that one looke of hers is able to put *all face Physicke* out of countenance. She knowes a fayre looke is but *a dumbe Orator* to commend vertue, therefore mindes it not. All her excellencies stand in her so silently, as if they had stolne upon her without her knowledge. The lining of her apparell (which is her selfe) is farre better then outsides *of Tissew:*[§] for though shee bee not arrayed in the spoyle of the *Silke-Worme,* shee is deckt in *innocence,* a farre better wearing. She doth not, with lying long a bed, spoyle both her *Complexion & Conditions;* nature hath taught her too *Immoderate sleepe is rust to the soule:* she rises therefore with *Chaunticleare,* her Dames Cocke; & at night makes the *Lambe* her *Courfew.* In milking a Cow, and strayning the Teates through her fingers, it seemes that so sweet a Milke-presse makes the Milke the whiter, or sweeter; for never came *Almond[§] Glove or Aromatique Oyntment* on her Palme to taynt it. The golden eares of Corne fall and kisse her feete when shee reapes them, as if they wisht to bee bound and led prisoners by the same hand fell'd them. Her breath is her owne, which sents[§] all the yeere long of *June,* like a new made Hay-cocke. She makes her hand hard with labour, and her heart soft with pittie: and when winter evenings fall early (sitting at her merry wheele) she sings a defiance to the giddy *Wheele of Fortune.* Shee doth all things with so sweet a grace, it seemes *ignorance* will not suffer her to doe ill, being her minde is to do well. She bestowes her yeeres wages at next Faire; and in choosing her Garments, counts no bravery[§] i'th' worlde like decency. The *Garden* and *Bee-hive* are all her *Physicke[§] & Chyrurgery,[§]* & she

lives the longer for't. She dare goe alone, and unfold sheepe
i'th'night, and feares no manner of ill, because she means none:
yet to say truth, she is never alone, for she is still accompanied
with *old songs, honest thoughts,* and *prayers,* but short ones; yet
they have their efficacy, in that they are not pauled[§] with insuing
idle cogitations. Lastly, her dreames are so chaste, that she dare
tell them: only a Frydayes dreame is all her *superstition:* that
shee conceales for feare of anger. Thus lives she, and all her
care is, She may dye in the *Spring time,* to have store of flowers
stuck upon her winding sheete.

AN EXCELLENT ACTOR

Whatsoever is commendable in the grave Orator, is most ex-
quisitly perfect in him; for by a full and significant action of
body, he charmes our attention: sit in a full Theater, and you
will thinke you see so many lines drawne from the circumference of so many eares, whiles the *Actor* is the *Center.* He doth
not strive to make nature monstrous, she is often seen in the
same Scaene with him, but neither on Stilts nor Crutches; and
for his voice tis not lower then the prompter, nor lowder then
the Foile[§] and Target. By his action he fortifies morall precepts
with example; for what we see him personate, we thinke truely
done before us: a man of a deepe thought might apprehend,
the Ghosts of our ancient *Heroes* walk't againe, and take him
(at severall times) for many of them. Hee is much affected to
painting, and tis a question whether that make him an excellent
Plaier, or his playing an exquisite painter. Hee addes grace to
the Poets labours: for what in the Poet is but ditty,[§] in him is
both ditty and musicke. He entertaines us in the best leasure
of our life, that is betweene meales, the most unfit time, either
for study or bodily exercise: the flight of Hawkes, and chase of
wilde beastes, either of them are delights noble: but some think
this sport of men the worthier, despight all *calumny.* All men
have beene of his occupation: and indeed, what hee doth fainedly
that doe others essentially: this day one plaies a Monarch, the
next a private person. Heere one Acts a Tyrant, on the morrow
an Exile: A Parasite this man to night, too morow a Precisian,[§]
and so of divers others. I observe, of all men living, a worthy

Actor in one kind is the strongest motive of affection that can be: for when he dies, we cannot be perswaded any man can doe his parts like him. Therefore the imitating Characterist was extreame idle in calling them Rogues. His Muse it seemes, with all his loud invocation, could not be wak't to light him a snuffe[§] to read the Statute:[1] for I would let his malicious ignorance understand, that Rogues are not to be imploide as maine ornaments to his Majesties Revels; but the itch of bestriding the Presse, or getting up on this wodden Pacolet,[§] hath defil'd more innocent paper, then ever did Laxative Physicke: yet is their invention such tyred stuffe, that like the Kentish Post-horse they can not go beyond their ordinary stage, should you flea[§] them. But to conclude, I valew a worthy Actor by the corruption of some few of the quality, as I would doe gold in the oare; I should not minde the drosse, but the purity of the metall.

WHAT A CHARACTER IS

If I must speake the Schoole-masters language I will confesse that Character comes of this infinitive moode χαράξω which signifieth to ingrave, or make a deepe Impression. And for that cause, a letter (as A. B.) is called a Character.

Those Elements which we learne first, leaving a strong seale in our memories.

Character is also taken for an Egiptian Hierogliphicke, for an impresse,[§] or shorte Embleme; in little comprehending much.

To square out a Character by our English levell, it is a picture (reall or personall) quaintlie[§] drawne in various collours, all of them heightned by one shadowing.

It is a quicke and softe touch of many strings, all shutting up in one musicall close: It is wits descant[§] on any plaine[§] song.

1 A statute of 1572 directed that all strolling players who had not been licensed by a lord be treated as vagabonds. Additional legislation against rogues and vagabonds was passed in 1597 and in 1603.

John Earle

FROM

Micro-cosmographie

A CHILDE

Is a Man in a small Letter, yet the best Copie of *Adam* before hee tasted of *Eve*, or the Apple; and hee is happy whose small practice in the World can only write this Character. Hee is natures fresh picture newly drawne in Oyle, which time, and much handling, dimmes and defaces. His Soule is yet a white paper unscribled with observations of the world, wherewith at length it becomes a blurr'd note booke. Hee is purely happy, because he knowes no evill, nor hath made meanes by sinne to bee acquainted with misery. Hee arrives not at the mischiefe of being wise, nor endures evils to come by foreseeing them. He kisses and loves all, and when the smart of the rod is past, smiles on his beater. Nature and his Parents alike dandle him, and tice§ him on with a bait of sugar to a draught of worme-wood. He playes yet like a young Prentice the first day, and is not come to his taske of melancholy. His hardest labour is his tongue, as if he were loath to use so deceitfull an Organ; and he is best company with it when hee can but prattle. Wee laugh at his foolish sports, but his game is our earnest: and his drums, rattles and hobby-horses, but the Emblems, & mocking of mans businesse. His father hath writ him as his owne little story, wherein hee reades those dayes of his life that he cannot re-member; and sighs to see what innocence hee has out-liv'd. The elder hee growes, he is a stayer§ lower from God; and like his first father much worse in his breeches. Hee is the Christians ex-ample, and the Old-mans relapse: the one imitates his purenesse, and the other falls into his simplicitie. Could hee put off his body with his little coate, he had got eternity without a burthen, and exchang'd but one Heaven for another.

A DOWNE-RIGHT SCHOLLER

Is one that has much learning in the Ore, unwrought and untryde, which time and experience fashions and refines. He is good mettal in the inside, though rough & unscour'd without, and therefore hated of the Courtier, that is quite contrary. The time has got a veine§ of making him ridiculous, and men laugh at him by tradition, and no unlucky absurdity, but is put upon his profession, and done like a Scholler. But his fault is only this, that his mind is somewhat much taken up with his mind, and his thoughts not loaden with any carriage§ besides. He has not put on the quaint garbe of the Age, which is now become a mans Totall. He has not humbled his meditations to the industry of Complement, nor afflicted his braine in an elaborate legge.§ His body is not set upon nice pinnes, to bee turning and flexible for every motion, but his scrape§ is homely, and his nod worse. He cannot kisse his hand and cry Madame, nor talke idly enough to beare her company. His smacking of a Gentle-woman is somewhat too savorie, and he mistakes her nose for her lippe. A very Woodcocke would puzzle him in carving, and hee wants the logicke of a Capon. He has not the glib faculty of sliding over a tale, but his words come squeamishly§ out of his mouth, and the laughter commonly before the jest. He names this word Colledge too often, and his discourse beats too much on the University. The perplexity of mannerlinesse will not let him feed, and he is sharpe set at an Argument when hee should cut his meate. He is discarded for a gamester at all games but one§ and thirty, and at tables§ he reaches not beyond doublets.§ His fingers are not long and drawn out to handle a Fiddle, but his fist is clunch't with the habite of disputing. He ascends a Horse somwhat sinisterly, though not on the left side, and they both goe jogging in griefe together. He is exceedingly censur'd by the Innes a Court men, for that hainous vice being out of fashion. Hee cannot speake to a dogge in his owne dialect, and understands Greeke better then the language of a Falconer. Hee has beene used to a darke roome, and darke clothes, and his eyes dazzle at a Sattin Doublet. The Hermitage of his study, has made him somwhat uncouth in the world, and men make him worse by staring on him. Thus is he silly and ridiculous, and it continues with him for some quarter of a yeare, out of the University. But practise him a little in men, and brush him ore with good companie, and hee shall out-ballance those glisterers as much as a solid substance do's a feather, or Gold gold-lace.

A PLAINE COUNTRY FELLOW

Is one that manures his ground wel, but lets himselfe lie fallow, and until'd. He has reason enough to doe his businesse, and not enough to bee idle or melancholy. Hee seemes to have the judgement of *Nabuchadnezzar* for his conversation[§] is among beasts, and his tallons none of the shortest, onely he eates not grasse, because he loves not sallets.[§] His hand guids the Plough, and the Plough his thoughts, and his ditch and land-marke is the very mound of his meditations. He expostulates with his Oxen very understandingly, and speakes Gee[§] and Ree better than English. His mind is not much distracted with objects, but if a good fat Cowe come in his way, he stands dumbe and astonisht, and though his hast bee never so great, will fixe here halfe an houres contemplation. His habitation is some poore thatcht roofe, distinguisht from his Barne, by the loope-holes that let out smoak, which the raine had long since washt thorow, but for the double seeling[§] of Bacon on the inside, which has hung there from his Grandsires time, and is yet to make rashers for posterity. His Dinner is his other work, for he sweats at it as much as at his labour; he is a terrible fastener on a piece of Beefe, & you may hope to stave the Guard off sooner. His Religion is a part of his Copy-hold, which hee takes from his Land-lord, and referres it wholly to his discretion. Yet if hee give him leave, he is a good Christian to his power (that is) comes to Church in his best cloaths, and sits there with his neighbours, where hee is capable onely of two prayers, for raine, and faire weather. Hee apprehends Gods blessings onely in a Good Yeare, or a fat Pasture, and never praises him but on good ground. Sunday hee esteemes a day to make merry in, and thinkes a Bag-pipe as essentiall to it, as Evening-Prayer, where hee walkes very solemnly after service with his hands coupled behind him, and censures[§] the dauncing of his parish. His complement with his Neighbour, is a good thumpe on the backe; and his salutation, commonly some blunt Curse. Hee thinkes nothing to be vices but pride and ill husbandry, from which hee wil gravely disswade youth and has some thrifty Hobnaile Proverbes to clout[§] his discourse. He is a niggard all the weeke except onely market day, where if his corne[§] sell well, hee thinkes hee may be drunke with a good conscience. His feete never stinke so unbecommingly, as when hee trots after a Lawyer in West-minster-hall, and even cleaves the ground with hard scraping, in beseeching his Worship to take his money. Hee is sensible of no calamity but the burning of a stacke of Corne, or the overflowing of a Medow, and thinkes *Noahs* Flood the greatest Plague that ever was, not because it drowned the World, but spoyl'd the grasse. For Death hee is never troubled, and if hee get in but his Harvest before, let it come when it wil he cares not.

A PRETENDER TO LEARNING

Is one that would make others more fooles then himselfe; for though hee know nothing, hee would not have the World know so much. He conceits[§] nothing in Learning but the opinion, which he seekes to purchase without it, though hee might with lesse labour cure his ignorance, then hide it. Hee is indeed a kind of Scholler-Mountebank, and his Art, our delusion. Hee is trickt out in all the accoutrements of Learning, and at the first encounter none passes better. He is oftner in his study, then at his Booke, and you cannot pleasure him better, then to deprehend[§] him. Yet he heares you not til the third knocke, and then comes out very angry, as interrupted. You find him in his Slippers, and a Pen in his eare, in which formality he was asleepe. His Table is spread wide with some Classicke Folio, which is as constant to it as the Carpet,[§] and hath laid open in the same Page this halfe yeare. His Candle is alwayes a longer sitter up then himselfe, and the boast of his Window at Midnight. He walkes much alone in the Posture of Meditation, and has a Booke still before his face in the fields. His pocket is seldome without a Greeke Testament, or Hebrew Bible, which hee opens only in the Church, and that when some stander by looks over. He has his sentences[§] for Company, some scatterings of *Seneca* and *Tacitus*, which are good upon all occasions. If hee read any thing in the morning, it comes up all at dinner; and as long as that lasts, the discourse is his. Hee is a great *Plagiarie* of Taverne-wit: and comes to Sermons onely that hee may talke of *Austin*.[§] His Parcels are the meere scrapings from Companie, yet hee complaines at parting what time he has lost. He is wondrously capricious to seem a judgement,[§] and listens with a soure attention, to what hee understands not: He talkes much of *Scaliger* and *Causabone*, and the Jesuites, and prefers some unheard-of Dutch name before them all. Hee has Verses to bring in upon these and these hints, and it shall goe hard but he will wind in his opportunity. He is criticall in a language hee cannot conster,[§] and speaks seldome under[§] *Arminius* in Divinity. His businesse and retirement and caller away is his Study, and he protests no delight to it comparable. Hee is a great Nomen-clator of Authors, which hee has read in generall in the Catalogue, and in particular in the Title,[§] and goes seldome so farre as the Dedication. Hee never talkes of any thing, but learning, and learnes all from talking. Three incounters with the same men pumpe him, and then hee onely puts[§] in, or gravely sayes nothing. He has taken paines to be an Asse, though not to bee a Scholler, and is at length discovered and laught at.

A BLUNT MAN

Is one whose wit is better pointed then his behaviour, and that course, and impollisht not out of ignorance so much as humour. He is a great enemy to the fine Gentleman, and these things of Complement, and hates ceremony in conversation, as the Puritan in Religion. Hee distinguishes not betwixt faire and double-dealing, and suspects all smoothnesse for the dresse of knavery. Hee starts at the encounter of a salutation, as an assault, and beseeches you in choler to forbeare your courtesie. Hee loves not any thing in Discourse that comes before the purpose, and is alwaies suspicious of a Preface. Himselfe falls rudely still on his matter without any circumstance,[§] except hee use an old Proverbe for an Introduction. Hee sweares olde out-of-date innocent oths, as by the Masse, by our Lady, and such like; and though there bee Lords present, hee cryes my masters. Hee is exceedingly in love with his humour, which makes him alwaies professe and proclaime it, and you must take what he sayes patiently, because he is a plaine man. His nature is his excuse still and other mens Tyrant for he must speake his mind, and that is his worst, and craves your pardon most injuriously§ for not pardoning you. His Jests best become him, because they come from him rudely and unaffected: and hee has the lucke commonly to have them famous. Hee is one that will doe more then he will speake, and yet speake more then he will heare: for though hee love to touch others, hee is teachy§ himselfe, and seldome to his own abuses replyes but with his fists. Hee is as squeazy§ of his commendations as his courtesie, and his good word is like an Elogie in a Satyre. Hee is generally better favour'd then hee favours, as being commonly well expounded§ in his bitternesse, and no man speaks treason more securely. He chides great men with most boldnesse, and is counted for it an honest fellow. Hee is grumbling much in the behalfe of the Commonwealth, and is in prison oft for it with credit. Hee is generally honest, but more generally thought so, and his downrightnesse credits him, as a man not well bended and crookned§ to the times. In conclusion, hee is not easily bad, in whom this qualitie is Nature, but the counterfeit is most dangerous since hee is disguis'd in a humour, that professes not to disguise.

A BOWLE-ALLEY

Is the place where there are three things throwne away beside Bowls, to wit, time, money and curses, and the last ten for one. The best Sport in it is the Gamesters,§ and he enjoyes it that lookes on and bets not. It is the Schoole of wrangling, and worse then the Schooles,§ for men will cavill heere for an haires breadth, and make a stirre where a straw would end the controversie. No Anticke screwes mens bodies into such strange flexures, and you would think them here senslesse to speak sense to their Bowle, and put their trust in intreaties for a good cast. The Betters are the factious noise of the Alley, or the gamesters beadsmen that pray for them. They are somewhat like those that are cheated by great Men, for they lose their mony & must say nothing. It is the best discovery of humours, especially in the losers, where you have fine variety of impatience, whilst some fret, some raile, some sweare, and others more ridiculously comfort themselves with Philosophy. To give you the Morall of it; It is the Embleme of the world, or the worlds ambition: where most are short, or over, or wide, or wrong-Byas't, and some few justle in to the Mistris§ Fortune. And it is here as in the Court, where the nearest are most spighted, and all blowes aym'd at the Toucher.§

A SHEE-PRECISE§ HYPOCRITE

Is one in whom good Women suffer, and have their truth mis-interpreted by her folly.

She is one, she knows not what her selfe if you aske her, but she is indeed one that ha's taken a toy§ at the fashion of Religion, and is enamour'd of the New-fangle. Shee is a Nonconformist in a close stomacher and Ruffe of Geneva Print, and her purity consists much in her Linnen. She ha's heard of the Rag of Rome, and thinks it a very sluttish Religion, and rayles at the Whore of Babylon for a very naughty Woman. Shee ha's left her Vir-ginity as a Relique of Popery, and marries in her Tribe without a Ring. Her devotion at the Church is much in the turning up of her eye, and turning downe the leafe in her Booke when shee heares nam'd Chapter and Verse. When she comes home, shee commends the Sermon for the Scripture, and two houres. She loves Preaching better then Praying, and of Preachers, Lec-turars,§ and thinkes the Weeke-dayes Exercise farre more edify-ing then the Sundaies. Her oftest Gossipings§ are Sabaoth-dayes journeyes, where (though an enemy to Superstition) shee will goe in Pilgrimage five mile to a silenc'd§ Minister, when there is a better Sermon in her owne Parish. Shee doubts of the Virgin Marie's Saluation, and dare not Saint her, but knowes her own place in heaven as perfectly, as the Pew shee ha's a key to. Shee is so taken up with Faith, shee ha's no roome for Charity, and understands no good Workes, but what are wrought on the Sampler. Shee accounts nothing Vices but Superstition and an Oath, and thinkes Adultery a lesse sinne, then to sweare by§ my

Truely. Shee rayles at other Women by the names of *Jezabel* and *Dalilah:* and calls her owne daughters *Rebecka* and *Abigail,* and not *Anne* but *Hannah.* She suffers them not to learne on the Virginalls,§ because of their affinity with the Organs, but is reconcil'd to the Bells for the Chymes sake, since they were reform'd to the tune of a Psalme. She overflowes so with the Bible, that she spils it upon every occasion, and will not cudgell her Maides without Scripture. It is a question whether she is more troubled with the Divell or the Divell with her: she is alwayes challenging and daring him, and her weapons are Spels no lesse potent then different, as being the sage Sentences of some of her owne Sectaries.² Nothing angers her so much as that Woemen cannot preach, and in this point onely thinks the Brownist erroneous: but what shee cannot at the Church, she do's at the Table, where she prattles more then any against sense, and Antichrist, till a Capon wing silence her. She expounds the Priests of *Baal* Reading Ministers, and thinkes the Salvation of that Parish as desperate as the Turkes. Shee is a maine derider to§ her capacity of those that are not her Preachers, and censures all Sermons but bad ones. If her Husband be a Tradesman, she helps him to Customers, howsoever to good cheere, and they are a most faithfull couple at these meetings, for they never faile. Her conscience is like others lust never satisfied, and you might better answer *Scotus* then her Scruples. Shee is one that thinkes she performes all her duty to God in hearing, and shewes the fruites of it in talking. Shee is more fiery against the May-pole then her Husband, and thinkes he might doe a Phinehas his Act to breake the pate of the Fiddler. She is an everlasting Argument; but I am weary of her.

A CONTEMPLATIVE MAN

Is a Scholler in this great University the World; and the same his Booke and Study. Hee cloysters not his Meditations in the narrow darknesse of a Roome, but sends them abroad with his Eyes, and his Brayne travels with his Feete. He looks upon Man from a high Tower, and sees him trulyer at this distance in his Infirmities and poorenesse. He scornes to mixe himselfe in mens

---

² Changed in 5th ed. (1629) to "and her weapon is the *Practice of Piety.*"

actions, as he would to act upon a Stage; but sits aloft on the Scaffold⁵ a censuring Spectator. Nature admits him as a partaker of her Sports, and asks his approbation as it were of her owne Workes, and variety. Hee comes not in Company, because hee would not be solitary, but findes Discourse enough with himselfe, and his owne thoughts are his excellent play-fellowes. Hee lookes not upon a thing as a yawning⁵ Stranger at novelties; but his search is more mysterious and inward, and he spels Heaven out of Earth. He knits his observations together, and makes a Ladder of them all to climbe to God. He is free from vice, because he has no occasion to imploy it, and is above those ends that make men wicked. He ha's learnt all can heere be taught him, and comes now to Heaven to see more.

Joseph Hall

OF THE GOOD MAGISTRATE

He is the faithfull Deputie of his Maker, whose obedience is the rule whereby he ruleth: his brest is the Ocean whereinto all the cares of private men emptie themselves; which as hee receives without complaint and overflowing, so he sends them forth againe by a wise conveyance in the streames of justice: his doores, his eares are ever open to suters; and not who comes first speeds well, but whose cause is best. His nights, his meales are short and interrupted; all which hee beares well, because hee knowes himselfe made for a publique servant of peace and justice. Hee sits quietly at the sterne, & commands one to the top-saile, another to the maine, a third to the plummet, a fourth to the anchor, as hee sees the need of their course and weather requires; and doth no lesse by his tongue, than all the Mariners with their hands. On the bench hee is another from himselfe at home; now all private respects of blood, alliance, amitie are forgotten; and if his own sonne come under triall, hee knowes him not: Pitie, which in all others is woont to be the best praise of humanitie, & the fruit of Christian love, is by him thrown over the barre for corruption: as for Favour, the false Advocate of the gracious, he allowes him not to appeare in the Court; there only causes are heard speake, not persons: Eloquence is then only not discouraged, when she serves for a client of truth: meere Narrations are allowed in this Oratory, not Proemes, not Excursions, not Glosses: Truth must strip herselfe, and come in naked to his barre, without false bodies, or colours, without disguises: A bribe in his closet,§ or a letter on the bench, or the whispering and winks of a great neighbour are answered with an angry and courageous repulse. Displeasure, revenge, recompense stand on both sides the bench, but he scornes to turne his eye towards them; looking only right forward at Equitie, which stands full before him. His sentence is ever deliberate and guided with ripe wisdome, yet his hand is slower than his tongue; but when he is urged by occasion either to doome§ or execution, he shewes how much hee hateth mercifull injustice: neither can his resolution or act be reversed with partiall importunitie. His forhead is rugged and severe, able to discountenance villanie, yet his words are more awfull than his brow, and his hand than his wordes. I know not whether he be more feared or loved, both affections are so sweetly contempered in all hearts. The good feare him lovingly, the middle sort love him fearefully, and only the wicked man feares him slavishly without love. He hates to pay private wrongs with the advantage of his office, and if ever he be partiall it is to his enemy. He is not more sage in his gowne than valorous in armes, and increaseth in the rigor of his discipline as the times in danger. His sword hath neither rusted for want of use, nor surfeteth of blood, but after many threats is unsheathed, as the dreadfull instrument of divine revenge. He is the guard of good lawes, the refuge of innocencie, the Comet§ of the guiltie, the pay-maister of good deserts, the champian of justice; the patron of peace, the tutor of the Church, the father of his Countrey, and, as it were, another God upon earth.

John Stephens

A COMMON PLAYER

Is *a slow Payer, seldome a Purchaser, never a Puritan.* The
Statute[3] hath done wisely to acknowledge him a Rogue:[4] for his
chiefe Essence is, *A dayly Counterfeite:* Hee hath been familiar
so long with out-sides, that hee professes himselfe, (beeing unknowne) to bee an apparant Gentleman. But his thinne Felt,
and his Silke Stockings, or his foule Linnen, and faire Doublet,
doe (in him) bodily reveale the Broaker:[§] So beeing not sutable,
hee proves a *Motley:* his minde observing the same fashion of
his body: both consist of parcells and remnants: but his minde
hath commonly the newer fashion, and the newer stuffe: hee
would not else hearken so passionately after new Tunes, new
Trickes, new Devises: These together apparell his braine and
understanding, whilest hee takes the materialls upon trust, and
is himselfe the Taylor to take measure of his soules liking. If
hee cannot beleeve, hee doth conjecture strongly; but dares not
resolve upon particulars,[5] till he hath either spoken, or heard
the *Epilogue;* unlesse he be prevented:[§] neither dares hee entitle
good things *Good,* unlesse hee bee heartned on by the Multitude:
till then, hee saith faintly what hee thinkes, with a willing purpose to recant or persist: So howsoever he pretends to have a
royall Master, or Mistresse, his wages and dependance prove
him to bee the servant of the people.[6] The cautions of his judging humour (if hee dares undertake it) bee a certaine number
of lying[7] jests against the common Lawyer; hansome conceits

3 See note 1, p. 356.
4 2nd ed. adds "errant," and a marginal note says "*Erratum* in the last impression."
5 2nd ed. revises to "Hee doth conjecture somewhat strongly, but dares not
commend a playes goodnes. . . ."
6 2nd ed. adds, "When he doth hold conference[§] upon the stage; and should
looke directly in his fellows face; hee turnes about his voice into the assembly
for applause-sake, like a Trumpeter in the fields, that shifts places to get an
eccho."
7 2nd ed. replaces with "sawsie rude."

against the fine Courtiers; delicate quirkes[§] against the rich
Cuckold a Cittizen; shadowed glaunces for good innocent Ladies
and Gentlewomen; with a nipping scoffe for some honest Justice,
who hath once[8] imprisoned him: or some thriftie Trades-man,
who hath allowed him no credit: always remembred, his object
is, *A new Play,* or *A Play newly revived.* Other Poems hee admits, as good fellowes take Tobacco, or ignorant Burgesses give
a voyce, for company sake; as things that neither maintaine,
nor bee against him.[9] Hee can seeme no lesse then one in
honour, or at least one mounted:[§] for unto miseries which persecute such, hee is most incident.[§] Hence it proceedes, that in
the prosperous fortune of a Play frequented, hee proves immoderate, and falles into a Drunkards paradise, till it be *last*[§]
no longer. Otherwise when adversities come, they come together:
For Lent[1] and Shrove-tuesday bee not farre asunder: then hee
is dejected daily and weekely: his blessings be neither lame nor
monstrous; they goe upon foure legges;[2] but move slowly; and
make as great a distance betweene their steppes, as betweene
the foure Tearmes.[§][3] If he marries, hee mistakes the Woman
for the Boy in Womans attire, by not respecting a difference in
the mischiefe. But so long as hee lives unmarried, he mistakes
the Boy, or a Whore for the Woman; by courting the first on
the stage, or visiting the second at her devotions.[4] Take him at
the best, he is but a shifting companion; for he lives effectually
by putting on, and putting off. If his profession were single, hee
would thinke himselfe a simple fellow, as hee doth all professions besides his owne: His owne therefore is compounded of
all Natures, all Humours, all professions. Hee is politick enough[5]

8 2nd ed. omits.
9 2nd ed. adds, "To be a player, is to have a *mithridate* against the pestilence:
for players cannot tarry where the plague raignes; and therfore they be seldome infected."
1 In 1600, the Privy Council prohibited plays on Sunday and during Lent.
2 On horseback; probably a reference to a tour in the provinces.
3 2nd ed. adds, "Reproofe is ill bestowed uppon him; it cannot alter his conditions: he hath bin so accustomed to the scorne and laughter of his audience,
that hee cannot bee ashamed of himselfe: for hee dares laugh in the middest of
a serious conference, without blushing."
4 2nd ed. adds, "When hee is most commendable, you must confesse there is no
truth in him: for his best action is but an imitation of truth, and *nullum simile
est idem* [no likeness is the same]. It may be imagined I abuse his carriage, and
hee perhaps may suddenly bee thought faire-conditioned: for he *playes above
boord.*"
5 2nd ed. changes to "also."

to perceive the Common-wealths doubts of his licence, and therefore in spight of Parliaments or Statutes he incorporates[§] himselfe by the title of a Brother-hood.[6] I need not multiply his
character; for boyes and every one, will no sooner see men of
this Faculty walke along, but they will (unasked) informe you
what hee is by the vulgar denomination.[7]

Thomas Fuller

THE ELDER BROTHER

Is one who made hast to come into the world to bring his Parents
the first news of male-posterity, and is well rewarded for his tidings. His composition is then accounted most pretious when
made of the losse of a double Virginitie.

*He is thankfull for the advantage God gave him at the starting
in the race into this world.* When twinnes have been even
match'd, one hath gained the gole but by his length. S. Augustine saith, *That it is every mans bounden duty solemnly to cele-
brate his birth-day.* If so, Elder Brothers may best afford good
cheer on the festivall.

He counts not his inheritance a Writ *of ease to free him from
industry:* As if onely the Younger Brothers came into the world
to work, the Elder to complement. These are the Toppes of their
houses indeed, like cotlofts,[§] highest and emptiest. Rather he
laboureth to furnish himself with all gentile[§] accomplishment,
being best able to go to the cost of learning. He need not fear

---

6 2nd ed. adds, "Painting & fine cloths may not by the same reason be called
abusive, that players may not be called rogues: *For they bee chiefe ornaments of
his Majesties Revells.*" A marginal note says, "I would have the correcting
Pedant goe study *Logicke.*"
7 2nd ed. changes to "title." It then concludes, "Yet in the generall number of
them, many may deserve a wise mans commendation: and therefore did I prefix
an Epithite of *common*, to distinguish the base and artlesse appendants[§] of our
citty companies, which often times start away into rusticall wanderers and then
(like Proteus) start backe again into the Citty number."

to be served as Ulrick Fugger was (chief of the noble family of the Fuggers in Auspurg) who was disinherited of a great patrimony onely for his studiousnesse, and expensivenesse in buying costly Manuscripts.

He doth not so remember he is an Heire, that he forgets he is a Sonne. Wherefore his carriage to his Parents is alwayes respectfull. It may chance that his father may be kept in a charitable Prison, whereof his Sonne hath the keyes; the old man being onely Tenant for life, and the lands entaild on our young Gentleman. In such a case when it is in his power, if necessity requires, he enlargeth his father to such a reasonable proportion of liberty as may not be injurious to himself.

He rather desires his fathers Life then his Living. This was one of the principall reasons (but God knows how true) why Philip the second, King of Spain, caused in the yeare 1568. Charles his Eldest Sonne to be executed for plotting his fathers death, as was pretended.[§] And a Wit in such difficult toyes accommodated the numerall letters in Ovids verse to the yeare wherein the Prince suffered.

FILIVs ante DIeM patrIos InqVIrIt In annos.
1568.
Before the tIMe, the oVer-hasty sonne
Seeks forth hoVV near the fathers LIfe Is Done.
1568.

But if they had no better evidence against him but this poeticall Synchronisme,[§] we might well count him a martyr.

His fathers deeds and grants he ratifies and confirms. If a stitch be fallen in a lease, he will not widen it into an hole by cavilling, till the whole strength of the grant run out thereat; or take advantage of the default of the Clark in writing where the deed appears really done, and on a valuable consideration: He counts himself bound in honour to perform what by marks and signes he plainly understands his father meant, though he spake it not out.

He reflecteth his lustre to grace and credit his younger brethren. Thus Scipio Africanus, after his great victories against the Carthaginians and conquering of Hannibal, was content

to serve as a Lieutenant in the warres of Asia, under Lucius
Scipio his younger Brother.

He relieveth his distressed kinred,[§] *yet so as he continues
them in their calling.* Otherwise they would all make his house
their hospitall,[§] his kinred their calling. When one being an
Husbandman challenged kinred of Robert Grosthead Bishop of
Lincoln, and thereupon requested favour of him to bestow an
office on him, *Cousen* (quoth the Bishop) *if your cart be broken,
I'le mend it; if your plough old, I'le give you a new one, and
seed to sow your land: but an Husbandman I found you, and
an Husbandman I'le leave you.* It is better to ease poore kinred
in their Profession, then to ease them from their Profession.

He is carefull to support the credit and dignity of his family:
neither wasting his paternall estate by his unthriftinesse, nor
marring it by parcelling his ancient mannours and demesnes
amongst his younger children, whom he provides for by annuities, pensions, moneys, leases, and purchased lands. He re-
members how when our King Alfred divided the river of Lee
(which parts Hartfordshire and Essex) into three streams, it
became so shallow that boats could not row, where formerly
ships did ride. Thus the ancient family of the Woodfords (which
had long continued in Leicestershire and elsewhere in England
in great account, estate and livelihood) is at this day quite ex-
tinct. For when Sir Thomas Woodford in the reigne of King
Henrie the sixth made almost an even partition of his means
betwixt his five Grandchildren, the House in short space utterly
decay'd; not any part of his lands now in the tenure or name of
any of his male line, some whereof lived to be brought to a low
ebbe of fortune. Yet on the other side to leave all to the eldest,
and make no provision for the rest of their children, is against
all rules of religion, forgetting their Christian-name to remember
their Sir-name.

Edward Hyde, 1st Earl of Clarendon

[CHARLES I]

The severall unhearde of insolencyes which this excellent Prince was forced to submitt to, at the other tymes he was brought before that odious judicatory, his Majesticke behaviour under so much insolence, and resolute insistinge upon his owne dignity, and defendinge it by manifest authorityes in the lawe, as well as by the cleerest deductions from reason, the pronouncinge that horrible sentence upon the most innocent person in the worlde, the execution of that sentence by the most execrable murther that ever was committed, since that of our blessed Savyour, and the circumstances therof, the application and interposition that was used by some noble persons to prævent that wofull murther, and the hypocrisy with which that interposition was deluded, the Saintlike behaviour of that blessed Martir, and his Christian courage and patience at his death, are all particulars so well knowne, and have bene so much inlarged upon in treatises peculiarly applyed to that purpose, that the farther mentioninge it in this place, would but afflicte and grieve the reader, and make the relation it selfe odious, and therfore no more shall be sayd heare of that lamentable Tragedy, so much to the dishonour of the Nation, and the religion professed by it; but it will not be unnecessary to add the shorte character of his person, that posterity may know the inestimable losse which the nation then underwent in beinge deprived of a Prince whose example would have had a greater influence upon the manners and piety of the nation, then the most stricte lawes can have.

To speake first of his private qualifications as a man, before the mention of his princely and royall virtues, He was, if ever any, the most worthy of the title of an honest man; so greate a lover of justice, that no temptation could dispose him to a wrongfull action, except it were so disguysed to him, that he be-

lieved it to be just; he had a tendernesse and compassion of
nature, which restrayned him from ever doinge a hard hearted
thinge, and therfore he was so apt to grant pardon to Malefactors, that his Judges represented to him the damage and in-
security to the publique that flowed from such his indulgence,
and then he restrayned himselfe from pardoninge ether murthers
or highway robberyes, and quickly decerned the fruits of his
severity, by a wounderfull reformation of those enormityes. He
was very punctuall and regular in his devotions, so that he was
never knowne to enter upon his recreations or sportes, though
never so early in the morninge, before he had bene at publique
prayers, so that on huntinge dayes, his Chaplynes were bounde
to a very early attendance, and he was likewise very stricte in
observinge the howres of his private cabbinett[§] devotions, and
was so seveare an exactor of gravity and reverence in all mention of religion, that he could never indure any light or prophane
worde in religion, with what sharpnesse of witt so ever it was
cover'd; and though he was well pleased and delighted with
readinge verses made upon any occasyon, no man durst bringe
before him any thinge that was prophane or uncleane, that kinde
of witt had never any countenance then. He was so greate an
example of conjugall affection, that they who did not imitate
him in that particular, did not bragge of ther liberty, and he
did not only permitt but directe his Bishopps to prosequte those
skandalous vices, in the Ecclesiasticall Courtes, against persons
of eminence, and neere relation to his service.

His kingly virtues had some mixture and allay that hindred
them from shyninge in full lustre, and from producinge those
fruites they should have bene attended with; he was not in his
nature bountifull, though he gave very much, which appeared
more after the Duke of Buckinghams death, after which those
showers fell very rarely, and he paused to longe in givinge,
which made those to whome he gave lesse sensible of the bene-
fitt. He kept state to the full, which made his Courte very orderly,
no man præsuminge to be seene in a place wher he had no
pretence[§] to be; he saw and observed men longe, before he re-
ceaved any about his person, and did not love strangers, nor
very confident[§] men. He was a patient hearer of causes, which
he frequently accustomed himselfe to, at the Councell Board,

and judged very well, and was dextrous in the mediatinge parte,
so that he often putt an end to causes by perswasion, which the
stubbornesse of mens humours made delatory§ in courts of justice. He was very fearelesse in his person, but not enterpryzinge,
and had an excellent understandinge, but was not confident
enough of it: which made him often tymes chaunge his owne
opinion for a worse, and follow the advice of a man, that did
not judge so well as himselfe: and this made him more irreso-
lute, then the conjuncture§ of his affayres would admitt. If he
had bene of a rougher and more imperious nature, he would
have founde more respecte and duty, and his not applyinge
some seveare cures, to approchinge evills, proceeded from the
lenity of his nature, and the tendernesse of his conscience,
which in all cases of bloode, made him choose the softer way,
and not hearken to seveare councells how reasonably soever
urged. This only restrayned him from pursuinge his advantage
in the first Scotts expedition, when humanely speakinge, he
might have reduced that Nation to the most slavish obedyence
that could have bene wished, but no man can say, he had then
many who advized him to it, but the contrary, by a wounderfull
indisposition all his Councell had to fightinge, or any other fatigue.§ He was alwayes an immoderate lover of the Scottish
nation, havinge not only bene borne ther, but educated by that
people and besiedged§ by them alwayes, havinge few English
aboute him till he was kinge, and the major number of his
servants beinge still of those, who he thought could never fayle
him, and then no man had such an ascendent§ over him, by the
lowest and humblest insinuations, as Duke Hambleton had.

As he excelled in all other virtues, so in temperance he was
so stricte that he abhorred all deboshry§ to that degree, that at a
greate festivall solemnity wher he once was, when very many
of the nobility of the English and Scotts were entertayned, he
was told by one who withdrew from thence, what vast draughts
of wyne they dranke, and that ther was one Earle who had
dranke most of the rest downe and was not himselfe mooved
or altred, the kinge sayd that he deserved to be hanged, and
that Earle comminge shortly into the roome wher his Majesty
was, in some gayty to shew how unhurte he was from that battle,
the kinge sent one to bidd him withdraw from his Majestys

presence, nor did he in some dayes after appeare before the kinge.

Ther were so many miraculous circumstances contributed to his ruine, that men might well thinke that heaven and earth conspired it, and that the starres designed it, though he was from the first declension§ of his power, so much betrayed by his owne servants, that ther were very few who remayned faythfull to him; yett that trechery proceeded not from any treasonable purpose to do him any harme, but from particular and personall animosityes against other men; and afterwards the terrour all men were under of the Parliament and the guilte they were conscious of themselves, made them watch all opportunityes to make themselves gratious to those who could do them good, and so they became spyes upon ther master, and from one piece of knavery, were hardned and confirmed to undertake another, till at last they had no hope of præservation but by the destruction of ther master. And after all this, when a man might reasonably believe, that lesse then a universall defection of three nations, could not have reduced a greate kinge to so ugly a fate, it is most certayne that in that very howre when he was thus wickedly murthered in the sight of the sunn, he had as greate a share in the heartes and affections of his subjects in generall, was as much beloved, esteemed and longed for by the people in generall of the three nations, as any of his prædecessors had ever bene. To conclude, he was the worthyest gentleman, the best master, the best frende, the best husbande, the best father, and the best Christian, that the Age in which he lyved had produced, and if he was not the best kinge, if he was without some parts and qualityes which have made some kings greate and happy, no other Prince was ever unhappy, who was possessed of half his virtues and indowments, and so much without any kinde of vice.

[OLIVER CROMWELL]

It had bene observed in Englande, that though from the dissolution of the last Parliament all things seemed to succede at home and abroade, to his wish, and his power and greatnesse to be better established then ever it had bene, yett Crumwell never had

the same serenity of minde he had bene used to, after he had refused the Crowne, but was out of countenance, and shaggringe[§]
as if he were conscious of not havinge bene true to himselfe,
and much more apprehensive of daunger to his person then he
had used to be; insomuch as he was not so easy of accesse, nor
so much seene abroade, and seemed to be in some disorder when
his eyes founde any stranger in the roome, upon whome they
were still fixed. When he intended to go to Hampton Courte,
which was his principle delight and devertion, it was never
knowne till he was in the Coach which way he would goe, and
was still hemmed in by his guardes before and behinde, and
the Coach in which he went was always thronged as full as it
could be with his servants who were armed, and he never returned the same way he went, and rarely lodged two nights together in one chamber, but had many furnished and præpared,
to which his owne key convayed him, and those he would have
with him, when he had a minde to go to bedd; which made his
feares the more taken notice of and publike, because he had
never bene accustomed to those præcautions.

It is very true he knew of many combinations[§] to assassinate
him, by those who he knew wishd the kinge no good; and when
he had discover'd the designe of Sindercombe, who was a very
stoute man, and one who had bene much in his favour, and who
had twice or thryce by wounderfull and unexpected accidents
bene disappointed in the minute he made sure to kill him, and
caused him to be apprehended, his behavyour was so resolute
in his examination and tryall, as if he thought he should still
be able to do it; and it was manifest that he had many more
associates, who were undiscover'd and as resolute as himselfe;
and though he gott him condemned to dy, the fellowes carriage
and wordes were such, as if he knew well how to avoyde the
judgement, which made Crumwell believe that a party in the
Army would attempt his rescue; wherupon he gave stricte charge
that he should be carefully looked to in the tower, and three or
fourr of the guarde always with him day and night. And at the
day for his execution, those troopes he was most confident of
were upon the Tower hill, wher the gallowes were erected. But
when the guard called him to aryse in the morninge, they founde
him deade in his bedd, which gave trouble exceedingly to Crum-

well, for besydes that he hoped at his death that, to avoyde the
utmost rigour of it, he would have confessed many of his confederates, he now founde himselfe under the reproch of havinge
caused him to bee poysoned, as not daringe to bringe him to
publique justice. Nor could he suppresse that scandall, though
it did appeare upon examination, that the night before, when
he was goinge to bedd in the presence of his guarde, his Sister
came to take her leave of him, and whilst they spake together
at the bedd-syde, he rubb'd his nose with his hande, of which
they then tooke no notice, and she goinge awaye, he putt off
his clothes, and leaped into his bedd with some snufflinge in
his nose, and sayd this was the last bedd he should ever go
into, and seemed to turne to sleepe, and never in the whole
night made the least noyse or motion, save that he sneezed
once. When the Phisicians and Surgeons opend his heade, they
founde he had snuffed up through his nostrills some very well
prepared poyson, that in an instant curdled all the blood in
that region, which presently suffocated him. The man was
drawne by a horse to the gallowes wher he should have hanged,
and buryed under it with a stake dryven through him, as is
usuall in the case of selfe murtherers, yett this accident perplexed Crumwell very much, and though he was without the
particular discovery which he exspected, he made a generall
discovery by it that he was more odious in his army then he
believed he had bene.

He seemed to be much afflicted at the death of his friende the
Earle of Warwicke, with whome he had a fast frendshipp,
though neither their humours or their natures were like; and
the heyre of that house, who had marryed his youngest daughter, dyed aboute the same tyme, so that all his relation to, or
confidence in that family was at an ende, the other branches
of it abhorringe his Allyance. His domestique delights were
lesned every day, and he playnly discover'd that his sunn Fal-
conbridge his hearte was sett upon an interest destructive to
his, and grew to hate him perfectly.§ But that which broke his
peace, was the death of his daughter Claypole, who had bene
alwayes his greatest joy, and who had in her sicknesse, which
was of a nature the Phisicians knew not how to deale with, had
severall conferences§ with him, which exceedingly perplexed

him; and though no body was nere enough to heare the particulars, yett her often mentioning, in the paynes she indured, the bloode her father had spilte, made people conclude that she had presented his worst actions to his consideration; and though he never made the least shew of remorse for any of those actions, it is very certayne, that ether what she sayd or her death affected him wounderfully.

Whatever it was, aboute the middle of August he was seized on by a common tertian[§] Ague, from which he believed a little ease and divertisement at Hampton Courte would have freed him; but the Fitts grew stronger, and his spiritts much abated,[§] so that he returned agayne to Whitehall, when his Phisitians begann to thinke him in daunger, though the preachers who prayed alwayes aboute him, and told God Almighty what greate things he had done for him, and how much more neede he had still of his service, declared as from God that he should recover, and he himselfe did not thinke he should dy, till even the tyme that his spiritts fayled him, and then declared to them that he did appoint his Sunn to succeede him, his eldest Sunn Richard; and so expyred upon the third day of September, (a day he thought alwayes very propitious to him, and on which he had tryumphed for severall victoryes) 1658, a day very memorable for the greatest storme of winde that had bene ever knowne, for some houres before and after his death, which overthrew trees, houses, and made greate wrackes at sea, and was so universall that there [were] terrible effects of it, both in France and Flaunders, wher all people trembled at it, besydes the wrackes all alonge the coast, many Botes havinge bene cast away in the very rivers; and within few dayes after, that circumstance of his death, that accompanyed that storme, was knowne.

He was one of those men, quos vituperare ne inimici quidem possunt, nisi ut simul laudent,[8] for he could never have done halfe that mischieve, without greate partes of courage and industry and judgement, and he must have had a wounderfull understandinge in the natures and humours of men, and as greate a dexterity in the applyinge them, who from a private[§] and obscure birth, (though of a good family) without interest of estate, allyance or frendshipps, could rayse himselfe to such

8 Whom even foes are unable to censure unless they praise at the same time.

a height, and compounde and kneade such opposite and contradictory tempers humour and interests, into a consistence, that contributed to his designes and to ther owne destruction, whilst himselfe grew insensibly powerfull enough, to cutt off those by whome he had climed, in the instant, that they projected to demolish ther owne buildinge. What Velleius Paterculus sayd of Cinna, may very justly be sayd of him, Ausum eum quæ nemo auderet bonus, perfecisse quæ a nullo nisi fortissimo perfici possunt.[9] Without doubte no man with more wickednesse ever attempted any thinge, or brought to passe what he desyred more wickedly, more in the face and contempt of religion and morall honesty, yett wickednesse as greate as his could never have accomplish'd those trophees without the assistance of a greate spiritt, an admirable circumspection and sagacity, and a most magnanimous resolution. When he appeared first in the Parliament he seemed to have a person in no degree gratious, no ornament of discource, none of those talents which use to reconcile the affections of the standers by, yett as he grew into place and authority, his partes seemed to be renew[d], as if he had concealed facultyes till he had occasion to use them, and when he was to acte the parte of a greate man, he did it without any indecensy through the wante of custome.

After he was confirmed and invested Protectour by the humble petition and advize, he consulted with very few upon any action of importance, nor communicated any enterpryze he resolved upon, with more then those who were to have principle partes in the exeqution of it, nor to them sooner then was absolutely necessary. What he once resolved, in which he was not rash, he would not be disswaded from, nor indure any contradiction of his power and authority, but extorted obedyence from them who were not willinge to yeilde it.

When he had layed some very extraordinary tax upon the Citty, one Cony, an eminent Fanatique, and one who had heartofore served him very notably, positively refused to pay his parte, and lowdely disswaded others from submittinge to it, as an imposition notoriously against the law and the propriety of the Subjecte, which all honest men were bounde to defende. Crum-

9 He who dared what no good man would dare has achieved what none but the bravest can achieve.

well sent for him, and cajoled him, with the memory of the old kindnesse and frendshipp that had bene between them, and that of all men he did not expecte this opposition from him, in a matter that was so necessary for the good of the Commonwealth. But it was alwayes his fortune to meete with the most rude and obstinate behaviour from those who had formerly bene absolutely governed by him, and they commonly putt him in minde of some expressions and sayinge of his owne, in cases of the like nature; so this man remembred him how greate an enemy he had expressed himselfe to such grievances, and declared that all who submitted to them and payed illegall taxes were more to blame, and greater enemyes to ther Country, then they who imposed them, and that the tyranny of Princes could never be grievous, but by the tamenesse and stupidity of the people. When Crumwell saw that he could not converte him, he told him that he had a will as stubborne as his, and he would try which of them two should be master, and therupon with some tearmes of reproch and contempt, he committed the man to pryson, whose courage was nothinge abated by it, but as soone as the Tearme§ came, he brought his Habeas Corpus in the Kings Bench, which they then called the Upper Bench. Maynard, who was of Councell with the prysoner, demaunded his liberty with greate confidence, both upon the illegality of the commitment and the illegality of the imposition, as beinge layd without any lawfull authority. The Judges could not maynetayne or defende either, but enough declared what ther sentence would be, and therfore the Protectors Atturny requyred a farther day, to answer what had bene urged. Before that day, Maynarde was committed to the Tower, for præsuminge to question or make doubte of his authority, and the Judges were sent for, and severely reprehended for sufferinge§ that license, and when they with all humillity mentioned the law, and Magna Charta, Crumwell told them, ther Magna Farta should not controle his Actions, which he knew were for the safety of the Commonwealth. He asked them who made them Judges; wher they had any authority to sitt ther, but what he gave them, and that if his authority were at an end, they knew well enough what would become of themselves, and therfore advised them to be more tender of that which could only præserve them, and so dismissed them with caution, that they should not suffer the Lawyers to prate what it would not become them to heare.

Thus he subdewed a spiritt that had bene often troublesome to the most soveraigne power, and made Westminster Hall as obedyent and subservient to his commaunds, as any of the rest of his quarters. In all other matters which did not concerne the life of his jurisdiction, he seemed to have greate reverence for the law, and rarely interposed betweene party and party; and as he proceeded with this kinde of indignation and hawtinesse with those who were refractory and dared to contende with his greatnesse, so towards those who complyed with his good pleasure, and courted his protection, he used a wounderfull civillity, generosity, and bounty.

To reduce three nations which perfectly[§] hated him to an intyre obedyence to all his dictates, to awe and govern those Nations by an Army that was indevoted to him, and wished his ruine, was an instance of a very prodigious addresse;[§] but his greatnesse at home was but a shadow of the glory he had abroade. It was hard to discover which feared him most, France, Spayne, or the Low Countrys, wher his frendshipp was current at the value he putt upon it; and as they did all sacrifice ther honour and ther interest to his pleasure, so there is nothinge he could have demaunded that either of them would have denyed him . . .

He was not a man of bloode, and totally declined Machiavells methode, which prescribes upon any alteration of a goverment, as a thinge absolutely necessary, to cutt of[§] all the heades of those and extirpate ther familyes, who are frends to the old, and it was confidently reported that in the Councell of Officers, it was more then once proposed, that ther might be a generall massacre of all the royall party, as the only exspedient to secure the goverment, but Crumwell would never consent to it, it may be out of to much contempt of his enimyes. In a worde, as he had all the wickednesses against which damnation is denounced and for which Hell fyre is præpared, so he had some virtues, which have caused the memory of some men in all ages to be celebrated, and he will be looked upon by posterity, as a brave, badd man.

[JOHN EARLE]

Dr. Earles was at that tyme Chaplyne in the house to the Earle of Pembroke, Lord Chamberlyne of his Majestys household, and had a lodginge in the courte under that relation. He was a person very notable for his elegance in the Greeke and Latine tounges, and beinge fellow of Merton Colledge in Oxforde, and havinge bene Proctour of the University, and some very witty and sharpe discourses beinge published in printe without his consent,[1] though knowne to be his, he grew suddaynely into a very generall esteem with all men, beinge a man of greate piety and devotion, a most eloquent and powerfull preacher, and of a conversation§ so pleasant and delightfull, so very innocent, and so very facetious,§ that no mans company was more desyred, and more loved. No man was more negligent in his dresse, and habitt,§ and meene,§ no man more wary§ and cultivated in his behaviour and discourse, insomuch as he had the greater advantage when he was knowne, by promisinge so little before he was knowen. He was an excellent Poett both in Latine, Greeke, and English, as appeares by many pieces yett abroade, though he suppressed many more himselfe, especially of English, incomparably good, out of an austerity§ to those sallyes of his youth. He was very deere to the Lord Falkelande, with whome he spent as much tyme as he could make his owne, and as that Lord would impute the speedy progresse he made in the Greeke tounge, to the information and assistance he had from Mr. Earles, so Mr. Earles would frequently professe that he had gott more usefull learninge by his conversation at Tew (the Lord Falkelands house) then he had at Oxforde. In the first setlinge of the Prince his family, he was made on[e] of his Chaplynes, and attended on him when he was forced to leave the kingdome, and therfore we shall often have occasyon to mention him hereafter. He was amongst the few excellent men, who never had, nor ever could have an enimy, but such a one who was an enimy to all learninge and virtue, and therfore would never make himselfe knowne.

[1] *Micro-cosmographie* was published without Earle's name throughout the seventeenth century.

Anthony Ashley Cooper, 1st Earl
of Shaftesbury

[HENRY HASTINGS (1551–1650)]

Mr. Hastings by his quality§ being the sonn brother and uncle
to the Earls of Huntington, and his way of living had the first
place amongst us; he was peradventure an originall in our age
or rather the coppy of our nobility in antient dayes in hunting
and not warlick§ times. He was lowe§ very strong and very active
of a reddish flexon§ hayr, his clothes alwais green cloth and
never all worth when new five pound: his house was perfectly
of the old fashion in the middst of a large park well stocked
with deere and neer the house rabbets to serve his kitchen,
many fish ponds and great store of wood and timber; a bowling
green in itt long but narrow full of high ridges it being never
leveld since it was plowed; they used round sand§ bowles and
it had a banqueting house like a stand a large one built in a
tree; he kept all manner of sports hounds that rann buck fox
hare otter and Badger and haukes long and short winged, he
had all sorts of netts for fishing; he had a walke§ in the new
forrest and the mannor of Christchurch, this last supplyed him
with red deer, sea and river fish; and indeed all his neighbors
grounds and royaltyes§ were free to him who bestowed all his
time in these sports, but what he borrowed to caress his neighbors wifes and daughters there being not a woman in all his
walkes of the degree of a yeomans wife or under and under the
age of forty but it was extreamly her fault if he were not intimately acquainted with her; this made him very popular, alwais
speaking kindly to the husband brother or father who was to boot
very welcome to his house when ever he came; there he found
beef pudding and small§ beer in great plenty; a house not soe
neatly kept as to shame him or his durty shooes: the great hall

strewed with mary§ bones, full of Hawkes perches hounds span-
iels and terryers the upper sides of the hall hung with the fox
skinnes of this and the last yeares killing, here and there a
polcatt intermixt; gunns keepers and Huntsmans poles in abundance: the parlor was a large long Roome as properly furnished,
on a great hearth paved with brick lay some terryers and the
choycest hounds and spaniells; seldome but two of the great
chayres had litters of young catts in them which were not to
be disturbed, he having alwais three or fower attending him at
dinner, and a little white round sticke of fourteen inches long
lying by his trencher that he might defend such meat as he had
noe mind to part with to them. The windowes which were very
larg served for places to lay his arrowes crossbowes stone bowes
and other such like accoutrements; the corners of the roome full
of the best chose hunting and hawking poles, an oyster table
att the lower end, which was of constant use twice a day all the
year round, for he never fayld to eat oysters before dinner and
supper through all seasons, the neighbouring town of Pool[e]
supplyed him with them: the upper part of this roome had two
small tables and a deske on the one side of which was a church
Bible on the other the booke of Martyrs; on the tables were
hawkes hoods bells and such like, two or three old green hatts
with their crownes thrust in soe as to hold ten or a dosen eggs,
which were of a phesant kind of poultry he tooke much care of
and fed himself; tables dice cards and boxes were not wanting,
in the hole of the desk were store of tobaccoe pipes that had
ben used. On one side of this end of the roome was the doore
of a closett where in stood the strong beer and the wine, which
never came thence but in single glasses that being the rule of
the house exactly observed for he never exceeded in drinke or
permitted itt, on the other side was a doore in to an old chappel
not used, for devotion, the pulpit as the safest place, was never
wanting of a cold chine of bief pasty of venison gammon of
Bacon or great apple pye with thicke crust extreamly baked. His
table cost him not much though it was very good to eat att,
his sports supplying all but beef or mutton, except Fridayes
when he had the best sea fish as well as other fish he could gett;
and was the day that his neighbors of best quality most visited
him. He never wanted a london pudding and alwais sung it in;

with my part lyes therein a;[2] he drunke a glass or two of wine at meales very often sirrup of gillyflower in his sack and had alwais a tunn glass without feet stood by him holding a pint of small beer which he often stirrd with a great sprig of Rosemary. He was well natured, but soone angry calling his servants bastard and cuckoldy knaves in one of which he often spoke truth to his owne knowledg and sometimes in both though of the same man. He lived to an hundred never lost his eye sight but alwais writ and read without spectacles and gott to horse without help. Untill past fourescore he ridd to the death of a stagg as well as any.

2 Part of an old catch: "There lies a pudding in the fire, / and my part lies therein a."

IX

Short Lives

Thomas Fuller

SIR WALTER RAWLEIGH

The sons of Heth *said unto* Abraham, *thou art a great Prince amongst us, In the choice of our Sepulchres bury thy dead, none shall withold them from thee.* So may we say to the *memory* of this *worthy Knight, repose your self in this our Catalogue under what Topick you please, of States-man, Sea-man, Souldier, Learned Writer,* and what not? His worth *unlocks* our *closest Cabinets,* and provides both *room* and *wellcome* to entertain him.

He was born at *Budeley* in this County, of an Ancient Family, but decaied in Estate, and he the youngest brother thereof. He was bred in *Oriel Colledg* in *Oxford,* and thence comming to Court, found some hopes of the Queens favours reflecting upon him. This made him write in a glasse Window, obvious to the Queens eye,

> *Fain would I climb, yet fear I to fall,*

Her *Majesty* either espying, or being *shown* it, did under-write,

If thy heart fails thee, climb not at all.

However he at last *climbed* up by the *stairs* of his own desert. But his Introduction into the Court bare an elder date. From this occasion: This *Captain Raleigh* coming out of *Ireland* to the *English Court* in good habit (his Cloaths being then a considerable part of his estate) found the Queen walking, till meeting with a *Plashy place*, she seemed to scruple going thereon. Presently *Raleigh* cast and spred his new Plush Cloak on the ground, whereon the Queen trod gently, rewarding him afterwards with many *Suits*, for his so free and seasonable tender of so fair *a foot Cloath*. Thus an advantagious admission into the first notice of a *Prince*, is more than half a degree to preferment.

It is reported of the Women in the *Balear Islands*, that to make their Sons expert archers; they will not, when children, give them their break-fast before they had *hit the mark*. Such the dealing of the *Queen* with this *Knight*, making him to *earn his Honour*, and by pain and peril, to purchase what places of credit or profit were bestowed upon him. *Indeed it was true of him, what was said of* Cato Uticensis: *That he seemed to be born to that onely which he went about:* So dexterous was he in all his undertakings, In *Court*, in *Camp*, by *Sea*, by *Land*, with *Sword*, with *Pen*, witnesse in the last his *History of the World;* wherein the onely *default* or (*defect* rather) that it wanteth one half thereof. Yet had he many enemies (which worth never wanteth) at Court, his cowardly Detractors, of whom Sir *Walter* was wont to say, *If any man accuseth me to my face, I will answer him with my mouth; but my tail is good enough to return an answer to such who traduceth me behind my back.*

JOHN DONNE

John Donne was born in this City of wealthy parentage, extracted out of *Wales*, one of an excellent wit, large travail, and choice experience. After many vicissitudes in his youth, his reduced age was honoured with the Doctorship of Divinity, and Denary of Saint *Pauls*.

Should I endeavour to deliver his exact character, I (who willingly would not doe any wrong) should do a fourfold injury.

1. To his worthy memory, whose merit my pen is unable to express.
2. To my self, in undertaking what I am not sufficient to perform.
3. To the Reader, first in raising, then in frustrating his expectation.
4. To my deservedly honored friend Master *Isaac Walton,* by whom his life is so learnedly written.

It is enough for me to observe he died *March* 31. *Anno Dom.* 1631. and lieth buried in Saint *Pauls* under an ingenious[§] and choice monument, neither so costly as to occasion envy, nor so common as to cause contempt.

SIR FRANCIS BACON

Sir *Francis Bacon* Knight, youngest son to Sir *Nicholas Bacon* Lord Keeper, was born in *York house Anno* 1560. For being demanded his age by Queen *Elizabeth,* he returned, that *he was* two *years younger then her Majesties reign.* He was bred in *Trinity-colledge* in *Cambridge,* and there first fell into a dislike of *Aristotles Philosophy,* as *Barren* and *Jejune,* inabling *some* to *dispute, more* to wrangle, *few* to find out trueth, and *none,* if confining themselves to his Principles.

Hence it was that afterwards he traded[§] so largely in *experiments,* so that as *Socrates* is said to be the first, who stooped Towring Speculations into Practical Morality: Sir *Francis* was one of the first, who reduced *Notional* to *Real* and *Scientifical* Philosophy.

He was afterwards bred in *Grays-Inn* in the Study of our *Municipal Law,* attaining to great Eminency, but no Preferment therein, during the reign of Queen *Elizabeth;* Imputable to the envy of a *great Person,* who hindred his *rising,* for fear to be hindred by him if risen, and Eclipsed in his own profession. Thus the strongest wing of *merit* cannot mount, if a stronger *weight* of *malice* doth depress it. Yet was he even then *Favorite* to a *Favorite,* I mean, the Earl of *Essex,* and more true to him, then the Earl was to himself. For finding him to prefer *destructive* before *displeasing* Counsel, Sir *Francis* fairly forsook, not his person, (whom his pity attended to the grave) but practises, and herein was not the *worse* friend, for being the *better* subject.

By K. *James* he was made his *Solicitor,* and afterwards his *Atturney,* (then priviledged contrary to custome to sit a member in *Dom. Com.*[1]) and at last Lord Chancellor of *England.* His abilities were a clear confutation of *two vulgar*[§] *errors,* (*libells* on learned men) First, that *Judgement, Wit, Fancy,* and *Memory,* cannot eminently be in conjunction in the same person, whereas our Knight was a *rich Cabinet,* fill'd with all *four,* besides a *golden* key to open it, *Elocution.* Secondly, *That he who is something in all, is nothing in any one Art,* whereas he was singular[§] *in singulis,*[2] and being *In-at-all* came off with credit.

Such as condemn him for pride, if in his *place,* with the *fift part* of his parts, had been *ten times* prouder themselves; he had been a *better* Master if he had been a *worse,* being too bountiful to his servants, and either too *confident* of their *honesty,* or too *conniving* at their *falshood.* The story is told to his advantage, that he had *two Servants,* one in all causes Patron to the *Plantiffe,* (whom his charity presumed always injured,) the other to the *Defendant,* (pitying him as *compelled* to *Law,*) but taking bribes of both, with this condition, *to restore the money received if the Cause went against them.* Their Lord ignorant hereof, always did unpartial Justice, whilst his men (making people *pay* for what was *given* them) by compact shared the money betwixt them, which cost their Master the loss of his office.

Leading a private life, he much delighted to study in the shade of solitariness, and many useful discoveries in Nature were made by him, so that he may be said to have left *nothing to his Executors and all to his Heirs,* under which notion the learned of all ages may be beheld. His vast bounty to such who brought him presents from great persons occasioned his want afterwards, who in rewarding them so remembred that he had been *Lord Chancellor,* that he forgot that he was but the Lord *Verulam.*

A *Viscountry* that began and ended in him dying issu'less, it being remarkable, that though we have had *two* Earls (of *several*[§] *families*) of Saint *Albans,* yet was there no Lord *Verulam,* as if it

---

1 The House of Commons. Fuller attributes this specific bit of information to William Rawley's life of Bacon (first published in 1657), his source, in fact, for a number of details.
2 In particular ones.

were reserved for that antient Roman *Colony* to be buried in its own reverend ruins and in this peerless Lords everlasting memory, much admired by *English,* more by out-landish[§] men; Distance diminishing his faults to be invisible to forreign eyes, whilst we beheld his perfections abated with his failings.

He died *Anno Domini* 1626. in the house of the Earl of *Arundel* at *High-gate,* and was buried in Saint *Michaels* Church in Saint *Albans,* Master *Mutis* his grateful servant erecting a Monument for him. Since I have read that his grave being occasionally[§] opened, his scull, (the relique of civil veneration) was by one *King* a *Doctor of Physick* made the object of scorn and contempt, but he, who then derided the dead, is since become the laughing stock of the living.

John Aubrey

SIR WALTER RALEIGH

In his youth for severall yeares—quaere[§] Anthony Wood how long—he was under streights for want of money. I remember that Mr. Thomas Child of Worcestershire told me that Sir Walter borrowed a gowne of him when he was at Oxford (they were both of the same College), which he never restored, nor money for it.

He went into Ireland, where he served in the warres, and shewed much courage and conduct, but he would be perpetually differing with . . .[3] (I thinke, Gray) then Lord Deputy; so that at last the hearing was to be at councell table before the queen, which was that he desired; where he told his tale so well and with so good a grace and presence that the queen tooke especiall notice of him and presently preferred him. (So that it must be before this that he served in the French warres.)

Queen Elizabeth loved to have all the servants of her Court

3 *Quaere Mr. Justice Ball.

proper men, and (as beforesaid Sir W. R.'s gracefull presence
was no meane recommendation to him). I thinke his first preferment at Court was Captaine of her Majestie's guard. There came
a countrey gentleman (or sufficient yeoman) up to towne, who
had severall sonns, but one an extraordinary proper handsome
fellowe, whom he did hope to have preferred to be a yeoman of
the guard. The father (a goodly man himselfe) comes to Sir
Walter Raleigh a stranger to him, and told him that he had
brought up a boy that he would desire (having many children)
should be one of her majestie's guard. Quod Sir Walter Raleigh
'Had you spake for your selfe I should readily have graunted your
desire, for your person deserves it, but I putt in no boyes.' Said
the father, 'Boy, come in.' The son enters, about 18 or 19, but
such a goodly proper young fellow, as Sir Walter Raleigh had not
seen the like—he was the tallest of all the guard. Sir Walter
Raleigh sweares him immediately; and ordered him to carry-up
the first dish at dinner, where the Queen beheld him with admiration,[4] as if a beautifull young giant had stalked in with the
service.

Vide[§] lord Bacon's apothegms and letters. As the queen
(Elizabeth) was playing on the virginalls,[§] . . . made this observation, that 'when *Jack's*[§] went up, *keys* went downe,' reflecting
on Ralegh.

He was the first that brought tobacco into England, and into
fashion.—In our part of North Wilts, e.g. Malmesbury hundred,
it came first into fashion by Sir Walter Long.

I have heard my grandfather Lyte say that one pipe was
handed from man to man round about the table. They had first
silver pipes; the ordinary sort made use of a walnutshell and a
straw.

It was sold then for it's wayte in silver. I have heard some[5] of
our old yeomen neighbours say that when they went to Malmesbury or Chippenham market, they culled out their biggest shillings to lay in the scales against the tobacco.

Sir W. R., standing in a stand at Sir Robert Poyntz' parke at
Acton, tooke a pipe of tobacco, which made the ladies quitt it till
he had donne.

4 *Like Saul, taller by the head and shoulders then other men.
5 *Josias Tayler.

Within these 35 years 'twas scandalous for a divine to take tobacco.

Rider's Almanac (1682, scilicet[§])—'Since tobacco brought into England by Sir Walter Raleigh, 99 yeares, the custome whereof is now the greatest of all others and amounts to yearly . . .'

Mr. Michael Weekes of the Royall Societie assures me, out of the custome-house bookes, that the custome of tobacco over all England is 400,000 *li.* per annum.

He was a tall, handsome, and bold man: but his naeve[§] was that he was damnable proud. Old Sir Robert Harley of Brampton-Brian Castle, who knew him, would say 'twas a great question who was the proudest, Sir Walter, or Sir Thomas Overbury, but the difference that was, was judged on Sir Thomas' side.

His beard turnd up naturally.—I have heard my grandmother say that when she was young, they were wont to talke of this rebus, viz.,

> The enemie to the stomack, and the word of disgrace,
> Is the name of the gentleman with a bold face.[6]

Old Sir Thomas Malett, one of the justices of the King's Bench tempore Caroli I et II,[7] knew Sir Walter; and I have heard him say that, notwithstanding his so great mastership in style and his conversation with the learnedst and politest persons, yet he spake broad Devonshire to his dyeing day. His voice was small, as likewise were my schoolfellowes', his grandnephewes.

Sir Walter Ralegh was a great chymist; and amongst some MSS. reciepts, I have seen some secrets from him. He studyed most in his sea-voyages, where he carried always a trunke of bookes along with him, and had nothing to divert him.

Memorandum:—he made an excellent cordiall, good in feavers, etc.; Mr. Robert Boyle haz the recipe, and makes it and does great cures by it.

A person so much immerst in action all along and in fabrication of his owne fortunes, (till his confinement in the Tower) could have but little time to study, but what he could spare in the morning. He was no slug; without doubt, had a wonderfull waking spirit, and great judgment to guide it.

---

6 Raw + lie (lye) = Rawlye, a common spelling.
7 In the reigns of Charles I and Charles II.

Durham-house was a noble palace; after he came to his great-
nes he lived there, or in some apartment of it. I well remember
his study, which was a little turret that looked into and over the
Thames, and had the prospect which is pleasant perhaps as any
in the world, and which not only refreshes the eie-sight but
cheeres the spirits, and (to speake my mind) I beleeve enlarges
an ingeniose[§] man's thoughts.

Shirburne castle, parke, mannor, etc., did belong (and still
ought to belong) to the church of Sarum.[§] 'Twas aliened in . . .
time (quaere bishop of Sarum) to . . . ; then . . . ; then Sir
W. R. begged [it] as a bôn[§] from queen Elizabeth: where he built
a delicate[§] lodge in the park, of brick, not big, but very convenient
for the bignes, a place to retire from the Court in summer time,
and to contemplate, etc. Upon his attainder, 'twas begged by the
favorite Carr, earl of Somerset, who forfeited it (I thinke) about
the poysoning of Sir Thomas Overbury. Then John, earl of Bris-
towe, had it given him for his good service in the ambassade[§] in
Spaine, and added two wings to Sir Walter Ralegh's lodge. In
short and indeed 'tis a most sweet and pleasant place and site as
any in the West, perhaps none like it.

In his youth his companions were boysterous blades, but generally those that had witt; except otherwise uppon designe to gett
them engaged[§] for him,—e.g. Sir Charles Snell, of Kington Saint
Michael in North Wilts, my good neighbour, an honest young
gentleman but kept a perpetuall sott, he engaged him to build a
ship (the Angel Gabriel) for the designe for Guiana, which cost
him the mannor of Yatton-Keynell, the farme at Easton-Piers,
Thornhill, and the church-lease of Bishops Cannings; which
ship, upon Sir Walter Raleigh's attainder, was forfeited. No question he had other such young . . .

From Dr. John Pell:— In his youthfull time, was one Charles
Chester, that often kept company with his acquaintance; he was
a bold impertenent fellowe, and they could never be at quiet for
him; a perpetuall talker, and made a noyse like a drumme in a
roome. So one time at a taverne Sir W. R. beates him and seales
up his mouth (i.e. his upper and neather beard) with hard wax.
From him Ben Johnson takes his Carlo Buffono (i.e. 'jester') in
Every Man out of his Humour.

He was a second to the earle of Oxford in a duell. Was ac-

quainted and accepted with all the hero's of our nation in his
time.

Sir Walter Long, of Dracot (grandfather to this old Sir James
Long) maried a daughter of Sir John Thynne, by which meanes,
and their consimility[§] of disposition, there was a very conjunct[§]
friendship between the two brothers (Sir Carew and Sir Walter)
and him; and old John Long, who then wayted on Sir W. Long,
being one time in the Privy-Garden with his master, saw the
earle of Nottingham wipe the dust from Sir Walter R.'s shoes
with his cloake, in compliment.

In the great parlour at Downton, at Mr. Ralegh's, is a good
piece (an originall) of Sir W. in a white sattin doublet, all em-
brodered with rich pearles, and a mighty rich chaine of great
pearles about his neck, and the old servants have told me that
the pearles were neer as big as the painted ones.

He had a most remarkeable aspect, an exceeding high forehead, long-faced, and sour eie-lidded, a kind of pigge-eie.

N.B.[§]— At . . . an obscure taverne, in Drury-lane (a bay-
liff's), is a good picture of this worthy, and also of others of his
time; taken upon some execution[§] (I suppose) formerly.

I have heard old major Cosh say that Sir W. Raleigh did not
care to goe on the Thames in a wherry boate: he would rather
goe round about over London bridg.

My old friend James Harrington, esq. [Oceana] was well acquainted with Sir Benjamin Ruddyer, who was an acquaintance
of Sir Walter Ralegh's. He told Mr. J. H. that Sir Walter Ralegh
being invited to dinner to some great person where his son was to
goe with him, he sayd to his son 'Thou art expected to-day at
dinner to goe along with me, but thou art such a quarrelsome,
affronting . . . , that I am ashamed to have such a beare in my
company.' Mr. Walter humbled himselfe to his father, and
promised he would behave himselfe mighty mannerly. So away
they went (and Sir Benjamin, I think, with them). He sate next
to his father and was very demure at least halfe dinner time.
Then sayd he, 'I, this morning, not having the feare of God before my eies, but by the instigation of the devill, went to a Whore.
I was very eager of her, kissed and embraced her, and went to
enjoy her, but she thrust me from her, and vowed I should not,
"For your father lay with me but an hower ago." ' Sir Walter,

being so strangely supprized, and putt out of his countenance at so great a table, gives his son a damned blow over the face. His son, as rude as he was, would not strike his father, but strikes over the face the gentleman that sate next to him and sayd 'Box about: 'twill come to my father anon.' 'Tis now a common-used proverb.

He loved a wench well: and one time getting up one of the Mayds of Honour[8] against a tree in a Wood, who seemed at first boarding to be something fearfull of her honour, and modest, she cryed, 'sweet Sir Walter, what doe you me ask? Will you undoe me? Nay, sweet Sir Walter! Sweet Sir Walter! Sir Walter!' At last, as the danger and the pleasure at the same time grew higher, she cryed in the extasy, 'Switter Swatter, Switter Swatter.' She proved with child, and I doubt not but this Hero tooke care of them both, as also that the Product was more then an ordinary mortall.

I have now forgott (vide History) whether Sir Walter was not for the putting of Mary, queen of Scotts, to death; I thinke, yea. But, besides that, at a consultation at Whitehall, after queen Elizabeth's death, how matters were to be ordered and what ought to be donne, Sir Walter Raleigh declared his opinion, 'twas the wisest way for them to keep the government in their owne hands, and sett up a commonwealth, and not be subject to a needy beggerly nation. It seemes there were some of this caball who kept not this so secret but that it came to king James's eare; who at . . . (vide *Chronicle*) where the English noblesse mett and received him, being told upon their presentment to his majesty their names, when Sir Walter Raleigh's name was told ('Ralegh') said the king 'On my soule, mon, I have heard *rawly* of thee.'— He was such a person (every way) that (as King Charles I sayes of the lord Strafford) a prince would rather be afrayd of then ashamed of. He had that awfulnes[s] and ascendency in his aspect over other mortalls, that the king . . .

It was a most stately sight, the glory of that reception of his majesty, where the nobility and gentry were in exceeding rich equippage, having enjoyed a long peace under the most excellent of queens; and the company was so exceeding numerous that their obedience carried a secret dread with it. King James did not

8 *Quaere J. Ball, who? 'Twas his first Lady.

inwardly like it, and with an inward envy sayd that, though so
and so (as before), he doubted not but he should have been able
on his owne strength (should the English have kept him out)
been able to have dealt with them, and get his right. Sayd Sir
Walter Raleigh to him, 'Would to God that had been put to the
tryall.' 'Why doe you wish that?' sayd the king.—'Because,' said
Sir Walter, 'that then you would have knowne your friends from
your foes.' But that reason of Sir Walter was never forgotten nor
forgiven.[9]

He was *praefectus*[1] (. . .) of Jarsey (Caesaria).

Old major[2] Stansby of . . . , Hants, a most intimate friend
and neighbour and coetanean[s] of the late earle of Southampton
(Lord Treasurer), told me from his friend, the earle, that as to
the plott and businesse (vide *Chronicle*) about the lord Cobham,
etc., he being then governor of Jersey, would not fully, or etc.,
doe things unles they would goe to his island and there advise
and resolve about it; and that really and indeed Sir Walter's
purpose was when he had them there, to have betrayed them and
the plott, and to have them delivered-up to the king and made
his peace.

As for his noble design in Guiana, vide the printed bookes.
Vide a Latin voyage which John, lord Vaughan, showed me,
where is mention of captaine North (brother to the lord North)
who went with Sir Walter, where is a large account of these matters. Mr. Edmund Wyld knew him and sayes he was a learned
and sober gentleman and good mathematician, but if you happened to speake of Guiana he would be strangely passionate and
say 'twas 'the blessedst countrey under the sun,' etc., reflecting
on the spoyling that brave designe.

When he was attached by the officer about the businesse which
cost him his head, he was carryed in a whery, I thinke only with
two men. King James was wont to say that he was a coward to be
so taken and conveyed, for els he might easily have made his
escape from so slight a guard.

He was prisoner in the Tower . . . (quaere) yeares; quaere
where his lodgeings were?

9 *From Dr. Whistler.
1 Overseer or governor. It appears from the parenthesis that Aubrey was not
sure of Raleigh's official title.
2 *Quaere Sir R. Henley, if not colonel.

He there (besides his compiling his *History of the World*) studyed chymistry. The earle of Northumberland was prisoner at the same time, who was the patrone to Mr. . . . Harriot and Mr. Warner, two of the best mathematicians then in the world, as also Mr. Hues ([who wrote] *de Globis*). Serjeant Hoskins (the poet) was a prisoner there too.

I heard my cosen Whitney say that he saw him in the Tower. He had a velvet cap laced, and a rich gowne, and trunke§ hose.

He was scandalizd with atheisme; but he was a bold man, and would venture at discourse which was unpleasant to the church-men. I remember first lord Scudamour sayd ' 'twas basely sayd of Sir W. R., to talke of *the anagramme of Dog*.' In his speech on the scaffold, I heard my cosen Whitney say (and I thinke 'tis printed) that he spake not one word of Christ, but of the great and incomprehensible God, with much zeale and adoration, so that he concluded he was an a-christ, not an atheist.

He tooke a pipe of tobacco a little before he went to the scaffold,[3] which some formall persons were scandalized at, but I thinke 'twas well and properly donne, to settle his spirits.

I remember I heard old father . . . Symonds (è Societate Jesu) say, that . . . , a father, was at his execution, and that to his knowledge he dyed with a lye in his mouth: I have now forgott what 'twas. The time of his execution was contrived to be on my Lord Mayer's day (viz. the day after St. Simon and Jude) 1618, that the pageants and fine shewes might drawe away the people from beholding the tragoedie of one of the gallants wor-thies that ever England bred. Buryed privately under the high alter at St. Margaret's church, in Westminster, on . . . (vide Register); in which grave (or neer) lies James Harrington, esq., author of *Oceana*.

Mr. Elias Ashmole told me that his son Carew Ralegh told him he had his father's skull; that some yeares since, upon digging-up the grave, his skull and neck-bone being viewed, they found the bone of his neck lapped over so, that he could not have been hanged. Quaere Sir John Elowys for the skull, who married Mr. Carew Ralegh's daughter and heire.

Sir W. Raleigh—Baker's *Chronicle*, p. 441—'A scaffold was erected in the Old Palace Yard, upon which, after 14 yeares re-

3 *[Recorded by] J. Stowe, I thinke.

privement, his head was cutt off. At which time such abundance
of bloud issued from his veines that shewed he had stock of
nature enough left to have continued him many yeares in life
though now above 3-score yeares old, if it had not been taken
away by the hand of violence. And this was the end of the great
Sir Walter Raleigh, great sometimes in the favour of queen Elizabeth, and (next to Sir Francis Drake) the great scourge and hate
of the Spaniard; who had many things to be commended in his
life, but none more than his constancy at his death, which he
tooke with so undaunted a resolution that one might percieve he
had a certain expectation of a better life after it, so far he was
from holding those atheisticall opinions, an aspersion whereof
some had cast upon him.'

In the register of St. Margaret's, Westminster, in the moneth
of October, Sir Walter Raleigh is entred, and is the last of that
moneth, but no dayes of the moneth are sett downe, so that he
being beheaded on the Lord Mayer's day, was buryed the . . .
He was buryed as soon as you are removed from the top of the
steps towards the altar, not under the altar.—from Elias Ashmole, esq.

On Sir Walter Rawleigh

> Here lieth, hidden in this pitt,
> The wonder of the world for witt.
> It to small purpose did him serve;
> His witt could not his life preserve.
> Hee living was belov'd of none,
> Yet in his death all did him moane.[4]
> Heaven hath his soule, the world his fame,
> The grave his corps, Stukley his shame.

This I found among the papers of my honoured friend and
neighbour Thomas Tyndale, esq., obiit . . . 167–, aet. 85.[5] This
Stukely was . . .

I am promised the *very originall* examination of Sir Walter
Ralegh, in the Tower, by Lord Chancellor Bacon, George Abbot

---

[4] *Horat. ep. 1, lib. 2:—Extinctus amabitur *idem*. [Horace, *Epistles*, I.2: When
he is dead, the same man will be loved.]
[5] Died . . . aged.

(archbishop of Canterbury), and Sir Edward Coke, under their owne hands, to insert in my booke.

At the end of the *History of the World* (vide last folio, *Hist. World*), he laments the death of the most noble and most hopefull⁸ prince Henry, whose great favourite he was, and who, had he survived his father, would quickly have enlarged⁸ him, with rewards of honour. So upon the prince's death ends his first part of his *History of the World,* with a gallant eulogie of him, and concludes, *Versa est in luctum cithara mea; et cantus meus in vocem flentium.*⁶

He had an apparatus for the second part, which he, in discontent, burn't, and sayd, 'If I am not worthy of the world, the world is not worthy of my workes.' ⁷

His booke sold very slowly at first, and the bookeseller complayned of it, and told him that he should be a looser by it, which put Sir W. into a passion; and sayd that since the world did not understand it, they should not have his second part, which he tooke and threw into the fire, and burnt before his face.

Mr. Elias Ashmole saies that Degore Whear in his *Praelectiones Hyemales* gives him an admirable encomium, and preferres him before all other historians.

An attorney's father (that did my businesse in Herefordshire, before I sold it) maryed Dr. Burhill's widdowe. She sayd that he was a great favourite of Sir Walter Ralegh's (and, I thinke, had been his chaplayne): but all or the greatest part of the drudgery of his booke, for criticismes, chronology, and reading of Greeke and Hebrew authors, was performed by him for Sir Walter Ralegh, whose picture my friend haz as part of the Doctor's goods.

He was somtimes a poet, not often.—Before Spencer's Faery Q. is a good copie of verses, which begins thus:—

Methinkes I see the grave wher Laura lay; at the bottome W. R.: which, 36 yeares since, I was told were his.

His intimate acquaintance and friends were . . . , earle of Oxford, Sir Francis Vere, Sir Horatio Vere, Sir Francis Drake,

---

6 My harp also is turned to mourning, and my song into the voice of them that weep.

7 *From his grand-nephewes my school-fellowes.

Nicholas Hill, Cavendish, Mr. Thomas Hariot, Sir Walter Long, of Dracot in Wilts., Cavaliero Surff, etc., Ben: Johnson.

When Serjeant Hoskyns was a prisoner in the Tower, he was Sir Walter's Aristarchus.[§]

A copie[8] of Sir W. Ralegh's letter, sent to Mr. Duke, in Devon, writt with his owne hand.

MR. DUKE,

I wrote to Mr. Prideaux to move you for the purchase of Hayes,[9] a farme sometime in my father's possession. I will most willingly give whatsoever in your conscience you shall deeme it worth, and if at any time you shall have occasion to use me, you shall find me a thankefull friend to you and yours. I am resolved, if I cannot entreat you, to build at Colliton; but for the naturall disposition I have to that place, being borne in that house, I had rather seate myselfe there then any where els; I take my leave, readie to countervaile all your courtesies to the utter of my power.

Court, the xxvi   Your very willing friend,
of July, 1584.   In all I shall be able,

                                                          Walter Ralegh.

> Even such is tyme, which takes in trust
> Our youth, our joyes, and all we have,
> And payes us but with age and dust.
> Within the darke and silent grave,
> When we have wandered all our wayes,
> Shutts up the story of our dayes.
> But from which grave and earth and dust
> The Lord will rayse me up I trust.

These lines Sir Walter Ralegh wrote in his Bible, the night before he was beheaded, and desir'd his relations with these words, viz. 'Beg my dead body, which living is denyed you; and bury it either in Sherburne or Exeter church.'

---

8 *I thinke I sent the originall to Anthony Wood.
9 *Hayes is in the parish of East Budleigh. He was not buryed at Exeter by his father and mother, nor at Shirburne in Dorset; at either of which places he desired his wife (in his letter the night before he dyed) to be interred. His father had 80 yeares in this farme of Hayes, and wrote 'esquier.'

The bishop of Sarum saieth that Sir Walter Raleigh lyes interred in St. Marie's church at Exon, not the cathedral: but knowes not if any inscription or monument be for him.

Sir Walter Raleigh hath neither stone nor inscription. Mr. Ashmole was the first told me of Sir Walter Raleigh. His son was buryed since the king's restauration in his father's grave.

Anthony à Wood

SIR HENRY WOTTON

Henry Wotton, a person singularly accomplish'd, Son of *Tho. Wotton* Esq; by his second Wife *Elizabeth,* Daughter of Sir *Will. Finch* of the *Mote* in St. *Martins* Parish in the County of *Kent,* but the Widdow of one *Morton* of the same County Esq; was born at *Bocton* hall in *Kent* 30. *March* 1568. educated in Grammar learning in *Wykehams* School near to *Winchester,* and thence in the beginning of 1584. he was transplanted to *New* coll. where living in the condition of a Gent.§ Com. had his Chamber in *Hart* hall adjoyning, and to§ his Chamber-Fellow there *Rich. Baker* his Countryman, afterwards a Knight and a noted writer. But continuing there not long, he went to *Queens* coll. where, by the benefit of a good Tutor and severe discipline there practiced, he became well vers'd in Logick and Philosophy; and for a diversion now and then, he wrote a Tragedy for the private use of that house called *Tancredo.* On the 8. *June* 1588. he, as a Member of *Qu.* coll. did supplicate the venerable Congregation of Regents that he might be admitted to the reading of any of the books of the Logick of *Aristotle,* that is to be admitted to the degree of Bach. of Arts: which desire of his was granted conditionally that he should *determine*§ in the Lent following; but whether he was admitted, or did *determine,* or took any other degree, it doth not appear in any of the University Registers, which I have exactly searched, and the more for this reason, be-

cause the author of his life[1] saith, that at 19 years of age he
proceeded Master of Arts, and at that time did read three Lat.
Lectures *De Ocello;*[2] which being learned, caused a friendship
between him and *Alberic. Gentilis,* who thereupon ever after
called him *Henrice mi Ocelle.* The said author also saith, that the
University Treasury was rob'd by Townsmen and poor Scholars,
of which such light was given by a Letter written to *Hen. Wotton* from his Father in *Kent,* occasioned by a dream relating to
that matter, that the Felons were thereupon discovered and apprehended, &c. But upon my search into the University Registers,
Records, Accompts, &c. from 1584. to 1589. in which time our
author *Wotton* was resident in *Oxon,* I find no such robbery committed. To pass by other mistakes in the said life, especially as to
time, which are not proper to set down in this place, I shall go
forward. After our author had left *Oxon,* he betook himself to
travel into *France, Germany,* and *Italy;* and having spent about
9 years in those places, he returned into *England,* and became
Secretary to *Robert* Earl of *Essex,* with whom continuing till
towards[§] his fall, he left *England* once more, and retiring to *Florence,* became so noted to the Great Duke of *Tuscany,* that he was
by him privately dispatched away with letters to *James 6.* K. of
Scots, under the name of *Octavio Baldi* to advise him of a design
to take away his life. Which message being welcome to that K.
he was by him (when made K. of *England*) honoured with the
degree of Knighthood, sent thrice Embassador to the *Repub. of
Venice,* once to the *States of the United Provinces,* twice to
Charles Emanuel Duke of *Savoy,* once to the United Princes of
Upper Germany in the Convention at *Heylbrune,* also to the Arch-
duke *Leopald,* to the Duke of *Wittenbergh,* to the Imperial Cities
of *Strasburgh* and *Ulme,* as also to the Emperor *Ferdinando* the
second. On the 15. *July* 1619. he returned from his Embassie at
Venice with a vain hope of obtaining the office of Secretary of
State,[3] but missing his design, I cannot yet tell to the contrary
but that he was sent to *Venice* again. Sure 'tis, that about 1623.
he had the Provostship of *Eaton* coll. confer'd upon him, which
he kept to his dying day, being all the reward he had for the great

1 *Isaac Walton.
2 *On the Eye.*
3 *Camd. in *Annal. Jac.* 1. MS. sub an. 1619. [Camden's manuscript *Annals of
King James I,* under the year 1619.]

services he had done the Crown of *England*. He hath written
these things following. . . .[4] Other MSS. also of his composition
do go from hand to hand, which I have not yet seen. At length
after Sir H. *Wotton* had spent 72 years in this vain and transitory World, did conclude his last day in *Eaton* coll. near to
Windsore, in the month of *Decemb.* in sixteen hundred thirty and
nine, and was buried in the Chappel belonging to the said College. When he made his Will he appointed this Epitaph to be put
over his grave. *Hic jacet huius sententiæ primus author* Dis-
putandi pruritus, Ecclesiarum scabies. *Nomen aliàs quære.*[5] In
his Provestship of *Eaton* coll. succeeded *Rich. Steuart* Doctor of
the Civil Laws, and Clark of the Closet to King *Ch.* I. of whom I
shall make farther mention under the year 1651.

IZAAK WALTON

I desire the Reader to know, that he was born in the ancient
Borough of *Stafford*, in *Aug.* 1593. that he was by Trade a
Sempster in *Chancery-lane* in *London*, where continuing till
about 1643. (at which time he found it dangerous for honest
men to be there,) he left that City, and lived sometimes at *Stafford*, and elsewhere, but mostly in the Families of the eminent
Clergy-men of *England*, of whom he was much beloved. He hath
written the lives of Dr. *Joh. Donne*, Sir *Hen. Wotton*, Mr. *Rich.
Hooker*, Mr. *George Herbert*, and of Dr. *Rob. Sanderson* sometimes B. of *Lincoln:* All which are well done, considering the
education of the author; as also *The compleat Angler, or the contemplative Man's recreation*, &c. He ended his days (in the great
Frost) at *Winchester*, in the house of Dr. *Will. Hawkins*, Prebendary of the Church there, (who had married his Daughter,)
on the 15. *Dec.* 1683. and was buried in the Cath. Ch. at that
place.

---

4 The bibliography of works published and in manuscript is omitted here.
5 Here lies the first author of this sentence: The itch of disputation will prove
the scab of the Church. Inquire his name elsewhere.

X

Letters

Sir Walter Raleigh

TO DAY A MAN, TO MORROW NONE:
Or, Sir Walter Rawleighs Farewell to his Lady,
The night before hee was beheaded:
Together with his advice
concerning Her, and her Sonne[1]

DEAR WIFE,

You shall receive my last words in these my last lines; my love
I send you that you may keepe it when I am dead, and my counsel that you may remember it when I am no more. I would not
with my will present you sorrows (dear *Besse*); let them go to the
grave with me, and be buried in the dust. And seeing it is not the
will of God that ever I shall see you any more in this life, beare
my destruction gently, and with a heart like your selfe.

First, I send you all the thanks which my heart can conceive,
or my words expresse, for your many troubles and cares taken for
me, which though they have not taken effect as you wished, yet

1 The title, reproduced from the first printed version of the letter, is in error.
Copies of the letter in manuscript indicate that Raleigh wrote it when he expected to be executed in December, 1603.

my debt to you is not lesse, but I shall never recompence it in this world.

Secondly, I beseech you even for the love you bare me living, that you doe not hide your selfe many dayes, but by your travell[§] seek to helpe your miserable fortune, and the right of your poore childe: Your mourning cannot availe me that am but dust.

Thirdly, you shall understand that my Lands were conveied (*bona fide*[2]) to my childe, the writings were drawne at Mid-summer was twelve-month, as divers can witnesse, and I trust that my blood will quench their malice that desire my slaughter, and that they will not seek also to kill you and yours with ex-tream poverty.

To what friend to direct you I know not, for all mine have left me in the true time of tryall; most sorry I am (as God knoweth) that being thus surprised with death I can leave you no better estate; I meant you all my Office of wines[3] or that I should pur-chase by selling it, halfe my stuffe[§] and my jewels, (but some few for the boy) but God hath prevented all my determinations; The great God that worketh all in all.

But if you can live free from want, care for no more, for the rest is but vanity.

Love God, and begin betime to repose your selfe on him, therein shall you finde true and everlasting riches and endlesse comfort: for the rest when you have travelled[§] and wearied your thoughts over all sorts of worldly cogitations, you shall sit downe by sorrow in the end.

Teach your son also to serve and fear God whilst he is young, that the feare of God may grow up with him, then will God be a husband unto you, and a father unto him, a husband and a father that can never be taken from you.

Bayly oweth me 1000 l. *A[d]rion* 600 l. In *Jersie* also I have much owing me; the arrerages of the wines will pay your debts.

And howsoever (I beseech you for my soules sake) pay all poore men when I am gone: no doubt you shall bee sought unto, for the world thinks I was very rich.

But take heed of the pretence of men and of their affections,

---

2 In good faith; legitimately.

3 In 1583, Queen Elizabeth had bestowed on Raleigh the patent for wines; he received a large income from fines for infringement and from an annual fee levied on every vintner for a license to sell wine.

for they last but in honest and worthy men: and no greater misery can befall you in this life, then to become a prey, and after to bee despised: I speake it (God knoweth) not to disswade you from marriage, for that will be best for you, both in respect of God and the world.

As for me I am no more yours, nor you mine, death hath cut us asunder, and God hath divided me from the world, and you from me: Remember your poore childe for his fathers sake that comforted you, and loved you in his happiest times.

I sued for my life (but God knowes) it was for you and yours that I desired it: for know it (deare wife) that your sonne is the childe of a true man, and who in his owne heart despiseth death, and all his mishapen and ugly forms.

I cannot write much: God knoweth how hardly[§] I stole this time when all were asleep, and it is now time to separate my thoughts from the world. Beg my dead body which living was denyed you, and either lay it in *Sherborne* or in *Exeter* Church by my father and mother. I can say no more, time and death call me away. The everlasting God, infinite, powerfull, and inscrutable God, That Almighty God which is goodnesse it selfe, mercy it selfe, the true light and life, keep you and yours, and have mercy upon me.

[And] teach me to forgive my persecuters and false accusers, and send me to meet him in his glorious Kingdome.

My true wife farewell, God blesse my poore boy, pray for me, my true God hold you both in His Armes.

John Donne

I. [TO———[4]]

SIR.

Only in obedience I send you some of my paradoxes; I love you & myself & them to well to send them willingly for they

---

[4] The addressee is not known. Since the letter was sent with ten of Donne's paradoxes, which were written by 1600, the letter can be dated "about 1600."

carry with them a confession of there lightnes & your trouble
and my shame. But indeed they were made rather to deceave
tyme then her daughther truth: although they have beene written
in an age when any thing is strong enough to overthrow her: if
they make you to find better reasons against them they do there
office: for they are but swaggerers: quiet enough if you resist
them. If perchaunce they be pretyly guilt,§ that is there best for
they are not hatcht:§ they are rather alarums to truth to arme her
then enemies: & they have only this advantadg to scape from
being caled ill things that they are nothings: therfore take heed
of allowing any of them least§ you make another. Yet Sir though
I know there low price except I receve by your next letter an assurance upon the religion of your frendship that no coppy shal-
bee taken for any respect of these or any other my compositions
sent to you, I shall sinn against my conscience if I send you any
more. I speake that in playnes§ which becomes (methinks) our
honestyes; and therfore call not this a distrustfull but a free
spirit: I meane to aquaint you with all myne: and to my satyrs
there belongs some feare & to some elegies & these perhaps
shame. Against both which affections§ although I be tough
enough yet I have a ridling§ disposition to bee ashamed of feare
& afrayd of shame. Therfore I am desirous to hyde them with out
any over reconing§ of them or there maker. But they are not
worth thus much words in theyre disprayse. I will step to a better
subject your last letter to which I need not tell I made no answere
but I had need excuse it. All your letter I embrace & beleeve it
when it speakes of your self & when of me too if the good words
which you speake of me bee ment of my intentions to goodnes:
for else alas! no man is more beggerly in actuall vertue then I. I
am sory you should (with any great ernestnes) desyre any thing
of P. Aretinus not that he could infect; but that it seemes you are
alredy infected with the common opinion of him: beleeve me
he is much lesse then his fame & was to well payd by the Roman
church in that coyne which he coveted most where his bookes
were by the counsell of Trent forbidden which if they had beene
permitted to have beene worne by all long ere this had beene
worne out: his divinyty was but a sirrope§ to enwrapp his prophane bookes to get them passage yet in these bookes which have
devine titles there is least harme as in his letters most good; his

others have no other singularyty in them but that they are forbidden. The psalmes (which you aske) If I cannot shortly procure you one to poses I can & will at any tyme borrow for you:
In the meane tyme Sir have the honor of forgiving two faults to-
geather: my not writing last tyme and my abrupt ending now.

2. [TO SIR HENRY GOODERE[5]]

If you were here, you would not think me importune, if I bid
you good morrow every day; and such a patience will excuse my
often Letters. No other kinde of conveyance is better for knowledge, or love: What treasures of Morall knowledge are in *Sene-
caes* Letters to onely one *Lucilius*? and what of Naturall in
Plinies? how much of the storie of the time, is in *Ciceroes*
Letters? And how all of these times, in the Jesuites Eastern and
Western Epistles? where can we finde so perfect a Character of
Phalaris, as in his own Letters, which are almost so many writs
of Execution? Or of *Brutus,* as in his privie[§] seals[§] for monie?
The Evangiles and Acts, teach us what to beleeve, but the
Epistles of the Apostles what to do. And those who have en-
devoured to dignifie *Seneca* above his worth, have no way fitter,
then to imagine Letters between him and S. *Paul.* As they think
also that they have expressed an excellent person, in that Letter
which they obtrude,[§] from our B. Saviour to King *Agabarus.*
The Italians, which are most discursive, and think the world
owes them all wisdome, abound so much in this kinde of expressing, that *Michel Montaigne* saies, he hath seen, (as I remember) 400 volumes of Italian Letters. But it is the other
capacity which must make mine acceptable, that they are also
the best conveyers of love. But, though all knowledge be in those
Authors already, yet, as some poisons, and some medicines, hurt
not, nor profit, except the creature in which they reside, contribute their lively activitie, and vigor; so, much of the knowledge
buried in Books perisheth, and becomes ineffectuall, if it be not

[5] When the letter was first printed, it was headed *"To Sir* G. M.," probably to
give the impression that it was sent to Sir George More, Donne's father-in-law.
It was almost certainly intended for Donne's friend Goodere, whom he wrote to
weekly. (See Roger E. Bennett, "Donne's *Letters to Severall Persons of
Honour,*" *PMLA,* LVI [1941], 124.) Donne wrote most of his problems early in
the first decade of the century, and the letter probably belongs to those years.

applied, and refreshed by a companion, or friend. Much of their goodnesse, hath the same period,§ which some Physicians of *Italy* have observed to be in the biting of their *Tarentola*,§ that it affects§ no longer, then the flie lives. For with how much desire we read the papers of any living now, (especially friends) which we would scarce allow a boxe in our cabinet, or shelf in our Library, if they were dead? And we do justly in it, for the writings and words of men present, we may examine, controll, and expostulate, and receive satisfaction from the authors; but the other we must beleeve, or discredit; they present no mean. Since then at this time, I am upon the stage, you may be content to hear me. And now that perchance I have brought you to it, (as *Thom. Badger* did the King) now I have nothing to say. And it is well, for the Letter is already long enough, else let this probleme supply, which was occasioned by you, of women wearing stones; which, it seems, you were afraid women should read, because you avert them at the beginning, with a protestation of cleanlinesse. *Martiall* found no way fitter to draw the Romane Matrons to read one of his Books, which he thinks most morall and cleanly, then to counsell them by the first Epigram to skip the Book, because it was obscene. But either you write not at all for women, or for those of sincerer palates. Though their unworthinesse, and your own ease be advocates for me with you, yet I must adde my entreaty, that you let goe no copy of my Problems, till I review them. If it be too late, at least be able to tell me who hath them.

Yours,

J. Donne.

3. TO THE WORTHIEST LADY,
MRS. MAGDALEN HERBERT

MADAM,

Every excuse hath in it somewhat of accusation; and since I am innocent, and yet must excuse, how shall I do for that part of accusing. By my troth, as desperate and perplexed men, grow from thence bold; so must I take the boldness of accusing you, who would draw so dark a Curtain betwixt me and your purposes, as that I had no glimmering, neither of your goings, nor

the way which my Letters might haunt. Yet, I have given this
Licence to Travel, but I know not whether,§ nor it. It is therefore
rather a Pinnace to discover; and the intire Colony of Letters,
of Hundreds and Fifties, must follow; whose employment is
more honourable, than that which our State meditates to *Virginia,* because you are worthier than all that Countrey, of which
that is a wretched inch; for you have better treasure, and a
harmlessness. If this sound like a flattery, tear it out. I am to
my Letters as rigid a Puritane, as *Cæsar* was to his Wife. I can
as ill endure a suspitious and misinterpretable word as a fault;
but remember, that nothing is flattery which the Speaker be-
lieves; and of the grossest flatteries there is this good use, that
they tell us what we should be. But, *Madam,* you are beyond instruction, and therefore there can belong to you only praise; of
which, though you be no good hearer, yet allow all my Letters
leave to have in them one part of it, which is thankfulness
towards you.

Michin,   *Your unworthiest Servant,*
July 11.   *Except your accepting*
1607.   *have mended him,*
                                              John Donne.

4. TO SIR H[ENRY] G[OODERE]

SIR,

I hope you are now wel come to London, and well, and well
comforted in your fathers health and love,[6] and well contented
that we aske you how you doe, and tell you how we are, which
yet I cannot of my selfe; If I knew that I were ill, I were well;
For we consist of three parts, a Soule, and Body, and Mind:
which I call those thoughts and affections and passions, which
neither Soule nor Body hath alone, but have beene begotten by
their communication, as Musique results out of our breath and
a Cornet. And of all these the diseases are cures, if they be
knowne. Of our Soules sicknesses, which are sinnes, the knowledge is, to acknowledge, and that is her physick,§ in which wee

[6] Since Goodere's father probably died about 1611, the letter was written prior
to that year.

are not dieted by drams and scruples,§ for we cannot take too much. Of our bodies infirmities, though our knowledge be partly *ab extrinseco*,[7] from the opinion of the Physitian, and that the subject and matter be flexible, and various; Yet their rules are certaine, and if the matter be rightly applyed to the rule, our knowledge thereof is also certaine. But of the diseases of the minde, there is no Cryterium,§ no Canon, no rule; for, our owne tast and apprehension & interpretation should be the judge, and that is the disease it selfe. Therefore sometimes when I finde my selfe transported with jollity, and love of company, I hang leads at my heeles, and reduce§ to my thoughts my fortunes, my yeares, the duties of a man, of a friend, of a husband, of a father, and all the incumbencies§ of a family. When sadnesse dejects me, either I countermine it with another sadnesse, or I kindle squibs§ about mee againe, and flie into sportfulnesse and company. And I finde ever after all, that I am like an Exorcist, which had long laboured about one, which at last appeares to have the Mother,§ that I still mistake my disease. And I still vexe my selfe with this, because if I know it not, no body can know it. And I comfort my selfe because I see dispassioned men are subject to the like ignorances. For divers mindes out of the same thing often draw contrary conclusions, as Augustine thought devout Anthony to bee therfore full of the holy Ghost, because, not being able to read, he could say the whole Bible, and interpret it. And Thyræus the Jesuite for the same reason doth thinke all the Anabaptists to be possessed. And as often out of contrary things men draw one conclusion. As, To the Romane Church, Magnificence and Splendor hath ever beene an argument of Gods favour, and Poverty and Affliction, to the Greeke. Out of this variety of mindes it proceeds, that though all our Soules would goe to one end, Heaven, and all our bodies must goe to one end, the Earth: Yet our third part, the minde, which is our naturall Guide here, chuses to every man a severall§ way. Scarce any man likes what another doth, nor, advisedly, that which himselfe. But, Sir, I am beyond my purpose; I meant to write a letter, and I am fallen into a discourse, and I doe not only take you from some businesse, but I make you a new busi-

[7] Extrinsic; from the outside.

nesse by drawing you into these meditations. In which yet let
my opennes be an argument of such love as I would fain expresse in some worthier fashion.

5. TO SIR H. GOODERE

SIR,

Every tuesday I make account that I turn a great hour-glass,
and consider that a weeks life is run out since I writ. But if I
aske my self what I have done in the last watch, or would do
in the next, I can say nothing; if I say that I have passed it
without hurting any, so may the Spider in my window. The
primitive Monkes were excusable in their retirings and en-
closures of themselves: for even of them every one cultivated
his own garden and orchard, that is, his soul and body, by meditation, and manufactures; and they ought§ the world no more
since they consumed none of her sweetnesse, nor begot others
to burden her. But for me, if I were able to husband all my time
so thriftily, as not onely not to wound my soul in any minute
by actuall sinne, but not to rob and cousen§ her by giving any
part to pleasure or businesse, but bestow it all upon her in
meditation, yet even in that I should wound her more, and contract another guiltinesse: As the Eagle were very unnaturall if
because she is able to do it, she should pearch a whole day upon
a tree, staring in contemplation of the majestie and glory of
the Sun, and let her young Eglets starve in the nest. Two of the
most precious things which God hath afforded us here, for the
agony and exercise of our sense and spirit, which are a thirst
and inhiation§ after the next life, and a frequency of prayer
and meditation in this, are often envenomed, and putrefied, and
stray into a corrupt disease: for as God doth thus occasion, and
positively concurre to evill, that when a man is purposed to do
a great sin, God infuses some good thoughts which make him
choose a lesse sin, or leave out some circumstance which ag-
gravated that; so the devill doth not only suffer§ but provoke us
to some things naturally good, upon condition that we shall
omit some other more necessary and more obligatory. And this
is his greatest subtilty; because herein we have the deceitfull
comfort of having done well, and can very hardly§ spie our

errour because it is but an insensible omission, and no accusing
act. With the first of these I have often suspected my self to be
overtaken; which is, with a desire of the next life: which though
I know it is not meerly out of a wearinesse of this, because I
had the same desires when I went with the tyde, and enjoyed
fairer hopes then now: yet I doubt§ worldly encombrances have
encreased it. I would not that death should take me asleep. I
would not have him meerly seise me, and onely declare me to
be dead, but win me, and overcome me. When I must shipwrack,
I would do it in a Sea, where mine impotencie might have some
excuse; not in a sullen§ weedy lake, where I could not have so
much as exercise for my swimming. Therefore I would fain do
something; but that I cannot tell what, is no wonder. For to
chuse, is to do: but to be no part of any body, is to be nothing.
At most, the greatest persons, are but great wens, and excres-
cences; men of wit and delightfull conversation, but as moales§
for ornament, except they be so incorporated into the body of the
world, that they contribute something to the sustentation of the
whole. This I made account that I begun early, when I understood the study of our laws: but was diverted by the worst
voluptuousnes, which is an Hydroptique§ immoderate desire of
humane learning and languages: beautifull ornaments to great
fortunes; but mine needed an occupation, and a course which
I thought I entred well into, when I submitted my self to such
a service, as I thought might imploy those poor advantages,
which I had. And there I stumbled too, yet I would try again:
for to this hour I am nothing, or so little, that I am scarce subject and argument good enough for one of mine own letters:
yet I fear, that doth not ever proceed from a good root, that I
am so well content to be lesse, that is dead. You, Sir, are farre
enough from these descents, your vertue keeps you secure, and
your naturall disposition to mirth will preserve you; but lose
none of these holds, a slip is often as dangerous as a bruise,
and though you cannot fall to my lownesse, yet in a much lesse
distraction you may meet my sadnesse; for he is no safer which
falls from an high tower into the leads,§ then he which falls
from thence to the ground: make therefore to your self some
mark, and go towards it alegrement.§ Though I be in such a
planetary§ and erratique fortune, that I can do nothing con-

stantly, yet you may finde some constancy in my constant advising you to it.

Your hearty true friend
J. Donne.

I came this evening from M. Jones *his house in* Essex, *where*
M. Martin *hath been, and left a relation of Captain* Whitlocks
death,[8] *perchance it is no news to you, but it was to me; without doubt want broke him; for when M.* Hollands *company by
reason of the plague broke, the Captain sought to be at Mrs.*
Jones *house, who in her husbands absence declining it, he went
in the night, his boy carrying his cloakbag, on foot to the Lord of*
Sussex, *who going next day to hunt, the Captain not then sick,
told him he would see him no more. A Chaplain came up to him,
to whom he delivered an account of his understanding, and I
hope, of his beliefe, and soon after dyed; and my Lord hath
buryed him with his own Ancestors. Perchance his life needed a
longer sicknesse, but a man may go faster and safer, when he enjoyes that day light of a clear and sound understanding, then in
the night or twilight of an ague or other disease. And the grace of
Almighty God doth every thing suddenly and hastily, but depart
from us, it inlightens us, warms us, heats us, ravishes us, at once.
Such a medicin, I fear, his inconsideration needed; and I hope as
confidently that he had it. As our soul is infused when it is
created, and created when it is infused, so at her going out,
Gods mercy is had by asking, and that is asked by having. Lest
your* Polesworth *carrier should cousen me, I send my man with
this letter early to* London, *whither this Tuesday all the Court
come to a Christening at* Arondell *house, and stay in town so
that I will sup with the good Lady, and write again to morrow
to you, if any thing be occasioned there, which concerns you,
and I will tell her so; next day they are to return to* Hampton,
and upon friday the King to Royston.

[8] The reference to the death of Capt. Edmund Whitelocke dates the letter
shortly after mid-September, 1608.

6. [TO GEORGE GERRARD[9]]

SIR,

It is one ill Affection[§] of a desperate debtor, that he dares not come to an account, nor take knowledge how much he owes; this makes me that I dare not tell you how manie letters I have received from you since I came to this Towne; I had three the first by the Cooke,[1] who brought none but yours, nor ever came to me, to let me know what became of the rest: the two other of the 7. and 8. of *March,* came in a letter which Sir *H. Wotton* writ to me from *Amyens;* there is not a size of paper in the Palace, large enough to tell you how much I esteeme my selfe honoured in your remembrances; nor strong enough to wrap up a heart so ful of good affections towards you, as mine is. When any thing passes between Sir *Thomas Roe* and you, tell him I am not the lesse his Servant, for not saying so by often letters: for by my troth, I am that so much as he could desire I should be, when he began to love me. Sir *Thomas Lucies* businesse, and perchance sadnesse forbid me writing now. I have written to him (whilest I lived in darknesse,[§] whether my Letters came to you or no) by another way; and if my poore Letters were any degree of service, I should doe it often, and rather be mine own Post, then leave any thing undone, to which he would give such an interpretation, as that it were an Argument of my Devotion to him. For my purpose of proceeding in the profession of the Law, so far as to a Title, you may be pleased to correct that imagination where you finde it. I ever thought the study of it my best entertainment and pastime, but I have no ambition, nor design upon the Stile.[§] Of my Anniversaries the fault which I acknowledge in my selfe, is to have descended to print any thing in Verse, which though it have excuse, even in our times, by example of men, which one would

[9] The letter had no heading when it was printed as it appears here in Donne's *Letters to Severall Persons of Honour,* 1651. An edited version was printed in the 1635 edition of Donne's *Poems,* and that version was reprinted, along with this one, in 1651. The heading (*"To my honoured friend G. G. Esquire"*) and date (*"Paris the 14 of Aprill,* here, 1612) of the edited version almost certainly belong to the letter printed here.
[1] Perhaps Sir Robert Drury's servant, Bartholomew Cooke.

thinke should as little have done it, as I; yet I confesse I wonder how I declined to it, and doe not pardon my self. But for the other part of the imputation, of having said so much, my defence is, that my purpose was to say as well as I could: for since I never saw the Gentlewoman, I cannot be understood to have bound my selfe to have spoken just Truth: but I would not be thought to have gone about to praise any bodie in rime, except I tooke such a Person, as might be capable of all that I could say. If any of those Ladies think that Mistris *Drury* was not so, let that Ladie make her selfe fit for all those praises in the Booke, and it shall be hers. Nothing is farther from colour or ground of Truth, then that which you write of Sir *Robert Druries* going to Masse. No man of our Nation hath been more forward to apply himselfe to the Church of the Religion where he hath come, nor to relieve their wants, where that Demonstration hath beene needfull. I know not yet whether Sir *John Brookes* purpose of being very shortly here, be not a just reason to make me forbear writing to him. I am sure that I would fainest do that in writing or abstaining which should be most acceptable to him. It were in vain to put into this letter any relation of the Magnificence which have been here at publication[§] of these marriages; for at this time there come into *England* so many *Frenchmen,* as I am sure you shall heare all at least. If they speak not of above eight hundred horse well caparosond, you may believe it: and you may believe, that no Court in Christendome had beene able to have appeared so brave[§] in that kinde. But if they tell you of any other stuffe, then Copper, or any other exercise of armes then running at the Quintain, and the Ring,[§] you may be bold to say *Pardone moy.* Sir, this messenger makes so much haste that I cry you mercy for spending any time of this Letter, in other imployment, then thanking you for yours, and promising you more before my remove from hence. I pray venture no Letter to me by any other way then M. *John Bruer* at the Queens Armes a Mercer in *Cheapside,* who is always like to know where we are; And make me by loving me still, worthy to be

Your friend and servant
J. Donne.

Sir Henry Wotton

I. TO MARCUS VELSERUS,
One of the two Governours of AUSBURG.
HENRY WOTTON *wishing health*

SIR,

I have written to you heretofore sometimes in private, but have a concern upon me now to do it also in publick,[2] of which (with your permission) I desire thus to inform you.

At the last *Frankefurt Mart* there was set to sale a certain Book of Bulk (which often gives the value) not inconsiderable. And it bore this Inscription:

> *Jaspar Scioppius* his *Ecclesiasticus:* opposed to the Authority of the most Serene Lord King *James*——wherein as with Arguments for the most part new, and in a way hitherto by no man trac'd ——And so on with the like modesty.

The Composer of this Work, in his begging Scraps all about, I know not by what means, seems to have lighted on a merry definition of an Ambassador, which above eight years before passing by that way, I had chanced to set down at my Friend's Mr. *Christopher Fleckamor*, in his *Album* of Friends, after the *German* custome, (*a white Paper-Book used by the* Dutch *for such kind of Mottos*) which was worded thus:

> *Legatus est vir bonus peregrè missus ad mentiendum Reipub. causâ.* In English, being only this Jest; *An Ambassador is an honest man sent to lye abroad for the Commonwealth.*

A Definition perhaps so Catholick, that it may comprehend even the Popes Legates; Now, what, I pray, think you doth this

---

2 The original Latin letter, of which this is a translation, was apparently published in December, 1612. No copy of the first edition is known, but the Latin was printed in *Reliquiae Wottonianae*, 1651. The translation first appeared in the third edition of this book (1672).

Scioppius hereupon? Throws open the Cabinet of familiarity, after so many years, revives an obsolete conceipt,§ priviledg'd from disturbance even by its Antiquity, and according to his civility adorns me with a most gentle construction,§ as if I had written it not only in good earnest, but even with ostentation. Nor satisfi'd with this, he endeavours to draw a blemish from my merriment, upon the untainted reputation of the best of Kings; as if Masters were oblig'd to answer for their Servants triflings. Lastly, To varnish over his perversness, he puts in a passage or two out of *Esay* and *Solomon* pleasantly, as nothing is secure from a prophane wit.

This I confess befell me in a wondrous age; for, who could have imagin'd so ill humour'd a creature likely to be born, whom such a little fancy upon the Licence of Ambassadors (who act only in Politicks) should so grievously offend; whereas we daily see the severity it self of holy Writ, so foully adulterated by some that are Masters of equivocations, pious frauds, and mental reservations? And this not by the by, nor in jest, or in the *Album* of Friends, where idle things and truths us'd to be set down with equal security, but on set purpose, and from the Pulpit, with priviledge and Authority of Superiors? Yea but it is *Scioppius* that has rose up, and what answer from me doth he expect? I remember indeed that being at *Venice,* my Family was struck with an *Anathema* in *Baronius* his *Paraenesis;* I remember that then also some things of the like sort were cast at me by *Gomitulus,* a Jesuit of *Perugia,* and by *Anthony Possevin,* which, although they flow'd from galled spirits, yet however I bore in silence, for, these were men of no mean repute, at least at home, and, such eminency as they had, qualifi'd the injury. But when a hungry Renegado, a dirty Sharker about the *Romish* court, only scribbles that he may dine, and a raw Pedant, not at all vers'd in more solid Learning, falls to treating of Church-matters; when the spawn of a Sexton, and an Ammunition Trull,[3] rages with that irreverence against a King, whose eminent knowledge in things divine and humane, and constant evenness of Justice, would beget a veneration to any private person; when a *German* quitting the modesty and honesty of his Countrey, breathes nothing throughout his whole Book but the subversion of Kings

---

[3] **See what is published of the Life and Parents of* Scioppius, *pag.* 127.

and Kingdomes; when, finally, the same mouth which had called
the Society of the Jesuits, a company of Parricides; and now
having begun to smell the *Roman* Kitchins, styles them the
*Prætorian Band of Gods Militia: Quis iniquæ tam patiens Urbis,
quæ istud Animal pabulatur, tàm ferreus ut teneat se?* Who can
endure so base a City (that feeds the Beast) or is so insensible
as to contain himself?

Wherefore (setting aside all lightness) I commune with you
by this Letter seriously; and from my heart (most accomplished
Velserus) desiring and beseeching you by our common bond
of Humanity, by our conscience in the same Faith and Baptism,
that (according to the power I know you have amidst your
people) you would quell these *Scioppians,* that such scandals
of mankind, and shames even to the best Causes, being banished
from Christian Society, good men may retain their esteem, and
Princes their Dignity; that your Marts may not be pester'd with
the prostituted Pens of Parasites, nor the Press (the brave Invention of the *Germans*) be so miserably tormented; and lastly,
that (as much as in our weakness lyes,) the happy quiet of
Kingdomes and Churches may ensue, which the highest Teacher,
and example of peace hath commended to us. But if he cannot
leave off that impudent scurrility (which from his base extrac-
tion he has very suitably contracted) without great inconvenience to his Belly, surely he deserves at least to have his
Commons⁵ shortned, for that execrable subtilty, whereby he
seems to himself quicker-sighted then the Council of *Trent:* for
they, first of any (that I know of) decreed,⁴ that Traditions and
holy Scripture were with equal affection, only, of piety and
reverence to be received: But this new Ecclesiastick, not in the
Album of Friends, but in the 485th. Page of his *sine Syntagma,*⁵
pronounces with a blasphemous and shameless mouth, *that the
Authority of Tradition is above the written Word of God.* I
could produce six hundred such *Scioppieties,* but that were to
rake a Dunghill. Wherefore farewel most Noble Sir, and again
farewel.

From *London, Decemb.* 2. after the *Julian* Accompt, in the
Year of our onely Mediatour, 1612.

4 **April* 8. Ses[sion] 4.
5 *Treatise on the Rite of Worship.*

2. TO THE LORD [FRANCIS] BACON,
VICOUNT ST. ALBANS

RIGHT HONOURABLE, AND MY VERY GOOD LORD,

I have your Lordships Letters dated the 20th. of *October,* and I have withall by the care of my Cousin Mr. *Thomas Meawtis,* and by your own speciall favour, three Copies[6] of that Work wherewith your Lordship hath done a great and everliving benefit to all the Children of Nature; and to Nature herself in her uttermost extent and latitude: who never before had so noble, nor so true an Interpreter, or (as I am readier to style your Lordship) never so inward a Secretary of her Cabinet: But of your said Work (which came but this week to my hands) I shall finde occasion to speak more hereafter; having yet read only the first Book thereof, and a few Aphorismes of the second. For it is not a banquet, that men may superficially taste, and put up the rest in their pockets; but in truth, a solid feast, which requireth due mastication. Therefore when I have once my self perused the whole, I determine to have it read peice by peice at certain houres in my domestick Colledge,[7] as an ancient Author: For I have learn'd thus much by it already, that we are extreamly mistaken in the computation[8] of Antiquity, by searching it backwards, because indeed the first times were the youngest; especially in points of naturall discoverie and experience. For though I grant that *Adam* knew the natures of all Beasts, and *Solomon* of all Plants, not only more then any, but more then all since their time; Yet that was by divine infusion, and therfore they did not need any such *Organum* as your Lordship hath now delivered to the world; nor we neither, if they had left us the memories of their wisdom.

But I am gone further then I meant in speaking of this excellent Labour, while the delight yet I feel, and even the pride

6 Bacon's *Novum Organum,* published 1620. Wotton writes at the end of the same year from Vienna, where he had been sent as ambassador extraordinary to Emperor Ferdinand. The battle referred to in the letter is that of Weisser Berg near Prague on Nov. 8, 1620, where the hopes of Frederick, the Elector Palatine (and son-in-law of King James) to become King of Bohemia were completely shattered.

7 Wotton's customary term for the cultivated young Englishmen who were members of his household when he was in Venice as ambassador.

that I take in a certain Congeniality[8] (as I may term it) with your Lordships studies, wil scant[§] let me cease: And indeed, I ow your Lordship even by promise (which you are pleased to remember, thereby doubly binding me) some trouble this way: I mean by the commerce of *Philosophical* experiments, which surely, of all other, is the most ingenuous Traffick: Therefore, for a beginning, let me tell your Lordship a pretty thing which I saw coming down the *Danuby*, though more remarkable for the Application, then for the Theory. I lay a night at *Lintz*, the Metropolis of the higher *Austria;* but then in very low estate, having been newly taken by the Duke of *Bavaria:* who, *blandiente fortunâ*,[9] was gone on to the late effects:[§] There I found *Keplar*, a man famous in the Sciences, as your Lordship knowes, to whom I purpose to convey from hence one of your Books, that he may see we have some of our own that can honour our King, as well as he hath done with his *Harmonica*.[1] In this mans study I was much taken with the draught of a Landskip on a piece of paper, me thoughts masterly done: Whereof enquiring the Author, he bewrayed[§] with a smile it was himself, adding he had done it, *non tanquam Pictor, sed tanquam Mathematicus*.[2] This set me on fire: at last he told me how. He hath a little black tent (of what stuffe is not much importing[§]) which he can suddenly set up where he will in a field, and it is convertible[§] (like a Wind-mill) to all quarters at pleasure, capable of not much more then one man, as I conceive, & perhaps at no great ease; exactly[§] close and dark, save at one hole, about an inch and a half in the *Diameter*, to which he applies a long perspective-trunke,[§] with the convexe glasse fitted to the said hole, and the concave taken out at the other end, which extendeth to about the middle of this erected Tent, through which the visible radiations of all the objects without are intromitted, falling upon a paper, which is accommodated to receive them, and so he traceth them with his Pen in their natural appearance, turning his little Tent round by degrees till he hath designed

8 Logan Pearsall Smith, Wotton's biographer and editor, points out that the word is Wotton's coinage. This is its first appearance.
9 Flattered by Fortune.
1 *De Harmonice Mundi* [*The Harmony of the World*], dedicated to King James in 1619.
2 Not as a painter, but as a mathematician.

the whole aspect of the field: this I have described to your Lordship, because I think there might be good use made of it, for Chorography: For otherwise, to make Landskips by it were illiberall;§ though surely no Painter can do them so precisely. Now from these artificiall and naturall curiosities, let me a little direct your Lordship to the contemplation of *Fortune*.

Here, by a sleight Battel full of miserable errours (if I had leisure to set them down) all is reduced,§ or neer the point. In the Provinces there is nothing but of fluctuation§ and submission, the ordinary consequences of Victory; wherein the triumphs of the field do not so much vex my soul, as the triumphs of the Pulpit: For what noise will now the Jesuite disseminate more in every corner, then *victrix causa Deo placuit;*[3] which yet was but the Gospel of a Poet: No, my Lord, when I revolve what great things *Zisca* did in the first troubles of his Countrie, that were grounded upon conscience, I am tempted to believe the All-distinguishing-eye hath been more displeased with some humane§ affections§ in this business, then with the businesse it self.

I am now preparing my departing toward my other employment, for in my first instructions I had a power to go hence when this controversie should be decided, either by Treaty, or by Fortune; whereof now the worser meanes have perverted the better.

Here I leave the *French* Ambassadors upon the Stage, as I found them; being willing (*quod solum superest*[4]) to deale between the Emperour and *Bethlehem Gabor,* with whom I have nothing to doe as he is now singled.§

Betwixt this and *Italy* I purpose to collect the memorablest observations that I have taken of this great Affaire, and to present a copy thereof unto your Lordships indulgent, not to your severe Judgment.

The present I cannot end (though I have too much usurped upon your pretious time) without the return of my humble thanks unto your Lordship for the kind remembrance of my Cousin Mr. *John Meawtis* in your letter to mee, and of your recommendation of him before; being a Gentleman, in truth of sweet conditions§ and strong abilities: I shal now transport him

---

3 The victorious cause was pleasing to God.
4 Since that is all there's left to do.

over the Alps, where we will both serve your Lordship, and love
one another. And so beseeching God to blesse your Lordship with
long life and honour, I humbly rest,

> *Your Lordships, &c.*

3. [TO SIR DUDLEY CARLETON]

MY VERIE GOOD LORD.

We have at last a new Pope after many scrutinies[s] and enclosure of the Cardinals almost three weekes. He hath assumed
the name of Urbanus VIII out of an affectionat remembrance
(as some saye) of much frendship which passed betweene him
and the Cardinal Fachinetti who was Urbanus VII. By birthe a
Florentine of no great parentage. His owne name is Barberini.
About which I can not omitt a pleasant note. They have taken
a beleefe in Rome that Popes must have an R. in thei're names
alternatively: Uno si, l'altro no,[5] which having a so falen[s] out
for a good while some vacant witt did take it up for a rule. And
it hath gotten such credit that Borghese before his entring into
this last Conclave would needs consult with certayn Astrologers
(who as your Lordship knows abounde in that Court) whether
some of his Uncles Creatures and in particular Gimnasio might
spuntare[6] at this tyme. Now, Barbarini who hath two R. R.
having succeeded Ludovisio who had none will mightily au-
thorize that foolish conceyte[s] amongst them and putt Campori
(the Darling of Borghese) out of all hope for the next turne
likewise. Methinkes your Lordship should reade this with a
smile to see them choose Popes as we doe oysters at home when
the moneth hath an R. in it. But to retourne to some more
serious consideration of this Man. He was long since 4 yeares
Nuntio[s] in Fraunce and gott his Cardinalship by commendation
of Henry 4. So as the Frenche have an interest in his fortune
as no doubt the Spaniards will have in his person. He was made
by the concurrence as well of Ludovisio as Borghese not as the
most confident[s] to bothe or to eather; but as the least distrusted
by Ludovisio among the Borghesians, having been a kinde of
retired unmedling man. A good humanist, a great Canoniste,

5 One, yes; another, no.
6 Rise, prevail (*Ital.*).

and one of the best Poete's that since Nicolaus V hath been in that chayre: so as his tymes are likely to be somewhat elegant and his humours tractable and yet one of the most Poetical Spiritts that we have amongst thease Gentlemen heere is the harshest man. He hath three nephews and two Brothers. Of whom he is likely to dispose before he thincke of the Valtolina. And therefore your Count Mansfeldt may marche towards Burgundie at leasure. From hense they have deputed 4 to Congratulat with him, two Procuratori,$ Erizzo and Barbaro, and the other two, are Saranzo and Zen already at Rome. But heere we are sodaynly caled to a greater bussinesse. For yesternight the Duke after some fewe dayes retirement uppon his usual indispositions, was surprized with so sharpe a Catarre as tooke from him his speache: so as they have given him the extreame unction and his Physitians yeilde him gonn. This will holde me heere till the election of a newe and give me occasion to entertayne your Lordship a weeke or two more with the state of oure Broglio[7] when the Candidati shall appeare.

And for the present I rest

Your Lordship's ever affectionatly to serve you,

Henry Wotton.

Venice $\frac{2}{11}$ August.

1623.

4. [TO CHARLES I]

MY MOST DEAR AND DREAD SOVERAIGN,

As I gave Your Majesty fore-knowledge of my intention to enter into the Church, and had your Gracious Approvement therein, so I hold it a second dutie to Your Majesty, and satisfaction to my self, to inform you likewise by mine own hand, both how far I have proceeded, and upon what motives; that it may appear unto your Majesty (as I hope it will) an act of conscience, and of reason; and not of greedinesse and ambition. Your Majesty will be therefore pleased to know, that I have

[7] Intrigue, scheming (*Ital.*).

lately taken the degree of Deacon;[8] and so far am I from aiming at any high flight, out of my former Sphear, that there I intend to rest. Perhaps I want not some perswaders, that measuring me by their affections, or by your Majesties goodnesse, and not by mine own defects or ends, would make me think, that yet before I dye, I might become a great Prelat. And I need no perswasion to tell me, that if I would undertake the Pastorall Function, I could peradventure by casualty,[§] out of the Patronages belonging to your Royall Colledge,[9] without further troubling of your Majesty, cast some good Benefice upon my self, whereof we have one, if it were vacant, that is worth more then my Provostship. But as they were strucken with horrour, who beheld the majesty of the Lord descending upon the Mount *Sinai:* so, God knowes, the nearer I approach to contemplate his greatnesse, the more I tremble to assume any cure of souls even in the lowest degree, that were bought at so high a price: *premant torcular qui vindemiarunt:* Let them presse the grapes, & fill the vessels, and tast the wine, that have gathered the Vintage. But shal I sit and do nothing in the Porch of Gods House, whereinto I am entred? God himself forbid, who was the Supream Mover. What Service then do I propound to the Church? or what contentment to mine own mind? First, for the point of Conscience, I can now hold my place Canonically, which I held before but dispensatively,[§] & withal I can exercise an Archidiaconal Authoritie annexed thereunto, though of small extent, and no benefit, yet somtimes of pious & necessary use. I comfort my self also with this Christian hope, That Gentlemen and Knights Sons, who are trained up with us in a Seminary of Church-men, (which was the will of the holy Founder) will by my example, (without vanity be it spoken) not be ashamed, after the sight of Courtly Weeds,[§] to put on a Surplice. Lastly, I consider, that this resolution which I have taken, is not unsutable even to my civill imployments abroad, of which for the most part Religion was the subject; nor to my observations which have been spent that way in discovery of the *Roman* Arts and Practices, wherof I hope to yeild the World some account, though rather by my pen, then by my voice. For though I must

---

8 Wotton seems to have become deacon not long after July 10, 1627.
9 Wotton was Provost of the "College" of Eton from July, 1624.

humbly confesse, that both my Conceptions and Expressions be
weak, yet I do more trust my deliberation then my memory: or
if your Majesty will give me leave to paint my self in higher
terms, I think, I shall be bolder against the judgements, then
against the faces of men. This I conceive to be a piece of mine
own Character; so as my private Study must be my Theater
rather then a Pulpit; and my Books my Auditours, as they are
all my Treasure. Howsoever, if I can produce nothing else for
the use of Church and State, yet it shall be comfort enough to
the little remnant of my life to compose some Hymnes unto his
endlesse Glory, who hath called me (for which his Name be
ever blessed) though late to his Service, yet early to the knowledge of his truth, and sense of his mercy. To which ever commending your Majesty, and your Royall Actions, with most
hearty and humble prayers, I rest

> *Your Majesties most devoted poor Servant.*

5. TO THE AUTHOR [JOHN MILTON], UPON THE FOLLOWING POEM
[A MASK PRESENTED AT LUDLOW-CASTLE (COMUS)]

From the Colledge, this 13. of April, 1638

SIR,

It was a special favour, when you lately bestowed upon me
here, the first taste of your acquaintance, though no longer then
to make me know that I wanted more time to value it, and to
enjoy it rightly; and in truth, if I could then have imagined your
farther stay in these parts, which I understood afterwards by
Mr. *H.*, I would have been bold in our vulgar⁵ phrase to mend
my draught (for you left me with an extreme thirst) and to
have begged your conversation again, joyntly with your said
learned Friend, at a poor meal or two, that we might have
banded⁵ together som good Authors of the antient time: Among
which, I observed you to have been familiar.

Since your going, you have charg'd me with new Obligations,
both for a very kinde Letter from you dated the sixth of this

Month, and for a dainty peece of entertainment which came therwith. Wherin I should much commend the Tragical part, if the Lyrical did not ravish me with a certain Dorique[§] delicacy in your Songs and Odes, wherunto I must plainly confess to have seen yet nothing parallel in our Language: *Ipsa mollities*.[1] But I must not omit to tell you, that I now onely owe you thanks for intimating unto me (how modestly soever) the true Artificer. For the work it self, I had view'd some good while before, with singular delight, having receiv'd it from our common Friend Mr. *R.* in the very close of the late *R*'s Poems, Printed at *Oxford,* wherunto it was added (as I now suppose) that the Accessory might help out the Principal, according to the Art of *Stationers,* and to leave the Reader *Con la bocca dolce*.[2]

Now, Sir, concerning your travels, wherin I may chalenge a little more priviledge of Discours with you; I suppose you will not blanch[§] *Paris* in your way; therfore I have been bold to trouble you with a few lines to Mr. *M. B.* whom you shall easily find attending the young Lord *S.* as his Governour, and you may surely receive from him good directions for the shaping of your farther journey into *Italy,* where he did reside by my choice som time for the King, after mine own recess[§] from *Venice.*

I should think that your best Line[§] will be thorow the whole length of *France* to *Marseilles,* and thence by Sea to *Genoa,* whence the passage into *Tuscany* is as Diurnal as a *Gravesend* Barge: I hasten as you do to *Florence,* or *Siena,* the rather to tell you a short story from the interest you have given me in your safety.

At *Siena* I was tabled in the House of one *Alberto Scipioni* an old *Roman* Courtier in dangerous times, having bin Steward to the *Duca di Pagliano,* who with all his Family were strangled, save this onely man that escap'd by foresight of the Tempest: With him I had often much chat of those affairs; Into which he took pleasure to look back from his Native Harbour; and at my departure toward *Rome* (which had been the center of his experience) I had wonn confidence enough to beg his advice, how I might carry my self securely there, without offence of

1 Tenderness itself.
2 With a pleasant taste in his mouth.

others, or of mine own conscience. *Signor Arrigo mio* (sayes he) *I pensieri stretti, & il viso sciolto*³ will go safely over the whole World: Of which *Delphian* Oracle (for so I have found it) your judgement doth need no commentary; and therfore (Sir) I will commit you with it to the best of all securities, Gods dear love, remaining

> Your Friend as much at command
> as any of longer date
> *Henry Wootton.*

Postscript.

SIR, *I have expresly sent this my Foot-boy to prevent your departure without som acknowledgement from me of the receipt of your obliging Letter, having my self through som busines, I know not how, neglected the ordinary conveyance. In any part where I shall understand you fixed, I shall be glad, and diligent to entertain you with Home-Novelties; even for som fomentation of our friendship, too soon interrupted in the Cradle.*

6. TO IZ[AAK] WA[LTON]
In answer of a Letter, requesting him to performe his promise of Writing the Life of Dr. Dunne

MY WORTHY FRIEND,

I am not able to yeeld any reason, no, not so much as may satisfie my self, why a most ingenuous Letter of yours hath lyen so long by me (as it were in§ lavender) without an answer, save this only, The pleasure I have taken in your Stile and Conceptions, together with a Meditation of the Subject you propound, may seem to have cast me into a gentle slumber. But, being now awaked, I do herein returne you most heartie thanks for the kinde prosecution§ of your first motion,§ touching a just office,§ due to the memory of our ever memorable Friend: To whose good fame, though it be needlesse to add any thing, (and my age considered, almost hopelesse from my Pen); yet I wil

---

³ Wotton translates elsewhere, "Your thoughts close, and your countenance loose."

endeavour to perform my promise, if it were but even for this cause, that in saying somwhat of the Life of so deserving a man, I may perchance overlive mine own.

That which you add of Dr. *King*, (now made Dean of *Roches-ter*,[4] and by that translated[§] into my native soile,) is a great spur unto me. With whom I hope shortly to conferre about it in my passage towards *Boughton Malherb*, (which was my geniall[§] Aire) and invite him to a friendship with that Family where his predecessor was familiarly acquainted. I shall write at large to you by the next Messenger (being at present a little in businesse); and then I shall set down certaine generall heads, wherein I desire information by your loving diligence; hoping shortly to injoy your own ever welcome company in this approaching time of the *Flye* and the *Corke*. And so I rest,

Your very heartie poor Friend to serve You,
H. Wotton.

John Chamberlain

I. TO DUDLEY CARLETON

SIR,

Though I looked for you before this time, and have often wisht you here among your old schoolefellowes that are almost all come up to the Parliament: yet as matters are lately fallen out about your Lord,[5] I am well content you be absent. Not that your Lord (as I hope) can be any way toucht with this divelish conspiracie,[6] but that neerenes of name, bloude, longe and inward dependance, and familiaritie, cannot but leave some aspersion, that will not easilie or lightly be washt of without time: in which consideration I heare he is rather wisht then willed[§]

---

4 Henry King was made Dean of Rochester on Feb. 6, 1639. This reference and that to fishing in the last sentence date the letter in the early spring of 1639.
5 Henry Percy, 9th Earl of Northumberland.
6 The Gunpowder Plot.

to kepe his house. I cannot but remember what you have divers times told me touching Thomas Percie, that you suspected him to be a subtile flattering daungerous knave. He hath not only verefied your judgement, but exceeded all degrees of comparison, and gon beyond Nero and Caligula that wisht all Rome but one head that they might cut yt of at a stroke, for he at one blowe wold have ruined the whole realme. He had hired the house or lodging next to the Parliament, together with the seller or vault under the upper house: into which by the meanes of one John-son[7] his man a superstitious papist, (or rather a priest as is thought) he hath conveyed any time this twelvemoneth as much pouder in sachells, as fowre or five and thirty barrells, hogges-heads, and firkins could contein, with intent the first day of the parlement when the King shold be in his speach to blowe them all up: and had so cunningly covered them with billets, faggots and such trash, that without long search they could not be dis-covered, and but that God blinded him or some of his, to send this inclosed [8] without name or date to the Lord Mountegle, yt was very like to take effect. But the carieng yt to the Lord of Salisberie and so to the King, yt gave such light, that watch being set, the fellowe was taken making his traines[§] at midnight with a blinde[§] lanterne, and presently confessed the plot, yet with such shew of resolution that he seemed to be cheifly greved that yt had wanted successe. The next day he was caried to the Towre, but what Sir William Waade (that is lieutenant) and

7 Guy Fawkes gave his name as John Johnson for several days after his arrest.
8 Chamberlain enclosed a copy of the anonymous warning given to William Parker, 4th Lord Monteagle. The warning was one of the most widely circu-lated letters of the seventeenth century, and it has remained sufficiently in de-mand that the Public Record Office is able to furnish a print from a stock nega-tive. It is reprinted here from such a print of PRO SP./14/216/No. 2, through the kindness of the Keeper of Public Records:

my lord out of the love i beare to some of youere frends i have a caer of youer preservacion therfor i would advyse yowe as yowe tender youer lyf to devyse some exscuse to shift of youer attendance at this parleament for god and man hathe concurred to punishe the wickednes of this tyme and thinke not slightlye of this advertisment but retyere youre self into youre contri wheare yowe maye expect the event in safti for thowghe theare be no appar-ance of anni stir yet i saye they shall receyve a terrible blowe this parleament and yet they shall not seie who hurts them this cowncel is not to be con-temned because it maye do yowe good and can do yowe no harme for the dangere is passed as soon as yowe have burnt the letter and i hope god will give yowe the grace to mak good use of it to whose holy proteccion i comend yowe.

other examiners have wrange out of him I cannot learne: only
I heare Sir Edward Bainham come lately out of the Lowe Countries is sought for: and some five or sixe Jesuites and priests
taken in a privie[§] search. Percie comming up on a sleveles[§]
errand and before he was looked for to your Lord, durst not
tarry to see the event,[§] but went away that night that his man
was taken. Curious folkes observe that this deliveraunce hapned
to the King the fift of November aunswerable to the fift of
August, both Tewsdayes, and this plot to be executed by Johnson as that at Johnstowne. On Tewsday at night we had great
ringing and as great store of bonfires as ever I thincke was
seene. And this is all I can write or remember in this matter.
The Earle of Cumberland died of a flixe[§] the 30th of October
leaving the earledome to his brother, and fifteen or sixten
thousand pound to his daughter, so she make no further claime;
his Lady and he were reconciled not longe before his death, but
yt fell out odly that he desiring she shold receve[§] with him she
was not prepared. The Lord Knolles is newly become a widower
by the death of his old Lady Chandos. Dr. Andrewes was con-
secrated bishop of Chichester on Sunday last: the mariages of
the earle of Essex and the younge Lord Crambourne to the Lord
Chamberlaines daughters are put of till toward Christmas. Sir
Edwin Sands bookes were burnt on Satterday in Paules Church-
yard by order of the high commission and not without his owne
consent as is saide. Sir Fraunces Bacon hath set foorth a new
worke of the proficience and advancement of learning. Monsieur
Beaumont the French ambassador went homeward the first of
this moneth, and hath blotted his former reputation with very
mecanicall[§] tricks at parting: for having 2000 ounces of plate
geven him he cavilled for 500 more, as having seene a president[§]
of the like, which being graunted him, he begd two horses more
by name of the King, besides pictures great and small with
jewells at his owne appointment,[§] and not a noble man or other
of his neere acquaintaunce but he got horses, geldings or somwhat of him: and the impost[§] of 60 tunne[§] of wine of the Lord
Treasurer which he sold to French marchants for threescore
pound: with divers other such petti larceries,[§] as yf he made no
conscience to robbe the Egiptians. We heare that Master Win-
wod hath a sonne, and that the States[§] and the Lady Conway

were his gossipps.§ Thus praeng you to remember my satten and
the other trincketts I commit you to God in great haste. From
London this 7th of November 1605.

Yours most assuredly
John Chamberlain.

To my assured goode frend Master Dudley Carleton geve these
at Paris.

2. TO SIR DUDLEY CARLETON

MY VERY GOODE LORD:

Your new messenger brought me your letter of the 19th of
this present, but he could tell me no newes of the printed or
painted§ paper you write of. I remember that in my last letter I saide that Sir Walter Raleigh was not secure, but now
he is past all peradventure§ for upon Thursday morning he
was beheaded in the old palace at Westminster twixt the Parlement House and the church. On Wensday he was brought
from the Towre to the Kings-bench barre, (as they say the
manner is when a man lives above a yeare and a day after he
is condemned) and there demaunded what he could say for himself why the sentence pronounced against him at Winchester
shold not be put in execution. The summe of his aunswer was,
that the King had imployed him in his service and geven him
a commission wherin he stiled him his loyall subject, and withall
geven him *potestatem vitæ et necis*,[9] which did amount to a
pardon, for in all reason he must be master of his owne life that
hath power over other mens: the judges replied that there is no
pardon for treason by implication, wherfore he must find a better
plea or undergo the sentence. Then he spake of his triall at
Winchester and avowed that all or the far greater part of those
that were present did acquit him in theyre conscience, and that
the Kings gracious forbearing him so long, (and but for this late
accident longer wold have don, even to an hundred yeares yf
nature could have drawne out his life so long), did shew that
his Majestie approved his innocence. But in conclusion he was

---

[9] Power of life and death.

willed§ to prepare himself, and so was delivered to the sheriffes of London and conveyed to the Gatehouse, where he spent the rest of that day in writing letters to the King and others, and in prayer with the Deane of Westminster, who came the next morning at five a clocke and ministred to him the communion and when he had broken his fast about eight a clocke came to the scaffold, where he found the earles of Arundell, Oxford, Northampton, the Lord of Doncaster and divers others. He made a speach of more then halfe an howre, wherin he cleered himself of having any intelligence with Fraunce, (which had ben objected to him,) more then to save his life and hide himself from the Kinges indignation: then that he never had any yll intent towards his Majestie not so much as in thought, that he had no other pretence nor end in his last viage then the inriching of the King, the realme, himself and his followers: that he never had any undutifull speach concerning his Majestie with the runagate French phisician, nor ever offered to Sir Lewes Stukeley 10000ᵘ to go with him into Fraunce, nor told him that the Lord Carew had geven him advise to be gon, and that he and the Lord of Doncaster wold maintain him in Fraunce, of which points he had ben accused by them, and though he protested not only to forgeve them but to pray God to forgeve them, yet he thought fit to geve men warning of such persons. To all this and much more he tooke God so often and so solemnly to witnes, that he was beleved of all that heard him. He spake somwhat of the death of the earle of Essex and how sory he was for him, for though he was of a contrarie faction, yet he fore-saw that those who estemed him then in that respect, wold cast him of as they did afterward. He confessed himself the greatest sinner that he knew, and no marvayle as having ben a souldier, a sea-man and a courtier: he excused the disfiguring of himself [1] by the example of David who fained himself mad to avoide daunger: and never heard yt imputed to him for a sinne. In conclusion he spake and behaved himself so, without any shew of feare or affectation that he moved much commiseration, and all that saw him confesse that his end was *omnibus numeris*

[1] On Aug. 20, 1618, Chamberlain wrote Carleton about Raleigh, "the pittifull plight he was in with biles§ and botches was don by art, as likewise a counterfeiting a while to be distracted."

absolutus,[2] and as far as man can discern every way perfect. Yt will not be amisse to set downe some few passages of divers that I have heard. The morning that he went to execution there was a cup of excellent sacke brought him and beeing asked how he liked yt, as the fellow (saide he) that drincking of St. Giles bowle as he went to Tiburn, saide yt was goode drincke yf a man might tarrie by yt. As he went from Westminster Hall to the Gatehouse, he espied Sir Hugh Beeston in the thronge and calling to him prayed he wold see him dye to morow: Sir Hugh to make sure worke got a letter from Secretarie Lake to the sheriffe to see him placed conveniently, and meeting them as they came nere to the scaffold delivered his letter but the sheriffe by mishap had left his spectacles at home and put the letter in his pocket. In the mean time Sir Hugh beeing thrust by, Sir Walter bad him farewell and saide I know not what shift[§] you will make, but I am sure to have a place. When the hangman asked him forgivenes he desired to see the axe, and feeling the edge he saide that yt was a fayre sharpe medicine to cure him of all his diseases and miseries. When he was laide downe some found fault that his face was west-ward, and wold have him turned, wherupon rising he saide yt was no great matter which way a mans head stoode so his heart lay right. He had geven order to the executioner that after some short meditation when he stretcht forth his handes he shold dispatch him. After once or twise putting foorth his handes, the fellow out of timerousnes (or what other cause) forbearing, he was faine to bid him strike, and so at two blowes he tooke of his head, though he stirred not a whit after the first. The people were much affected at the sight insomuch that one was heard say that we had not such another head to cut of. Another wisht the head and braines to be upon S. N.[3] shoulders. There was great meanes made for his life, and I heare the Quene wrote very earnestly to the King as he tendered[§] her health to spare him for that she had receved great goode by his receits.[§] I heare not so much of her recoverie of late as when I wrote last, but rather that she goes *peggiorando*,[4] insomuch that yt is doubted whether the King come

2 Complete in every way.
3 Sir Robert *N*aunton, one of the *S*ecretaries of State.
4 Getting worse.

hither to day from Tiballs or go directly to Hampton-court where she lies. The Spanish Dominican lately come hither is saide like-wise to have laboured for Sir Walter Raleigh, as finding his death wold much alienate the mindes of our people as yf he were sacri-ficed to the malice of the Spaniards: but yt is verelie thought some unseemly speaches fathered upon him whether truly or falsly by those two fellowes were the principall motives of his ruine. Yt is saide we shold have some declaration set out touch-ing the causes of his execution at this time, but whether his protestations and manner of dieng may alter the case God knowes: for he died very religiously, and every way like a Christian, insomuch that the Deane of Westminster (they say) commends him excedingly and sayes he was as redy and as able to geve as take instruction. His execution was the more re-markeable for that yt fell out the day of the Lord Maiors triumph, though yt began with a tragedie, and beeing a reasonable fayre morning grew very fowle all the day after. Monsieur Clerc the French Agent went away this day sevenight and I heard yester-day that Master Beecher and the Lord Weems were come out of Fraunce. I am sory we shold have no body there to see how matters passe, for we are possessed here that the States[s] biais runs very strongly that way. On Wensday, Sir Humfrie Tufton was censured in the Star Chamber for bastinading Christofer Nevill the Lord of Abergavenies sonne, in a jealous humor that he made love to his wife, whom he caused to write him a letter and so drew him into the trap. His whole fine for himself and his men one way and other comes to almost 4000^{li}. Besides he is to make some submission in that court, and some satisfaction to Nevill as the earles marshalls shall awarde. His two men are to stand on the pillorie and to be whipt: Master Nevill is to have 1000^{li} of this fine for his costs. And so with the remem-brance of my best service to my goode Lady I commend you to the protection of the Almighty. From London this last of Octo-ber 1618.

Your Lordships to commaund
John Chamberlain.

John Milton

OF EDUCATION
TO MASTER SAMUEL HARTLIB

MASTER HARTLIB,

I am long since perswaded, that to say, or doe ought worth memory, and imitation, no purpose or respect should sooner move us, then simply the love of God, and of mankinde. Neverthelesse to write now the reforming of Education, though it be one of the greatest and noblest designes, that can be thought on, and for the want whereof this nation perishes, I had not yet at this time been induc't, but by your earnest entreaties, and serious conjurements;§ as having my minde for the present halfe diverted in the persuance of some other assertions, the knowledge and the use of which, cannot but be a great furtherance both to the enlargement of truth, and honest living, with much more peace. Nor should the lawes of any private friendship have prevail'd with me to divide thus, or transpose my former thoughts, but that I see those aims, those actions which have won you with me the esteem of a person sent hither by some good providence from a farre country to be the occasion and the incitement of great good to this Iland. And, as I hear, you have obtain'd the same repute with men of most approved wisdom, and some of highest authority among us. Not to mention the learned correspondence which you hold in forreigne parts, and the extraordinary pains and diligence which you have us'd in this matter both heer, and beyond the Seas; either by the definite will of God so ruling, or the peculiar sway of nature, which alsc is Gods working. Neither can I thinke that so reputed, and so valu'd as you are, you would to the forfeit of your own discerning ability, impose upon me an unfit and over ponderous argument, but that the satisfaction which you professe to have receiv'd from those incidentall discourses which we have wander'd into, hath prest & almost constrain'd you into a perswasion, that what you require from me in this point, I neither ought, nor can in conscience deferre beyond this time both of so much need at once, and so much opportunity to trie what God hath determin'd. I will not resist therefore, what ever it is either of divine, or humane obligement that you lay upon me; but will forthwith set down in writing, as you request me, that voluntary *Idea,* which hath long in silence presented it self to me, of a better Education, in extent and comprehension farre more large, and yet of time farre shorter, and of attainment farre more certain, then hath been yet in practice. Briefe I shall endeavour to be; for that which I have to say, assuredly this nation hath extreame need should be done sooner then spok'n. To tell you therefore what I have benefited herein among old renowned Authors, I shall spare; and to search what many modern *Janua's* and *Didactics*[5] more then ever I shall read, have projected, my inclination leads me not. But if you can accept of these few observations which have flowr'd off, and are as it were the burnishing of many studious and contemplative yeers altogether spent in the search of religious and civil knowledge, and such as pleas'd you so well in the relating, I here give you them to dispose of.

The end then of learning is to repair the ruins of our first parents by regaining to know God aright, and out of that knowledge to love him, to imitate him, to be like him, as we may the neerest by possessing our souls of true vertue, which being united to the heavenly grace of faith makes up the highest perfection. But because our understanding cannot in this body found it selfe but on sensible[§] things, nor arrive so cleerly to the knowledge of God and things invisible, as by orderly conning[§] over the visible and inferior creature, the same method is necessarily to be follow'd in all discreet[§] teaching. And seeing every nation affords not experience and tradition anough for all kinde of learning, therefore we are chiefly taught the languages of those people who have at any time been most industrious after wisdom; So that language is but the instrument convaying to us things usefull to be known. And though a lin-

---

5 Milton has in mind two works of John Amos Comenius, *Janua Linguarum Reserta* [*The Door of Languages Opened*] and *Didactica Magna* [*The Great Didactic* (or *Instructor*)].

guist should pride himselfe to have all the tongues that *Babel*
cleft the world into, yet, if he have not studied the solid things
in them as well as the words and lexicons, he were nothing so
much to be esteem'd a learned man, as any yeoman or trades-
man competently wise in his mother dialect only. Hence appear
the many mistakes which have made learning generally so unpleasing and so unsuccessfull; first we do amisse to spend seven
or eight yeers meerly in scraping together so much miserable
Latin, and Greek, as might be learnt otherwise easily and delightfully in one yeer. And that which casts our proficiency
therein so much behinde, is our time lost partly in too oft idle
vacancies§ given both to schools and Universities, partly in a
preposterous§ exaction, forcing the empty wits of children to
compose Theams, verses, and Orations, which are the acts of
ripest judgement and the finall work of a head fill'd by long
reading, and observing, with elegant maxims, and copious invention. These are not matters to be wrung from poor striplings,
like blood out of the nose, or the plucking of untimely fruit:
besides the ill habit which they get of wretched barbarizing§
against the Latin and Greek *idiom,* with their untutor'd *Angli-
cisms,* odious to be read, yet not to be avoided without a well
continu'd and judicious conversing§ among pure Authors digested, which they scarce taste, wheras, if after some preparatory
grounds of speech by their certain forms§ got into memory, they
were led to the praxis§ thereof in some chosen short book lesson'd
throughly to them, they might then forthwith proceed to learn
the substance of good things, and Arts in due order, which would
bring the whole language quickly into their power. This I take
to be the most rationall and most profitable way of learning languages, and whereby we may best hope to give account to God
of our youth spent herein: And for the usuall method of teaching
Arts, I deem it to be an old errour of universities not yet well
recover'd from the Scholastick grosnesse of barbarous ages, that
in stead of beginning with Arts most easie, and those be such as
are most obvious to the sence, they present their young unma-
triculated§ novices at first comming with the most intellective abstractions of Logick & metaphysicks: So that they having but
newly left those Grammatick flats & shallows where they stuck
unreasonably to learn a few words with lamentable construction,

and now on the sudden transported under another climat to be
tost and turmoild with their unballasted wits in fadomles§ and
unquiet deeps of controversie, do for the most part grow into
hatred and contempt of learning, mockt and deluded all this
while with ragged notions and babblements, while they expected
worthy and delightfull knowledge; till poverty or youthfull yeers
call them importunately their severall wayes, and hasten them
with the sway of friends either to an ambitious and mercenary,
or ignorantly zealous Divinity; Some allur'd to the trade of Law,
grounding their purposes not on the prudent, and heavenly contemplation of justice and equity which was never taught them,
but on the promising and pleasing thoughts of litigious terms,§
fat contentions, and flowing fees; others betake them to State
affairs, with souls so unprincipl'd in vertue, and true generous
breeding, that flattery, and court shifts§ and tyrannous aphorismes appear to them the highest points of wisdom; instilling
their barren hearts with a conscientious slavery, if, as I rather
think, it be not fain'd. Others lastly of a more delicious§ and airie
spirit, retire themselves knowing no better, to the enjoyments of
ease and luxury, living out their daies in feast and jollity; which
indeed is the wisest and the safest course of all these, unlesse
they were with more integrity undertak'n. And these are the
errours, and these are the fruits of mispending our prime youth
at the Schools and Universities as we do, either in learning meere
words or such things chiefly, as were better unlearnt.

I shall detain you now no longer in the demonstration of
what we should not doe, but strait conduct ye to a hill side,
where I will point ye out the right path of a vertuous and noble
Education; laborious indeed at the first ascent, but else so
smooth, so green, so full of goodly prospect, and melodious
sounds on every side, that the harp of *Orpheus* was not more
charming.§ I doubt not but ye shall have more adoe to drive
our dullest and laziest youth, our stocks§ and stubbs§ from the
infinite desire of such a happy nurture, then we have now to
hale and drag our choisest and hopefullest wits to that asinine
feast of sowthistles and brambles which is commonly set before
them, as all the food and entertainment of their tenderest and
most docible age. I call therefore a compleate and generous§
Education that which fits a man to perform justly, skilfully and

magnanimously[§] all the offices both private and publike of peace and war. And how all this may be done between twelve, and one and twenty, lesse time then is now bestow'd in pure trifling at Grammar and *Sophistry,* is to be thus order'd.

First to finde out a spatious house and ground about it fit for an *Academy,* and big enough to lodge a hundred and fifty persons, whereof twenty or thereabout may be attendants, all under the government of one, who shall be thought of desert sufficient, and ability either to doe all, or wisely to direct, and oversee it done. This place should be at once both School and University, not needing a remove to any other house of Scholler-ship, except it be some peculiar Colledge of Law, or Physick,[§] where they mean to be practitioners; but as for those generall studies which take up all our time from Lilly[6] to the commenc-ing, as they term it, Master of Art, it should be absolute. After this pattern, as many edifices may be converted to this use, as shall be needfull in every City throughout this land, which would tend much to the encrease of learning and civility[§] every where. This number, lesse or more thus collected, to the con-venience of a foot company, or interchangeably two troops of cavalry, should divide their daies work into three parts, as it lies orderly. Their studies, their exercise, and their diet.

For their studies, First they should begin with the chief and necessary rules of some good Grammar, either that now us'd, or any better: and while this is doing, their speech is to be fashion'd to a distinct and cleer pronuntiation, as neer as may be to the *Italian,* especially in the vowels. For we Englishmen being farre northerly, doe not open our mouthes in the cold air, wide enough to grace a Southern tongue; but are observ'd by all other nations to speak exceeding close and inward: So that to smatter[§] Latin with an english mouth, is as ill a hearing as law French. Next to make them expert in the usefullest points of grammar, and with-all to season them, and win them early to the love of vertue and true labour, ere any flattering seducement, or vain principle seise them wandering, some easie and delightfull book of Education would be read to them; whereof the Greeks have store as *Cebes,*

6 The various revisions of and additions to William Lily's introduction to Latin grammar, published in its first form in 1513, were prescribed by law to be used in all English schools; Lily's *Grammar* was still used exclusively in Milton's time.

Plutarch, and other Socratic discourses. But in Latin we have none of classic authoritie extant, except the two or three first books of *Quintilian,* and some select peeces elsewhere. But here the main skill and groundwork will be, to temper[§] them such lectures and explanations upon every opportunity, as may lead and draw them in willing obedience, enflam'd with the study[§] of learning, and the admiration of vertue; stirr'd up with high hopes of living to be brave men, and worthy patriots, dear to God, and famous to all ages. That they may despise and scorn all their childish, and ill taught qualities, to delight in manly, and liberall[§] exercises: which he who hath the Art, and proper eloquence to catch them with, what with mild and effectuall perswasions, and what with the intimation of some fear, if need be, but chiefly by his own example, might in a short space gain them to an incredible diligence and courage: infusing into their young brests such an ingenuous and noble ardor, as would not fail to make many of them renowned and matchlesse men. At the same time, some other hour of the day, might be taught them the rules of Arithmetick, and soon after the elements of Geometry even playing,[§] as the old manner was. After evening repast, till bed time their thoughts will be best taken up in the easie grounds of Religion, and the story of Scripture. The next step would be to the Authors of *Agriculture, Cato, Varro,* and *Columella,* for the matter is most easie, and if the language be difficult, so much the better, it is not a difficultie above their yeers. And here will be an occasion of inciting and inabling them hereafter to improve the tillage of their country, to recover the bad soil, and to remedy the wast that is made of good: for this was one of Hercules praises. Ere halfe these Authors be read, which will soon be with plying hard, and dayly, they cannot choose but be masters of any ordinary prose. So that it will be then seasonable for them to learn in any modern Author, the use of the Globes, and all the maps first with the old names; and then with the new: or they might be then capable to read any compendious method[§] of naturall Philosophy. And at the same time might be entring into the Greek tongue, after the same manner as was before prescrib'd in the Latin; whereby the difficulties of Grammar being soon overcome, all the Historicall[§] Physiology of *Aristotle* and *Theophrastus* are open before them, and as I may say, under contribution. The like accesse will be to

Vitruvius, to *Senecas* naturall questions, to *Mela, Celsus, Pliny,* or *Solinus.* And having thus past the principles of *Arithmetic, Geometry, Astronomy,* and *Geography* with a generall compact[§] of Physicks,[§] they may descend[§] in *Mathematicks* to the instrumentall science of *Trigonometry,* and from thence to Fortification, *Architecture,* Enginry,[§] or navigation. And in naturall Philosophy they may proceed leisurly from the History[§] of *Meteors,*[§] minerals, plants and living creatures as farre as Anatomy. Then also in course might be read to them out of some not tedious writer the institution[§] of Physick; that they may know the tempers, the humors, the seasons,[§] and how to manage a crudity:[§] which he who can wisely and timely doe, is not onely a great Physician to himselfe, and to his friends, but also may at some time or other, save an Army by this frugall, and expencelesse meanes only; and not let the healthy and stout bodies of young men rot away under him for want of this discipline; which is a great pitty, and no lesse a shame to the commander. To set forward all these proceedings in nature & mathematicks, what hinders, but that they may procure, as oft as shall be needfull, the helpfull experiences of Hunters, fowlers,[§] Fishermen, Shepherds, Gardeners, *Apothecaries;* and in the other sciences, *Architects,* Engineers, Mariners, *Anatomists;* who doubtlesse would be ready some for reward, and some to favour such a hopefull Seminary. And this will give them such a reall tincture of naturall knowledge, as they shall never forget, but dayly augment with delight. Then also those Poets which are now counted most hard, will be both facil and pleasant, *Orpheus, Hesiod, Theocritus, Aratus, Nicander, Oppian, Dionysius* and in Latin *Lucretius, Manilius,* and the rurall part of Virgil.

By this time, yeers and good generall precepts will have furnisht them more distinctly with that act of reason which in *Ethics* is call'd *Proairesis:*[§] that they may with some judgement contemplat upon morall good and evill. Then will be requir'd a speciall reinforcement of constant and sound endoctrinating to set them right and firm, instructing them more amply in the knowledge of vertue and the hatred of vice: while their young and pliant affections[§] are led through all the morall works of *Plato, Xenophon, Cicero, Plutarch, Laertius,* and those *Locrian* remnants; but still to be reduc't[§] in their nightward studies wherewith they close the dayes work, under the determinat[§] sentence[§] of *David,* or *Salomon,* or the Evangels and *Apostolic* scriptures. Being perfit in the knowledge of personall duty, they may then begin the study of Economics.[§] And either now, or before this, they may have easily learnt at any odde hour the *Italian* tongue. And soon after, but with warinesse, and good anti- dote, it would be wholsome anough to let them tast some choise comedies Greek, Latin, or *Italian:* Those tragedies also that treate of houshold matters, as *Trachiniæ, Alcestis* and the like. The next remove must be to the study of *Politics;* to know the begin- ning, end, and reasons of politicall societies; that they may not in a dangerous fit of the common-wealth be such poor, shaken, uncertain reeds, of such a tottering conscience, as many of our great counsellers have lately shewn themselves, but stedfast pil- lars of the State. After this they are to dive into the grounds of law, and legall justice; deliver'd first, and with best warrant by *Moses;* and as farre as humane prudence can be trusted, in those extoll'd remains of Grecian Law-givers, *Lycurgus, Solon, Zaleu- cus, Charondas,* and thence to all the Romane *Edicts* and tables[§] with their *Justinian;* and so down to the *Saxon* and common laws of England, and the Statutes. Sundayes also and every evening may be now understandingly spent in the highest matters of *The- ology,* and Church History ancient and modern: and ere this time the Hebrew tongue at a set hour might have been gain'd, that the Scriptures may be now read in their own originall; whereto it would be no impossibility to adde the *Chaldey,*[§] and the *Syrian*[§] dialect. When all these employments are well conquer'd, then will the choise Histories, *heroic poems,* and *Attic* tragedies of statliest, and most regal argument, with all the famous Politicall orations offer themselves; which if they were not only read; but some of them got by memory, and solemnly pronounc't with right accent, and grace, as might be taught, would endue them even with the spirit, and vigor of *Demosthenes* or *Cicero, Euripides,* or *Sopho- cles.* And now lastly will be the time to read with them those organic[§] arts which inable men to discourse and write perspicu- ously, elegantly, and according to the fitted[§] stile of lofty, mean,[§] or lowly. Logic therefore so much as is usefull, is to be referr'd to this due place with all her well coucht[§] heads and Topics,[§] untill it be time to open her contracted palm into a gracefull and ornate

Rhetorick taught out of the rule of *Plato, Aristotle, Phalereus, Cicero, Hermogenes, Longinus.* To which Poetry would be made subsequent, or indeed rather precedent,[§] as being lesse suttle[§] and fine,[§] but more simple,[§] sensuous[§] and passionate.[§] I mean not here the prosody of a verse, which they could not but have hit on before among the rudiments of grammar; but that sublime art which in *Aristotles poetics,* in *Horace,* and the *Italian* commentaries of *Castelvetro, Tasso, Mazzoni,* and others, teaches what the laws are of a true *Epic* poem, what of a *Dramatic,* what of a *Lyric,* what decorum is, which is the grand master peece to observe. This would make them soon perceive what despicable creatures our common rimers and play-writes be, and shew them, what Religious, what glorious and magnificent use might be made of Poetry both in divine and humane[§] things. From hence and not till now will be the right season of forming them to be able writers and composers in every excellent matter, when they shall be thus fraught with an universall insight into things. Or whether they be to speak in Parlament or counsell, honour and attention would be waiting on their lips. There would then also appear in Pulpits other visages, other gestures, and stuffe otherwise wrought then what we now sit under, oft times to as great a triall of our patience as any other that they preach to us. These are the studies wherein our noble and our gentle youth ought to bestow their time in a disciplinary way from twelve to one and twenty; unless they rely more upon their ancestors dead, then upon themselves living. In which methodicall course it is so suppos'd they must proceed by the steddy pace of learning onward, as at convenient times for memories sake to retire back into the middle ward, and sometimes into the rear of what they have been taught, untill they have confirm'd, and solidly united the whole body of their perfeted[§] knowledge, like the last embattelling of a Romane legion. Now will be worth the seeing what exercises, and what recreations may best agree, and become these studies.

Their Exercise.

The course of study hitherto briefly describ'd, is, what I can guesse by reading, likest to those ancient and famous schools of *Pythagoras, Plato, Isocrates, Aristotle* and such others, out of which were bred up such a number of renowned Philosophers, orators, Historians, Poets and Princes all over *Greece, Italy,* and *Asia,* besides the flourishing studies[§] of *Cyrene* and *Alexandria.* But herein it shall exceed them, and supply a defect as great as that which *Plato* noted in the common-wealth of *Sparta;* whereas that City train'd up their youth most for warre, and these in their Academies and *Lycæum,* all for the gown,[§] this institution of breeding which I here delineate, shall be equally good both for Peace and warre. Therefore about an hour and a halfe ere they eat at noon should be allow'd them for exercise and due rest afterwards: But the time for this may be enlarg'd at pleasure, according as their rising in the morning shall be early. The exercise which I commend first, is the exact use of their weapon;[§] to guard and to strike safely with edge, or point; this will keep them healthy, nimble, strong, and well in breath, is also the likeliest meanes to make them grow large, and tall, and to inspire them with a gallant and fearlesse courage, which being temper'd with seasonable lectures and precepts to them of true fortitude, and patience, will turn into a native and heroick valour, and make them hate the cowardise of doing wrong. They must be also practiz'd in all the locks[§] and gripes of wrastling, wherein English men were wont to excell, as need may often be in fight to tugge, to grapple, and to close. And this perhaps will be anough, wherein to prove and heat their single[§] strength. The interim of unsweating themselves regularly, and convenient rest before meat may both with profit and delight be taken up in recreating and composing their travail'd spirits with the solemn and divine harmonies of musick heard, or learnt; either while the skilfull *Organist* plies his grave and fancied[§] descant,[§] in lofty fugues, or the whole Symphony with artfull and unimaginable touches adorn and grace the well studied cords[§] of some choise composer; some times the Lute, or soft organ stop waiting on elegant voices either to Religious, martiall, or civill ditties;[§] which if wise men & prophets be not extreamly out,[§] have a great power over dispositions and manners, to smooth and make them gentle from rustick harshnesse and distemper'd passions. The like also would not be unexpedient after meat to assist and cherish nature in her first concoction,[§] and send their mindes backe to study in good tune and satisfaction. Where having follow'd it close under vigilant eyes till about two hours before supper, they are by a sudden alarum or watch word, to be call'd out to their military motions, under skie or covert, according to the season, as was the Romane wont; first on foot, then as their age permits, on horse back, to all the art of cavalry; That having in sport, but with much exact-nesse, and dayly muster, serv'd out the rudiments of their Soul-diership in all the skill of embattailing, marching, encamping, fortifying, beseiging and battering, with all the helps of ancient and modern stratagems, *Tactiks* and warlike maxims, they may as it were out of a long warre come forth renowned and perfect Commanders in the service of their country. They would not then, if they were trusted with fair and hopefull armies, suffer them for want of just and wise discipline to shed away from about them like sick feathers, though they be never so oft sup-pli'd: they would not suffer[s] their empty & unrecrutible Colo-nells of twenty men in a company, to quaffe out, or convay into secret hoards, the wages of a delusive list, and a miserable rem-nant: yet in the mean while to be overmaster'd with a score or two of drunkards, the only souldiery left about them, or else to comply with all rapines and violences. No certainly, if they knew ought of that knowledge that belongs to good men or good gover-nours, they would not suffer these things. But to return to our own institute, besides these constant exercises at home, there is another opportunity of gaining experience to be won from pleas-ure it selfe abroad; In those vernal seasons of the yeer, when the air is calm and pleasant, it were an injury and sullennesse against nature not to go out, and see her riches, and partake in her rejoycing with heaven and earth. I should not therefore be a perswader to them of studying much then, after two or three yeer that they have well laid their grounds, but to ride out in companies with prudent and staid guides, to all the quarters of the land: learning and observing all places of strength, all com-modities[s] of building and of soil, for towns and tillage, harbours and Ports for trade. Somtimes taking sea as farre as to our Navy, to learn there also what they can in the practicall knowl-edge of sailing and of sea fight. These wayes would trie all their peculiar gifts of nature, and if there were any secret excellence among them, would fetch it out, and give it fair opportunities to advance it selfe by, which could not but mightily redound to the good of this nation, and bring into fashion again those old admired vertues and excellencies, with farre more advantage now in this puritie of Christian knowledge. Nor shall we then need the *Mounsieurs* of *Paris* to take our hopefull youth into thir slight and prodigall custodies and send them over back again transform'd into mimics, apes & Kicshoes.[§] But if they desire to see other countries at three or four and twenty yeers of age, not to learn principles, but to enlarge experience, and make wise observation, they will by that time be such as shall deserve the regard and honour of all men where they passe, and the society and friendship of those in all places who are best and most eminent. And perhaps then other Nations will be glad to visit us for their breeding, or else to imitate us in their own Country.

Now lastly for their diet there cannot be much to say, save only that it would be best in the same house; for much time else would be lost abroad, and many ill habits got; and that it should be plain, healthfull, and moderat I suppose is out of controversie. Thus Master *Hartlib*, you have a generall view in writing, as your desire was, of that which at severall times I had discourst with you concerning the best and Noblest way of Education; not beginning, as some have done from the cradle, which yet might be worth many considerations, if brevity had not been my scope. Many other circumstances also I could have mention'd, but this to such as have the worth in them to make triall, for light and direction may be anough. Only I believe that this is not a bow for every man to shoot in[§] that counts himselfe a teacher; but will require sinews almost equall to those which Homer gave Ulysses, yet I am withall perswaded that it may prove much more easie in the assay,[§] then it now seems at distance, and much more illustrious: howbeit not more difficult then I imagine, and that imagination presents me with nothing but very happy and very possible according to best wishes; if God have so decreed, and this age have spirit and capacity anough to apprehend.

The end.

James Howell

SIR,

It was a quaint difference the Ancients did put twixt a *Letter*, and an *Oration*, that the one should be attird like a Woman, the other like a Man: The latter of the two is allowd large *side*§ robes, as long periods,§ parenthesis, similes, examples, and other parts of Rhetorical flourishes: But a *Letter* or *Epistle*, should be short-coated, and closely couchd;§ a Hungerlin§ becomes a *Letter* more hansomly then a gown. Indeed we should write as we speak; and that's a true familiar Letter which expresseth ones mind, as if he were discoursing with the party to whom he writes in succinct and short terms. The *Toung* and the *Pen* are both of them Interpreters of the mind; but I hold the *Pen* to be the more faithful of the two: The *Toung in udo posita*, being seated in a moyst slippery place may fail and falter in her sudden extemporal expressions; but the *Pen* having a greater advantage of premeditation, is not so subject to error, and leaves things behind it upon firm and authentic record. Now, *Letters*, though they be capable of any subject, yet commonly they are either *Narratory*, *Objurgatory*, *Consolatory*, *Monitory*, or *Congratulatory*. The first consists of *relations*,§ The second of *reprehensions*, The third of *comfort*, The last two of *counsel* and *joy*: There are some who in lieu of Letters write *Homilies*, they Preach when they should Epistolize; There are others that turn them to tedious *tractats*; this is to make Letters degenerat from their tru nature. Some modern Authors there are, who have expos'd their *Letters* to the world, but most of them, I mean among your Latin Epistolizers, go fraighted with meer *Bartholomew*§ ware, with trite and trivial phrases only, listed§ with pedantic shreds of School-boy verses. Others ther are among our next transmarin§ neighbours Eastward, who write in their own language, but their stile is so soft and easie, that their *Letters* may be said to be like bodies of loose flesh without sinews, they have neither joynts of art, nor *arteries* in them; They have a kind of simpering and lank hectic[§] expressions made up of a bombast of words and finical affected complements only: I cannot well[§] away with such sleazy stuff, with such cobweb-compositions, where there is no strength of matter, nothing for the Reader to carry away with him, that may enlarge the notions of his soul: One shall hardly find an apothegm, example, simile, or any thing of Philosophy, History, or solid knowledg, or as much as one new *created* phrase, in a hundred of them; and to draw any observations out of them, were as if one went about to distil cream out of froth; Insomuch that it may be said of them, what was said of the Eccho, *That she is a meer sound, and nothing else.*

I return you your *Balzac*[7] by this bearer, and when I found those Letters, wherein he is so familiar with his King, so flat, and those to *Richelieu,* so puff'd with prophane hyperboles, and larded up and down with such gross flatteries, with others be-sides which he sends as Urinals[§] up and down the world to look into his water, for discovery of the crazie condition of his body, I forbore him further: so I am

Your most affectionate servitor,

J. H.

Westminster, 25. Julii., 1625.

2. TO SIR JAMES CROFTS, KNIGHT, AT S. OSITH

SIR,

I could not shake hands with *England,* without kissing your hands also: and because, in regard of your distance now from *London,* I cannot do it in person, I send this Paper for my deputy.

The News that keeps greatest noise here now, is the return of Sir *Walter Raleigh* from his myne of Gold in *Guiana* the South parts of *America,* which at first was like to be such a hopefull

---

7 Jean Louis Guez de Balzac, the first of whose numerous collections of *Lettres* was published in 1624 and translated into English a decade later.

boon§ Voyage, but it seems that that golden myne is proved a
meer *Chymera,* an imaginary airy myne; and indeed his Majestie
had never any other conceipt§ of it: But what will not one in
Captivity (as Sir *Walter* was) promise, to regain his Freedom?
who would not promise not onely mynes, but mountains of Gold,
for Liberty? and tis pity but such a knowing well-weigh'd§ Knight
had not had a better Fortune; for the *Destiny* (I mean that brave
Ship which he built himself of that name, that carried him
thither) is like to prove a *fatall* Destiny to him, and to some of
the rest of those gallant Adventurers which contributed for the
setting forth of thirteen Ships more, who were most of them his
kinsmen and younger brothers, being led into the said Expedition
by a generall conceipt the world had of the wisedom of Sir *Walter
Raleigh;* and many of these are like to make *Shipwrack* of their
estates by this Voyage. Sir *Walter* landed at *Plymouth,* whence
he thought to make an escape; and some say he hath tampered
with his body by Phisick, to make him look sickly, that he may be
the more pitied, and permitted to lie in his own house. Count
Gondamar the *Spanish* Ambassador speaks high§ language, and
sending lately to desire Audience of his Majestie, he said he had
but one word to tell him, his Majestie wondring what might be
delivered in one word; when he came before him, he said onely,
Pyrats, Pyrats, Pyrats, and so departed.

Tis true that he protested against this Voyage before, and
that it could not be but for some prædatory designe: And if it
be as I hear, I fear it will go very ill with Sir *Walter,* and that
Gondamar will never give§ him over, till he hath his head off
his shoulders; which may quickly be done, without any new
Arraignment, by vertue of the old Sentence that lies still dormant
against him, which he could never get off by Pardon, notwithstanding that he mainly laboured in it before he went; but his
Majestie could never be brought to it, for he said he would keep
this as a Curb to hold him within the bounds of his Commission,
and the good behaviour.

Gondamar cries out, that he hath broke the sacred Peace
twixt the two Kingdoms, That he hath fired and plundred *Santo
Thoma* a Colony the *Spaniards* had planted with so much blood,
neer under the *Line,*§ which made it prove such a hot service§
unto him, and where, besides others, he lost his eldest son in

the Action; and could they have preserved the Magazin⁵ of *Tobacco* onely, besides other things in that Town, something mought⁵ have bin had to countervail the charge of the Voyage. *Gondamar* alleadgeth further, that the enterprise of the myne failing, he propounded to the rest of his Fleet to go and intercept some of the Plate-Galeons,⁵ with other Designes which would have drawn after them apparant acts of Hostility, and so demands Justice: besides other disasters which fell out upon the dashing⁵ of the first designe, Captain *Remish,* who was the main Instrument for discovery of the myne, pistol'd himself in a desperat mood of discontent in his Cabin, in the *Convertine.*

This return of Sir *Walter Raleigh* from *Guiana,* puts me in minde of a facetious⁵ tale I read lately in *Italian* (for I have a little of that Language already) how *Alphonso* King of *Naples* sent a *Moor* who had been his Captive a long time, to *Barbary,* to buy horses, and to return by such a time. Now there was about the King a kinde of *Buffon* or Jester who had a Table-book, wherein he was used to register any absurdity, or impertinence, or merry passage that happened about the Court. That day the *Moor* was dispatched for *Barbary,* the said Jester waiting upon the King at supper, the King call'd for his Journall, and askt what he had observed that day: thereupon he produced his Table-book, and amongst other things, he read how *Alphonso* King of *Naples* had sent *Beltran* the *Moor,* who had been a long time his Prisoner, to *Morocco* (his own Countrey) with so many thousand Crowns, to buy horses. The King asked him why he inserted that: Because, said he, I think he will never come back to be a Prisoner again, and so you have lost both man and money. But if he do come, then your Jest is marr'd, quoth the King: No Sir; *for if he return I will blot out your name, and put him in for a* Fool.

The Application is easie and obvious: But the world wonders extremely, that so great a wise man as Sir *Walter Raleigh* would return to cast himself upon so inevitable a Rock, as I fear he will; and much more, that such choice men, and so great a Power of Ships, should all come home, and do nothing.

The Letter you sent to my Father, I conveyed safely the last week to *Wales.* I am this week, by Gods help, for the *Netherlands,* and then I think for *France.* If in this my forren employment I may be any way serviceable unto you, you know what power you have to dispose of me; for I honor you in a very high degree, and will live and die,

Your humble and ready Servant, J. H.

London, 28. *of March,* 1618.

3. TO THE HONOURABLE SIR ROBERT MANSELL, VICE-ADMIRALL OF ENGLAND, FROM VENICE

SIR,

As soon as I came to *Venice,* I applied my self to dispatch your businesse according to instructions, and Mr. *Seymor* was ready to contribute his best furtherance: These two *Italians* who are the Bearers hereof, by report here, are the best Gentlemen-Workmen that ever blew Crystall, one is allied to *Antonio Miotti,* the other is Cousin to *Mazalao;* for other things they shall be sent in the Ship *Lion,* which rides here at *Malamocca,* as I shall send you account by conveyance of Mr. *Symns:* Herewith I have sent a Letter to you from Sir *Henry Wotton,* the Lord Ambassador here, of whom I have receiv'd som favours. He wish'd me to write, that you have now a double interrest in him; for wheras before he was onely your Servant, he is now your Kinsman by your late§ marriage.

I was lately to see the Arsenall of *Venice,* one of the worthiest things of Christendom; they say ther are as many Gallies, and Galeasses of all sorts, belonging to Saint *Mark,*⁸ either in Cours, at Anchor, in Dock, or upon§ the Carine, as ther be dayes in the yeer; here they can build a compleat Gally in half a day, and put her a float in perfect Equippage, having all the ingredients fitted before hand, as they did in three hours, when *Henry* the third pass'd this way to *France* from *Poland,* who wish'd, that besides *Paris,* and his Parliament Towns, he had this Arsenall in exchange, for three of his chiefest Cities: Ther are three hundred people perpetually here at Work, and if one comes young, and grows old in Saint *Marks* service, he hath a Pension from the State during life. Being brought to see one of the *Clarissimos*§

⁸ The patron saint of Venice.

that governs this Arsenall, this huge Sea Store-House, amongst other matters reflecting upon *England,* he was saying, That if *Cavaglier Don Roberto Mansell* were now here, he thought verily the republic would make a proffer to him to be Admirall of that Fleet of Gallies and Galeons, which are now going against the Duke of *Ossuna,* and the Forces of *Naples,* you are so well known hear.

I was, since I came hither, in *Murano,* a little Island, about the distance of *Lambeth* from *London,* wher Crystall-Glasse is made, and 'tis a rare sight to see a whole Street, where on the one side ther are twenty Furnaces together at work; They say here, that although one should transplant a Glasse-Furnace, from *Murano* to *Venice* her self, or to any of the little assembly of Islands about her, or to any other part of the Earth besides, and use the same Materials, the same Workmen, the same Fuell, the self same Ingredients evry way, yet they cannot make Crystall Glasse in that perfection, for beuty and lustre, as in *Murano;* som impute it to the qualitie of the circumambient Ayr, that hangs ore the place, which is purified and attenuated by the concurrence of so many fires, that are in those Furnaces night and day perpetually, for they are like the *Vestall* fire which never goes out; And it is well known, that some Ayrs make more qualifying impressions then others, as a *Greek* told me in *Sicily,* of the Ayr of *Egypt,* wher ther be huge common Furnaces to hatch Eggs by the thousands in *Camels* Dung; for during the time of hatching, if the Ayr happen to come to be overcast, and grow cloudy, it spoyls all; if the Skie continue still serene and clear, not one Egg in a hundred will miscarry.

I met with *Camillo* your Consaorman§ here lately, and could he be sure of entertainment,§ he would return to serve you again, and I beleeve for lesse salary.

I shall attend§ your commands herein§ by the next, and touching other particulars, wherof I have written to Captain *Bacon:* So I rest

Your most humble
and ready Servant *J. H.*

Venice, May the 30. 1621.

4. TO DR. [THOMAS] PRICHARD,
[VICE-PRINCIPAL OF JESUS COLLEGE, OXFORD]

SIR,

Since I was beholden to you for your many favours in *Oxford,*
I have not heard from you, (*ne* γρῦ *quidem*).⁹ I pray let the
wonted correspondence be now reviv'd, and receive new vigour
between us.

My Lord Chancelor *Bacon* is lately dead of a long languishing
weaknes; he died so poor, that he scarce left money to bury him,
which though he had a great *Wit,* did argue no great *Wisdom,*
it being one of the essentiall properties of a Wiseman to provide
for the main chance. I have read, that it hath bin the fortunes
of all *Poets* commonly to die Beggars; but for an *Orator,* a
Lawyer, and *Philosopher,* as he was, to die so, 'tis rare. It seems
the same fate befell him, that attended *Demosthenes, Seneca,*
and *Cicero,* (all great men) of whom, the two first fell by *corruption;* the fairest Diamond may have a flaw in it, but I beleeve he died poor out of a contempt of the pelf of Fortune, as
also out of an excesse of generosity, which appear'd, as in divers
other passages, so once when the King had sent him a Stag, he
sent up for the Underkeeper, and having drunk the Kings health
unto him in a great Silver-Guilt⁵-Bowl, he gave it him for his
fee. He writ a pitifull Letter to King *James,* not long before his
death, and concludes, *Help me dear Soverain Lord and Master,
and pity me so far, that I who have bin born to a Bag,*⁵ *be not
now in my age forc'd in effect to bear a Wallet;*⁵ *nor I that desire
to live to study, may be driven to study to live:* Which words, in
my opinion, argued a little abjection⁵ of spirit, as his former
Letter to the Prince did of prophanes,⁵ wherin *he hoped, that as
the Father was his Creator, the son will be his Redeemer.* I write
not this to derogat from the noble worth of the Lord Viscount
Verulam, who was a rare man, a man *Reconditæ scientiæ, &
ad salutem literarum natus,*¹ and I think the eloquentest that
was born in this Isle. They say he shall be the last Lord Chancelor, as Sir *Edward Coke* was the last Lord Chief Justice of

⁹ Not even a syllable.
¹ Of profound knowledge, and born for the advancement of learning.

England; for ever since they have bin term'd Lord Chief Justices of the Kings Bench; so hereafter ther shall be onely *Keepers* of the Great Seal, which for Title and Office, are deposable; but they say the Lord *Chancelors* Title is indelible.

I was lately at *Grayes-Inne* with Sir *Eubule,* and he desir'd me to remember him unto you, as I do also *Meum* Prichardum *ex imis* præcordiis, *Vale* κεφαλή μοι προσφιλεστάτη.[2]

Yours most affectionatly while *J. H.*

London, Jan. 6. 1625.

5. TO MY HONOURABLE FRIEND SIR C. C.

SIR,

I was upon point of going abroad§ to steale a solitary walk, when yours of the twelfth current§ came to hand; the high researches, and choice abstracted notions I found therein seem'd to heighten my spirits, and make my fancy fitter for my intended retirement and meditation; adde hereunto that the countenance of the weather invited me, for it was a still evening, it was also a cleer open sky, not a speck, or the least wrinkle appear'd in the whole face of heaven, 'twas such a pure deep azur all the hemisphere over, that I wondred what was become of the three Regions of the aire with their meteors, so having got into a close§ field, I cast my face upward, and fell to consider what a rare prerogative the *optic* vertue of the *eye* hath, much more the *intuitive* vertue of the *thought,* that the one in a moment can reach Heaven, and the other goe beyond it: Therefore sure that Philosopher was but a kind of frantic§ foole, that would have pluck'd out both his eyes because they were a hinderance to his speculations: Moreover I began to contemplat as I was in this posture the vast magnitude of the Universe, and what proportion this poore globe of earth might beare with it, for if those numberlesse bodies which stick in the vast roofe of Heaven, though they appeare to us but as spangles, be, some of them, thousands of times bigger then the earth take the *Sea* with it to boot (for they both make but one spheare) surely, the Astronomers had reason to tearme this spheare an indivisible point,

2 My Prichard from the bottom of my heart; farewell, my dear fellow.

and a thing of no dimension at all being compar'd to the whole world; I fell then to thinke that at the second generall destruction it is no more for God Almighty to fire this earth, then for us to blow up a small squibb,§ or rather one grain of gunpowder: As I was musing thus, I spyed a swarme of gnatts waving up and downe the aire about me, which I knew to be part of the Universe as well as I, and me thought 'twas a strange opinion of our Aristotle to hold that the least of those small insected ephemerans§ shou'd be more noble then the sun, because it had a sensitive soule in it. I fell to thinke that the same proportion which those animalillios bore with me in point of bignes, the same I held with those glorious spirits which are neare the throne of the Almighty: what then should we thinke of the magnitude of the Creatour himselfe, doubtles 'tis beyond the reach of any humane immagination to conceive it; In my private devotions I presume to compare him to a great mountaine of light, and my soule seemes to discerne some glorious forme therein, but suddenly as she would fix her eyes upon the object, her sight is presently dazled and disgregated§ with the refulgency and coruscations thereof.

Walking a little further I spyed a young boysterous bull breaking over hedge and ditch to a heard of kine in the next pasture, which made me thinke that if that fierce strong animall, with others of that kind knew their owne strength, they would never suffer man to be their Master; Then looking upon them quietly grasing up and downe, I fell to consider that the flesh which is daily dish'd upon our tables is but concocted§ grasse, which is recarnifyed§ in our stomacks, and transmuted to another flesh; I fell also to thinke what advantage those innocent animalls had of man, who, as soone as nature casts them into the world, find their meat dress'd,§ the cloath layed, and the table cover'd, they find their drinke brew'd and the buttery open, their beds made, and their cloathes ready; And though man hath the faculty of reason to make him a compensation for the want of these advantages, yet this reason brings with it a thousand perturbations of mind, and perplexities of spirit, griping cares, and anguishes of thought, which those harmeles silly creatures were exempted from: Going on I came to repose my selfe upon the trunk of a tree, and I fell to consider further what advantage that dull *vegetable* had of those feeding animalls, as not to be so troublesome and beholden to nature, nor to be so subject to starving, to diseases, to the inclemency of the weather, and to be far longer liv'd: I then spyed a great stone, and sitting a while upon't, I fell to weigh in my thoughts that that stone was in a happier condition in some respects, then those *sensitive* creatures and *vegetables* I saw before, in regard that that stone, which propagates by *assimilation* as the philosophers say, needed neither grasse nor hay, or any aliment for restauration of nature, nor water to refresh its roots, or the heat of the sun to attract the moisture upwards to encrease the growth: As I directed my pace homeward, I spyed a kite soaring high in the aire, and gently gliding up and downe the cleare Region so far above my head I fell to envy that bird extreamely and repine at his happines that he should have a priviledge to make a nearer approach to Heaven then I.

Excuse me that I trouble you thus with these rambling meditations; they are to correspond with you in some part for those accurat fancies of yours you lately sent me. So I rest.

Your entire and true servitor.

J. H.

Holborn, 17 *Mar.* 1639.

6. TO THE HON. MASTER CAR[EW] RA[LEIGH]

SIR,

Yours of the 7th current§ was brought me, wherby I find that you did put your selfe to the penance of perusing some *Epistles,* that goe imprinted lately in my name; I am bound to you for your *paines* and patience (for you write, you read them all thorough) much more for your candid *opinion* of them, being right glad that they should give entertainment to such a choice and judicious Gentleman as your selfe: But wheras you seem to except against somthing in one *Letter,* that reflects upon Sir *Walter Raleigh's* voyage to *Guyana,* because I terme the gold Mine he went to discover, an *ayrie and supposititious Mine,* and so inferre that it toucheth his honour; Truly sir, I will deale clearly with you in that point, that I never harbour'd in my

brain the least thought to expose to the world any thing that
might prejudice, much lesse traduce in the least degree that
could be, that rare and renowned Knight, whose fame shall contend in longævity with this Island it selfe, and with that great
World which he *Historiseth* so gallantly; I was a youth about
the town when he undertook that expedition, and I remember
most men suspected that *Mine* then to be but an imaginary
politick§ thing, but at his return, and missing of the enterprise,
these *suspitions* turn'd in most to reall *beliefs* that 'twas no
other. And King *James* in that Declaration which he commanded
to be printed and published afterwards touching the circumstances of this action (upon which my Letter is grounded, and
which I have still by me) termes it no lesse; And if we may
not give faith to such publick regal instruments, what shall wee
credit? besides, there goes another printed kind of Remonstrance
annex'd to that Declaration which intimates as much; And there
is a worthy Captain in this towne, who was a coadventurer in
that expedition, who, upon the storming of St. *Thoma,* heard
young Mr. *Rawligh* encouraging his men in these words, come
*on my noble hearts, this is the Mine we come for, and they who
think there is any other, are fooles.* Add hereunto that Sir *Richard Baker* in his last Historicall collections intimates so much,
therfore 'twas far from being any opinion broach'd by my selfe, or
bottom'd§ upon weak grounds, for I was careful of nothing more,
then that those *Letters,* being to breath open ayre, should relate
nothing but what should be derived from good fountaines; And
truly sir, touching that Apologie of Sir *Walter Raligh's* you write
of, I never saw it, and I am very sory I did not, for it had let in
more light upon me of the cariage§ of that great action, and
then you might have been well assur'd that I would have done
that noble Knight all the right that could be.

But sir, the severall arguments that you urge in your Letter
are of that strength, I confesse, that they are able to rectifie
any indifferent§ man in this point, and induce him to believe
that it was no Chymera, but a reall Mine; for you write of divers
pieces of gold brought thence by Sir *Walter* himselfe: and Captain *Kemys,* and of some ingotts that were found in the Governors Closet at St. *Thoma,* with divers crusibles, and other refining instruments; yet, under favour, that might be, and the

benefit not countervaile the charge, for the richest Mines that
the King of *Spain* hath upon the whole Continent of *America*,
which are the Mines of *Potosi*, yeild him but six in the hundred
all expences defrayed. You write how King *James* sent privately
to Sir *Walter* being yet in the Tower, to intreat and command
him, that he would impart his whole designe unto him under
his hand, promising upon the word of a King to keep it secret,
which being done accordingly by Sir *Walter Raleigh*, that very
originall paper was found in the sayd Spanish Governours closet
at St. *Thoma;* whereat, as you have just cause to wonder, and
admire the activeness of the Spanish Agents about our Court
at that time, so I wonder no lesse at the miscariage of some
of his late Majesties Ministers, who notwithstanding that he had
pass'd his royall word to the contrary, yet they did help Count
Gondamar to that Paper, so that the reproach lieth more upon
the English then the Spanish Ministers in this particular: Wheras
you alledge that the dangerous sicknes of Sir *Walter* being
arrived neere the place, and the death of (that rare spark of
courage) your brother upon the first landing, with other circumstances discourag'd Captain *Kemish* from discovering the
Mine, but to reserve it for another time, I am content to give as
much credit to this as any man can; as also that Sir *Walter*,
if the rest of the Fleet according to his earnest motion⁵ had gone
with him to revictuall in *Virginia* (a Country where he had
reason to be welcome unto, being of his owne discovery) he
had a purpose to return to *Guyana* the Spring following to pursue his first designe: I am also very willing to believe that it
cost Sir *Walter Rawleigh* much more to put himselfe in equipage
for that long intended voyage, then would have payed for his
liberty, if he had gone about to purchase it for reward of money
at home, though I am not ignorant that many of the co adventurers made large contributions, and the fortunes of some of
them suffer for it at this very day. But although *Gondamar*, as
my Letter mentions, calls Sir *Walter* Pyrat, I, for my part am
far from thinking so, because as you give an unanswerable
reason, the plundering of St. *Thoma*, was an act done beyond
the Equator, where the Articles of Peace 'twixt the two Kings
doe not extend; yet, under favour, though he broak not the
Peace, he was sayed to break his *Patent* by exceeding the bounds

of his Commission, as the foresayd Declaration relates, for king *James* had made strong promises to Count *Gondamar,* that this fleet should commit no outrages upon the King of *Spaine's* subjects by land, unlesse they began first, and I believe that was the maine cause of his death, though I think if they had proceeded that way against him in a legall course of tryall, he might have defended himselfe well enough. Whereas you alledge that if that Action had succeeded, and afterwards been well prosecuted, it might have brought *Gondamar's* great Catholick Master to have bin begg'd for at the Church dores by Fryars, as he was once brought in the latter end of Queen *Elizabeths* dayes; I beleeve it had much damnified⁵ him, and interrupted him in the possession of his West Indies, but not brought him, under favour, to so low an ebb; I have observed that it is an ordinary thing in your popish Countreys for Princes to borrow from the Altar, when they are reduc'd to any streights, for they say, *the riches of the Church are to serve as anchors in time of a storme;* Divers of our Kings have done worse, by pawning their Plate and Jewels: Whereas my Letter makes mention that Sir *Walter Rawleigh* mainly laboured for his Pardon before he went, but could not compasse it, this is also a passage in the foresayed printed relation, but I could have wish'd with all my heart he had obtain'd it, for I believe, that neither the transgressing of his Commission, nor any thing that he did beyond the *Line,*⁵ could have shortned the line of his life otherwise, but in all probability we might have been happy in him to this very day, having such an Heroic heart as he had, and other rare helps, by his great knowledge, for the preservation of health; I beleeve without any scruple what you write that Sir *William St. Geon* made an overturre unto him of procuring his pardon for 1500. 1.⁵ but whither⁵ he could have effected it I doubt a little, when he had come to negotiat it really: But I extreamely wonder how that old sentence which had layn dormant above sixteene yeares against Sir *Walter Rawleigh* could have been made use of to take off his head afterwards, considering that the Lord chancelour *Verulam,* as you write, told him positively, (as Sir *Walter* was acquainting him with that proffer of Sir *William St. Geons* for a pecuniary pardon) in these words, *Sir, the knee timber of your voyage is money, spare your purse in this particular, for upon my life*

you have a sufficient pardon for all that is passed already, the
King having under his broad Seale made you Admiral of your
Fleet and given you power of the Martiall law over your officers
and Souldiers; One would think that by this royall patent, which
gave him power of life and death over the Kings liege people Sir
Walter Rawlegh should become *Rectus in curia,*[3] and free from
all old convictions; but Sir, to tell you the plaine truth Count
Gondomar at that time had a great stroke in our Court, because
there was more then a meere overture of a match with *Spain*
which makes me apt to belive that that great wise Knight being
such an *Anti-Spaniard,* was made a sacrifice to advance the
matrimoniall treaty: But I must needs wonder, as you justly
do, that one and the same man should be condemned for being
a friend to the *Spaniard,* (which was the ground of his first condemnation) [and] should afterwards lose his head for being
their enemy by the same sentence: Touching his return I must
confesse I was utterly ignorant that those two noble Earls
Thomas of *Arundell* and *William* of *Pembrook* were ingaged[s]
for him in this particular, nor doth the printed relation, make any
mention of them at all; therefore I must say that envy her self
must pronounce that return of his, for the acquitting of his
fiduciary pledges to be a most noble act, and waving[s] that of
King *Alphonso's Moore,* I may more properly compare it to the
act of that famous *Roman* Commander (*Regulus* as I take it)
who to keep his promise and faith return'd to his enemies where
he had been prisoner, though he knew he went to an inevitable
death: But well did that faithlesse cunning Knight who betrayed
Sir *Walter Rawlegh* in his intended escape being come a shore,
fall to that contemptible end, as to dy a poore distracted beggar
in the Isle of *Lyndey,* having for a bag of money falsified his
faith confirm'd by the ty of the holy Sacrament as you write, as
also before the yeare came about to be found clipping the same
coyn in the Kings own house at *White Hall* which he had receiv'd as a reward for his perfidiousnesse, for which being condemned to be hang'd, he was driven to sell himself to[s] his shirt,
to purchase his pardon of two Knights.

And now Sir, let that glorious and gallant Cavalier Sir *Walter*
Rawlegh (who *lived long enough for his own honor though*

3 Outstandingly upright (a pillar in the senate).

not for his country, as it was said of a *Romane* Consull) rest quietly in his grave and his vertues live in his posterity, as I find they do strongly, and very eminently in you; I have heard his enemies confesse that he was one of the weightiest[§] and wisest men that this Island ever bred; Mr. *Nath. Carpenter* a learned and judicious authour was not in the wrong when he gave this discreet character of him, *who hath not known or read of that prodigie of wit and fortune Sir* Walter Rawlegh *a man infortunate in nothing els but in the greatnesse of his wit and advancement, whose eminent worth was such both in domestick policy, forreine expeditions & discoveries, in Arts and literature, both practic[§] and contemplative, that it might seem at once to conquer[§] both example and imitation.*

Now Sir, hoping to be rectified in your judgement touching my opinion of that illustrious Knight your *father*, give me leave to kisse your hands very affectionately for the respectfull mention you please to make of my *brother* once your neighbour; he suffers, good soule, as well as I, though in a differing manner; I also much value that favourable censure[§] you give of those rambling letters of mine, which indeed are nought els then a legend of the cumbersome life and various fortunes of a *Cadet;*[§] but whereas you please to say *that the world of learned men is much beholden to me for them and that some of them are freighted with many excellent and quaint[§] passages delivered in a masculine and solid stile, adorn'd with much eloquence, and stuck with the choicest flowers pick'd from the Muses garden; whereas you also please to write that you admire my great travells, my strenuous endeavours, at all times and in all places to accumulate knowledge, my active laying hold upon all occasions, and on every handle[§] that might (with reputation) advantage either my wit or fortune:* These high gallant straines of expressions, I confesse, transcend my merit, and are a garment too gawdy for me to put on, yet I will lay it up among my best reliques whereof I have divers sent me of this kind: And whereas in publishing these Epistles at this time you please to say, *that I have done like Hezekiah when he shewed his treasures to the Babylonians, that I have discovered my riches to thieves who will bind me fast and share my goods;* To this I answer, that if those innocent letters (for I know none of them but is such) fall among such thieves they will have no great prize to carry away, it will be but *petty larceny;* I am already, God wot, bound fast enough, having been a long time coopt up between these walls, bereft of all my meanes of subsistence and employment, nor do I know wherefore I am here, unlesse it be for my sinnes; For I beare as upright a heart to my King and Countrey, I am as conformable and well affected to the government of this land, specially to the high Court of Parliament as any one whatsoever that breaths air under this meridian, I will except none; And for my Religion I defie any creature 'twixt heaven and earth that will say, I am not a true *English* Protestant: I have from time to time employ'd divers of my best friends to get my liberty, at least wise leave to go abroad upon bayl (for I do not expect, as you please also to believe in your letter, to be delivered hence as Saint *Peter* was by miracle) but nothing will yet prevail.

To conclude, I doe acknowledge in the highest way of recognition, the free and noble proffer you please to make me of your endeavours to pull me out of this dolefull sepulcher, wherein you say I am entomb'd alive; I am no lesse oblig'd to you for the opinion I find you have of my weake abilities which you *please to wish heartily may be no longer eclypsed;* I am not in despair but a day will shine that may afford me opportunity to improve this good opinion of yours (which I value at a very high rate) and let the world know how much I am

Sir,

Your real and
ready Servitor

J. H.

Fleet,§ 5 *May,* 1645.

7. TO MR. T[HOMAS] V[AUGHAN]
AT BRUSSELLS

MY DEARE TOM.

Who would have thought poore *England* had been brought to this passe? could it ever have entred into the imagination of man that the scheme and whole frame of so ancient and well molded a government should be so suddenly struck off the hinges, quite put out of joynt and tumbled into such a horrid confusion? who would have held it possible that to fly from *Babylon,* we should fall into such a *Babel?* that to avoid superstition some people should be brought to belch out such horrid profanenesse, as to call the temples of God the tabernacles of Sathan;§ the Lords Supper a two penny Ordinary,§ to make the Communion table a manger, and the Font a trough to water their horses in; to term the white desent§ robe of the Presbiter the whores smock; the pipes through which nothing came but Anthemes and holy hymnes, the devills bagpipes, the Liturgy of the Church though extracted most of it out of the sacred text call'd by some another kind of *Alchoran,* by others raw porredge, by some a piece forg'd in hell; who would have thought to have seen in *England* the Churches shut and the shops open upon *Christmas* day? could any soule have imagined that this Isle would have produced such monsters, as to rejoyce at the *Turks* good successes against Christians, and wish he were in the midst of *Rome:* who would have dreamt tenne yeares since when Archbishop *Lawd* did ride in state through *London* streets accompanying my Lord of *London* to be sworn Lord high Treasurer of *England,* that the *mitre* should have now come to such a scorn, to such a national kind of hatred, as to put the whole Island in a combustion; which makes me call to memory a saying of the Earle of *Kildare* in *Ireland,* in the raigne of *Henry* the 8, which Earl, having deadly feud with the Bishop of *Cassiles,* burnt a Church belonging to that Diocesse, [and] being ask'd upon his examination before the Lord Deputy at the Castle of *Dublin,* why he had committed such a horrid sacriledge as to burn Gods Church? he answered, I had never burnt the Church unlesse I had thought the Bishop had been in't: Lastly, who would have imagin'd that the *Accise*§ would have taken footing here? a word I remember in the last Parliament save one, so odious that when Sir *D. Carleton* then secretary of State, did but name it in the house of Commons he was like to be sent to the Tower; although he nam'd it to no ill sense but to shew what advantage of happinesse the people of *England* had or'e other nations having neither the gabells§ of *Italy,* the tallies§ of *Frannce,* or the *Accise* of *Holland* layd upon them, upon this he was suddenly interrupted and call'd to the barre; such a strange

Metamorphosis poore *England* is now come unto, and I am afraid our miseries are not come to their height, but the longest shadows stay till the Evening.

The freshest newes that I can write unto you is, that the *Kentish* Knight of your acquaintance whom I writ in my last had an *apostacy* in his braine, dyed suddenly this week of an *impostume*§ in his breast, as he was reading a pamphlet of his owne that came from the presse, wherein he shew'd a great mind to be nibling with my Trees; but he only shew'd his teeth, for he could not bite to any purpose.

Willi: Ro: is return'd from the warres, but he is growne lame in one of his armes, so he hath no mind to beare *armes* any more; he confesseth himselfe to be an egregious foole to leave his mercership,§ and goe to be a musqueteer: It made me thinke upon the tale of the *Gallego*§ in *Spaine,* who in the civill warrs against *Aragon* being in the field he was shot in the forehead, and being carried away to a tent, the surgeon search'd his wound and found it mortal; so he advis'd him to send for his Confessor, for he was no man for this world in regard the braine was touch'd; the soldier wish'd him to search it againe, which he did, and told him that he found he was hurt in the braine and could not possibly scape, whereupon the *Gallego* fell into a chafe, and sayed he lyed, for he had no braine at all *porque si tuviera seso, nunca huviera venido a esta guerra,* If I had had any brain, I would never have come to this Warre; All your friends here are well, except the maymd Souldier, and remember you often, specially Sir *J. Brown,* a good gallant Gentleman who never forgets any who deservd to have a place in his memory. Farewell my deare *Tom:* and God send you better daies then we have here, for I wish you as much happines as possibly man can have; I wish your mornings may be good, your noones better, your evenings and nights best of all; I wish your sorrowes may be short, your joyes lasting, and all your desires end in successe; let me heare once more from you before you remove thence, and tell me how the squares§ goe in *Flanders;* So I rest.

Your entirely affectionat Servitor

J. H.

Fleet, 3 *Aug.* 1644.

Dorothy Osborne

Letters to William Temple

1. [JUNE 2–4, 1653]

SIR

I have bin reckoning up how many faults you lay to my charge in your last letter, and I finde I am severe, unjust, unmercifull, and unkinde; O mee how should one doe to mende all these? 'tis worke for an Age and tis to bee fear'd I shall bee soe olde before I am good, that 'twill not bee considerable to any body but my self whither I am soe or not. I say nothing of the Pritty humor you fancy'd mee in, in your dream, because 'twas but a dream, Sure if it had bin any thing else, I should have rememberd that my Lord L[isle] loves to have his Chamber, and his Bed to himself. but seriously now, I wonder at your Patience, how could you heare mee talke soe sencelessly (though twere but in your sleep) and not bee redy to beate mee? what nice, mistaken points of honnor, I prettended to and yet could allow him a roome in the same bed with mee! well dream's are pleasant things to People whose humor's are soe, but to have the Spleen and to dreame upont is a punnishment I would not wish my greatest Enemy. I seldome dream, or never remember them unlesse they have bin soe sad as to put mee into such disorder as I can hardly recover when I am awake, and some of those I am confident I shall never forgett.

You aske mee how I passe my time heer, I can give you a perfect accounte not only of what I doe for the present, but what I am likely to doe this seven yeare if I stay heer soe long. I rise in the morning reasonably Early, and before I am redy⁵ I goe rounde the house till I am weary of that, and then into the garden till it grows to hott for mee. about ten a clock I think of makeing mee redy, and when that's don I goe into my

fathers Chamber, from thence to dinner, where my Cousin
[Henry] Molle and I sitt in great State, in a Roome and at a
table that would hold a great many more. After dinner wee sitt
and talk till Mr B.[4] com's in question and then I am gon. the
heat of the day is spent in reading or working and about sixe
or seven a Clock, I walke out into a Common that lyes hard^s
by the house where a great many young wenches keep Sheep
and Cow's and sitt in the shade singing of Ballads; I goe to
them and compare theire voyces and Beauty's to some Ancient
Shepherdesses that I have read of and finde a vaste difference
there, but trust mee I think these are as innocent as those could
bee. I talke to them, and finde they want nothing to make them
the happiest People in the world, but the knoledge that they are
soe. most comonly when wee are in the middest of our discourse
one looks aboute her and spyes her Cow's goeing into the Corne^s
and then away they all run, as if they had wing's at theire heels.
I that am not soe nimble stay behinde, & when I see them drive-
ing home theire Cattle I think tis time for mee to retyre^s too.
when I have supped I goe into the Garden and soe to the syde
of a small River that runs by it where I sitt downe and wish
you with mee, (You had best say this is not kinde neither) in
Earnest tis a pleasant place and would bee much more soe to
mee if I had your company. I sitt there somtimes till I am lost
with thinking, and were it not for some cruell thoughts of the
Crossenesse of our fortun's that will not lett mee sleep there, I
should forgett there were such a thing to bee don as goeing to
bed. Since I writt this my Company is increased by two, My
Brother Harry, and a faire Neece, the Eldest of my Brother^s
Peytons Daughter's, she is soe much a woman, that I am almost
ashamed to say I am her Aunte, and soe Pritty that if I had
any designe to gaine a Servant I should not like her company.
but I have none, and therfore, shall indeavor to keep her heer
as long as I can perswade her father to spare her, for she will
easily consent to it haveing soe much of my humor (though it
bee the worst thing in her) as to like a melancholy place, and
litle company.

My Brother John is not come downe againe nor am I certaine

---

4 Levinus Bennet, Sheriff of Cambridgeshire, was Cousin Molle's choice for
Dorothy's hand.

when hee will bee heer, hee went from London into Gloucester-shyr to my Sister§ who was very ill, and his youngest Girle of which hee was very fonde is since dead, but I beleeve by that time his wife has a litle recoverd her sicknesse and the losse of her Childe, hee will bee comeing this way. My Father is reason-ably well but keeps his Chamber still, and will hardly I am affrayde Ever bee soe perfectly recoverd as to come abroade againe. I am sorry for Poore Walker, but you need not doubt§ of what hee has of yours in his hands, for it seems hee do's not use to doe his worke himself (I speake seriously), hee keeps a french man that setts all his Seal's and Ring's. if what you say of my Lady Lepington bee of your owne knoledge I shall beleeve you, but otherwise I can assure you I have heard from People that prettend to know her very well, that her kindenesse to Compton was very moderate, and that she never liked him soe well, as when hee dyed and gave her his Estate. but they might bee deceived, and tis not soe strange as that you should imagin a Coldenesse and an indifference in my letter where I soe litle meant it, but I am not displeased you should desyre my kinde-nesse, enough to aprehende§ the losse of it, when it is safest, Only I would not have you aprehende it soe farr as to belie[ve] it posible. that were an injury to all the assurances I have given you and if you love mee you cannot think mee unworthy. I should think my self soe, if I founde you indifferent to mee, that I have had soe long and soe perticuler a freindship for. but sure this is more then I need to say, you are Enough in my heart to know all my thoughts, and if soe, you know better then I can tell you how much I am

Yours

2. [OCTOBER, 1653]

SIR

Why are you soe sullen, and why am I the cause? can you beleeve that I doe willingly deffer my Journy? I know you doe not. why then should my Absence now bee lesse suportable to you then heretofore? it cannot, nay it shall not bee long (if I can help it) & I shall break thorough all inconvency's [sic] rather then deny you any thing that ly's in my power to grant; but by your owne rules then may not I Expect the same from you? is it posible that all I have sayed cannot Oblige you to a care of your Selfe? what a pleasant distinction you make when you say tis not melancholy makes you doe these things but a carelesse forgetfulnesse, did ever any body forget themselv's to that degree that was not melancholy in Extreamity? good God how are you Alter'd! and what is it that has don it? I have knowne you when of all the things in ye^s world you would not have bin taken for a discontent,^{s} you were as I thought perfectly pleased with your condition, what has made it soe much worse since? I know nothing you have lost and am sure you have gained a friend, A friend that is capable of the highest degree of friendship you can propounde, that has already given an intire heart for that wch she received, and tis noe more in her will then in her power ever to recall it or devide it; if this bee not Enough to sattisfye you, tell mee what I can doe more, I shall finde lesse difficulty in the doeing it then in imagining what it may bee; and will not you then doe soe much for my sake as to bee carefull of a health I am soe infinitly concern'd in and wch these Courses^s must need's distroy? if you Loved mee you would, I am sure you would, and Let mee tell you, you can never bee that perfect friend you describe if you can deny mee this.

but will not your wife⁵ beleeve there is such a friendship? I am not of her opinion at all but I doe not wonder neither that she is of it. Alas, how few there are that ever heard of such a thing, and ffewer that understand it, besyd's it is not to bee taught or Learn'd, it must come Naturaly to those that have it and those must have it before they can know it. but I admire,^{s} since she has it not, how she can bee sattisfyed with her condition, nothing else sure can recompence the Alteration you say is made in her fortune. what was it took her? her husbands good face? what could invite her where there was neither fortune, witt nor good usage and a husband to whome she was but indifferent? wch is all one to mee, if not worse, then an Aversion and I should sooner hope to gaine upon one that Hated mee

---

⁵ It is not clear whether this is some particular lady who is so called in jest or whether it is a playful reference to an imagined wife.

then upon one that did not consider mee enough either to Love
or hate mee; i'le swere she is much Easyer to please then I
should bee. there are a great many ingredients must goe to the
makeing mee happy in a husband, first, as my Cousin [Elizabeth]
Fr[anklin] say's, our humors must agree, and to doe that hee
must have that kinde of breeding that I have had and used that
kinde of company, that is hee must not bee soe much a Country
Gentleman as to understand Nothing but hawks and dog's and
bee fonder of Either then of his wife, nor of the next sort of
them whose aime reaches noe further then to bee Justice of
peace and once in his life high Sheriff, who read no book but
Statut's and study's nothing but how to make a speech inter-
larded with Latin that may amaze his disagreeing poore Neighbours and fright them rather then perswade them into quiet-
nesse; hee must not bee a thing that began the world in a free
scoole, was sent from thence to the University, and is at his
farthest when hee reaches the Inn's of Court, has noe acquaintance but those of his forme§ in these places, speaks the french
hee has pickt out of Old Law's, and admires nothing but the
Storry's hee has heard of the Revells§ that were kept there before
his time; hee must not bee a Towne Gallant neither that lives in
a Tavern and an Ordinary,§ that cannot imagin how an hower
should bee spent without company unlesse it bee in sleeping,
that makes court to all the Women hee sees, thinks they beleeve
him and Laughs and is Laught at Equaly; Nor a Traveld Moun-
sieur whose head is all feather inside and outside, that can talk
of nothing but dances and Duells, and has Courage Enough to
were§ slashes§ when every body else dy's with cold to see him;
hee must not bee a foole of noe sort, nor peevish nor ill Natur'd
nor proude nor Coveteous and to all this must bee added that
he must Love mee and I him as much as wee are capable of
Loveing. Without all this his fortune though never soe great
would not sattisfye mee, and with it a very moderat one would
keep mee from ever repenting my disposall.§ I have bin as large
and as perticular in my discriptions as my Cousin Molle in his
of Moore Park; but that you know the place soe well I would
send it you, nothing can come neer his Patience in writeing it
but my reading ont.§ but would you had sent mee your fathers
letter, it would not have bin lesse welcome to mee then to you,

and you may safely beleeve that I am Equaly concern'd with
you in any thing.

I should bee pleased too to see somthing of my Lady Carlisles
writeing because she is soe Extreordinary a Person. I have bin
thinking of sending you my Picture till I could come my self,
but a Picture is but dull company and that you need not, besyd's
I cannot tell whither it bee very like mee or not, though tis the
best I have ever had drawne for mee and Mr Lilly[6] will have it
that hee never took more pain's to make a good one in his life.
and that was it I think that spoiled it; hee was condemned for
makeing the first hee drew for mee a litle worse then I, and
in makeing this better hee has made it as unlike as tother. hee
is now I think at my Lord Pagetts at Marloe where I am promised hee shall draw a Picture of my Lady for mee, she giv's it
mee she say's as ye greatest testimony of her friendship to mee,
for by her owne rule she is past the time of haveing Pictur's
taken of her, After Eighteen shee say's there is noe face but
decay's aparantly. I would faine have had her Excepted such
as had never bin beauty's, for my comfort, but she would not.

When you see your friend Mr Heningham You may tell him
in his Eare there is a Willow Garland comeing towards him. hee
might have sped better in his suite if hee made court to mee
as well as to my La[dy Grey de] Ru[thin], shee has bin my wife
this Seven year and who soever pretends there must ask my
Leave; I have now given my consent that she shall marry a Very
pritty litle Gentleman, Sr Chr[istopher] Yelverton's Son, and I
think wee shall have a wedding ere it bee long. my Lady her
Mother in great kindenesse would have recomended Hen[ry Yel-
verton] to mee and told mee in a Complement that I was fitter
for him then her daughter whoe was younger and therfore did
not understand the world soe well, that she was certain if hee
knew mee hee would bee Extreamly taken, for I would make
just that kinde of wife hee looked for. I humbly thankt her but
sayed that without knowing him (more then by relation[5]) I
was certain hee would not make that kinde of husband I looked
for, and soe it went noe further.

I Expect my Eldest brother heer shortly whose fortune is well

---

6 Peter Lely, who, after the death of Sir Anthony Van Dyck in 1641, was the
most fashionable portrait painter in England for almost forty years.

mended by my Other brothers death, soe as if hee were sattisfyed himself with what hee has don, I know noe reason why hee might not bee very happy, but I am affrayd hee is not. I have not seen my Sister[§] since I knew shee was soe, but sure she can have lost noe beauty, for I never saw any shee had but good black Ey's wch cannot Alter. hee Lov's her I think at the Ordinary rate of husbands, but not enough I beleeve to marry her soe much to his disadvantage if it were to doe again, and that would kill mee were I as shee. for I could bee infinitly better sattisfyed wth a husband that had never Loved mee in hope hee might, then wth one that began to Love mee lesse then hee had don.

I am   Yours

3. [FEBRUARY 4, 1654]

Tis well you have given over your reproches; I can allow you to tell mee of my faults kindly and like a friend; Posibly it is a weaknesse in mee, to ayme at the worlds Esteem as if I could not bee happy without it; but there are certaine things that custom has made Almost of Absolute necessity, and reputation I take to bee one of those; if one could bee invisible I should choose that, but since all people are seen and knowne, and shall bee talked of in[§] spight of theire Teeth's, whoe is it that do's not desyre at least that nothing of ill may bee sayed of them whither Justly, or Otherwise? I never knew any soe sattisfied with theire owne innocence as to bee content the worlde should think them Guilty; some out of pride have seem'd to contemme ill reports when they have founde they could not avoyde them; but none out of strengh of reason though many have prettended to it; noe not my Lady New Castle with all her Philosophy;[7] therfore you must not Expect it from mee; I shall never bee ashamed to owne that I have a particuler Valew for you above any Other, but tis not the greatest merritt of Person will Excuse a want of fortune; in some degree I think it will, at least with the most

---

[7] Margaret Cavendish, Duchess of Newcastle, eccentric poetess, philosopher (*Philosophical Fancies*, 1653), and biographer. In another letter, Dorothy Osborne wrote that "there are many soberer People in Bedlam, i'le swear her friends are much to blame to let her goe abroade."

rationall part of the worlde, and as farr as that will reach I
desyre it should; I would not have the worlde beleeve I marryed
out of Interest§ and to please my friends, I had much rather
they should know I chose the Person, and took his fortune because twas necessary and that I preffer a competency with one
I esteem infinitly before a Vaste Estate in Other hands; Tis
much Easier sure to get a good fortune then a good Husband,
but whosoever marry's without any consideration of fortune
shall never bee allowed§ to doe it out of soe reasonable an apre-
hension;§ the whole worlde (without any reserve) shall pronounce they did it meerly to sattisfie theire Giddy humor. Besides
though you imagin twere a great argument of my Kindenesse
to consider nothing but you, In Earnest I beleeve twould bee
an injury to you, I doe not see that it putts any Valew upon
men, when Women marry them for Love (as they terme it), 'tis
not theire merritt but our ffolly that is alway's presumed to
cause it, and would it bee any advantage to you to have your
wife thought an indiscreet person? All this I can say to you, but
when my Brother disputes it with mee I have Other Arguments
for him, and I drove him up soe close t'other night that for want
of a better gap to gett out at, hee was faine to say that hee
feard as much your haveing a fortune as your haveing none,
for hee saw you held my Lord L[isle's] principles, that Religion
or honnour were things you did not consider att all, and that
hee was confident you would take any Engagement, serve in any
employment or doe any thing to advance yourself. I had noe patience for this, to say you were a begger, Your Father not worth
4000ʹⁱ in the whole world, was nothing in comparison of haveing noe Religion nor noe honnour. I forgott all my disguise and
wee talked our selves weary, hee renounced mee againe and I
defyed him, but both in as Civill Language as it would permitt,
and parted in great Anger with the Usuall Ceremony of a Leg§
and a Courtesy,§ that you would have dyed wᵗʰ Laughing to
have seen us. the next day I not beeing at dinner saw him not
till night; then hee cam into my Chamber, where I supped but
hee did not. Afterwards Mʳ Gibson and hee and I talked of indifferent things till all but wee two went to bed, there hee sate
halfe an hower and sayde not one word nor I to him, at Last in
a pittifull Tone, Sister say's hee, I have heard you say that when

any thing troubles you, of all things you aprehend[§] goeing to bed, because there it increases upon you and you lye at the mercy of all your sad thoughts which y[e] silence and darknesse of y[e] night adds a horror to; I am at that passe now, I vow to God I would not indure another night like the last to gaine a Crowne. I whoe resolved to take noe notice what ayled him, sayd twas a knoledge I had raised from my Spleen only; and soe fell into a discourse of Melancholy and y[e] Causes, and from that (I know not how) into Religion, and wee talked soe long of it and soe devoutely´that it layed[§] all our anger, wee grew to a calme and peace with all the world; two hermitts conversing in a Cell they Equaly inhabitt, never Expressed more humble Charritable Kindenesse one towards another then wee, hee asked my Pardon and I his, and hee has promised mee never to speak of it to mee whilest hee liv's but leave the Event[§] to God Almighty, and till hee sees it don, hee will bee always the same to mee that hee is; then hee shall leave mee, hee say's, not out of want of Kindenesse to mee, but because hee cannot see the Ruine of a Person that hee lov's soe passionatly and in whose happinesse hee had layed up all his. These are the Term's wee are at, and I am confident hee will keep his word wth mee; soe that you have noe reason to fear him in any respect, for though hee should break his promise hee should never make mee break mine; noe let mee assure you, this Rivall nor any other shall Ever Alter mee. Therfor spare your Jelousy or turne it all into Kindenesse.

I will write Every week, and noe misse of letters shall give us any doubts of one another, Time nor accidents shall not prevaile upon our hearts, and if God Almighty please to blesse us, wee will meet the same wee are, or happyer. I will doe all you bid mee, I will pray, and wish and hope, but you must doe soe too then; and bee soe carfull of your self that I may have nothing to reproche you with when you come back. That vile wench[8] let's you see all my Scribles I beleeve, how doe you know I tooke care your haire should not bee spoyled? tis more then Ere you did I think, You are soe necgligent on't and keep it soe ill, tis pitty you should have it. may you have better luck in the Cutting it then I had with mine, I cutt it two or 3 year

8 Nan Stacy, a young woman who had perhaps once been in Miss Osborne's service and who was employed by Temple in London.

agon and it never grew since; Looke to it, if I keep the Lock you give mee better then you doe all the rest, I shall not spare you, Expect to bee soundly Chidden. what doe you mean to doe with all my Letters? leave them behinde you? if you doe it must bee in safe hands. some of them concerne you, and mee, and Other People besydes, very much, and they will almost loade a horse to carry.

Dos not My Cousins at M[oor] P[ark] mistrust us a little? I have a great beleife they doe, I'me sure Robin C[heke] tolde my Brother of it since I was last in Towne. of all things I admire[s] my Cousin Molle has not gott it by the End, hee that frequents that Famely soe much and is at this instant at Kimbolton. if hee has, and conceals it, hee is very discreet, I could never discerne by any thing that hee knew it. I shall indeavor to accustome my self to the noyse on't and make it as Easy to mee as I can, though I had much rather it were not talked of till there were an absolute nescessity of discovering it, and you can oblige mee in nothing more then in concealing it.

I take it very kindly that you promise to use all your interest in your F[ather] to perswade him to indeavor our happinesse, and hee apears soe confident of his power that it gives mee great hopes. Deare, shall wee ever bee soe happy, think you? Ah I dare not hope it, yet tis not want of love gives mee these fear's. noe, in Earnest, I think, (nay I am sure) I love you more then Ever, and tis that only gives mee these dispaireing thoughts, When I consider how small a proportion[s] of happines is allowed in this worlde, and how great mine would bee in a person for whome I have a passionate Kindenesse and whoe has the same for mee; As it is infinitly above what I can deserve, and more then God Almighty usually allotts to the best People, I can finde nothing in reason but seems to bee against mee, and mee thinks tis as vaine in mee to Expect it as twould bee to hope I might bee a Queen (if that were realy as desyrable a thing as tis thought to bee). And it is Just it should bee soe; Wee complaine of this world and the Variety of Crosses and afflictions it abound's in, and yet for all this whoe is weary on't (more then in discourse)? whoe thinks with pleasure of leaveing it, or preparing for the next? Wee see olde folkes that have ou[t]lived all ye comforts of life, desyre to continue it, and nothing can wean

us from the ffolly of preffering a mortall beeing subject to great
infirmity's and unavoydable decays, before an immortall one
and all ye Glorry's that are promised with it. Is not this very like
preaching? well tis too good for you, you shall have noe more
on't, I am affrayde you are not mortified[§] Enough for such discourses to worke upon, though I am not of my Brothers opinion
neither (that you have noe religion in you), in Earnest I never
tooke any thing hee ever sayd halfe soe ill, as nothing sure
is soe great an injury, it must suppose one to bee a Divell in
human Shape. O mee now I am speaking of Religion lett mee
aske you is not his Name Bagshaw that you say railes on Love
& Women? because I heard one tother day speaking of him &
comending his witt but withall sayed hee was a Perfect Atheist,
if soe I can allow him to hate us, and love, which sure has somthing of devine in it, since god requir's it of us; I am comeing
into my preaching vaine againe, what think you? were it not
a good way of prefferment as the times are? if you advise mee
to it ile venture. the woman at Somercett house was Cryed[§] up
mightily, think on't;

Deare I am　　Yours

John Aubrey

TO MY WORTHY FRIEND MR. ANTHONIE
À WOOD, ANTIQUARIE OF OXFORD

Sir!

I have, according to your desire, putt in writing these minutes[§]
of lives tumultuarily,[§] as they occurr'd to my thoughts or as
occasionally I had information of them. They may easily be
reduced[§] into order at your leisure by numbring them with red
figures, according to time and place, &c. 'Tis a taske that I never
thought to have undertaken till you imposed it upon me, sayeing

that I was fitt for it by reason of my generall acquaintance, having now not only lived above halfe a centurie of yeares in the world, but have also been much tumbled up and downe in it which hath made me much knowne; besides the moderne advantage of coffee-howses in this great citie, before which men knew not how to be acquainted, but with their owne relations, or societies. I might add that I come of a longaevous[§] race, by which meanes I have imped[§] some feathers of the wings of time, for severall generations; which does reach high.[§] When I first began, I did not thinke I could have drawne it out to so long a thread.

I here lay-downe to you (out of the conjunct friendship between us)[9] the trueth, and, as neer as I can and that religiously as a poenitent to his confessor, nothing but the trueth: the naked and plaine trueth, which is here exposed so bare that the very *pudenda* are not covered, and affords many passages that would raise a blush in a young virgin's cheeke. So that after your perusall, I must desire you to make a castration (as Raderus to Martial) and to sowe-on some figge-leaves—i. e., to be my *Index expurgatorius*.

What uncertainty doe we find in printed histories? they either treading too neer on the heeles of trueth that they dare not speake plaine, or els for want of intelligence (things being antiquated) become too obscure and darke![1] I doe not here repeat any thing already published (to the best of my remembrance) and I fancy my selfe all along discourseing with you; alledgeing[§] those of my relations and acquaintance (as either you knew or have heerd of) *ad faciendam fidem:*[2] so that you make me to

9 In a marginal note, Aubrey dates their first acquaintance in 1665, and he adds, quoting not quite accurately, "Utrumque nostrum admirabili modo / Consentit astrum. *Horat.* lib. 2, ode 17; Nescio quod certe est, quod me tibi temperet, astrum. *Pers. Sat.* v. v. 50 [The stars of the two of us are wondrously linked together—Horace, Book 2, ode 17; Surely, one star governs us both—Persius, Satire 5, line 50 (properly 51)]."

1 Aubrey probably has in mind a passage in the last paragraph but one of the preface to Raleigh's *Historie of the World* (1614): ". . . who-so-ever in writing a moderne Historie, shall follow truth too neare the heeles, it may happily[§] strike out his teeth. There is no Mistresse or Guide, that hath led her followers and servants into greater miseries. He that goes after her too farre off, looseth[§] her sight, and looseth him-selfe: and hee that walkes after her at a middle distance; I know not whether I should call that kinde of course Temper[§] or Baseness."

2 To command belief.

renew my acquaintance with my old and deceased friends, and to *rejuvenescere*[3] (as it were) which is the pleasure of old men. 'Tis pitty that such minutes had not been taken 100 yeares since or more: for want wherof many worthy men's names and notions are swallowd-up in oblivion; as much of these also would, had it not been through your instigation: and perhaps this is one of the usefullest pieces that I have scribbeld.

I remember one sayeing of generall Lambert's, that the best of men are but men at the best: of this, you will meet with divers examples in this rude and hastie collection. Now these *arcana* are not fitt to lett flie abroad, till about 30 yeares hence; for the author and the persons (like medlars) ought to be first rotten. But in whose hands must they be deposited in the mean time? advise me, who am,

Sir,
Your very affectionate friend
to serve you,

John Aubrey.

London,
June 15,
1680.

Sir George Etherege

TO HIS GRACE THE DUKE OF BUCKINGHAM

Ratisbone, October 21, 1686.

MY LORD,

I never enjoy my self so much, as when *I* can steal a few Moments, from the Hurry of public Business, to write to my Friends in *England;* and as there is none there to whom *I* pay a profounder Respect than to your Grace, wonder not if *I* afford my

[3] To regain youth.

self the Satisfaction of conversing with you by way of Letters,
(the only Relief I have left me to support your Absence at this
distance) as often as I can find an opportunity.

You may guess by my last, whether I don't pass my Time very
comfortably here; forc'd as I am by my Character, to spend the
better part of my time in Squabling and Deliberating with Persons of Beard and Gravity, how to preserve the Ballance of Christendome, which would go well enough of its self, if the Divines
and Ministers of Princes would let it alone: And when I come
home spent and weary from the *Diet*,§ I have no Lord *D—t*'s, or
Sir *Charles S—y*'s to sport away the Evening with; no Madame
I—, or my Lady *A—*'s; in short, none of those kind charming
Creatures *London* affords, in whose Embraces I might make my
self amends for so many Hours murdered in impertinent Debates; so that not to magnifie my sufferings to your Grace, they
really want a greater stock of Christian Patience to support
them, than I can pretend to be Master of.

I have been long enough in this Town (one would think) to
have made Acquaintance enough with Persons of both Sexes, so
as never to be at a loss how to pass the few vacant Hours I can
allow my self: But the terrible Drinking that accompanies all
our Visits, hinders me from Conversing with the Men so often as
I would otherwise doe; and the *German* Ladies are so intollerably
reserv'd and virtuous, (with Tears in my eyes I speak it to your
Grace) that 'tis next to an impossibility to carry on an Intrigue
with them: A Man has so many Scruples to conquer, and so
many Difficulties to surmount, before he can promise himself the
least Success, that for my part I have given over all Pursuits of
this Nature: Besides, there is so universal a Spirit of Censorious-
ness reigns in this Town, that a Man and a Woman cannot be
seen at *Ombre* or *Piquet* together, but 'tis immediately concluded
some other Game has been played between them; and as this
renders all manner of Access to the Ladies almost impracticable,
for fear of exposing their Reputation to the Mercy of their ill-
natur'd Neighbours, so it makes an innocent Piece of Gallantry
often pass for a criminal Correspondence.

So that to deal freely with your Grace, among so many noble
and wealthy Families as we have in this Town, I can only pretend to be truly acquainted but with one: The Gentleman's Name

was Monsieur *Hoffman,* a frank, hearty, jolly Companion; his Father, one of the most eminent Wine-Merchants of the City, left him a considerable Fortune, which he improved by marrying a *French* Jeweller's Daughter of *Lyons:* To give you his Character in short, he was a sensible ingenious§ Man, and had none of his Country Vices, which I impute to his having travelled abroad and seen *Italy, France* and *England.* His Lady is a most accomplish'd ingenious Person, and notwithstanding she is come into a Place, where so much Formality and Stiffness are practiced, keeps up all the Vivacity, and Air, and good Humor of *France.*

I had been happy in my Acquaintance with this Family for some Months, when an ill favour'd Accident rob'd me of the greatest Happiness I had hitherto enjoy'd in *Germany,* the loss of which *I* can never sufficiently regret. Monsieur *Hoffman,* about three Weeks ago, going to make merry with some Friends (at a Village some three Leagues from this Place) upon the *Danube,* by the Unskilfulness or Negligence of the Watermen, the Boat, wherin he was, unfortunately chanced to over-set, and of some twenty Persons, not one escaped to bring home the News but a Boy that miraculously saved himself by holding fast to the Rudder, and so by the Rapidity of the Current was cast upon the other Shore.

I was sensibly afflicted at the Destiny of my worthy Friend, and so indeed were all that had the Honour of knowing him; but his Wife took on so extravagantly, that she (in a short Time) was the only talk both of City and Country; she refus'd to admit any Visits from her nearest Relations, her Chamber, her Antichamber, and Pro-antichamber were hung with Black, nay the very Candles, her Fans, and Tea-table wore the Livery of Grief; she refus'd all manner of Sustenance, and was so averse to the Thoughts of Living, that she talk'd of nothing but Death; in short, you may tell your injenious Friend *Monsieur de Saint Evremont,* that *Petronius*'s *Ephesian* Matron, to whose Story he has done so much Justice in his noble Translation, was only a Type of our more obstinate, as well as unhappy *German* Widow.

About a Fortnight after this cruel Loss (for I thought it would be Labour lost to attack her Grief in its first Vehemence) I thought my self obliged, in Point of Honour and Gratitude to the Memory of my deceased Friend, to make her a small Visit, and condole her Ladyship upon this unhappy Occasion: And tho' I had been told that she had refused to see several Persons who had gon to wait on her with the same Errand, yet I presumed so much upon the Friendship her late Husband had always express'd for me, (not to mention the particular Civilities I had received from her self) as to think I should be admitted to have a sight of her: Accordingly I came to her House, sent up my Name, and word was immediately brought me, that if I pleas'd I might go up to her.

When I came into the Room, I fancy'd my self in the Territories of Death, every thing looked so gloomy, so dismal, and so melancholly. There was a grave *Lutheran* Minister with her, that omitted no Arguments to bring her to a more composed and more Christian Disposition of Mind. Madam (says he) you don't consider that by abandoning your self thus to Despair, you actually rebel against Providence; I cann't help it, (says she) Providence may e'en thank it self, for laying so insupportable a Load upon me: O fye, Madam, (cries the other) this is down right impiety; What would you say now, if Heaven should punish it by some more exemplary§ Visitation? That is impossible, replies the Lady sighing, and since it has rob'd me of the onely Delight I had in this World, the only Favour it can do me is to level a Thunderbolt at my Head and put an end to all my Sufferings. The Parson finding her in this extravagant Strain, and seeing no likelihood of Perswading her to come to a better Temper, got up from his Seat and took his leave of her.

It came to my turn now to try whether I was not capable of comforting her, and being convinced by so late an Instance that Arguments brought from Religion were not like to work any extraordinary Effects upon her, I resolved to attack her Ladiship in a more sensible part, and represent to her the great inconveniences (not which her Soul, but) her Body received from this inordinate Sorrow.

Madam, saies *I* to her, next to my Concern for your worthy Husband's untimely Death, I am griev'd to see what an Alteration the Bemoaning of his Loss has occasion'd in you: These Words raising her Curiosity to know what this Alteration was, *I* thus continu'd my Discourse; In endeavouring, Madam, to extinguish, or at least to alleviate your Grief, than which nothing can be more prejudicial to a beautiful Woman, I intend a publick Benefit, for if the Public is interested, as most certainly it is, in the preserving of a beautiful Face, that Man does the Public no little Service who contributes most to its Preservation.

This odd Beginning operated so wonderfully upon her, that she desired me to leave this general Road of Complements, and explain my self more particularly to her. Upon this (delivering my self with an unusual Air of Gravity, which your Grace knows I seldom carry about me in the Company of Ladies) I told her, that Grief ruines the finest Faces sooner than any thing whatever; and that as envy it self could not deny her Face to be the most charming in the Universe, so if she did not suffer⁵ her self to be comforted, she must soon expect to take her Farewel of it. I confirm'd this Assertion, by telling her of one of the finest Women we ever had in *England* who did her self more injury in a Fortnight's time by lamenting her only Brother's Death, than ten Years could possibly have done; that I had heard an eminent Physician at *Leyden* say, That Tears (having abundance of saline Particles in them) not only spoild the Complexion, but hastned Wrinkles: But, Madam, concluded I, why should I give my self the trouble to confirm this by foreign instances, and by the Testimonies of our knowing Doctors, when alas! your own Face so fully justifies the Truth of what I have said to you.

How! reply'd our disconsolate Widow, with a Sigh that came from the Bottom of her Heart, And is it possible that my just concern for my dear Husband, has wrought so cruel an Effect upon me in so short a Time? With that she order'd her Gentlewoman to bring the Lookinglass to her, and having survey'd her self a few Minutes in it, she told me she was perfectly convinced that my Notions were true; but, cries she, what would you have us poor Women do in these Cases? For something, continues she, we owe to the Memory of the Deceased, and something too to the World, which expects at least the common Appearances of Grief from us.

By your leave, Madam, saies I, all this is a Mistake, and no better; you owe nothing to your Husband, since he is dead, and knows nothing of your Lamentation; besides, could you shed an Ocean of Tears upon his Hearse, it would not do him the least

Service; much less do you lye under any such Obligations to the
World, as to spoil a good Face only to comply with its tyrannic
Customs: No, Madam, take care to preserve your Beauty, and
then let the World say what it pleases, your Ladyship may be
revenged upon the World whene'er you see fit. I am resolved,
answers she, to be intirely govern'd by you, therefore tell me
frankly what sort of a Course you'd have me steer? Why, Madam,
saies I, in the first place forget the Defunct; and in order to bring
that about, relieve Nature, to which you have been so long un-
merciful, with the most exquisit Meats and the most generous
Wines. Upon Condition you'll sup with me, cries our afflicted
Lady, I will submit to your prescription. But why should I trouble
your Grace with a Narration of every Particular? In short, we had
a noble Regale§ that Evening in her Bed-chamber, and our good
Widow push'd the Glass so strenuously about, that her Comforter
(meaning my self) could hardly find the way to his Coach. To
conclude this Farce, (which I am afraid begins now to be too
tedious to your Grace) this *Phœnix* of her Sex, this Pattern of
Conjugal Fidelity, two Mornings ago was marry'd to a smooth-
chind Ensign of Count *Trautmandorf*'s Regiment, that had not a
farthing in the World but his Pay to depend upon: I assisted at
the Ceremony, tho' I little imagin'd the Lady would take the
Matrimonial Receit so soon.

I was the easier perswaded to give your Grace a large Account
of this Tragi-comedy, not only because I wanted better Matter to
entertain you with at this Lazy Conjuncture, but also to show
your Grace, that not only *Ephesus* in ancient, and *England* in
later Times, have afforded such fantastical Widows, but even
Germany it self; where, if the Ladies have not more Virtue than
those of their Sex in other Countries, yet they pretend at least a
greater Management of the outside of it.

By my last Pacquet from *England,* among a heap of nauseous
Trash, I received the *Three Dukes of Dunstable,* which is really
so monstrous and insipid, that I am sorry *Lapland* or *Livonia* had
not the Honour of producing it; but if I did Penance in reading it,
I rejoyced to hear that it was so solemnly interr'd to the Tune of
Catcalls. The *'Squire of Alsatia* however, which came by the following Post, made me some amends for the cursed impertinence

of the *Three Dukes;* and my witty Friend Sir *C— S—y's Bella mira* gave me that intire Satisfaction that I cannot read it over too often.

They tell me my old Acquaintance Mr. *Dryden* has left off the Theatre, and wholly applies him self to the Study of the Controversies between the two Churches. Pray Heaven! this strange alteration in him portends nothing disastrous to the State; but I have all along observed, That Poets do Religion as little Service by drawing their Pens for it, as the Divines do Poetry by pretending to Versification.

But I forget how troublesome I have been to your Grace, I shall therefore conclude with assuring you that I am, and to the last Moment of my Life shall be ambitious of being,

My LORD,

Your Grace's most obedient,
and most obliged Servant,
G. Etherege.

Biographical and Bibliographical Notes

The following abbreviations have been used in these notes:

JEGP *Journal of English and Germanic Philology*
MLN   *Modern Language Notes*
MLR   *Modern Language Review*
MP   *Modern Philology*
N&Q   *Notes and Queries*
PMLA *Publications of the Modern Language Association of America*
PQ   *Philological Quarterly*
RES   *Review of English Studies*
SP   *Studies in Philology*
STC   A. W. Pollard and G. R. Redgrave, *A Short-Title Catalogue of Books . . . , 1475–1640* (1926)
TLS   [London] *Times Literary Supplement*

JOHN AUBREY
1626–1697

"This yeare all my business and affaires ran Kim§ Kam. Nothing tooke effect," Aubrey wrote under the year 1666 in his scrap of an autobiography. The statement accurately describes his life and works. Pressed for money even at Trinity College, Oxford, and at the Middle Temple, Aubrey finally settled down to bankruptcy and dependence on the generosity of many friends. The only book of his published in his lifetime, *Miscellanies* (1696), a codification of tales of occult phenomena under twenty-one headings, is unrepresentative in its seeming completeness and structure. It is representative, however, in that it reveals the lifelong folkloristic and antiquarian interest that drew him to membership in the Royal Society at its founding and that led to many manuscript pages on the topography of Wiltshire and Surrey and on the remains of Gentilism and Judaism.

In a life spent in recording topographical and biographical details, the most important event was not personally guiding Charles II about the prehistoric remains at Avebury but meeting Anthony à Wood in 1667. From 1669 until his death, Aubrey gathered information for Wood's projected work on the writers and bishops of Oxford, at the same time following his interest in collecting information about English mathematicians from the time of Henry VIII and about Thomas Hobbes. He left behind a jumble of over 400 lives, some only a few words long, that of Hobbes over 20,000 words. "Never any in England were delivered so faithfully and with so good authority," he wrote, and he tried to provide for publication independent of Wood's work by getting his notes deposited in the library of the Ashmolean Museum at Oxford. Four lives were published in 1797 and others in 1813, but Aubrey's work was first given proper treatment in 1898 with the publication of Andrew Clark's two-volume edition, which remains the basic text of the *Brief Lives*. By permission of the Clarendon Press, Oxford, Aubrey's notes for the life of Sir Walter Raleigh are here printed from Clark's edition. Clark's order has been changed in two places; notes containing a few references for Wood to examine, a coat of arms, a pedigree and some family history, Raleigh's epigram on Sir Robert Cecil, and a small list of Raleigh's works have been omitted; two racy stories not present in Clark's edition have been added from MS. Aubrey 6 (ff. 74ᵛ and 77ʳ) through the kindness of the Librarian, Bodleian Library, Oxford. Aubrey's letter to Wood is printed from Clark, I, 10–12.

John Collier's *The Scandal and Credulities of John Aubrey* (1931) is a small collection of lives, with some passages printed for the first time and with an appreciative introduction. For an edition of *Brief Lives* (1949; 3rd ed. 1960), Oliver Lawson Dick selected 134 lives and included excerpts from others in his long biographical introduction. Some of the lives and some passages from other works by Aubrey are in *Brief Lives and Other Selected Writings* (1949), edited by Anthony Powell, who had published in 1948 a biographical study, *John Aubrey and His Friends* (new rev. ed., 1963).

FRANCIS BACON
1561–1626

"Scarcely any man has been entitled to be called a thorough man of the world," wrote Macaulay in his extraordinary 100-page review of Basil Montagu's new edition of Bacon's *Works* (*The Edinburgh Review*, LXV [July, 1837]). The assessment holds good: after education at Trinity College, Cambridge, and at Gray's Inn, after a long career in the House of Commons, Bacon became James I's Solicitor-General in 1607, Attorney-General in 1613, Lord Keeper in 1617, and

Lord Chancellor in 1618. One of the great figures in English law,
he was knighted in 1603, made Baron Verulam in 1618 and Viscount
St. Alban in 1621. But Bacon had opposed Aristotle long before he
tangled with Sir Edward Coke, and he is the primary articulator of
the importance of induction, experimentation, and utilitarianism in
scientific learning. *The Two Bookes . . . Of the proficience and advancement of Learning, divine and humane* (1605) and its enlarged
Latin version, *De Dignitate & Augmentis Scientiarum* (1623) point
out the inadequacies of existing knowledge and consider the need
and possibility of its advancement; the *Novum Organum,* printed
under the title *Instauratio Magna,* in 1620, discusses the hindrances
to advancement and provides the empirical and rational tool for
securing it. After his fall from power in 1621, Bacon found time to
write his fine *Historie of the Raigne of King Henry the Seventh*
(1622).

Macaulay thought that Bacon's works on science *indirectly* "moved
the intellects which have moved the world," that only in the *Essays*
was "the mind of Bacon brought into immediate contact with the
minds of ordinary readers." ("Bacon's Essaies . . . first opened my
Understanding as to Moralls," wrote Aubrey of himself at the age
of twelve.) Ten essays, starting with "Of Studies" and "Of discourse"
and ending with "Of Negociating," were published in 1597 in a
little volume that included also a few Latin religious meditations
and a fragment on the appearances of good and evil. With the exception of the essay "Of Honour and reputation," these essays were revised and printed in 1612 with twenty-nine new ones. In 1625 Bacon
revised and amplified all the essays, and added nineteen for the first
time. The text used here is that of *The Essayes or Counsels, Civill
and Morall,* 1625; a few changes have been made in the text of the
Cornell copy in the light of W. Aldis Wright's collation of ten copies
on pp. 351–353 of his edition of 1885 in the Golden Treasury Series,
an edition that remains outstanding. The text of the first edition of
"Of Studies" follows, so that Bacon's original aphoristic approach
may be compared with his later method.

Studies serve for pastimes, for ornaments & for abilities. Their
chiefe use for pastime is in privatenes and retiring; for orna-
mente is in discourse, and for abilitie is in judgement. For expert
men can execute, but learned men are fittest to judge or censure.
⁌ To spend too much time in them is slouth, to use them too
much for ornament is affectation: to make judgement wholly by
their rules, is the humour of a Scholler. ⁌ They perfect *Nature,*
and are perfected by experience. ⁌ Craftie men contemne them,
simple men admire them, wise men use them: For they teach not
their owne use, but that is a wisedome without them: and above
them wonne by observation. ⁌ Reade not to contradict, nor to

believe, but to waigh and consider. ❧ Some bookes are to bee tasted, others to bee swallowed, and some few to bee chewed and disgested: That is, some bookes are to be read only in partes; others to be read, but cursorily, and some few to be read wholly and with diligence and attention. ❧ Reading maketh a full man, conference a readye man, and writing an exacte man. And therefore if a man write little, he had neede have a great memorie, if he conferre little, he had neede have a present wit, and if he reade little, he had neede have much cunning, to seeme to know that he doth not. ❧ Histories make men wise, Poets wittie: the Mathematickes subtle, naturall Phylosophie deepe: Morall grave, Logicke and Rhetoricke able to contend.

The standard edition of Bacon's works remains that by James Spedding, R. L. Ellis, and D. D. Heath (7 vols., 1857–1859), supplemented by Spedding's *The Letters and the Life* (7 vols., 1861–1874). The Spedding texts of the *Essays* and *The Advancement of Learning* are available in Hugh G. Dick's *Selected Writings of Francis Bacon* (Modern Library, 1955). "The Relation of Bacon's *Essays* to his Program for the Advancement of Learning" is examined by Ronald S. Crane in *Schelling Anniversary Papers* (1923), pp. 87–105. Bacon's style is the subject of another article in this volume, Morris W. Croll's "Attic Prose: Lipsius, Montaigne, Bacon," pp. 117–150; see, too, George Williamson's *The Senecan Amble* (1951). Bacon's ideas are analyzed in Fulton H. Anderson's *The Philosophy of Francis Bacon* (1948); his influence on the rise of science is set forth in Richard Foster Jones's *Ancients and Moderns* (1936; 2nd ed., 1961). There are many biographies, among them David Mallet's (1740), R. W. Church's (1884), Fulton H. Anderson's (1962), and Catherine Drinker Bowen's (1963).

SIR THOMAS BROWNE
1605–1682

After some years at Winchester School and at Oxford, Browne studied medicine at the leading schools on the continent, at Padua, at Montpellier, and at Leyden (where he took a degree). Incorporated M.D. at Oxford in 1637, he settled down in the same year to practice medicine in Norwich, then perhaps the second largest town in England. By this time he had already written *Religio Medici*, which circulated widely enough in manuscript that eight copies have survived and that an additional one was the basis of two unauthorized editions in 1642. These led to an authorized edition in 1643, a Latin edition in 1644, and to the seventeen other editions printed in Browne's lifetime which gave him an international reputation. This was enhanced in 1646, with the publication of *Pseudodoxia Epidemica: or, Enquiries into very many Received Tenents, and commonly Presumed Truths;* the familiar title, *Vulgar Errors,* may have been sanctioned by Browne since the running title on the pages reads "Enquiries into Vulgar and Common Errors." By 1672, this volume, which reveals Browne's marveling temper almost as clearly as it does his philosophical skepticism, had gone through seven editions or impressions. Browne's next work was *Hydriotaphia, Urne-Buriall, or, A Discourse of the Sepulchrall Urnes lately found in Norfolk. Together with The Garden of Cyrus, or the Quincunciall, Lozenge, or Net-work Plantations of the Ancients, Artificially, Naturally, Mystically Considered. With Sundry Observations* (1658). Here and in the posthumously published *A Letter to a Friend* (1690) and in *Christian Morals* (1716), Browne returned to the theme of life and death which preoccupied him in his religion and his practice as a physician.

Hydriotaphia was twice printed in 1658, and editions appeared in 1659 and 1669. The text printed here is that of the first (octavo) edition of 1658. This has been corrected by the *Errata* in that edition; by the *Errata* in the 1658 quarto (where *Hydriotaphia* and *The Garden of Cyrus* were printed as an appendage to the "fourth" edition of *Pseudodoxia Epidemica*), and by its list of "Marginall Illustrations omitted, or to be added to the Discourses of *Urn-Burial,* and of the *Garden of Cyrus*" (sig. [b4^r]); and by Browne's autograph or authorized alterations in a number of copies of the 1658 octavo (as these have been described by John Carter and Jeremiah S. Finch). Of Browne's 140 marginal notes, the forty which are of most intrinsic importance to the text are printed. Most of those omitted are citations of sources (and complimental references to friends); these can be found, with more precise references than Browne ordinarily gives, in L. C. Martin's *Sir Thomas Browne: Religio Medici and Other Works* (1964), which is the best edition of Browne's major works (exclusive of the *Pseudodoxia*).

The most readily available edition of Browne's complete works is that by Geoffrey Keynes (6 vols., 1928–1931; rev., 4 vols., 1964). Particularly useful editions of *Hydriotaphia* are those by W. A. Greenhill in 1896 and by John Carter in 1932. Samuel Johnson wrote a life of Browne for the second edition of *Christian Morals* (1756); among the best lives of Browne are Olivier Leroy's *Le Chevalier Thomas Browne: Médecin, Styliste & Metaphysicien* (1931), Jeremiah S. Finch's *Sir Thomas Browne: A Doctor's Life of Service and Faith* (1950), and Frank L. Huntley's *Sir Thomas Browne: A Biographical and Critical Study* (1962). Huntley's Chap. XIII (a revision of his "Sir Thomas Browne: The Relationship of *Urn Burial* and *The Garden of Cyrus*," *SP*, LIII [1956], 204–219) is a fine essay. Chap. 4 of F. P. Wilson's *Seventeenth Century Prose* (1960) is a delightful appreciation and Joan Bennett's *Sir Thomas Browne, a Man of Achievement in Literature* (1962) is a useful guide to Browne's work.

JOHN BUNYAN
1628–1688

By the age of twenty or twenty-one, Bunyan had attended a grammar school of some kind; had spent three years in the Commonwealth army, where he was exposed to a variety of radical preachers; had, like his father, become a tinker; and had married. The rest of his life received its focus from the open-communion separatist Church at Bedford, a mile from his native village of Elstow. Here he had been baptized by immersion before 1654 and had been received into the congregation; here he began to preach in 1656, and here he was elected pastor on January 21, 1672. On this day he was still in prison. He had been there since November, 1660, when he had been charged with unauthorized preaching and refusal to conform to the Church of England, and he stayed there until May, 1672, a few months after Charles II had signed the Declaration of Indulgence, though he had been allowed to visit his friends and family from time to time and even, occasionally, to address meetings. Bunyan saw himself and was viewed by sympathizers as elected by God to point out the road to salvation in spite of, or, more accurately, because of his small formal education and his low social station. In a style that combined ordinary speech with the phrase of the Bible, Bunyan turned out a great stream of argumentative and hortatory works. *Grace Abounding* was written during his long imprisonment. *The Pilgrim's Progress* may have been partly written then, though it was perhaps finished in Bunyan's second imprisonment during the first half of 1677; it was published in 1678. These are his greatest works, along with *The Life and Death of Mr. Badman* (1680), *The Holy War* (1682), and the second part of *The Pilgrim's Progress* (1684).

Bunyan's spiritual autobiography differs from the customary work of this kind not only in its quality but in its emphasis on conversion. Of the 339 paragraphs in the body of *Grace Abounding* in its final form, the first 264 relate Bunyan's condition before and during his conversion; separately entitled sections on his call to ministry and on his imprisonment start at ¶265 and at ¶318. Slightly less than half of the book is printed here: ¶'s 1–56 (his state before conversion and the beginning of conversion); ¶'s 89–105 (the effect of Scripture on him, and his hardheartedness); ¶'s 128–160 (his satisfaction, and the introduction of the major temptation episode); ¶'s 290–339 (his ministry, the slander directed at him, and his imprisonment). The selections allow the reader to compare the effect of the world of man on Bunyan with the greater reality and intensity of conscience and Scripture. Of the five editions of *Grace Abounding* published after the first (1666) in Bunyan's lifetime, no copies of the 2nd and 4th are known. The 3rd, undated but probably published between 1672 and 1674, is "Corrected and much enlarged"; the 5th (1680) also bears this announcement on its title page; the 6th (1688) differs from the 5th only in a few minor points. The text printed here by permission of the Clarendon Press, Oxford, is that in the fine edition by Roger Sharrock (1962), who based his text on the first edition for the original body of the narrative and on the 3rd and 5th for the additional passages which first appeared in them. In the selections here printed, ¶'s 12–14, 33–36, 43–45, 105, 129–131, 138, 142, 145, 153, 160, 291, 295, and 301–305 are from the 3rd ed.; ¶'s 32, 142, 149, 157, and 306–317 are from the 5th.

The standard complete edition of Bunyan's works remains that of George Offor (3 vols., 1853, repr. 1860–1862). Bunyan studies are much indebted to the work of Dr. John Brown, for many years minister of Bunyan's Church at Bedford, who edited *The Life and Death of Mr. Badman* (1905), *The Holy War* (1905), *The Pilgrim's Progress* (1907), and *Grace Abounding* (1907), and who wrote a fine biography, *John Bunyan, His Life, Times, and Work* (1886, rev. ed. by Frank M. Harrison, 1928). The best edition of *The Pilgrim's Progress* is that by James B. Wharey (1928); this was revised in 1960 by Roger Sharrock, who had previously written a fine piece on "Spiritual Autobiography in *The Pilgrim's Progress*," *RES*, XXIV (1948), 102–120, and a biography (1954). There are distinguished books by Henri Talon, *John Bunyan, l'Homme et l'Oeuvre* (1948; trans. 1951), and by W. Y. Tindall, *John Bunyan, Mechanick Preacher* (1934); interesting studies by Robert Southey, J. A. Froude, G. B. Shaw, Charles H. Firth, and F. R. Leavis; and a bibliography of Bunyan's works by Frank M. Harrison (1932).

ROBERT BURTON
1577–1640

Burton matriculated at Brasenose College, Oxford, in 1593, transferred to Christ Church College in 1599, and, after taking his B.A. in 1602, M.A. in 1605, and B.D. in 1614, spent the rest of his life there as tutor and librarian. He had a modest income from his appointment in 1616 as vicar of St. Thomas's, in the suburbs of Oxford, and, later, from benefices which he held *in absentia*. Except for a Latin comedy, *Philosophaster* (written in 1606 and revised for performance in 1618), and for nineteen Latin poems, all his efforts went into *The Anatomy of Melancholy*.

The *Anatomy* was first published in 1621, and Burton made revisions and additions for editions in 1624, 1628, 1632, and 1638. The 6th ed. (1651) also has authority, for the publisher explained in a postscript that Burton had left with him a copy of the book "exactly corrected, with severall considerable Additions by his own hand." Between the 1st and 6th editions, the book grew from about 300,000 words to about 485,000; the preface of Democritus Jr. is seventy per cent longer in the 6th ed. than in the 1st. About two-thirds of the 1651 preface is printed here (pp. 1–40, 46–47, 59–68, and 76–78). All of Burton's main subjects are covered or suggested except for his lengthy examination of the sorts and conditions of men, of which his words on critics (pp. 71–72) may serve as an example:

Your supercilious Criticks, Grammatical triflers, Note-makers, curious Antiquaries, finde out all the ruines of wit, *ineptiarum delicias* [charming absurdities], amongst the rubbish of old writers; *Pro stultis habent nisi aliquid sufficiant invenire, quod in aliorum scriptis vertant vitio,* all fools with them that cannot find fault; they correct others, & are hot in a cold cause, puzzle themselves to finde out how many streets in *Rome,* houses, gates, towers, *Homers* countrey, *Aeneas* mother, *Niobes* daughters, *an Sapho publica fuerit? ovum prius extiterit an gallina? &c. & alia quæ dediscenda essent scire, si scires* [whether Sappho was a whore, whether the egg or the hen came first, and other things which ought to be unlearned if they're known], as *Seneca* holds. What clothes the Senators did wear in *Rome,* what shoes, how they sat, where they went to the close stool, how many dishes in a messe,§ what sauce; which for the present for an historian to relate, according to *Lodovic. Vives,* is very ridiculous, is to them most precious elaborate stuff, they admired for it, and as proud, as triumphant in the mean time for this discovery, as if they had won a city, or conquered a province; as rich as if they had found a Mine of Gold ore. *Quosvis authores absurdis commentis suis percacant & stercorant,* one saith, they bewray and dawb a company of books and good Authors, with their absurd Comments, *correctorum sterquilinia* [dung-heaps of improvers] *Scaliger* cals them, and shew their wit in censuring others, a company of foolish note-makers, humble-bees, dors§ or beetles, *inter stercora ut plurimum versantur,* they rake over all those rubbish and dunghils, and prefer a manuscript many times before the Gospel it self, *thesaurum criticum* [a critical collection], before any treasure, and with their *deleaturs, alii legunt sic, meus codex sic habet* [omit this, omit that, some read thus, my MS. reads thus], with their *postremæ editiones* [last editions], annotations, castigations, &c. make books dear, themselves ridiculous, and do no

body good, yet if any man dare oppose or contradict, they are
mad, up in arms on a sudden, how many sheets are written
in defence, how bitter invectives, what apologies? *Epiphilledes
hæ sunt ut meræ nugæ* [these are poor grapes and mere
trifles]. But I dare say no more of, for, with, or against them,
because I am liable to their lash, as well as others. Of these and
the rest of our Artists and Philosophers, I wil generally conclude they are a kind of mad men, as *Seneca* esteems of them,
to make doubts & scruples, how to read them truly, to mend
old authors, but will not mend their own lives, or teach us
*ingenia sanare, memoriam officiorum ingerere, ac fidem in
rebus humanis retinere,* to keep our wits in order, or rectifie
our maners. *Numquid tibi demens videtur, si istis operam
impenderit?* is not he mad that draws lines with *Archimedes,*
whiles his house is ransacked, and his city besieged, when the
whole world is in combustion, or we whilst our souls are in
danger, (*mors sequitur, vita fugit*) [death follows, life flies]
to spend our time in toyes, idle questions, and things of no
worth?

To save space, the marginal notes which swarm over Burton's pages
have been omitted, except for those on his first two pages. Though
most of them document his sources or repeat in Latin what he says
in the text in English, they are an intrinsic part of his text; chance
and the patience of the printer seem to have dictated what went
into the text and what into the margin.

The 7th ed. of the *Anatomy* was published in 1660; the 8th in
1676; the 9th was not published until 1800. Sterne, Johnson, Keats,
and Lamb are among those who have used and admired the book.
The 3-volume edition of the Rev. A. R. Shilleto (1893), though based
on the 7th ed. and deficient in other ways, is a considerable scholarly
accomplishment, still useful. The best available edition is that of
Holbrook Jackson (3 vols., Everyman Library, 1932), though spelling
and punctuation are modernized. Lawrence Babb, whose *Sanity in
Bedlam* (1959) is the best study of the *Anatomy,* has edited a copious
selection from the *Anatomy* (1965). Burton's *Philosophaster,* first
printed in 1862, has been re-edited and translated by Paul Jordan-
Smith (1931). Useful matter about Burton will be found in several
articles in *Oxford Bibliographical Society Proceedings and Papers,*
I (1922–1926), 159–246; in Paul Jordan-Smith's *Bibliographia Bur-
toniana* (1931); and in William R. Mueller's *The Anatomy of Robert
Burton's England* (1952).

JOHN CHAMBERLAIN
1554–1628

A City gentleman of means, Chamberlain never pursued a profession or held public office but was content to be a spectator of life about him. His view was not wide. He had attended Trinity College, Cambridge, and Gray's Inn; in his fifties he passed several months in Venice; but he spent almost all his life in London, and in the thirty years covered by his letters, he lived within a few minutes' walk of St. Paul's. Always a bachelor, he filled his life with friends, among them prominent men like William Gilbert, William Camden, Sir Henry Savile, Sir Thomas Bodley, Lancelot Andrewes, and Sir Ralph Winwood.

All but a handful of Chamberlain's 480 extant letters were written to a friend twenty years younger than he. He was the trusted adviser of a distant relation by marriage, Dudley Carleton, who was knighted a few months before he became ambassador to Venice in 1610. (Carleton was ambassador to The Hague from 1616 to 1625, and then to France until 1628, when he was created Viscount Dorchester and made Secretary of State; some of his letters to Chamberlain have survived.) Chamberlain's letters to Carleton are unsurpassed as a record of what was on the minds and tongues of Londoners between 1597 and 1626. For all their gossipy news, they reveal an observer who was moderate, even cautious, a shrewd and sometimes caustic commentator on the ways of the London world. The letters were intended to be read only by their recipients, but nineteen of them were first printed in 1725, many others were published from time to time, and in 1939 all of them were edited in two volumes, with an introduction, by Norman E. McClure. McClure's fine text is used here with the generous permission of the publisher, The American Philosophical Society.

There is a fine essay about Chamberlain and his circle in Wallace Notestein's *Four Worthies* (1956), pp. 27–119.

ANTHONY ASHLEY COOPER,
1ST EARL OF SHAFTESBURY
1621–1683

Shaftesbury was the most eminent politician of his time. He succeeded his father as 2nd baronet in 1631, and, despite the litigation which diminished his estate, inherited great wealth. A member of Parliament before he was of age, he supported the Royalist cause until 1644, went over to the Parliamentary side, and broke with it in 1654. One of the men appointed to invite Charles to assume the kingship, he was made a member of the Privy Council in 1660, Chancellor of the Exchequer in 1661, and Lord Chancellor in 1672. (He had been created Earl of Shaftesbury earlier in 1672 for supporting Charles's Declaration of Indulgence.) His distinction shone only more brightly when he was dismissed from office after a year and became the leader of the opposition. As a primary advocate of parliamentary government, religious toleration, and trade and colonial expansion, Shaftesbury was the organizing genius behind the Country party which became the Whig party of the next hundred years. His accomplishment in party politics was matched by another: he was largely responsible for the passage of the Act of Habeas Corpus in 1679.

Shaftesbury wrote very little. The character of Henry Hastings appears in the fragment of an autobiography (to 1639) which he wrote late in his life. There, in describing the gentry who resorted weekly to the bowling-green at Hanley, near his country house in eastern Dorsetshire, Shaftesbury included the picture of Hastings before he gave a catalogue of other men in the area. The character was first printed several times in the 1750's and became well known through its appearance in David Nichol Smith's *Characters from the Histories & Memoirs of the Seventeenth Century* (1918). (Smith also printed the characters of Shaftesbury himself in Gilbert Burnet's *History of My Own Time* and Dryden's *Absalom and Achitophel.*) Smith used the text given by William D. Christie in his *Memoirs, Letters, and Speeches of Anthony Ashley Cooper* (1859). The character is printed here, with the permission of the Keeper of Public Records, from a Xerox copy of the original in the Shaftesbury Papers in the Public Record Office (PRO 30/24/18).

Shaftesbury has been derogatively immortalized by Dryden in *Absalom and Achitophel* (1681) and in *The Medal* (1682). The standard life remains that by William D. Christie (2 vols., 1871). H. D. Traill's *Shaftesbury* (1886) presents an unsympathetic view; this is counteracted by Osmund Airy's account in the *Dictionary of National Biography*. Louise Fargo Brown's *The First Earl of Shaftesbury* (1933) stresses Shaftesbury's commercial and colonial interests.

SIR WILLIAM CORNWALLIS
1579?–1614

Sir Charles Cornwallis, appointed ambassador to Spain in 1605, wrote of his son, "Of all sorts of people I most dispaire of those of his sorte, that are Philosophers in their wordes and fooles in their workes." His judgment is severe but not inaccurate. His son William "the younger" (by which he is distinguished from an uncle of the same name) married at sixteen, went through his money in two years, served under Essex in Ireland (where he was knighted), tried for a short time to have a career in public life, and settled for a life of reading and writing in the midst of a constantly growing family. His *Essayes* (twenty-five of them) were published in 1600, and in the following year *A Second part of Essayes* (containing twenty-four) appeared, together with *Discourses upon Seneca, the Tragedian,* moral commentaries on a dozen passages. After his death, two volumes of his paradoxes, *Essayes or rather Encomions* and *Essayes of Certaine Paradoxes,* were published, both in 1616.

Despite Bacon's earlier publication, Cornwallis has some right to the title of the first English essayist, for his essays achieved a form which Bacon's did not take until his revisions of 1612. He seems to have written them after he had seen a manuscript in which some of Montaigne's were translated, and he used them to reveal what he had discovered about himself in the light of his reading of Seneca and Plutarch. Acquainted with Donne, he wrote the first of his paradoxes at the time Donne, too, was interested in the form, and in his last two books the wit and ingenuity of the paradox are tempered by his Stoic seriousness. His essays were reprinted with some revisions in 1606 and again in 1610, when three new ones were added; *Of Adversitie* is one of these, and it is here printed from the 1610 volume, where it is "Essay. 50."

The standard edition of the essays is that of Don Cameron Allen (1946), where the 1606 text is followed for the first twenty-five and the 1610 text for the other twenty-seven. Allen has, with considerable justification, repunctuated the essays. Cornwallis's earliest paradoxes were printed with an introduction in R. E. Bennett's "Four Paradoxes by Sir William Cornwallis, the Younger," *Harvard Studies and Notes in Philology and Literature,* XIII (1931), 219–240. Allen's introduction succinctly provides biographical information; see, too, P. B. Whitt's "New Light on Sir William Cornwallis, the Essayist," *RES,* VIII (1932), 155–169. Bennett examines Cornwallis's debt to Montaigne in *PMLA,* XLVIII (1933), 1080–1089; Cornwallis's essays are discussed in E. N. S. Thompson's *The Seventeenth-Century English Essay* (1926) (*University of Iowa Studies,* III, no. 3 [1926], 34–37), and in W. L. MacDonald's "The Earliest English Essayists," *Englische Studien,* LXIV (1929), 34–44.

ABRAHAM COWLEY
1618–1667

Cowley was a schoolboy of fifteen at Westminster when his *Poetical Blossomes* was published, in the same year as Donne's *Poems;* he had

not yet received the B.A. from Trinity College, Cambridge, when the
third edition of his poems appeared in 1637. Ejected in 1644 from his
Cambridge fellowship, he spent the next ten years mainly in Paris
in the service of Lord Jermyn, secretary to Queen Henrietta Maria.
He returned to London in 1654, and after his imprisonment in 1655
his allegiance to the Crown seems to have wavered. He studied medicine and botany for a couple of years and was granted the degree of
M.D. at Oxford in 1657, but he never practiced medicine. At the
Restoration he was merely reinstated in his fellowship; through the
kindness of Lord Jermyn and the Queen Dowager he was able to
retire as an amateur gardener and country gentleman. For his love
poems and his Anacreontics, as the author of the first religious epic
in English and of the first Pindaric odes in English, Cowley won
renown as the leading poet of his time. For Milton, he ranked with
Shakespeare and Spenser; he was buried near Chaucer and Spenser
in Westminster Abbey; he was the darling of Dryden's youth; and for
Dr. Johnson he was undoubtedly the best of the metaphysical poets.

Until his retirement, Cowley had written little prose: critical
prefaces to his *Poems,* 1656, and to the Pindaric odes published
here; a partisan political pamphlet, and *A Proposition For the Advancement of Experimental Philosophy* (1661). His essays, which
have been admired since Cowper's time for their limpid style, their
Horatian view of life, and their Montaigne-like stamp of personalness,
were written during his last years and were first published in his
Works (1668). The last section of this volume is entitled *Several
Discourses by way of Essays, in Verse and Prose;* it contains eleven
essays, of which "Of Solitude" is the second and "Of My self" the
last. The 1668 text is followed here; three marginal notes which
are mere citations are omitted.

Almost all of Cowley's work is available in *The Complete Works*
edited by A. B. Grosart (2 vols., 1881). *The English Writings* have
been edited by A. R. Waller (2 vols., 1905–1906). The essays are
available in several editions; one of the best is Alfred B. Gough's
The Essays and Other Prose Writings (1915). There is a fine selection of Cowley's poetry and prose in L. C. Martin's little volume
(1949). The first biography is that by Thomas Sprat (1668); Johnson's life (1779) is mainly based on Sprat and on Anthony à Wood
and is mainly interesting for its critique of metaphysical poetry; the
standard lives are Jean Loiseau's *Abraham Cowley: Sa Vie, Son
Oeuvre* (1931) and Arthur H. Nethercot's *Abraham Cowley, The
Muse's Hannibal* (1931). Nethercot has an essay on "Abraham Cowley's Essays," *JEGP,* XXIX (1930), 114–130. Cowley's prose style is
discussed on pp. 998–1001 of Richard F. Jones's "Science and English Prose Style in the Third Quarter of the Seventeenth Century,"
PMLA, XLV (1930) and in an exchange of views in *PMLA,* XLVI
(1931), 962–967. The bibliography in Loiseau's life has been supple-

mented by that in Robert B. Hinman's *Abraham Cowley's World of Order* (1960), which examines Cowley's poetry in the light of his speculative thought.

JOHN DONNE
1572–1631

Donne was born after January 23 and before June 19, 1572. He entered Hart Hall, Oxford, in 1584, studied there and at Cambridge for several years, and may have traveled abroad before he entered Thavies Inn in 1591. He was at Lincoln's Inn from 1592 to 1594 or 1595. He served under the Earl of Essex in the expedition against Cadiz (1596) and took part in the expedition against the Azores in the following year. Soon after his return, he became secretary to Sir Thomas Egerton, the Lord Keeper, and he held this post until his marriage to Ann More in December, 1601. In 1601 and again in 1614 he was a Member of Parliament, and throughout these years he hoped for a political career. He was ordained deacon and priest on January 23, 1615, by John King, Bishop of London; was made Reader in Divinity at Lincoln's Inn in 1616, where he served until 1622; was appointed Dean of St. Paul's on November 19, 1621, and Vicar of St. Dunstan's-in-the-West in 1624. He died March 31, 1631. During his lifetime, little of his work was published: *Pseudo-Martyr* (1610); *An Anatomie of the World* (1611), reprinted with *The Second Anniversarie, Of the Progres of the Soule* (1612); *Ignatius his Conclave* (1611); *Devotions upon Emergent Occasions* (1624); and six sermons. His *Poems* were published after his death (1633, 1635, 1639, 1649, 1650 [reissued 1654], 1669), as were *Juvenilia* (1633), *LXXX Sermons* (1640), *Biathanatos* (1646 or 1647), *Fifty Sermons* (1649), *Essayes in Divinity* (1651), *Letters to Severall Persons of Honour* (1651), and *XXVI. Sermons* (1660–1661).

Donne's interest in fashionable prose genres is clear in his having written nineteen problems, twelve paradoxes (and part of another), two characters, and an essay. Most of these were written before the turn of the century; in 1616, thirteen of the problems were published in Holland in a Latin translation without their being identified as his, and his character of a dunce and his essay "Of Valour" were first printed in the 11th impression of the Overburian collection (1622). Eleven paradoxes and ten problems were printed in *Juvenilia: or Certaine Paradoxes, and Problems* (1633); the text of "That only Cowards dare dye" (the ninth paradox) is printed from the first edition of this volume. Most of the other pieces were added in *Paradoxes, Problems, Essayes, Characters, Written by Dr. Donne* (1652).

About two hundred of Donne's letters have survived, three-quarters of which were printed in two books, *Letters to Severall Persons of Honour*, 1651 (129 letters) and *A Collection of Letters, Made by Sir Tobie Mathews* (1660). Of the letters printed here, the text of three is from the 1651 volume: Letter 2 (pp. 105–108), Letter 5 (pp. 48–54), and Letter 6 (pp. 253–257). Letter 1 was first published in Evelyn M. Simpson's *A Study of the Prose Works of John Donne* (1924), and it is printed here from pp. 316–317 of the 2nd ed. (1948) by permission of the Clarendon Press, Oxford. Letter 3 is printed from the appendix to the *Life of Herbert* in Walton's *Lives*, 1670 (last pagination, pp. 98–99), and Letter 4 from *Poems, By J. D.*, 1633 (pp. 370–373).

The best complete edition of Donne's poems is that of Sir Herbert Grierson (2 vols., 1912, reprinted many times); Helen Gardner has superbly edited *The Divine Poems* (1952) and *The Elegies and The Songs and Sonnets* (1965). The standard edition of the sermons is that by George R. Potter and Evelyn M. Simpson (10 vols., 1953–1962). The Nonesuch Press published the *Paradoxes and Problems* (1923) with a bibliographical preface by Geoffrey Keynes. They are the subject of Paul N. Siegel's "Donne's *Paradoxes and Problems*," *PQ*, XXVIII (1949), 507–511; R. C. Bald's "A Latin Version of Donne's Problems," *MP*, LXI (1964), 198–203; and Chap. VI of Mrs. Simpson's *A Study of the Prose Works of John Donne*, which is the best guide to all the prose. There is no modern edition of the letters, but I. A. Shapiro's edition is nearly ready for publication. The letters are most readily available in Sir Edmund Gosse's *The Life and Letters of John Donne* (2 vols., 1899; repr. 1959); Charles E. Merrill, Jr., has edited *Letters to Severall Persons of Honour* (1910). The most useful articles about the letters are I. A. Shapiro's "The Text of Donne's *Letters to Severall Persons*," *RES*, VII (1931), 291–301; R. E. Bennett's "Donne's Letters from the Continent in 1611–12," *PQ*, XIX (1940), 66–78, and "Donne's *Letters to Severall Persons of Honour*," *PMLA*, LVI (1941), 120–140; Stanley Johnson's "Sir Henry Goodere and Donne's Letters," *MLN*, LXIII (1948), 38–43; and a long correspondence in the *TLS* which starts on August 22, 1952, p. 556, and continues on pp. 597, 613, 629, 645, 700, 743, and 837. Biography since Gosse's has been undistinguished psychology and fiction. Edward Le Comte's *Grace to a Witty Sinner* (1965) incorporates scholarship since Gosse's time, but is more accurate in details than penetrating in interpretation and is, in the main, a popular introduction; his bibliography is a good guide to important biographical contributions. R. C. Bald's long-awaited life, very nearly finished when he died in 1965, will undoubtedly be printed. There is a bibliography by Geoffrey Keynes (1914; 3rd ed., 1958) and a fine study of Donne's prose style (exclusive of the letters), Joan Webber's *Contrary Music* (1963).

JOHN EARLE
1600?–1665

While Earle was yet alive, Walton wrote that he had long ago begun and had recently finished a translation of the *Ecclesiasticall Polity* into Latin, and he described Earle in words that are everywhere corroborated: "Since Mr. *Hooker* died, none have liv'd whom God hath blest with more innocent Wisdom; more sanctified Learning, or a more pious, peaceable, primitive Temper: so that this excellent person seems to be only like himself & our venerable *R. Hooker.*" The first part of Earle's life was spent at Oxford (Christ Church and Merton); here he took his B.A. and M.A.; here he wrote *Micro-cosmographie. Or, a Peece of the World Discovered; in Essayes and Characters* (1628); here, in 1631, he was made one of the proctors of the University and chaplain to Philip, Earl of Pembroke, then the Chancellor. In the thirties, he was among the "men of eminent parts and faculties" (William Chillingworth, Gilbert Sheldon, Henry Hammond, Edward Hyde, Thomas Barlow, Robert Sanderson, George Morley) who frequently visited Great Tew, the hospitable estate of young Lucius Cary, later Viscount Falkland. Unlike these friends who guided the Church during its darkest days and re-established it in 1660, Earle always retained his sweet reasonableness of temper, his liberal and conciliatory outlook, his depth of discernment. In 1641, he was appointed tutor to Prince Charles; he became Charles's chaplain on the Continent, was with him during the interregnum, and was probably always the churchman closest to him. In 1649, his translation of *Eikon Basilike* into Latin was printed. At the Restoration, Hyde placed in his hands (and those of Sheldon and Morley) control of the presentation of the bulk of the crown benefices. He was also appointed Dean of Westminster; in 1662, he became Bishop of Worcester, and the following year he was translated to Salisbury. A few of his poems survive; his Latin translation of the *Polity* was neglected and destroyed.

Three editions of *Micro-cosmographie*, which is generally considered the best of the character books, were printed in 1628 (fifty-four characters). No copy of the 4th ed. has survived. The 5th ed. (1629) adds twenty-three new characters; the "6th" of 1633 is the last edition to make an addition (one new character). The text used here is that of the first edition (*STC* 7439), with the incorporation of the few verbal changes and additions made in the 2nd ed. (*STC* 7440) and its placement of the sentence "His Table is spread wide . . . ." in "A Pretender to Learning."

The best editions of *Micro-cosmographie* are those by Alfred S. West (1897), Gwendolyn Murphy (1928), and Harold Osborne (1933). The editions are described in Murphy's *A Bibliography of*

English Character-Books, 1608–1700 (1925), pp. 35–44 (Suppl. 4 of *Transactions of the Bibliographical Society*, VI [1926]). Earle's life is sketched in prefaces of the editions and in George G. Perry's account in the *Dictionary of National Biography*.

SIR GEORGE ETHEREGE
1635?–1692?

Many of the details about Etherege's life are vague, but the most important event was the production and publication of *The Comical Revenge; or, Love in a Tub* in 1664. The play was not only the precursor of the Restoration comedy of manners, but its dedication to Lord Buckhurst (later the Earl of Dorset) was Etherege's entree into the fashionable world ruled over by Dorset, Sedley, Rochester, and Buckingham. *She wou'd if she cou'd* (1668), though a better play, was not so successful, but this hardly diminished Etherege's reputation. Six months after it was produced, he was off for Turkey, as secretary to the English embassy; he was there for three years. His third, last, and best play, *The Man of Mode or, Sir Fopling Flutter,* was produced and published in 1676. About 1679 or 1680, Etherege married a rich widow, and he seems to have been knighted either in preparation for his marriage or as a result of it. In August 1685, he left for Ratisbon as James II's envoy to the Diet of the German Empire; there, despite one episode with a touring actress, which only for a moment dispelled the general diplomatic dullness, he pined for the London he never saw again. Etherege's firmest commitments were to urbanity and courtliness; he was pleased to confess that he was a fop at heart, that he was so used to affectations that nothing natural could touch him without the help of the air of the court. He nourished the legend of his idleness and was probably more pleased by Rochester's and Dryden's references to it than he was by Rochester's attributing "Fancy, Sense, Judgment, and Wit" to him or by Dryden's complimentary statement, "I will never enter the lists in Prose with the undoubted best author of it which our nation has produc'd."

Etherege's absences from England resulted in voluminous correspondence. Some of it was gathered up in a *Letterbook* which was edited by Sybil Rosenfeld in 1928; some of it, now at Harvard, was described by Rosenfeld in "The Second Letterbook of Sir George Etherege," *RES*, III (1952), 19–27. More than 200 holograph letters in the British Museum have never been printed. The letter printed here is taken from *The Miscellaneous Works of George Villiers, Duke of Buckingham* (1704), pp. 131–140. The date it bears there—October 21, 1689—is wrong: Buckingham died April 16, 1687, and Etherege left Ratisbon no later than April 25, 1689. If the paragraph which mentions D'Urfey's *A Fool's Preferment, or The Three Dukes of Dunstable* (1688), Shadwell's *The Squire of Alsatia* (1688), and Sedley's *Bellamira* (1687) is treated as an interpolation from some later letter, the rest of this one fits all the circumstances of October 21, 1686. Etherege starts by suggesting that he has written or intends to write a number of letters to Buckingham (there is a fine one dated November 12, 1686, in the 1704 volume); he has been long enough in Ratisbon (eleven months) to become acquainted with the natives, but not so long that he has become hardened to their ways; he seems to have heard that Dryden is at work on *The Hind and the Panther,* which was published in the spring of 1687.

Etherege's *Dramatic Works* have been edited by H. F. B. Brett-Smith (2 vols., 1927), and the *Poems* by James Thorpe (1963). Biographical material is in the introductions to Rosenfeld's and Brett-Smith's volumes. Most of the standard books on the Restoration stage describe Etherege's drama, as does Dale Underwood's *Etherege and the Seventeenth-Century Comedy of Manners* (1957).

OWEN FELLTHAM
1602?–1668

Most of Felltham's life was spent in the service of the Earl of Thomond at Great Billing in Northamptonshire; he became steward of Thomond's estate and accumulated some wealth himself. Of his earlier life we know only that he visited the Low Countries in the twenties, that he had some acquaintance with the literary circles of London in the twenties and thirties, that he was a staunch Anglican and Royalist. To his contemporaries he was best known for his *Resolves,* for his poem in memory of Immortal Ben in *Jonsonus Virbius* (1638), and for his *Brief Character of the Low-Countries,* which appeared in pirated editions in 1648 and 1652 (and in several authorized editions from 1652 on) and which inaugurated a small vogue for the character that described a nation.

Felltham says that he wrote the first hundred *Resolves Divine, Morall, Politicall* at the age of eighteen. In these, which were probably published in 1623, meditation of a moral proposition was generally followed by its development or expansion and by resolution in personal terms, all done in a spare and pointed Senecan style. The 2nd ed. (1628) reprints these resolves on pp. 1–93; a new century of resolves covers 294 pages and reflects some slight change of purpose in its greater discursiveness, in Felltham's particular reference to the "Essay, *which of all writing, is the neerest to a running* Discourse," and in such titles as "Of Fame," "Of Dissimulation," "Of Death," "Of Marriage and single life," and "Of Travel." The 3rd ed. (1628–1629) reverses the order of the two centuries and provides titles for the original century. The 1661 folio of the *Resolves* contains forty-one of Felltham's poems in a section called *Lusoria,* some letters, the *Brief Character,* and the 8th ed. of the resolves, with the fifty-seven kept from the original century considerably enlarged so that they are much more essayistic and with twenty-eight added for the first time. The text of the three resolves printed here follows the earliest printing: that for *"A Rule in reading Authors"* is from the 1st ed. (where it is numbered XXVII on pp. 81–85), with the title provided by the 3rd ed.; *"Of Puritans"* and *"Of the worship of Admiration"* are from the new century in the 2nd ed. (no. V, pp. 9–12, and no. XIIII, pp. 39–41).

The only modern edition of the *Resolves* is by Oliphant Smeaton (1904). McCrea Hazlett has a good article on the development of the form of the *Resolves* in *MP,* LI (1953), 93–101. Ronald Bayne's account of Felltham's life in the *Dictionary of National Biography* has been corrected and supplemented by M. D. Cornu, "A Biography and Bibliography of Owen Felltham with Some Notes on his Poems and Letters," *University of Washington Digests of Theses,* I (1931), 134–142; Jean Robertson, "Owen Felltham of Great Billing," *N&Q,* CLXXIII (1937), 381–384; and Fred S. Tupper, "New Facts Regarding Owen Feltham," *MLN,* LIV (1939), 199–201.

THOMAS FULLER
1608–1661

At thirteen, Fuller entered Queens' College, Cambridge, where the President was his uncle John Davenant, the Lady Margaret Professor of Divinity. By the time he was twenty, he was B.A. and M.A.; within two years, he had been ordained and had become curate of St. Benet's Church, Cambridge. Through the interest of Davenant, who had become Bishop of Salisbury, he was made a prebendary of Salisbury Cathedral and vicar of Broadwindsor; in 1635, he was granted the B.D. at Cambridge. In 1642, he was made curate of the Savoy Chapel in London, but the troubled times affected even moderate Anglicans and Fuller left London to become an army chaplain at Oxford and then chaplain to the infant Princess Henrietta Anne at Exeter. Back in London in 1646, he preached where he could, and his reputation as a preacher led to his frequent presence in London after he had been made curate at Waltham Abbey in Essex by the Earl of Carlisle in 1649 and rector of Cranford by the Earl of Berkeley in 1658. At the Restoration he was made D.D. at Cambridge by royal mandate and was appointed Chaplain in Extraordinary to the King. The list of his prose works is longer than that of his clerical positions. Though none of them is of the first rank or characterized by great depth and penetration, all of them show his good sense, charm, and pleasant wit, even when their subjects seem to allow little scope for such things. His best known books are *The Historie of the Holy Warre* (1639, 5th ed. 1651), a history of the crusades; *The Holy State* (1642, 4th ed. 1663), a conduct book; *Good Thoughts in Bad Times* (1645) and *Good Thoughts in Worse Times* (1647), devotional manuals which were often reprinted and which led to a third volume, *Mixt Contemplations in Better Times* (1660); *A Pisgah-Sight of Palestine* (1650, repr. 1662), a descriptive geography; *Abel Redivivus* (1651), a collection of biographies of modern churchmen, edited and partly written by Fuller; *The Church-History of Britain* (1655), the first attempt of this kind since Bede's, to which Fuller appended *The History of the University of Cambridge* and *The History of Waltham-Abby in Essex*; and *The History of the Worthies of England* (1662).

The *Holy State* is divided into five books. The first explores family relations and the second various occupations and professions; the "Generall Rules," Fuller said, "we have placed in the middle, that the Books on both sides may equally reach to them"; the fourth deals with the governing class and the fifth with the vile persons who make up *The Profane State*. The lessons set forth in the discursive characters and anecdotal biographical sketches are summed up in the essays in Book III. The text used here is the 1st edition. "The Elder Brother" is Chap. 14 of Book I, and *"Of Books"* is Chap. 18 of Book III; the few marginal notes in which Fuller identifies his sources have been omitted.

Fuller died before his *History of the Worthies* was printed, and his son John summed up the purpose of the book in his dedication to the King: "The matter . . . is the description of such native and particular Commodities as the several Counties of Your Kingdom afford, with a revival of the Memories of such Persons which have in each County been eminent for Parts or Learning." Though the portrait of Fuller in the book bears the Latin motto "Method is the mother of memory," the *Worthies* is difficult to use. Fuller finally placed Raleigh under *Devonshire* (Sea-men), pp. 261–262; Donne is found in *London* (Writers, since the Reformation), p. 221; and Bacon is in *Westminster* (Statesmen), pp. 241–242. The text printed here omits two marginal notes in the account of Raleigh and two in that of Bacon.

Fuller's reputation flourished in the nineteenth century since he was a favorite with Southey, Coleridge, and Lamb, and many of his works, including his poems (ed. A. B. Grosart, 1868) and his sermons (2 vols., ed. John E. Bailey and W. E. A. Axon, 1891) were made available. Particularly useful are editions of the *Church-History* by J. S. Brewer (6 vols., 1845) and of the *Worthies* by P. Austin Nuttall (3 vols., 1840). The *Worthies* was edited in 1952 by John Freeman; the text is abridged, modernized, and re-ordered. The first volume of Maximilian G. Walten's edition of *The Holy State* (1938) is a facsimile of the text of 1642; the second volume contains an introduction and notes. A fine study of this book is Walter E. Houghton, Jr.'s *The Formation of Thomas Fuller's Holy and Profane States* (1938). Biography of Fuller starts with an anonymous life in 1661. John E. Bailey's 800-page life was published in 1874. The most recent biographies are Dean B. Lyman's *The Great Tom Fuller* (1935) and William Addison's *Worthy Dr. Fuller* (1951). A *Bibliography of the Works of Thomas Fuller* was edited by Strickland Gibson, with an introduction by Geoffrey Keynes, in *Oxford Bibliographical Society Proceedings & Papers*, IV (1936), 63-161; there is a small supplement in *ibid.*, N. S. I (1948), 44.

JOSEPH HALL
1574-1656

Raised in an atmosphere of Calvinistic Puritanism, Hall entered Emmanuel College, the center of Puritanism at Cambridge, in 1589. He was made a Fellow in 1595 and took orders in 1600. From December 1601, he spent several unhappy years at Hawstead in Suffolk, where he was ill-treated as rector by Sir Robert Drury. In 1608, he was appointed one of Prince Henry's domestic chaplains, and the same year he was presented the living at Waltham Holy Cross in Essex. Here he stayed twenty-one years. Made Dean of Worcester in 1616, and appointed one of James's representatives at the Synod of Dort in 1618, he was finally rewarded with the bishopric of Exeter in 1627. In 1641, he was translated to Norwich, where he was forced into retirement by the Act of Sequestration in 1643. The works for which Hall is known were written early in his career, probably to call attention to his abilities, though he told Sir Robert Drury that he was "forced to write books to buy books." He was still at Cambridge, where he was for two years University Lecturer in Rhetoric, when he established his reputation with *Virgidemiarum . . . First three Bookes, Of Tooth-lesse Satyrs* (1597) and *The three last Bookes. Of byting Satyres* (1598). Hall found in Juvenal a way of expressing his interest in morality, and he was one of the first to write satires on the classical model in English. His next excursion into satire was a Latin prose burlesque of travelers and utopias, *Mundus Alter et Idem,* published anonymously about 1605 and translated about 1609 by John Healey as *The Discovery of A New World.* In the next half dozen years, Hall wrote the works, all of them in modish genres, which gained him the name of the "English Seneca" or the "Christian Seneca" and which earned him an international reputation. His *Meditations and Vowes* was published in 1605 and republished the next year with large additions. *Heaven upon Earth, Or Of true Peace, and Tranquillitie of Minde* (1606) is made up of twenty-seven short

Senecan essays logically structured to support a thesis. Seneca is joined to Theophrastus in *Characters of Vertues and Vices* in 1608. In the same year appeared *Epistles, The First Volume: Conteining two Decads* and by 1611 six decades of epistles had been published. Though Hall continued to write voluminously, his other works are forgotten except for *Episcopacie by Divine Right* (1640). This book drew him into a pamphlet war with the group of Puritans known as the Smectymnuans and finally with John Milton, who not only countered his arguments for episcopacy but remembered his satiric work and answered in kind.

Two editions of the *Characters of Vertues and Vices* were published in 1608; these contained twenty-four characters, nine of good types and fifteen of evil ones. Hall added two characters in 1614 when the others were printed in his *Recollection of such Treatises as have been heretofore severally published*. The characters went through several editions in this volume and in the several editions of Hall's *Works*. The French translation of 1610 was often reprinted, and references exist to a Latin translation in 1619 and a German one in 1628. *"Of the Good Magistrate"* is here printed from the first edition ("to be sold at the sign of the Bul-head"), with two changes in punctuation taken over from the 2nd edition.

Hall's works are most readily available in the edition by Philip Wynter (10 vols., 1863). The *Poems* have been edited by A. Davenport (1949); *The Discovery of A New World* by Huntington Brown (1937); and *Heaven upon Earth* and *Characters of Vertues and Vices* by Rudolf Kirk (1948). Kirk's book has a useful introduction, though his discussion of Hall's neo-Stoicism has been variously supplemented and qualified. The best life remains that by George Lewis (1886).

JAMES HOWELL
1593/4–1666

Born and raised in Wales, Howell naturally migrated to Jesus College, Oxford, where he received the B.A. in 1613. During the next years, he was employed as a steward in the glass factory of Sir Robert Mansel in London, and in the spring of 1617 he was sent abroad on business. In the midst of travels through Holland, Spain, Italy, France, and Switzerland, Howell resigned his job; he did not return to England until the winter of 1620. In the next years, he tried, with little success, to use his foreign experience to gain a public post. Between 1622 and 1624, he was in Spain as a special envoy to negotiate for the release of an English merchant ship. In 1626, he became secretary to Lord Scrope, Lord President of the North, and remained in

his service until 1630. He visited Denmark in 1632 as secretary and
orator to a special embassy, and he was abroad occasionally during
the next ten years, when he was almost certainly a Royalist intelli-
gencer. On August 30, 1642, he was appointed one of the clerks of
the Privy Council, but in November he was arrested by Parliamentary
order; he was confined to the Fleet until the general amnesty of 1650.
Before his imprisonment he had written two books: *Dodona's Grove*
(1640), a political allegory about affairs in Europe and in England
in the first third of the century; and *Instructions for forreine Travell*
(1642), a practical guide for travelers to the Continent. During and
after his imprisonment, he had to support himself by his pen, and
he produced a large number of books and pamphlets (many of them
heavily dependent on the published works of others) for the enter-
prising publisher, Humphrey Moseley. Among them are his *Letters,*
a continuation of the popular *Dodona's Grove* (1650), an enlarged
version of the *Instructions* (1650), a survey of Venice (1651), a
translation of Josephus' *History of the Jews* (1652), a history and
"perambulation" of London (1657), an English-French-Italian-Spanish
dictionary (1659), and a collected volume of historical discourses
(1661). In February 1661, he was rewarded for his services to the
Crown by the new post of Historiographer Royal.

The first volume of Howell's familiar letters, *Epistolae Ho-Elianae,*
was published in 1645. The second volume was published in 1647
with the title *A New Volume of Letters.* In 1650, the "second" edition
of *Epistolae Ho-Elianae* appeared; this contained the letters printed
in 1645 and in 1647, with an additional (third) volume of letters
and with dates added to all the letters. The "third" edition of *Epistolae Ho-Elianae* (1655), the last published in Howell's lifetime,
added a fourth volume of letters. With the exception of Letter 1, all
the letters are printed here as they first appeared. Letter 1 was first
printed as the opening letter in 1647; Howell made interesting additions to it when he printed it in 1650 at the beginning of volume I,
and that text is used here. Letters 2, 3, and 4 are from the 1645
volume, where they appear, respectively, as no. III of Section I (pp.
5–8), no. XXVII of Section I (pp. 52–54), and no. VIII of Section 4
(pp. 8–9). Letters 5, 6, and 7 are from the 1647 volume, pp. 121–125,
196–206, 206–210. The dates are, of course, from the edition of 1650.

The genuineness of the letters has been much debated. The most
likely explanation for the many discrepancies of time and event
which they contain is that they are frequently pastiches. Verona M.
Hirst has suggested in "The Authenticity of James Howell's Familiar
Letters," *MLR,* LIV (1959), 558–561, that Howell put together the
letters from copies in his possession just as he did many of his other
works—by editing and combining. In the later volumes, when he was
running short of genuine material, he wrote the more literary and
essayistic epistles specifically for publication. The most useful edition

of the letters is that by Joseph Jacobs (2 vols., 1890–1892), which is, however, based on the "tenth" edition (1737). Jacobs' annotation has been corrected and expanded by Edward Bensly in a haphazardly arranged series of articles in *Aberystwyth Studies*: III (1922), 27–42; IV (1922), 39–48; V (1923), 43–73; VI (1924), 23–45; VIII (1926), 17–35; IX (1927), 17–33. Jacobs' bibliography of Howell's works has been corrected in a useful little volume by William H. Vann, *Notes on the Writings of James Howell* (1924).

EDWARD HYDE, 1ST EARL OF CLARENDON
1609–1674

Another great historian wrote that Clarendon was one of the chief founders of the system of church and state on which the English constitution has rested since the Restoration, and he attributed Clarendon's statesmanship to his study and writing of history. Even as a young man down from Oxford and enrolled at the Middle Temple, Hyde moved comfortably in the circle of poets, wits, and scholars who surrounded Ben Jonson, and one of his first compositions was a sequel to Sir Henry Wotton's *Parallell betweene Robert late Earle of Essex, and George late Duke of Buckingham* in which he pointed out the difference and disparity between the men. Admitted to the bar in 1633, Hyde was equally at home in legal company and in the brilliant group at Great Tew. The tolerant rationality of Tew informed his actions as a new member of Parliament in 1640, and he supported the popular party in its attempts to control Charles's violations of law. Parliament's desire to assimilate the English ecclesiastical system to that of Scotland and to exclude the clergy from secular offices turned him to the Crown, and he became an informal adviser to the King. In February 1643, he was made a member of the Privy Council and was knighted, and, shortly after, he was appointed Chancellor of the Exchequer. In February 1646, after the last Royalist army had been defeated in Cornwall, he fled with Prince Charles to Scilly. There, on March 18, he started writing a history of recent events which would be didactic and advisory, and, once settled in Jersey, he brought his narrative, now increasingly patterned on the histories of Tacitus and Livy, down to 1644. His writing was interrupted when he was called, in the spring of 1648, to join the Prince on the continent. Within three years, he had become Charles's chief political adviser, and in January 1658 he was made Lord Chancellor of the government in exile. At the Restoration, he was made Baron Hyde of Hindon and assumed power as Lord Chancellor of England. As the Earl of Clarendon, a title given him at the coronation, he was the most powerful man in England, but increasingly he antagonized court, Parliament, and King, and he was dismissed from office in 1667. Anticipating Parliament's charge that he was a traitor, he fled to France and spent his remaining years vindicating himself by his pen. On July 23, 1668, he started writing his autobiography; by August 1, 1670, when he had brought his story down to 1660, his manuscript was over 600,000 words long. The following year, his son Laurence was allowed to visit him and he brought from England the manuscript of the "History." Clarendon spent about a year combining the "History" and the "Life," adding new sections for the coherence and completeness of his narrative to produce the *True Historical Narrative of the Rebellion and Civil Wars* as we now know it. During his years in France, he also wrote a separate discourse of vindication and a series of essays reflecting on Christian duties, and he finished an earlier work of contemplations on the Psalms. Nor was this all. He wrote a reply to Hobbes's *Leviathan*, and he continued the story of his life through his chancellorship and fall.

After Clarendon's death, Laurence Hyde supervised the making of a generally faithful transcript of the *History*, and this text was printed in three volumes at Oxford in 1702–1704. The profits of the copyright were used to provide a building for the University press, and the Clarendon printing-house was erected in 1713, a fitting memorial to Clarendon, who had been Chancellor of the University from 1660 to 1667. Clarendon's continuation of the "Life" and portions of the manuscript "Life" which he had left out of the *History* were published by the University Press in 1759 as *The Life of Edward Earl of Clarendon*. In 1888, W. Dunn Macray produced a superb modern-spelling edition (6 vols.) of the *History* from the original manuscripts, indicating which parts came from the "History" and which from the "Life." In 1918, David Nichol Smith, in *Characters from the Histories & Memoirs of the Seventeenth Century*, printed thirty-seven characters as they appear in the manuscripts. The text of the three characters printed here is based on film of the manuscripts, through the kindness of the Librarian, Bodleian Library. The character of Charles I is from pp. 383–384 of the manuscript "Life," MS. Clarendon 123 (first printed in *History*, 1702–1704, III, 197–199; Macray, IV, 488–492; Smith, pp. 48–53). The *Cromwell* is from pp. 547–550 of the manuscript "Life," with ¶'s 6–8 from the manuscript "History," MS. Clarendon 112, p. 33 (*History*, 1702–1704, III, 500–509; Macray, VI, 88–97; partly printed in Smith, pp. 139–140). The *Earle* is from the manuscript "Life," p. 57 (first printed in *The Life*, 1759, pp. 26–27 of the folio edition; Smith, pp. 168–170).

The *History* is most readily available in Macray's edition, mentioned above. The standard biography is Sir Henry Craik's *The Life of Edward Earl of Clarendon* (2 vols., 1911); there is a good short life by C. H. Firth in the *Dictionary of National Biography*. The most useful commentary on the *History* is by Firth: "Clarendon's 'History of the Rebellion,'" *English Historical Review*, XIX (1904), 26–54, 246–262, 464–483; see, too, David Nichol Smith's introduction, pp. xxx–xliv. L. C. Knights praises Clarendon's political wisdom in "Reflections on Clarendon's History of the Rebellion," *Scrutiny*, XV (1948), 105–116. The focus of B. H. G. Wormald's *Clarendon* (1951, repr. 1964) is, as its subtitle suggests, on *Politics, Historiography, and Religion, 1640–1660*.

BEN JONSON
1572/3–1637

If Dr. Johnson deserves the title "last of the Romans," Ben Jonson may properly be called the first of them. Though he was not a distinguished student at Westminster School, he never forgot what he learned from his eminent teacher, William Camden, and though he never went to a university, he knew that "hee that was onely taught by himselfe, had a foole to his Master." Jonson's masters were Aristotle and the Roman poets, moralists, historians, and rhetoricians; not only did they make him a full man, but he read them so well that he could convert their substance to his own use. By the time Jonson was twenty-two, he had served enough of an apprenticeship as a bricklayer so that he was later made a member of the Tilers' and Bricklayers' Company, he had seen military service in Flanders, and he had married. He had already had some experience as actor and playwright when he went to work for Philip Henslowe and the Admiral's Company about 1597. His first great success was *Every Man in His Humour*, put on the stage in 1598 not by Henslowe but by the Chamberlain's Company, which was to produce most of his great plays. Jonson's next plays were interesting experiments to adapt formal satire to the stage, and they failed. Their failure turned him to tragedy (though an enigmatic reference puts him among "our best for Tragedie" in 1598), and *Sejanus* appeared in 1603. The greatest plays followed *Eastward Ho*, a collaboration with old friends and rivals, Marston and Chapman, late in 1604: *Volpone* (1606), *Epicoene* (1609), *The Alchemist* (1610), and *Bartholomew Fair* (1614). In 1616 appeared *The Workes of Benjamin Jonson*, a carefully supervised collection of Jonson's work to about 1612; it contains, in addition to the plays Jonson wished to preserve, 133 *Epigrammes*, a smaller collection of lyrics and occasional verses called *The Forrest*, and a number of masques and entertainments. The volume demonstrates not only the classical virtues of perspicuity of style and strength of structure, but also Jonson's rational intelligence as he stresses the didactic and ethical function of poetry, and it shows him to be, to quote from the dedication of *Volpone,* "*the interpreter, and arbiter of nature, a teacher of things divine, no lesse then humane, a master of manners: and can alone (or with a few) effect the businesse of man-kind.*" Jonson's great days were over, though his work after this time would have made the reputation of any man smaller than himself. For almost two decades he continued to write poems and masques and to experiment occasionally on the stage. He was the literary dictator of London, "Saint Ben" or "father" to a whole tribe of sons that included Robert Herrick, Thomas Carew, Thomas Randolph, Sir Lucius Cary, and William Cartwright. In 1618–1619, he walked to Scotland and visited William Drummond, who left a record of his conversation; in 1623, a fire destroyed his papers; in 1628, he was laid low by a paralytic stroke. After his death, his friend Sir Kenelm Digby saw through the press in 1640–1641 a second folio volume of *Workes.* This contains more plays and masques; poems, in a section called *The Under-woods;* a translation of *Horace, His Art of Poetrie; The English Grammar;* and *Timber.*

Timber was obviously put together from loose papers which Jonson wrote after his fire. The first part is made up of apothegms and small essays on morals, manners, and statecraft; the larger pieces at the end are on the art of writing and on types of literature. Almost all is derivative, the result of Jonson's reading, but everything has his stamp. C. J. Sisson has suggested (*TLS,* September 21, 1951) that *Timber* contains lecture notes which deal in a systematic way with the main problems in the theory and practice of rhetoric, that Jonson served as a deputy for the Professor of Rhetoric at Gresham College from 1619 to 1623 or 1627, and that the honorary degree of M.A. which he was granted by Oxford in 1619 was given him so that he might teach. A separate title page, dated 1641, in the *Workes,* says only *Timber: or, Discoveries; Made upon Men and Matter: As They have flow'd out of his daily Readings; or had their refluxe to his peculiar Notion of the Times;* the text is on pp. 85–132. The two selections printed here are on pp. 115–117; their titles are marginal notes in the original.

The standard edition of Jonson's complete works is *Ben Jonson,* ed. C. H. Herford and Percy and Evelyn Simpson (11 vols., 1925–1952, repr. 1954); vols. 1 and 2, *The Man and his Work,* provide a biography and an introduction to each work. William B. Hunter, Jr., edited *The Complete Poetry* in 1963; good modern-spelling editions of the individual plays are being issued in *The Yale Ben Jonson.* Editions of *Timber* which cite Jonson's sources are those by Felix E. Schelling (1892) and Maurice Castelain (1906); the most recent edition is by Ralph S. Walker (1953). Swinburne's *A Study of Ben Jonson* (1889) is still worth reading; Jonas A. Barish has edited a good group of critical essays, mainly on the dramatic work, in *Ben*

Jonson (1963). Of particular interest to readers of *Timber* are Walker's "Ben Jonson's *Discoveries:* a New Analysis," *Essays and Studies of The English Association,* V (1952), 32–51, and Frank B. Fieler's "The Impact of Bacon and the New Science upon Jonson's Critical Thought in *Timber,*" *Renaissance Papers, 1958, 1959, 1960* (1961), pp. 84–92. Maurice Castelain's *Ben Jonson, l'Homme et l'Oeuvre* (1907) has 953 pages; a good short biography is Marchette Chute's *Ben Jonson of Westminster* (1953).

JOHN MILTON
1608–1674

"My father," Milton wrote (in Latin), "destined me from a child to the pursuits of literature; and my appetite for knowledge was so voracious, that, from twelve years of age, I hardly ever left my studies, or went to bed before midnight." Milton's education was a long one: he may have entered St. Paul's School as early as 1615–1616; he was the most distinguished student at Christ's College, Cambridge, from 1625 to 1632; until 1638 he put himself through a rigorous course of study in his father's house at Hammersmith and then at Horton in Buckinghamshire; he ended his formal education with a fifteen-month journey abroad, chiefly in Italy. Only then, in his early thirties, did he become a schoolmaster. If Milton was not so precocious as Cowley, he outstripped him, certainly, in "On the Morning of Christ's Nativity," written at twenty-one, and in "L'Allegro" and "Il Penseroso," probably written at twenty-two, and Cowley was never to attain the heights of *Comus* (1634) and *Lycidas* (1637). Milton probably published *Poems,* 1645, because between the date of *Epitaphium Damonis* (late in 1639 or early in 1640) and the publication of the poems, he was so busy with other matters that he had found time to write in verse only three sonnets. The years 1641–1660 are the years of his prose tracts. In 1654, he wrote of those in print, "When, therefore, I perceived that there were three species of liberty which are essential to the happiness of social life—religious, domestic, and civil; and as I had already written concerning the first, and the magistrates were strenuously active in obtaining the third, I determined to turn my attention to the second, or the domestic species. As this seemed to involve three material questions, the conditions of the conjugal tie, the education of the children, and the free publication of the thoughts, I made them objects of distinct consideration." In 1641–1642, Milton had written five pamphlets against prelacy. In 1643–1645, he wrote four pamphlets on the subject of divorce; *Of Education* appeared (in June 1644) after the first of these, *The Doctrine and Discipline of Divorce,* and *Areopagitica* after the second (in November 1644). Milton did not leave the subject of civil liberty to the magistrates for long. In 1649, he wrote *The Tenure of Kings and Magistrates*, which led to his appointment as Secretary for Foreign Tongues to the Council of State, and *Eikonoklastes*. For some time his sight had been failing, and the first of his two Latin defenses of the English people (1651, 1654) cost him his eyes. In the year of the Restoration, he was still concerned with the *Ready and Easy Way to Establish a Free Commonwealth*. His other prose works do not fit so neatly into categories. Among them are a Latin grammar (written in English) and a treatise on logic (written in Latin), a history of Britain and a brief history of Russia, and an examination of Christian doctrine. *Paradise Lost* was published in 1667 (2nd ed., rev., 1674); *Paradise Regained* and *Samson Agonistes* were published together in 1671; the minor poems were reprinted with additions in 1673.

Milton had begun to oppose traditional university education during his Cambridge years, but his letter *Of Education* to Samuel Hartlib was probably not entirely to Hartlib's liking. Hartlib was at the center of a movement to adapt education to the middle-class world of trade and technology by making it more popular and more scientific, and, as a disciple of the eminent continental educator, John Amos Comenius, he was largely responsible for Comenius' visit to England in 1641–1642. Hartlib would have liked the importance Milton attached to the study of science, but he would not have been sympathetic to an aristocratic view of education which re-emphasized the tradition of Renaissance humanism and the centrality of the study of the classics. Though his own aims were not incongruous with Milton's conception of a complete and generous education and with his emphasis on true virtue derived from knowledge to repair the ruins of our first parents, Hartlib would have preferred a more democratic, pragmatic, and pietistic statement. *Of Education* was anonymously published without a title page in June 1644, and the text printed here follows that edition. A second edition, with a few minor corrections, was printed in 1673, at the end of the second edition of the minor poems.

The Works of John Milton (Columbia University Press, 18 vols. [in 21], 1931–1938, and 2-vol. Index, 1940) is the only complete edition with original spelling. Of the eight projected volumes in the Yale edition of the *Complete Prose Works*, the first four volumes have appeared (1953, 1959, 1962, 1966), covering the works through 1655. The most useful one-volume edition of the *Complete Poems and Major Prose* is probably that by Merritt Y. Hughes (1957). The best edition of *Of Education* is the massively annotated one by Donald C. Dorian in Vol. II of the Yale *Prose Works* (Introduction by Ernest Sirluck). Oliver M. Ainsworth's *Milton on Education* (1928) pulls together Milton's most important statements on various aspects of education. A good recent article is John F. Huntley's "*Proairesis, Synteresis,* and the Ethical Orientation of Milton's *Of Education*," *PQ*, XLIII (1964), 40–46. The most useful introductions to Milton's life and career are James Holly Hanford's *A Milton Handbook* (1926; 4th ed., 1946), Marjorie H. Nicolson's *John Milton: A Reader's Guide to His Poetry* (1963), and Douglas Bush's *John Milton, a Sketch of His Life and Writings* (1964). The first biographies of Milton have been edited by Helen Darbishire in *The Early Lives of Milton* (1932, repr. 1965). The most voluminous life is that by David Masson (6 vols., 1859–1880 [with rev. edns. of the first three vols., 1881, 1894, 1896], and an Index, 1894; repr. 1946). J. Milton French has collected and edited *The Life Records of John Milton* (5 vols., 1949–1958). A good modern life is Hanford's *John Milton, Englishman* (1949). There is a fine selective bibliography of Milton in Bush's *English Literature in the Earlier Seventeenth Century 1600–1660* (2nd ed., rev., 1962), pp. 615–622 (and a fine chapter on Milton, too). Fuller bibliographies of Milton scholarship and criticism are David H. Stevens' *Reference Guide to Milton from 1800 to the Present* (1930), with Harris F. Fletcher's addenda, *Contributions to a Milton Bibliography, 1800–1930* (1931), and Calvin Huckabay's *John Milton: A Bibliographical Supplement, 1929–1957* (1960).

DOROTHY OSBORNE
1627–1695

When on December 24, 1652, Dorothy Osborne wrote the first of her letters to William Temple, she was a spinster of twenty-five, living at Chicksands in Bedfordshire, forty miles from London. Her mother had died the year before, and she, the youngest of nine children and the only daughter among the four still alive, supervised the household and the care of her father, now at sixty-seven the shadow of the gallant royalist who had held Castle Cornet on Guernsey for years against the Parliament. Her letters reveal an extraordinary view of upper-class provincial life in difficult times, and they reveal, too, an extraordinary woman. She has often been compared to Jane Austen; she resembles even more the aunt who died in the year she was born —Magdalen Herbert, wife of Sir John Danvers. The gravity and the drollery which are in the letters, the melancholy and the sharp wit, the delicacy of feeling and the outspoken expression, the poise and independence made her attractive to many suitors, including Henry Cromwell, son of the Protector, and her cousin Thomas Osborne, the future Earl of Danby and Lord Treasurer. Her passionate kindness for William Temple, whom she had met when she was twenty-one, and his for her, prevailed over the objections of both families to a match which was not financially advantageous: after her father's death and after her recovery from the smallpox which marred her beauty, she married Temple on Christmas Day, 1654. For several years they lived quietly in Ireland, and then Temple embarked on the distinguished diplomatic career that culminated in the forging of the Triple Alliance in 1668 and in ambassadorships to The Hague in 1668–1671 and 1674–1676. In the context of the letters, it is only fitting that Lady Temple should have helped her husband arrange the marriage of William of Orange to Mary, niece of Charles II. Her life with Temple was happy and busy, but she knew how small a proportion of happiness is allowed in this world: seven of their children died in infancy, one daughter at fourteen, and the only son to reach adulthood took his own life. During the years of retirement at Moor Park in Surrey, she was mild, peaceful, wise, and great; the adjectives were used by an astute observer, her husband's young amanuensis, Jonathan Swift.

Extracts from Dorothy Osborne's letters were first published in Thomas P. Courtenay's *Memoirs of the Life, Works, and Correspondence of Sir William Temple* (II, 273–337). The letters were published separately in an edition by E. A. Parry in 1888, and again, with corrections and additions, in 1903. The series of letters written before the marriage numbers seventy-six; about a dozen later letters by Dorothy Osborne have been published. Temple's replies are lost, except for one fragment (three volumes of his letters were edited by Swift, 1700–1703, and many others have been published). The best edition of Dorothy Osborne's letters to Temple is that by G. C. Moore Smith (1928), who added only a little punctuation to the originals. The three letters printed here are numbered 24, 44, and 57 by Moore Smith. They follow his text, with the permission of the Clarendon Press, Oxford; proper names in brackets are additions to the text.

There are appreciative essays by Virginia Woolf in *The Second Common Reader* (1932) and by F. L. Lucas in *Studies French and English* (1934), and a psychograph by Lord David Cecil in *Two Quiet Lives* (1948). In Homer E. Woodbridge's *Sir William Temple: The Man and his Work* (1940), the best life of Temple, Chaps. 2 and 3 are particularly relevant to Dorothy Osborne.

SIR THOMAS OVERBURY
1581–1613

Overbury's name is attached to characters, most of which he did not write; it is not attached to many political maneuvers which he probably set in motion. After taking his B.A. at Oxford in 1598 and after studying law at the Middle Temple, Overbury entered public life in the employ of the Secretary of State. As early as 1601, he had met Robert Carr, a Scot five years younger than he, and when Carr became a favorite of King James in 1607, Overbury tied himself to Carr's star.

Carr was knighted in December 1607, and Overbury six months later. As Carr's adviser, Overbury was probably one of the most influential men in English politics for half a dozen years. Able and shrewd, he was also proud and insolent, and Ben Jonson, who had addressed a poem to him, later called him a mortal enemy. Opportunistically, he welcomed Carr's affair with Frances Howard, Countess of Essex, insofar as it might benefit Carr's career, but he opposed Carr's wish to marry her, for he was fearful that the Howards would usurp his influence. His opposition cost him his life: he was imprisoned in the Tower in April 1613, and, poisoned through the machinations of the Countess, he died there in September.

Overbury's poem called "A Wife" was entered on the Stationers' Register two weeks before the newly divorced Countess of Essex married the newly created Earl of Somerset on December 26, 1613. Whether it was written by Overbury to ingratiate himself with the Countess of Rutland or to provide an ideal picture by which Carr might measure his Frances is not known. It is doubtful that the merits of the poem itself called forth a second impression some time after May 16, 1614. Rumors about Overbury's scandalous death gave the poem some notoriety, and the title page of the new impression reads, *A Wife now The Widdow of Sir Thomas Overburye. Being A most exquisite and singular Poem of the choice of a Wife. Whereunto are added many witty Characters, and conceited Newes, written by himselfe and other learned Gentlemen his friends.* The publisher added to the poem twenty-one characters. Of these Overbury may have written the first three, "A good Woman," "A very very Woman," and "Her next part," and perhaps half a dozen more; "An affected Traveller" may possibly be his, but not "An elder Brother." The 3rd, 4th, and 5th impressions were also published in 1614; the 4th added nine characters, among them "A Puritane" and Sir Henry Wotton's verse "Character of a happie life." The 6th impression (1615) was so greatly enlarged that it was given a title different from that of all others, *New and Choise Characters, of several Authors.* Forty-two new characters are first printed here. Of these, three, including "A Tinker," were claimed by "J. Cocke" in a poem which prefaces the second impression of the characters of John Stephens (1615). A group of thirty-two, including "A fayre and happy Milke-mayd" and "An excellent Actor," were preceded by a separate title page, and these have been attributed on good evidence to the playwright, John Webster. "An excellent Actor" is a reply to Stephens' "A common Player," published earlier in the year; it caused Stephens to revise his portrait in his second impression, and the revision mollified Webster sufficiently so that in later impressions of "An excellent Actor" he omitted the words from "Therefore the imitating Characterist" through "should you flea them." Of the three impressions printed in 1616, only the 9th impression adds a group of new characters, the last of which is "What a

Character is"; six "prison" characters here, dealing with the life of a debtor, may have been written by Thomas Dekker. The last additions to the Overburian volume were made in the 11th impression (1622), when Donne's essay on valor and his character of a dunce were included. The text of each of the characters printed here is based upon the text of the impression in which it first appeared.

The best edition of *The Overburian Characters* is that by W. J. Paylor (1936), with good introduction and notes. The case for Webster's authorship of 32 characters, first set forth (1913–1915) in articles by H. D. Sykes and Baron A. F. Bourgeois, is discussed in Paylor's introduction (pp. xvii–xix) and in F. L. Lucas's edition of *The Complete Works of John Webster* (4 vols., 1937), where these characters are reprinted (IV, 5–61). The impressions of the Overburian characters are described in Gwendolyn Murphy's *A Bibliography of English Character-Books, 1608–1700* (1925), pp. 15–26 (Suppl. 4 of *Transactions of the Bibliographical Society*, VI [1926]); there is a brief supplement by Paylor in *ibid.*, XVII (1936), 340–348. The most comprehensive studies of the character are Benjamin Boyce's *The Theophrastan Character in England to 1642* (1947) and *The Polemic Character 1640–1661* (1955). Works generally attributed to Overbury are printed in Edward F. Rimbault's *The Miscellaneous Works in Prose and Verse of Sir Thomas Overbury* (1856, 1890), which also has a short life. The best account of the Overbury scandal is William McElwee's *The Murder of Sir Thomas Overbury* (1952).

SAMUEL PEPYS
1633–1703

One of the many children of an impoverished tailor, Pepys was raised in a Puritan household; he came naturally by his industry, his highly developed conscience, his drive for money and good living. He attended St. Paul's School and took his B.A. at Magdalene College, Cambridge, in 1653. Two years later he married Elizabeth de St. Michel, the fifteen-year-old daughter of a feckless Huguenot exile. He was first employed to manage the affairs of his cousin, Edward Montagu, a member of the Admiralty Commission who became Joint-Commander of the English fleet in 1656 and Earl of Sandwich in 1660, and Montagu continued to help him. When he started to keep his diary on January 1, 1660, he had been a clerk to one of the Tellers of the Exchequer for a year and a half; his salary was £50 a year, and besides his house and goods he was "not clearly worth £25." In March, he joined the Navy Office as Montagu's secretary; in July, he became Clerk of the Acts of the Office at a salary of £350. This position, which he held throughout the years of the diary, made Pepys, with the

Treasurer, the Comptroller, the Surveyor, and the Independent Commissioners, one of the chief officers of the Navy; his house on Seething Lane was an official residence which overlooked the gardens and courtyards of the Navy Office; at the end of 1666, he wrote, "I pray God make me thankful for it, I do find myself worth in money, all good, above £6,200." This is the Pepys known to the nineteenth century: the careerist in his early thirties, the perfect type, as James Russell Lowell called him, of the philistine bourgeois, with all the commonness and vulgarity of interest of the type, but also a very likable young man, naive, sincere, and utterly honest as he reported his feelings, motives, and actions. Even in the diary, however, there is the picture of the extraordinarily competent civil servant; on March 5, 1668, Pepys's three-hour defense of the Navy Office before the bar of the House of Commons won him universal acclaim. His later career has been properly assessed only in our own century. When, in 1673, the Duke of York was forced by the Test Act to resign as Lord High Admiral, the King replaced him by a Commission and appointed Pepys Secretary to the Office of Lord High Admiral. He was in command of the Navy until May 1679, when he was falsely charged with piracy, popery, and treachery, and committed to the Tower. He had built the finest peacetime fleet that England had ever possessed, only to see it and the Navy service disintegrate in the next five years. In May 1684, he resumed his position at the King's request, this time with even more power as Secretary for the Affairs of the Admiralty, and, under his old master, James II, he pushed through a large program of naval reconstruction. He voluntarily resigned his place shortly after William and Mary came to the throne. For more than a decade, then, Pepys superintended the rebuilding and the reform of the Navy, and he has been called the architect of the naval machine which ultimately gave England dominion of the seas and of a great empire. During his last years of retirement, Pepys was able to indulge in the pursuits of a virtuoso. He had been a member of the Royal Society since 1665 and had been elected President in 1684; now he could follow interests which were not professional.

Whether his motive was self-examination, self-protection, or retrospective pleasure, Pepys put great store in the diary he kept for over nine years: he postponed writing an entry until the next day when he "began to write idly and from the purpose"; he had it bound and preserved it though he destroyed other papers and records; when his failing eyesight forced him to discontinue it, he wrote that it was "almost as much as to see myself go into my grave." He used a popular system of shorthand, probably for both convenience and secrecy, and occasionally a hodge-podge of foreign words, but he bequeathed his collection of shorthand manuals along with his diary and 3,000 books to his nephew with the proviso that his collection would one day be permanently housed at Magdalene College. The diary, which contains about 1,300,000 words on 3,012 quarto pages bound in six volumes, was transcribed by a Cambridge undergraduate, John Smith, in 1819–1822. A little more than a quarter of it was edited and published in two volumes by Richard Neville, 3rd Lord Braybrooke, in 1825 (3rd ed., enlarged, 1848–1849). The Rev. Mynors Bright transcribed the whole diary and published about seventy per cent of it in 1875–1879. All of Bright's transcription, except for a few indelicate passages, was printed in a 9-volume edition by Henry B. Wheatley (1893–1899), which remains the standard text. Part of that text is reprinted here, with the permission of the publishers, G. Bell and Sons, Ltd., who hope to publish in a couple of years the first volumes of a definitive edition, newly transcribed and annotated by William Matthews and Robert Latham.

The only work by Pepys published in his lifetime was *Memoires Relating to the State of the Royal Navy of England, For Ten Years, Determin'd December 1688* (ed. J. R. Tanner, 1906). Part of his papers and correspondence has been made available: *Private correspondence and Miscellaneous Papers . . . 1679–1703* (1926) and *Further Correspondence . . . 1662–1679* (1929), ed. J. R. Tanner; *Letters and the Second Diary* (1932), ed. R. G. Howarth, who used John Smith's untrustworthy text (1841) for the diary, which covers July 30, 1683–Mar. 29, 1684; *Shorthand Letters . . . 1662–1679* (1933) and *The Tangier Papers* (1935), ed. Edwin Chappell; *The Letters of Samuel Pepys and His Family Circle* (1955), ed. Helen T. Heath; his correspondence with John Evelyn in Clara Marburg's *Mr. Pepys and Mr. Evelyn* (1935). Pepys's collection of "Sea" manuscripts, his early printed books to 1558, his medieval manuscripts, and his shorthand books have been described in the four volumes of *Bibliotheca Pepysiana, A Descriptive Catalogue of the Library of Samuel Pepys* (1914–1940); the broadside ballads he collected have been edited by Hyder E. Rollins in *A Pepysian Garland* (1922) and *The Pepys Ballads* (8 vols., 1929–1932). A fine article on Pepys's shorthand and its effect on the style of the diary is W. Matthews' "Samuel Pepys, Tachygraphist," *MLR*, XXIX (1934), 397–404. The best biography is Arthur Bryant's *Samuel Pepys*: vol. 1, *The Man in the Making* (1933) covers 1633–1669; vol. 2, *The Years of Peril* (1935), 1669–1683; vol. 3, *The Saviour of the Navy* (1938), 1683–1689.

SIR WALTER RALEIGH
1554?–1618

Fuller properly added "and what not" to the categories of *"State-man, Sea-man, Souldier, Learned Writer"* under which he might have placed Raleigh; merely to add explorer, colonizer, poet, and patron of poetry to the list is still to omit his dramatic force, the personality which kept men's eyes on him and the character which won him men's affection and loyalty. Raleigh was briefly at Oxford, but left to fight with the Huguenots against the Catholics in France. He was even more briefly at the Middle Temple, where he was more interested in poetry and in courtly pursuits than in law. In 1578, he joined his half-brother, Sir Humphrey Gilbert, in a piratical expedition against the Spaniards, and in 1580, as captain of an infantry company, he helped suppress rebellion in Ireland. At the end of 1581, he returned to England and was for a decade Elizabeth's favorite. Knighted in 1584, he grew rich and powerful by such appointments as Warden of the Stannaries, Lieutenant of Cornwall, Vice Admiral of the West, and Captain of the Guard. He fell from favor because of his marriage to one of the Queen's maids-of-honor, Elizabeth Throckmorton. Always a strong advocate of sea power (though he had no active role in the repulse of the Spanish Armada), Raleigh tried for years to establish colonies in what was to be called 'Virginia"; he was the prime mover behind the settlement of Roanoke Island in 1584, and in later attempts. In 1595, he planned and commanded an expedition to Guiana to search for gold and he explored the valley of the Orinoco; in 1596, he led one of the four squadrons which captured and sacked Cadiz; in the following year, he led a squadron in the futile expedition to the Azores. During the last years of the century, Raleigh's power at court was overshadowed by that of Essex, but with the execution of Essex his influence was at its peak. He had not, however, established close relations with James of Scotland, and in July 1603, he was committed to the Tower for alleged complicity in plots against James. In November, he was tried at Winchester, sentenced to death, reprieved, and sent to the Tower, where he was confined in fairly comfortable circumstances for twelve years. Before this time, Raleigh's writing had been occasional: even the nymph's words to the passionate shepherd were a reply. He had written in 1591 a stirring account of the heroism of Sir Richard Grenville, in a pamphlet called *A Report of the Truth of the fight about the Iles of Açores, this last Sommer. Betwixt the Revenge, one of her Majesties Shippes, And an Armada of the King of Spaine.* In 1596, after his voyage to South America, he published a volume to vindicate his endeavors and to stir up interest in a colonial empire, *The Discoverie of the Large, Rich, and Bewtiful Empyre of Guiana, with a relation of the great and Golden Citie of Manoa,* which was frequently reprinted and translated. In the Tower, encouraged by the patronage of Henry, Prince of Wales, and by the aid of many friends, he embarked on his *History of the World.* The book was printed in 1614; Raleigh had started with Creation and got down to the Roman conquest of Macedon. Since the whole was didactic and informed by the concept that history showed the workings of God's providence in the affairs of men, King James did not find its matter remote and he had it suppressed for a while. Raleigh was finally released from the Tower in March 1616, on the condition that he sail to Guiana for gold, and a year later he set out with thirteen ships and 1,000 men. His search did not succeed, and he was accused of piracy by the Spanish Ambassador because his men had sacked the settlement at San Thomé. He was executed for high treason on October 29, 1618.

The interest of the seventeenth century in Raleigh is shown not only in the many editions of his *History* and of his *Remains*, but even in his letter printed here, which was deemed worthy of independent publication as a pamphlet twenty-six years after his death. The text used here is the one first given to seventeenth-century readers in 1644. Its heading is wrong; the letter was not written the night before he was beheaded (on that night, his Bess was with him till midnight), but in December 1603, on the night before he expected to be executed in Winchester. The printer got hold of an edited manuscript (all but one of the four surviving manuscripts show signs of editing), and then edited it further, adding at its close the eight lines which Aubrey says were written by Raleigh in his Bible just before his execution. The text of the most authoritative manuscript of the letter has been printed in *Sir Walter Raleigh: Selections,* ed. G. E. Hadow (1917), pp. 181–184.

The most nearly complete edition of Raleigh's works was published in 1829 by the Oxford University Press; vol. 1 has biographies by William Oldys and Thomas Birch; vols. 2–7 contain the last reprint of the complete *History;* vol. 8 has most of the miscellaneous works. *A Report of the . . . Revenge,* omitted from the 1829 *Works,* is printed in Hadow's fine *Selections. The Discoverie of . . . Guiana* was edited by V. T. Harlow in 1928. The best edition of Raleigh's poems (1929, rev. and suppl. 1951) is by Agnes M. C. Latham, who is now editing the letters. The 2-volume life and letters (1868) by Edward Edwards remains a standard work. Among many biographies, the following may be singled out: W. Stebbing, *Sir Walter Ralegh* (1891, 2nd ed. 1899); Edward Thompson, *Sir Walter Raleigh, Last of the Elizabethans* (1936); Willard M. Wallace, *Sir Walter Raleigh* (1959); A. L. Rowse, *Ralegh and the Throckmortons* (1962). Philip Edwards' *Sir Walter Ralegh* (1953) stresses the literary attainments and Ernest A. Strathmann's *Sir Walter Ralegh: A Study in Elizabethan Skepticism* (1951) stresses Raleigh's thought. John Racin, Jr., "The Early Editions of Sir Walter Ralegh's *The History of the World*," *Studies in Bibliography,* XVII (1964), 199–209, discusses the suppression of the *History* and corrects T. N. Brushfield's *Bibliography* (2nd ed., rev., 1908).

JOHN STEPHENS
fl. 1615

Little is known about John Stephens. He was admitted to Lincoln's Inn in 1611, and was called "the yonger, of Lincolnes Inn, Gent." on the title page of the second edition of his characters. He may perhaps be considered one of the stepsons of Ben Jonson. In the dedication of his play, *Cinthias Revenge: or Maenanders Extasie* (1613), he is contemptuous toward "the vaine mercenary rout of Bastard-poets," associates himself with those who would instruct and delight, and differentiates readers from understanding readers; Jonson may have written the prefatory verses "To his much and worthily esteemed friend the Author," which are signed "B. I."

Stephens may have been one of the learned gentlemen who contributed to the Overburian collection. The earlier impressions contain a poem, "A Morning Sacrifice," signed "I. S. Lincolniensis," which was dropped from the 6th and later impressions; the 6th is the impression in which John Webster replied to Stephens' *A common Player.* That was first published in *Satyrical Essayes Characters and Others* (1615), for which Stephens wrote three satirical essays in verse, four prose essays, and 43 characters. In the same year, a second edition was published, called *Essayes and Characters. Ironicall, and Instructive* (re-issued as *New Essayes and Characters* in 1631); seven characters and a satirical verse essay, "a defence for common Law & Lawyers mixt with reproofe against the Lawyers common Enemy," were added, and *"A common Player"* was substantially changed. The text printed here is that of the first edition, pp. 244–249; all the changes and additions made in the 2nd ed. (pp. 295–301) are in the notes, but two of the marginal notes have been omitted.

There is a very short life of Stephens by A. F. Pollard in the *Dictionary of National Biography,* and an article by Percy Simpson on "The Authorship and Original Issue of 'Cinthia's Revenge,'" *MLR,* II (1907), 348–350.

IZAAK WALTON
1593–1683

Over 300 editions of *The Compleat Angler* have made Walton's name synonymous with angling, but he is also the first professional biographer of stature in England, and his proficiency as biographer allowed him to play an active minor role in the re-establishment of the High Church and what it stood for. Walton had little formal education; born in Stafford, he was apprenticed to his brother-in-law, a prospering sempster of London, and in 1618 he was admitted to membership in the Ironmongers' Company. Until the middle of 1643, he was a successful merchant, probably a draper, in the parish of St. Dunstan's-in-the-West. His literary interests may have stemmed from the closeness of his shop to the Inns of Court and to the presence of booksellers in his neighborhood: he was a friend of Michael Drayton's, he had met Ben Jonson, and he knew some of the sons of Ben. He may have met Donne in 1624 when the eminent Dean of St. Paul's became also the vicar of his parish church, but the acquaintance may have started only after December 1626, when he married Rachel Floud, whose family connections with Archbishop Thomas Cranmer and with Dr. John Spenser (once president of Corpus Christi College, Oxford) would have recommended the Waltons to Donne. During the wars and the interregnum, Walton lived in Clerkenwell and also on a small estate he owned in Staffordshire, and he devoted himself increasingly to writing. In 1661–1662, he helped his old friend George Morley, now Bishop of Worcester, by acting as his personal steward. When his second wife, Anne Ken, died in 1662, leaving him with two small children, he followed Morley, who had just been translated, to Winchester. For the last twenty years of his life he resided mainly with Morley, who now exerted even greater influence on his career than he had in the past. In dedicating his *Lives*, 1670, to Morley, Walton wrote, *"If I had been fit for this Undertaking, it would not have been by acquir'd Learning or Study, but by the advantage of forty years friendship, and thereby the hearing of and discoursing with your Lordship, which hath inabled me to make the relation of these Lives passable in an eloquent and captious age."*

The publication of Walton's biographies has been described on pp. 31–32 of the Introduction. The life of Donne is here reprinted from *Lives*, 1675, where Walton substantially revised it for the third and last time; the main addition is the story of Donne's vision of his wife.

The Compleat Angler was first published in 1653; it was revised and enlarged in 1655; new editions appeared in 1661 (re-issued 1664), in 1668, and in 1676 (with the addition of instructions on trout-fishing by Charles Cotton and with Col. Robert Venables' *The Experienced Angler*, which had first been published in 1662). Peter Oliver's *A New Chronicle of The Compleat Angler* (1936) describes 284 editions and impressions. Since 1876, many facsimiles of the first edition have appeared; the best was published by A. & C. Black in 1928. The *Everyman's Library* edition is mainly a reprint of the 5th ed. (1676), and it follows Andrew Lang's 1896 edition. The *Modern Library* edition follows Geoffrey Keynes's *The Compleat Walton* (1929) in printing the 4th ed. (1668); Keynes's volume is the best available edition of all Walton's works. The most useful essays about *The Compleat Angler* are James Russell Lowell's Introduction to his edition of 1889; Austin Dobson's "On Certain Quotations in Walton's 'Angler,'" in *Miscellanies, Second Series* (1901); H. J. Oliver's "The Composition and Revision of *The Compleat Angler*," *MLR*, XLII (1947), 295–313; and B. D. Greenslade's "*The Compleat Angler* and the Sequestered Clergy," *RES*, N.S. V (1954), 361–366. Walton's *Lives* are most readily available in the *World's Classics* edition (1927), which, however, reprints the first rather than the revised *Life of Sanderson*. David Novarr's *The Making of Walton's "Lives"* (1958) examines Walton's biographic technique through study of his purposes, sources, and revisions; see, too, R. C. Bald, "Historical Doubts Respecting Walton's *Life of Donne*," in *Essays in English Literature . . . Presented to A. S. P. Woodhouse*, ed. Millar MacLure and F. W. Watt (1964), pp. 69–84. John Butt has done "A Bibliography of Izaak Walton's *Lives*," *Oxford Bibliographical Society Proceedings and Papers*, II (pt. IV, 1930), 327–340. Most of what we know of Walton's life comes from accounts by Sir John Hawkins (ed. *Angler*, 1760), by Thomas Zouch (ed. *Lives*, 1796, 1807, 1817), and by Sir Harris Nicolas (ed. *Angler*, 1836). The fullest and most accurate life is Arthur M. Coon's unpublished dissertation (Cornell University, 1938).

ANTHONY À WOOD
1632–1695

Anthony Wood (the "à" is his own invention) was born, he tells us, "in an antient stone-house opposite to the forefront of Merton Coll.," Oxford; there he lived and worked in a zealously guarded garret study, and there he died. An undistinguished student at Merton, he took his B.A. in 1652, but he was never invited to become a Fellow. His patrimony was just large enough so that he could indulge his historical and antiquarian interests, and between 1657 and 1659 he collected inscriptions and took notes on antiquities for a proposed description of Oxfordshire. In 1660, he obtained access to the University archives, and for a decade he compiled material for a history of the city of Oxford, the University, and the colleges. His treatise on the University was accepted by the University Press in 1669, and after five years of revisions, additions, and arguments with Dr. John Fell, Dean of Christ Church, who paid both Wood and the publication charges and who insisted on translation into Latin (not by Wood) and on revisions of his own, Wood saw in print *Historia et Antiquitates Universitatis Oxoniensis* (1674). Part I is an annalistic history; the second part describes buildings and institutions, includes historical notices of the colleges and their famous men, and adds "Fasti" (mainly lists of important University officials). Wood did not like the volume, and he re-wrote it in English. (His revision was published, with a continuation by John Gutch, in 1786–1790.) At Fell's request, Wood had somewhat expanded his original sketches of writers in the *Historia;* he continued his researches, and on June 18, 1691, the first volume of his biographical dictionary, *Athenae Oxonienses,* was published. Within a week, Wood heard that the President of Trinity College had said that Wood "*collected* it but not *writ* it," and that it was thought in London that "a great deal of ill nature" was in the book. The second volume was published on July 18, 1692, and a year later Wood was prosecuted in the vice-chancellor's court at Oxford for the libelous statement that Clarendon had received money from office-seekers at the Restoration. He was convicted, fined, and deprived of the privileges of the University. Unpublished at his death were his autobiography (through 1672) and his diary or journal-notes (1673–1695), and his survey of the antiquities of the city of Oxford. Wood left his books and manuscripts to the Ashmolean Museum, and they passed to the Bodleian Library in 1858.

Athenae Oxonienses is subtitled *An Exact History of all the Writers and Bishops Who have had their Education in The most ancient and famous University of Oxford, from The Fifteenth Year of King Henry the Seventh, Dom. 1500, to the End of the Year 1690. Representing The Birth, Fortune, Preferment, and Death of all those Authors and Prelates, the great Accidents of their Lives, and the Fate and Character of their Writings. To which are added, The Fasti or Annals, of the said University, For the same time.* Volume I spends 546 columns on the writers and 87 columns on the bishops who died before 1641; volume II devotes even more space to the writers. The lives are distinguished because of Wood's industry and accuracy, not because of his ability as a writer, though his bluntness and peevishness, his cantankerousness and spleen frequently give his statements and opinions a very sharp edge. The *Athenae* is not exclusively about Oxonians; Wood included men who were merely incorporated at Oxford, and he added others when they were somehow connected to a life he was writing. For instance, the sketch of Walton is appended to the life of Hooker because Wood had depended heavily on Walton's *Life of Hooker* in writing his own account; so, Marvell can be found attached to Samuel Parker, and Waller to Sidney Godolphin. Wood was at work on a third volume when he died, and an edition of the *Athenae* published in 1721 incorporates his additions and corrections in edited form. The text used here is that of the first edition, I, 264–265, 530–532.

The best edition of *Athenae Oxonienses* is an annotated one, based on the 1721 edition, by Philip Bliss (4 vols., 1813–1820). Wood's autobiography was published in 1730, and again, with the diary, in 1772. The autobiography and diary are most readily available at the beginning of Bliss's edition of *Athenae.* They have been transcribed more accurately in Andrew Clark's *The Life and Times of Anthony Wood* (5 vols., 1891–1900), but here other papers of Wood's have been incorporated chronologically. Clark describes Wood's collection of printed books in I, 6–21, and his manuscripts in IV, 228–250. Llewelyn Powys's abridgement (1932, repr. 1961) of Clark's *Life and Times* must be used with great care. Wood's *Survey of the Antiquities of the City of Oxford* has also been edited by Clark (3 vols., 1889–1899); there is a short life of Wood in I, 1–25. William R. Parker, in "Wood's Life of Milton: Its Sources and Significance," *Papers of the Bibliographical Society of America*, LII (1958), 1–22, finds the life "almost wholly worthless as biographical source material." J. Milton French comes to the conclusion that Wood's trustworthiness is astonishing in "The Reliability of Anthony Wood and Milton's Oxford M.A.," *PMLA*, LXXV (1960), 22–30.

SIR HENRY WOTTON
1568–1639

Wotton was affectionately known to King James as Ottavio Baldi; John Chamberlain referred to him, with less affection, in his letters as Signor Fabritio; and it is quite possible that Ben Jonson had him in mind when he created Sir Politic Would-be. The pre-eminent exemplar of the Italianate Englishman, Wotton was, in fact, a wilder projector than Sir Pol: on the one hand, he worked with daring and ingenuity to try to win the Venetians to Protestantism as the first step in bringing reformation to religion in Italy, and, on the other, he tried to introduce the best of Italian culture into England. Even at Oxford, Wotton seems to have prepared himself for a diplomatic career, and, at twenty-one, he journeyed abroad for five years in pursuit of learning, languages, and friendships. When he returned to England, he entered the service of the Earl of Essex and accompanied him on his ventures to Cadiz, to the Azores, and even to Ireland in 1599. He left Essex in the nick of time and spent four more years abroad, during which he ingratiated himself to men of position in Italy and to James in Scotland. James knighted him in 1604, just before he made him ambassador to Venice. Until 1610, and again from 1616 to 1619 and from 1621 to 1623, Wotton was in charge of the embassy in Venice, and he served, too, as ambassador to The Hague in 1614 and as ambassador extraordinary on several missions. In 1624, the King rewarded him with the Provostship of Eton, and, despite his disappointment that greater place was not his, he pursued the life of cultivated retirement for which his intellectual and artistic interests had prepared him. Wotton projected many literary works, generally when he thought that publication might further his career;

he never wrote his proposed account of the Venetian quarrel with the Pope, his history of Venice, his life of Luther, and his history of England, and his philosophical survey of education remained a fragment. Most of his short prose pieces and his few poems were first published in *Reliquiae Wottonianae* (1651), the volume of remains which Walton edited and for which he wrote a prefatory life. Wotton's best little book is *The Elements of Architecture,* published in 1624. Its concern is the building of a great country house; the first book in English on the subject, it is interesting both for its advocacy of Palladian architecture and for its discussion of such general aesthetic problems as symmetry and the representation of nature.

About a thousand of Wotton's letters and dispatches have survived; they include familiar letters, news-letters to political correspondents, and reports to the King and the Secretary of State. Fifty-eight letters were printed in *Reliquiae Wottonianae* (1651), and in each succeeding edition (1654, 1672, 1685), the number was increased; the 1685 edition has 173. The text of three of the six letters reprinted here is taken from *Reliquiae Wottonianae,* 1651 (no. 2 is on pp. 411–416, no. 4 on pp. 384–388, and no. 6 on pp. 511–513), and that for Letter 1 is from the third edition (1672), sigs. e8ʳ–f2ʳ. Letter 3 is printed from a copy of the holograph in the State Papers, Foreign, Venice, in the Public Record Office (SP 99/25) through the courtesy of the Keeper of Public Records. Letter 5 follows the text in Milton's *Poems,* 1645, pp. 71–73.

Logan Pearsall Smith's *The Life and Letters of Sir Henry Wotton* (2 vols., 1907) contains the best modern biography, 511 of the letters, and a useful chronological table of all Wotton's letters (II, 417–454). The table lists the letters and dispatches edited by George Tomline in *Letters and Dispatches from Sir Henry Wotton to James the First and his Ministers, in the years MDCXVII–XX* (1850), and the 15 printed in C. Knight Watson's "Letters from Sir Henry Wotton to King James I. and others," *Archaeologia,* XL (1866), 257–284. In "Lettere autografe inedite di Sir Henry Wotton nell'Archivio di Stato di Firenze," the first section of *Fatti e Figure del Seicento Anglo-Toscano* (1957), Anna M. Crinò prints 32 Italian letters written between 1601 and 1607. The best edition of Wotton's poems remains John Hannah's *Poems by Sir Henry Wotton, Sir Walter Raleigh, and Others* (1845, 1857; *The Courtly Poets,* 1870; *The Poems of Sir Walter Raleigh . . . with those of Sir Henry Wotton,* 1875, 1892). S. T. Prideaux edited *The Elements of Architecture* in 1903; it appears also among the tracts in *Complaint and Reform in England 1436–1714,* ed. William H. Dunham, Jr., and Stanley Pargellis (1938). H. S. Kermode edited *A Philosophical Survey of Education or Moral Architecture and The Aphorisms of Education* in 1938. Frederick Hard's "Sir Henry Wotton: Renaissance Englishman," *Pacific Spectator,* VII (1953), 364–379, is a good introductory essay.

Glossary

Glossed words are, in the main, listed under their modern spelling; where a word has no familiar modern equivalent or where the seventeenth-century spelling may mislead, listing is by old spelling. The main purpose has been to gloss (1) words which look familiar but have changed in customary meaning and (2) words which have a special meaning in a given context. A word sometimes appears more than once, when it is used as more than one part of speech or when its spelling may lead to confusion. Wherever a semi-colon appears in a gloss, only one of the meanings will generally be relevant for a particular context.

abated   weakened
abjection   abjectness
abortion   miscarriage
abroad   out
absurd   unreasonable
absurdly   irrationally
abuseth   misleads
accise   excise
ace   a point, a jot (*one*, at dice)
adamant   loadstone, magnet
address   skill, adroitness
admire   be filled with wonder at, be amazed at
adverse   opposite
aequinox   mid-point
affect   like; use; prefer
affecting   liking, liking to use
affection   disposition
affections   feelings, emotions; passions
affects   produces an effect
against   in anticipation of; before
aggravates   adds weight to, makes worse

agreeably   fittingly
alegrement   cheerfully
aliened   alienated, transferred
alledging   citing, adducing as evidence
allow   approve
allowed   credited, believed
almond glove   probably a glove impregnated with oil of almonds
ambassade   embassy, ambassadorship
ambodexters   opportunists
analyseth   separates
answer   act in conformity with, correspond
answering   corresponding to
antick   playing the part of a clown; grotesque
Anticyra   one of several towns so named in Greece, famous for cures
        for madness
appendants   extras, hired men, not full members of a company
appointment   choice
apposed   questioned
apprehend   fear
apprehension   concern
arable   arable land
arches   arcs
arefaction   drying
arietations   uses of the battering ram
Aristarchus   a severe critic (originally, of the Homeric poetry)
arraying   setting in order
artillery gardens   archery grounds
as one would   such as please one
ascendent   influence
assay   trial, experiment
attend   await, wait for
attenuable   that which can be made thinner
audacities   reckless men
austerity   severity in judgment
Austin(e)   Augustine
aversation   aversion, turning away
avoided   made void, shown to be invalid
away   put up with
awfulness   sublime majesty, impressiveness
babies   dolls, puppets
bables   baubles
bag   purse, money-bag
banded   bandied, talked about

barbarism   rudeness of language, deviation from the classical standard
   of a language
barbarizing   writing unidiomatically
barriers   a tournament in which combatants fought on foot with a
   railing (barrier) between them
Bartholomew ware   cheap, flimsy merchandise of the kind sold at Bartholomew Fair
bassa   pasha
Battle Abbey   Hastings
baulks   intentional omissions, stumbling-blocks
bear out   successfully sustain
beare   beer; March beer—strong ale
beares-foot   hellebore
beat over   treat thoroughly
beats down   depresses, devaluates
bedlam   the hospital of St. Mary of Bethlehem in London, a hospital
   for lunatics
been in pain   taken pains
beholding   indebted
bent   bent grass
besieged   surrounded
bestead   assist
bestowing   placing, settling in life
bewrayed   betrayed, revealed
biles   boils
blanch   avoid, turn away from
blind   dark
blush   glance
boisterous   violent, clamorous
bôn   boon, gift, favor
boon   prosperous, fortunate, successful
bottomed   supported, founded
box   boxwood
brave   gorgeous
bravery   ostentation, bravado; finery, ostentatious display; show,
   splendor
braves   runs counter to
break up   shine forth
breeding   education
broaker   pawnbroker, second-hand dealer
broken   arranged for different instruments
broken my mind   confided
brother   brother-in-law

Bullen　Boulogne
bullises　bullaces, wild plum
bumbast　bombast, inflated, puffed up
burses　bourses, merchants' exchanges
by my truly　a very mild oath
by-respects　reasons which are subsidiary, at one side
cabinet　a private chamber
cadet　a younger son
Cales　Cadiz
called　summoned by Divine authority
calling　vocation; sometimes, a divine call, or the inward conviction of such a call
callosities　insensibility to feeling
can　be able
canting　jargon (of thieves and vagabonds)
canvasses　intrigues, discussions
caps　square-caps, the sign of the scholar
card　chart, map
care not　do not use care
careful　full of cares
carpet　covering of a table, tablecloth
carriage　baggage, burden; the manner of carrying out or performing
cast　cast away, rejected, dismissed from good opinion
castle-soap　Castile soap
casualty　chance, accident
cat　tipcat, a game in which a small pointed piece of wood is raised from the ground (or "hole") by striking one end with a stick and then hit while it is in the air
catches　rounds, each singer catching up his part in turn
catching　arresting
censure　judgment, opinion; criticism
censures　passes judgment on
Chaldey　Aramaic, Semitic language dominant in southern Babylonia, in which small parts of the Old Testament were written
chamaïris　dwarf iris
champion　champaign, open country, common land
character　symbol, letter of the alphabet
chargeable　costly
charming　enchanting
check　interfere
chop　chop logic, split hairs
chyrurgery　surgery

circumstance   setting the scene, introductory qualification
circumstances   preliminary details
civilians   authorities on civil law
civility   good citizenship
Clarissimo   a Venetian grandee
close   an enclosed field, a farmyard
close   secret; enclosed
closet   a private room, a small study; sometimes, the private apartment of a monarch
clot   clod of earth
clout   piece out, patch
clouts   pieces of cloth
coetanean   contemporary, companion
cogging   cheating
coldly   without warmth of feeling
colone   a farmer on shares, a serf
colorably   having the appearance of truth
combination   collusion
combinations   people associated in plotting
comely   decorous, aesthetically pleasing
comet   omen, portent
commanded   controlled by force
commodities   conveniences, advantages
commons   rations
compact   treatise
compage   coherence, compaction
composition   temperament
compound   settle
compoundeth   makes by the combination of elements
computation   reckoning, estimation
concealed   (with *land*) holding land without proper title
conceipt   conceit, witticism
conceit   conception, idea; fanciful, ingenious notion; worth, value
conceits   values, cares for
concocted   digested
concoction   digestion
conditioned   stipulated, provided for by law or agreement
conditions   classes, ranks; personal qualities
conferences   meetings, interviews
conferred   compared
confident   over-bold, forward, presumptuous; having trust or confidence in
confounded   destroyed

congress   meeting, interview, encounter
conjunct   close
conjuncture   combination of circumstances, crisis
conjurements   solemn appeals
conning   studying, examining
conquer   to be beyond
consaorman   house-steward
conscience   consciousness
consent   concent, accord of several parts
consequence   logical sequence
conservatories   repositories
consimility   similarity
conster   construe
construction   interpretation
consumption   decline
contract   contracted, in smaller compass
contradict   oppose
conversation   conduct; social conduct; manner of life
converse in   deal with, be engaged in
conversing   associating
convertible   capable of being turned
convict   convicted, proved
convince   refute
cook's   cook's shop, eating-house
copels   cupels, porous vessels used to refine gold and silver
copes   cope, canopy
cordial   invigorating, hearty
cords   chords
corn   grain, wheat
corographical   chorographical, delineating regions on a map
corrivations   structures which make possible the confluence of streams
corsives   corrosives, vexations
cosening   cheating
cost   expenditure of time and thought
cotloft   cockloft; a small upper loft, usually reached by a ladder
couched   formulated, expressed; put together
countenances   wry faces
country   native, of one's country
courses   practices, lines of action
courtesy   curtsy
courtship   courtly manner of persuading
cousen   cozen, cheat, defraud
Crassians   grossly stupid men

cried up   proclaimed to be excellent, extolled

cringes   kneelings

crookned   crook-kneed, pliant

crotchets   characters indicating the duration of a tone by its shape, and the pitch by its position on the staff; a prop with a forked top which serves as a support

crudity   indigestion

cryterium   criterion

curious   skillful; exquisite, choice; careful

curiously   carefully; closely

currantoes   newspapers

current   of this month, or, of last month

cut   make a woodcut

dammasin   damson plum

damnified   injured, caused loss to

dark   in the dark, ignorant

darkness   ignorance

dashing   frustrating, destroying

day-net   a net which can be closed suddenly by pulling a string

deboshed   debauched

deceive   rob of nourishment

declension   decline

decline   avoid, shun

decretory   decreed, ordained

deducted   deduced, derived from

defalcations   deductions

delatory   dilatory, causing delay, time-consuming

delicacy   pleasure

delicate   charming, pleasant

delicious   pleasure-loving; addicted to sensuous indulgence

deliver   speak

delivered   recorded

demeans   demesnes

depend   hang on, remain unsettled

deposed   disposed of, placed, buried

deposition   burial

deprehend   catch in the act

descant   a melodious accompaniment, sung or played; improvisation on a set theme

descend   proceed from the general to the specific

desent   decent

desperateness   rashness

despised   looked down on, viewed with contempt

destruction   the power of destroying

determinate   definitive

determine   adjudicate; maintain a thesis in a disputation (by which a student entered upon the degree of B.A.)

determined   fixed beforehand, decided

device   plot, contrivance; something fancifully or emblematically designed

devolved   entrusted

Diet   the parliamentary assembly of the German Empire

dilate   stretch

discipline   learning

discomposed   disturbed, unsettled

discontent   malcontent

discoursing   talkative

discover   uncover, disclose

discovering   disinterring

discreet   showing discernment, judicious

disgregated   confused (by the scattering of visual rays)

disparage   undervalue

dispensatively   by dispensation

dispensed with   excused, exempted

dispirits   extracts and transfuses the essence of

disposal   bestowal, the act of disposing or placing (oneself)

disputations   formal philosophical debates

dissertion   desertion, spiritual despair

distastes   annoyances, disgusts

ditty   a little poem, intended to be sung; a simple song (but sometimes solemn)

diuturnity   long duration

doctor   a learned man

dominicals   dominical letters; a letter used to denote the Sundays in a particular year with respect to the dates on which they fall

donaries   donations

doom   judgment

Doric   pastoral

dorpes   villages

dors   hornets, bees

doublets   an old form of backgammon

doubt   fear

doubtful   indistinct

draught   drawing, sketch

dread   revered, held in awe

drean   drain

dressing   preparing for the oven

drie   ironic, scornful

drive   aim, attack

druggers   druggists

dry   uncolored by emotion

Dutch   German

economics   the management of the household or family

effects   deeds, accomplishments

effectually   wholly

elaborate   highly finished

Elias   Elijah

embrious   embryonic, merely a beginning

eminent   high, towering over all

empiricks   quacks

endite   indite, compose, write

engaged   bound by legal obligation, mortgaged, made security for

enginry   mechanical engineering

enlarged   released, freed

enormous   monstrous, excessively wicked

entertainment   employment

entrals   entrails, internal parts

ephemerans   insects that live for a day or a few days

equal   just

errand   purpose, intention

escapes   mistakes

escapes   escapes notice

evacuate   get rid of

event   outcome, result

exactly   completely

execution   occasion (?)

exemplary   remarkable, extraordinary

exenteration   disembowelling, evisceration

exercise   the performance of religious duties or of worship

exility   thinness, weakness

exolution   setting free of the spirit

exornations   embellishments

expert   experienced

expilators   pillagers

explode   hiss, hoot off stage, reject with scorn

expounded   interpreted

express   specially dispatched message

express   precise

exquisite   highly elaborate, *recherché*
extasis   ecstasy
extenuate   disparage
exuccous   exsuccous, sapless
facetious   witty
facile   pliable
facility   pliability, weakness
fact   deed, act
faculty   ability, facility
fadomles   fathomless
faint   lose heart, get discouraged
fallen out   happened
falls   conclusions, outcomes
fancied   fanciful
fast   not easily extricated
fatigue   work, toil, what causes fatigue
faulkner   falconer
favour   face
feign   to relate in fiction, invent
fel-mongers   dealers in skins or hides (mainly of sheep)
ferity   cruelty, barbarity
figure   a set pattern; shape
figured   represented, expressed metaphorically
fine   set fee
fine   pay a fee for leased property
fine   refined in reasoning, overmeticulously discriminated
firm   secure
fitted   appropriate to speaker, subject, and audience
flagges   flags, iris
flashy   insipid, tasteless
flea   flay, whip
Fleet   a prison in London
flexon   flaxen
flixe   flux, dysentery
flos Africanus   African marigold
Flower-de-lices   fleur de lis, iris
flowers   powder
fluctuation   change (of sides or loyalties)
foil   a light, blunt sword for fencing
fond   foolish
fondness   foolishness
foot-pace   dais
form   class at school, at college, at the Inns of Court

forms   paradigms

forwards   prone, quick

foul   unattractive, ugly

found   base

fowler   one who hunts wild birds

frantic   insane

frettellaria   fritillaria, lilies

froward   perverse, cross, stubborn

fume   smoke dream, empty fancy

fumes   perfumes (with overtone of smoke, which beclouds, and of vapor, which vanishes quickly)

funge   a soft-headed fellow, a mushroom

furniture   trappings, equipment

fustian   inflated, bombastic, pretentious

gabells   taxes

Gallego   a Galician (from northwest Spain)

gamester   player

gate   gait

gave place   retreated

gee and ree   commands given to an animal or team to turn right and left, or go forward, or move faster

generous   appropriate to one of noble birth or spirit

genial   natural, pertaining to birth or to family

gentile   genteel, gentlemanly

gentleman-commoner   one of a privileged class of undergraduates formerly recognized at Oxford and Cambridge; they wore special academic dress, dined at a separate table, were exempt from some lectures, and paid higher fees

gingle   jingle

ginnitings   jennetings, variety of early apple

give   make good, measure up to

give out   desist, leave off

give over   leave off, give up

given over   passed over

glister   clyster, enema

globe   mass, crowd

goaler   gaoler, jailer

gossipings   meetings with friends

gossips   godparents, sponsors

gown   symbol of the activities of peace (the legal, clerical, and governmental professions)

gracing   compliment

grandy grandee, man of elevated rank

great year the period during which the stars and planets return in their revolution to the position they had at the creation of the world

gripers extortioners

grutching begrudging, grumbling

guilt gilt

gymnicks gymnastics

habit dress, demeanor

handle means

hap luck, fortune

happily haply

hard close

hardly with difficulty

hatched brought to full development; engraved or cut or drawn in lines to give a shaded effect

health drinking healths, toasts

heavy hard to bear

hectic feverish

help put a favorable construction on

herba muscaria grape hyacinth

herein in this matter

Hierom St. Jerome

high early, long ago, far back in antiquity; strong, angry, arrogant

high-place altar

his its

his . . . his one's . . . another's

historical systematic, though not necessarily chronological, presentation

history a systematic account (without reference to time) of a set of natural phenomena

hollyokes the evergreen or holm-oak

hopeful promising

horse pads tracks in a muddy road made by horses' hoofs

hospital place of rest and entertainment; a charitable institution for housing and maintaining the needy, aged, or sick

hottest most violent

housekeepers householders, landed gentry

humane human

humorous eccentric, unbalanced

hungerlin a short fur coat, introduced from Hungary

hydroptic thirsty, insatiable

hyssop the type of a lowly plant

I aye

illiberal   not befitting a liberally educated person

illiberality   stinginess

immanitie   monstrous cruelty

impatiency   restlessness, lack of endurance

imped   fastened on or engrafted wings to improve power of flight

impertinences   matters of no concern

impertinent   without pertinence

importing   important, of consequence

importunate   troublesome

importune   importunate, urgent

imposeth   places restrictions upon

impost   tax

impostume   cyst, abscess, swelling

impress   impresa, a motto or device, the meaning of which is frequently veiled

in   on the part of; with

in a mean   moderately, plainly

in lavender   to put aside carefully for future use

in spite of their teeth   notwithstanding one's opposition

incensed   burned

incident   apt to fall into, subject to

incommixed   unmixed

incorporates   gets admitted as a member of a company or guild (brotherhood)

incremable   incombustible

incult   uncultivated, rough

incumbencies   heavy duties and obligations

indifferent   impartial, unbiased

indignities   unworthy acts

ingaged   *see* engaged

ingeniose   ingenious, intelligent, talented

ingenious   clever in invention or construction; intelligent; wellbred

ingenuity   ingenuousness, candor

ingrossings   monopolies

inhiation   the act of opening the mouth wide, gaping after

iniquity   inequity, lack of perspective

injuriously   offensively

inquisition   inquiry

insinuation   way of getting into company

institution   beginning, original form; an introduction or elementary book on a subject

intempestive   unseasonable

interest   advantage (pecuniary)

interlace   intermix, insert

interlocution   a speech of reply, conversing well

inward   intimate

jack   upright piece of wood fixed to the back of the key-lever, and fitted with a quill which plucked the string as the jack rose when the key was pressed down

judgment   man of judgment

jument   beast of burden

juncture   joining together, coherence

Justice   Justice of the Peace

justs   jousts, mock combat between two horsemen armed with lances

kennels   gutters, the surface drains of a street

kicshoes   kickshaws; fantastical, frivolous persons

kim kam   badly, perversely

kinred   kindred

l.   pounds (*abbr.*)

labored   carefully wrought

laborious   diligent

lacrymatories   tear-bottles

lap   wrap, tie up

larceries   larcenies

larix   larch

last   lasting

late   recent

Lauretta   Loretto

layed   allayed, subdued

leads   a flat roof

lear   look away or aside

least   lest

lecture   lectureship, appointment to deliver discourses or sermons on occasions outside the regular order of church services

lecturer   a preacher who delivers an occasional sermon or lecture

leg   a bow made by drawing back one leg and bending the other

legal   concerned with the law of works, with salvation by works, not by faith

legge   bow

letting   blocking, stopping

li.   pounds (*abbr.*)

liberal   worthy of a free man; necessary to the making of a gentleman

lighters   boats, flat-bottomed barges

lilium convallium   lily of the valley

line   route; equator
listed   embellished
lively   accurately, to the life
livor   liver, violent passion
lixivious   impregnated with alkaline salts, having the ability to leach
locks   holds
longaevous   long-lived
loose   lose
loose   discharge of the shaft
loose   release from restraint
looses   discharges; with *pretty*—lucky shots
low   late in time, recent, recently; short in height
Lucina   the goddess of childbirth
lust   desires
luxuriate   indulge in lust
Macaronicon   a work which is a jumble, medley (Macaronic poetry is
            verse in which two or more languages are jumbled to-
            gether, or verse which contains in a Latin context
            vernacular words with Latin endings and in Latin con-
            structions)
magazens   magazines, arsenals
magazine   storehouse
magnanimity   magnificence, grandeur
magnanimously   highmindedly
maintained   backed up, supported
maketh   is for the advantage of
male-content   discontent
Mare del Zur   Pacific Ocean
marishes   marshes
mary   marrow
mates   checkmates, overcomes
maul   a heavy blow
mean   middle
meat   food
mecanicall   mean, vulgar
meene   mien
meet with   approaches, comes close to
mercership   the trade of a mercer, a dealer in textile fabrics
mercies   blessings, gifts of God
meridian   the point halfway between the creation and the last day
mess(e)   meal
metal   the "stuff" of which man is made
meteors   meteorology

method　systematic arrangement or treatment, methodical exposition

mettle　metal

mind　remind

minutes　rough drafts, memoranda, brief summaries

mirth　joy, happiness

mistress　in the game of bowls, a jack, the small ball used as a mark

Mizraim　Egypt (*Hebr.*); the son of Ham who is considered the ancestor of the Egyptians

melo-cotones　a variety of peach

mezerion　mezereon, a small shrub with lilac-colored flowers

moales　moles, spots or marks on the skin

moderate　sum up

monomachies　duels, single combats

mortified　brought to a holy life through self-denial and abstinence

mother　hysteria

motion　proposal, suggestion

mought　might

mounted　elevated in position or power

mummy　a liquid or gum derived from an embalmed body and used as a drug

N.B.　*nota bene,* note well

naeve　nevus, birthmark

naturally　in nature

naught　naughty, immoral

necessity　inevitability

nice　delicate

niceness　the quality of being not easily pleased, finely discriminative

night-gown　dressing gown

non-residents　ministers who held benefices *in absentia*

Nuntio　Nuncio, permanent official representative of the Roman See at a foreign court

obtrude　present, set forth

occasionally　on a particular occasion

occupation　the taking up of one's time

oes　round bright spots, sequins

of　between; off

of course　in due course

of touch　touching, having personal reference to

offend　hurt, pain

offers　attempts

office　duty, service

officious　zealous

omniscious　omniscient

one and thirty a card game

ont on it, of it

opinative opinionative

opprobrious disease disease stemming from shameful conduct, prob-
        ably syphilis

ordinairie an eating house, or tavern

organic constructive, broadly instrumental

ought owed

out wrong, mistaken

out of without

outlandish foreign

over-live outlive

overween over-esteem

Pacelot in the romance *Valentine and Orson,* a dwarf who had a
        magical horse

packs unopened packets

painful painstaking

painted drawn or printed freehand (?)

paires impairs

parcels particles

parlours conferences, colloquies, conversations

particular an inventory of possessions

partlets old-fashioned collars

passengers travelers, wayfarers

passionate arousing feelings and stirring emotions; impassioned, ex-
        pressive of strong emotion

patent license, certificate

patera broad flat dish, used in pouring out libations at sacrifices

pauled palled, weakened

Paul's St. Paul's Church, London, the precincts of which were a pop-
        ular place for transactions, appointments, and gossip

peculiar chosen, special

peece piece, unite, join

peevishness perverseness

peradventure uncertainty, doubt

perdue in an advanced outpost or in a lonely post; (with *sentinel*)
        the post of a sentinel in a very dangerous position

perfect improve

perfectly completely, utterly

perfeted perfected

period conclusion, end; a complete sentence or unit, usually of sev-
        eral clauses, grammatically connected and rhetorically con-
        structed

personate   masked, impersonating
perspectives   telescopes
philology   speculative philosophical writing
physick   medicine
picture   statue
pine-apple-trees   pines
places   Scriptural texts
plain song   a simple musical theme
planetary   wandering, erratic
plate galleons   Spanish ships which brought yearly tribute of gold
     from America
platform   plan
plausible   courting applause
playing   the use of games and of amusements (in learning)
playnes   plainness
playstered   plastered
plunge   dilemma
poling   seizing, exacting fees
politic   expedient
ponderation   weighing
pory   porous
poser   an examiner, one who poses questions
practic   practical, active
practise   good management
prank   dress showily
praxis   practice, practical application
praying in aid of   being an advocate for
prebends corps   property, from the revenue of which a prebendary or
     canon of a cathedral gets his stipend
precedent   to come before (in value)
precipitate   rash, headstrong
precise   puritanical
Precisian   Puritan
prefer   to put forward in status, rank, or position
pre-occupateth   anticipates
preposterous   putting the last first; in reversed order
prescription   title, claim
presidents   precedents
pressed   punished
presses   bookcases
prest   impressed, forced to serve in the army or navy
pretence   claim
pretended   alleged

pretendeth is used as an excuse for

prevent anticipate

prevention anticipation

prick in plant; embroider

prickt planted, set

private common (as opposed to noble)

privateness retirement

privie private, secret

proairesis intelligent choice between good and evil; action based on reasoning and full understanding (Aristotle, *Nicomachean Ethics,* II and III)

Procuratori senators of the Venetian Republic, charged with high administrative functions

production birth (being led into)

profession declaration of belief in and obedience to a religion

professors those who declare their sentiments openly; open advocates of religion

progress a state journey made by a royal or a noble person or by a church dignitary

proletaries Roman citizens of the lowest class

proling prowling

promiscuous mixed, heterogeneous

propension propensity

prophanes profaneness

proportion amount

propugner defender, supporter

prosecute carry out, follow up with a view to completing

prosecution following up

prospectives telescopes

proyning pruning, cultivating

publication public announcement (of the banns of marriage)

purprise environs

pusle puzzle, confusion

putid foul, stinking

puts in makes an occasional comment

quadlins codlings, a variety of apple

quaere query

quaere ask (*Lat.*)

quaint ingeniously contrived; polished

qualified trained

quality rank, status, social position

quarrel excuse

quarter proper place

quean　wench, slut

quich　quitch grass (couch grass)

quickneth　hastens

quire　choir

quirkes　quips

rabbine　rabbi, a learned Jewish commentator on law or doctrine

racked　wracked, broken

rampiers　ramparts

ranges　rows

ranging　arranging

ranking　ordering

Ranters　the most fanatic of the Nonconformist sects; believed that the elect were completely outside moral law

raspes　raspberries

rated　controlled through rates fixed by authorities

ready　quick, speedy

recarnified　converted into flesh again

receipt　recipe, formula, prescription; receptacle

receits　prescriptions, remedies

recess　departure

receve　take holy communion

recited　quoted

reconing　valuing, estimating

recreative　refreshing

redress　cure, remedy

reduce　bring back

reduced　brought; led back; brought within bounds; brought to a state of gravity and composure; brought down to a bad condition

redy　dressed

regale　a fine meal, a choice feast

reins　kidneys

relate　tell, narrate

relation　narration, relating, telling

relentment　dissolution, softening

reluct for　strive to (hide)

remiss　relaxed, loose

repaired　gone, resorted

re-saluting　being greeted

resent　feel injured

resented　felt

reserved　saved

resolution　solution

resolve   determine (the size of)

resorts   conclusions, ends

respect   cause

respects   considerations

resume   take up again, recover

resumed   taken from

retire   leave

revels   informal merrymaking and entertainment, or more formal ritual and ceremony

revoke   recall

ribes   currants

ridling   riddling, puzzling

right   straight

right descensions   vertically

rigid   unyielding in belief

ring   a circlet of metal suspended from a post which a rider tried to carry off on the point of his lance

Rosie cross men   Rosicrucians, Utopian reformers

roughness   undue severity

round   square, straightforward

royalties   domains or manors in possession of royal rights or privileges

ruffle   swagger

run   pitch, popularity

saciety   satiety

safe   safely

St. Ellen's   St. Helen's, Isle of Wight

St. Martin's   district of London where manufacture of counterfeit ware flourished

salamander's wool   asbestos

sallets   salads, greens

sallow   willow

salutation   a kiss, by way of greeting

salute   greet, greet with a kiss

salve   provide a remedy for, save

sand   sandstone

Sarum   Salisbury

sarza   sarsaparilla

Sathan   Satan

satyrian   butterfly orchis

Satyrs   satires

scaffold   the place or structure which holds the audience

scandal   discreditable behavior

scandalous   in a disgraceful position

scant scarcely, hardly

scape transgression, error

scelestique wicked

school the Schoolmen or Scholastics, medieval scholars

sciences fields of knowledge

scilicet namely, that is to say (*Lat.*)

scrabling scrambling

scrape bow

scruple a very small quantity; the smallest unit of weight (Roman)

scrutinies the formal taking of individual votes, as a method of electing to an office

scurvie hardened

seals authenticated documents, pledges, guarantees

seared incapable of feeling

seasons the effects of seasonal change on the body

seeling ceiling

sense feeling

sensible sensitive; accessible to the senses

sensuous affecting the senses directly

sent scent

sentence a statement or maxim full of thought, an aphorism, a moral reflection; a Scriptural passage

sententious full of intelligence or wisdom

sepulture burial

service the duty of a soldier, participation in warfare

services trees like the mountain ash but with larger and edible fruit

set a bar fix limits

several separate, distinct

severe accurate, rigorous, exact

shaggringe chagrined

sharer stockholder

shift a fraudulent or evasive device; stratagem, expedient; effort

shift to change one's clothing

shoreless boundless

side take sides

side robes long robes

silenced debarred from a regular charge

silly of humble rank

simple straightforward, comprehensible at once

Sinai Mt. Sinai represents legalistic adherence to religion before the oncoming of grace

single of each one, individual

singled set apart, solitary

singular   outstanding

sirrope   syrup

sister   sister-in-law

slashes   vertical slits made in a garment to expose a lining or undergarment of a different color

sleveles   sleeveless, futile

small   weak

smallage   wild celery or water parsley

smart   sharp, severe

smartly   thoroughly, vigorously

smatter   talk ignorantly, chatter

snuff   candle-end

sort   consort, lead, agree

sorts   ranks, conditions

sot   blockhead, dolt

span   the distance between the tip of the thumb and the tip of the little finger when the hand is fully extended; a short space of time

spangs   spangles

specious   beautiful

spectrums   specters

squalor   roughness

squares   affairs, matters

squeamishly   shyly, awkwardly

squeazy   niggardly

squibs   firecrackers

stand   loss, standstill

standards   raised objects

staples   commercial centers, principal market for some kind of merchandise

States   States General (legislative assembly) of Holland

stayer   stair

steal   do by stealth

steel   iron used for purpose of flavor or impregnation in a medicine

steeple house   the tower of a church, sometimes detached from the church; used by Quakers to describe any church building

steering   (may be an error for "veering")

stereometry   the science of measuring solids

stick   hesitate, hold back; resist; scruple

stile   a distinguishing title or name

still   ever

stocks   stupid people

stond　obstruction

stool　commode, toilet

stooved　stoved, put in a hothouse

stounded　stunned

strong　masculine; compressed; signifying or implying much

stubbs　blockheads

studied　been eager for

studies　schools, centers of learning

study　zeal, eagerness

stuff　property, especially household goods

stupend　stupendous

subject　substance, material

suffer　allow

sufficiency　ability

sullen　sluggish

superannate　superannuate, render obsolete

superintendent　officer in charge, overseer

survey　surveillance, supervision

surviving　of survival

sute　order, sequence

suttle　subtle; thin (as well as the customary meaning)

synchronism　coincidence in time

Syrian　Syriac, a form of Aramaic used by Christians; the language of the oldest manuscripts of the Synoptic Gospels

Table Laws　the tablets on which collections of ancient Greek and Roman laws were inscribed, especially the Twelve Tables (c. 450 B.C.) embodying the most important rules of Roman law

tables　games played on boards

take in　consider

take of(f)　remove

take up　borrow

tallies　taxes, receipts for taxes

tarentola　tarantula

target　a small shield

taskers　piece-workers

tax　censure; traduce

teachy　tetchy, touchy

tearmes　terms, the periods appointed for the sitting of certain courts of law

tedious　disagreeable, painful

temper　a middle course

temper　adapt to particular needs

tender   delicate

tendered   treated with proper concern

tenent   tenet

term   end; a period appointed for the sitting of certain courts of law

terse   refined, cultured

tertian ague   an acute intermittent fever which returns every other day

tests   cupels, or the iron containers in which cupels were heated

theater   scene of action; a book giving a view or conspectus of some subject

thorow   through

thrust   thirst for

tice   entice

tinct   tint, color

tires   attires, clothes

tissew   tissue; a sheer fabric, usually silk

title   title page

to   in comparison with; up to; down to; as

Tom of Bedlam   a non-violent madman, licensed to beg about the country

topics   the classes of materials suitable for conducting argument

toucher   the bowl which is close to the jack

tourneys   knightly sports and exercises; mock contention between two groups of horsemen

towards   close to the time of

toy   fancy

tract   length

traded in   occupied one's self with, habitually practiced

trains   trick, stratagem, treachery

transcorporating   believing in the transmigration of souls to new bodies

translated   transferred (especially from one bishop's see to another)

transmarine   across the sea

travalleth   travaileth, works

travel   travail, effort, work

travelled   travailed, worked

trench to   encroach on

trimmed   shaved

triumphed   celebrated a Roman triumph

triumphs   spectacular public entertainments, celebratory in nature (with processions, pageants, speeches)

trivant   truant, idler

trunk   tube

trunk-hose   baggy breeches covering hips and upper thighs, sometimes stuffed or padded

tuition   care

Tully   Marcus Tullius Cicero

tumultuarily   haphazardly

tunne   large casks, barrels

tunnels   shafts or flues of chimneys

turgent   inflated

turn over   consider, search into

turn the buckle of his girdle   show his anger

Turquets   little Turks (?)

under   below the level of

undoing   destroying

unmatriculated   inexperienced in what goes on in a university

unpartial   impartial

unready   intractable, restive

unrecrutible   incapable of getting recruits, or, perhaps, losing recruits because of dishonest practices

upon the careen   turned on one side for repair

urinals   glass vessels for medical examination of urine

use   interest; treatment

uses   customarily is

vacancies   days on which studies were suspended (vacations); in Milton, probably holy days, on which secular studies were suspended

Vacuna   goddess of rural leisure

vaine   vein, tendency

Vatinius   a partisan of Caesar

vein   habit

version   direction

vessel   container, bottle, pot

Vide   see (*Lat.*)

virginal *or* **pair of virginals**   rectangular keyed musical instrument (like a spinet), set in a case without legs

virtue   capacity, ability, power

vizars   visors, masks

voluntaries   volunteers

vulgar   common

waited upon   watched, examined; accompanied

walk   a part of a forest or a game preserve supervised by a keeper

wallet   container; a beggar's bag or a peddler's pack

wardens   a variety of pear

warlick   warlike

warm set   planted in a sunny location
wary   careful
wave   waive
weapon   sword
wearish   sickly, wizened
weeds   garments
weight   specific gravity (in a non-technical sense)
weightiest   ranking very high in value or importance
well away   put up with, tolerate, endure
well-weighed   well esteemed
welts   borders, edging
were   wear
whether   whither; why
whifflers   triflers, contemptible fellows (sometimes, smokers of tobacco)
whited   whitewashed
whitethorn   hawthorn
whither   whether
willed   compelled; commanded
winch   wince
without   outside; about, around
wittal   wittol, cuckold
woman   a person prone to tears and weakness
work   influence
would   should
writing fair   making a clean copy
yawning   open-mouthed, gaping
ye   the

ABOUT THE EDITOR

DAVID NOVARR, Professor of English at Cornell University, received his B.A., M.A., and Ph.D. from Yale University. Most of his teaching and writing is in seventeenth-century literature. He is the author of The Making of Walton's "Lives" *and of articles on Donne, Dekker, Milton, Dryden, and others.*

A NOTE ON THE TYPE

The text of this book was set on the Linotype in a new face called Primer, designed by Rudolph Ruzicka, earlier responsible for the design of Fairfield and Fairfield Medium, Linotype faces whose virtues have for some time now been accorded wide recognition.

The complete range of sizes of Primer was first made available in 1954, although the pilot size of 12 point was ready as early as 1951. The design of the face makes general reference to Linotype Century (long a serviceable type, totally lacking in manner or frills of any kind) but brilliantly corrects the characterless quality of that face.

The book was designed by Betty Anderson and was composed, printed, and bound by H. Wolff, New York.